F

Not

AN ENCYCLOPEDIA OF
Swearing

AN ENCYCLOPEDIA OF
Swearing

THE SOCIAL HISTORY OF OATHS, PROFANITY, FOUL LANGUAGE, AND ETHNIC SLURS IN THE ENGLISH-SPEAKING WORLD

GEOFFREY HUGHES

M.E.Sharpe
Armonk, New York
London, England

Library of Congress Cataloging-in-Publication Data

Hughes, Geoffrey, 1939–
  An encyclopedia of swearing : the social history of oaths, profanity, foul language, and
ethnic slurs in the English-speaking world / Geoffrey Hughes.
    p. cm.
Includes bibliographical references and index.
ISBN–13: 978-0-7656-1231-1 (alk. paper)
ISBN–10: 0-7656-1231-3
    1. English language—Obscene words—Dictionaries. 2. English language—Slang—
Dictionaries. 3. Blessing and cursing—Dictionaries. 4. Invective—Dictionaries.
5. Swearing—Dictionaries. I. Title.

PE3724.O3H84 2006
427'.09—dc22   2005012793

Printed in the United States of America

The paper used in this publication meets the minimum requirements of
American National Standard for Information Sciences
Permanence of Paper for Printed Library Materials,
ANSI Z 39.48-1984.

BM (c)   10   9   8   7   6   5   4   3   2

CONTENTS

CONTENTS

PREFACE

Today swearing and foul language are an established part of the linguistic environment, occasionally invading even the best mannered and most controlled circles. There is hardly a domain where "bad language" is not to be heard, and there are now several genres of popular culture, such as rap, reggae, "celebrity" channels, and those of shock jocks, which are largely dependent on the lower registers. The old saying that there is money in muck is being validated in yet another way. Are such utterances and outlets part of a new barbarism, yet another sign that nothing is taboo? The argument for a decline to the lowest common denominator seems strong. It is hard to believe that Thomas Jefferson and Abraham Lincoln spoke in the White House in the way that their successor Richard Nixon is recorded as having done, or that previous members of the British Royal Family used the strong language for which the Duke of Edinburgh and his daughter Princess Anne are notorious. The utterances of Beowulf, Lancelot, and Guinevere have a dignified purity subsequently lost, just as within a few recent decades of modern popular culture the dignified altruistic nobility of Superman has given way to the barbarous punk rock group, the Sex Pistols, and the inarticulate cynicism of Bart Simpson, the denizens of "South Park," and so on.

Yet, in fact, Queen Elizabeth I "swore like a man," and was no stranger to coarse jests. Six hundred years ago the English were known to the French as *les goddems* ("the goddams") just as their modern successors are known as *les fuckoffs*. These collective abilities led William Hazlitt to the generalization that "the English, it must be owned [admitted], are rather a foulmouthed nation" (1821, *Table Talk,* xxii). Attitudes toward this proliferation are changing and complex. "Four-letter" words were used with unembarrassed frequency in medieval medical texts, before the current opaque, euphemistic, and abstract terms like "genitalia" and "private parts" became the essential mode of professional discourse. Yet in Chaucer only the crudest and most exhibitionist of the pilgrims use taboo words. Shakespeare generally avoided them, his contemporary Ben Jonson paraded several, John Aubrey scandalously observed in the mid-seventeenth century that John Selden "got more with his prick than his practice," and his demure contemporary Samuel Pepys recorded reluctantly words like "shit."

Lexicographers were caught in a dilemma between inclusiveness and "decency": Dr. Samuel Johnson (1755), the *Oxford English Dictionary* (*OED* 1884–1928), and even *Webster III* (1961) omitted the crudest words. Yet underground, slang, and even polite dictionaries had included them from the sixteenth century. The reputations of major novelists like James Joyce and D.H. Lawrence were first sullied and then rehabilitated by legal process for using in print words heard in the street. Today "four-letter" words are in "the dictionary," on "the street," and used increasingly in "the media." They even proliferated in books awarded the prestigious Booker Prize for 1994 and 2003. Yet a curious double standard prevails: *fuck* and *cunt* are designated as "taboo," but are commonly used, as any data on currency show. What then is taboo? In reality it is a new category, the ethnic slur.

The social history of swearing and foul language is fascinating. But much of the data has been buried, hidden, or deliberately ignored as "unworthy of preservation," as Dr. Johnson called "cant" or underground slang. Maybe the doughty Doctor was right, since dredging the linguistic sewer is an unedifying exercise. There is a problem of contamination in dealing with dirt, which can lead to a double standard, shown in this fastidious evasion: "There is a certain adjective, most offensive to polite ears, which plays apparently the chief role in the vocabulary of large sections of the community." That was Professor H.C. Wyld, in his *History of Modern Colloquial English,* discoursing knowingly for half a page on a word without ever mentioning it. What was the word? Contemporary readers surely would have known. Now only the social context and the date of publication lead us to it. Since the book came out in 1920 in England, it must have been *bloody,* then supposedly taboo. Indeed, the whole odd evasion would make sense only in England, since in the United States it would have been nonsensical, while in Australia it would have been laughable. Today such reticence has long passed away. A recent survey showed that the name of Jesus was familiar to the majority of British children, but as a swearword.

Fifty years ago a work such as this would have been difficult to write, since taboos still operated even in lexicography, the one area that should have been free of such restraints. Today that has all changed, with the publication of the *Supplement* to the *Oxford English Dictionary* (1972–1986) and the *Random House Historical Dictionary of American Slang* (1994–currently in production and retitled *Historical Dictionary of America Slang* with Oxford University Press). Material is now so abundant that it is difficult to select and maintain a balance between the differing categories and the varieties of global English. But as Dr. Johnson wisely observed, while the dictionary is hastening to publication, "some words are budding, and some falling away." And as he reflected on his progress through "the treadmill of the alphabet," "to the weariness of copying I was condemned to add the vexation of expunging." A work of this kind is easier to start than to finish, since bizarre verbal outrages are now commonplace. Though no work on swearing can be comprehensive without becoming very tedious, this should give the reader an awareness that there are fundamental historical changes in swearing and foul language, as well as a sense of *Plus ça change; c'est plus la même chose* ("The more things change, the more they stay the same").

Although the entries are arranged in alphabetical order, this is not a dictionary. Readers will find a greater range of headings with cross-references in the main text than appear in the Contents. Thus Film is discussed under two headings, namely Cinema and Hollywood; terms for Foreigners are discussed under Ethnic Slurs and numerous specific terms; Lesbians are subsumed under Homosexuals; and so on. The material has been organized under various categories: the words themselves; historical periods; strategies or conventions, such as euphemisms, "minced oaths," and disguise mechanisms; reprehensible behaviors, such as cowardice, cuckoldry, and prostitution; as well as significant authors and major lexicographers, those creators and retrievers of what Lord Acton called "the absorbing past."

Geoffrey Hughes

ACKNOWLEDGMENTS

A work of this complexity and range cannot be achieved by a single person. Accordingly I am happy to recognize those scholars, researchers and philologists who ventured into "the dark continent of words," in John S. Farmer's phrase, and recorded their findings, some more willingly than others. They are surprisingly numerous and extend from the predecessors of the ebullient Francis Grose through Farmer and Henley to Murray, Craigie, Bradley and Onions of the unique *OED*, Robert Burchfield of the worthy *OED Supplement*, Eric Partridge, down to Jonathan Lighter and his team at the magnificent *Historical Dictionary of American Slang*, currently in production. I owe a special debt of thanks to Grant Barrett and the *HDAS* team for sharing with me some of their unpublished data.

I must also record my thanks to Blackwell Publishers for allowing me to re-use some of the material from *Swearing* (1991), my earlier venture into the field. Professor Kader Asmal was kind enough to supply me with some data on unparliamentary language and Tanya Barben of the Rare Books Collection at the University of Cape Town assisted me enthusiastically in some exotic searches. Peter Knox-Shaw and Christopher Hope gave me the benefit of their views

This work was the brainchild of Todd Hallman, who approached me several years ago with a proposal for this improbable and challenging enterprise. Todd has been a model editor, supportive, patient, encouraging, generous, wise, and flexible, but uncompromising on the important issues. Cathleen Prisco, Amy Odum and Mel Wolfson managed the problems of editing with extraordinary punctiliousness and patience. I should also like to thank my beloved wife, Letitia, for help with the proofreading and my dear son Conrad for the loan of his sharp critical mind and his computer. The University of Cape Town English Department granted me temporary use of an office and a computer, prior to the generous assistance of Professor Joan Hambidge at a critical stage of the project.

INTRODUCTION

Words cannot be unsaid, any more than blows can be taken back, and both can have serious repercussions. Swearing is a perennial source of fascination for those interested in language and society, continuously provoking controversy and raising topical issues. An extraordinary range of style and content has evolved in oaths, profanity, foul language, and ethnic slurs over the centuries, on a scale from the most sacred utterances to the most taboo. Formal swearing is a ritual of social compliance and obligation: in marriage, in court, for high office, and as allegiance to the state. On the other hand, informal swearing constitutes a transgression of social codes ranging from the merely impolite to the criminal. This work seeks to introduce students and word lovers to this diversity and its historical evolution.

Swearing now includes so many varied and developed forms that some broad distinctions need to be made at the outset. Let us start with differences between mode and content. In terms of mode, we swear *by* some higher force or somebody; we swear *that* something is so; we swear *to* do something; we swear *at* something or somebody; and we swear simply out of anger, disappointment, or frustration. These different modes can be retermed by various unfamiliar classical terms, such as asseveration, invocation, imprecation, malediction, blasphemy, profanity, obscenity, and ejaculation (in its old sense of "exclamation"). The figure Varieties of Swearing and Word Magic is designed to give the reader a basic map of the territory, showing the hierarchical separation between the binary opposites of "sacred," "profane," and "taboo," divided by the "line of acceptability" on which stands "oaths," since they can be either sacred or profane. The categories of "obscenity," "foul language," and "ethnic slurs" stand below the line because they are purely secular and have no sacred equivalent. As the entries for these major categories show, several of the terms have complex histories and unstable meanings. "Taboo" itself also contains a binary opposition, referring to human experiences, words, or deeds that are unmentionable because they are either ineffably sacred (like the name of God) or unspeakably vile (like incest). Although we are familiar with most of these modes of swearing now, they have not been constantly present in the past. They represent a growth or accumulation that has evolved over centuries. Nevertheless, the crude and simple history of swearing, however named, is that people used mainly to swear *by* or *to*, but now they swear mostly *at*.

Variations of Swearing and Word Magic

SACRED

	Prayers	Attestations		Charms	Oaths

Line of Acceptability ――――――――――――――――――――――――――――

Curses	Profanity		Spells	Obscenity
Malediction	Perjury		Foul Language	
Blasphemy			Ethnic Slurs	

PROFANE   TABOO

At base, swearing is governed by "sacral" notions of word magic; that is to say the belief that words have the power to change the world. These beliefs tend to be very powerful at primitive stages of society, manifesting themselves in charms, spells, invocations, and curses, so that taboos or prohibitions have grown up around dangerous or offensive usages. Swearing is, in one sense, a violation of these taboos: the "high" varieties violate the taboo of invoking the name of the deity, while the "low" are often violations of sexual taboos, especially those concerning copulation and incest. This dualistic juxtaposition of the binary opposites of the sacred and the profane, the high and the low, symbolically represents the angelic and the diabolical potentialities of man. This binary can be related to that between the ancient Apollonian and Dionysiac impulses toward wisdom and to erotic or drunken orgy, respectively. From the "high" dualistic perspective, it is language in its most highly charged state, infused with a religious force recognizable in the remote modes of the spell and the charm, but also present in the prayer, forms of words seeking to invoke a higher power to change the world or validate the truthfulness of a claim. Hence the multitudinous variations of the form *by God!* such as the medieval *by God that sitte above!, for Cristes swete tree!* (by Christ's dear cross!), *zounds!* (by God's wounds!), *by Jove!,* and so on. At base these varieties are profoundly serious, though some in time became merely fashionable. The same is true of curses, even the most far-fetched: "God damn your eyes!" is quite explicit. But the same mode is found in disguised forms: *drat,* for example, is an abbreviation for "God rot," usually "God rot your bones!"—or any other part of the anatomy. There is always the alarming possibility of the words coming true.

Let us now narrow the focus to the formal mode of swearing *by* something or somebody, or *that* something is so, or *to do* something. We should bear in mind that the oldest sense of "to swear" was simply "to take an oath" or "to give a solemn undertaking," and that for several centuries (from about 900 to 1400) this was the only sense. In other words, swearing *at* did not exist in Anglo-Saxon times: at any rate, there are no survivals of this mode. Swearing *by* is still apparent in the formal oaths taken by witnesses, officeholders, and so on.

The important point is that the form of words is traditional, as in "I solemnly swear to tell the truth, the whole truth, and nothing but the truth, so help me God." This mode, termed *asseveration* or *attestation,* can be extended to include all kinds of religious referents—for example, the Lord, Jesus, the holy Cross, God's wounds, Mary, the heavens, as well as objects regarded as sacred, such as "on my mother's grave." This mode forms the basic structure of verbal trust on which all society is based, for every culture has some form of binding oath, as it has some form of verbal taboo.

However, when these sacred names, figures, or objects of veneration are invoked in an unsanctioned way, lightly and irreverently, and especially when they are used to swear *at* somebody or simply out of exasperation, then the mode changes to *profanity, blasphemy, imprecation,* or *malediction.* The distinction between profanity and blasphemy is quite complex and hinges largely on intention, in that profanity is usually regarded as habitual, whereas blasphemy is more obviously intentional or deliberate. However, both involve the violation of the taboos against the use of holy names and referents.

In the cases of imprecation and malediction, the mode changes to cursing, since the intention is to call down divine or diabolical forces against the object or person concerned. These forms may be very serious, such as "May you rot in hell!" running through a whole gamut of ejaculations such as "God damn your eyes!" or "the Devil take it!" to the comparatively trivial as in "Blast it!" A quotation from Philip Stubbes's notable work *An Anatomie of Abuses* (1583) shows the overlapping of the categories: "Then fell she to sweare and teare, to curse and banne" (72). (*Ban* is an old word, now archaic, meaning "to curse.") A curious form is that of the "self-immolating oath," in which the speaker, not some outsider, becomes the focus. These range from rather quaint formulations such as "Strike me dead!" or "Well, blow me down!" to the nautical "Shiver me timbers!" or "I'll be buggered!" or "Well, I'm damned!"

As one moves down the modes from the higher to the lower, so the problematic and unstable category of obscenity emerges. This broadly involves the terms referring to the "lower" functions of defecation, copulation, references to the genitalia, and especially the taboos relating to incest. There is also a virtually indiscriminate range of usage, from the profoundly shocking to the comparatively trivial, from "Jesus fucking Christ!" to "piss off!" from "motherfucker" to "tit." What is paradoxical about obscenity is that although the forms of words are among the most insulting, they cannot be taken literally. Thus "God rot your bones!" could potentially come true, whereas "son of a bitch!" is a physical impossibility.

Historically a major shift has occurred in comparatively recent times, in that the "lower" physical faculties of copulation, defecation, and urination have come very much to the fore as referents in swearing. Though these may be deeply wounding, many of these forms of words, such as *son of a bitch, bugger off!, go take a flying fuck,* and so on deal with literal or practical impossibilities. In this respect they are obviously different in literal potential from the "high" variety. However, there is a recurring problem of interpretation and analysis concerning the degree to which any person (other than the swearer of an oath) can know how literally to interpret forms of swearing. Although there is invariably some difference in interpretation in any form of words, this divergence between literal and metaphorical meaning is greatest of all in the case of swearing. The point can be emphasized by comparing bizarre but established oaths in other languages, such as French "putain de merde!" (literally "whore of shit!") and Italian "porca Madonna!" (literally "the sow Madonna!").

In the realm of the physical there is the interestingly exact correlation between what one can do in public and what one can say, without causing a breach of the peace or incurring a lawsuit. Consider the following graphic scale of infractions:

Action	Acceptability	Word
farting	barely acceptable in public	*fart*
urination	barely acceptable in public	*piss*
defecation	totally unacceptable in public	*shit*
copulation	totally unacceptable in public	*fuck*

This degree of correlation between taboo action and related word is rare. The paradigm is a particular feature of Anglo-Saxon society from post-medieval times up to the recent past. But it is not universal, either historically or geographically. *Gropecuntlane* was a London street name recorded from the thirteenth century, later joined by *Pissynglane* and *Shitteborrowlane,* all so called for obvious reasons, prior to the conveniences of modern privacy. These English names have all been changed or euphemized, but in French society, for example, the equivalents of all the unacceptable words are in common use. George Santayana offered this brilliant insight into the binary division of the English vocabulary: "As the Latin languages are not composed of two diverse elements, as English is of Latin and German, so the Latin mind does not have two spheres of sentiment, one vulgar and the other sublime" (*Interpretations of Poetry and Religion* 1916, 131–32). Public evidence endorses but also questions the Freudian view in *Civilization and Its Discontents* that civilization depends on the repression of basic individual urges, provoking the decadent infractions of the Restoration and more recently the manifesto of the underground *Oz* magazine of 1970 endorsing "dope, rock 'n' roll, and fucking in the streets."

VARIETIES OF CONTENT

Given the diversity of speech communities, the range of content is remarkable for its protean diversity and poetic creativity, but also shocking in its ugliness and cruelty. Swearing draws upon very powerful but incongruous resonators. These include the following: the use of religious reinforcers (*by God!, the devil take it!*) and sacred references (*by my father's soul, on my mother's grave*); family origins (*son of a bitch, whoreson*); the attribution of various reprehensible behaviors and violations of moral codes, including treachery (*traitor, turncoat*), idleness (*bum, layabout*), promiscuity (*whore, slut*), dishonesty (*liar, cheat*), theft (*crook, swindler*), lack of courage or martial commitment (*coward, chicken*), sycophancy (*toady, brownnose*), meanness (*parsimonious, miser*), dirt (*filthy, scum*); social stigmas, such as illegitimacy (*bastard, whoreson*), perversion (*bugger, butt-fucker*); social conditions, such as poverty (*poor, miserable*); insulting names, demeaning labels, and unflattering comparisons, such as the animal (*cow, pig*), the sexual (*prick, tit*), the intellectual (*imbecile, ignoramus*), the excretory (*turd, shit*), the racist (*whitey, yid*), and the political (*fascist, nazi*).

Because nonformal swearing is essentially figurative and metaphorical, the categories often overlap and the same terms can be used in different areas. In addition, some terms are used simply as counters, such as *old* and *little,* in "the stupid old fart!" or "you silly little twit!" Similarly, "destinational phrases" like "piss off!" or "get lost!" cannot be taken literally. Furthermore, many other terms have become so generalized that they no longer have any relationship with their original literal sense: *punk* started its semantic history meaning "a prostitute," *bugger* meant "a heretic," while *harlot* meant "a rascal." The force of many vituperative terms thus depends on the context in which they are used, especially their acceptability or otherwise in a given speech community. The wide range of terms encompasses an extraordinary variety of attitudes, including the violent, the amusing, the shocking, the absurd, the casual, and even the impossible.

Historically, modes of swearing and societal taboos show quite different emphases at different stages and sectors of the same basic culture. It would seem, for example, that feces are universally used in oaths and insults, while sex is used in a culture-specific variety of ways, emphasizing, for example, incest in terms like *motherfucker* in some cultural groupings, adultery in *cornuto* in others, and a polymorphous variety in the application of the terms for the genitalia.

Swearing, however, is also strongly governed by fashion, so that at any given time the current modes are seldom taken literally. Few people now would stop to consider the protean uses of *hell* in, say, "hell's bells!," "the hell it is!," "to hell with it!," "I've got the hell in with him," "we drove like hell," and "we had a helluva good meal." The point is that these have become established idioms and so cannot be subjected to simple semantic analysis, anymore than can the phrase "come hell or high water." Even those who find *hell* an offensive term would have to agree that its infernal force is weakened or diluted in these phrases. It is usually only when a new mode is coming into fashion or an established mode is becoming anachronistic that it attracts comment. Thus when Daniel Defoe noted (in 1712) the ironic inappropriateness of certain oaths ("They call dogs the sons of whores and men the sons of bitches"), he was commenting on idioms long established. One should be aware that *bitch* then was still a word of force: Francis Grose commented in his slang dictionary *A Classical Dictionary of the Vulgar Tongue* (1785) that it was "the most offensive word that can be given to an English woman." Today, of course, it has lost much of its impact and can be applied to a man, a thing, or a situation.

Just as there are differences in the degree of provocation carried by certain swearwords, depending on one's culture, age, gender, and so on, so there are degrees of directness in swearing. These range from the directly personal ("You——!") or ("——you!"), through the personal by reference ("X is a——!"), the personal rejection: ("——off!"), to general expressions of anger, frustration, or annoyance ("——it!" or plain "——!"). Obviously the person addressed or within earshot will respond differently, with a verbal riposte, a physical gesture, or even a lawsuit. In the past, duels were fought over insults, some of them apparently very slight hints that impugned a person's or a family's honor.

In trying to reconstruct the verbal past, we are obviously dependent on written documents, which in the nature of things do not always reflect the contemporary oral situation in terms of currency or rarity of usage. The study of the language of swearing is frustrated by the obstacles of suppressed or garbled historical evidence, notably in uncertain etymologies (verbal origins of several of the major swearwords) and incomplete semantic histories. However, an analysis of origins is revealing in certain respects. It gives the lie to the popular misconception (perpetuated even in academic circles) that the "four-letter words" are exclusively Anglo-Saxon in origin. In fact only about half of them have these remote roots. Equally popular errors are found in "folk etymologies," appealing but fanciful explanations of word origins, such as deriving *crap* from Dr. Thomas Crapper and *bloody* from "by our lady!" Even though disproved, these myths remain surprisingly tenacious.

TABOOS

Since taboos are to be found wherever swearing exists, suppression of offensive words or euphemistic variations are perennial features. Thus *blooming* and even plain *b* were common substitutes when *bloody* was regarded as a serious swearword. Another strategy is to take refuge in what the great historian Edward Gibbon called "the decent obscurity of a learned language," namely classical alternatives like *defecation* and *copulation*. Garbled, mangled, or "minced" oaths are far more common than is generally realized. Some are reasonably obvious, such as *darned* and *durned* for *damned* and *tarnation* for *damnation*. *Gorblimey!* is an instance similar to *drat!* cited previously being a corruption of *God blind me!*, mainly London Cockney in use, dating from about 1870. As a response to Puritan prohibitions against profanity on the stage in the early seventeenth century, the name of God was omitted, leaving only an apostrophe, thus generating forms like *zounds!* (for "God's wounds!") and *snails!* (for "God's nails!"), gruesome memorials of the Crucifixion.

Taboos typically make themselves felt through substitutions, such as "the f-word" or "a four-letter word," which are transparent. But sometimes these occur in a covert fashion. Among several curious by-products of collective, and seemingly unconscious, censorship, there is the mysterious appearance of the word *donkey* surprisingly late in the history of the language, about 1785. The original and ancient term *ass* started to fall into disrepute through its uncomfortable phonetic proximity to *arse*. In bawdy poems Jonathan Swift and the Earl of Rochester had already rhymed *asses* with *passes*. And Francis Grose observed in his slang dictionary (1785): "A lady who affected to be extremely polite and modest would not say ass because it was indecent." It has remained displaced by *donkey* as the common term for the animal in British English, even though *ass* and *arse* have since diverged in pronunciation. In American English, of course, both words are pronounced with a short "a," which has had the effect of driving the sense of "donkey" out of use. Another instance is to be found in the relative absence of the word *cock* in earlier American parlance, and the substitution of various polite forms, such as *rooster* (a soporific euphemism that censors out any sexual suggestion), *faucet* for *cock* in the sense of "tap," and *roach,* the emasculated form of *cockroach*. However, in recent decades the taboo has been comprehensively broken, with *cocksucker* developing a vigorous currency.

Taboos often reveal divisions within a society, there being different conventions according to class, social position, sex, and age. In some societies, taboo terms may be uttered only by the priestly class (as in formal cursing or the uttering of an anathema), while in others they are the sole class prohibited from taboo utterances: it would obviously be most inappropriate, for example, for a priest to indulge in genital swearing. The relationship between class and swearing in England is fascinatingly complex. Broadly speaking, swearing has flourished most in the upper and lower or working classes, but not in the bourgeoisie or middle class. Queen Elizabeth I reportedly "swore like a man," while in medieval times foul language was designated as "cherles termes," or peasant talk.

Contrary to the norms in the West, swearing is not universal. According to a number of authorities, several substantial speech communities, including the American Indians, the Japanese, the Malayans, and most Polynesians do not swear. In several religions, such as Brahmanism, Judaism, and Islam, direct reference to the name of God is taboo. At the other extreme, some societies have curious modes of obligatory swearing. Donald F. Thompson showed, in his researches among the Australian aborigines in northern Queensland, that an elaborate etiquette of swearing existed among the tribes of the area, one based more on social position than content. A curious Chinese perspective is offered by Alasdair Milne in his study, *The Heart of the Dragon:*

> In some parts of China it was customary for a bride to curse her new in-laws and her husband-to-be for three days before the wedding. There was an established genre of cursing-songs, passed on between the girls of the villages and elaborated on by each new bride as she came near her wedding day. . . . But it was above all the future mother-in-law who bore the brunt of the curses. (1984, 67)

However, these cultures and their remarkable conventions stand outside the scope of this study.

The history of swearing clearly shows oscillations between periods of repression and counterbalancing reactions of license and excess. Thus the medieval period was marked by extraordinary freedom in the use of religious oaths, which authorities in the Renaissance sought to reduce and inhibit by various legal constraints and fines. The strict repression of the Puritan Commonwealth was followed by the extreme decadence of the Restoration, which in turn led to the restrained rational mode of the early eighteenth century, epitomized by the formidable Dr. Johnson. The censorship and widespread euphemism of the Victorian era have in turn given way to the increasing latitude of the twentieth century. Significantly, the United States has shown a long legacy of the Puritanism of the Pilgrim Fathers, which it has vigorously thrown off, especially in the period since the 1960s. Indeed, American English is now the variety showing the most innovation in swearing and foul language. However, within this speech community there has developed the censoring force of political correctness.

Yet within the global English speech communities, swearing and obscenity are not constant in their modes, styles, and referents. Some modes of swearing appear to be universal, while others are more specific to a culture. Within some speech communities, variants emerge over time on the basis of nationality, class, and gender. Swearing is taken more seriously in some periods than in others, even being raised at some stages of the culture to the verbal art form known as "flyting." This practice survives in a modified form as the ritual verbal dueling found on the streets of the United States, where it is known variously as "sounding," "signifying," and "playing the dozens." At other phases swearing is driven underground and is subject to fines and legal reprimands.

As English has become a world language with strongly defined regional varieties, so certain modes of swearing and matching taboos have emerged. To a large extent the character and nature of the founding populations have determined the style and the extent of swearing. Thus in America the strong Puritan elements in the Pilgrim Fathers and later Quaker immigration led to a generally reticent and disciplined mode of speech: the Quakers refuse to utter oaths of any kind, on principle. On the other hand, the founding convicts (so to speak) of Australia established a verbal environment in which swearing and underground criminal slang flourished. Furthermore, taboos are not constant across what has become a globally dispersed language. Thus the taboo against the use of *bitch* has diminished across the Atlantic, so that *son of a bitch* has always been more in vogue in American English than British English. Similarly, the taboo against *bloody* had no force in the Outback, so that the word was recognized as "the great Australian adjective" as far back as 1894. Yet modes of swearing are not clearly predictable: there is no obvious reason why *whoreson* has always been more confined to England, or that the same word, for example *bastard,* should have very different meaning and social impact in Britain, America, and Australia. In recent decades there has been much discussion over the extent of "the semantic derogation of women," that is, the predominance of negative female terms, and the related question of whether terms of female anatomy, such as *cunt* and *tit,* or animal terms like *bitch* and *cow,* have greater currency and potency than the equivalent male terms *prick* and *balls, pig* and *swine.*

Foul language, by its very nature, tends not to be used freely in written or printed form, so that survival of evidence is often haphazard. The lines below were written about 1790 in a satirical poem by St. G. Tucker called "The Discontented Student":

Our scholar every night
Thinks of his books, and of his bride by light . . .
"G—D—your books!" the testy father said,
"I'd not give—— for all you've read."

The last line suggests a first instance of the common coarse phrase "not give a fuck," otherwise first recorded about 1917. But the poem was first published only in 1977. Many of Robert Burns's bawdy works were also published after his death. The true historical extent of coarse language in private use is similarly difficult to determine. The correspondence of many modern authors has now been published: that of E.E. Cummings, Ernest Hemingway, William Faulkner, John Dos Passos, and F. Scott Fitzgerald reveals plenty of foul language, in some cases quite at variance with their published work. In the case of Philip Larkin, the racism that surfaced in his private letters caused a radical downgrading of his status as a poet. On the other hand, the correspondence of Charles Dickens, the Brontë sisters, Henry James, and other major Victorians is largely of the same register as their novels. The same is true of Samuel Johnson, yet the journals of his contemporaries Jonathan Swift and James Boswell are filled with colloquialism and profanity. Sadly, from the pens of Shakespeare and Chaucer nothing private has survived.

There is a time-honored difference between the "language of the street" and what is "fit to print." Yet the boundaries are always shifting and being tested. In the furor following George Bernard Shaw's sensational use of the word *bloody* in his play *Pygmalion* in 1914,

Shaw himself commented: "I don't know of anything more ridiculous than the refusal of some newspapers . . . to print the word 'bloody,' which is in common use as an expletive by four-fifths of the English nation, including many educated persons." Shaw was being slightly mischievous, as was Kenneth Tynan when he casually uttered the word *fuck* on B.B.C. television in 1965. These two instances have become notorious verbal milestones, but one should be aware that both Shaw and Tynan were men of the theater and considerable self-publicists. The same is true of many modern celebrities and media personalities, especially radio talk-show "shock jocks" and rappers. Swearing is also increasingly used as a political weapon to provoke outrage and gain publicity for a cause.

LEXICOGRAPHICAL STRATEGIES

Dictionaries have been put in a difficult situation in the face of modern laws against obscenity. For the past two centuries or so they have maintained a division of usage into the decent bourgeois standard and the less acceptable varieties of profanity. But this division has not always existed. All the most taboo words were recorded in the works of John Florio (1598) and Nathaniel Bailey (1721 and 1730). Samuel Johnson (1755) and the usually irrepressible Francis Grose (1785) showed varying degrees of censorship, as did the founder of American lexicography, Noah Webster (1806). Even the astoundingly comprehensive *Oxford English Dictionary* (1884–1928) omitted the two most taboo terms, *fuck* and *cunt,* though it found a place for *windfucker, twat,* and *bugger.* There was then the real possibility of prosecution for what was termed "obscene libel," yet this did not deter J.S. Farmer and W.E. Henley in their major work, *Slang and Its Analogues* (1890–1904). Even the landmark Third Edition of *Webster* (1961), which outraged many by its adoption of an oral standard of acceptability, did not feel secure enough from protests and boycotts to include both terms; nor, in 1963, did the *Dictionary of American Slang,* edited by Harold Wentworth and Stuart Berg Flexner. The *Penguin English Dictionary* (1965) was the first standard reference work published in this century to include all the "four-letter words," a euphemism that itself dates from 1934. However, slang dictionaries are currently showing a resurgence, with a variety of works appearing virtually on an annual basis and the *Random House Historical Dictionary of American Slang* (1994–) establishing a new standard of comprehensiveness.

To modern ears most swearwords are now usually "demystified" into mere forms of words. Yet they remain a major source of complaint in broadcasting. Statements are now made "under oath" in formal, for instance, legal proceedings, or in such necessary rituals of social and political continuity as taking an oath of allegiance. In the past, however, they were often invoked as required tests of loyalty to the current regime. Formal oaths have rigid formulas of words, as do curses, anathemas, and exorcisms. Thus the form of the wedding pledge in the *Book of Common Prayer* has become the archaic mode "I plight thee my troth" ("I pledge you my faith"). The more "informal" swearing becomes, the more the language becomes elastic, malleable, and flexible, generating forms like *absobloodylutely.* Consequently, idiomatic and grammatical complexity become remarkable features. Indeed, in some contexts word choice seems to be almost totally random and variable, as in "I couldn't give a damn/shit/fuck/two hoots." In other contexts word choice has to be very precise to be effective. Thus a condemnatory comment like "He's an obsequious little prick!" achieves its effect through the contrast of the high register *obsequious* with the low register *prick*, but if one were to substitute, say *penis* or *cock*, the impact would be lost. This instance illustrates an important point about linguistic usage peculiar to swearing; namely, that all synonyms in a given word-field do not function equally and interchangeably as swearwords.

Are there common phonetic features and alliterating formulas in swearing? Many of the most used swearing terms in English start with the letters "b" and "f," for reasons that are not easily explained. Could it be that what are termed in phonetics "bilabial plosives" (like "b") and "bilabial fricatives" (like "f") are the most satisfactory phonetic expressions of emotional release? The great Danish scholar Otto Jespersen noted alternatively, "a whole family of words with an initial *d*" (1962, 229). Alliteration plays a powerful role, possibly as a survival from flyting. It certainly figures largely in medieval swearing, essentially because of the dominance of the alliterative scheme in the poetics of the period. Rhyme is also apparent in some of the cruder exclamations in general currency, such as *hell's bells!*, *fuck a duck!*, and—imperfectly—*shit a brick!* and *stone the crows!* A similar form is *poppycock*, which actually originates in crude Low Dutch *pappa kak*, literally "soft shit."

The great diversity of style and content so apparent in the history of swearing makes its evolution difficult to encapsulate into a coherent framework. An unexpected source lies in the brilliant insight of the great Italian philosopher Giambattista Vico in *The New Science* (1712). In Vico's analysis, language evolves through three stages, being originally sacred, then poetic, and finally conventional (1948, 306–7). His evolutionary framework is highly germane to the history of swearing, which has followed the same pattern. It also points up the problem of knowing exactly what degree of literalism and seriousness is being invoked in a particular form of words, without an intimate knowledge of the period involved. Are the words sacred, poetic, or profane? Hamlet's furious denunciation of "marriage vows as false as dicer's [gambler's] oaths" (III iv 44–45) juxtaposes the two modes of vows and oaths memorably. Today swearing is highly indiscriminate in its references, drawing on a whole range of sources mentioned earlier, from the personal, sexual, and excretory to the religious and the political. In many ways this extreme diversity is a manifestation of the sociological concept of *anomie* or "normlessness," diagnosed by Émile Durkheim as the distinctive malaise of modern society in his study *Suicide* in 1897.

Questions are often asked about the future of swearing, more especially if there are any taboos left or anything sacred left to swear by. Robert Graves in his notable study *The Future of Swearing and Improper Language* (1936) took this view: "Of recent years in England there has been a decline of swearing and foul language, and this shows every sign of continuing indefinitely." Clearly, Graves was being slightly provocative when he opined that "I cannot believe that it has a future, at least, one worth setting besides its past." However, in Graves's defense, we should remember that the medieval English were so noted for their swearing that the French referred to them in the fifteenth century by the derogatory soubriquet of *les goddems* ("the goddams"). Contradicting Graves's slightly cavalier prediction, there has been a veritable explosion of swearing, and a wholesale violation of decorum in the past half century, especially since the 1960s, and notably in the United States. There are many reasons for this upsurge, but in itself it is nothing new, since history shows many instances of oscillations from puritanism to decadence. The modern English, following their medieval ancestors, are now termed *les fuckoffs* ("the fuckoffs") by the French of modern times.

Graves certainly had a point in stressing that swearing does have an illustrious past. The vigor, creativity, and exuberance exemplified in the vituperative oaths uttered by such notable Renaissance figures as Queen Elizabeth, William Dunbar, Walter Kennedy, and Sir David Lindsay have never been surpassed. The same is true of the astonishingly licentious obscenity given free reign in the verse by the Earl of Rochester, the most brilliant wit and most accomplished rake in the court of Charles II. There is likewise no modern equivalent of that bizarre encyclopedia of humorous obscenity, François Rabelais's *Gargantua and Pantagruel* (1533–1564). Reading the robust and inventive seventeenth-century translation of Thomas Urquhart and Peter Anthony Motteux, one wonders if adequate resources exist in the modern English vocabulary for a similar undertaking at the present.

In short, although we may think that we live in risqué or decadent times when profanity and obscenity are encountered so frequently in the street (and with increasingly monotonous regularity on the television and at the movies) the fact is that these boundaries of decorum were breached centuries ago. The unexpected impact of political correctness has obviously exercised a censoring influence and affected the choice of terms. Furthermore, there is no doubt that modern swearing, profanity, and foul language are characterized by a notable paucity of vocabulary and lack of invention. If the characters of Chaucer (who were created in religiously strict but comparatively uncensored times) or even those of Shakespeare (who was subjected to the censorship of the ill-named Master of the Revels) were to materialize among us now, we would surely be impressed by the remarkable power and range of their oaths, profanity, and foul language.

AN ENCYCLOPEDIA OF
Swearing

ABBREVIATIONS

Abbreviations in swearing are common, not for the usual reason of convenience, but because they provide a useful form of euphemism or disguise mechanism. They may be partial, as in *bug* for *bugger*, or use the initial letter as a code, as in "b" for *bloody*. Today they are common in forms like "the f-word," "effing," and so on. The practice has increased in print, where the taboos against the use of improper language were severely policed in the past.

Historically the practice can be traced back at least to Elizabethan times, in the form of **minced oaths**, discussed below. Some forms are no longer readily comprehensible. In their *Dictionary of Slang and Its Analogues* (1890–1904) Farmer and Henley have an odd entry under the heading *B.C.*:

> A young woman complained [to a magistrate] of having been abused by a woman who called her a B.C. On being asked the meaning, the young woman said that C meant "cat," but the B——, well, it was too shocking to utter, and the magistrate allowed her to whisper the word in his ear. It was a well-known word of sanguinary sound [sic]; but though B.C. was hardly a pretty epithet, yet his lordship could hardly grant a summons for libel against the person of whom complaint was made for using it.

This highly amusing Victorian anecdote (dated ca. 1888) is revealing, but frustrating now. It shows that the "sanguinary" word (*bloody*) was clearly taboo, as various contemporary authorities have stated. The other offending term (*cat*) carried an underground sense of "prostitute" from Elizabethan times until about 1910. (The sense has continued as *cathouse*, a slang term for "brothel" in both British and American English.) It now seems very incongruous that a word meaning "whore" could be uttered in court, but *bloody* could not. As a consequence, the abbreviation "B.C." became established in the legal profession for a person bringing a flimsy case for libel.

The *Oxford English Dictionary* entry for *bloody* notes that the word was regarded (ca. 1887) "by respectable people" as being "on a par with obscene or profane language, and usually printed in the newspapers (in police reports, etc.) as "b——y." As a consequence, the abbreviation "b" became established for several decades, especially as "b.f." for "bloody fool," from about 1925. The abbreviation probably did not assist the political party called the British Fabians (originally founded 1884) since they were jocularly referred to as "the B.F.s"

Laurence Sterne contrived a wonderfully absurd situation exploiting evasions of taboo language via abbreviation in his highly eccentric (and popular) novel *Tristram Shandy* (1760–1767). In Book VII, chapters 20–25, the carriage of two French nuns is mired in a bog, and it is only by uttering two unmentionable words that they can encourage their mules to pull them out. Sterne plays with the taboo and teases the reader by hinting that in "the two words ****** and ****** there is as much sustenance as if you gave [the mules] a peck of corn." There follow embarrassed whisperings between the nuns (which the reader cannot overhear), and it transpires that the two taboo terms are *bouger* (*bugger*) and *fouter* (*fucker*). However, the nuns ingeniously solve the problem by splitting the terms into two inoffensive halves, one nun uttering first half and the other the second:

Abbess.   {bou—bou—bou—
Margarita. {—ger—ger—ger

Sterne extracts the maximum humor from the situation by showing the reader in print format the disguise that the nuns contrive orally, so that the joke is transparent throughout. He goes further, wickedly adding the detail that "the old mule let a f–" ("let off a fart"). The use of the abbreviation for this natural animal function is a form of mock politeness, since the author did not have to add the embarrassing detail at all.

Although this fictional anecdote seems far-fetched, the artful solution arrived at by the nuns dramatizes the process of **disguise mechanisms** that in fact takes place within a speech community over time. Most euphemisms and disguise mechanisms are really a form of connivance. The use of asterisks or dashes is a transparent disguise or obvious evasion of the offending form. In his *Classical Dictionary of the Vulgar Tongue* (1785), Francis Grose resorted to the forms *c**t*, *a-se*, and *a—e*. Yet neither Nathaniel Bailey nor Dr. Johnson showed the same prissiness in their dictionaries of 1728 and 1755, respectively.

However, in time the abbreviated forms become entrenched as independent forms. The classic instance is the development of what are called **minced oaths**, in which the offending term has been removed. Thus the gruesome medieval oath *God's wounds!* was reduced ca. 1600 to plain *zounds!* by the excision of the name of God, while *drat!* is the survivor of the formula "God rot——." As the original serious import is lost, so the words take on new, independent, and trivial meanings. *Zounds* is now obsolete, while *drat* is mild and passé. The name *Jesus* also has very ancient forms of abbreviation, found in *Jis* from as far back as ca. 1528, and *Jeez* and *Gee* ca. 1900.

Generally speaking, the greater the "taboo violation," the larger the number of euphemistic abbreviations. Within the American provenance, the most powerful example lies in *motherfucker*, still most taboo to respectable people. Consequently, it has generated a great diversity of abbreviations, ranging from *M.F.*, *mo'-fo'*, *muh-fuh*, and the "purified" forms *mother*, *momma*, and *muther*, recorded as far back as 1975 by the humorist Irma Bombeck referring to unmanageable shopping trolleys as "these little mothers." However, an amazing earlier instance comes from Ezra Pound, who in 1948 wrote scabrously of "all them g.d.m.f. generals c.s. all of 'em fascists" (Canto LXXIV). This decodes into "goddam mother-fucking generals cocksuckers."

Another strategy of recent decades is to use the formula "the f- word" (from ca. 1973), "the "the n- word" (from ca. 1985), "the k- word" (from ca. 1985), and so on. These are not equally transparent, since they come from different speech-communities: the taboo words in question are *fuck, nigger,* and *kaffir,* respectively. The phonetic rendition of the initial letters is also used to generate other forms, such as the word *fuck* being abbreviated to *eff* (from ca. 1950), *effing* (from ca. 1929), and *eff off!* (from ca. 1958). Other manifestations are *HN* in Black American parlance for "house nigger," *Af* for *African* and *K* for *Kaffir* in South African slang. Abbreviations are also a feature of **ethnic insults,** found in *jap, chink, eyetie, paki,* and *yank.*

See also: Bloody; Disguise Mechanisms; Ethnic Insults; Minced Oaths; Motherfucker; Zounds.

Bibliography
Partridge, Eric. *A Dictionary of Slang and Unconventional English.* London: Routledge & Kegan Paul, 1970.

ABJURATION

Abjuration denotes the formal renunciation upon oath of previously held views, particularly the forswearing of heretical opinions. Deriving from Latin *abjurare,* "to deny," the term dates from about 1500 and was regrettably common in the volatile religious climate of the Reformation, but is now virtually obsolete.

See also: Recantation; Renegade.

AFFIDAVIT

A declaration made by a person under oath and signed before a person empowered to administer oaths. The word in Latin means "He/she declares on oath," from *affidare,* "to trust oneself," from *fidus,* "faithful." The dramatist Ben Jonson first used the term in the late sixteenth century. The form of an affidavit is standardized, and a form of words must be uttered in which the deponent declares that the statement is binding, in order for the document to be admissible in a court of law.

See also: Asseveration; Attestation.

ALIENS

Since xenophobia, or hatred of strangers, is a feature of most societies, terms for aliens tend to form a notable word stock in the vocabulary of swearing and vituperation. Various stereotypical behaviors are attributed to aliens. These include barbarism, savagery, sexual perversion, paganism, stupidity, lack of hygiene, dishonesty, unscrupulous business practices, strange clothes and eating habits, inarticulateness, and incompetence in using the speaker's language. These present various degrees of threat to the "home" culture, which stigmatizes outsiders accordingly. Thus terms like *macaroni, frog,* and *limey* derive from fairly trivial notions or myths about diet, whereas the derogatory use of *jew* in phrases like *to jew down,* meaning "to cheat," is a far more profound criticism.

The prime forces driving the early generation of xenophobic attitudes are religious and

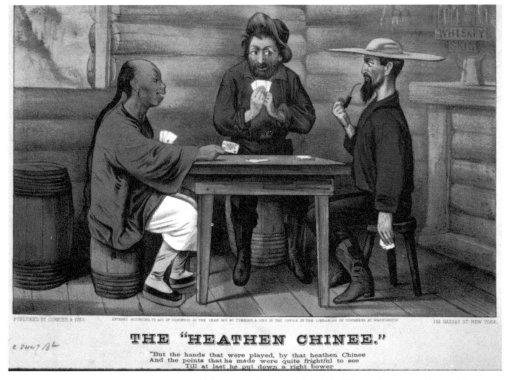

THE "HEATHEN CHINEE."

"But the hands that were played, by that heathen Chinee
And the points that he made were quite frightful to see
Till at last he put down a right bower

Like aliens everywhere, nineteenth-century Chinese immigrants to the United States became objects of fear, stereotyping, and disparaging epithets. An 1871 lithograph by Currier and Ives depicts the poker game in Bret Harte's famous poem, "The Heathen Chinee." The image endured for decades. *(Library of Congress, LC-USZC2-2563)*

martial rivalry. Thus the earliest hostile terms are *heathen,* derived from Anglo-Saxon *hæpen,* followed in medieval times by *infidel* and *paynim,* the old form of *pagan.* As the age of European exploration developed in subsequent centuries, a whole group of new terms emerged around 1600, namely *savage, alien, intruder, interloper, barbarian,* and *foreigner.*

See also: Barbarian; Blason Populaire; Ethnic Insults.

Bibliography
Allen, Irving Lewis. *The Language of Ethnic Conflict.* New York: Columbia University Press, 1983.

ALITERATION

Swearing employs various kinds of phonetic emphasis, notably alliteration (the repetition of a particular consonant) and rhyme (the repetition of a vowel sound). Historically, alliteration, not rhyme, was the staple poetic arrangement of words in Anglo-Saxon and much medieval poetry. Although it no longer has this literary status, alliteration continues to be a notable feature of swearing.

A number of Geoffrey Chaucer's contemporaries used the alliterative scheme, notably William Langland in his huge spiritual poem *Piers Plowman,* creating many powerful satirical effects: thus in the section on the Seven Deadly Sins, Gluttony "pissed in a potel [a large bottle] a *pater noster* while" (Passus B V l. 348). In a memorable condemnation of the corrupt clergy of his time, Chaucer refers to "a shitten shepherd" (*General Prologue* l. 504). This is the only use of a four-letter word in the *Prologue,* and in this context means "corrupt." In the *Chester Play* (ca. 1500) a character is denounced as "a shitten-arsed shrew" (l. 157), although by this time alliteration was generally passé in England. However, as the entry on **flyting** demonstrates, the alliterative tradition was still thriving in Scotland in the sixteenth century in vituperative contexts. *The Flyting of Dunbar and Kennedy* (1503) is liberally stocked with couplings such as "Fantastik fule" (l. 35), "Fals tratour, feyndis gett [bastard]" (l. 244), and "Suir swappit swanky, swynekeper for swatis," which translates very tamely into Modern English as: "Lazy great smart-arse, perpetual pig-keeper for small beer" (l. 77).

Alliteration has clearly atrophied as a literary feature in modern times. Furthermore, whereas previously alliteration covered almost the whole range of the alphabet, nowadays only certain letters are favored above others in swearing. Many of the most commonly used modern terms start with the letters "b," "d," and "f," found in *bloody, blooming, blasted, bastard* and *bugger, damn, darn, devil* and *drat, frigging, footling, fart, fuck* and its euphemistic variants. It is a speculation that the consonants "b" and "f," which are, respectively, bilabial plosives and bilabial fricatives, offer an effective vehicle for emotive release because of the physical release of air. As Otto Jespersen noted appositely of the others nearly a century ago: "Thus we have here a whole family of words with an initial *d,* allowing the speaker to begin as if he were going to say the prohibited word, and then turn off into more innocent channels" (1962, 229).

See also: Flyting; Rhyme.

Bibliography

Jespersen, Otto. *Growth and Structure of the English Language* (1905). Oxford: Blackwell, 1962.
Turville-Petre, Thorlac, ed. *Alliterative Poetry of the Later Middle Ages.* London: Routledge, 1989.

AMELIORATION. *See:* Semantic Changes and Trends.

ANATHEMA

The modern sense of *anathema,* namely "a detested person or thing," is nowhere near as powerful as the original meanings, which were "something accursed," "the curse of God," or "the ritual form of excommunication." These senses, all containing the notion of a curse, were common in the sixteenth and seventeenth centuries. Thus Francis Bacon wrote in his essay on Goodness (1625): "He wished to be an anathema to Christ," while John Donne explained in his *Biathanatos* (1619) that anathema was "utter damnation." Subsequently the word became much used in the sectarian vituperation of the Reformation, thus explaining the comment in the *OED* that "the weakening of the sense has accompanied the free use of *anathemas* as weapons of ecclesiastical rancour." The original sense is perhaps best preserved now in the verb *anathematize,* but in general terms the word shows the trend of **loss of intensity**.

See also: Curse and Cursing; Damn; Hell; Religious Oaths.

ANATOMICAL INSULTS

Today the use of names of parts of the body as lexical items in swearing and in strong language is so entrenched that it is natural to assume that it has always been so. (One is focusing here on the direct usage, such as "You prick!," and the personal insult by indirect reference, as in "major league asshole!") In fact, this is a comparatively recent convention, historically speaking, even though the words themselves have in some cases been in the language since ancient times. Generally, terms like *arse, arsehole/asshole* are recorded as personal vituperation only from the early decades of the twentieth century. According to the *Oxford English Dictionary* and the *Random House Historical Dictionary of American Slang,* the first recorded insulting applications of sexual terms are as follows: *prick* (1928), *cunt* (1929), *twat* (1929), and *tit* (1947). *Dick* is unique in its development, since the sense of "fool" is recorded from the sixteenth century, but that of "penis" only from about 1888.

See also: Ass/Arse; Cock; Cunt; Genitalia; Twat.

ANGLO-SAXON PERIOD

The Anglo-Saxon (or Old English) period is broadly defined as extending from the earliest written records (ca. 500) to 1100, when the social and linguistic effects of the Norman Conquest started to become apparent. This was the period when the Germanic peoples traditionally called the Angles, Saxons, and Jutes invaded and settled Britain. The literary materials that have survived are of a high moral tone, including the epic poem *Beowulf* (ca. 900), various heroic lays or narrative poems, saints' lives, the *Anglo-Saxon Chronicle,* the laws of some of the Saxon kings, charms, and gnomic verses or "wisdom literature." The sole exception lies in the miscellaneous **riddles**, some of which are certainly obscene.

Consequently what the Anglo-Saxon "language of the street" was like is not known. However, there are numerous instances of maxims that stress the importance of using language in a disciplined and responsible way, as in this quotation from *The Wanderer:* "A wise man must be patient, not over-passionate nor over-hasty in speech" (ll. 65–68). Such prescriptions stress the vital, indeed sacred link between words and deeds. The *Gnomic Verses* contain much proverbial material endorsing loyalty, such as "Faith shall be in an earl" (Gordon 1954, l. 314). Numerous warnings concern the punishment awaiting the man who breaks faith and is thus ostracized to the feared condition of exile, movingly depicted as the state of a solitary wanderer.

The epic, heroic, and moralizing qualities of the surviving Anglo-Saxon poetry limit the kind of swearing encountered there to **asseverations**. Oaths are reserved for the serious commitments of the warrior ethic. When Beowulf makes a public undertaking to the Danish King Hroðgar and his followers to rid them of the threat of the cannibalistic monster Grendel (ll. 636–38), his word is taken not merely as a statement of intent but as an article of faith. Perhaps most revealing is the point that when this extraordinary hero, slayer of monsters and a dragon, lies dying, Beowulf reflects modestly that he kept faith: "I did not pick treacherous quarrels, nor have I sworn unjustly any oaths" (ll. 2736–39). A revealing moral insight is also provided by the etymology of the word *warlock,* which is Anglo-Saxon *wærloga,* meaning "oath breaker." Black magic was thus seen as a form of false swearing. When the monster Grendel incapacitates the swords of the Danish warriors by evil spells, the term used is *forsworen,* "forsworn" (ll. 801–5).

Furthermore, the name of God is mentioned some thirty times in *Beowulf,* but always in a solemn fashion; it is never "taken in vain." Religious swearing, which was to become so common from the Middle English period onward, is a rarity. The typical heroic response in a moment of exasperation is dignified, cool, and measured, similar to the convention in the old western films. When Beowulf's sword breaks in his crucial confrontation with the dragon, he responds with philosophical dignity, not with an expletive typical of his modern equivalent (ll. 2680–87).

While one would expect Beowulf to be an ideal exemplar or role-model, the importance of the self-binding oath is an essential feature of the whole verbal culture. In the *Germania* (written ca. 55), the Roman historian Tacitus especially noted the prime importance accorded loyalty among the Germanic tribes, some of whom were to become the English. The poem *The Battle of Maldon,* based on an actual battle between the men of Essex and some marauding Vikings in 991, provides a striking ethical example. When the Vikings arrogantly ask for treasure, assuming that the people of Maldon will buy them off with *danegeld,* or protection money, rather than fight, the local leader Byrhtnoth gives them a savagely ironic answer: the Vikings can expect spears and swords for tribute (ll. 46–47). (The term *answer* is significant here, since this now mundane word derives from Anglo-Saxon *andswarian,* meaning literally "to swear against," to make a formal legal reply to a charge.) Byrhtnoth was an *ealdormann* or nobleman, but the acute sense of verbal honor is by no means limited to his class. As the poem unfolds every man in his station from Byrhtnoth, who is "Æþelredes eorl," King Ethelred's earl or viceroy, down the social hierarchy via Aescferth, the hostage from Northumbria, to the humble churl Dunnere, each man is given his dramatic moment to make good the English boast. It is some nobles, in fact, who treacherously flee when Byrhtnoth falls and the battle seems lost. They embody the ignominy Tacitus had noted a thousand years previously: "As for leaving a battle alive after your chief has fallen, *that* means lifelong infamy and shame" (chapter 14).

The Anglo-Saxon laws corroborate a similar underlying rigor and discipline in the matter of insults. (They also indicate that such language was indeed to be heard, even if it has not survived in the existing texts.) "If anyone in another's house calls a man a perjurer, or shamefully accosts him with insulting words, he is to pay a shilling to him who owns the house, and six shillings to him to whom he spoke that word, and to pay twelve shillings to the king." (Laws of Hlothhere and Eadric, kings of Kent [673–685?], no. 11). The Laws of Alfred (900) contain an interesting injunction: "Do not ever swear by the heathen gods." (This constraint comes some 300 years after Christianity was first brought to England.)

The end of the Anglo-Saxon period shows, however, a sad degeneration of the old traditions of verbal honor. As the land was invaded by the marauding Vikings, so a general demoralization set in. Wulfstan, Archbishop of York at the time of the worst Viking depredations, denounced a wholesale breaking of faith in his jeremiad *Sermo Lupi ad Anglos* (1025): "Many are forsworn, and grievously perjured, for pledges are broken over and over again" (ll. 87–88).

See also: Anglo-Saxon Terms; Asseveration; Charms; Riddles; Word Magic.

Bibliography

Alexander, Michael. *The Earliest English Poems.* Harmondsworth: Penguin, 1966.

————. *Old English Literature.* London: Macmillan, 1983.

Gordon, R.K. *Anglo-Saxon Poetry.* Everyman's Library. London: Dent, 1954.

Mitchell, Bruce. *An Invitation to Old English.* Oxford: Blackwell, 1995.

Tacitus, Cornelius. *Tacitus on Britain and Germany.* Trans. H. Mattingly. Harmondsworth: Penguin, 1964.

ANGLO-SAXON TERMS

In relation to the language of swearing, the epithet "Anglo-Saxon" is commonly used to mean "four-letter." This equation of the most powerful swearwords with the most ancient word-stock is strictly a misconception, at best a half-truth, although it continues to be found in both learned and popular usage. Thus on July 21, 1959, a U.S. federal judge, Frederick van Pelt Bryan, handed down a judgment in favor of *Lady Chatterley's Lover,* noting that "Four-letter Anglo-Saxon words are used with some frequency" (cited in Craig 1962, 158). More recently Ronald Pearsall observed: "The English language of sex is curt and Anglo-Saxon" (1969, 368). The reader will be aware of many similar instances in popular usage.

In fact what are now the most wounding and obscene terms in English swearing are first recorded long after the Anglo-Saxon period, which is broadly defined in historical terms as extending from the earliest written records to about 1100. It turns out that the true Anglo-Saxon terms are confined to common "lavatorial" words, while the strongest terms are of unknown origin and recorded much later. The following table sets out the field in terms of etymological origin and historical evolution:

Anglo-Saxon	Norman French	Unknown
shit	piss	cunt (ca. 1203)
turd	cock	fuck (ca. 1503)
arse		bum (ca. 1387)
fart		twat (ca.? 1660)
	crap (ca.? 1780)	

This tabulation demonstrates that "Anglo-Saxon" is used as a simplistic misnomer, the full picture being developed in the entry for **rude words**. All the terms listed in the table have their own entries, showing their etymological origins and semantic evolution, which are often quite complex.

See also: Anglo-Saxon Period; "Four-Letter" Words; Rude Words, Semantic Field of.

Bibliography

Craig, Alec. *The Banned Books of England.* London: Allen & Unwin, 1962.

Partridge, Eric. *Origins.* London: Routledge, 1958.

Pearsall, Ronald. *The Worm in the Bud: The World of Victorian Sexuality.* London: Weidenfeld and Nicolson, 1969.

ANIMAL TERMS

Animal terms figure notably in the history of swearing, although they were not a major feature of Anglo-Saxon literature. The major exception was *wulf*, used to refer to a cruel, rapacious, or evil person, often in the title "the Devil's wolf." Otherwise, the chosen animals themselves are not especially dangerous or repulsive, though some are poisonous, such as the snake, and others malodorous, such as the skunk and polecat. For some cultural reason the pig provides the richest verbal field, together with the variants *sow* and *swine*. (The same pattern is seen, interestingly, in the dominance of French *cochon* and German *schweinhund*.) *Swine* is the oldest term in the field, being recorded in Chaucer's richest swearing resource, the Wife of Bath, who condemns "Metellius, the foule cherl, the swyn" (*Prologue* l. 460). Unlike *sow*, *swine* continues to have resonance in swearing in the British Isles, especially among the older generation, while *pig* has become more a feature of U. S. swearing, having been especially fashionable among radical youth in the 1960s as an opprobrious term for the police.

Dogs also feature strongly in the field. *Dog* itself was much used in medieval times as a term of reproach, abuse, or contempt for what the *Oxford English Dictionary* calls "a worthless, despicable, surly or cowardly fellow." It is so recorded from about 1325, but the opprobrious sense died out in the nineteenth century. Cur and **bitch** are terms of such power that they have their own entries, as does **son of a bitch**, now well established in American English. Contemptuous terms for horses, such as *jade* and *hack,* have also lost currency and power.

In English parlance *rat* is a term of deep contempt, meaning essentially one who has betrayed a party, a close confidant, or a lover. The original uses, dating from the late eighteenth century, referred to political deserters, alluding to the behavior of rats leaving a sinking ship. The currency has continued to the present, but is now frequently applied to personal relationships. The English press generally referred to Princess Diana's former lover, Major James Hewitt, as "the love rat," while the tabloid *Sun* newspaper castigated a journalist who had accused a dead scientist of lying, filling its front page with the headline "You rat!" (July 22, 2003).

In the category of snakes, the oldest term is *worm*, memorably applied in 1402 to the ecclesiastical reformer, John Wycliffe: "Sith [since] that wickide worme, Wiclyf be his name, began to sow the seede of cisme [schism] in the erthe" (Friar Daw in *Political Poems* II, l. 45). *Viper* is similarly recorded in association with treachery from 1596, *snake* from 1593, and *reptile* from 1749.

Other terms include *cow, monkey, baboon, ape, skunk, polecat,* and *shrew*, which has for centuries been used in a metaphorical fashion of both a disreputable man and an unpleasant woman, long after the animal term ceased to be familiar. *Polecat* was originally applied contemptuously to courtesans and prostitutes, most strikingly in this first instance from Shakespeare's *Merry Wives of Windsor* (1597): "Out of my door, you witch, you rag, you baggage, polecat, you runnion [bitch], out! out!" (IV ii 195). It has since become generalized, as has *skunk*, first used metaphorically in 1840. The field shows a typical concentration of female terms.

See also: Bitch; Dogs; Feminization of Opprobrious Terms; Shrew; Son of a Bitch.

Bibliography

Leach, Edmund. "Anthropological Aspects of Language: Animal Categories and Verbal Abuse." In Lenneberg, Eric H. (ed.), *New Directions in the Study of Language*. Cambridge, MA: M.I.T. Press, 1964.

ASS/ARSE

These two terms are now phonetic variants, in American and British English respectively, of the ancient word for the backside, fundament, posteriors, or buttocks, animal or human. This part of the anatomy and its emissions are, of course, a fruitful area for vituperation. *Arse,* derived from late Anglo-Saxon *ears,* was in common use up to the eighteenth century, the medlar fruit having been called the *open-ears* from the earliest times. Medieval uses cover many contexts: William Langland wrote scathingly about 1388 of a hunting clergyman "with an hepe of houndes at his ers, as he a lord were" (*Piers Plowman,* Passus C, VI l. 161), and Chaucer used the word in risqué contexts in the *Canterbury Tales,* notably *The Summoner's Tale.* However, in John Wycliffe's contemporary translation of the Bible we find the graphic compound *arse-ropes* used for "intestines." Equally unexpected is this definition from a medieval medical text: "Emoroides ben fiue veynes whyche stretche out atte the arse" ("Hemorrhoids are five veins which stretch out at the arse," from John of Trevisa 1398).

Because of its general acceptability in medieval times, the term did not have any great personal animus. In subsequent demotic use it generated many compounds like *arse-crawl, arse-hole, ars-versy* (head over heels), and the insulting phrase "kiss my arse!" meaning "get lost!," found in late medieval drama and still current in American English, also compounded to *ass-kisser.* However, Francis Grose in his *Classical Dictionary of the Vulgar Tongue* (1785) euphemized the form of the word to *a-se,* an indication that it was becoming indelicate. During the same period the ancient word *ass* (meaning donkey) started to take on a pronunciation that was uncomfortably close to *arse.* In bawdy poems **Jonathan Swift** and the **Earl of Rochester** had already rhymed *asses* with *passes,* and Grose observed: "A lady who affected to be extremely polite and modest would not say ass because it was indecent." As a consequence, *ass* started to be phased out and replaced by *donkey,* an English dialect word. *Ass* (in the animal sense) had, of course, acquired associations of stupidity in uses like *silly ass* and *complete ass.* These associations continued in both varieties but were applied indiscriminately to both words, still found in British *stupid arse* and American *dumb ass.* However the two terms continued as homophones (words with the same sound but different meaning) in American pronunciation.

The *Oxford English Dictionary* took the view (in 1888) that *arse* was "obsolete in polite use," and that the phrase "ignorant ass" was "now disused in polite literature and speech." There is an amusingly disguised reference to *arsehole* in the august periodical *The Times Literary Supplement* (February 24, 1905), where a reviewer of *De Profundis* (Oscar Wilde's account of his term of imprisonment for sodomy) wrote: "It is impossible, except very occasionally, to look upon his testament as more than a literary feat. Not so, we find ourselves saying, are souls laid bare."

Although *ass* has continued on its route to obsolescence, *arse* regained its general currency in British English from the time of World War I. This included its use as a mild swearword in phrases like "You stupid Arse!" or expressions of contempt, such as "that arse Snooks." Today both *arse* and *ass* are in fairly common but impolite use, on both sides of the Atlantic, especially in the compounds *arsehole/asshole* and *arse-creeper/ ass-licker.* There is a remarkable anticipation of modern idiom in William Blake (1784):

"If I have not presented you with every character in the piece call me Arse—" (*Complete Poetry & Prose*, 451).

Both terms have also extended their sexual meanings in contemptuous terms for homosexuals, such as *arse bandit* and *ass-fuck*, but especially in the chauvinist phrase "a piece of ass," meaning a woman regarded as a sexual object. (There is an interesting anatomical association here with *tail*, which in Middle English could refer to both male and female genitalia, but was not used as a personal insult.) It would appear that *ass* is being increasingly used in British English, possibly to the point of becoming the dominant form. Hence the headline "Kick Ass, Tony!" (Mr. Blair, the Prime Minister) in the British tabloid *The Sun* in 2001. In Australian English *arse* is the exclusive form, but the main meaning is "effrontery" or "cheek."

See also: Anatomical Insults.

Bibliography
Lighter, Jonathan, ed. *Random House Historical Dictionary of American Slang*. New York: Random House, 1994–.
Partridge, Eric. *A Dictionary of Slang and Unconventional English*. London: Routledge & Kegan Paul, 1970.
Rawson, Hugh. *A Dictionary of Invective*. London: Hale, 1989.

ASSEVERATION

A solemn affirmation or emphatic assertion endorsing a particular view or the truth of a statement. It lacks, however, the formality of a sworn oath. Archbishop Thomas Cranmer wrote in 1564 of "such abominable and beastly asseverations as you ever heard." The term is now virtually obsolete.

See also: Attestation.

ATTESTATION

To *attest* is to bear witness or to testify under oath, while *attestation* is the process of so doing. Both terms, together with *testify, testament, testator, testimonial, testimony,* and many others, derive from Latin *testis,* "a witness," in turn related to Latin *stare,* "to stand," still surviving interestingly, in the *witness stand,* taking the *stand,* and so on.

See also: Asseveration.

AUSTRALIA

Of all the global varieties of English, the Australian is most noted for the liberal use of swearing and profane language. This is, no doubt, a reflection of the nature of the founding population, which was made up principally of 160,000 convicts, very unlike the Pilgrim Fathers of the United States. A mere half-century after the establishment of the penal colonies in Australia, H.W. Haygarth commented in now-familiar terms on Antipodean verbal fashions: "Profane swearing prevails throughout the interior of New South Wales to an extent hardly conceivable but by those who have actually witnessed it" (*Bush Life in Australia* 1848, cited in Hornadge 1980, 134). This remains the dominant characteristic of Australian English, but there are surprising anomalies.

It has been estimated that within two generations of the arrival of the First Fleet in Botany Bay (Sydney) in 1788 "a staggering 87 per cent of the Australian population were either convicts, ex-convicts or of convicts descent" (McCrum et al. 1986, 288). The convicts had a distinctive dialect or criminal argot called *flash,* a term that had been current in England from about 1700, and was defined by Francis Grose in his *Classical Dictionary of the Vulgar Tongue* (1785) as "the language used by thieves." The use of this dialect in Australia was commented on as early as 1793, while Edward Gibbon Wakefield, in his *Letter from Sydney* (1829), claimed that "terms of slang and flash are used from the gaols to the Viceroy's palace, not excepting the Bar and the Bench. No doubt [he prophesied] they will be considered quite parliamentary, as soon as we have a parliament" (cited in Hornadge 1980, 76).

The most common epithet in the dialect was *bloody,* which Grose also noted was "a favourite word used by thieves in swearing." Numerous observers and visitors to Australia subsequently commented on the extraordinary currency enjoyed by the word: Alexander Marjoribanks noted in his *Travels to New South Wales* (1847) that a bullock driver used the word twenty-seven times in an hour, extrapolating the instance to show that over fifty years the man would have used "this disgusting word no less than 18,200,000 times" (57–58). As the entry in the *Oxford English Dictionary* for *bloody* shows, the word was "in general colloquial use from the Restoration [1660] to ca. 1750," but then became increasingly stigmatized by respectable English people. However, in Australia the word was regarded quite differently, since as far back as August 18, 1894, the *Sydney Bulletin* claimed *bloody* as "the Australian adjective." The criminal provenance of the flash language also contributed the deadliest Australian insult, namely *bludger,* which originally meant a street bully or prostitute's pimp, but has become extended through army usage to mean a parasite, idler, skiver, or freeloader.

The Aborigines

This term is used uniquely of the original native population of Australia, who have suffered the common indignities of insult visited upon colonized native populations, notably by William Dampier, the English buccaneer, who described them in 1688, as "the miserablest people in the World . . . and setting aside their humane shape, they differ but little from Brutes" (1906, 350). The usual catalog of terms like *savage* and *barbarian* was current in the early accounts. Robert Hughes was the first historian to style them "the first Australians" (1987, 8).

Aborigine, deriving from the Latin phrase *ab origines,* meaning "from the beginning," has replaced the earlier term *aboriginal,* used by Charles Darwin in 1858. The people were originally termed *natives* or *blacks,* then stigmatized as *niggers,* a term that gained currency during the nineteenth century, and was in turn slowly replaced in the following century by the abbreviation *abo* and by *boong,* itself an aboriginal term. One of the earliest terms, now largely obsolete, is *myall,* an aboriginal word (pronounced "mile") meaning "stranger," originally applied to the colonists from about 1798, but then used by them to refer to "wild blacks," as opposed to the Aborigines. Curiously, *coon* was also borrowed from America, but "not extensively used by white Australians," though "sometimes used by Aborigines to describe other Aborigines of whom they disapprove" (Hornadge 1986, 136). These are the principal terms, as a quotation from M. Terry's *Sand and Sun* (1937) explains: "My word, we've got plenty of names for 'em too. Let's see. There's nigger, boong, coon, blackfellow, myall" (269).

Like most ethnic abbreviations used by outsiders, *abo* conveys both familiarity and contempt. As a sense of national pride and identity has been assumed by the community, so the term has become less acceptable. As G.A. Wilkes puts it in his *Dictionary of Australian Colloquialisms* (1990), *abo* is "not always intended as derogatory, but is increasingly taken to be so." The same is true of *boong,* which during World War II was taken over by whites and used generally, as in this glossary entry: "*Boong:* Any Asiatic or colored person; *Boongs with boots on:* Japanese" (Rohan Rivett, *Behind Bamboo* 1946, 395). The contentiousness of the term is partly dependent on the user: "On the eve of Aboriginal National Week, the Victorian Aboriginal community is divided in its reaction to the Premier, Mr. Hamer, referring to Aborigines as 'boongs' at a press conference last Friday" (*The Australian,* July 8, 1980). Developments in later decades show that *Aborigine* and *Aboriginal* are being reclaimed by the population.

Aborigines are of special interest to this study since they have in their own verbal culture a convention of compulsory insult. Donald F. Thompson showed, in his researches among the Australian Aborigines in northern Queensland, that an elaborate etiquette of swearing existed among the tribes of the area, based more on social position than content. Thompson found that except in the presence of certain relatives, "there is no restriction upon reference to the genitalia or the physical functions of reproduction, defecation, and micturition" (1935, 465). He also observed a clear distinction between "unorganized" and "organized" swearing. In the first category, swearing and obscenity fall under no sanction and are "used by both sexes in quarrels and taunts to goad an enemy to fight" (1935, 469). Thompson's alternative category (of "organized" or "licensed" swearing) is stranger, since it involves "swearing and obscenity that is not only permissible, but obligatory, between those who stand in certain relationships under the classificatory system" (1935, 469).

Opprobrious terms for foreigners are also common. The richest resource seems to be reserved for the Chinese and includes *chows, chinks, opium smokers, quangs, slants, slit-eyes, yellow bastards,* and for some odd reason *paddies* (normally used of the Irish), which in the past has caused especial offense among the target community. In addition, there is the common derogatory term for an Englishman, namely **pom**, dating from about 1912.

A Robust and Colorful Variety

The prophecy of Edward Gibbon Wakefield, cited earlier, that "terms of slang and flash . . . will be considered quite parliamentary" has been fulfilled. Parliamentary exchanges in Australia are often laced with highly insulting language, such as this from the House of Representatives in 1975:

Dr. R.T. Gun (Labour):   "Why don't you shut up, you great poofter?"
Mr. J.W. Bourchier (Liberal):   "Come round here, you little wop, and I'll fix you up."
                                      (cited in Hornadge 1980, 166)

Two other British terms with wide currency are *bastard* and *bugger.* G.A. Wilkes notes of the first that the variety of applications, ranging from "derogatory, but not suggesting illegitimacy" through to "compassionate" and "friendly affectionate" is "remarked on by overseas visitors." A former prime minister, Paul Keating, was quoted as saying: "I'm a bastard. But I'm a bastard who gets the mail through. And they appreciate that" (*Sunday Telegraph*, November 20, 1994). *Bugger* has a similar range, and is often found in *bugger all* and *burnt to buggery.*

Australian English is unusual in having the self-critical term *ocker*, a derisive nickname in use from the late 1960s for a rough and uncultivated Australian male, also for a person who exploits an exaggerated Australian nationalism. A surprisingly large lexical input derives from the Australian satirist and comedian Barry Humphries, originator of the stereotypical comic figure of Barry McKenzie in the satirical magazine *Private Eye* (1964–1973). Humphries created for this innocent abroad a comic compendium of idioms deriving from picturesque metaphors for his principal activities, namely urination (*drain the dragon* and *syphon the python*), vomiting (*technicolor yawn* or *liquid laugh down the great white telephone* or *chunder,* explained below), and defecation (*strangle a darkie*). Copulation is alluded to by humorously graphic (and uncomplicatedly chauvinist) figures of speech, such as *sink the sausage* and *spear the bearded clam;* or coy euphemisms, such as *to feature* or *exercise the ferret;* while *flog the lizard* or *jerking the gerkhin* are the preferred terms for masturbation. "Bazza" McKenzie avoids the obscenities and blasphemies of the coarser London set, his most powerful ejaculations being *stone the crows!, Jeez!, bloody oath,* or the ambivalent *bastard.* Humphries described McKenzie as "a pastiche figure" some of whose "standard" Australianisms are "a sop to Pommy readers" (1988, 134). But several have gained a considerable currency among readers and even institutional status in Australia. Thus the *Australian National Dictionary* (1988) lists *liquid laugh, technicolour yawn,* and *syphon the python*—all directly attributable to Humphries. *Chunder,* a general term for "to vomit" is probably derived from Chunder Loo, rhyming slang for "spew." Rhyming slang has a considerable currency in Australia, serving in part to disguise coarse terms, such as Edgar Britts for "shits"—that is, diarrhea.

As these features indicate, Australian English has several areas of surprising verbal reticence. For example, *oath* is widely used as a general-purpose euphemism. The curious phrase "my bloody oath" is recorded as far back as 1848, and the variant "my colonial oath" from 1859 (*Australian National Dictionary*). Both still enjoy vigorous currencies. Similarly, the expression "my word!" is a very common expression of emphatic agreement or endorsement, rather than one of surprise, as in British English. Two other euphemisms are survivals from earlier phases of British English. The first is *naughty* for sexual intercourse, as in "Until I met Thelma, I always thought sheilas [girls] had to be talked into a bit of naughty" (1959, cited in the *Australian National Dictionary*). Curiously, the use of both *naughty* and *naught* as clear sexual innuendo extend back to Elizabethan English, when a *naughty-house* was a brothel. In Shakespeare's *Richard III,* Gloucester makes a "man of the world" allusion to King Edward's notorious affair with Mistress Shore (I i 98–100). Other instances are to be found in *Troilus and Cressida* (IV ii 25, 32–33) and *Measure for Measure* (II i 75–76). These explicit senses have largely died out in British English, surviving only in the senses of "risqué, mildly indecent, or titillating." The other surprising Australian survival is *nasty* for the feminine genitals, found in Grose (1785): "a nasty name for a nasty thing." It also reappears in the phrase "dry as a nun's nasty" in the Barry McKenzie series (1988). Interestingly, *nasty* in the sense of "sexual intercourse" and *do the nasty* for "to copulate" are both recorded in American English from the 1930s.

The unconventional roots of Australian English are still apparent in a variety full of colorful and lively slang. Many terms are distinctive, such as *chromo* for "prostitute," *giggle house* for "lunatic asylum," *shirtlifter* for "male homosexual," and *frog* for "condom," as are the picturesque idioms, such as "ugly as a hatful of arseholes," "scarce as rocking-horse manure," and "to bang like a dunny [outdoor lavatory] door" for to copulate furiously. The general lack of restraint characterizing the variety is evident in the unusual policy adopted by the editors of the *Australian National Dictionary* (1988) concerning the omission of usage labels:

> It should be clear from the citations if a word is mainly colloquial or the slang of a particular group, and equally clear if it is for some reason taboo in some contexts. Labels like *coarse, colloq., derog.,* and *slang,* which tend unnecessarily to categorize, have therefore been omitted. (Preface, vii)

This policy makes the dictionary unique in modern times, when usage label "warnings" are now *de rigueur* in areas of sex, obscenity, blasphemy, and especially racist slurs. More surprisingly, the dictionary gives no such indication under the entries for *boong* and *chink,* which contain a number of savagely racist quotations. Furthermore, it simply omits *slant, opium smoker, slit-eyes, paddy,* even *bugger* and *flash.* The Australian sense of freedom to appropriate a variety of epithets is shown in this extraordinary outburst: "You rotten, bloody, poofter, commo, mongrel bastard!" (Wilkes 1985, 259).

See also: Bloody; Pom, Pommy.

Bibliography

Dampier, William. *Dampier's Voyages.* Edited by John Masefield. London: Grant Philips, 1906.

Hornadge, Bill. *The Australian Slanguage.* North Ryde, New South Wales: Cassell, 1980.

Hughes, Robert. *The Fatal Shore.* New York: Knopf, 1987.

Humphries, Barry. *The Complete Barry McKenzie.* London: Methuen, 1988.

McCrum, R., et al. *The Story of English.* London: Faber/B.B.C., 1986.

Ramson, W.S., ed. *The Australian National Dictionary.* Melbourne: Oxford University Press, 1988.

Thompson, Donald F. "The Joking Relationship and Organised Obscenity in North Queensland." *American Anthropologist* N.S. 37 (1935): 460–90.

Wilkes, G.A. *A Dictionary of Australian Colloquialisms.* 2nd ed. Sydney: Sydney University Press, 1985.

B

BARBARIAN

In modern times *barbarian* has fallen into relative disuse, but in previous centuries it carried great potency, as *savage* still does. Although the term is rooted in Barbary, the area of North Africa southwest of Egypt, the basic sense has always been "an uncivilized person." Furthermore, it has been used in a culturally exclusive fashion to stigmatize successively those who were "non-Hellene," then "non-Roman," then "non-Christian," then "one of a nation outside Italy," that is to say, foreigners whose language and customs differed from those of the speaker or writer. In addition to these xenophobic denotations, the word usually implied one who was an infidel and cruel, embodying *barbaric* behavior. The earliest citation in the *Oxford English Dictionary*, dated 1549 and in Scots dialect, is revealing in its admission of prejudice: "Euere nation reputis vthers nations to be barbarians" ("All nations regard others as barbarians").

Barbarian also has a linguistic aspect, being a Greek form of the Latin term *balbus*, meaning "stammering." It is thus rooted in demeaning attitudes toward foreign languages, seeking to belittle them by making them sound like infantile babbling through derisive imitation. A classic instance is *Hottentot*, which according to Olfert Dapper in his description of the people in 1670 "is a word meaning 'stutterer' or 'stammerer' on account of their clicking speech."

See also: Aliens; Hottentot; Xenophobia.

BASTARD

The early use of *bastard* was literal, alluding to the fact of illegitimacy, while the subsequent potency of the term as a swearword obviously derives from the stigma of the condition. Originally the word referred to a child of a nobleman born out of wedlock but acquiring some paternal status. It is derived from Old French *fils de bast*, interpreted alternatively as a "child born in a barn" or "child of the packsaddle." (Packsaddles were used as makeshift beds for men on the move, who might share their beds with local women.) The term is recorded as a surname, notably in the case of Geoffrey the Bastard Plantagenet, Chancellor of England from 1181–1189, and is still occasionally encountered. The most distinguished bastard in English history, William the Conqueror, was known by his disreputable title well into the Middle Ages. The term has subsequently generalized greatly in meaning and tone.

One of the most savage instances of personal insult occurs in John Ford's *Tis Pity She's a Whore* (1633) in the denunciation: "Thy corrupted bastard-bearing womb!" (IV iii). However, in Shakespeare's *King Lear* (ca. 1605), Edmund the Bastard famously interrogates this derogatory sense, asking: "Why bastard? wherefore base?"(I ii 6–9). François Rabelais attacked his critics in *Pantagruel* (1533): "As for you, little envious prigs, snarling bastards . . . go hang yourselves" (in the translation of 1737 by Peter A. Motteux). By the early nineteenth century it was being used as a word of reproach; in 1833, Charles Lamb, normally a mild-mannered person, complained in a letter about a sick child who had kept him awake: "The little bastard is gone."

Eric Partridge comments in his annotated edition of Grose's *Classical Dictionary of the Vulgar Tongue* (1931): "During the War [World War I] it was very frequent among British troops of all countries and most counties." He noted that even then it could express opprobrium, affection, and sympathy or simply be used in a neutral fashion. Class differences in usage were noted by Robert Graves in his study *The Future of Swearing:*

> Among the governed classes one of the unforgivable words of abuse is "bastard." . . . Whereas in the governing classes there is always far greater tolerance towards bastards, who often have noble or even royal blood in their veins, and who, under the courtesy title of "natural sons and daughters," have contributed largely to our ancestral splendours. (1936, 15)

In Modern English *bastard* has almost entirely lost its original literal sense, having been replaced by the euphemism "love child." Furthermore, in the global varieties of the language, *bastard* has acquired very different connotations: in American and British English the traditional virulence is still apparent in direct personalized usage, such as "you bastard!" It can also be used of something unpleasant or difficult, as in "This thing's a real bastard." However, in Australian English, where the wide currency of the term has been commented on since World War I, it is used with a considerable variety of tones. A previous prime minister, Gough Whitlam, said in an address to his party in 1974 that he did not mind his political opponents "calling me a bastard. . . . But I hope that you will not publicly call me a bastard as some bastards in the Caucus have" (*Sunday Telegraph,* June 9). Sir Edmund Hillary, co-conqueror of Mt. Everest in 1953, memorably announced the achievement: "We knocked the bastard off!" The term can express compassion ("the poor bastard") or even affection ("he's a good bastard").

Bibliography
Graves, Robert. *The Future of Swearing.* London: Kegan Paul, Trubner, 1936.
Rawson, Hugh. *A Dictionary of Invective.* London: Robert Hale, 1989.
Wilkes, G.A. *A Dictionary of Australian Colloquialisms.* Sydney: Sydney University Press, 1990.

BAWDY

Bawdy, meaning "naughty, sexually suggestive or obscene talk or behavior," derives from *bawd,* a medieval term for a procurer, later a procuress of prostitutes. The term, recorded from the early sixteenth century, is essentially rooted in the underworld and its coded speech, *double-entendres* or sexual puns, current in *bawdy houses* or brothels. Hawkers of indecent literature were then termed *bawdy baskets*, while a *bawdy banquet* meant "whoremongering." *Bawdry* was an earlier, now obsolete relative, defined by Dr. Johnson (1755) as "Obscenity; unchaste language." Previously Roger Ascham had criticized Malory's *Morte Darthur* as containing "open manslaughter and bold bawdry."

The general term for this bawdy underground language, which thrived in Elizabethan times and was surprisingly elaborate, was *cant.* One of the first guides to cant, Robert Greene's racy *A Notable Discovery of Coosnage* (1591), glosses various key terms in this fashion:

The bawd, if it be a woman, *a pander*
The bawd, if it be a man, *an apple-squire*
The whore, *a commodity*
The whore-house, *a trugging-place.*
(in Salgado 1972, 176)

Cant has survived, but it now has a quite different meaning, namely "hypocritically self-righteous speech or pious platitudes." Although *bawdy* has retained its original meaning, the term is becoming obsolescent.

See also: Dictionaries.

Bibliography

Salgado, Gamini, ed. *Cony-Catchers and Bawdy Baskets.* Harmondsworth: Penguin, 1972.

BEGGAR

The condition of poverty is generally viewed, in the West at any rate, with a mixture of contempt and sympathy. *Beggar* has shifted in meaning over time, in a fashion similar to *bastard,* from being a social description, recorded from the early thirteenth century, to a general emotive term. As a consequence of natural disasters, pandemics, and famines, medieval society had a great mass of destitute people reduced to begging. With the subsequent "enclosure," or buying up of common land (previously accessible to all), this number greatly increased. However, in Elizabethan times there emerged a less genuine underclass consisting of idlers and confidence tricksters, "a vast army of wandering parasites" (Salgado 1972, 140). Hence the term *beggar* (which probably derives from a mendicant or begging religious order called the Beghards) changed from being a literal description to a term of reproach. Those who were physically fit but work-shy and often aggressive in their manner were called *sturdy beggars,* a term recorded from 1538. The social problem they embodied is starkly alluded to in Act 39 of Queen Elizabeth (1597): "For the suppressing of rogues, vagabonds and sturdy beggars."

Beggar is recorded as a term of contempt from about 1300 and is so used in Shakespeare in *Richard III* (1592) in a reference to "a beggarly denier [small coin]" (I ii 253). The word became quite common as a mild insult in phrases like "the cheeky beggar!" in Victorian terms, and could even be used playfully and familiarly, as in Thomas Hughes's famous novel *Tom Brown's School Days* (1857): "You're an uncommon good-hearted little beggar!" (Chapter 1). The modern equivalent is "you lucky beggar!" These usages have had little currency outside British English (being unrecorded in American and Australian dictionaries of slang).

See also: Bum; Poverty.

Bibliography
Salgado, Gamini, ed. *Cony-Catchers and Bawdy Baskets.* Harmondsworth: Penguin, 1972.

BERK

An exclusively British slang term for a fool or stupid person. It now carries little impact (like English *twit* or *wally*) and thus is usually reinforced by the adjective *stupid.* However its origins in Cockney rhyming slang were far more insulting, for in this coded language *berk* is the abbreviated form of *Berkeley Hunt,* rhyming with *cunt.*

See also: Rhyming Slang; Stupidity.

BIBLE

The Bible is the central authority enshrining prohibitions against swearing, but it is also a storehouse of curses and strong language, which has attracted bowdlerism. Biblical injunctions against swearing are frequent and punitive, especially in the Old Testament. The third commandment (Exodus 20:7) is quite explicit: "Thou shalt not take the name of the Lord thy God in vain, for the Lord will not hold him guiltless that taketh his name in vain." Equally explicit is the prescription in Leviticus, chapter 24, where a young man has "blasphemed the name of the LORD and cursed":

13. And the Lord spake unto Moses and saying,
14. Bring forth him that hath cursed . . . and let all that heard him lay their hands upon his head, and let all the congregation stone him.
15. And thou shall speak unto the children of Israel, saying, whoever curseth his God shall bear his sin.
16. And he that blasphemeth the name of the LORD, he shall surely be put to death, and all the congregation shall certainly stone him: as well as the stranger as he that is born in the land, when he blasphemeth the name of the LORD, shall be put to death.

This injunction clearly gives divine sanction to the death penalty for blasphemy, even placing an obligation on witnesses to take action. The text formed the basis for many stringent and punitive responses to blasphemy and profanity from the Middle Ages to the Renaissance.

However, the seminal New Testament text, Christ's Sermon on the Mount (Matthew, chapter 5), advocates a less vengeful attitude toward swearing as well as other aspects of human sinfulness. Nevertheless, the prohibition is very clear:

34. But I say unto you, Swear not at all; neither by Heaven: for it is God's throne:
35. Nor by earth: for it is his footstool: neither by Jerusalem; for it is the city of the great King.
36. Neither shalt thou swear by thy head, for thou canst not make one hair white or black.
37. But let your communication be, Yea, yea; Nay, nay: for whatsoever is more than these cometh of evil.

This remarkable text advocates a total ban on swearing, making no distinction between blasphemy in its most extreme sense, the use of the Lord's name, and less heinous asseverations. Significantly, no punishments are prescribed. The ban has been put into practice only by one Christian sect, the Quakers.

Modern attitudes toward swearing, even among people who are not religious, tend to be divided between Old Testament disapproval and New Testament acceptance. Most would regard a complete ban on swearing as being unrealistic. The Bible is also a source of strong language. This is especially apparent of the older translations, such as those by Wycliffe (1380), Tyndale (1535), and the King James Version (1611), produced at a time when robust language was not considered inappropriate in Holy Writ and before modern taboos had set in.

Examples from Wycliffe's Version include the following:

Luke 11:27: "Blessed be the teetis which thou hast sokun [sucked]."

Examples from the King James Version include the following:

I Kings 14:10 and II Kings 9:8: "I will cut off . . . him that pisseth against the wall."
II Kings 18:27 and Isaiah 36:12: "they may eat their own dung and drink their own piss with you?"

See also: Bowdlerization; Quakers and Shakers; Webster and His Dictionaries.

BILLINGSGATE

Billingsgate was the site of a noted London fish market of which there are records from about 1250. The name became especially associated from as far back as 1652 with the coarse and scolding language of the fishwives who worked there, when Nicholas Culpeper alluded ironically to "down-right Billingsgate Rhetoric." Nathaniel Bailey defined *Billingsgate* in his Dictionary of 1721 as "a scolding impudent Slut," while John Wesley used the traditional sense in the phrase "low Billingsgate invectives" (*Works* 1750). The term has an exclusively

The word *billingsgate* (meaning coarse, abusive language) comes from an eponymous market in London. The fishwives who worked there in the seventeenth century were known for their crude invectives. (*Graphic Works of George Cruikshank*, Richard A. Vogler, Dover Publications)

British provenance, but is seldom encountered nowadays. The fish market was moved to Docklands in 1982.

See also: Bywords of Swearing; Fishwife; Women, Swearing in.

BITCH

Bitch has the longest history among animal terms as an insult, extending from the fourteenth century to the present, during which time it has steadily lost force through generalization. Although the etymology lies in late Old English *bicche,* a female dog, the word was not used demeaningly in the earliest period of the language, as the cognate Old Norse

23

term *bikkja* was. (The same pattern applies to other animal terms of abuse in Anglo-Saxon.) The early applications were to a promiscuous or sensual woman, a metaphorical extension of the behavior of a bitch in heat. Herein lies the original point of the powerful insult *son of a bitch,* found as *biche sone* ca. 1330 in *Arthur and Merlin* (l. 333), while in a spirited exchange in the *Chester Play* (ca. 1400) a character demands: "Whom callest thou queine, skabde bitch?" ("Who are you calling a whore, you miserable bitch?") (l. 181). However, in a contemporary reference in Chaucer's *Pardoner's Tale,* during a denunciation of gambling, dice are referred to as "the bicched bones" (l. 656). Henry Brinklow, a savage polemicist of the Reformation, referred sarcastically to his Catholic opponents in 1542 as being "as chast as a sawt bitch," or "as pure as a randy bitch" (*The Complaynt of Roderick Mors,* xxiv, 63).

Male application is not exclusively modern, being recorded from about 1500. Perhaps the most arresting instance occurs in Thomas Hobbes's translation of the *Odyssey* (1675): "Ulysses looking sourly answered: 'You bitch'" (Book xviii, l. 310). However, the term could be used with considerable flexibility; in *Tom Jones* (1749), Fielding has the genial comment: "I can tell you landlord is a vast comical bitch." (Book xvii, chapter 3). Although Farmer and Henley commented in their *Slang and Its Analogues* (1890–1904) that the opprobrious application to a man "has long since passed out of decent usage," it has again became fashionable in recent decades.

During the eighteenth century the virulent female sense became dominant. Thus, Francis Grose noted in his *Classical Dictionary of the Vulgar Tongue* (1785) that "the most offensive appellation that can be given to an English woman, even more provoking than that of whore, as may be gathered from the regular Billingsgate or St. Giles's answer—'I may be a whore, but can't be a bitch.'" Dr. Johnson (1755) quoted a very modern idiom from Dr. John Arbuthnot's *History of John Bull* (1712): The principal character has "an extravagant bitch of a wife" (chapter 9). The growth of the insulting sense drove the literal sense of *bitch* out of currency, resulting in various euphemistic formations, such as *doggess, lady dog, she dog,* and *puppy's mother.* Mrs. Piozzi recounted Dr. Johnson's anecdote: "I did not respect my mother, though I loved her; and one day, when in anger she called me a puppy, I asked her if she knew what they called a puppy's mother" (*Anecdotes of the Late Samuel Johnson,* 1786).

Today the term can be used as a wounding personal insult in both British and American English, but is less prominent in Australian and other global varieties. The overall semantic trend in modern English has been generalization, since it can also be applied to a man, to a difficult situation or a complaint, and used as a verb meaning "to complain or criticize." In American slang a "shift to opposite" is also apparent in that *bitching* and *bitchin'* can be used to mean "very, wonderful or excellent," a sense recorded from about 1957.

See also: Animal Terms; Dogs; Shrew; Son of a Bitch.

Bibliography

Lighter, Jonathon, ed. *Random House Historical Dictionary of American Slang.* New York: Random House, 1994–.

Partridge, Eric. *A Dictionary of Slang and Unconventional English.* London: Routledge & Kegan Paul, 1970.

THE TWO PLATFORMS

Every **RADICAL** in Congress **VOTED** for **NEGRO SUFFRAGE**. Every **RADICAL** in the Pennsylvania Senate **VOTED** for **NEGRO SUFFRAGE**. **STEVENS, FORNEY & CAMERON** are for **NEGRO SUFFRAGE**; they are all Candidates for the **UNITED STATES SENATE**. **NO RADICAL NEWSPAPER OPPOSES NEGRO SUFFRAGE**. **GEARY** said in a Speech, at Harrisburg, 11th of August, 1866—"**THERE CAN BE NO POSSIBLE OBJECTION TO NEGRO SUFFRAGE**."

CLYMER'S
Platform is for the White Man.

GEARY'S
Platform is for the Negro.

READ THE PLATFORMS

CONGRESS says, **THE NEGRO MUST BE ALLOWED TO VOTE, OR THE STATES BE PUNISHED**.
[POST THIS UP.]

No group of Americans has been more denigrated by ethnic slur than blacks. In this poster from the 1866 Pennsylvania gubernatorial campaign, the image of a thoughtful young white man symbolizes the candidate's white-supremacist platform, while the caricature of a black man represents his opponent's "Negro suffrage" platform. *(Library of Congress, LC-USZ62-32498)*

BLACKS

Given the cultural histories of the dominant English-speaking communities, black people have consistently been seen as outsiders. Although initially perceived as exotic, they have been subject to various kinds of negative stereotyping, deriving from the roles in which they have been variously placed, as barbarians, heathens, warriors, mercenaries, colonial subjects, and slaves. The assumption that all blacks are the same, although they have major differences in culture and religion, let alone pigmentation, reinforces these stereotypes, as does the word-field. Virtually without exception, the major literary treatments of blacks focus on their status as outsiders or their problems of identity. The religious conflicts of the Crusades and the Moorish invasion of Europe clearly served to intensify these negative roles. However, the early terms in the word field, such as *ethiop* and *blackamoor,* suggest an exotic, even romantic quality. It was only from about 1800 that words such as **nigger, kaffir, hottentot**, and **coon**, which were originally only mildly insulting, started to acquire such animus and force that they have become genuinely taboo. In recent decades there has been a concerted reclamation of these stigmatizing terms and a reassertion of the positive qualities of *black*.

Although *black* is an Anglo-Saxon term, it was not used demographically. Charles II was described in "wanted" posters as "a tall black man, over two yards high"—a reference to his hair color. Furthermore, all the word's modern negative associations of evil, wicked, portentous, malign, and so on are recorded later, from the sixteenth century. The earliest use of *black* to refer to "a black person" dates from only about 1625. In the American context the source term *African* had an early currency in New England, and was widely used in the United States in the nineteenth century, as was the compound *African-American*. The latter was resuscitated by Black Americans as the preferred term from the late 1960s.

An early European name for Africa was *Ethiopia:* in the first English atlas to show Africa, John Speed's *The Prospect of the World* (1627), the continent is called "Aethiopia" and the Atlantic is termed "The Aethiopian Ocean." *Ethiop,* deriving from Greek *æthiopos* meaning "burnt face," had been used by John Wycliffe in his Bible of 1382: "The Ethiopian cannot change his skin" (Jeremiah 13:23). It survived, mainly as a euphemism, well into the nineteenth century: "There are [in London] 50 ethiopian minstrels," wrote Henry Mayhew in *London Labour and the London Poor* (1852, III, 190). He was referring to "black-face" minstrels.

John Speed also introduced the more enduring term *Colored* in his curiously titled *Theatre of the Empire of Great Britaine* (1611), describing "their coloured countenances and their curled hair" (xxv, 49). The term was to have a long currency in America as a euphemism for *black,* institutionalized in the form of the N.A.A.C.P. (National Association for the Advancement of Colored People), founded in 1909 by white Americans. The name has been kept, despite the preferences for *African-American* or *Black* in recent decades, as a continuing political reminder of the status of black people.

Moor, dating from the fourteenth century as a consequence of the religious wars against the heathen in North Africa and the Middle East, referred to dark-skinned people, often Muslims, originally from Mauritania, but was not originally a critical or hostile term. The first element of the related word *blackamoor,* which dates from the sixteenth century, is one of the first uses of *black* to refer to a person of African descent. Andrew Boorde in his *Introduction to Knowledge* (1547) noted that "there be whyte mores and black moors" (chapter xxxvi). According to the Shakespearean scholar Philip Brockbank, "The black or tawny soldier-hero was a figure in festivals [in London] long before he reached the Elizabethan stage. . . . These Moorish shows were resplendent, soldierly and sensual" (1989, 200). A similar sense of exotic power is found in the earlier martial portraits of Lycurgus and Emetrius in Chaucer's *Knight's Tale* (ll. 2129–84).

The plays of Christopher Marlowe (1564–1593) and Shakespeare (1564–1616) provide an illuminating range of these exotic stereotypes. The barbaric hero of Marlowe's *Tamburlane the Great* (ca. 1587), who immodestly styled himself "the Scourge of God and Terror of the World," was historically a Scythian or Tartar warlord, but given the inexact geographical notions of the time, would be simply regarded as a foreigner of color. Aaron the Moor, the villain of the early Shakespearean tragedy *Titus Andronicus* (1592), is presented as a total outsider, showing exultant villainy, diabolical humor, and "motiveless malignity," in the phrase that Coleridge applied to Iago. Aaron's alienation is racial, social, and psychological. The Romans speak of his "satanic" blackness and of the "devil" child he has fathered on

Tamora, the Queen of the Goths. He features in the only contemporary depiction of a Shakespeare play. In *The Merchant of Venice* (1596) the Prince of Morocco is a contrasting vignette role, an understudy for Othello. Presenting himself in the role of suitor to Portia after traversing "the Hyrcanian deserts and the vasty wilds of wide Arabia," Morocco is proud but alludes defensively, albeit poetically, to his color:

Mislike me not for my complexion,
The shadow'd livery of the burnish'd sun
(II i 1–2).

When he picks the wrong casket, he is distraught, exclaiming "O hell!," but Portia is openly relieved: "Let all of his complexion choose me so" (II vi 76–77).

Othello (1604) is the classic study in racial stereotyping with tragic consequences. Styled as "The Moor of Venice," the hero is a double cultural outsider, possibly based on Leo Africanus, a scholarly North African Arab whose *History and Description of Africa* Shakespeare evidently drew on. Throughout the play Othello is called "the Moor," or simply "Moor." The contemporary English view of Italy as a den of vice and deviousness is discussed further in the entry for **Italians**. Like the Prince of Morocco, Othello is open about coming from an alien and barbarous locale, peopled by "the Cannibals that each other eat, / The anthropophagi" (I iii 143–44). These stereotypes and myths have been the subject of research by Hall (1995), Loomba (2002), Hadfield (2003), and others. This "otherness" attracts Desdemona, but is exploited cynically and destructively by the "demi-devil" Iago, who dismisses the union as that between "an erring barbarian and a supersubtle Venetian" (I iii 362–63). Iago consistently uses and even thinks in stereotypes, claiming "these Moors are changeable in their wills" (I iii 350), then conceding that "the Moor . . . is of a constant, loving, noble nature," then switching to the opposing view of the sexually potent, dangerous predator: "I do suspect that the lusty Moor / Hath leapt into my seat" [i.e. cuckolded me] (II i 301, 307–8). He rouses Brabantio, Desdemona's father, in crude agricultural terms: "an old black ram is tupping your white ewe" (I i 88–89). Other stereotyping references are "the thicklips" (I i 66), similar to "the thicklipped," used of Aaron the Moor in *Titus Andronicus* (IV ii 175) and still surviving in American English.

The special horror of Othello's tragedy is that as Iago torments him with the suspicion of his wife's infidelity, he becomes so enraged that he starts to conform to the stereotype of the barbarian and the savage. Samuel Taylor Coleridge put the case with amazing crudity in 1848: "A similar error has turned Othello into a rank, wooly-pated, thick-lipped nigger" (*Essays* I, 64). Othello's furious threat "I will chop her into messes . . . Cuckold me!" (IV i 211) possibly implies cannibalism, since *messes* means "gobbets," echoed in *King Lear* in relation to "the barbarous Scythian" (I i 119–20). Likewise, the theme of witchcraft and magic returns disturbingly, from Brabantio's original accusations (I ii 65, I iii 64), leading to Othello's denial (I iii 169), but resurfacing in the nature of the handkerchief, the crucial evidence. Originally an innocent love token, it becomes an object of sorcery: "'Tis true, there's magic in the web of it." (III iv 68–73). Its making incorporates *mummy*, a liquor supposedly derived from embalmed bodies (used only here and in *Macbeth* IV i 23). The final act is full of polarized images. Othello speaks of Desdemona's skin as "whiter than snow / And smooth as monumental alabaster" (V ii 4–5), while Emilia is more outspoken: "The more angel she / And thou the blacker devil" (V ii 131). Othello's theatrical and problematic suicide is a final re-enactment of a brutal "service" to the state, when another outsider, "a malignant and a turbaned Turk," beat a Venetian and criticized Venice, whereupon

I took by the throat the uncircumcised dog,
And smote him thus. [stabs himself]
(V ii 344–45)

Part of Othello's "strange eventful history" is being "sold to slavery" (I iii 138). Although *slave* is rooted in *slav*, during the seventeenth century the term came to connote a black. Furthermore, slavery was increasingly regarded as an acceptable practice in Britain and its colonies, and in Restoration times it became quite fashionable to own Blackamoor slaves. It seems that the Quakers were the first religious group to object to slavery, in 1741. Socially there are some signs of genuine affection and attraction, although patronizing attitudes abound, and subsequent references are increasingly to black servants and slaves. Samuel Pepys, a considerable flirt, wrote affectionately on January 23, 1667, of "Mrs. Hall, which is my little Roman-nose black girl, that is mighty pretty," while John Aubrey noted that Sir William Davenant "got a terrible clap of a Black handsome wench" and hints at a liaison between John Selden and "my Lady's Shee Blackamore." Generally speaking, it is only from the eighteenth century that words like **nigger** start to be used consistently as expressions of contempt.

Within the American provenance, by far the greatest lexicon of nicknames and ethnic slurs relates to blacks. In his major study, *The Language of Ethnic Conflict* (1983), Irving Lewis Allen lists some 240 such terms, arranged under eleven headings. These are the name *Negro* and its modifications (e.g., *nigger*); *black* and its modifications (e.g., *black fellow*); other color allusions (e.g., *blue*—also found in Francis Grose's dictionary of 1785); ironic color allusions (e.g., *spook*); allusions to physical differences (e.g., *burr-head*); given personal names (e.g., *Leroy*); occupational stereotypes (e.g., *cotton picker*); allusions to African origin (e.g., *zulu*); other cultural allusions (e.g., *jim crow*); animal metaphors (e.g., *jungle bunny*); stereotypes of low intelligence (e.g., *rock*); status diminution (e.g., *boy*).

The reclamation of *Black* as a positive and unifying term was part of the program of Black Consciousness during the 1960s (although the formulation originally referred to a religious movement in Jamaica in the 1930s). The movement generated the American semantic correlatives *Black Power* (1966), *Black Panther* (1965), and *Black Caucus* (1967), recorded in this encounter; "When I tried to get into the black caucus, they said, 'No peckerwoods allowed in here, Sonny'" (*New York Times*, September 7, 1967). All these formulations were given wide currency in the writings of Eldridge Cleaver, Stokely Carmichael, and Malcolm X (Malcolm Little).

In the United States perceived racial disloyalty is increasingly stigmatized among Blacks. Thus *Jim Crow* became popularized as the title of a song by "the father of American minstrelsy," Thomas Dartmouth Rice, in 1828, but took on the sense of "a turncoat" from as early as 1837. The name became highly politicized, denoting segregationist legislation from 1904. **Uncle Tom** in the "disloyal" sense emerged still later, about 1921, seventy years after Harriet Beecher Stowe's famous novel. In American literature, ethnic slurs for Blacks have continued to feature both in themselves and in effects on the critical reputations of important works. The entry for **Mark Twain** covers the continuing reactions to the term *nigger* in *Huckleberry Finn*. More recently, the plot of Philip Roth's acclaimed novel *The Human Stain* (2000) stems from the devastating effects on the career of an academic of the casual use of the term *spooks*.

In other predominantly Anglo-Saxon communities there are fewer terms—for example, *Aborigine* in Australia—but they often carry great animus. Two important witness-words stigmatizing and stereotyping blacks as aliens on religious and racial grounds are **kaffir** and **hottentot**, which have their own entries. The curious semantic history of **coon** is also treated separately. In recent decades all these terms have became taboo.

See also: Australia; Coon; Ethnic Insults; Hottentot; Kaffir; Nigger; Uncle Tom.

Bibliography

Allen, Irving Lewis. *The Language of Ethnic Conflict.* New York: Columbia University Press, 1983.
Brockbank, Philip. *On Shakespeare.* Oxford: Blackwell, 1989.
Fryer, Peter. *Staying Power.* London: Pluto Press, 1984.
Hadfield, Andrew. *Amazons, Savages and Machiavels.* Oxford: Oxford University Press, 2001.
———, ed. *William Shakespeare's Othello.* London: Routledge, 2003.
Hall, Kim F. *Things of Darkness.* Ithaca: Cornell University Press, 1995.
Jones, Eldred. *Othello's Countrymen: The African in English Renaissance Drama.* Oxford: Oxford University Press, 1965.
Loomba, Ania. *Shakespeare, Race and Colonialism.* Oxford: Oxford University Press, 2002.
Said, Edward. *Orientalism.* New York: Vintage Books, 1979.

BLASON POPULAIRE

A stereotypical characterization of a group of which one is not a member. The term means literally a "popular emblem or badge," but it is given to a group by outsiders, not worn spontaneously by them. Although the term has an international currency in scholarship, it is not in general use. The stereotypes are based on folklore and on prejudice, since the characterizations are invariably negative, typically focusing on such behavioral features as idleness, dirtiness, inefficiency, stupidity, meanness, cowardice, aggressiveness, drunkenness, sexual promiscuity, and perversion. Even virtues that are traditionally admired can become the source of criticism, as in the hyperefficiency attributed to the Germans or extreme cleanliness attributed to the Swiss. Outgroups or those incompletely assimilated are typically targeted, as William M. Clements argues: "Hence in ethnic jokes in the United States, where such virtues as efficiency, cleanliness and orderliness are valued, the target of exoteric folklore, no matter what the particular group, is depicted as inefficient, dirty and disorganized" (Green, ed., 1997).

The basic assumption of blasons populaires is that nations are homogeneous and share national characteristics—for example, "Scots are mean," "Poles are stupid," "English are reserved," and so on. Such prejudice is manifestly absurd, denying individuality, ignoring regional variations within the society, and conflating national components such as "the English" with "the British." In the past these characterizations have generally been retailed without opposition, except in the United States, on the part of Jewish groups. Furthermore, on October 18, 2004, President Mbeki of South Africa specifically raised in Parliament the blason populaire that black people are perceived as "lazy, liars, foul-smelling, diseased, corrupt, violent, amoral, sexually depraved, animalistic, savage and rapist."

The role of language is crucial, serving to endorse and reinforce a stereotype, making it into a cliché. Hence the development of formulations like *Latin lover, Indian giver, to go Dutch, to turn Turk,* and so on. The attribution of lechery to other nations is shown in formulations like *French letter* (for the prophylactic) and *Spanish fly* (for the aphrodisiac). Farmer and Henley's *Dictionary of Slang* (1890–1904) defines "French Vice" as "a euphemism for all sexual malpractices." (Incidentally *French letter,* recorded from ca. 1856, was returned with compliments by the French as *capote anglaise* [English raincoat], and the earlier phrase *French leave,* dating from ca. 1770, was similarly returned as *filer à l'anglaise.*) Among the numerous ironic or contemptuous uses of *Dutch* are *Dutch courage* (alcoholically induced), *Dutch feast* (where the host gets drunk before his guests), *Dutch auction* (descending in value), *Dutch treat* (i.e., *going Dutch*), *Dutch wife,* a bolster, *Dutch widow,* a prostitute. The *Oxford English Dictionary* entry stresses the sociolinguistic connections: "Characteristic or attributed to the Dutch, often with an opprobrious or derisive application, largely due to the rivalry and enmity between the English and the Dutch in the seventeenth century. Often with allusion to the drinking habits ascribed to the 'Dutch.'" Yet only *Dutch widow* is recorded prior to 1700, in a play by Middleton in 1608. Puns using *the netherlands* and the *low countries* to refer to the genital area were common in Elizabethan times.

Also effective are ethnic slurs and ethnic jokes, or *ethnophaulisms,* to use the professional term. Some of these have gained proverbial status: for example *timeo danaos dona ferentes* (Virgil, *Aeneid,* II, 48), popularized as "Beware of Greeks bearing gifts," or "The only good Indian is a dead Indian," (attributed to Philip Henry Sheridan at Fort Cobb, Oklahoma, January 1869). As B.J. Whiting showed in his monumental study *Proverbs, Sentences, and Proverbial Phrases from English Writings Mainly before 1500* (1968), many xenophobic (and also misogynist) sentiments are to be found in medieval writings. These sentiments can take other forms, such as group nicknames: for example, *frogs* for the French, *squareheads* for Scandinavians, *yellow bellies* for Asians, and *curry munchers* for Indians. Significantly, these national nicknames are not entirely stable: *frog,* apparently derived from French cuisine, was also applied to the Dutch and to the Jesuits in the past.

These mechanisms extend to ethnic jokes, such as the myriad examples concerning an Englishman, an Irishman, and a Scotsman, and to group jokes, such as those about women drivers, mothers-in-law, and dumb blondes. Ethnic jokes are, paradoxically, often most savage and intense when retailed by "in group" tellers or authors against their own group. Jewish humor, as exemplified in Leo Rosten's classic collection *The Joys of Yiddish* (1968), illustrates this point on virtually every page, often in the witty definitions of the rich store of disparaging terms for social types like *schmuck, schlemiel, schmegegge, yenta,* and so on. The same is true of Irish humor, much of which is self-directed. This feature of making a joke out of an insult would seem to be a characteristic of groups who see themselves as marginalized, as threatened, or as outsiders. It is not a feature for example, of British humor, which is outer-directed at foreigners generally, or across class barriers.

Folk etymologies (plausible but inaccurate explanations of the origins of words) are also revealing, since they are in themselves popular misconceptions. Among numerous examples are *spic,* supposedly from "no spika da Inglish," *wog* from "worthy oriental gentleman," and *wop* from "without papers." Even true etymologies should not be underrated: thus *kaffir* is truly derived from Arabic *kafir,* "an infidel," while *bugger* is ultimately derived from *Bulgarus,* "a Bulgarian," originally meaning "a heretic," later "a sodomite."

In modern times blasons populaires and ethnophaulisms have come to be seen as potentially dangerous propagandist weapons, in view of the persecution of the Jews and other minorities in Europe, leading to the Holocaust and genocide. The rise of political correctness has certainly served to drive overt statements expressing xenophobic sentiments, ethnic slurs, and similar prejudices underground.

See also: Bugger; Ethnic Insults; Folk Etymology; Hottentot; Kaffir.

Bibliography
Allen, Irving Lewis. *The Language of Ethnic Conflict.* New York: Columbia University Press, 1983.

Aman, Reinhold, ed. *Maledicta: The International Journal of Verbal Aggression.* Philadelphia: Running Press, 1977–.

Green, Thomas A., ed. *Folklore: An Encyclopedia.* Santa Barbara, CA: Clio Books, 1997.

BLASPHEMY

Blasphemy is the contemptuous use of religious symbols or names, either by swearing or abuse. A distinction is often made between blasphemy and profanity on the grounds that blasphemy is intentional, whereas profanity is more habitual. Thus the rituals of black magic would fall under blasphemy, whereas most swearing would be categorized as profanity. The distinction, though valuable, is not absolute. The seriousness of blasphemy as an offense has declined with the secularization of Western society.

The root notion is linguistic, lying in Greek *blasphemia,* meaning "profane speech or evil slander." First recorded ca. 1200 in the *Ancrene Riwle* ("Rule for Nuns") in Middle English, it meant "to utter impious or profane words" and was usually followed by *against,* as in John Wycliffe's anticlerical comment that "freres by gabbings [gabbling] blaspheme upon Christ." From considerable overuse in the religious divisions of the sixteenth century, it became generalized to mean simply "abuse." However, Dr. Johnson defined it (1755) as "strictly and properly, an offering of some indignity, or injury, unto God himself, either by words or writing."

The category in English Law of Blasphemous Libel refers to the crime committed if a person insults, offends, or vilifies the deity, Christ, or the Christian religion. In earlier times, when Christianity was considered to be part of the law itself, blasphemy was construed as subversion, thus incurring numerous prosecutions. Christopher Marlowe (1564–1592) allegedly propagated various heretical views, one "that Christ was the bedfellow of John the Baptist and used him after the manner of Sodom," although the allegations were never proved (Gill 1989, x). His play *The Tragicall History of Dr. Faustus* (ca. 1590) certainly proved the most daring

The Tragicall Hiſtorie of the Life and Death of Doctor Fauſtus.

With new Additions.

Written by Cʜ. Mᴀʀ.

Printed at London for *Iohn Wright*, and are to be ſold at his ſhop without Newgate. 1631.

Christopher Marlowe's *Doctor Faustus* (ca. 1590) invokes infernal powers, necromancy, and satanism in dramatizing the damnation of its title character. T.S. Eliot later observed that blasphemy—a crime severely punished in the playwright's time—was central to Marlowe's work. *(The Art Archive)* and illuminating dramatic text on black magic, also called necromancy, Satanism, and devil worship, involving the use of spells and the blasphemous exploitation of Holy Writ. Faustus calls up the devil Mephostophilis onstage in an explicit conjuring ritual including a magic circle:

Within this circle is Jehovah's name
Forward and backward anagrammatised
Th'abbreviated names of holy saints
(I iii 8–10)

The powers Faustus invokes are infernal ("Belzbub, monarch of burning hell") and sacred ("the holy water which I now sprinkle and the sign of the cross"). The invocation is in Latin, the language of the Church and of scholarship, showing his sacrilegious abuse of his knowledge. He persists in his necromancy, saying: "I'll conjure, though I die therefore" and signs with his own blood the formal contract or pact with the devil: ("I, John Faustus, by these presents, do give both body and soul to Lucifer."). During twenty-four years of limited power and pleasure, he at one point "fetches the Pope a box of the ear," provoking the papal curse "Damned be this soul for ever for this deed" and the enactment of the whole ritual of the **anathema**.

Blasphemy could attract the most severe punishments. Up to 1677 it was punishable by burning at the stake, and the death penalty remained in force in Scotland until 1825. Over the past two centuries the blasphemy law has been invoked only at irregular intervals. Thus Shelley's joint publication of a notorious pamphlet, *The Necessity of Atheism* (1811), did not lead to a prosecution, although he was sent down from Oxford. The same happened to Mark Boxer, editor of the Cambridge literary magazine *Granta,* for publishing in 1952 a poem beginning "God, God, the silly sod." However, a case was brought by the Crown in 1882 for the publication of comic cartoons ridiculing Christianity.

There have been two controversial cases in recent times. The first was the private prosecution (the first for fifty years in the United Kingdom) brought in 1977 by **Mrs. Mary Whitehouse,** a moral crusader, against the editor of *Gay News* for the publication of a poem ("The Love That Dares to Speak Its Name") by Professor James Kirkup, in which a Roman centurion enjoys sexual fantasies about the crucified Christ, who, it is implied, was a promiscuous homosexual. She won the case, which was tried at the Old Bailey: the editor was fined £500 and given a prison sentence of eighteen months, suspended for nine months, and the poem may not be printed in the United Kingdom. The advocate John Mortimer, who conducted the defense, subsequently observed: "At the trial it was ruled that we could call no evidence on the poem's literary merit (so blasphemers are treated far more harshly than pornographers)" (*Spectator* April 21, 1990, 7).

In 1989 an attempt to invoke the law against Salman Rushdie's controversial novel *The Satanic Verses* failed on the grounds that the blasphemy law covers only Christianity, its personages, and articles of belief. This led to two opposed initiatives, one to extend the law to include other religions; the other to abolish it entirely. In April 1989 a bill for abolition introduced in the House of Commons fell without debate. However, *The Satanic Verses* was immediately banned in India and South Africa on the grounds of blasphemy against Islam and was burned on the streets of Bradford, Yorkshire. In February 1989 the Ayatollah Khomeini, the Iranian spiritual leader, issued a *fatwa,* or death sentence, against Rushdie, his publishers, and translators. This led to attacks and even murders.

In the United States religious tolerance is endorsed by the First Amendment to the Constitution, stipulating that "Congress shall make no law respecting an establishment of religion . . . or abridging the freedom of speech or the press."

See also: Curse and Cursing; Formal Oaths.

Bibliography

Gill, Roma, ed. *Doctor Faustus.* London: A.C. Black, 1989.

Henningsen, G. "Witchcraft." In *Medieval Folklore,* eds. C. Lindahl, J. McNamara, and J. Lidow. Santa Barbara, CA: ABC Clio Books, 1997.

Kieckhefer, R. "Witchcraft." In *Folklore,* ed. Thomas A. Green. Santa Barbara, CA: ABC Clio Books, 1997.

Ruthven, Malise. *A Satanic Affair.* London: Hogarth Press, 1990.

Sprenger, Jacobus, and Heinrich Kramer. *Malleus Maleficarum.* 1486.

BLAST

The root sense of this ancient word, recorded from Anglo-Saxon times, is "a strong gust of wind," which in the sixteenth century extended to "a sudden infection destroying vegetable or animal life," in those times thought to be the consequence of lightning or a malignant wind or planet. The verbal sense of "to curse with imprecations" or "to wish the wrath or curse of heaven upon," with an appeal to God implied, is recorded from about 1634 in the curse "Blast you all" in George Chapman's play *Revenge for Honour* (v). Thereafter the word follows the same basic development as *damn,* being used by writers such as Henry Fielding: "blast my reputation" (1752); Oliver Goldsmith: "Blast me!" (1762); and Thomas Babington Macaulay: "Calling on their Maker to curse them, blast them, and damn them" (1849, *English History* I iii). The participial form *blasted* follows the same route, from the barren "blasted heath" in *Macbeth* (I iii 77) to Lord Chesterfield's view in 1750 that "Colonel Chartres . . . was I believe, the most notorious blasted rascal in the world" (*Letters,* January 8). The semantic history thus shows the familiar pattern of generalization and **loss of intensity**. The word is generally more current in British than American English.

See also: Damn.

BLOODY

An expletive much used in the past four centuries, although its impact and currency in global varieties of English have varied considerably. It is common in British English, essential in Australian English, but rare in American English. In general it shows **loss of intensity**, having become a mere intensifier through overuse.

Discussions of the origins of *bloody* have been confused by a frequently retailed "folk etymology," deriving the word from a corruption of "by our lady." While this explanation is plausible phonetically, it is clearly not logical grammatically, since "by our lady" would not fit the adjectival function. ("By our lady hell!" would be a bizarre conjunction.) As is common with underground or slang usage, original written instances are difficult to trace. The *OED* cites an example from the Scots poet Gavin Douglas as far back as 1513, but most authorities trace the meaning much later. Samuel Pepys described the Fire of London in his *Diary* as "a most horrid, malicious, bloody flame, not like the fine flame of an ordinary fire" (September 2, 1666), while the playwright Thomas Otway uses the phrase "a bloody Cuckold-making scoundrel" in 1681 (*Works* II, 137). The metaphorical connection with literal *bloody* seems to have started with the phrase "bloody drunk," originally meaning "fired up and ready to shed blood," still surviving in "bloody minded." **Samuel Johnson** (1755) condemned "bloody drunk" as "very vulgar," but **Jonathan Swift** used a very modern idiom in a letter to Stella: "It was bloody hot walking today" (May 8, 1711).

The *Oxford English Dictionary* entry for *bloody* (originally published in a fascicle or small volume in March 1887) makes some pointed comments on class usage:

> In general colloquial use from the Restoration [1660] to about 1750; now constantly in the mouths of the lowest classes, but by respectable people considered "a horrid word," on a par with obscene or profane language, and usually printed in the newspapers (in police reports, etc.) as "b——y."

In the same year, Gilbert and Sullivan's new operetta *Ruddygore* was rapidly renamed *Ruddigore*. (This euphemistic practice was extended, generating forms like *blooming, blinking,* and *ruddy,* as well as the abbreviation of plain *b,* as in "The b thing won't work.") Professor H.C. Wyld in his *History of Modern Colloquial English* (1920) showed a similar attitude to that of the *Oxford English Dictionary,* but was more coy: "There is a certain adjective, most offensive to polite ears, which plays apparently the chief role in the vocabulary of large sections of the community." In his *Universal Dictionary of the English Language* (1934) he was more explicit: "meaningless adjective much used among very low persons." The novelist Nevil Shute recalled receiving in 1926 a pointed ultimatum from a publisher: "The House of Cassell does not print the word 'bloody.'" The word was changed to *ruddy* and the novel (*Marazan*) duly appeared (Montagu 1973, 264).

In the colonial varieties of English, usage and impact have varied greatly. As the entry for **Australia** shows, *bloody* has always been highly current, reflecting the convict origins of the settlers. As Francis Grose noted in his *Classical Dictionary of the Vulgar Tongue* (1785), *bloody* was "a favourite word used by thieves in swearing." From the early years of the penal settlement, many observers commented on the extraordinarily prolific use of the word, so that for over a century it has been regarded as "the Australian adjective," acquiring the institutional status of "the great Australian adjective" (A. Haskell, *Waltzing Matilda* 1940, 35). Its acceptability was certainly enhanced when it was popularized in a marching song during World War I called "the Australaise." The printed version (written by J.C. Dennis) appeared with ironic omissions of the supposedly "unprintable" but obvious word:

Fellers of Australier
    Blokes an' coves an' coots
Shift yer——carcasses,
    Move yer——boots.

The chorus showed another interesting feature in the use of those swearwords that become familiarized or banalized:

Get a——move on,
　　Have some——sense,
Learn the——art of
　　Self de——fense.

The slang historian J.A. Farmer had noted in 1895 that *bloody* was "interlarded by every Cockney into every remark, suitably or unsuitably" (cited in *Random House*). The practice has become very common: "Shootin' kanga-bloody-roos at Tumba-bloody-Rumba" (1976, cited in the *Australian National Dictionary*). The process, known as "infixing" shows that the epithet has lost semantic force and is being used simply as a makeweight for syncopation. Also a feature of American English, as H.L. Mencken noted many decades ago (1936, 315), it is discussed in the entry for **flexibility**.

Bloody continues to be the staple epithet of Australian English. As far back as 1942, a judge ruled in the Sydney Divorce Court that "the word *bloody* is so common in modern parlance that it is not regarded as swearing" (cited in Hornadge, 1980, 144). In 1970 a member of the House of Representatives announced to a wondering audience: "I never use the word 'bloody' because it is unparliamentary. It is a word I never bloody well use" (cited in Hornadge 1980, 145). The minister of transport was less reticent in his comments on a forthcoming budget in 1973: "There is going to be some bloody mammoth changes—some changes which the Budget will disclose. Bloody mammoth changes, that is the only way you can describe them. I think that Frank Crean has done a bloody good job standing up to the pace. Bloody oath, he has done a marvellous job in standing up to the pace" (*Sydney Morning Herald* August 18, 1973, 2). The *Australian National Dictionary* defines it as "an intensive, ranging in force from 'mildly irritating' to 'execrable.'"

In the United States, by contrast, *bloody* has never attracted the currency of Australia nor the opprobrium of the United Kingdom. Mencken observed in *The American Language:* "Perhaps the most curious disparity between the two tongues is presented by *bloody*. The word is entirely without improper significance in America, but in England it is regarded as indecent, with overtones of the blasphemous" (1936, 311–12). As the entry for **Pygmalion** shows, George Bernard Shaw's provocative use of the term in his comedy in 1914 provoked a scandal in London, but had no impact in New York.

Bloody now has very different currencies and severity of impact in global varieties of English. It continues to have only limited use in the United States, being unlisted in most dictionaries of slang. In British and South African English it is now a mild and somewhat passé intensifier. "It's a bloody good budget" commented Trevor Manuel, the South African minister of finance, on the front page of *This Day* (February 19, 2004). The usage raised no objection.

See also: Australia; Folk Etymology; *Pygmalion.*

Bibliography

Hornadge, Bill. *The Australian Slanguage*. North Ryde, NSW: Cassell Australia, 1980.

Mencken, H.L. *The American Language*. New York: Knopf, 1936.

Montagu, Ashley. *The Anatomy of Swearing*. London and New York: Macmillan and Collier, 1973.

Partridge, Eric. "The Word Bloody." In *Words, Words, Words*. London: Methuen, 1933.

Rawson, Hugh. *Devious Derivations*. New York: Crown, 1994.

Wyld, H.C. *A History of Modern Colloquial English*. Oxford: Blackwell, 1920.

BODY LANGUAGE AND GESTURE

Although swearing is generally regarded as an exclusively verbal practice, blasphemy, profanity, and obscenity cover a wide variety of modes, including violations of taboos through insulting signs or outrageous actions. These modes can be highly developed in what were traditionally called "primitive" cultures. Thus the ritualistic action of pointing the finger among the Australian aborigines can in itself have fatal consequences for the victim, the equivalent of the curse. It is a viable speculation that in the remote stages of a culture, gesture increasingly accompanies and even replaces language (see Sapir 1921, 21 and Barber 1964, 24–34). Consequently, a historical survey shows that various modes of body language continue to thrive up to modern times, some of them sufficiently provocative to lead to legal consequences.

The most unambiguous and wounding gesture of personal contempt, short of actually laying hands on someone, is to spit at them, notably recorded in the humiliation of Christ in the Gospels (Mark 10:34 and Matthew 26:67). Secular references abound from the Middle English period onward, and there are powerful instances in Shakespeare, such as Shylock's complaint in *Merchant of Venice* that the Gentiles "spit upon my Jewish gaberdine" (I iii 109) and the Lady Anne's rejection of the outrageous advances of Richard Gloucester at her husband's funeral (*Richard III*, I ii 148). Elsewhere in Shakespeare about a dozen similar instances are to be found. One of the last references recorded in the *Oxford English Dictionary* is from *Uncle Tom's Cabin* (1852), chapter xxxviii.

Offensive body language, or what Ashley Montagu calls "gesticulatory swearing" (1973, 344), has become the focus of considerable discussion in modern times, often carrying the misleading implication that it is a modern phenomenon. Although little evidence exists in the surviving Anglo-Saxon and Middle English literature, there are highly developed instances in the Renaissance. François Rabelais's *Gargantua and Pantagruel* (1533–1535) has a whole farcical chapter in which Panurge indulges in a contest of insulting sign language with an Englishman (Book II, chapter 19). Absurdly and tantalizingly, the signs are described in detail, but their meaning is not. The famous exchanges of coded provocation between the servants of the Capulets and the Montagus in *Romeo and Juliet* (1594) provide a notable early example. Since the actions are derived from Continental practices, they need to be explained in the text to the English audience:

Sampson: I will bite my thumb at them; which is a disgrace to them, if they do bear it.

Abram: Do you bite your thumb at us, sir?

Sampson: I do bite my thumb, sir.

Abram: Do you bite your thumb at us, sir?
Sampson (aside to Gregory): Is the law on our side if I say ay?
Gregory (aside to Sampson): No.
Sampson: I do not bite my thumb at you, sir; but I do bite my thumb, sir.
(I i 47–57)

First, the servants seek to perpetuate the feud between the great families of Verona, but use a lower form of currency, the gesture; second, they are uncertain of the codes, wishing both to provoke and remain ambiguous, even using "sir" in an ironic fashion. Their actions are explained in Randle Cotgrave's *Dictionarie of the French and English Tongues* (1611) under the entry for *nique*: "To threaten or defie by putting the thumbe naile into the mouth and with a jerke (of the upper teeth) make it to knack [make a cracking sound]."

Cotgrave's entry is quoted by the *Oxford English Dictionary* in relation to another gesture, "to give the 'fico', to insult." Dr. Johnson defined *fico* in 1755 in both linguistic and physical terms as "An act of contempt done with the fingers expressing 'a fig for you.'" (*Fico* is Italian for *fig*.) The action is defined more specifically by the *OED* as "A contemptuous gesture which consisted of thrusting the thumb between two of the closed fingers or into the mouth," supported by quotations from the Elizabethan period, such as Thomas Lodge's in 1596: "Giving me the Fico with his thombe in his mouth" (*Wits Misery,* 23). Other continental idioms, such as French *faire la figue* and Spanish *dar la higa,* denote the same action. Among slang dictionaries, Grose (1785) curiously has no reference, but Farmer and Henley (1890–1904) carry a long colorful etymological account, alluded to by Ben Jonson and others, concerning the emperor Barbarossa, who avenged an insult to his empress by making prisoners use only their teeth in "the extraction of a fig from the fundament of a mule." Two of the braggart Pistol's numerous bellicose ejaculations in Shakespeare's *Henry V* are "Die and be damned and figo for your friendship!" and "The fig of Spain!" (III vi 62). In another piece of bluster he vows, with obvious emphatic gesture:

> I speak the truth:
> When Pistol lies, do this; and fig me, like
> The bragging Spaniard.
> (*Henry IV, Part II,* V iii 120–22)

However a sexual aspect is suggested by the use of *fig* in Elizabethan slang to mean *fuck.* Charmian certainly puns on this sense, saying to the Soothsayer: "I love long life better than figs" (*Antony and Cleopatra,* I i 34). A modern survival is the idiom "not to give a fig" for something.

The Italian term *cornuto* contains a powerfully insulting complex of symbolic actions implying adultery, discussed in the entry for **cuckoldry**. During the fifteenth and sixteenth centuries, when the term was borrowed into English, the related word *horn* came to acquire strong associations of cuckoldry, but neither the term nor the symbolic gesture has ever conveyed the gravity of insult surrounding them in Italy, where the repertoire is notable and the subject of several works—for example, Desmond Morris, *Gestures* (1979). Peter Burke in his article, translated from the French as "The Art of Insult in Italy," records the outrageous response of a famous sixteenth-century Roman courtesan, Isabel de Luna, to a demand for debt: she wiped her backside with it (1989, 53).

The degree of symbolic gesticulation used in communication is often derived from cultural factors. When Captain James Cook arrived in Oceania in 1774, he recorded this greeting from the natives: "One fellow shewed us his back side in such a manner that it was not necessary to have an interpreter" (Beaglehole 1961, 485). On her visits to New Zealand, Queen Elizabeth has often been subjected to this insult or gesture of protest, known by the Maori name of the *whakapohane*, described by a local expert as "the ultimate culturally sanctioned way of registering opprobrium" (Mort 1986, 212). The same practice has become well known on college campuses in the United States as *mooning*, recorded from 1965, although it is more of a prank or taunt, intended variously to impress, register protest, or affront. *Moon* in the slang sense of "buttocks" is recorded as far back as 1756, but the subsequent history is disjunctive.

The related practice of "flashing" has a longer continuous history, starting as underworld slang in the eighteenth century, and defined by Grose (1785) as: "To shew ostentatiously. To flash one's ivory; to laugh and shew one's teeth." The modern genital sense is first recorded in Farmer and Henley (1890–1893), but was then applied to both sexes: "To flash a bit (venery) . . . to permit examination; to 'spread' . . . said of women only" and "To flash it or to flash one's meat—to expose the person . . . said usually of men." The modern practice invariably has the motive to shock and usually occurs in a public place. The more recent action of "streaking" (running naked in public) seems to date from a sudden craze in late 1973 in Los Angeles, often performed as a communal act. Desmond Morris wryly commented: "The phenomenon of 'streaking' is a strange example of an act that only has value as an Overexposed Signal" (1977, 210).

More than half a century ago R.G. Collingwood made these observations about cultural differences in communication: "A dispute between Italian peasants is conducted hardly more in words than in a highly elaborated language of manual gesture. . . . Italians do not possess more sensitive fingers than northern Europeans. But they do have a long tradition of controlled finger-gesture, going back to the ancient game of *micare digitis*" (1938, 242). (The "ancient game" is that of guessing how many fingers one has raised or hidden.) It is a common observation by visitors to the Latin parts of Europe that the indigenous population uses gestures to a marked degree. Thus the *Larousse Dictionnaire du Français Argotique* (*Dictionary of French Slang*) includes three pages of provocative gestures (2001, 261–63). However, one must be cautious about such generalizations, as the following extract shows:

> Some cried, some swore, and the tropes and figures of Billingsgate were used without reserve in all their native zest and flavour; nor were those flowers of rhetoric unattended with significant gesticulation. Some snapped their fingers, some forked them out, some clapped their hands, and some their backsides.

This wonderfully graphic description of rude exchanges and robust body language has a timeless zest. But the source is unexpected, being Tobias Smollett's description of a party in Bath, a fashionable upper-class enclave, in his novel *Humphry Clinker* (1771, 53–54). The allusion to

Billingsgate is thus ironically amusing, normally referring to the crude language notoriously used by the fishwives in that London market. The passage also indicates that insulting gestures were well developed in the eighteenth century, a period traditionally regarded as highly formal. Snapping of fingers would not now qualify as a mode of insult, but is alluded to in Philip Stubbes's *Anatomie of Abuses* (1583): "Then snap go the fingers ful brauely [very stylishly] God wot" (II, 50). There is this memorable altercation in Dickens's *Martin Chuzzlewit* (1843–44):

> [Mrs. Prig] leaned forward, and snapped her fingers once, twice, thrice, each time nearer to the face of Mrs. Gamp; and then rose to put on her bonnet, as one who felt that there was now a gulf between them, which nothing could ever bridge across.
>
> The shock of this blow was so violent and sudden, that Mrs. Gamp sat staring at nothing with uplifted eyes, and her mouth open as if she was gasping for breath. (chapter xlix)

We are certainly familiar with fingers used in other insulting modes. Indeed the phrase "to fork the fingers" is recorded, remarkably, as far back as 1640, in a collection called *Witts Recreations*: "His wife . . . behind him forks her fingers" (C ii).

Body language shows considerable instability over time, as well as the capacity to transfer to different cultures. Even the clapping of hands, now the traditional sign of applause and approval, was in earlier times a gesture of derision. Miles Coverdale (1535) translated Job 27:23 as: "Than [Then] clappe men their hondes at him, yee and ieaste [jest] of him." The King James Version (1611) is more contemporary in its symbolism: "Men shall clap their hands at him and shall hiss him out of his place." The wagging of the head was also a gesture of contempt in earlier times: "They that passed by revyled him waggynge ther heeddes" is in the William Tyndale Version (1526) of the mocking of Christ on the Cross. All three modes are found in the King James Version of Lamentations 2:15: "All that pass by clap their hands at thee; they hiss and wag their head at the daughter of Jerusalem." To *hiss* someone is far older, recorded in John Wyclif's translation of the Bible in 1388. Now the action is usually confined to public disapproval of a performance, known in stage parlance as "getting" (or being given) the bird, previously "the big bird" (i.e., the goose), recorded from about 1825. The verb *to goose* dates from the same period, but has probably been driven out of use by the rival sense from rhyming slang whereby *goose = goose and duck = fuck*, and more recently, "to grope," recorded from about 1906.

Sticking out one's tongue, another overt gesture of contempt, is related to the more disguised action of sticking one's tongue in one's cheek, or speaking "tongue in cheek," recorded from about 1768, to which a derisive significance was previously attributed. (Today, of course, this action is metaphorical and simply denotes irony.) The literal action has become prevalent in sports in recent decades as a form of provocation and contempt. The tennis champion in the women's French Open (2004), Anastasia Myskina, stuck out her tongue at her opponent upon receiving the trophy at the award ceremony.

Body language obviously continues to supply significant forms of aggressive and insulting behavior. While some gestures, like mooning, flashing, and streaking, have no semantic correlatives, others show a cross-fertilization between gesture and language. Continuing the tradition of *figo* and *cornuto,* the insulting phrase "Up yours!" is a verbalization of what the

OED coyly terms "an impolite gesture, a shortened form of 'Up your arse!,' itself an abbreviated imperative of 'Shove [it] up your arse!'" For the uninitiated, Norman Moss's *British/American Dictionary* (1984) illustrated the British style (forked fingers) and the American (single finger). The *Random House Historical Dictionary of American Slang* (1994) defines the action more accurately as "an obscene gesture of contempt," referring to the semantic analogue of Latin *digitis impudicus*, and giving the earliest instance as 1938. Although "giving the finger" is a deliberately provocative and insulting action, only flashing and streaking are legal offenses per se, no doubt because they involve exposing the genitalia.

See also: Billingsgate.

Bibliography

Barber, Charles L. *The Story of Language*. London: Pan, 1964.

Beaglehole, J.C. ed. *The Journals of Captain James Cook*. Vol. II. Cambridge: Cambridge University Press, 1961.

Burke, Peter. "L'art d'insulte en Italie." In *Injures et Blasphemes,* edited by Jean Delumeau. Paris: Editions Imago, 1989.

Caradec, François. *Larousse Dictionnaire du Français Argotique*. Paris: Larousse, 2001.

Collingwood, R.G. *The Principles of Art*. Oxford: Oxford University Press, 1938.

Montagu, Ashley. *The Anatomy of Swearing*. London and New York: Macmillan and Collier, 1973.

Morris, Desmond. *Manwatching*. London: Cape, 1977.

————. *Gestures*. London: Jonathan Cape, 1979.

Mort, Simon. *Longman Guardian New Words*. London: Longman, 1986.

Sapir, Edward. *Language*. London: Hart-Davis, 1921.

BODY PARTS. *See:* Anatomical Insults

BOWDLER, DR. THOMAS

Dr. Thomas Bowdler (1754–1825), a retired physician turned country gentleman, became a self-appointed censor with the uncompromising view that "Words that give an impression of obscenity should not be spoken, written or printed." He put his views into practice by publishing major texts in *bowdlerized* or clearly expurgated versions. The most famous of these was *The Family Shakespeare* (1818), in which, according to the title page, "nothing is added to the original text; but those words and expressions are omitted which cannot with propriety be read aloud in a family." Reading aloud was then an important family entertainment. The Preface was quite frank: "Many words and expressions occur which are of so indecent a nature as to render it highly desirable that they should be erased . . . neither the vicious taste of the age, nor the most brilliant effusions of wit, can afford an excuse for profaneness or obscenity" (viii). Continuing in this vein of total assurance, Bowdler announces: "The most sacred Word in our language is omitted in several instances, in which it appeared as a mere expletive; and it is changed into the sacred word Heaven in a still greater number" (1827, xvii). In fact, the work was more of a family enterprise, since Bowdler's sister Harriet (Henrietta Maria, 1750–1830) had already produced an earlier edition in 1807 and she continued to be the major collaborator. She

THE

FAMILY SHAKSPEARE,

In Eight Volumes;

IN WHICH

NOTHING IS ADDED TO THE ORIGINAL TEXT;

BUT THOSE WORDS AND EXPRESSIONS ARE OMITTED

WHICH CANNOT WITH PROPRIETY BE READ

ALOUD IN A FAMILY.

———— exemit labem purumque reliquit
Æthereum sensum, atque aurai simplicis ignem.
VIRGIL.

BY

THOMAS BOWDLER, Esq. F.R.S. & S.A.

THE FIFTH EDITION.

VOL. I.

CONTAINING

TEMPEST;
TWO GENTLEMEN OF VERONA;
MERRY WIVES OF WINDSOR;
TWELFTH-NIGHT: OR, WHAT YOU WILL;
MEASURE FOR MEASURE;
MUCH ADO ABOUT NOTHING.

LONDON:

PRINTED FOR

LONGMAN, REES, ORME, BROWN, AND GREEN.
PATERNOSTER-ROW.

1827.

English editor Thomas Bowdler produced *The Family Shakespeare* in 1818, omitting "words and expressions . . . which cannot with propriety be read aloud in a family." *Bowdlerization* became synonymous with the prudish expurgation of a literary text.

"endeavoured to remove everything that could give just offence to the religious and virtuous mind." The first edition, which included only twenty of the thirty-seven plays, appeared without an editor's name, and only after a few years did Bowdler's "authorship" begin to be known.

The Family Shakespeare was to become the most famous, subsequently the most notorious, of all expurgated books. The excisions from the first edition were drastic, including the whole of *Romeo and Juliet* as well as large sections of *Hamlet* and *Timon of Athens*. Although Thomas Bowdler included all the plays, like most censors he was inconsistent. In *Othello* he retained, somewhat surprisingly, such powerful condemnations as "impudent strumpet," "cunning whore of Venice," and "demi-devil," although he predictably excised "an old black ram is tupping your white ewe" (I i 88–89). Oddly, Lady Macbeth's famous line "Out damned spot!" is retained, while in *Hamlet* an old word for prostitute, *drab,* is deleted but *whore* is kept. In the following savage curse upon Athens by Timon as he leaves the city for good, the lines in italics were excised from *The Family Shakespeare.* They indicate the rationale for expurgation and retention: Bowdler's clear policy was to excise sexual references, but he has kept alarming images of violence and social disintegration:

Let me look back upon thee. O thou wall,
That girdlest in those wolves, dive in the earth,
And fence not Athens! Matrons turn incontinent [promiscuous]!
Obedience fail in children! slaves and fools,
Pluck the grave wrinkled senate from the bench,
And minister in their steads! *To general filths*
Convert, o' the instant, green [innocent] *virginity!*
Do't in your parents' eyes! Bankrupts, hold fast;
Rather than render back; out with your knives,
And cut your trusters' throats! Bound servants, steal!
Large-handed robbers your masters are,
And pill by law. Maid to thy master's bed;
Thy mistress is o' the brothel! Son of sixteen,
Pluck the lin'd crutch from thy old limping sire,
With it beat out his brains!
(*Timon of Athens* IV i 1–15)

The Family Shakespeare proved highly popular, generating five editions in twenty years. When the copyright lapsed (in 1860), a rival edition was immediately brought out by another publisher, and by 1894 there were some forty expurgated editions of Shakespeare on the market. The Bowdlers became something of an institution. Thomas went on to produce with even less justification a "purified" text of Gibbon's *Decline and Fall of the Roman Empire* (1826), "with the careful omission of all passages of an irreligious or immoral tendency." When young Thomas wrote his uncle's obituary in the 1825 edition, he made two predictions, one reassuring, the other disturbing:

the readers of Shakespeare will henceforth probably increase tenfold; the Family Shakespeare will be the edition which will lie on the table of every drawing-room; and the name of the editor will be remembered, as one who has contributed more than any other individual to promote the innocent and rational enjoyment of well-educated families.

See also: Bowdlerization; Shakespeare, William.

Bibliography

Perrin, Noel. *Dr. Bowdler's Legacy.* London: Macmillan, 1969.

BOWDLERIZATION

The publication of a text that has been expurgated, doctored, or castrated, to accommodate "family values," following the practice of **Dr. Thomas Bowdler** (1754–1825) and his family, who produced expurgated or sanitized texts of major works, most notably *The Family Shakespeare* (1807). The related eponymous terms are *bowdlerize* (1836), *bowdlerism* (1869), and *bowdlerization* (1882). Thomas's learned mother, Elizabeth S. Bowdler, had already produced in 1775 her *Commentary on the Song of Solomon Paraphrased*. In this she objected to the word *bed*, preferring a euphemism such as "bridal chariot," and commented on the amorous Bride's effusion, "He shall lie all night between my breasts," that this "would be impossible," proposing that "he" should be changed to "it," meaning a bundle of myrrh.

However, the practice of bowdlerism was already established well before the Bowdler family started to wield the blue pencil. Charles Wesley in 1744 published his *Collection of Moral and Sacred Poems, from the most Celebrated Authors*, in which about 100 poems have lines missing or substituted. Subsequent decades saw "pruned" or "purged" collections of poets as diverse as the Earl of Rochester, Abraham Cowley, and Matthew Prior. (Further details are to be found in Noel Perrin 1969.) In 1805 the publisher Tabart issued a *Robinson Crusoe* "Revised for the Use of Young Persons," even though the original text is almost entirely innocent.

The year 1807 was a watershed year, with the publication of a parallel work of bowdlerism, *Tales from Shakespear,* by Charles and Mary Lamb. As the title suggests, it dealt more with the plot outlines of Shakespeare's plays, but in a simplified and purified form, appropriate for children. Thus the barbaric curses that Lear unleashes on Cordelia are simply paraphrased: "The plainness of speech, which Lear called pride, so enraged the old monarch . . . that in a fury of resentment he retracted a third part of the kingdom." In *Romeo and Juliet* the two major sources of bawdy, Mercutio and the Nurse, become virtually silent parts.

There is a distinction between bowdlerism proper, the acknowledged modification or paraphrasing of texts to avoid embarrassment in a juvenile or family audience, such as the Bowdlers and the Lambs produced, and the surreptitious doctoring or expurgating of texts. The date of these founding expurgating enterprises is significant, since bowdlerism is generally regarded as a symptom of Victorian prissiness and preciousness, but these volumes actually anticipated the Victorian era by several decades. However, expurgation certainly became established during the Victorian period.

In the United States one of the prime exponents of bowdlerism was Noah Webster (1758–1843), whose career in expurgating started with spelling books, continued with his famous dictionaries, and finished with his Bible (1833), of which he said: "I consider this . . . the most important enterprise of my life" (Perrin 1969, 133). The work showed Webster's policy of replacing the franker Anglo-Saxon terms with the more opaque classical vocabulary. Thus, *stink* is replaced by "offensive in smell," "putrify," "ill savor," and "odious scent"; Job's poignant lament "Why died I not from the womb? Why did I not give up the ghost when I came out of the belly?" is changed to "Why did I not expire at the time of my birth?"

Bowdlerism really took hold in the nineteenth century, with expurgated editions of major authors becoming *de rigueur*. The victims included the poets Geoffrey Chaucer, William Dunbar, John Donne, John Dryden, Robert Herrick, Alexander Pope, Robert Burns, and Walt Whitman as well as William Wycherley, Aphra Behn, John Cleland, Jonathan Swift, Daniel Defoe, and Samuel Pepys, whose amazingly frank *Diary* was first published in 1848. Not all editors were draconian; some were simply deceptive. Thus James Paterson's edition of Dunbar (1860) included *terse*, a Middle Scots word for "penis," but glossed as "tail"; similarly *swyfe* was glossed as "sing and play" when in fact it meant "copulate." Although most of these established authors were restored in the course of the twentieth century, many new books were banned or bowdlerized, a topic covered under **censorship**. Others were first banned and then expurgated. These included D.H. Lawrence's *The Rainbow* (1915) and his **Lady Chatterley's Lover** (1928).

Although bowdlerism is regarded as something of a joke from a contemporary "liberated" viewpoint, it has proved far more tenacious and widespread than is generally realized. Many works lacking any tincture of obscenity, some at the heart of the English literary tradition, are bowdlerized. It is only fairly recently that school editions of Shakespeare have become unexpurgated. An American study by James Lynch and Bertrand Evans, *High School English Textbooks: A Critical Examination* (1963) showed that all of the eleven prescribed editions of *Macbeth* were bowdlerized. Most editions of *Gulliver's Travels* still excise the grosser physical details. In the United States hardly a year passes without some protest over prescribed school texts regarded as blasphemous or profane in some way.

See also: Bible; Bowdler, Dr. Thomas; Censorship; *Lady Chatterley's Lover;* Victorian Age.

Bibliography
Craig, Alec. *The Banned Books of England.* London: Allen & Unwin, 1962.
Perrin, Noel. *Dr. Bowdler's Legacy.* London: Macmillan, 1969.

BROADCASTING

This section concerns radio and television broadcasting, since film is covered under the headings of **cinema** and **Hollywood**. Both media have in the course of their development tested the parameters of what is considered "decent" or "unacceptable" in the realm of broadcast language. However, the basic understandings, assumptions, and constitutional rights concerning broadcasting differ considerably between the United Kingdom and the United States and accordingly are treated separately in this entry. Radio has special features, coming directly into the home, where privacy and "family values" are paramount, where children have unsupervised access to the medium and often without advance warning of its content. Furthermore, stations have very different audiences and target markets, which a listener may traverse simply by turning a dial.

The nature of radio has changed in both content and range. Initially British radio was essentially institutional, confined to the B.B.C. (the British Broadcasting Corporation, founded 1922 and a monopoly until 1973). The corporation saw its role as essentially institutional, educational, and enlightening, as well as conveying the core values of the nation. In the United States this role was assumed by the V.O.A. (the Voice of America, founded in 1942 to counter Nazi propaganda in Germany). American radio was essentially competitive from the outset, so that to prevent a monopoly Congress passed the Radio Act of 1927, setting up the Federal Communications Commission. However, with the advent of independent and therefore competitive radio stations, entertainment became a major priority, with increasing appeal to the lowest common denominator. There has been a dramatic increase in the number of "talk radio" stations, some frankly exploiting the shock value of strong language, with corresponding increase in the number of complaints. The B.B.C. and the British Broadcasting Standards Council currently receive more complaints about bad language than about violence and other forms of offensive behavior. When I was interviewed by the B.B.C. about my book *Swearing* (1991), it was spelled out before the broadcast started that "the four-letter words" could not be used. Fiona Pitt-Kethley's poem "Censorship" deals with the topic ironically:

The BBC does not like certain words.
Dildoes and buggery are always out.
"Cocks are OK, as long as they're not sucked"—
    a young researcher telephoned me back.
        (in Ricks and Michaels 1990, 422–23)

Although religious sensitivities have generally hardened, the television broadcast by the B.B.C. of "Jerry Springer—The Opera" in January 2005 provoked a major demonstration of public outrage, with threats of lawsuits for blasphemy, since the production included a swearing tirade between Jesus and the Devil, journalists calculating that in all there were 3,168 "f" words and 297 "c" words.

The issue of broadcasting standards in the United States is problematized by the protection of freedom of speech under the First Amendment to the Constitution. Accordingly, under the Communications Act (Section 326) it is stated that:

> Nothing in this Act shall be understood or construed to give the power of censorship over the radio communications or signals transmitted by any radio station, and no regulation or condition shall be promulgated or fixed by the Commission which shall interfere with the right of free speech by means of radio communications.

However, under section 1464 of the same Act it is determined that:

> Whoever utters any obscene, indecent or profane language by means of radio communication shall be fined not more than $10,000, or imprisoned not more than two years, or both.

A *Report on the Broadcast of Violent, Indecent, and Obscene Material* to the Federal Communications Commission in 1975 addressed "specific positive action taken and planned by the Commission to protect children from excessive programming of violence and obscenity" (1). The Report noted that complaints about violent or sexually oriented programs rose from over 2,000 in 1972 to nearly 25,000 in 1974. The NAB and the three major television networks established a programming schedule whereby the "Family Viewing" period would extend from 7.00 P.M. to 9.00 P.M.

The report continues: "The Congress has authorized the Commission to enforce . . . Section 1464 which prohibits utterance of 'any obscene, indecent or profane language by means of radio communication'" (7). Recognizing that the "problem of 'indecent' language" and its definition has persisted, the report puts forward another definition:

> The new definition of "indecent" is tied to the use of language that describes, in terms patently offensive as measured by contemporary community standards for broadcast media, sexual and excretory activities and organs, at times of the day when there is a reasonable risk that children may be in the audience. (8)

These remarks can be placed in context alongside those of the comedian Milton Berle, who inaugurated "Texaco Star Theatre" in 1948. Berle recalls that "We had tremendous censorship in those days. You couldn't say 'hell' or 'damn.'" (Wheen, 1985, 212).

In Britain initiatives to control the content and language of broadcasting derived from various quarters, including the Clean Up TV campaign started in 1965 by **Mrs. Mary Whitehouse**. In 1991 the Broadcasting Standards Council in the United Kingdom issued a report under the title of *A Matter of Manners? The Limits of Broadcasting Language*. The Introduction asked the question: "Why, in the face of such sustained criticism of bad language, does it continue to appear, without apparent justification, in a multitude of programs providing, therefore, a potential source of offense to large numbers of people" (1991, 1). The Council set up a panel of carefully selected respondents from the broadcasting audience and monitored their responses to a variety of programs, extracts, and lists of words. The resulting findings formed the basis of the Council's report.

A curious finding of the report was that more than 15 percent of the respondents did not know the words *motherfucker, cocksucker,* and *tosser,* presumably because the first two terms are predominantly American in usage. In this provenance, the most offensive were the taboo words *fuck* and *cunt*, with *nigger,* the only racial epithet in the list, being rated fifth. Notably, over half the panel regarded the traditional religious oaths such as *blast, damn, hell,* and *God* as "not at all" strong or offensive.

A demographic analysis within the panel showed that generally women and older people rated bad language as more offensive than men and younger people. However, young people were more sensitive to racist epithets. The panel were given a list of eighteen racist epithets, of which the four most unacceptable were those referring to persons of African or Asian descent, namely *nigger, wog, coon,* and *paki,* broadly speaking those who are called "the new Britons." The "middle range" were those referring to Continental and Asian people, namely *dago, chink, nip, kraut, frog, jap,* and *honky,* the one term referring to white people. The least unacceptable terms were those referring to other nationals in the British Isles, those from Wales, Scotland, and Ireland, namely *taffy, jock, mick,* and *paddy* (1991, 17). This indicates a direct relationship between the extent to which a person is considered an outsider and the strength of the epithet applied to them.

A separate test showed sharp discrimination between derogatory terms for women, homosexuals, and those suffering from disability and limited intelligence. Of the ten terms used, by far the least acceptable were *spastic* and *cripple,* followed in increasing order by the terms for homosexuals, namely *dyke, queer, poof,* and *nancy boy.* Of the two terms for women, *slag* (a relatively new British term for a promiscuous woman) was third on the list, but *bitch* was second to last. The high rating of unacceptability accorded *spastic* and *cripple* shows a new sensitivity to disability, possibly related to the growth of political correctness. Both terms are now increasingly replaced by *cerebral palsy* and *disabled.*

The report did not offer specific recommendations, but also contained the views of various scriptwriters and professionals in the field of television production. These research-based insights into audience responses to various categories of offensive language are valuable. A familiar witness word for censoring obscenity is *bleep,* originally an echoic term for a radio signal, but from about 1966 meaning to delete an offensive word from a broadcast, generating *bleeping,* used as an intensifier from about 1970.

See also: Whitehouse, Mrs. Mary.

Bibliography

Hargreave, Andrea Millwood, ed. *A Matter of Manners? The Limits of Broadcasting Language.* London: John Libbey, 1991.
Ricks, Christopher, and Leonard Michaels, eds. *The State of the Language 1990s Edition.* London: Faber & Faber, 1990.
Wheen, Francis. *Television.* London: Century, 1985.

BUGGER

The original senses of *bugger,* a predominantly British term, were powerfully xenophobic. Derived from French *Bougre,* from Latin *Bularus* meaning "a Bulgarian," it meant "a heretic" from the fourteenth century and "a sodomite" from the sixteenth. However, in the modern period it shows generalization and **loss of intensity**, its original critical sense giving way to a wide variety of tones, also seen in *bastard* and *bitch.*

The cultural stereotyping behind the original meanings is illuminating. The sense of "heretic" derives largely from the Bulgarians belonging to the Greek Orthodox Church and subscribing to the Albigensian heresy. The medieval English church writer Dan Michel (ca. 1340) condemns "false Christians," who in following their unorthodox belief are like "the bougre and the heretik and the apostate" (1866, 19). However, Robert of Brunne's contemporary *Chronicle* (ca. 1330) retails this subversive view: "The King said & did crye the pape [Pope] was heretik and lyued in bugerie" (320). The sexual sense appears to be a malicious extension of the idea of perversion. The attribution of "filthy" sexual practices to freethinkers and religious "deviants" is an ancient and ingrained propagandist stereotype. (A similar relation lies in the semantic development of *libertin,* originally "a free thinker," into *libertine,* a sexually decadent person.) A specific ascription of sexual deviancy to heathens is found in *Fardel Facions* (1555): "as rancke bougers with mankinde, and with beastes, as the Saracenes are" (II x 224). There is also the accusation directed against foreign usurers by Edward Chamberlayne in 1667: "The sin of Buggery, brought into England by the Lombards" (*On the Present State of England* I, 41). The "sin of Buggery" is technically a problematic concept under English law, since it covers both sodomy (anal intercourse) and bestiality (sex with animals). In general usage the first meaning is dominant. Thus John Florio's *Worlde of Wordes* (1598), an English/Italian dictionary, defines Italian *bardascia* as "a bardash, a buggering boy, an ingle."

The shift to a general term of abuse, insult and as an expletive is apparent in two quotations in the *Oxford English Dictionary:* the first from Thomas D'Urfey in 1719: "From every trench the bougers fly"; the second from the Court Sessions in 1794: "She said, b-ast and b-gg-r your eyes. I have got none of your money." This is also an early use of the verbal sense, now general in modern phrases like "bugger you!," "bugger off!," "bugger all," and the less virulent sense of "bugger up," meaning "mess up" or "destroy."

In contemporary global English the distribution of *bugger* among different speech communities is surprisingly varied. It is generally prevalent in the British, Australian, and South African varieties. (Afrikaans even has *boggeral,* a "calque" or loan translation of "bugger all.") In all of these it can even be used playfully and affectionately, as in "he's a nice old bugger" or "you lucky bugger!" Australian English has the common phrase *burnt to buggery.* The word has also been taken into **pidgin English**, where it has no stigma and is therefore widely used in the forms *baga,* "person" and *lesbaga,* "lazy bugger." The highly generalized verb *bagarap,* from "bugger up," in its intransitive use carries all the senses of "break, have an accident, become injured or exhausted, disintegrate." The transitive form is *bagarapim,* meaning variously "to destroy, break, rape, render useless." *The Australian* newspaper reported in 1975 that "Prince Charles broke into Pidgin at the end of his speech [in Papua New Guinea] saying: 'Af de ren I bagarap mi nau arait,' which meant 'Unfortunately rain caused me some inconvenience yesterday, but now everything is all right.'" (September 19, 1). However, the term has not really taken root in American English: Mencken noted that *bugger* was "not generally considered obscene in the United States" (1936, 314), a situation that still seems to obtain. The pronunciation is often different (as "booger"), and the main survivors are the euphemized forms "bug off!" and "bugged up."

See also: Aliens; Loss of Intensity, Weakening, or Verbicide.

Bibliography

Mencken, H.L. *The American Language.* New York: Knopf, 1936.
Wilkes, G.A. *A Dictionary of Australian Colloquialisms.* 2nd ed. Sydney: Sydney University Press, 1985.

In this fanciful etching of the shop of "Monsieur Derriere" (1785), ladies are fitted with the padded bustles fashionable at the time. Derriere claims to spare no pain or expense in meeting clients' needs in the "bottom department." *(Library of Congress, LC-USZ62-85714)*

BUM

Since this complex term has a wide variety of meanings and tones, this entry focuses on the more critical. There are three basic senses in American English—namely as a noun, meaning "an idler, layabout, or loafer"; as a verb, "to beg"; and as an adjective, "of low quality, substandard, or not right." All ultimately originated in German *bummler,* "an idler," and *bummeln,* "a leisurely stroll," found in Jerome K. Jerome's *Three Men on the Bummel* (1900). The earliest appearance of *bum* in America in the first sense ("he's just an idle bum") is about 1830, and it has remained the strongest, but is not common in British usage. However, the term in previous decades was applied to a promiscuous woman or cheap prostitute, and is still current in more sophisticated types like *tennis bum* or *ski bum,* "a person who lives or tries to live by his or her sports talent and charm without being genuinely professional" (Chapman 1986). From this meaning it was a short semantic step to the verbal usage "to bum a ride" or "to bum around," and a number of varied uses, such as *stumblebum* (an alcoholic derelict) and *bummer* (originally, from the mid-nineteenth century, an idler, but from the 1960s a disappointing narcotic experience, and subsequently a bad time generally).

Historically, British usage has included a considerable number of these derogatory senses, but the oldest is "a bum card," meaning "a marked playing card," recorded in John Northbrook's *Treatise Against Dicing, Dancing, Plays, and Interludes* (1577). An early eighteenth-century verse (Tom Brown, *The Poet's Condition*) complains: "My levee's all duns / Attended by bums" ("My party's full of bailiffs attended by loafers"). Many other contemporary and later uses are found, such as plain *bum*, meaning "disreputable," and *bum bailiff*, defined by Dr. Johnson as "a bailiff of the meanest kind; one that is employed in arrests."

The principal sense in British usage is anatomical, defined by Dr. Johnson as "the buttocks; the part on which we sit." Recorded from Middle English, it was in general use until about 1800 when, in Eric Partridge's words, "it began to lose caste" (*Dictionary of Historical Slang* 1972). It accordingly generated a great number of compounds, such as *bum thrasher* for a school master, *bum sucker* for a toady or sponger, and *bum fodder* for trashy literature. This last appears to have been coined in a satire on the Rump Parliament written about 1660, probably by one Alexander Brome, memorably titled "Bumm-Fodder; or, Waste Paper proper to wipe the nation's rump with, or your own." The term immediately caught on and has continued to the present in the euphemized forms *bumf* and *bumph*.

Like the related terms *tail* and *arse*, *bum* has also carried a sexual sense, found in *bum shop*, a brothel; *bum boy*, a catamite; and *bum fuck* for sodomy (current in American English, although the euphemism *buns* is preferred for *buttocks*). The term thus shows in its various semantic histories a variety of disreputable associations, namely idleness, dishonesty, and promiscuity. Outside American and British usage, in Australia and South Africa, for example, the term is not greatly used.

See also: Beggar.

Bibliography

Lighter, J.E., ed. *Random House Dictionary of American Slang*. New York: Random House, 1994–.
Partridge, Eric. *A Dictionary of Slang and Unconventional English*. London: Routledge & Kegan Paul, 1937.

BURNS, ROBERT

Although Robert Burns (1759–1796) is Scotland's national poet, famous for such lyrics as "My luve is a like a red, red rose" and the globally institutional "Auld Lang Syne," he wrote a considerable volume of bawdy lyrics, some published after his death under the title of *The Merry Muses of Caledonia* (1799/1800). This collection contains some surprising anticipations of modern obscenity. His "Ode to Spring" inverts hierarchy by starting earthily:

When maukin bucks [male hares], at early f—ks,
In dewy glens are seen, sir;

before introducing mythological figures like Latona, who waits

Till his p-go [pego, i.e., penis] rise, then westward flies
To r-ger Madame Thetis.
(ll. 1–8)

"Libel Summons" describes a male lover who "Defrauds her wi' a frig or dry-bob" (l. 22). (A *dry-bob* is defined by Burns's friend Francis Grose [1785] as "copulation without emis-

The best-known of all Scottish poets, Robert Burns wrote in the vernacular of romantic love, natural simplicity, and the pride of the common man. Less known is his substantial body of bawdy lyric verse. (Library of Congress, LC-DIG-ppmsc-07528)

sion.") Many poems adopt the persona of a brazen chauvinist under titles such as "The Fornicator" and the scorned "Hen-peck'd Husband," the "I" claiming that "I'd kiss her maids and kick the perverse b——h" (l. 10). "A Fragment" to the chorus of "Green grow the rushes O" jauntily recalls "I fairly fun [found] her c-ntie, O" (l. 16). The song "I'll tell you a tale of a Wife" has eleven quatrains in which the last word (unprinted) rhymes with "runt" and "brunt." Following the tradition of **William Dunbar**, Burns includes a sexually eager woman who frankly states that "Nine inch will please a lady," continuing:

> But for a koontrie c-nt like mine,
>> In sooth, we're nae sae gentle;
> We'll tak tway [two] thumb-bread to the nine,
>> And that's a sonsy pintle [handsome penis]
> ("Come rede me, dame," ll. 9–12)

Rightly regarded as the poet of the common man, Burns audaciously comments on the philandering of the European aristocracy in a poem named after its chorus, which runs "And why should na poor folk mowe mowe mowe." *Mow* is a northern dialect and Scots word, now rare, meaning "copulate," juxtaposed in the following couplet with a more modern formation:

> She mowes like reek thr' a' the week,
> But finger f——s on Sunday O.

Burns also wrote a quite lengthy poetic "Address to the Deil" [Devil] with a mocking tone, of how "Ye cam to Paradise incog" to "Eden's bonie yard," using a whole range of honorific titles, covered in the entry for **Devil**.

See also: Devil, the; Dunbar, William.

Bibliography
Burke, J., and S.G. Smith. *The Merry Muses of Caledonia.* Edinburgh: Macdonald Publishing Co., 1982.
Kinsley, James, ed. *The Poems and Songs of Robert Burns.* Oxford: Oxford University Press, 1968.

BYWORDS OF SWEARING

According to the received wisdom of English folklore, certain occupations are especially associated with swearing. Interestingly, they are not exclusively male or working class. Among these proverbial attributions are tinkers, troopers, and fishwives (see under **fishwife**) as does the related name **Billingsgate**. The saying that something lacking in value "is not worth a tinker's curse" is still current, as is the comment that someone "swears like a fishwife." John Dekker commented in his play *The Honest Whore* (1608): "He swore like a dozen of drunken tinkers" and his contemporary Randle Cotgrave translated a French saying *Il jure comme un abbé* as "He swears like a tinker say we" (1611). The *Oxford English Dictionary* noted: "The low repute in which [tinkers], especially of the itinerant sort, were held in former times is shown by the expressions *to swear like a tinker, a tinker's curse or damn, as drunk* or *as quarrelsome as a tinker,* etc." The third byword, trooper, is first recorded much later in a comment in the *Sporting Magazine* of 1810: "The fellow swore . . . like a trooper." The association of the armed forces with swearing is endorsed by a number of authorities, including **Eric Partridge** and **Robert Graves**, as well as the numerous personal records.

An earlier locale of bad language generating a specific historical term is *bear-garden*. The original Bear Garden was a theater built in Elizabethan times on the south bank of the Thames; it was especially associated with bearbaiting and other cruel and rowdy sports of the time. The foul language emanating from there was recorded in a number of sayings, such as "He speaks Bear-garden" in John Ray's collection *English Proverbs* (1678).

The attribution of foul language to artisans and the lower classes is typical and traditional, found in the medieval phrase for foul language, namely **cherles termes**, meaning "peasant talk" or "low-class language." In *Hamlet* (1600) the hero berates himself at one point that he should lose verbal control

And fall a-cursing like a very drab [prostitute]
A scullion! [kitchen servant]
(II ii 616–24)

However, there is an important counterbalancing attribution in one of the earliest comments on class and swearing in Sir Thomas Elyot's *The Governour* (1531): "They will say that he that swereth depe, swereth like a lorde" (chapter xxvi). The saying confirms the observation of many of his contemporaries, that the nobility swore freely, and even Queen Elizabeth, according to one contemporary, "swore like a man," a form of upper-class *insouciance* or disregard for traditional restraints. These aspects are covered in **class and swearing**. Elyot also follows **Chaucer** and other medieval writers in regarding gambling as a great provoker of oaths.

These traditional sayings are, of course, significant indicators of historical observations and values. But today there are virtually no fishwives or tinkers in existence, and lords have always been in a minority. Outside the armed forces there are no longer modern equivalents or specific callings especially associated with swearing. In the American provenance the principal example of a tradition of swearing lies not in specific occupations but in the practice of "sounding" and "playing **the dozens**," a form of ritual insult practiced by African Americans.

See also: Billingsgate; Cherles Termes; Dozens, the; Fishwife; Soldiers and Sailors.

Bibliography

Cameron, Paul. "Frequency and Kinds of Words in Various Social Settings, or What the Hell's Going On?" *Pacific Sociological Review* XII (1969), 101–4.
Flexner, Stuart Berg. *I Hear America Talking.* New York: Van Nostrand Reinhold, 1976.

C

CANADA

Canada is a vast and socially diverse country, so that the emphasis of this entry is on the English-speaking communities, which comprise some 45 percent of the population. In *The American Language,* Mencken discussed Canadian English under "Dialects," derived variously from "a continuous flow of immigration from the British Isles" and from "currents of migration from the United States" (1963, 469). Modern Canadian English is generally highly influenced by the cultural dominance of the United States, from which some 345 television channels are beamed. The opening essay of the collection *Canadian Writing Today,* entitled "Broadcasting and Canadian Culture," made this concession: "The bitter fact is that most Canadians have formed their taste in entertainment from the most popular American network shows" (Richler, ed., 1970, 31).

The distinguished academic Northrop Frye observed: "The Canadian sensibility has been profoundly disturbed not so much by our famous problem of identity as by some such riddle as 'Where is here?'" (cited in Atwood 1972, 10). Different authorial voices confront that riddle and express their identity. In general they have retained the bourgeois decencies of earlier English literary models, as is apparent in the major exponents of its literature, such as Alice Munro, Margaret Atwood, and Michael Ondaatje. Munro deals subtly with the banalities and frustrations of everyday feminine life, into which crudity only occasionally erupts. In "Gold Man" the poet Elizabeth Brewster articulates the laconic Canadian idiom:

I come from a country
Of slow and diffident words
Of broken rhythms
Of unsaid feelings.
(quoted in Atwood 1972, 180)

Others are more abrasive. Atwood has always tested the margins, but clearly does not see a virtue in obscenity. However, she makes fun of macho idioms, observing "Work by a male writer is often spoken of admiringly as having 'balls'; ever hear anyone speak admiringly of a work by a woman as having 'tits'?" (1982, 198). John Herbert's play *Fortune and Men's Eyes* (1967), depicting a homosexual rape in a Canadian reformatory, used an appropriate range of crude homosexual slang before it became fashionable. However, the unique publishing scandal involving a Canadian author occurred in 1968, when Mordecai Richler's satirical and scatological novel *Cocksure* was banned by W.H. Smith in Britain. Racial exclusivity is pointedly satirized by Earle Birney, whose poem "Anglosaxon Street" uses the ancient alliterating scheme with neat irony:

Here is a ghetto gotten for goyim
O with care denuded of nigger and kike
No coonsmell rankles reeks only cellarrot.
(ll. 5–7)

Although the variety is not as marked by obscenity and profanity as is American English, sexual and scatological terms are used quite freely in everyday discourse. Yet the recent *Guide to Canadian English Usage* (1997) included no blasphemous or obscene terms, even in the entry on *euphemism*. Likewise, the symposium *Focus on Canada* (1993) focused largely on phonetic and regional variations. There was no discussion of taboo or obscene language beyond a passing comment from John Sandiland's *Western Canadian Dictionary and Phrase Book* (1913) that taboo expressions were "often avoided" by initials (e.g., B.S. for "bullshit") and that racist terms are entered without any reference to their derogatory implications (Gregg in Clarke, ed., 1993, 28).

"Two Solitudes" was Hugh MacLennan's pointed title, now a proverbial observation, of "the nervous coexistence of the two founding cultures: French and English" (cited in Waterston, 1973, 35). The French-speaking population of Quebec is, however, distinctive in its blasphemy, being noted for using religious terms as powerful swearwords. As René Hardy has observed: "The French-speaking Québécois never cease to amaze by the abundant generation of original swearwords, frequently borrowed from the Catholic religion" (author's translation; 1989, 99). Hardy traces the origins of this attitude to the periods of strict control by the French/Catholic authorities in the past. However, the marked explosion of swearing that has occurred in the past few decades in American English has not had much impact on the Canadian variety. Consequently, euphemistic variants such as *freaking* and *frigging* remain more common than the root term *fucking*.

The principal nickname for a Canadian, especially a French-Canadian, is *Canuck,* recorded from 1835. It is usually considered derogatory, especially when used by an outsider. The term became an inflammatory turning point in the U.S. 1972 presidential election when it was used in a letter ("we don't have blacks, but we have Cannocks [sic]") attributed to an aide of the Democratic senator from Maine, Edmund Muskie (Bernstein and Woodward, *All the President's Men,* 1972, 132). The "Canuck letter," as it came to be known, was published in the New Hampshire *Union Leader* two weeks prior to the primary election, and the subsequent fallout damaged Muskie's campaign.

Bibliography

Atwood, Margaret. *Survival.* Toronto: Anansi, 1972.
———. *Second Words.* Boston: Beacon, 1982.

Barber, Katherine, ed. *The Canadian Oxford Dictionary*. Toronto: Oxford University Press, 1988.

Clarke, Sandra, ed. *Focus on Canada*. Amsterdam: John Benjamins, 1993.

Fee, Margaret, and Janice McAlpine, eds. *Guide to Canadian English Usage*. Toronto: Oxford University Press, 1997.

Hardy, René. "Ce que sacrer veut dire: à l'origine du juron religieux au Québec," in Delumeau, *Injures et Blasphèmes*. Paris: Imago, 1989.

Mencken, H.L. *The American Language*. Raven I. McDavid Jr., ed. New York: Knopf, 1963.

Waterston, Elizabeth. *Survey: A Short History of Canadian Literature*. Toronto: Methuen, 1973.

CANT. *See:* Dictionaries

CARIBBEAN

The Caribbean archipelago stretches in an arc of some 2,000 miles from Trinidad, only seven miles off the coast of Venezuela, to the Bahamas, not far from Florida. Within it, English is used in a continuum from a relatively standardized form to many varieties of local dialects or creoles, reflecting the diverse origins of the islanders, ranging from the English colonists, the owners of plantations, to their slaves, who were of African, Spanish, and Indian origins. Not all of these island varieties have been described with equal detail.

In his classic study *Jamaica Talk* (1961) Frederic G. Cassidy notes the complexity of the relations between color and labor: "No simple division between master and servant or black and white was ever made. From the beginning of English settlement there were indentured white servants very close to slavery; on the other hand, many blacks earned or were granted their freedom." He quotes Edward Long, who observed in 1742: "The Creole Blacks hold the Africans in the utmost contempt, stiling [sic] them 'salt-water Negroes' and 'Guiney birds,' but value themselves on their own pedigree" (1961, 156). He notes that the term *Creole* has shifted substantially in meaning. The earliest attributive use (dated 1740) refers to "the Creole Negroes," but by the following century the sense was "an individual born in the West Indies, of white parents," before taking on a general sense of "native." Furthermore, in the Jamaican variety of English, "The word [niega], which the *OED* enters under *neger,* but which is usually spelled *nayga* or *naygur* in the dialect literature, is used by black people to condemn those of their own colour. . . . *Naygur* is often tantamount to 'good for nothing' and *neegrish* is 'mean and dispicable'" (1961, 156). Degrees of blackness were, furthermore, significant, as Long pointed out: "The nearest to a Negro is a Sambo, the next a Mulatto, next a Quadroon, next a Mustee, and next a Mustaphino" (Cassidy 1961, 162). The collection *Voices in Exile: Jamaican Texts of the 18th and 19th Centuries* contains a number of insights—for example, *brown* was used for people of mixed race, who "formed a relatively privileged class between the black, dispossessed majority and the ruling white minority" (D'Costa and Lalla 1989, 143). A popular jaunty local song recorded in 1793 by J.B. Moreton describes the sexual adventures of a slave girl and her white "massa" and how she is beaten by the "misses":

My massa curse her, "lying bitch!"
And tell her, "buss my rassa" ("kiss my arse").
(ibid., 14)

Moreton also records the cruelty and contempt with which freed mulatto women ("these African queens") treat their slaves and former companions: "the yellow snake says to her poor black wench . . . : "*You damn'd [s]corpion! You black vipa! . . . Kackkaw foa you!* [shit for you!]" (ibid., 17).

Buckra, which in the American South has become a term of contempt for a poor white, has always had an elevated status in Caribbean English. Deriving from an African language, probably Ibo or Efik in Nigeria, in which *mbakara* means "he who surrounds or governs," it is first found, according to Cassidy, in Antigua in 1736, and four years later in Jamaica (1961, 155). Although used since the eighteenth century to mean a white man, it could in the past be used more generally: "it is not used exclusively in referring to the white man; a brown or black gentleman is also called so in acknowledgement of his gentility, or genteel appearance" (1961, 155).

Effeminacy is specifically despised. "A *mama* or *mama-man* is one who does woman's work, is woman-like or mean, worthless as a man. The word said to be the highest possible insult among the Jamaican folk is [mampaalo], which may be spelled *mampalo*. It means a man who is unmanly, abusive to women; also one who indulges in abnormal sexual relations of any kind. (Cf. Colombian *mampaalo,* a cock without fighting spirit)" (Cassidy 1961, 182). This complex of ideas and symbols runs across various cultures, being also apparent in the American English taunting use of *chicken* and Middle Scots *crawdon,* meaning a cock that will not fight, used by William Dunbar in his *flyting* with Kennedy about 1500.

Since the 1960s there has been an entirely new development, as the United Kingdom has accommodated many immigrants from the Caribbean with the typical problems of assimilation and alienation faced by communities dealing with such demographic changes. A number of Caribbean poets in the United Kingdom have started to use Creole forms in protest poetry, which establishes the black immigrant identity by ironically reclaiming ethnic slurs. One powerful instance is Mikey Smith's "Nigger Talk" poem, from *News for Babylon*:

Funky talk
Nitty gritty grass-root talk
. . .
Dis na white talk;
Na white talk dis.
It is coon, nignog, sambo, wog talk.

This is quoted in David Dabydeen's article "On Not Being Milton: Nigger Talk in England Today," which begins: "It is hard to put two words together in creole without swearing. Words are spat out from the mouth like live squibs" (in Ricks and Michaels 1990, 1–14). This is a powerful expression of the oral tradition in Caribbean poetry. The other, usually termed the literary tradition, is finely exemplified in the remarkable work of Derek Walcott, winner of the Nobel Prize for Literature in 1992.

See also: Dunbar, William.

Bibliography

Allsopp, Richard, ed. *Dictionary of Caribbean Usage.* Oxford: Oxford University Press, 1996.

Cassidy, Frederic G. *Jamaica Talk.* London: Macmillan, 1961.

Cassidy, Frederic G., and Robert B. Le Page, eds. *Dictionary of Jamaican English.* 2nd ed. Cambridge: Cambridge University Press, 1980.

D'Costa, Jean, and Barbara Lalla, eds. *Voices in Exile: Jamaican Texts of the 18th and 19th Centuries.* Tuscaloosa: University of Alabama Press, 1989.

Ricks, Christopher, and Leonard Michaels, eds. *The State of the Language 1990s Edition.* London: Faber & Faber, 1990.

CATHOLICS

The schism in the Christian Church brought about by the Reformation in the sixteenth century involved fundamental redefinitions in the notions of authority, as well as radically changed attitudes among those who had traditionally been termed "even Christians" or "fellow Christians." As the various sects competed for power, what had previously been a vocabulary of solidarity split into labels of vilification. This was especially evident in the enduring prejudicial terms applied to the Pope, to Roman Catholics, and to Rome.

In England, Henry VIII engineered the break with Rome by defying the authority of the Pope and creating in 1534 through "the Act of Supremacy" the new "Church of England called *Anglicana Ecclesia.*" This and subsequent acts demoted the Pope to "the Bishop of Rome," thus reducing his authority and making him a mere foreign ecclesiastic. This action intensified vehement anti-Catholic feeling, bred of xenophobia, chauvinism, and incipient nationalism. (The title *Pope* had been used from the fourteenth century to the nineteenth, to mean "the spiritual head of a Mohammedan or pagan religion.") In the Litany of the *Book of Common Prayer* (1549) the people prayed to be delivered from "the Bishop of Rome and his detestable enormities." Some of the vocabulary had been generated during the fourteenth century Wycliffite movement for reform: *Pope-holy,* a sarcastic formulation with strong suggestions of hypocrisy, is first recorded in William Langland's *Piers Plowman* about 1387; equally old is *Rome-runner,* referring to agents of direct papal taxation, which was obviously unpopular.

There was a rapid expansion of terms such as *papish* and *Romish,* laden with hostile overtones of a kind familiar to modern readers in political labels ending in *-ism* and *-ist,* such as *fascism* and *racist.* A sense of this semantic growth can be gauged from this sample, with dates of first recorded usage: *papist* (1521), *popish* (1528), *popery* (1534), *papistical* (1537), *papistic* (1545), *papish* (1546), *papism* (1550), *popestant* (1550), and *popeling* (1561).

Most of these terms have become obsolete. But some continued to be current for centuries. "Hatred of Roman Catholicism ran like a fever through English society in the seventeenth century, and to call a man a papist was to accuse him of treachery and perfidy" (Lockyer 1967, 11). Guy Fawkes Day (commemorating the Gunpowder Plot, an unsuccessful Catholic conspiracy to blow up the Houses of Parliament in 1605) was previously called Pope Day, since the Pope was burnt in effigy, a practice that continued up to the early twentieth century. Though the Popish Plot (1678) turned out to be a fabricated conspiracy concocted by Titus Oates, who was subsequently found guilty of perjury, the intensity of anti-Catholic suspicion made it initially credible. Joseph Addison's *Spectator* No. 125 (1714) records this revealing anecdote: "This knight had

Anti-Catholic xenophobia in America is starkly reflected in this 1855 cartoon. With the rise in Irish immigration and the spread of Catholic education, nativists perceived Roman Catholic influence as a growing threat. *(Library of Congress, LC-USZ62-30815)*

occasion to enquire the way to St. Anne's Lane; upon which the person whom he spoke to called him a young popish cur, and asked him, who made Anne a saint?" The slogan "No popery!" still survives, especially in the political rhetoric of Northern Ireland. Indeed both *popery* and *papist* are still recorded in standard dictionaries of British English. The *Pope's nose,* insultingly used of "the rump of a fowl," dates from post-Reformation times, being first recorded in 1796. The more domestic variant, the *parson's nose,* emerges about a hundred years later.

The Gunpowder Plot served to aggravate the prejudices against Catholics generally and especially the Jesuit order, already denounced by Philip Stubbes in his *Anatomie of Abuses* (1583) as "the diuels agents." The order's reputation for casuistry and prevarication have, in the words of the *Oxford English Dictionary,* "rendered the name odious, not only in English, but in other languages." One of the conspirators, the Jesuit Father Garnet, notoriously continued to equivocate under oath when being interrogated, a point further discussed in the entry for **Shakespeare**. Thus by 1640 the sense of "dissembling person or prevaricator" was well established. Associations of sodomy and masturbation also developed, the first found in the Earl of Rochester's ironic vision (ca. 1687) of a Utopia in which

The Jesuits Fraternity
Shall leave the use of Buggery.
("A Ramble in Saint James's Park," ll. 145–46)

The second occurs later, recorded in Francis Grose's *Classical Dictionary of the Vulgar Tongue* (1785), as *to box the Jesuit:* "A sea term for masturbation; a crime, it is said, much practised by the reverend fathers of that society." Related opprobrious terms implying casuistry (with dates from the *OED*) were *jesuit* (vb) (1601), *jesuitish* (1600), *jesuitism* (1609), *jesuitic* (1640), and *jesuitize* (1644). *Jesuitical* (from 1600) is still in use.

Grose also recorded *craw-thumper* as a term for Catholics, "so called from their beating their breasts in the confession of their sins." The same term is applied from 1845 to early Catholic settlers in Maryland. Of the other words that developed in England, only *papist* appears to have crossed the Atlantic, although *poper* is also recorded. Among other exclusively American terms are the contemptuous epithets *bead-puller, fish-eater,* and *mackerel-snapper.* The modern composite title *Roman Catholic* is recorded from 1605, since in the words of the *OED,* the alternatives "simple *Roman, Romanist,* and *Romish* had become too invidious."

See also: Religious Oaths.

Bibliography

Allen, Irving Lewis. *The Language of Ethnic Conflict.* New York: Columbia University Press, 1983.
Hillerbrand. H.J., ed. *The Reformation in Its Own Words.* London: S.C.M. Press, 1964.
Lockyer, Roger, ed. *Clarendon's History of the Great Rebellion.* Oxford: Folio Society, 1967.

CAXTON, WILLIAM

William Caxton (?1422–1491) is famous in English history for his revolutionary contribution in starting the first printing press in England in 1476. Whereas the previous manuscript culture naturally reflected regional and cultural diversity, the uniformity of the new print format brought with it the expectation of a standard in usage. Caxton thus found himself having to make many decisions about what was linguistically "correct," a new notion. In the Prologue to his *Eneydos* (ca. 1490), he complained with a note of exasperation, "Certaynely it is harde to playse every man bycause of dyversitie and chaunge of langage."

Caxton also contributed to the bourgeois standard notion of "language which is fit to print." As the entry on the **medieval period** shows, language now regarded as coarse and obscene thrived in common sayings and even in names. Although he made no overt comment about the propriety of coarse language in print, Caxton certainly had bowdlerizing tendencies. In the earlier Winchester manuscript of Sir Thomas Malory's *Morte Darthur,* the sufferings of Lancelot in "The Fair Maid of Astolat" are graphically described: "the blood burst out, nigh a pint at once, that at last he sank down upon his arse, and so swooned down, pale and deadly" (1947, III, 1074). In Caxton's version *arse* is edited out, and the decent synonym *buttocks* takes its place. This was a practice to be repeated many times over the centuries.

See also: Medieval Period; Press, the.

Bibliography

Vinaver, Eugene, ed. *The Works of Sir Thomas Malory.* Oxford: Oxford University Press, 1947.

CENSORSHIP

Censorship basically takes two forms, namely preventive interference by the state prior to publication, or subsequent punitive prosecution, dealt with more fully under **fines and penalties** and **lawsuits**. There are also less direct interventions, from bodies such as the Press Council, the Church, as well as less obvious forms like self-censorship deriving from general cultural expectations within society or from unsourced pressures, such as political correctness. Censorship has a dismayingly long record in English literary history and came to a formal end only comparatively recently with changes in the definition of **obscenity** in 1959 and the abolition of the office of the **Lord Chamberlain** in 1968. However, a vigorous debate continued in the United Kingdom and the United States, with authorities such as Lord Patrick Devlin and Professor Irving Kristol arguing for the right of the community to protect its moral standards, and others, like Professors Horace Hart and Ronald Dworkin arguing for the primacy of individual rights. The situation in the United States is more complex, in view of the rights enshrined in the First Amendment, and is treated toward the end of this entry. Film censorship is dealt with under the entries for **cinema** and **Hollywood.**

Although censorship is usually associated with repressive regimes, some form of it is found in comparatively democratic societies, especially in relation to the stage, the cinema, and literature. Furthermore, it was absent from comparatively conservative and controlled societies in the past. The Middle Ages, for example, is regarded as being a period of strict ecclesiastical control and censorship. Yet the example of **Chaucer** shows that it was possible for a writer to use the full extent of obscenity and profanity without censure or punishment. In fact, Henry VIII (1491–1547) was the first European monarch to limit the freedom of expression by publishing a list of banned books in 1529. As the drama became more secular and popular, stringent policing of plays began through the institution by the Crown in 1545 of the ill-named **Master of the Revels**, a Court officer in the service of the Lord Chamberlain, the most powerful minister in the land. The Master's powers included the licensing of playhouses and the preemptive right to censor plays, which actors had to present or recite to him prior to public performance.

Another preemptive source was the *Index* (short for *Index Librorum Prohibitorum* or List of Forbidden Books) derived from rules agreed at the Council of Trent (1564), formulated by the Catholic Church as part of the Counter-Reformation. This was a list of books that Roman Catholics were forbidden to read. The first *Index* was published in 1564, the second in 1596, and subsequent editions continued up to 1948. In addition, the Vatican published the *Index Expurgatorius,* listing books not to be read without correction—that is, after passages had been deleted or altered. This category gave rise to the modern sense of *expurgate,* meaning "to cleanse or remove impurities," recorded from 1678 in the comment of Thomas Jones: "The Catholic Church ... hath ... cracked her credit by forgeing, expurgating, etc." (*Rome No Mother,* chapter 64). In 1966 the Vatican agreed not to publish further editions.

Initially, theatrical censorship was exercised mainly on the grounds of doctrine and politics: an ordinance of 1599 had specified "matters of religion, or the governance of the estate of the common weale." The scene in Shakespeare's *Richard II* (1595) depicting the deposition of the King was banned from being performed during the reign of Queen Elizabeth, and omitted even from the early printed quartos. Linguistic grounds were instituted only in 1606, three years after the end of Elizabeth's reign, the relevant legislation being "An Act to Restrain Abuses of Players" (1606):

> If . . . any person or persons doe or shall in any Stage play, Interlude, Shewe, Maygame or Pageant jestingly or prophanely speake or use the holy name of God or of Christ Jesus, or of the Holy Ghoste or of the Trinitie . . . [they] shall be forfeite for everie such Offence by him or by them committed Tenne pounds. (3 Jac. I. c.21)

Like most restrictive legislation, censorship encouraged ingenious evasions. First, there was a marked increase in the use of pagan deities. Second, "minced oaths" or substitutions avoiding direct references to foul or profane terms, suddenly sprang up in great profusion. Both varieties are still current. Although "by Jove!" is now a dated British exclamation, an early form is found in Shakespeare's *Twelfth Night* (IV ii 13). Similarly, when Faustus blasphemously calls up the devil in Christopher Marlowe's *Doctor Faustus* (1592), within the magic circle used in the ritual "is Jehovah's name," not the name of the Christian God. Ben Jonson created some wonderfully absurd pagan exclamations in his comedy *Everyman in his Humour* (acted in 1598 with Shakespeare in the cast): Bobadill swears *by the foot of Pharaoh* and exclaims *Body o' Caesar!*

As the entry for **minced oaths** shows, this disguise mechanism had been in existence from the time of Chaucer. However, in the years immediately prior to the legislation against Profanity on the Stage, some self-censorship was evidently taking place, since Shakespeare and other dramatists used many newly minced oaths such as *'sblood* (for *God's blood*) from 1598 onward. These were deliberate evasions, as opposed to the usual process of steady erosion over time, such as *God blind me!* becoming *Gor blimey!* and finally plain *blimey!* The older forms have all passed away, the only survivor being *'struth,* respelled as *strewth.* Apart from philologists, the speech community generally does not recognize the original profane meanings of minced oaths. Later, in King James I's reign, in 1623, a more general prohibition was enacted, covered under **fines and penalties**, specifying a penalty of one shilling per oath.

The Master of the Revels continued with his excisions, which early in James's reign extended from the performance of plays to include their printing. Comparison of texts shows precisely how some authors under pressure changed their texts for publication. Thus Ben Jonson toned down the oaths in his play *The Magnetic Lady* (1632), which had been subjected to an investigation into a charge of blasphemy, altering *by Jesu* to "believe me," *by heaven* to "by these hilts" ("by this sword"), and *faith* to "marry" or "indeed." The entry for **Shakespeare** details many similar substitutions in the posthumous *First Folio* (1623).

When the Civil War broke out in 1642, the Puritan army under Oliver Cromwell took up arms, not only against the king, but against "popery, prelacy, superstition, heresy, schism, and profaneness." One of the first pieces of legislation passed by the Puritans, on September 2, 1642, was the closing of the theatres for, among other things, "too commonly expressing lascivious Mirth and Levitie." In this generally repressive atmosphere, numerous tracts were written against swearing, such as Walter Powell's *A Summons for Swearers* (1645), but *A Free Discourse against Customary Swearing and a Dissuasive against Cursing,* written ca. 1647 by Robert Boyle, the famous scientist, was published only in 1695, nearly a half century later and four years after his death. In 1645 the Scottish Parliament determined that cursing or blaspheming should be "censurable" and the fine should be according to rank: a nobleman should pay 20 pounds Scots, a baron 20 marks (about £7), and a gentleman 10 marks (about £3.5).

The **Restoration** of the Monarchy, in 1660, involved the simultaneous restoration of the theaters and the innovation of women actors, in both of which the new king, Charles II, took an active interest. However, the new theatrical regime was tightly but shrewdly controlled: the Letters Patent or Royal Licences permitted only two theaters in London, and the managers, Thomas Killigrew and Sir William Davenant, were to be responsible for censoring the plays performed there. The new Restoration drama was both a rebellion against Puritanism and a mirror of the decadence and open sexuality of the Court. There were oaths in profusion, but in general they were either minced or secular.

Although there were attacks on the stage as a corrupting institution, notably by Jeremy **Collier** in 1698, and even assaults on actors, there was little official intervention. But in the early part of the eighteenth century, there emerged fearless satirists such as Jonathan Swift, Alexander Pope, and Henry Fielding. Pope's poetic satires pilloried the most powerful in the land using substitute names, some of them transparent, such as "Anna" for Queen Anne, but his attacks provoked no retaliation. When, however, the same technique was used in theatrical satires such as John Gay's *The Beggar's Opera* (1728), a thinly-disguised attack on the prime minister, Sir Robert Walpole, and in Fielding's *The Welsh Opera* (1731), which lampooned the Royal Family, Walpole himself took action. In 1737 he claimed to have received the manuscript of a scurrilous, anonymous, but unperformed play, enigmatically titled *The Golden Rump,* allegedly full of scandalous abuse of the King and his ministers. The actual origins of the play are still uncertain, but the parliamentary consequence was the introduction of a Licensing Act of unparalleled restrictiveness.

The powers of the Lord Chamberlain, exercised via officials called Examiners of Plays, remained virtually as defined by the Act of 1737 for well over two centuries. In the interim various attempts were made to limit the Chamberlain's authority, most notably in 1842 and 1843, resulting in the limiting directive that the Lord Chamberlain was forbidden to withhold his license unless on the grounds of "the preservation of good manners, decorum and of the public peace." Petitions by dramatic authors of note, especially George Bernard Shaw, achieved some flexibility, but the powers and responsibilities of the Lord Chamberlain for theatrical censorship ended only with abolition of the office in terms of the Theatres Act in 1968.

However, between 1737 and 1968 something of a double standard continued to exist, for in the new and expanding field of fiction very few prosecutions occurred initially. The publication of what is termed an "obscene libel" was made into a common-law offence in 1727. As the entry for **John Cleland** shows, punishments for pornography were not necessarily severe. The growth of pornography in Victorian times led to the Obscene Publications Act of 1857, with a number of prosecutions and withdrawals of works for fear of prosecution, notably that of Algernon Charles Swinburne's *Poems and Ballads* in 1866. The crucial comments made by Lord Chief Justice Alexander Cockburn, in a case in 1868, are discussed further in the entry for **obscenity**.

By far the greatest number of prosecutions and suppressions of literary works have been on the grounds of obscenity rather than profanity. In the past century censorship has been exercised to prevent or ban the publication of numerous books, including Charles Baudelaire's *Fleurs du Mal* (1857), Mark Twain's *Tom Sawyer* (1876) and *Huckleberry Finn* (1885), James Joyce's *Ulysses* (1922), Radclyffe Hall's *The Well of Loneliness* (1928), Henry Miller's *Tropic of Cancer* (1934) and *Tropic of Capricorn* (1939), as well as D.H. Lawrence's *The Rainbow* (1915) and **Lady Chatterley's Lover** (1928), to name the most famous cases. The last-named work attracted the greatest notoriety. (Incidentally, in France the ban on Baudelaire's *Fleurs du Mal,* also instituted in 1857, was raised only in 1949.)

Under the laws of the United States at the time of the Revolution, the status of obscene libel was unclear, but in the early nineteenth century a number of states in New England strengthened their laws in this regard. After 1868 the Cockburn definition of obscenity started to carry weight. However, the moral crusader who was to prove highly influential was Anthony Comstock (1844–1915). In 1873 he and the Y.M.C.A. Committee for the Suppression of Vice managed to get through Congress an act bearing his name that greatly increased the restrictions on obscene publications, which were taken to include even contraceptive literature.

As the entry for **lawsuits** shows, the determination of Comstock and his followers led to some extraordinary successes, notably in Boston in the 1920s. Indeed the phrase "Banned in Boston" became something of a cliché. The prosecutors took advantage of a clause in the Massachusetts statute forbidding the public sale of any book "containing obscene indecent language." (It was the Concord Public Library that first banned Mark Twain's *Huckleberry Finn,* in 1885). However, **Comstockery** suffered major setbacks in failed prosecutions, most significantly, of James Joyce's *Ulysses* in 1933 and *Lady Chatterley's Lover* in 1959.

While official censorship has declined radically, challenges and bannings continue on a surprising scale. According to the American Civil Liberties Union, among the ten most challenged books of 1990–2000 were Mark Twain's *Huckleberry Finn,* John Steinbeck's *Of Mice and Men,* and the *Harry Potter* series by J.K. Rowling. In the same period the three most common grounds for banning were "sexually explicit" material (1,607), "offensive language" (1,427), and material considered "unsuited to age group" (1,256). This was out of a total of 6,364 challenges.

Self-censorship continued, usually on the grounds of obscenity, real or imagined. Even after the *Chatterley* judgments, Lawrence Durrell's Preface to an American edition of *Lady Chatterley's Lover* in 1968 resorted to a "reverse code" for the offending words "kcuf," "tnuc," "kcirp" and "sllab." Furthermore, a number of American major dictionaries omitted the most taboo of what Judge van Pelt Bryan called (not with complete accuracy) the "four-letter Anglo-Saxon words." These included the third edition of *Webster* (1961) and its derivatives, and even the *Barnhart Dictionary of Etymology* (1988).

Of a different order was E.M. Forster's homosexual novel *Maurice,* which he wrote between 1910 and 1913, but did not feel able to publish during his lifetime (1879–1970), even when the laws governing homosexuality were revised in 1967. Two instances from very different authors are open about self-censorship. Alluding to an incident of exposure in her novel *The Pargiters* (written in 1932 but published only in 1977), Virginia Woolf conceded: "There is, as the three dots used after the sentence 'He unbuttoned his clothes . . . ' testify, a convention, supported by law, which forbids, whether rightly or wrongly, any plain description of the sight that Rose, in common with many other girls, saw" (cited in Smith, ed., 1993, 119). In *The Moon and Sixpence* (1930) the explosive comment "Get out, you bloody swine" is followed by Somerset Maugham's ironic confession that "since this book is meant for family reading, I thought it better—at the expense of truth—to put into [Strickland's] mouth language familiar to the domestic circle" (chapter 47).

Under the apartheid regime in South Africa writers had to deal with a strict Censorship Board proscribing the traditional topics of obscenity and blasphemy and ordering the whole-sale banning of books. Other taboos peculiar to the period were miscegenation or what was called "sex across the color line." Virtually every major author experienced some difficulty.

See also: Blasphemy; Bowdlerization; Collier Controversy; *Lady Chatterley's Lover;* Minced Oaths; Obscenity; Restoration, the.

Bibliography

Craig, Alec. *The Banned Books of England.* London: Allen & Unwin, 1962.
Devlin, Patrick. *The Enforcement of Morals.* Oxford: Oxford University Press, 1968.
Gurr, Andrew. *The Shakespearean Stage.* Cambridge: Cambridge University Press, 1980.
Hart, H.L.A. *Law, Liberty and Morality.* Stanford, CA: Stanford University Press, 1963.
Kristol, Irving. "Pornography, Obscenity, and the Case for Censorship." *The New York Times Magazine,* March 28, 1971. Reprinted in Kristol, *On the Democratic Idea in America.* New York: Harper & Row, 1972.
Rolph, H.C. *The Trial of Lady Chatterley.* Harmondsworth: Penguin, 1960.
Shirley, Frances A. *Swearing and Perjury in Shakespeare's Plays.* London: Allen & Unwin, 1979.
Smith, Nigel, ed. *Essays and Studies 1993: Literature and Censorship.* Cambridge: D.S. Brewer, 1993.
United States v. *One Book Called "Ulysses,"* S.D.N.Y., 1933.

CHARMS

The most remote linguistic usage invariably contains some form of **word magic**. Charms, spells, exorcisms, and runes represent in their different ways the ancient and primal belief in the power of words over physical objects and the invisible powers in nature. Being the opposite of spells and curses, charms seek to harness the energy of word magic and the hidden virtues of objects in a positive way, to prevent or cure various afflictions. In earlier times this belief system was termed "natural magic." To this day idioms like "it worked like a charm" are relics of this belief. Curiously, *charm* is not an Anglo-Saxon word, being borrowed about 1300 from Old French *charme,* meaning a charm or enchantment, being ultimately related to Latin *carmen,* "a song." The Anglo-Saxon term was *galdor,* derived from *galan,* "to sing," which reinforces the important relationship with *chant* and *enchantment.* Instructions for ancient charms frequently specify that the form of words must be sung, usually many times and commonly with some ritual action.

These ancient fragments of folk memory preserved in oral tradition are to be found in great numbers in Anglo-Saxon manuscripts; some "are probably among the oldest lines in the English language" (Gordon 1954, 85). Even a pagan deity is invoked in a charm for infertile land: "Erce, Erce, Erce, mother of Earth," although most of the piece is Christian in its references. Some, with quite complex and lengthy incantations, are directed against wens (harmless cysts of the skin), swarms of bees, convulsions, and even the theft of cattle.

One, a charm for a safe journey, refers explicitly to word magic: "I chant a charm of victory, I bear a rod of victory / word-victory, work-victory" (Gordon 1954, 91).

The post-medieval growth of science and rational inquiry, allied with the authority of the Church, served largely to discredit charms or to stigmatize them by associating them with witchcraft or heretical practices. Today they are generally regarded as part of folklore or popular superstition.

See also: Blasphemy; Spells; Word Magic.

Bibliography
Cockayne, O. *Leechdoms, Wortcunning, and Starcraft of Early England.* Revised ed. London: Holland Press, 1961.
Gordon, R.K. *Anglo-Saxon Poetry.* London: Dent, 1954.
Grattan, J., and C. Singer. *Anglo-Saxon Magic and Medicine.* London: Oxford University Press, 1952.
Kieckhefer, R. *Magic in the Middle Ages.* New York: Cambridge University Press, 1989.

CHAUCER, GEOFFREY

The works of Geoffrey Chaucer (ca. 1340–1400) contain unexpected volumes of blasphemy, profanity, foul language, and xenophobic insult. Furthermore, Chaucer gives us many insights into swearing, namely class differences, gender factors, and different levels of awareness of the seriousness of oaths. Although he lived in a totally different society six centuries ago, Chaucer makes the modern reader aware of the vitality, creativity, continuity, and dangers of swearing. We would not expect these qualities from the preeminent English poet of the medieval era, "the first finder of our fair language," as Thomas Hoccleve called him, the first commoner to be buried in Westminster Abbey and praised by all his peers, both English and European. The *Canterbury Tales* (1386–1400) draws on diverse literary influences, notably the spirituality of Dante, the idealism of Petrarch, and the realism of Boccaccio, as well as his extensive human experience, as an envoy, ambassador, and senior civil servant.

Chaucer's great frame narrative encapsulates the diversity of the Middle Ages and forms a wonderful *tour de force* of medieval literary genres. It explores the polarities of the sacred and the profane: from the most spiritual genres, the saint's life, homily and sermon, obviously befitting a pilgrimage, through the elevated epic and chivalric romance, the dream vision, tales of faery and magic, the love debate, the beast fable and complex allegory down to the frankest amorous memoirs and the crudest imaginable bedroom farces. This diversity reflects variously the idealism, spirituality, worldliness, crudity, and corruption of the tellers: they range from the Knight, whose whole life has been devoted to campaigns against the heathen all over the known world; the Parson, the one "good man of religion"; the frankly physical Miller; the sexually omnivorous and much married Wife of Bath; down to the most corrupt spiritual confidence tricksters. The bawdy tales, unexpected entertainments on a pilgrimage, belong to the genre of the medieval French ***fabliaux:*** cleverly plotted narratives treating sexual infidelity and even profanity in a comic, often cynical, fashion. Their conclusions embody a rough justice that seldom squares with Christian morality. The prime examples are the tales of the Miller, Merchant, Shipman, and Reve.

Less predictably, the tales are seldom purely generic in the mixture of style and content.

The Nun's Priest's beast fable is very philosophical and learned; the coarse Miller's adulterous farce is surprisingly literary; the saint's life of the Prioress is full of anti-Semitism; the Pardoner's grim hellfire sermon has unintentional sexual revelations in its hysterical denunciations. The opposing criteria of *ernest* and *game* (seriousness and fun) are teasingly intertwined, as are high and low language. The realistic link-pieces between the tales contain a similar range of register, from formal compliment, bawdy *double-entendre,* down to furious verbal brawls and wounding insults. From all of them echo an amazing range of oaths, exclamations, ejaculations, lamentations, and curses.

Chaucer is the only major author prior to the modern era who used the whole gamut of the lexis, from the most technical and philosophical to the most vulgar and obscene. In his work can be found the whole range of "four-letter" words: *ferte, erse, pisse, shiten, queynte, collions* (testicles), and *swyve,* which predates the arrival of *fuck* around 1500 and thrived from the medieval period before suffering a curious demise around the end of the Victorian era. The authors who came after Chaucer were all restrained by censorship of one form or another. Although there was no actual censorship, many tracts and major texts were extremely censorious about swearing. These included Robert of Brunne's *Handlyng Synne* (ca. 1300) and Dan Michel's *Ayenbite of Inwit,* or "The Remorse of Conscience" (ca. 1340).

These admonitory texts make the profusion of oaths in the *Canterbury Tales* particularly astonishing. Herbert Starr, in what is probably a conservative estimate, calculated that there are two hundred different oaths in Chaucer (Elliott 1974, 263). Ralph Elliott noted that "It is the vulgar characters who swear most and most profanely, with Harry Bailly [the Host of the Tabard Inn] well out in front, the Wife of Bath some way behind, followed by the Pardoner and the Miller" (Elliott 1974, 253). Chaucer's early poem *The Parlement of Foulys* (ca. 1382), a comic debate with vigorous exchanges between the different orders of birds, makes a similar discrimination between the "polite language" of the aristocracy and "cherles termes" of the lower-class birds. In the scheme of the *Canterbury Tales,* the hierarchical correlation between class and language is equally apparent, as the entries for the **medieval period** and **cherles termes** make clear.

Chaucer the author, who has created the whole ingenious scheme of storytelling, presents a narrative *persona,* another Chaucer, the pilgrim-narrator, who refers to the problems of obscenity and profanity in the *Prologue* (ll. 725–42). In a slightly embarrassed fashion he hopes that the reader will not ascribe the bad language to his *vileynye* ("ill-breeding"), since he is obliged to repeat the tales truthfully, even though people will speak *rudeliche and large* ("rudely and freely"). From these modest protestations, he moves to a quite different level of argument, reminding us firstly that "Crist spak himself ful brode in hooly writ" ("Christ himself spoke very plainly in Holy Writ") and that Plato prescribed that "The wordes moot be cosyn for the dede" ("The language must be appropriate to the action").

Although oaths seem to cascade indiscriminately from the lips of the pilgrims as they make their pilgrimage to Canterbury, Chaucer is clearly making a judgment on the characters on the basis of their swearing and "brode" language. Even Madame Eglentine, the prim, class-conscious Prioress, swears mildly by St. Loy, appropriately the patron saint of jewelers. At one end of the scale is the pious modesty of the Knight, "who never in his life said anything ill-bred" (*vileynye*), telling a romance of chivalry virtually free of oaths. At the other are a variety of foul-mouthed and profane exhibitionists who seem to have no business on the pilgrimage. These include the Miller, Reeve, Pardoner, Summoner, Wife of Bath, and the Host of the Tabard Inn in London, the self-appointed master of ceremonies. The principal theme of the corrupt Friar's tale is swearing, more especially whether grievous curses like "The feend yow fecche!" ("The Devil take you!") used by a furious carter as he flays his horses should be taken literally as invocations, or regarded with more toleration as expressions of frustration in which "The carl spak oo thing, but he thoght another" ("The chap said one thing but he meant another," l. 1568).

The Parson, an idealized figure, is aggressively judgmental against swearing. When the Host invites him to tell his tale, using provocative language:

"Sir Parrishe Prest," quod he, "for Goddes bones
Telle us a tale. . . . by Goddes dignitee!"

the Parson immediately retorts:

"Benedicitee!
What eyleth the man so synfully to swere?"
("What is wrong with the man that he swears so grievously?")

The Host stands his ground, but warns the pilgrimage to expect a *predicacioun* (sermon). Into the confrontation quite unexpectedly comes the Shipman (skipper), a ruthless and unChristian man, who also has strong views, insisting that the Parson shall not preach.

"Nay, by my fader soule, that schal he nat!"
Seyde the Shipman, "heer schal he nat preche;
He schal no gospel glosen [interpret] here ne teche."
(ll. 1166–80)

These three characters express different attitudes then current toward profane and religious language. The Parson is severely against all swearing, the Host regards it more broad-mindedly as a venal (minor) sin, but the Shipman is hostile to preaching and represents a growing fundamentalist suspicion of priests and "glosing" (ingenious interpretation) of the Gospel. This attitude was to harden into Protestantism and Nonconformity in the following centuries.

The originality of the swearing in the *Canterbury Tales* is difficult to appreciate now. Disparaging secular uses of *foul, lousy, old, shrew, swine,* and *idiot* were then new, but have lost their impact in the intervening centuries through the semantic trend of **loss of intensity**. Several of them emerge from the lips of the formidable Wife of Bath, who in her amorous and violent memoir, her remarkably extensive *Prologue,* castigated her elderly spouses in wickedly insulting phrases like *olde bareful of lies* and *sire oulde lecchour,* dismissing Metellius as *the foule swyn.* In the *Friar's Tale* the devil-figure speaks of *a lowsy jogelour* ("a lousy juggler"), using *lousy* for the first recorded time. The Pardoner extends the currency of the ancient term *bitch* in condemning dice as *the bicched bones two.* Even the Man of Law, a conservative practitioner of

69

the language, launches the fascinating word **virago** as a new misogynist term, while the disillusioned Merchant refers to his wife as a **shrew**, a term newly applied to a woman. Both terms have their own entries.

Most of the swearing is, expectedly, religious and traditional. The Parson, the one "good man of religion" on the pilgrimage, tells the final "tale," but in the form of a lengthy discourse on the Seven Deadly Sins. He condemns swearing in a literal fashion, although he opens with an appeal that sounds to us like an oath:

> For Cristes sake, ne swereth nat so synfully in dismembrynge of Crist by soule, herte, bones and body. For certes it semeth that ye thynke that the cursed Jewes ne dismembred nat ynough the preciouse persone of Crist, but ye dismembre hym more. (l. 590)

The Parson's strict interpretation condemns much of the profanity that has been uttered on the path of pilgrimage. His view is echoed in the pseudo-sermon delivered by the corrupt simoniac bogus evangelist, the Pardoner. His own hellfire diatribe is schizophrenic; one mode is the standard denunciation of swearing, setting out three modes:

> Gret sweryng is a thing abhominable,
> And fals sweryng is yet more reprevable [reprehensible]. . . .
> But ydel sweryng is a cursednesse [wickedness].
> (ll. 631–38)

The other mode is the orgy of swearing indulged in by the revelers in his tale in their drunken frenzy, indiscriminately garbling dicers' oaths and invocations to holy relics:

> "By Goddes precious herte," and "by his nayles,"
> and "by the blood of Crist which is in Hayles [a sacred relic],
> Sevene is my chaunce, and thyn is cynk [five] and treye [three]!"
> "By Goddes armes, if thou falsly pleye,
> This daggere shal thurghout thyn herte go!"
> Thys fruyt cometh of the bicched bones two
> Forsweryng, ire, falseness, homycide.
> (ll. 651–57)

The revelers, too, in the words of the Parson, "dismember" Christ:

> And many a grisly ooth thanne han they sworn
> And Cristes blessed body they to-rente [tore to pieces]
> (ll. 708–9)

This idiom, which is to modern readers the most shocking, is reiterated throughout the work. The body of Christ, the wounds and torture of the Crucifixion, become a grim motif. Thus the drunken Miller announces himself almost incoherently: "By armes, by blood and bones" (3125). The Host reacts to the *Physician's Tale* in a similar way, giving us an indication of what Chaucer considered outrageous swearing to be:

Our Host gan to swere as he were wood [mad];
"Harrow!" quod he, "by nayles and by blood!"
(ll. 287–88)

("Harrow!" is an almost untranslatable medieval cry of pain and distress; it is secular, surviving only in the adjective *harrowing*.)

The most sacred Christian symbols take on different meanings, not all of them expected in an age of faith. The Cross is strangely transfigured into "Cristes sweete tree" (*Miller's Tale*, l. 3767) and the sufferings of the Crucifixion are made into exclamations, such as "for Cristes peyne," "for Cristes passioun." (*Tree* was used of the Cross from Anglo-Saxon English through to late Middle English; *passioun* in Chaucer's time meant "the sufferings of Christ on the Cross.") However, the Cross is also used in a way we would consider blasphemous in the Wife of Bath's retaliation for her young husband's dalliances: "I made him of the same wood a croce [cross]." Protestations range from the Latin *corpus dominus* ("by God's body") to "by Godes herte!," "God help me so. . ." and "God it woot," which later became "God wot," the ancestors of "God knows."

Blessings are usually general, as in "God save al the route" ("God save all the company"), sometimes reinforced to "God bless us, and oure lady Seinte Marie!" But some are profane or even blasphemous. The Shipman ends his cynical tale relating ledger-sheets and bedsheets with a naughtily ambiguous blessing: "God us sende / Taillynge ynogh unto our lyves ende" ("May God give us plenty of bonking/accounting until the end of our lives").

Invocations follow the same pattern, including "by thilke [the same] God that yaf me soule and lyf!," "by heighe God!," "by God and by Saint John!," "by hevene king!," and "for verray God, that nys but oon" ("By the true God, of which there is only one"). This is, of course, the top of the scale. Lesser known saints such as St. Note and St. Ronyan make their appearances, as do ancestors, some of them surprisingly remote in "by my fader soule!" and even "by my moodres sires soule!" and related artifacts, such as "by seint Poules belle!" The comparatively mild are "Benedicitee!" ("The Lord bless you!"). Some are completely personal and secular, such as "so theech!" ("so may I prosper!") and "nevere in my lyf, for lief ne looth" ("never in my life, whether I wish to or not").

This miscellany suggests that oaths spring indiscriminately from the pilgrims' lips—the light, the heavy, and the absurd. Yet in some cases Chaucer clearly seeks to individuate swearing to make oaths, curses, and blessings an indicator of character and values. A notable example is the Wife of Bath's outrageous mixture of sentiments expressed toward her old husband: "O leeve sire shrew, Jhesu shorte thy life!" ("Oh dear master villain, may Jesus shorten your life!"). Likewise, the outraged husband in the *Merchant's Tale*, catching his wife and her lover *in flagrante dilecto*: "God yeve yow bothe on shames deth to dyen" ("May God give you both a shameful death!"). Similar is the Host's furious response to the charlatanism of the eunuch Pardoner hawking bogus relics:

"By the cros which that Seint Eleyne fond
I wolde I hadde thy collions [testicles] in my hond.
They shal be shryned [enshrined] in an hogges toord!"

(ll. 951–52)

Two final examples show the individuated use of oaths. The *Man of Law's Tale* shows a conservative, dignified formality appropriate to the teller's character and station: "But oon avow to grete God I heete" ("But one oath I promise to great God"). *Heete* was an archaic term, even in Chaucer's time. Other formal archaisms are *parfay* (by my faith), *thanked be Cristes grace!, God and all his halwes brighte!* (*halwes* being an archaic word for "saint" and the root of *Halloween*). However, from this highly respectable legal pillar of the establishment emanate two strains of opprobrious language, namely xenophobia and misogyny. In his denunciation of the devious sultaness in his tale (ll. 358–61) he launches a new term of misogynist abuse, **virago**.

Xenophobic swearing is an important and troubling aspect of the *Canterbury Tales*. The anti-Semitic phrase *the cursed Jewes* occurs in the dour sermon of the Parson, being repeated in the *Pardoner's Tale* and also in the motif of the dismembering of Christ. However, the most surprising context is the gruesome anti-Semitic tale told by the Prioress, discussed more fully in the entry for **Jews**.

The *Nun's Priest's Tale*, a brilliant compendium of narrative techniques and a comic tour de force, makes an artfully humorous comment on swearing by its absurd placing of standard oaths in an animal fable. The vain cock Chantecleer protests: "By God! I hadde rather than my sherte" ("I'd give my shirt"). His favorite wife, Pertelote, implores him to take some homeopathic medicine: "For Goddes love, taak some laxatyf!" Even the wily fox, who has already consumed Chantecleer's father, speaks in an aristocratic fashion; "My lord, your father—God his soule bless!" At the crisis when Chantecleer is abducted by the fox, Chaucer's "swete prest" makes splendid fun of the extravagant exclamations typical at such points of a narrative: he appeals to "Destinee," to "Venus," and to "Gaufred" (Geoffrey de Vinsauf, the master of medieval rhetoric), all in vain. He himself utters only the mildest of oaths "Benedicitee!" at a moment of frantic excitement and rural panic. But suddenly the farmyard chase is compared to a grimmer reality of xenophobic hostility (ll. 3394–97), the massacre of Flemish immigrants during the Peasants' Revolt of 1381. Chroniclers reported that many lost their lives because they said *brood* and *kaas* instead of *bread* and *cheese*. At the conclusion of his tale the Host compliments him on his manly physique and virile manner, naughtily adding "I-blessed be thy breche and every stoon" which translates incongruously in Modern English as "Blessed be your buttocks and both testicles" (ll. 3448).

The epithet "Chaucerian" has come to mean "risqué," "naughty," or "crude," unfairly and simplistically on the basis of the coarse tales told by the few vulgar tellers. For the structure of the *Canterbury Tales* shows a complete range of human types and characters, as well as a medieval encyclopedia of narrative. Chaucer's genius consisted not only in creating a microcosm of medieval society, but also in matching the tellers and the tales. Centuries before Freud, Chaucer had intuitively grasped the truth that when people speak, especially in an extended narrative, their values, ideals, fantasies, insecurities, and aggressions are subconsciously revealed, and that their expletives are crucial revealers.

Chaucer's great scheme, although apparently unfinished, is actually complete, since it ends with Chaucer taking leave of his readers as a pious and God-fearing Christian facing the Last Judgment. This conclusion, called the Retractions, is crucial to the understanding of the work, since Chaucer the author finally unmasks himself and separates his own literary output into the wheat and the chaff, the works of ultimate spiritual value and those that "soonen into sinne," those that derive from baser materials and instincts. Among these are the fabliaux, the crude and profane tales. Chaucer's final words show him to be profoundly earnest in his hope "that I may be oon of hem at the day of doom that shulle be saved."

See also: Cherles Termes; Fabliau; Jews, the; Medieval Period; Minced Oaths; Saints' Names; Shrew; Virago.

Bibliography

Benson, Larry, ed. *The Riverside Chaucer.* Oxford: Oxford University Press, 1988.
Benson, Larry D., and Theodore M. Andersson. *The Literary Context of Chaucer's Fabliaux.* Indianapolis: Bobbs–Merrill, 1971.
Brewer, D.S. "The Fabliaux." In Rowland, Beryl, ed., *A Companion to Chaucer Studies.* Oxford: Oxford University Press, 1968.
Elliott, Ralph W.V. *Chaucer's English.* London: André Deutsch, 1974.
Howard, Donald. *The Idea of the Canterbury Tales.* Berkeley: University of California Press, 1976.
Muscatine, Charles. *Chaucer and the French Tradition.* Berkeley: University of California Press, 1957.
Ross, Thomas. *Chaucer's Bawdy.* New York: E.P. Dutton, 1972.

CHERLES TERMES

This designation was used in medieval times to refer to "low-class" language, predicated on the assumption that bad language was more prevalent among the lower orders. The Anglo-Saxon form *ceorl* meant "a peasant or laborer," and has yielded the modern form *churl,* meaning "a surly, ill-bred person," now virtually obsolete, chiefly surviving in *churlish,* meaning "ungenerous," applied to a man of any class.

In Anglo-Saxon times the word of a *ceorl* carried little weight in the eyes of the law. According to the Laws of Ine (688–94) ¶18: "A twelve hundred man's oath stands for six *ceorl's* oaths. If a *ceorl* is often accused, and if at last he is taken [in the act], his hand or foot is to be stuck off." The bias in favor of the man of property is blatant: a *hundred* was an ancient division of a county. The same bias is apparent in the Laws of Hlothhere and Eadric (673–85) ¶16: "If a man of Kent buys property in London, he is to have two or three honest *ceorls,* or the king's town-reeve, as witness."

Medieval *cherle* implied various behaviors, notably that of bad language. The debate poem *The Owl and the Nightingale* (ca. 1250) contains the first instance of *shit-word,* meaning crude language associated with rustics, in that case herdsmen. In Chaucer's early poem *The Parlement of Foulys* (ca. 1382), a comic debate, this verbal association is made explicit in some vigorous exchanges between the different orders of birds:

"Now fy, cherl! . . .
Out of the donghil cam that word ful right!"
(ll. 596–97)

In the scheme of the *Canterbury Tales,* the correlation between class and language is very clear. Chaucer the Pilgrim-Narrator apologizes in advance for the crudity of the Miller's and Reve's tales by saying that the tellers were "cherles" and that they told tales of "harlotry"—that is, "wickedness" or "smut" (l. 3182). Neither is strictly a *cherl* in class terms, both being fairly prosperous tradesmen, but both qualify, especially the Miller, since he has the manners of an oaf and clearly revels in shocking "the gentils," or the well-bred among the pilgrims. The Reve says in advance that he will requite the Miller "right in his cherles termes" (l. 3917).

See also: Billingsgate; Bywords of Swearing; Class and Swearing.

Bibliography

Brewer, D.S. "The Fabliaux." In Rowland, Beryl, ed., *A Companion to Chaucer Studies.* Oxford: Oxford University Press, 1968.

CHILDREN, SWEARING IN

Generally speaking, it is assumed rightly that children learn to swear. Consequently, there are typical prohibitions against adults swearing in front of children, summed up in the French dictum *pas devant les enfants* ("not in front of the children"). However, in modern times, swearing has clearly become common among children, so the stage has almost been reached that the dictum should be reversed to *pas devant les parents* ("not in front of the parents").

Historically, there is little evidence of children swearing, possibly because of pre-Freudian notions that children are "innocent," strangers to cruelty, violence, sexuality, and foul language. In the literature of the past children seldom feature as individuals, more as the objects of value or obstacles in the lives of grown-ups. Dedicated social researchers, such as Henry Mayhew, the author of the classic study *London Labour and the London Poor* (1851–1862) commented on the terrible exploitation of children in Victorian society but not on their verbal behavior.

However, there is some literary evidence to the contrary. In Ben Jonson's comedy *Everyman in His Humour* (1598), the elder Kno'well observes ironically that the education of infants is marked, not by repression of swearing but by encouragement:

> Their first words
> We form their tongues with, are licentious jests
> Can it call whore? Cry bastard? Oh then kiss it,
> A witty child! Can't swear? The father's darling!
> Give it two plums.
> (II iii 19–23)

Sir Thomas Elyot advised in *The Boke of the Governour* (1531) that the children of a gentleman should be brought up exclusively by clean-spoken women and that men should not be allowed in the nursery (I xxvi). Furthermore, assumptions of swearing in children can be drawn from some of the earlier prohibitions against swearing. For instance, the law of 1623 stipulated a penalty of one shilling and, further, that the offender was to be whipped if younger than twelve years old. In 1649 the Scottish Parliament made the offense of cursing a parent punishable by death, although a grown-up child was presumably envisaged for this extreme penalty.

Previous notions about swearing in children were wrongly grounded in the assumption that they learned to swear exclusively from adults. However, common experience shows that children usually learn to swear as a behavior of conformity in school. In the United States there has been considerable sociolinguistic research into various forms of verbal dueling practiced by black male youths, known variously as "sounding," "signifying," and "playing the dozens." William Labov showed that "the activity is remarkably similar throughout the various black communities" (1972, 302). Timothy Jay's study *Cursing in America* (1992) has a lengthy chapter on the emergence of an obscene lexicon. One field study showed that this starts surprisingly early and is more prevalent among young boys. However there was a consistent pattern of increase to a peak at ages 7–8 and then a trailing off around ages 11–12 (1992, 44–60). The incidence of *fuck,* for example, rises from a figure of 13 at ages 5–6 to a peak of 26 at ages 7–8, falling first to 16 at ages 9–10 and further to 2 at ages 11–12. The implication of this pattern is that the early acquisition is imitative, while the later reduction reflects awareness of the seriousness and taboo quality of the words.

In the United Kingdom the University of Bergen Corpus of London Teenage Language, or COLT Corpus, compiled in 1993 focuses on the spoken language of thirteen- to seventeen-year-old teenagers from different boroughs of London. The word-frequency list shows that obscenities rank high, the top ten being *fucking* (with a ranking of 482), *god, shit, fuck, bloody, crap, bastard, bitch, piss,* and *bollocks* ("testicles" or "rubbish," with a ranking of 94). Parental class notions of what is offensive can color the issue, as Jilly Cooper amusingly noted "I once heard my son regaling his friends: 'Mummy says that *pardon* is a much worse word than *fuck*'" (1981, 39).

See also: Dozens, the.

Bibliography

Bergen Corpus of London Teenage Language (COLT).
Cooper, Jilly. *Class.* New York: Knopf, 1981.
Jay, Timothy. *Cursing in America.* Philadelphia: Benjamins, 1992.
Labov, William. *Language in the Inner City.* Oxford: Basil Blackwell, 1972.

CHINESE, THE

Since Britain as a colonial power did not engage with China even on a diplomatic level until 1793, and Chinese visitors were rare in Britain, there are comparatively few terms for them in British English. However, Chinese indentured laborers arrived in numbers in America during the California Gold Rush of 1849 and shortly after that in Australia. Because of their low immigrant status, economic competitiveness, and obvious cultural differences, the Chinese were given a great variety of nicknames. Of these, *chink,* recorded from about 1880 in America and from the 1890s in Australia, has become dominant.

Describing the community's sociolinguistic status in the United States, Irving Lewis Allen observed: "The Chinese are so various nicknamed [Allen documents 38 different names] because in the nineteenth century they were the largest Asian immigrant minority in the nation and they were thought to be the 'ultimate alien.' The terms, many of them dating from the 1870s and 1880s, clearly echo the resentments toward the mass immigration of cheap industrial labor, which forced competition with white, native-born labor. Compounding these conflicts with the native-born, the Chinese often settled in big cities and into large and pertinacious enclaves, which heightened their visibility" (1983, 94).

The terms range from ironic cultural references, such as *buddha-head, celestial,* and *little-brown-brother* to the overtly hostile *moon-eyed leper, squint-eyes, yellow-belly, yellow-peril,* and *yellow-bastard.* Even apparently innocent terms provoke anger in the target community, as H.L. Mencken noted: "The Chinese greatly dislike the terms *Chinaman* and *Chinee,* just as the Japanese dislike *Jap*" (1945, 374).

The Chinese community has in typical fashion attracted many ethnic stereotypes and jokes. In his *Dictionary of Invective* (1989), Hugh Rawson lists sixteen phrases using *Chinese* as an epithet, suggesting incompetence, fraud, or disorganization. They include *Chinese ace,* "an inept aviator"; *Chinese deal,* "a pretended deal"; and *Chinese fire drill,* "sheer chaos." However, *not a Chinaman's chance*—that is, no chance at all—reveals their disadvantageous situation.

In Australia a remarkably similar situation developed. Even the basic term *Chinaman* carried considerable hostility, as is seen in the Sydney *Bulletin* in 1887: "No nigger, no Chinaman, no lascar, no kanaka [laborer from the South Sea Islands], no purveyor of cheap labour, is an Australian." *Chink* is recorded from about 1890, *chinkie* from about 1876, followed by a whole host of terms—namely *chows, opium smokers, quangs, slants, paddies,* and *yellow bastards.* In *Our Australian Cousins* (1879), James Inglis noted that, for some reason, the Chinese were especially incensed by the label of *paddy,* commonly used of the Irish. On a geopolitical front, the ominous formulation *yellow peril* dates from about 1900.

See also: Blason Populaire; Ethnic Insults; Xenophobia.

Bibliography

Allen, Irving Lewis. *The Language of Ethnic Conflict.* New York: Columbia University Press, 1983.
Mencken, H.L. *The American Language.* New York: Knopf, 1945.
Rawson, Hugh. *A Dictionary of Invective.* London: Hale, 1989.

CHRIST

The First Commandment has obviously made the name of God taboo even in nonreligious contexts, leading to phonetic erosions such as *gog* and *cokk* recorded as far back as the fourteenth century. In the case of the name of Christ, these forms emerged far later than those for God and Jesus. The reason would seem to be that the name of Christ was in fact freely used in the medieval period, notably in the works of **Chaucer** and William Langland. A poignant secular lyric, "Western Wind," dated from the early sixteenth century, deals with the separation of lovers and has this powerful invocation:

Christ if my love were in my armes,
And in my bed againe.

In comparison with the other sacred names, the word field of euphemisms is also surprisingly short. Together with the dates of first recorded usage, it is as follows: *Criminy* (1680), *Crikey* (1839), *Cripes* (1840s), *Jiminy Christmas* (1897), *Christmas* (1898), and *for crying out loud* (1924). The last example is of the "diversion" type, in which the sacred name is turned into an inoffensive term that leads the rest of the phrase.

As can be seen, there have not been any additions for nearly a century. Most are traditional and used on both sides of the Atlantic. The American contributions are not notable: the "executive" style, *Jesus H. Christ,* dates from 1924. The reason for the brevity of the field would seem to be that, as in medieval times, the use of the name of Christ may be offensive, but it is not strictly taboo.

See also: Chaucer, Geoffrey; God, Euphemisms for; Jesus.

CINEMA

This entry focuses on the British film industry, to distinguish it from the material covered under **Hollywood**. The distinction is not absolute, since there have been considerable and increasing collaboration and migration of talented filmmakers and scriptwriters, especially in the direction of Hollywood, and many films have been hybrids. Furthermore, while the name *Hollywood* usually denotes the major studios, there are also a number of independent filmmakers operating there and elsewhere.

Notions about what is proper to see and hear in public will usually be more rigorous than what can be read in private. While the British film industry has never been subject to the preemptive American Production Code, it has obviously been constrained by the laws governing obscenity and the notions of public decency as interpreted by the Lord Chamberlain, which have profoundly affected the history of the theater in the United Kingdom. The authority for distributing films rests with the national British Board of Film Censors, set up in 1912 to standardize ratings, but local authorities may override the board's decisions. In 1916 the board drew up a list of forty-three topics for deletion, ranging from "scenes laid in disorderly houses," "cruelty to animals," and "'First Night' scenes" to "excessively passionate love scenes," but there was no prohibition on language *per se*. With the introduction of the X certificate (1951) came changes of language, such as "lust" to "passion" and "lecherous fantasies" to "unspeakable dreams" (in Ingmar Bergman's *Smiles of a Summer Night*). John Trevelyan, who was involved in the licensing and rating of films from 1951 to 1971, has given valuable insights into his *modus operandi* in his memoir *What the Censor Saw* (1973). He valued collaboration with the filmmakers, encouraging them to show him unfinished scripts so that he could advise on whether acceptance was likely and which certificate they might expect.

Up to the 1960s the dominant tenor of British cinema was that of restraint: in language, in sexuality, and in crime and violence. There was also a curious disjunction between content and style, in that even serious topics were treated with a light touch. Films came in fairly predictable genres, namely comedy, which was formulaic, situational, and witty; gritty war films and stylized crime stories, in which the detectives (and often the criminals) were upper-class, urbane, and well-spoken in the manner of Agatha Christie's Hercule Poirot and Miss Marple, and Leslie Charteris's the Saint. Most crime was treated in a comic or absurd fashion, most notably in the classic *Kind Hearts and Coronets* (1949), a comedy of revenge in which an entire unsympathetic upper-class family is murdered in bizarre ways by a unsuspected distant relative. The absurdity of the plot was emphasized by having Alec Guinness playing all eight victims. *The Lavender Hill Mob* (1951) and *The Ladykillers* (1955) were typical in their comic depiction of incompetent criminals, leading to the farcical detective Clouseau of Peter Sellers's *Pink Panther* series of the 1960s. *Captain's Paradise* (1953) presented adultery in a similar light vein, with a plot of a ship's captain who bigamously maintains two wives in different ports. Sexual passion was either suppressed or idealized, notably in David Lean's early classic *Brief Encounter* (1945), scripted by Noel Coward. Even in the early war films strong language did not truly feature: *The Cruel Sea* (1953), *The Dam Busters* (1954), and *The Battle of Britain* (1970) maintained the stereotype of the stoical British hero.

Farce, with its long stage history in England, continued in films, indecent language being disguised by double-entendres of the "slap and tickle" or "wink wink, nudge nudge" variety, or Cockney rhyming slang codes, as in "Up the Khyber" (which decodes as Khyber Pass = arse). An alternative mode was the dilution of serious content into a genre of the musical, notably in *Oliver!* (1968), a saccharine version of Charles Dickens's grimly realistic novel of underworld crime, *Oliver Twist* (1837–1839), previously made into a classic by David Lean in 1948. In *Oliver!* the sinister criminal godfather Fagin becomes a largely comic figure, leading his apprentices in crime in jaunty choruses like "You've got to pick a pocket or two." However, the film won an Academy Award.

A major landmark of realism was the British Lion screen adaptation of John Braine's novel *Room at the Top* (1959). In an article in the *Saturday Review* (April 11, 1959), Arthur Knight noted that the term "adult" applied to the film in a number of new ways: "Its characters swear, curse, connive, commit adultery like recognizable (and not altogether unlikable) human beings. And the effect is startling" (cited in Wolf, 1979, 239). More significantly, although the film broke most of the Production Code rules, it won two Oscars, one by Simone Signoret as the mistress. Other British films reflecting "the permissive society" in showing more candor in sex and coarse speech were *Look Back in Anger* (1959), *Saturday Night and Sunday Morning* (1960), *A Taste of Honey* (1961), and *The Loneliness of the Long Distance Runner* (1962). The scripts, however, were tame in comparison with those of subsequent decades, since they had been doctored by the British Board of Film Censors and the Lord Chamberlain's Office. Anthony Aldgate's study *Censorship and the Permissive Society* (1995) details these interventions, which were numerous.

Furthermore, there were still major cases of banning or suppression. Joseph Strick's film of *Ulysses* appeared in 1967, nearly half a century after James Joyce had published his controversial novel, and provides a revealing case history. Although the initial ban on the book had been lifted in the United States in 1933, more than a hundred theaters canceled their bookings. The British censor John Trevelyan ordered the excision of two scenes and 400 words of dialogue in twenty-nine sections. Strick called a press conference, threatening to distribute a press release with the excised words, which were broadcast in an interview he gave on the B.B.C. television program "24 Hours." He arrived at an ingeniously drastic solution: "I complied with the cuts Trevelyan had ordered by making them intolerable, by screeches on the sound track and the film going blank" (Wolf 1979, 283). Trevelyan subsequently wrote: "I could not understand why he had done this since I thought it very unlikely that anyone would show the film like this" (1973, 114). The film was granted an X certificate. More astonishingly, at the Cannes Film Festival, the sound track was replaced with subtitles approved by the Académie Française and the screening committee. At the jury showing, even these had been obliterated. Strick tried to stop the projection by switching off the power, and then withdrew the film when the jury refused to intercede on his behalf. The festival director, Favre-Le Bret, argued that it was quite different to hear the words than to read them (Wolf 1979, 283).

The main area of censorship was, expectedly, Molly Bloom's long soliloquy concluding the novel, a remarkable piece of stream of consciousness, mainly an erotic reverie of extraordinary frankness, recalling an adulterous liaison with a British soldier. The ending thus becomes an ironic parody of Homer's *Odyssey* and the enduring fidelity of Penelope, Ulysses's wife. Although the sound track was censored (in terms of "word count" only one four-letter word, *fuck,* had been admitted), in the words of Alexander Walker, "There was also the vocal virtuosity of Barbara Jefford . . . bringing the film to an amazing close of pure aural orgasm" (1977, 221).

Many film critics have observed that the visual and verbal suggestiveness of earlier films is more effective than the blatant nudity, copulation, crudity, and obscenity of their more recent successors. This is evident in many of the most admired and awarded films of both the American and British tradition, such as *Rebecca* (1940), *Citizen Kane* (1941), *Casablanca* (1943), *Gone with the Wind* (1949), *The Third Man* (1949), *The Bridge on the River Kwai* (1957), *Lawrence of Arabia* (1962), *My Fair Lady* (1964), *A Man for All Seasons* (1966), *Bonnie and Clyde* (1967), *Butch Cassidy and the Sundance Kid* (1969), *Chariots of Fire* (1981), *Gandhi* (1982), *Amadeus* (1985), *Shakespeare in Love* (1998), and *American Beauty* (1999). Virtually none of the films of Alfred Hitchcock has any salacious or obscene features in the scripts. All the enormously successful James Bond films, originally derived from the plots of Ian Fleming, follow the stylistic formula of the earlier British detective films, with both hero and villain being well spoken and verbally restrained and using witty puns rather than coarse abuse, which would demean them.

However, since the 1990s profanity and obscenity have become almost the order of the day in major British-based films, such as the Irish political drama *The Commitments* (1991), *Trainspotting* (1996), and the comedy *Four Weddings and a Funeral* (1994), in which the "dialogue" started with the word *fuck* being reiterated four times in different contexts. In many ways the development of the modern cinema is epitomized in the two treatments of *The Ladykillers:* The original British production (1955) was a clean-spoken farce; the remake by the Cohen Brothers (2004), set in the Deep South, is gratuitously foul-mouthed. Yet both the original reticence and the subsequent excess are unrealistic.

See also: Censorship; Hollywood.

Bibliography

Aldgate, Anthony. *Censorship and the Permissive Society.* Oxford: Clarendon, 1995.

Hunnings, Neville M. *Film Censors and the Law.* London: George Allen and Unwin, 1967.

Manvell, Roger. *Films and the Second World War.* Cranbury: A.S. Barnes, 1974.

Phelps, Guy. *Film Censorship.* London: Gollancz, 1975.

Trevelyan, John. *What the Censor Saw.* London: Michael Joseph, 1973.

Walker, Alexander. *Double Takes.* London: Elm Tree Books, 1977.

Wolf, William, and Lilian Kramer Wolf. *Landmark Films.* New York & London: Paddington Press, 1979.

CLASS AND SWEARING

According to notions of "received wisdom" concerning the sociolinguistic modes of English society, which still preserves its traditional class structure to a surprising degree, swearing is a low-class habit. Phrases like "the language of the gutter" can still be heard. Historical study shows, however, that this is a popular oversimplification. The consistent pattern emerging historically in English society is that swearing is more prevalent among the upper and the lower classes but is generally avoided by the middle class. As the entry for **"U" and "Non-U"** also shows, verbal gentility is more the preserve of the bourgeois. The dynamic in America is naturally more complex.

There is no evidence of class differences in linguistic behavior in Anglo-Saxon times, probably because of the limited survival of texts. However, the medieval word *cherle* meaning a peasant (still surviving as *churl*) had an explicit association with bad language shown in the phrase **cherles termes**, meaning foul or coarse language. As the entry for **Chaucer** shows, the correlation between class and language in the *Canterbury Tales* is very clear. The Knight tells a romance of chivalry in appropriately decorous language, whereupon the drunken Miller responds with a scurrilous bawdy farce, provoking the Reeve into a riposte. Both use the whole available range of "four-letter" words and some scandalous oaths, for which Chaucer apologizes, saying that they were both "cherles." However, the Parson in his discourse on the Seven Deadly Sins makes a different correlation between swearing and class. He criticizes those who "holden it a gentrie or a manly dede to swere grete oaths" ("regard it as a classy or macho thing to swear powerfully," l. 601). This observation on *gentrie* indicates a mode of fashionable upper-class swearing that was to become established in later centuries.

According to certain quaint medieval notions of genealogy, the churls of the world were descended from Cain. This idea is clearly dramatized in the religious plays known as the Wakefield Pageants in the Towneley Cycle (acted ca. 1554–1576), in which Cain is a lively character, and his speech is larded with obscenity and blasphemy. As the entry for **medieval period** shows, he tells his brother Abel to "kys the dwillis toute!" ("kiss the devil's backside"), is rude to the Almighty, and bids the audience a crude farewell: "By all men set I nat a fart." This tradition has continued and was endorsed by H.C. Wyld in his *Universal Dictionary of the English Language* (1934), in which he defined *bloody* as a "meaningless adjective much used among very low persons."

However, the freedom of swearing enjoyed by the upper classes is famous, or notorious. Alluded to in Chaucer and in the entry for **God's wounds**, it becomes a social feature of comment in the Renaissance. The most spectacular examples come from the swearing matches indulged in by the Scottish nobility and covered under the entry for **flyting**. South of the border Sir Thomas Elyot in *The Governour* (1531) recorded the disapproving saying that "They will say that he that swereth depe, swereth like a lorde" (I, xxvi). Henry VIII swore freely, and his son Edward VI, upon ascending the throne at the age of ten in 1547 "is said to have delivered himself of a volley of the most sonorous oaths" (Montagu 1973, 132). More surprising, Henry's daughter, Queen Elizabeth I, is said to have sworn "like a man." On her abilities in this regard Nathan Drake observed: "A shocking practice seems to have been rendered fashionable by the Queen . . . for it is said that she never spared an oath in public speech or private conversation when she thought it added energy to either" (Shirley 1979, 10). Ashley Montagu asserts (without authority) that "*God's wounds* was a favorite oath of Queen Elizabeth's, and it is said that the corruption *'Zounds* first originated with the ladies of her court, who also used it in the form *zooterkins*" (1973, 139). In addition, numerous anecdotes attest to her blunt speech and her relish of the vulgar jest or naughty story (Shirley 1979, 10). John Aubrey, the first collector and publisher of anecdotal biography in England, retails the following episode:

> This Earle of Oxford [Edward de Vere] making his low obeisance [bow] to Queen Elizabeth, happened to let a Fart, at which he was so abashed and ashamed that he went to Travell, 7 yeares. On his returne the Queen welcomed him home, and sayd, "My Lord, I had forgot the Fart." (*Brief Lives*)

This was a time when the *insouciance* or carefree attitude of the nobility was expressed in various forms of exhibitionism, in magnificent codpieces, and in spectacular but also crude language. Shakespeare creates a particularly revealing scene in *Henry IV, Part I*, where Harry Hotspur, a bold and outspoken aristocrat, lectures his wife on the swearing appropriate to her station:

Swear me Kate, like a lady as thou art
A good mouth-filling oath.
(III i 257–58)

This context, revealing of expectations of both class and gender, is discussed more fully in the entry for **swearing in women**. But at the heart of Hotspur's speech is the assumption that the upper classes are not bound by bourgeois prissiness, norms, and expectations.

This emphasis on upper-class swearing in Shakespeare should not obscure the equally clear awareness that swearing was also despised as low-class behavior. The strongest example is Hamlet, who in his state of frenzied frustration swears furiously, but is simultaneously disgusted, that he

Must, like a whore, unpack my heart with words
And fall a-cursing like a very drab [prostitute]
A scullion! [kitchen servant]
(II ii 616–24)

Hamlet is the most verbally sensitive and acute character in Shakespeare, and thus the social markers he chooses for swearing, whores and scullions, are highly significant. (Scullions were the lowest rank of kitchen servants, and notorious for their foul language; in 1592, Thomas Nashe accused Gabriel Harvey of being a "kitchen-stuff wrangler [quarreler]" in *Strange News*, I, 229, 31–35.)

Queen Elizabeth's successor, James I, was something of a linguistic anomaly. On the one hand his diatribe in 1604 against the evils of smoking, "A Counterblaste to Tobacco" (then a new vice), ends in the mode of a hell-fire sermon: "and in the black stinking fume thereof most resembling the horrible Stygian smoke of the pit that is bottomless" (James avoids "Hellish," preferring the classical *Stygian*). But his correspondence with his favorite, George Villiers, Duke of Buckingham, "is astonishing, swapping four-letter words" (Stone 1987, 104). (More details are given in the entry for **homosexuals**.) Likewise, he commissioned the Authorized Version of the Bible (1611), yet the language he used to describe his passion for Buckingham was blasphemous. He told his council in 1617: "Jesus Christ did the same and therefore I cannot be blamed. Christ had his John and I have my George" (Fraser 1974, 168).

Upon the Restoration of the monarchy in 1660 after the Puritan Commonwealth, aristocratic liberty became license, embodied in the decadent example of Charles II. Using his favorite oath, the king commented on the portrait of him painted by Sir Peter Lely: "Odd's fish, I am an ugly fellow." (*Odd's fish* is a "minced oath" for "God's face.") A more fulsome response was that of a gentleman, upon being bitten by one of the king's spaniels: "God bless your Majesty! And God damn your dogs!" Anecdotes abound of what the diarist John Evelyn called the king's "unexpressable luxury and profanenesse, gaming and all dissolution" —that is, lust, profanity, gambling, and decadence. The license of the court and the contemporary stage is covered in the entries for **Restoration** and the **Collier Controversy**.

After this nadir, the behavior of royalty became more becoming, at least in the verbal domain. Queen Victoria was famous for her severity and Puritanism, and although Edward VII was notorious for his sexual scandals, the Royal Family was virtually oath-free until the latter part of the twentieth century. One famous anecdote concerns George V's convalescence at Bognor in 1929. When the local council requested some recognition of his stay, the king reportedly responded curtly to his aides: "Bugger Bognor!" But the town did gain the title of royal recognition, namely Bognor Regis.

While Queen Elizabeth II has remained a model of decorum, her husband, the Duke of Edinburgh, and their daughter, Princess Anne, show much of the verbal insouciance of their Renaissance ancestors. The Duke is notorious for his abrasive remarks, often about foreigners, and even came out with the archaism "Gadzooks!" Ever impatient of the intrusions of the British press, Princess Anne told them to "Naff off!" in one episode in 1982. (The equivalent would be "Get lost!" or "Bugger off!") Responding to a security scandal at Buckingham Palace in 2003 when a reporter gained entrance by pretending to be servant, the Princess allegedly described him as "a fucking incompetent twat" (*Daily Mirror,* November 21, 2003). Even Prince Charles, generally more restrained in verbal matters, explained the low standards of English in his office by commenting in 1989 that "English is taught so bloody badly." The publicity given to such episodes is partly based, like the revelations of sexual impropriety, on their media value as scandal, but also on the modern egalitarian assumption that such language is inappropriate to those in high office.

It is notable that those British prime ministers noted for using coarse or strong language in public derive almost entirely from noble families, such as William Pitt and Charles James Fox from an earlier era, the last being Sir Winston Churchill. He famously combined acerbity and even cruelty in his denunciations. Adolf Hitler he castigated as "this bloody guttersnipe," Benito Mussolini was "this whipped jackal," while socialism was "Government of the duds, by the duds for the duds" (Montagu 1973, 338). Always frank, he said to Hugh Foot, governor of Jamaica, on the prospect of continuing immigration to Britain: "We would have a magpie society. That would never do" (Roberts 1994, n.p.).

In the United States notions of class are ostensibly at variance with the democratic ethos of the nation, although the prevalence of the terms *class* and *classy* in various phrases suggests that the notion is not entirely alien. Studies into profanity such as those of Cameron (1969) and Jay (1992) have different social foci, such as schoolchildren and college students, who are assumed to be homogeneous in class terms. There are, naturally, general expectations of status. It is indisputable that, like any nation, Americans expect their leaders to speak with the dignity appropriate to high office. Consequently, one of the most damaging revelations of the Watergate tapes was that President Richard Nixon, the successor of such articulate and dignified presidents as Thomas Jefferson and Abraham Lincoln, spoke like a gangster, even using such banal terms and phrases as *crap, bullshit, asshole, I don't give a shit,* and *a bunch of crap* (Nixon 1974). The ironic linguistic memorial to Nixon's presidency was the phrase used in editing the incriminating tapes he had so carefully and furtively preserved: "Expletive deleted."

At the other end of the scale was the extraordinary disjunction between language and action characterizing the sexual scandal concerning President Bill Clinton and his aide Monica Lewinsky (1999–2000). As the evidence of sexual misconduct mounted, so the president's language became more bizarrely euphemistic, reiterating phrases like "inappropriate action." Throughout the whole affair, no oaths or vituperation were uttered in public. The fact that Clinton lied in public became an open secret.

However, there is also little doubt that presidents who show "the common touch" by using low-register language usually achieve a genuine affection with the populace. Harry Truman's popularity in part derived from this trait: his wife once commented that he "liked to call horse-manure horse-manure," adding mischievously that it had taken her a long time to get the president to use this polite version. Truman commented in 1961: "I fired [General Douglas] MacArthur because he wouldn't respect the authority of the President. I didn't fire him because he was a dumb son of a bitch, although he was" (Flexner 1976, 233). Merle Miller's oral biography *Plain Speaking* (1974) shows that Truman used the epithet quite freely. More public was John F. Kennedy's comment on price increases proposed by U.S. Steel: "My father always told me that all businessmen were sons of bitches, but I never believed it till now" (April 1962; quoted in Arthur M. Schlesinger, *A Thousand Days: John F. Kennedy in the White House*, New York: Houghton Mifflin, 1965, 635).

A less expected example comes from President Lyndon Johnson. During the Vietnam War there was some shocking television coverage (on CBS in August 1965) showing Vietnamese villagers being burned alive through the actions of some U.S. marines. Frank Stanton, the president of CBS, received a phone call from Johnson early the following morning. "Frank, are you trying to fuck me?" Johnson asked, adding, "Yesterday your boys shat on the American flag" (Wheen 1985, 88–89).

Although class categorizations are increasingly problematic to establish, it is still a tenable generalization that swearing is more prevalent among the upper and the lower echelons of British society, but is less frequent in the middle class.

See also: Cherles Termes; "U" and "Non-U."

Bibliography

Cameron P. "Frequency and Kinds of Words in Various Social Settings, or What the Hell's Going On?" *Pacific Sociological Review* 12 (1969), 101–4.

Flexner, Stuart Berg. *I Hear America Talking.* New York: Van Nostrand Reinhold, 1976.

Fraser, Antonia. *King James.* London: Weidenfeld & Nicolson, 1974.

Jay, Timothy. *Cursing in America.* Philadelphia/Amsterdam: Benjamins, 1992.

Miller, Merle. *Plain Speaking.* London: Gollancz, 1974.

Montagu, Ashley. *The Anatomy of Swearing.* London and New York: Macmillan and Collier, 1973.

Nixon, Richard. "Transcripts of Eight Recorded Presidential Conversations." Hearings Before the Committee of the Judiciary, House of Representatives, 93rd Congress, 2nd Session, May–June 1974.

Roberts, Andrew. *Eminent Churchillians.* New York: Simon and Schuster, 1994.

Shirley, Frances A. *Swearing and Perjury in Shakespeare's Plays.* London: Allen & Unwin, 1979.

Stone, Norman, ed. *The Makers of English History.* London: Weidenfeld & Nicolson, 1987.

Wheen, Francis. *Television.* London: Century, 1985.

CLELAND, JOHN

John Cleland (1709–1789) was a minor eighteenth-century writer, now famous chiefly on account of his *succès de scandale,* the notoriously successful pornographic novel *The Memoirs of a Woman of Pleasure.* Being no stranger to the debtor's prison, Cleland actually completed the manuscript in the Fleet Prison between February 1748 and March 1749. The book's history of controversy began with warrants being issued against the author, printer, and publisher on its original publication, and ended in litigation when it was eventually reissued in the United States in 1966. Brought before the Privy Council, Cleland pleaded poverty, was merely reprimanded, but given a comparatively light fine, on condition that he did not repeat the offense. While the bookseller reportedly made some £10,000, Cleland's royalty was £20. He nevertheless prepared a heavily expurgated version, *Memoirs of Fanny Hill,* after the name of the heroine, published in March 1750. This too was prosecuted. He proceeded with *Memoirs of a Coxcomb* (an idiot) (1751) and *Memoirs of an Oxford Scholar* (1755), both written in a similar vein. He eventually died in poverty.

Despite the content of his works, Cleland's style is entirely typical of its period, preferring high register or formal vocabulary to coarse "four-letter" words. It is thus, paradoxically, pornography without "dirty words." In this extended description of one of her many sexual encounters, Fanny is "loath to leave the tender partner of my joys behind me." Accordingly:

I not only tightened the pleasure-girth around my restless inmate by a secret spring of suction and compression that obeys the will in those parts, but stole my hand softly to that store-bag of nature's prime sweets, which is so pleasingly attached to its conduit pipe from which we receive them; there feeling, and most gently indeed, squeezing those tender globular reservoirs; the magic touch took instant effect, quickened, and brought on upon the spur the symptoms of that sweet agony, the melting moment of dissolution, when pleasure dies by pleasure, and the mysterious engine of it overcomes the titillation it has raised in those parts, by plying them by the stream of a warm liquid that is itself the highest of all titillations, which they thirstily express and draw in like the hot-natured leech, which to cool itself, tenaciously attracts all the moisture within its sphere of exsuction.
(1994, 106)

This typical description of sexual congress shows the unintentional comedy arising from using a scientific, more especially hydraulic, register (words like *suction, compression, globular reservoirs, engine,* and *exsuction*) to a vital and passionate activity.

Cleland also uses metaphors of a high poetic quality, sometimes straining a little for their effect; for example: "The platform of his snow-white bosom, that was laid out in a manly proportion, presented, on the vermilion [scarlet] summit of each pap the idea of a rose about to blow" (1994, 63). The curious use of *pap* instead of the more direct *nipple* shows Cleland's essential delicacy. The coarse sexuality of the underworld is as steadfastly avoided as its argot: "Avoiding the company of jades [prostitutes] and——s, I was thus constant in my fidelity," writes his decadent Oxford scholar in his *Memoirs* (1969, 99). Only occasionally does he descend to incongruously direct words such as *rod* or *clit.* Yet Cleland covers the taboo subject of masturbation, alluded to by such euphemisms as *the solitary vice, inferior gratification, digitation,* in addition to the common word at the time, *pollution.* Such latinized terms were *de rigueur* during the period for "rude" topics. Cleland even uses the word *pego* (thought to be a Greek word for "fountain") for "penis," although his more preferred terms are *machine* and *engine.*

Bearing in mind that the original manuscript was read out at a meeting of the notorious Hell Fire Club in 1737, it is possible that Cleland is occasionally indulging in deliberate exaggeration in such robust sexual metaphors as *battering ram, weapon, stiff gristle of "amour,"* and *volvanic eruptions.* His use of the formal *Venus Mound* is a direct translation of Latin *Mons Veneris,* which could be more coarsely rendered as "Fanny Hill."

See also: Fanny; Pornography; Rude Words, Semantic Field of.

Bibliography

Cleland, John. *Fanny Hill, or The Memoirs of a Woman of Pleasure.* Harmondsworth: Penguin, 1994.
———. *Memoirs of an Oxford Scholar.* London: Sphere, 1969.
Wagner, Peter. *Eros Revived: Erotica of the Enlightenment in England and America.* London: Secker and Warburg 1988.

COCK

The early history of *cock* essentially derives from a series of symbols of maleness or virility, often with overtones of dominance. The subsequent interweaving of the senses of "rooster" and "penis" is interestingly complex, making it difficult to pinpoint the first clear use of the phallic sense. The term has developed a remarkable diversity of meanings in a long and vigorous history in British English, during much of which it was not taboo. In the entry for *cock* in the *Oxford English Dictionary* in 1893, Sir James Murray admitted a double standard in the sense of "penis": "The current name among the people, but *pudoris causa* [for reasons of modesty], not permissible in polite speech or literature; in scientific language the Latin is used." In American English *cock* was largely driven underground by the taboo against the sense of "penis" until comparatively recently. Still more interesting is that the term has thrived in a broad range of genital and copulatory senses in African-American slang.

The root sense, the "male farmyard fowl," goes back to Anglo-Saxon; the "plumbing" sense of a "tap or spout" can be traced back to the late fifteenth century; and the sense of the hammer or firing pin of a gun to the mid-sixteenth century. However, the origin of the sense of "penis" is more difficult to trace, precisely because it is a metaphorical extension of these other meanings. In the comment quoted above, Murray noted that the sense was "in origin perhaps intimately connected with sense 12," that is, "a short tap for the emission of fluid." Two Shakespearean contexts are definitely suggestive. In this exchange from *The Taming of the Shrew* (1594) there is clearly a wordplay between the senses of "fowl" and "penis":

Katharina: What is your crest? A coxcomb?
Petruchio: A combless cock, so Kate will be my hen.
(II ii 224–25)

The other occurs in the melodramatic warning of Pistol, the braggadocio pseudo-warrior in *Henry V* (1599), who exclaims: "Pistol's cock is up, and flashing fire will follow" (II i 56). Pistol having been provoked, "cock" is usually taken to be a pistol, his namesake, cocked and ready to fire. However, the stage context (in which both Pistol and Nym have drawn swords) invites another metaphor, that of a sword. This link is found elsewhere in Shakespeare, in the exchange between Hamlet and Ophelia in the Play Scene, which contains a great deal of sexual innuendo: when Ophelia comments, "You are keen, my lord, you are keen," Hamlet's rejoinder is, "It would cost you a groaning to take off my edge" (III ii 262–63). There is clearly a wordplay here between "edge" in the sense of "sword" and "sexual appetite," implying "penis."

The connection between *weapon* and "penis" is itself ancient, being established in Anglo-Saxon, where *wæpen* is glossed in Bosworth and Toller's *Anglo-Saxon Dictionary* (1898) in Victorian terms as "membrum virile," and a boy was termed a *wæpened cild,* "a weaponed child." The aggressive metaphor was clearly still thriving in *Burlesque Homer* (1772) by a Mr. Bridges: "If you meet the whoring goddess, / Drive your stiff weapon through her bodice" (l. 178). It has continued to the present, with related metaphors like *tool, chopper,* and less well known variants such as *beef bayonet, dagger,* and *ramrod,* all recorded in Jonathon Green, *The Slang Thesaurus* (1986). *Vagina* in Latin means "a sheath," although the original usage by the Roman comedian Plautus in his play *Pseudolis* (1181) seems to have been facetious.

While *weapon* has had a continuous currency for over a thousand years, other ancient terms for the penis have become obsolete. They are *tarse* (from Anglo-Saxon *teors*), rhymed with *arse* by the Earl of Rochester, before dying out in the eighteenth century; *pintle,* which became obsolete about 1600; and *limb* and *yard* (from Middle English *yerde*), basically meaning "a stick." Thus Priapism was defined as "the vnwilful stondynge of the yerde" ("the involuntary erection of the penis") in the English translation of *The Cyrurgie of Guy de Chauliac* (ca. 1425). Shakespeare puns on the sense in *Love's Labour's Lost* (1595):

Boyet: He loves her by the foot.
Dumaine: He may not by the yard.
(V ii 675–76)

Eric Partridge commented that "In the approximate period 1590–1780, *yard* was perhaps the most generally used literary term for 'penis,' and obsolete by ca. 1850" (1947, 225). A later metaphorical relative is *prick,* used with wicked humor by Mercutio in *Romeo and Juliet* (1595): "the bawdy hand of the dial is now upon the prick of noon" (II iv 121). *Cock* was used similarly for a number of suggestively erect or pointed objects, such as the pointer on a balance and the gnomon or marker of a sundial (from 1613). We shall return to the copious range of metaphors later.

These Elizabethan instances are, however, antedated by an anonymous saucy lyric of the early fifteenth century: "I have a gentle [noble] cock." The cock in question is described for four verses in brilliant terms like *crystal, coral,* and *azure,* so that the singular fowl resembles the psychedelic Chauntecleer in Chaucer's *Nun's Priest's Tale,* but in the final pair of lines there is a sudden switch in metaphor to an undoubtedly phallic denouement:

And every night he percheth him
In mine lady's chaumber.

The sophisticated humor of the lyric certainly suggests that the term then carried both senses of "fowl" and "penis" without strain.

The relationship between the "fowl" and the "penis" senses is also found in German *hahn.* An unexpected source linking the two with the "tap" sense is found in a woodcut made by Albrecht Dürer around 1497 called *Männerbad,* depicting a group of naked men in a public bath. As the illustration shows, one man is placed strategically so that his genitals are obscured by a water tap with a stopcock in the shape of a small ornamental barnyard cock. Lorrayne Y. Baird referred to this conjunction in *Maledicta* (1981) as "a triple visual pun"—that is, an image linking tap, rooster, and penis, obscured but implied. This compositional arrangement, whereby *hahn* is visible as water tap and rooster but hidden as penis, seems clearly to acknowledge symbolically the use of the various meanings. Dozens of idiomatic phrases abounding in earlier centuries attest to the use of *cock* in a sexual sense in British English, either directly or by association. In his *Classical Dictionary of the Vulgar Tongue* (1785), Francis Grose includes *cock ale* for "a provocative drink" and *cock alley* or *cock lane* for "the private parts of a woman." The sense of "sexually forward" is found in *a cockish wench* for "a forward coming girl," while *cock bawd* refers to a man keeping a brothel, a variant of *cock pimp,* "the supposed husband to a bawd" in the *Canting Dictionary* of the unidentified

"B.E." (1690). Most of these instances are, of course, vulgar rather than obscene. Many others denote confidence or dominance, such as *cock of the walk* and *cock-sure, cock house, cock of the school,* although some are neutral, like *cock a hoop. Weathercock* and *cockade* are also still in common use, although some now prefer the euphemized *weathervane* and *rosette.*

All of these idiomatic uses have maintained a vigorous currency in British English, but their number and frequency are greatly diminished in American English. The underlying reason is that a taboo against *cock* has been generally prevalent in America for centuries, no doubt a reflection of its Puritan origins. Thus the term *rooster* (recorded from only ca. 1772) has continued to be generally preferred, since "to roost" suggests sleep rather than rampant sexual activity. Likewise *faucet* is preferred for *cock* in the sense of "tap," and instead of the full form *cockroach,* the emasculated abbreviation *roach* is standard. In the first record of the term in 1624 in his *Description of Virginia* (V 171), Captain John Smith referred to an "Indian Bug called by the Spaniards *cacarootch*" (now *cucaracha*). The first element (*caca-*) in fact derives from the creature's annoying habit of defecation, indicating that the development to the form *cockroach* must have occurred when there was no taboo against *cock.* (A parallel case is *poppycock,* which derives from Dutch *pappa kak,* "soft shit.") A brief comparison between any standard British and American dictionary demonstrates the far greater tolerance for *cock-* forms in British over American English.

However, in recent decades this "deficit" has been dramatically reduced in the lower registers, a point taken up in the entry for **innovation.** Seemingly the most powerful word in terms of its obscenity and insult-impact is *cocksucker.* Although first recorded simply as "a feliatrix" in Farmer and Henley's *Slang and Its Analogues* (1890–1904), the term has developed almost entirely in the United States. In the African-American provenance where the term developed from the 1950s and continues to be more general, it is, as Clarence Major points out, an "abusive, all-purpose, male-to-male term with no special reference to sexual activity" (*A Dictionary of African-American Slang*). This is a classic instance of a term having very different degrees of insult or provocation depending on the speech community, since outsiders tend to take such terms more literally than insiders. E.E. Cummings, in an early adjectival use, wrote of "members of the cocksucking leisure classes" (Letter, July 28, 1923). It is not clear what he had in mind. A still earlier term is *cockteaser,* a variant of *cockchafer,* also recorded in *Slang and Its Analogues* (1890–1904) and defined as "a girl in the habit of permitting all familiarities but the last." It has become current only in recent decades, predominantly in the United States.

Perhaps the least expected sense is that of the female genitals. The *Dictionary of African-American Slang* (1994) gives "vagina; female genitalia" as the primary sense, pointing out that the main term for "penis" in the speech community is *dick.* It also lists *cock-opener* for "penis," as well as *cockhound* and *cocksman* for sexually predatory males. *Random House* (1994) categorizes the sense as "Southern and Black English," giving supporting quotations back to 1867. It speculates plausibly that this sense perhaps derives from the obsolete English dialect use of *cock* to mean "cockle or shell fish," quoting an observation in Northall's *English Folk-Rhymes* (1892): "It is significant that the *labia minora* are still termed "cockles" in vulgar parlance."

As has been seen, great numbers of metaphors abound in the genital area. Farmer and Henley (1890–1904) list approximately six hundred synonyms, ranging from nursery terms such as *dicky,* classical references such as *Priapus,* physical metaphors such as *beard-splitter,* and topical allusions like *Old Rowley,* a famous stallion, for Charles II, who was famously well-endowed. The Earl of Rochester paid Charles the chauvinist compliment that "His Sceptre and Prick are of a length" in his "Satire on Charles II" (1680, l. 11). A more familiar slang term, *tool,* has a surprisingly long history, being first recorded in Thomas Becon in 1553 in a reference to "All his toles that appertayne to the Court of Venus" (*Reliques of Rome,* 18). Shakespeare has a comic stereotypical reference in *Henry VIII* (1612): "Have we some strange Indian with the great tool, come to court, [since] the women so besiege us?" (V iii 131–32). It has a continuous history up the present.

Earlier in the discussion it was shown that *prick* was used as a bawdy allusion to the penis as far back as Shakespeare's *Romeo and Juliet* (1595). Touchstone the Clown in *As You Like It* (1599–1600) was certainly playing on the penile sense, also used by various contemporary dramatists, in this couplet:

He that sweetest rose will find
Must find love's prick and Rosalinde.
(III ii 117–18)

Henrietta Maria Bowdler showed that she understood the allusion by cutting the offending lines from *The Family Shakespeare* (1807). The excision stood through subsequent editions, while *The Household Edition of the Dramatic Works of Shakespeare* (1861), edited by William Chambers and Robert Carruthers, pointedly replaced *prick* with "thorn."

The semantic association between terms for the penis and stupidity is notably strong. *Prick* started to take on the sense of "fool" or "contemptible person," usually preceded by *silly* from the nineteenth century, and has maintained the sense to the present. A notable instance was the comment attributed to John F. Kennedy: "I didn't write S.O.B. [on a confidential memorandum in 1961]. . . . I didn't think Diefenbaker [the Canadian prime minister] was a son of a bitch. I thought he was a prick" (quoted in Hook and Kahn, 1980).

A comparative newcomer to the field, *dick* is given an early citation in *Slang and Its Analogues* (1890–1904), where it is simply categorized as "military," a view corroborated by Barrère and Leland's *Dictionary* of 1889. The term is usually regarded as having an American provenance, and it should be remembered that J.S. Farmer was an American. In American usage *dick* can also be used as a verb meaning "to copulate," but in the phrasal verb *dick with* or *dick around,* means "to potter or meddle." The association with stupidity is clear in *dickhead* (from ca. 1962) and *dick-brain* (from ca. 1971).

A similar tripartite semantic history, albeit exclusively British, is *pillock,* previously *pillcock* or *pillicock,* first a vulgar term for the penis recorded from medieval times. A character in Sir David Lindsay's Play, *The Satire of the Three Estates* (1539) notes: "Methink my pillock wil nocht ly doun" (l. 4419). As a term of endearment for a boy it is charmingly defined by John Florio (1598) as "a darlin, a beloved lad." (Curiously *prick* is also recorded in this affectionate sense from about 1540.) The extension to *pillicock hill* for the female genitalia is graphically alluded to by the Fool in *King Lear* (1605): "Pillicock sat on pillicock hill" (III iv 75). The old sexual senses faded away during the eighteenth century, but *pillock* has revived in modern British slang (from the 1960s) to mean "a fool."

Cock has other, quite diverse critical senses, such as that of "rubbish" or "nonsense," as in "cock and bull story" or as in "the salesman spoke a lot of cock" and a *cock-up,* a common British term for a *foul-up.* In other global varieties, the term is used with the kind of freedom still apparent in British English. Australian English has two vulgar additions: *cockrag* for a loincloth worn by Aborigines, and *cock it up,* used of a woman offering herself sexually. The South African variety has no special semantic extensions. Overall, *cock* has never been used as a term of direct personal insult as is the case with *cunt.*

See also: Genitalia.

Bibliography

Ayto, John. *Bloomsbury Dictionary of Word Origins.* London: Bloomsbury, 1991.
Baird, Lorrayne Y. "O.E.D. Cock 20: The Limits of Lexicography of Slang." In *Maledicta* 5 (1981), 213–26.
Barrère, Albert, and Charles G. Leland. *Dictionary of Slang, Jargon, & Cant.* Edinburgh: Ballantyne Press, 1889.
Burchfield, Robert. "Four-letter Words and the *OED.*" *Times Literary Supplement,* October 13, 1972.
———. "An Outline History of Euphemisms in Old English." In *Fair of Speech,* edited by D.J. Enright. Oxford: Oxford University Press, 1986.
Chapman, Robert L. *New Dictionary of American Slang.* New York: Harper & Row, 1986.
Farmer, J.S., and W.E. Henley. *Slang and Its Analogues.* London: Routledge and Kegan Paul, 1890–1904. Reprint, Oxford: Wordsworth Press, 1987.
Flexner, Stuart Berg. *I Hear America Talking.* New York: Van Nostrand Reinhold, 1976.
Green, Jonathan. *The Slang Thesaurus.* Harmondsworth: Penguin, 1988.
Grose, Francis. *A Classical Dictionary of the Vulgar Tongue.* London: S. Hooper, 1785.
Hook, Donald, and Lothar Kahn. *Book of Insults and Irreverent Quotations.* Middle Village, NY: Jonathan David Publishers, 1980.
Jay, Timothy. *Cursing in America: A Psycholinguistic Study of Dirty Language in the Courts, in the Movies, in the Schoolyards and on the Streets.* Philadelphia: J. Benjamins, 1992.
Lighter, J.E., ed. *Random House Historical Dictionary of American Slang.* New York: Random House, 1994–.
Major, Clarence. *Juba to Jive: A Dictionary of African-American Slang.* Harmondsworth: Penguin, 1994.
McDonald, James. *Dictionary of Obscenity, Taboo and Euphemism.* London: Sphere Books, 1988.
Maurer, David W. *Language of the Underworld.* Lexington: University Press of Kentucky, 1981.
Partridge, Eric. *Shakespeare's Bawdy.* London: Routledge & Kegan Paul, 1947.
Sagarin, Edward. *The Anatomy of Dirty Words.* New York: Lyle Stuart, 1962.
Spears, Richard A. *Slang and Euphemism.* New York: Signet, 1991.

COLLIER CONTROVERSY

Jeremy Collier (1650–1726) was a nonjuring clergyman who responded vehemently to what he regarded as the decadence and profanity of the **Restoration** drama in a broadside with the defiant title: *A Short View of the Immorality and Profaneness of the English Stage* (1698). Collier condemned, in an articulate but puritanical manner, not just the immorality and wholesale profanity of current stage productions, but also the satirizing of the clergy and gross breaches of poetic justice, in that libertines were rewarded and vice flourished. In all these characteristics, he pointed out, the contemporary drama was totally different from classical theater. The Puritan revolution had included the closing of the theaters as vehicles of immorality, so that their restoration in 1660 naturally prompted comparisons with the great dramatic achievements of the Elizabethan age. Collier's attack, the most notable of several on the contemporary theater, proved to be the opening salvo in a major controversy involving a number of the dominant playwrights of the time, some of whom then withdrew from the stage.

Collier devotes a large proportion of his work (nearly 300 pages long) to vulgar swearing and blasphemous language:

> And as for Swearing, 'tis used by all Persons and upon all Occasions: By Heroes, and by Poltroons [cowards and scoundrels]; by Gentlemen, and Clowns; Love and Quarrels; Success and Disappointment; Temper and Passion; must be varnish'd, and set with *Oaths*.

Collier was no hysterical puritanical sermonizer. He freely acknowledges that swearing has its place: "At some times, and with some *Poets*, Swearing is no ordinary Relief. It stands up in the Room of Sense, gives Spirit to a flat Expression, and makes a Period [sentence] Musical and Round." But like a shrewd preacher, he penetrates the disguise mechanisms used in oaths, using two analogies, that of the spirit and the letter, and that of debasing the currency by the contemporary practice of "coin-clipping" or shearing the edges off silver coins and melting the metal down for profit:

> Sometime they mince the matter; change the Letter and keep the Sense, as if they had a mind to steal a Swearing (*Gad* for *God*), and break the Commandments without Sin. At another time, the Oaths are clipt, but not so much within the Ring, but that the *Image and Superscription* are visible.

Throwing down the gauntlet, Collier then identifies his targets in person:

> Instances of all these kinds may be mette with in the *Old Batchelour, Double Dealer,* and *Love for Love* [all by William Congreve]. And to mention no more, *Don Quixot* [by Henry Fielding], the *Provok'd Wife,* and the *Relapse* [both by Sir John Vanbrugh], are particularly Rampant and Scandalous.

Collier's attack lacks any sense of irony or humor and seems indiscriminate. But his criticisms do not lack validity: it should be realized, for example, that Vanbrugh's *The Provok'd Wife* originally contained a scene in which the decadent aristocrat Sir John Brute goes on the rampage disguised as a clergyman.

The *Short View* was widely read, immediately provoking ripostes from the authors named and others, to which Collier peremptorily responded, so that within three months it had gone through as many editions. Vanbrugh's response was more appropriately called *A Short Vindication of the Relapse and the Provok'd Wife* (London, 1698). His defense was simple and witty: he assumed that Collier's mind had been corrupted by reading too many decadent plays, arguing that he was simply reflecting the manners of the age:

> Whether such Words are entirely justifiable or not, there's at least this to be said for 'em; That People of the Nicest Rank [highest calibre] both in their Religion and their Manners throughout *Christendom* use 'em.
>
> . . . And in England, we meet with an Infinity of People, Clergy as well as Laity, and of the

best Lives and Conversations who use the words *I-God, I-faith, Cods fish, Cot's my Life,* and many more, which all lye liable to the same objection.

Now whether they are right or wrong in doing it, I should think at least their Example is Authority enough for the Stage; and shou'd have been enough to have kept so good a Christian as Mr. *Collier* from loading his Neighbour with so foul a Charge as Blasphemy and Profaneness, unless he had been better provided to make it good.

John Dryden (who wrote over forty plays) used the stage for his reply, penning an epilogue to John Fletcher's *The Pilgrim* (originally written in 1621), pointing out that the tone of immorality had been set, not by the stage but by the court of King Charles II:

He tells you that this very moral age
Received its first infection from the stage;
But sure a banisht Court, with lewdness fraught,
The seeds of open vice, returning, brought.

Congreve also replied (*Amendments of Mr. Collier's False and Imperfect Citations,* 1698), as did Thomas D'Urfey, but their responses were less telling than expected. Collier immediately replied with *A Defence of the Short View* (1699) and then pressed on with *A Second Defence* (1700) and *Maxims and Reflections Upon Plays* (1701).

Although Collier is usually characterized as a puritanical theater hater, the cogency of his criticism, the determination of his onslaught, and his insistence that "the Stage must either reform, or not thrive upon profaneness" undoubtedly affected views of the theater, as well as its practitioners. Congreve, for example, gave up the stage after the failure of his most brilliant play, *The Way of the World* (1700). The standard work on this significant episode of English theater is still that by Sister Rose Anthony.

See also: Censorship; Restoration, the.

Bibliography

Anthony, Sister Rose. *The Jeremy Collier Controversy 1698–1726.* Milwaukee: Marquette University Press, 1937.
Collier, Jeremy. *A Short View of the Immorality and Profaneness of the English Stage.* London: 1698.
Krutch, Joseph Wood. *Comedy and Conscience after the Restoration.* New York: Columbia University Press, 1924.
Ridpath, George. *The Stage Condemn'd.* London: 1698.
Thompson, Peter, and Gamini Salgado. *The Everyman Companion to the Theatre.* London: Dent, 1985.

COMICS

The comic strip has diversified greatly as a genre from its original focus of innocent humor to include "war comics," "adventure comics," "cowboy comics," and those dealing with politics, space exploration, and social questions. Thus the generic name *comic* (recorded from ca. 1889) is now a misnomer. The language has changed, in concert with that of popular culture, Western society at large, and to match the topic in question. Up to the 1960s the language of comics was fairly sanitized, but since then there has been an explosion of taboo terms. This has been more obvious in British comics than in the American variety, most of which are certified "Approved by the Comic Codes Authority." Instituted in 1954, the Code had the same basic aims and restrictions of the Hollywood Production Code (1930), the section on Dialogue insisting that "Profanity, obscenity, smut, vulgarity, or words or symbols which have acquired undesirable meanings are forbidden."

Traditionally, the language of comics was decent and proper, in keeping with the social environment, well described by George Orwell in 1940 in his classic essay "Boys' Weeklies": "Everything is safe, solid and unquestionable" (1958, 131). In the British tradition the settings were commonly boarding schools or football teams, so that the most extreme breach of verbal decorum was exclamations such as "Crumbs!," "Heck!" or "What the . . ." Orwell notes the "stylized cries of pain 'Oooogh!,' 'Grooo!' and 'Yaroo!,'" also commenting: "The slang ('Go and eat coke [coal]!,' 'What the thump!,' 'You frabjous ass!,' etc., etc.) has never been altered, so that the boys are now using slang which is at least thirty years out of date" (1958, 120). He quotes an instance of the "extraordinary, artificial, repetitive style" from the *Gem:* "Arthur Augustus sat up dizzily. He grabbed his handkerchief and pressed it to his damaged nose. . . . 'Bai Jove! This is a go, deah boy!' gurgled Arthur Augustus. I have been thwown into quite a fluttah! Oogh! The wottahs! The wuffians! The feahful outsidahs! Wow!' etc. etc. etc." (1958, 120).

Insulting ethnic stereotypes and labels were *de rigueur.* As Orwell commented: "In the *Gem* of 1939, Frenchmen are still Froggies and Italians are still Dagoes. If a Spaniard appears, he is still a 'dago' or 'greaser' who rolls cigarettes and stabs people in the back" (1958, 128, 137). "Sex is completely taboo," Orwell observed, adding knowingly, "especially in the form in which it actually arises in public schools" (1958, 121). He was referring to homosexuality, notoriously rife in English public schools in what was known as "the fagging system." "Religion is also taboo; in the whole thirty years' issue of the *Gem* and *Magnet,* the word 'God' probably does not occur, except in 'God Save the King.'"

Since World War II there have been enormous changes, from monumentally handsome heroes like Superman, Batman, and Captain America to grotesque and cynical antiheroes like Bart Simpson and Andy Capp, with a consequent change of idiom. In the late 1960s in United States there emerged underground comics dealing with social and political subjects, such as sex, drugs, rock and roll, and protests against the Vietnam War. The alternative spelling "comix" was used (as in *Zap Comix,* 1968) to distinguish them from mainstream comics and possibly to emphasize "X" for "X-rated." There was an increasing degree of black humor and a visual style of graphic ugliness. Reacting against the restrictions of the Comics Code and Dr. Frederic Wertham's highly influential study *The Seduction of the Innocent* (1954), there emerged parodic numbers like *Dr. Wirtham's Comix* with full-frontal nudity and *Wimmen's Comix,* with stories like "Tits and Clits" and "Twisted Sisters."

The major development from about 1980 in Britain was the similar growth of "adult" or "mature" comics such as *Viz, Crisis, Brain Damage,* and *Gas.* These have demolished most of the older taboos. The character of "Paul Wicker the tall vicar" (from *Viz*) has been described as a "malevolent, hard-drinking cleric who abuses his Bible class, holds 'Fuck the Pope' rummage sales, and tries to bribe an investigating bishop, who responds: 'Never mind the bullshit Whicker, I've been hearing some complaints about you'" (D.J. Taylor 1990, 22).

Two samples from *Crisis* (no. 46, June 22, 1990) show the descent into a sewer of low invective. "Sinergy" [sic] shows some explicit sex, followed by this tirade from a betrayed black woman: "Bloody ugly bitch! Cow! Whore! How could he do it with such an empty-head, no-brain slut? A bimbo . . . I can feel the violence coming on!" An episode from "For a Few Troubles More" (set in contemporary Ireland) plumbs the depths of the local idiom: "it was like hooer's piss," "sod off y'undead bastard!," "Ah piss off, y'oul witch!," "Ferfrigsake mate! she's a face on her like a well-skelped [slapped] arse!," and a coy euphemism, "Oh fug!" *Viz* now carries the warning "Not for sale to children," includes all the four-letter words, a "profanisaurus" of obscene vocabulary, and a homophobic spoof, "Robin Hood and Richard LittleJohn," featuring "Queerwood Forest" signposted as "Public Cottaging Area" and "Strictly No Heterosexuality Allowed" (no. 114, May 2002).

The language of comics has changed fundamentally from the artificial idiom of dated euphemism to the argot of various savage underworlds and satirical parodies. Although comics are increasingly analyzed by some modern scholars, it is notable that within three years of Mickey Mouse being launched by Disney in 1928, the derogatory use of *Mickey Mouse* as an epithet to dismiss a person or thing as lacking value, authenticity, and seriousness was starting to gain currency.

See also: Popular Culture.

Bibliography

Cook, William. *The Silver-Plated Jubilee—25 Years of Viz*. London: Boxtree, 2004.
Jackson, Kevin. *Planet Simpson*. London: Ebury, 2004.
Orwell, George. "Boys' Weeklies." In *George Orwell: Selected Writings,* edited by George Bott. London: Heinemann, 1958. (Originally published in *Horizon* No. 3, March 1940.)
Sabin, Roger. *Adult Comics: An Introduction*. London: Routledge, 1993.
Taylor, D.J. "Capricious Sphincters." *The Spectator,* May 26, 1990.
Wertham, Frederic. *The Seduction of the Innocent*. London: Museum Press, 1954.

COMMUNISM

The use of political labels as terms of abuse is usually more intense at the extremes of the political spectrum. As the entry for **political names** shows, some are thrown up spontaneously by crises; others are generated systematically. Thus *radical* was a term of great animus in earlier times, as *fascist* has become more recently. In the rhetoric of the Communist Party, terms like *capitalist* and *bourgeois* had particular virulence, as can be seen on virtually any page of the *Communist Manifesto* (1848) by Karl Marx and Friedrich Engels. They were subsequently joined by *imperialist* and *lackey*. However, *communist* and its synonyms have had very different currencies in American and British English. In America *communist,* and especially the abbreviation *commie,* have for several decades been virulent terms, but have virtually no such currency in British English. The difference in the emotive quality in the two varieties is thus largely a reflection of the degree of the perceived threat of the political philosophy to the prevailing system. One of the first recorded uses (in 1849) is Ebenezer Elliott's ironic rhyming definition: "What is a communist? One that yearnings / For equal division of unequal earnings" (*Poetical Works* II, 202). Apart from **red**, the communist term with the greatest currency in British English has been *bolshy,* derived from the militant Bolshevik party in the Russian Revolution. While *Bolshevist* was used, in the words of the *Oxford English Dictionary* as "a term of reproach for an out-and-out revolutionary" from 1917, *bolshy* rapidly gained currency from the following year in the more general sense of "uncooperative, recalcitrant or difficult" as well as "left wing." It is now dated and obsolescent. The currency of *communist* itself has radically declined with the collapse of the soviet communist empire in the 1990s.

The American Communist Labor Party was founded in 1919 (two years after the Russian Revolution) and reached the zenith of its electoral strength in 1932 when its presidential candidate, William Z. Foster, polled almost 103,000 votes. Although Russia was technically on the side of the Allies in World War II, the federal government put in place a legislative program to destroy the party. This included the Smith Act (1940), the McCarran Act (1950), and the Communist Control Act (1954). However, the principal anti-Communist crusader was Senator Joseph McCarthy, who in 1950 gained the national spotlight when he made this sensational (but unsubstantiated) charge: "I have here in my hand a list of 205 [people] that were known to the Secretary of State as being members of the Communist Party and who are working and shaping policy of the State Department" (*Intelligencer,* February 10, 1950). McCarthy's campaign gathered force and ruthlessness, notably in the form of the House Un-American Activities Committee (originally instituted in 1938), which sought in public hearings from 1953 to 1955 to coerce from those subpoenaed the names of communists. Feelings of revulsion against these methods led to the term *McCarthyism* appearing contemporaneously in 1950. Two years later the *American Historical Review* wrote of "the McCarthyite 'witch hunting'" (57, 386). In a memorable correction, the black singer and actor Paul Robeson simply denounced the committee, saying "You are un-American."

At the time of the "red scare" or "communist threat," the hysteria surrounding the Rosenberg trial and the consequent communist witch-hunt, *communist* and *commie* came to carry the senses in American English of "traitor," "enemy," "foreigner," "outsider," or "liberal." But far earlier, in 1933, Jack Warner denounced leaders of the Hollywood Screen Writers Guild as "communists, radical bastards and soap-box sons of bitches." His brother Harry went even further: "They want blood," he screamed. "They want to take my goddamn studio. . . . You goddamn Communist bastards! You dirty sons of bitches! All you'll get from me is shit!" (Behlmer 1985, 9–10). Quotations in the *Random House Historical Dictionary of American Slang* (1994) show an eerie sense of stereotyping: "a bunch of Commie intellectuals" (1949); "a bunch of atheist commie professors" (1968); and "You're all a bunch of . . . commie pinkos" (1972–1975). Reflecting the current sense of guilt by association, *communist sympathizer, fellow traveler* and *card-carrying* became terms of abuse. Robert Welch, the founder of the John Birch Society, even coined the portmanteau form *comsymp,* generated from *communist sympathizer.* Yet both *communist* and *commie* underwent radical generalization of meaning, the original political sense being increasingly ignored. These semantic developments far outlived the communist threat. The *New Dictionary of American Slang* (1986) defines *communist* as, simply, "any despised person = bastard," as in "some communist swiped my typewriter." The word has no special currency in African-American English.

Communist and its derivatives have never acquired the same virulence in British English, largely because communism has never been taken seriously as a political threat, let alone a viable philosophy. In the apartheid era in South Africa the Communist Party was banned and *Communist* acquired a powerful sense of "traitor" similar to that in America, while in Australia *commo* has become a term of hostility but limited currency. Yet a comment like "the commo bastard!" would not have the same force there as in American English.

See also: Political Names; Red.

Bibliography

Behlmer, Rudy. *Inside Warner Brothers (1935–51)*. New York: Simon & Schuster, 1985.
Corker, Charles. *The Communist Problem in the United States.* New York: Fund for the Republic, 1955.
Fried, Richard M. *Men Against McCarthy.* New York: Columbia University Press, 1976.

COMSTOCKERY

The term refers to immoderate censorship, especially of literary texts, on the grounds of assumed immorality. *Comstockery* is now the equivalent in American English for *Bowdlerism* in British English, both terms deriving from the censoring activities of individuals. But whereas Dr. Thomas Bowdler (1754–1825) and his immediate family were self-appointed censors who took it upon themselves to *bowdlerize* or expurgate major texts like Shakespeare and the Bible, Anthony Comstock (1844–1915) was a radical moral crusader who founded the Society for the Suppression of Vice and operated constitutionally by prosecuting or seeking to suppress the publication of numerous literary works. *Comstockery* was coined in 1905 by George Bernard Shaw as an ironic riposte when Comstock attacked Shaw's play *Mrs. Warren's Profession* as "one of Bernard Shaw's filthy productions" by "this Irish smut dealer." In a letter to the *New York Times* (September 26, 1905), Shaw responded: "Comstockery is the world's standing joke at the expense of the United States." As censorship has become less entrenched, the term has become increasingly dated.

Comstock and his followers represented a resurgence of the extreme puritanism that had flourished in England in the seventeenth century. His early career was devoted to making arrests for obscenity; he then worked for the Young Men's Christian Association, which had set up a Committee for the Suppression of Vice, subsequently the Society for the Suppression of Vice. In 1873 he got through Congress an act popularly termed the Comstock Act, the "Act for the Suppression of the Trade in, and Circulation of Obscene Literature and Articles for Immoral Use." The act was comprehensive in its restrictiveness, closing the mails to "obscene and indecent matter," and expanding the definition of "literature" to include even publications dealing with contraception, such as Margaret Sanger's *The Woman Rebel* (1914) and Mary Ware Dennett's pamphlet *The Sex Side of Life, an Explanation for Young People* (1919).

Comstock took his duties very seriously, personally conducting raids, and was not above acting as an *agent provocateur,* inducing booksellers to acquire obscene or banned books, thus becoming liable to prosecution. He prosecuted more than 3,500 people (although less than ten per cent were found guilty) and destroyed more than 160 tons of allegedly obscene literature. He once boasted that he had driven fifteen people to their deaths. He was appointed a special agent in the Post Office for enforcing the Act, a position he held until his death. Of his publications, *Morals Versus Art* (1887) most summed up his philosophy.

The successes and failures of Comstock and his followers are summed up in the entry for **censorship**. What finally brought Comstockery into disrepute was the indiscriminacy of prosecutions for obscenity and the arbitrary interventions of the U.S. Postal Service and U.S. Customs, whose confiscations included works by Aristophanes, Petronius, Giovanni Boccaccio, François Rabelais, Daniel Defoe, Voltaire, Jean-Jacques Rousseau, and Henri Balzac. The bans on these works remained in force until 1930, when a notable legal victory led to some relaxation of the Tariff Act. There was also a slow liberalization of attitude toward censorship, encouraged by the articulate opposition of some robust individuals. These included Theodore Schroeder, a lawyer and a champion of literary freedom, who attacked Comstock directly in 1906, arguing that "there is no organized force in American life which is more pernicious than Comstockery." Schroeder argued ingeniously that "Mr. Comstock is also an unconscious witness to the harmlessness of obscenities," since "he has for forty years 'stood at the mouth of a sewer,' searching for and devouring 'obscenity' for a salary," but has been left or made "so much purer than all the rest of humanity" (1911, 101–3). His successor, John S. Sumner, was not nearly so successful in his tenure. Vestiges of the Comstock Act survived into the 1990s. The legacy of Comstock is somewhat ironic: the 15,000-volume collection of pornography held in the Library of Congress is based on material confiscated by the U.S. Post Office and Customs in terms of the Comstock Act of 1873.

See also: Bowdlerization; Censorship.

Bibliography

Craig, Alec. *The Banned Books of England and Other Countries.* London: Allen & Unwin, 1962.
Schroeder, Theodore A. *Obscene Literature and the Constitutional Law.* New York: privately printed, 1911.

COOLIE

From its original denotative sense of a laborer in India or China, *coolie* has become a highly insulting label for an Indian or Asian person. Its origins are disputed, being either in *Koli,* the name of a low-caste people of Western India, or in the South Indian Dravidian word *quli,* "a day laborer," probably influenced by Tamil *kuli,* meaning "daily hire." Although the term was borrowed into English about 1598, British colonists started to use it in various slighting ways, such as "a common fellow of the lowest class" and "a private soldier."

With the export of Indian labor to plantations in South Africa and the West Indies, the term has come to be widely used disparagingly for an Indian in British English and several varieties. In South Africa it was used in a broad sense of any menial laborer of color. The

INDIAN OCEAN.— A COOLIE OPERATIC PERFORMANCE AT CEYLON — THE " GURU " SINGING THE PROLOGUE.

The performer in this Ceylonese opera (1878 woodcut) is identified as a "coolie"—a derogatory term for any person from India or an unskilled laborer from the Far East. *(Library of Congress, LC-USZ62-119342)*

Rev. Charles Pettman noted in *Africanderisms* (1913), the first study of borrowings into South African English, that "as used in Cape Dutch, *coolie* is applied to Coloured porters and labourers and not to Hindu or Chinese laborers exclusively." It still carries great opprobrium. *Coolie* is also recorded in American English from 1854 for a Chinese or East Asian. In 1907, Johnson remarked in *Discrimination Against Japanese* (56) that "the name 'coolie'... is applied to all Orientals." In contemporary American street-gang use the term refers to an unaffiliated youth.

Coolie is now an offensive mode of address for an Indian in England, as well as in South Africa and Jamaica. Although not used of immigrant Indians in the United States, the term became commonly applied to Chinese laborers, especially during the boom years of railroad construction during the mid-nineteenth century. The word has followed the typical semantic pattern of race terms by acquiring a highly emotive and derogatory meaning through being used by out-group speakers.

See also: Kaffir.

Bibliography
Pettman, the Rev. Charles. *Africanderisms.* London: Longmans Green, 1913.

COON

Coon has had an unpredictable semantic history, largely but not exclusively confined to the United States. Supposedly derived from *raccoon,* the abbreviated form was current from at least 1742. Originally a term for a white rustic, from the 1820s it was used of a cunning or remarkable man, as in the description of Davy Crockett as "a right smart coon" (M. St. C. Clarke, *Sketches of Crockett* 1832, 144). Two minstrel songs seem to have initiated and consolidated the association with blacks, the first in 1834 being "O ole Zip Coon." By the Civil War it was being generally used as a term of derogation for blacks, as in *Uncle Tom's Cabin* (1852): "Well, Tom, yer coons [escaped slaves] are fairly treed" (130). H.L. Mencken quotes the curious story of Ernest Hogan, a black, who wrote a song in 1896 under the stereotyping title of "All *Coons* Look Alike to Me," apparently not regarding the word as offensive, and was "amazed and crushed by the resentment it aroused among his people" (1963, 386). As the song increased in popularity and provocation, so it greatly accelerated the currency of the term, which is now taboo.

In its British currency *coon* has become an ethnic insult for a black person, although like *wog,* it is often used more generally of a person of color. Thus Philip Larkin wrote in a private letter, "Thanks for the postcard from Coonland [Morocco]" (1992, 690). In Australian English it has been used disparagingly to refer to an Aborigine, at least from about 1899: "Australia is a elova fine place for coons, and the blacker and uglier they are the better they seem to be treated" (1905, from *Truth,* Sydney, 24). The strangest survival is in South Africa, where the term traditionally refers to the Cape Colored revelers who celebrate the New Year holiday in "the Coon Carnival," with blackened faces in the minstrel style, elaborate costumes, parades, and dancing. Although originating in the emancipation of the slaves in 1838, the first recorded use is only in 1924. The black-and-white makeup supposedly explains the derivation from *raccoon.* Although the derogatory meaning of *coon* is also current, it has failed to displace this special celebratory sense.

See also: Blacks; Ethnic Insults; Hottentot; Kaffir; Nigger.

Bibliography

Brandford, J. *A Dictionary of South African English.* Cape Town: Oxford University Press, 1987.
Mencken, H.L. *The American Language.* Abridged ed. by R. McDavid. New York: Knopf, 1963.

COPROLALIA

This arcane term, which would translate literally from Greek into demotic English as "talking shit," refers to a psychological condition whereby victims are overcome with a perverse desire to utter socially inappropriate or unacceptable words such as swearwords and racial epithets. The condition is regarded as part of Tourette's syndrome, named after Giles de la Tourette, who coined the word in its French form *coprolalie* in *Archives de Neurologie* 1885 (IX, 19). The word rapidly gained psychological currency, an article in the *Journal of Nervous and Mental Disorders* in 1886 commenting that "Echolalia (the meaningless repetition of words

Originally a term for country whites in the United States, *coon* is believed to have been associated with African Americans for the first time in an 1834 minstrel song, "O ole Zip Coon." *(Library of Congress, LC-USZ62-126131)*

and phrases) and coprolalia may form part of the symptoms of insanity." (XIII, 412). Have-lock Ellis in his *Affirmations* (1898) was more specific: "These extremes are of two kinds: the first issuing in a sort of coprolalia, or inclination to dwell on excrement. . . . The other is that of pruriency, or the perpetual itch to circle round sexual matters" (147). About a third of sufferers from Tourette's syndrome show coprolalia, interpreted more broadly as manifest-ing itself by involuntary muscular tics, gesticulations, and vocal outbursts.

As with many technical psychological terms, coprolalia has tended to be popularized and trivialized, as in the instance from W. Gaddis, *Recognitions* (1955): "When you have Tourette's disease you go around repeating dirty words all the time. Coprolalia. Everybody below Four-teenth Street has coprolalia" (II v 531). Coprolalia is also a form of sexual gratification, now recognized in the simpler formulation of "talking dirty." Notable sufferers of coprolalia were Jonathan Swift (1667–1745) and Wolfgang Amadeus Mozart (1756–1791), although both used obscenities in writings.

See also: Swift, Jonathan.

Bibliography

Brown, Norman O. *Life Against Death.* London: Routledge & Kegan Paul, 1959.

Kushner, Howard I. *Cursing Brain?: The Histories of Tourette's Syndrome.* Cambridge, MA: Harvard University Press, 1999.

Leckman, James F., and Donald J. Cohen. *Tourette's Syndrome.* New York: John Wiley, 1998.

COPULATION

In all cultures copulation has a special binary status, being viewed alternatively as sacred and profane, depending on context. The process gives man access to divine life-giving powers, but via basic animal functions, thus uniting the two aspects of humanity's dualistic nature. Yeats's observation that "Love has pitched his mansion in / The place of Excrement" (from "Crazy Jane Talks with the Bishop") is a poetic rendering of the stark Latin *inter urinas et faeces nascimur* ("We are born between urine and feces"), quoted by Freud in *Civilization and Its Discontents* (1930, 78). Historically, English terms for copulation have come to be re-garded as obscene and therefore highly taboo, forming a potent element in swearing and profanity. Their public use is still regarded as unacceptable and highly controversial in all speech communities, despite exploitation in various forms of popular culture. In this re-spect English differs from other languages, for example French, in which the verbs of copulation, *foutre* and *baiser,* are in common currency.

The public status of these terms has varied. Curiously, English has had three basic terms for copulation in its historical development, all of disputed origin and all at some time regarded as taboo. In consequence, enormous numbers of euphemisms and synonyms have grown up. The earliest and least-known term was the verb *sard,* recorded from Anglo-Saxon times to the seventeenth century; it coexisted with *swive,* recorded from medieval times to the Renaissance, but thereafter with diminishing frequency. The origins of *swive* are in Anglo-Saxon *swifan,* "to revolve," also "to sweep," although sexual instances are hard to trace. *Sard* has the notable distinction of being the only word in the field used in formal contexts. Both *sard* and *swive* have now been archaic for over a century. The modern term **fuck** is recorded only from the early sixteenth century. All the early recorded instances are from the North, and several of them are found in *flytings* or swearing matches, a form of entertainment carried on, surprisingly, by the Scottish nobility and literati. Since then it has had an underground or disreputable currency, although some authors have tried to rehabilitate it.

Swive in its clear sexual sense is first recorded in the *Canterbury Tales* (1386–1400), when the Miller ends his bawdy tale of adultery with this coarse summary:

Thus swyved was the carpenteres wyf,
For al his keping and his ialousye
[In spite of all his watchfulness and suspicion].
(ll. 666–67)

Although Chaucer apologizes in advance for the Miller's tale as being that of a *cherle* or lowclass person, *swyve* is found in a variety of contexts. In a fifteenth-century verse a magpie vows to reveal an affair, using a medieval oath into the bargain:

A, seyde the pye, by Godes wylle,
How thou art swyved y [I] shalle telle.

John Florio's *A Worlde of Wordes* (1598), the first comprehensive English/Italian dictionary, translated the relevant Italian verb via the whole gamut of available English synonyms with Renaissance exuberance:

Fottere: To iape [jape], to sard, to fucke, to swive, to occupy.

We notice that out of this extensive word field, only one term has survived into Modern English in the copulatory sense. Most of the recorded instances of *swive* are scurrilous: John Fletcher's translation of a passage of Martial, published in 1656, carries the line: "I can swive four times a night; but thee once in four years I cannot occupye" (xi 98). Eric Partridge cited in 1937 the naughty title of *The Queen of Swiveland* for Venus. However, the word was never as taboo as *fuck*, being included in the dictionaries of Nathaniel Bailey (1730), Francis Grose (1785), and the great *Oxford English Dictionary* (1884–1928). But during the nineteenth century its currency started to peter out, ending with this piece of quasi-medical Victorian advice: "Don't bathe on a full stomach, nor swive" (1898). Throughout its history the term stayed semantically stable and did not develop related idioms such as *swive about* or *swive off!*

Sard, as has been mentioned, is an ancient word found in formal contexts in AngloSaxon, such as the translation of St. Matthew 5:27 ("Do not commit adultery") in the *Lindisfarne Gospels* as: "Ne serð þu oðres mones wif." By the medieval period *sard* was being used in less elevated contexts. The character of Gluttony in the morality play *The Castle of Perseverance* (ca. 1425) urges Mankind to be "serðyn gay gerlys," which would approximate to "screwing good-time girls" (l. 1163). Before it died out it became a fairly rare regional word found more in the North: "Go, teach your grandam [grandmother] to sard" was "a

Nottingham proverb," according to Howell's *English Proverbs,* dated 1617. Its existence in a proverb shows that the word was not then taboo.

"To jape" meant both "to play and "to deceive," but the sexual sense surfaces in the anonymous *Political Poems* (1382) in this shockingly Oedipal comment: "Sle thi fadre and jape thi modre and they will thee assoile" ("Kill your father and fuck your mother, and they will forgive you," I, 270). A late medieval extract from the play *Hyckescorner* (1510) runs: "he japed my wife and made me cuckold" (i 171). A pointed comment on the word's semantic change was made by George Puttenham in *The Arte of English Poesie* (1589): "Such wordes as may be drawen to a foule and unshamefast sense, as one that should say to a young woman, 'I pray you let me jape with you, which is indeed no more than let me sport with you' . . . for it may be taken in another perverser sense" (Book III, chapter 22). Thereafter the sexual sense faded away as the modern meaning established itself.

The sexual sense of *occupy* provides an even stronger example of how one meaning can affect the general currency of a word. The primary sense of "to take possession of; take for one's own use or seize" is recorded from about 1380. However the sexual sense of "to copulate" (*OED* 8) appeared about 1432 in this amusing passage from Ranulph Higden's *Polychronicon:* "Men of Lacedemonia [Sparta], fatigate and weary through the compleyntes of their wifes beenge at home, made a decre and ordinaunce that they sholde occupye many men, thenkenge the nowmbre of men to be encreesed by that." An explicit comment on the semantic deterioration of the word is found in Shakespeare's *Henry IV, Part II* (1597), ironically in the mouth of Doll Tearsheet: "as odious as the word 'occupy', which was an excellent word before it was ill sorted" (II iv 159). The contemporary dramatist Ben Jonson noted in his *Discoveries* (1637): "Many, out of their own obscene Apprehensions, refuse proper and fit words, as *occupie, nature,* and the like." The comment in the *Oxford English Dictionary* bears this out: "The disuse of this verb in the 17th and most of the 18th c. is notable. . . . This avoidance appears to be due to its vulgar employment in sense 8." This sexual sense is last recorded in 1660.

In common with other word fields dealing with the genitalia and excretion, the taboo has generated a great number of euphemisms, as well as a division of registers between the coarser native words and classical terms. Thus *copulation* itself (first used in the sexual sense ca. 1632) and *intercourse* (from ca. 1798) have histories similar to *occupy,* but now have primary sexual meanings. *Conversation* meant "adultery" from ca. 1511, surviving in the formula *criminal conversation* subsequently abbreviated in legal jargon to *crim. con.,* recorded from 1809, but now obsolete. In addition to the euphemistic phrase *to sleep with,* discussed under **Euphemisms,** is *cover,* now confined to agricultural contexts, but first recorded as an official euphemism in 1535 in *Act 27 Henry VIII* c. 6. It appears grossly in Shakespeare's *Othello* (I i 111) and pompously in Sir Thomas Urquhart's delightful translation of Rabelais (1653): "Madam, it would be a very great benefit to the commonwealth, delightful to you, honourable to your progeny, and necessary for me, that I cover you for the propagating of my race" (Book II, chapter 21).

The field contains a huge variety of slang terms, like modern *screw, shag, hump,* and *bonk,* several of them of surprising duration. Thus the copulatory sense of *screw* is first recorded in the *New Canting Dictionary* (1725), but then seemingly dropped out of usage until it was revived about 1937. *Shag* is similarly first found in Francis Grose's *Classical Dictionary of the Vulgar*

Tongue (1785) but had an apparent hiatus of usage until the 1950s. Grose also includes *hump*, noting that it was "once a fashionable word for copulation." *Bonk* is an exclusively modern British word, recorded in the sexual sense from the 1950s. Jonathon Green's *Slang Thesaurus* (2nd edition, 1999) has approximately two hundred such terms.

In many ways the division of registers shows the split between the polarities of the mystical and the grossly physical, with the preponderance on the latter. Walt Whitman's phrase "the divine work of fatherhood" is a rare example of the first mode. The dysphemisms (which allude to the physicality of the act with gross directness) are far more numerous, including the current *poke, stuff, screw,* preceded by *making the beast with two backs* (notably used in *Othello* I i 116).

See also: Comstockery; Frig, Frigging; Fuck; *Lady Chatterley's Lover; Oxford English Dictionary.*

Bibliography

Ayto, John. *Bloomsbury Dictionary of Word Origins.* London: Bloomsbury, 1991.
Burchfield, Robert. "Four-letter words and the *OED.*" *Times Literary Supplement,* October 13, 1972.
————. "An Outline History of Euphemisms in Old English." In *Fair of Speech,* ed. D.J. Enright. Oxford: Oxford University Press, 1986.
Chapman, Robert L. *New Dictionary of American Slang.* New York: Harper & Row, 1986.
Farmer, J.S., and W.E. Henley. *Slang and Its Analogues.* London: Routledge and Kegan Paul, 1890–1904. Reprint, Oxford: Wordsworth Press, 1987.
Flexner, Stuart Berg. *I Hear America Talking.* New York: Van Nostrand Reinhold, 1976.
Green, Jonathan. *The Slang Thesaurus.* Harmondsworth: Penguin, 1988.
Grose, Francis. *A Classical Dictionary of the Vulgar Tongue.* London: S. Hooper, 1785.
Jay, Timothy. *Cursing in America: A Psycholinguistic Study of Dirty Language in the Courts, in the Movies, in the Schoolyards and on the Streets.* Philadelphia: J. Benjamins, 1992.
Lighter, J.E., ed. *Random House Historical Dictionary of American Slang.* New York: Random House, 1994.
McDonald, James. *Dictionary of Obscenity, Taboo and Euphemism.* London: Sphere Books, 1988.
Maurer, David W. *Language of the Underworld.* Lexington: University Press of Kentucky, 1981.
Partridge, Eric. *Origins.* 3rd ed. London: Routledge & Kegan Paul, 1977.
Sagarin, Edward. *The Anatomy of Dirty Words.* New York: Lyle Stuart, 1962.
Spears, Richard A. *Slang and Euphemism.* New York: Signet, 1991.

COWARDICE

At the warrior stage of culture, physical courage was the most esteemed virtue, and correspondingly the greatest social ignominy was the stigma of cowardice. Today, however, the social value of courage is modified by notions of political or diplomatic skills in avoiding confrontation. As the entry for the **Anglo-Saxon period** shows, the value of absolute loyalty to the clan and to the chief was celebrated, both in battle poems and those poignantly depicting the life of disgraced exiles. The primary term in the ancient language for "cowardly" was *earg,* which had the subsidiary meanings of "evil, wretched, vile."

The modern term *coward* entered the language around 1250. Interestingly derived from Old French *coart,* ultimately Latin *cauda,* "a tail," the base meaning alludes, according to the *Oxford English Dictionary,* to the habit of an animal "turning tail" in fright. It was previously a highly emotive and provocative term that could be grounds for a duel. Cowardice and treachery are obviously related to a degree, as is shown in the entry for **renegade**, meaning one who deserts a cause. *Runagate,* a "vagabond, fugitive or renegade" is an anglicized form showing the same link, notably in an early use from *Richard III* (1591), where Richard dismisses Richmond as a "white-livered runagate" (IV iv 465).

The allusion to the white liver derives from a whole series of terms in medieval physiognomy explaining courage and cowardice as having physical origins. Specifically it was believed that the liver was the seat of the passions, and that a liver lacking color indicated weakness or lack of courage. (The term *courage,* incidentally, is rooted in Latin *cor,* meaning "heart.") This folklore led to the scornful epithet *lily-livered,* found in *Macbeth* (V iii 17). Despite its fanciful origins, the term is still current.

Other terms showing the same association are *stomach* and *guts,* both perpetuating the folklorish notion of the stomach as the seat of courage and strong emotions. The first still survives principally in the idiom to have "the stomach for a fight," memorably used by Queen Elizabeth when she addressed her troops on the eve of the Spanish Armada in 1588: "I know I have the body of a weak and feeble woman, but I have the heart and stomach of a king." *Guts* was previously not a low-register word, being used by Sir Philip Sidney in his translation of the Psalms in 1580. Jonathan Swift was one of the first to incorporate the sense of "courage" in his *Polite Conversation* (1738): "The fellow's well enough, if he had any guts in his brain." Now well established, *guts* has the related forms *gutsy, gutsiness,* and the condemning *gutless,* first used by Ezra Pound in a letter of 1900.

American English has absorbed many of these terms and idioms, and added its own. A compound linking the old world with the new is *chicken-hearted,* meaning "fearful" and "cowardly" in Grose's *Classical Dictionary of the Vulgar Tongue* (1785). Other compounds, notably *chicken-livered,* preceded the development of the free-standing *chicken* about 1933. This has extended to the idioms derived from teenage car duels, of *playing chicken* and *chickening out,* and the contemptuous *chickenshit,* euphemized to *C.S.* The other principal term is *yellow,* recorded in P.T. Barnum's *Struggles and Triumphs:* "We never thought your heart was yellow" (1856, 400). It was extended to *yellow-belly,* possibly associated with a Mexican, from the color of a Mexican soldier's uniform. This introduces the stereotypical association of cowardice with certain nationalities on the basis of recent war experience. Although the terminology of cowardice has generally become more physical and less moral in its focus, it still retains a stinging and insulting edge in personal use.

See also: Anglo-Saxon Period; Renegade.

Bibliography
Rawson, Hugh. *A Dictionary of Invective.* London: Hale, 1991.
Tacitus, Cornelius. *Tacitus on Britain and Germany.* Translated by H. Mattingly. Harmondsworth: Penguin, 1964.

CRAP

As a less vulgar synonym for *shit,* the term covers almost exactly the same basic semantic areas of "feces," "nonsense," "rubbish," or "insincere talk" in both American and British English, though more widely used in the former. However, unlike *shit* it has never been used as a direct personal insult. The sense of "rubbish" leads back to the origins of the term in Medieval Latin *crappa*, meaning "chaff" or possibly Old Dutch *krappen*, "to harvest." It is first recorded in the fifteenth century in the sense of "chaff, residue, or dregs." While it is not easy to distinguish between the various senses of "rubbish" or "waste" that accumulate around *crap*, they seem to have solidified into the main sense of "excrement" by the eighteenth century, especially in the forms *crapping-casa, crapping-castle,* and *crapping-ken,* various terms for a toilet. (A related form, *cropping-ken,* is recorded in Elisha Coles's dictionary of 1676.)

This evidence for the term's antiquity is significant, if only because it questions the basis of the frequently retailed explanation of the origin of *crap* in the name of a famous innovator, Thomas Crapper. Several popular studies treat the word as an eponym, or term derived from a personal name. This is a typical example:

> To *crap* is to defecate and derives from Crapper's Valveless Water Waste Preventor which was the name under which the first flush lavatory was sold in England. The inventor, Thomas Crapper, who was borne in Thorne, near Doncaster, in 1837, delivered England from the miserable inconvenience the garderobe. (Boycott 1982, 35)

Unfortunately, this appealing story turns out to be a **folk etymology**, or a plausible but unsubstantiated explanation of the origin of a term. It is unsupported by any major reference work, since the meaning had evolved before the appropriately named Crapper was born.

The modern short form of the word did not appear in print in the sense of defecation until the mid-nineteenth century. Hugh Rawson cites the interesting instance of Mark Twain using the form *crap* for *crop* when imitating the East Tennessee dialect in *The Gilded Age* (1873), commenting: "It is unlikely that either Twain or his collaborator on the novel, Charles Dudley Warner, would have committed this word to paper if the coarse meaning were widely known at the time" (*Dictionary of Invective* 1991).

Perhaps because the term did not have the same level of taboo as *shit,* it was used more freely and extended semantically to accommodate more meanings, especially in the United States. In the course of the twentieth century, there have developed numerous compounds such as *crapbrain, craphead,* and the punning *crapshooter,* as well as the main senses of "pretentious talk," "nonsense," "bold and deceitful absurdities," "offensive or disrespectful treatment," and "anything of poor or shoddy quality." Many of these senses have filtered back into British English. Of the usages that remain peculiarly American, there is the exclamatory sense: "O crap, it's broken again!"; the verbal sense of "to lie or exaggerate": "Don't try and crap me!"; and various idiomatic uses such as "a bunch of crap," a locution of President Nixon's preserved on the Watergate tapes.

See also: Folk Etymology.

Bibliography

Boycott, Rosie. *Batty, Bloomers and Boycott.* London: Hutchinson, 1982.
Lighter, Jonathan, ed. *Random House Historical Dictionary of American Slang.* New York: Random House, 1994–.
Rawson, Hugh. *A Dictionary of Invective.* London: Hale, 1991.

CRIMEN INJURIA

The formula refers to a category under South African law defined as an action seriously injuring the dignity of another person. Although it can cover such offenses as making obscene gestures or exposing oneself, it is most commonly invoked in prosecutions for swearing, especially for using highly offensive ethnic slurs, such as *kaffir* or *coolie.* Prosecutions are not common, but regular. The formulation preserves an old sense of *injury,* namely "intentionally hurtful or offensive speech," recorded from the sixteenth century.

CUCKOLDRY

The state of marital infidelity has always attracted scorn for the deceived husband rather than for the adulterous wife. This general feature of European society derives from the earlier notion that the wife was the man's property or servant and was thus expected to obey him. (Revealingly, the original sense of *seduce* was not sexual, but wrongfully to persuade another man's labor to leave him.) The humiliating words associated with cuckoldry have always been too sensitive to become personal insults in English, and even their currency has diminished in modern times. It is important, as with most sexual matters, to distinguish between the action and the word. Writers may be sensitive about the use of the words *cuckold* and *unfaithful,* but adultery is a major motif of medieval literature, both in tragic contexts, such as Tristan and Isolde and Lancelot and Guinevere, and in the comic worlds of the **fabliau.**

Cuckold derives from *cuckoo,* alluding to the parasitic habit of the female bird in changing its mate frequently and laying its eggs in other birds' nests. The association is common in medieval folklore, literature, and iconography. The old form *kukewold,* borrowed from Old French *cuccault,* made up of *cuccu* plus the pejorative suffix *-ault,* first appears about 1250 in the satirical and polemical poem *The Owl and the Nightingale* (l. 1544). The term was clearly regarded as embarrassingly direct, even in John Lydgate's *Fall of Princes* (ca. 1440): "To speke plaine Englishe, made him cokolde. Alas I was not auised wel before Vnkonnyngly to speake such language: I should haue sayde how that he had an horne. . . . And in some land *Cornodo* men do them call." (The references to "horn" and "Cornodo" (*cornuto*) are clarified later in this entry.)

The verbal extension of "to cuckold" is recorded from about 1589, exclusively applied from a male perspective, explained in Dr. Johnson's definition: "To corrupt a man's wife; to bring upon a man the reproach of having an adulterous wife; to rob a man of his wife's fidelity." Johnson adds a note about alerting a husband of his wife's infidelity: "it was usual to alarm [provoke] a husband at the approach of an adulterer by calling *cuckoo.*" Shakespeare alludes to this practice in a song in *Love's Labour's Lost* (1588–1590):

The cuckoo then on every tree,
Mocks married men; for thus sings he—
   Cuckoo
Cuckoo cuckoo! Oh word of fear,
Unpleasing to the married ear!
(V ii 906–10)

A Contented Cuckold in the new fashion.

How blest am I and what a happie life.   *In my conceit; hees more then mad that scornes*
DoeI injoy but.I may thank my Wife   *To weare such pretious, profitable Hornes.*
Tis shee that rais'd my fortune all this store   *To be a Cuckold why should I repine*
Her.occupation brings:and tenn times more   *The disgrace is my Wifes; the profit mine.*
sold by John Overton at the white horse without Newgate

This seventeenth-century English print depicts a cuckold counting the jewelry that his unfaithful wife—shown in a window at the upper right—received from her suitors. *Cuckold* derives from *cuckoo*, alluding to the habit of the female bird of changing its mate. A contented cuckold was called a *wittol*. *(Library of Congress, LC-USZ62-132019)*

These references show that the term and the name of the symbolic bird were articulated openly in the Renaissance. However, the literary association between the bird and the cuckold is far older, for in Chaucer's *Knight's Tale* (ca. 1386) the figure of Jalousye [Suspicion] is depicted with "a cukkow sittynge on his hand." Shakespeare deals with the theme frequently in both comedy and tragedy, notably in *Othello,* when Iago encourages Roderigo: "If thou canst cuckold him, thou do'st thyself a pleasure, and me a sport" (I iii 375), and worse, when Othello rages: "I will chop her into messes! Cuckold me! (IV i 197).

A curious related term, rare and generally unknown, is *wittol,* meaning a conniving cuckold or one resigned to his wife's infidelity. The term originates in the fifteenth century as *wetewold,* from *witen,* "to know" and the suffix *-wold,* probably from *cukewold.* In Shakespeare's *The Merry Wives of Windsor* (1597), Ford rants furiously at his imagined disgrace: "See the hell of having a false woman! My bed shall be abused, my coffers ransacked and my reputation gnawn at . . . Cuckold! Wittol! Cuckold! the devil himself hath not such a name" (II ii 312–18).

The cuckold's horns form a curious motif widely found in European iconography and literature. This evolved into the practice of placing a set of horns on the deceived husband's head as a sign of public humiliation, found in the stage direction to a quarto text of *The Merry Wives of Windsor* (1597): *Enter Sir John Falstaff with a Buck's head upon him* (V v). The symbolism is, however, far older in both European and English literature. In Geoffrey of Monmouth's romance *Vita Merlini* (ca. 1150), Merlin is betrayed sexually and in a fit of rage tears off the antlers of a stag he has been riding and throws them at his former mistress and her lover. There was even an odd superstition that horns would spontaneously sprout from the husband's head, alluded to in *The Collier of Croydon* (ca. 1580): "My head groweth hard, my horns will shortly spring." This motif in turn led to great numbers of puns and compounds, notably *horn-mad* (frantic with sexual suspicion), also first found in Shakespeare, in *The Comedy of Errors* (II i 57).

These English references to the humiliating horns are paralleled by the Italian term for a cuckolded husband, namely *cornuto,* meaning "horned," which in that language is a grievous and highly provocative insult. So is the well-known two-fingered gesture of the "horned hand," formed with the index and little finger erect, suggestively symbolizing the horns of the cuckold. This gesture has been traced as far back as ancient Etruscan and Pompeiian wall paintings, although these contexts are not necessarily adulterous. As has been seen, the term *cornuto* had been borrowed long before Elizabethan English, no doubt as a witness word reflecting Italian corruption. *The Merry Wives of Windsor* (1597) carries this comment: "The peaking *cornuto* her husband, dwelling in a continual larum of jealousy" ("The snooping cuckold her husband living in a continual panic of sexual suspicion," III v 71). Dr. Johnson defined the term in his *Dictionary* (1755) in a literal fashion as "a man horned; a cuckold."

Cuckoldry is much associated with stereotypical acts of tragic frenzy and revenge in the context of Latin countries. This convention is endorsed by the highly popular melodramatic operas *Cavalleria Rusticana* (1890) and *I Pagliacci* (1892). However, in English literature cuckoldry is also presented humorously, albeit with a degree of *schadenfreud.* In the acerbic comedies of Ben Jonson, generally set in Italy, the theme of marital infidelity abounds. Furthermore, in the later **Restoration** comedy, saturated with sexual intrigue and adultery, there are even characters called Wittol and Horner in William Wycherley's *The Country Wife* (1672).

Adultery continues to be a major theme in literature and popular culture. Yet the open and direct uses of *cuckold, wittol,* and *cornuto* have steadily diminished in currency. *Cornuto* is no longer regarded as an English word, *wittol* is virtually obsolete, and *cuckold* is not commonly heard. Despite the shame of the condition, the term has not become a swearword, nor has it ever been a legal term. At most it is usually uttered *sotto voce,* or behind the deceived husband's back, the condition being alluded to by some euphemism or circumlocution. The fact of cuckoldry, rather than the word, is the most likely grounds for a crime of passion.

See also: Folk Etymology; Restoration, the.

Bibliography

"Cuckold." In *Medieval Folklore,* ed. Carl Lindahl, John McNamara, and John Lindow. Santa Barbara: ABC–CLIO, 2000.

O'Donoghue, Bernard, ed. *The Courtly Love Tradition.* Manchester: Barnes & Noble, 1982.

Tanner, Tony. *Adultery in the Novel.* Baltimore: Johns Hopkins, 1979.

CUNT

Cunt has always been a specific term, unlike *cock,* and has been the most seriously taboo word in English for centuries, remaining so for the vast majority of users. (However, the *Random House Historical Dictionary of American Slang* [1994] categorizes the term as "usually considered vulgar," its general broad formula for words as diverse in their impact as *fart* and *ass.*) As is typical of powerfully taboo terms, it has generated a number of variant forms, such as *queynte, cunny,* and *quim,* as well as numerous synonyms. This entry focuses first on the word itself and then on the variants.

Astonishingly to modern readers, *cunt* was used with far greater openness in earlier times in popular, idiomatic, and even technical currency. It is a startling discovery that its first recorded appearance is in *Gropecuntlane,* an Oxford street name, about 1230. Whether this arresting name was a warning or an encouragement is hard to say, but the term was clearly acceptable publicly. (The name, previously found in other cities, was subsequently changed to Magpie Lane.) Even more remarkable are the recorded personal names of women such as Gunoka Cuntles (1219), Bele Wydecunthe (1328), and even men's names such as Godwin Clawecuncte (1066), John Fillecunt (1216), and Robert Clevecunt (1302). Medieval medical texts such as the English translations of Lanfrank's *Cirurgerie* [Surgery] (ca. 1400) and *The Cyrurgie of Guy de Chauliac* (ca. 1425) use core words now regarded as obscene or grossly impolite as terminology. "In wymmen," we read in Lanfrank, "þe necke of the bladdre is schort & is maad fast to the cunte" (1894, 172). There was even a proverbial saying, *drunk as a cunt,* apparently the first contemptuous use. The *Survey of English Dialects* carried out in the 1950s and 1960s showed the word to be still in common rural use for the vulva of a cow.

The first recorded instance occurs well after the Anglo-Saxon period, which ended about 1100. Although there are many ancient cognate Germanic forms, such as Old Norse *kunta,* Old Frisian, Middle Low German, and Middle Dutch *kunte,* the word is not general in Old English: Eric Partridge claims that it is recorded once as *kunte (Dictionary of Historical Slang,* 1937). This paucity certainly suggests a taboo. Furthermore, Robert Burchfield, in an "Outline

History of Euphemisms in Old English," does not mention *cunt* in the context of Old English at all, observing that "the normal term for the female genitalia was *gecyndlic*" (1986, 22). Bosworth and Toller's *Anglo-Saxon Dictionary* (1898) has the entry *gecyndlim*, literally "birth-limb" for "vulva." During the latter part of the Anglo-Saxon period the extensive invasions by the Scandinavian peoples speaking Old Norse might have provided the source. The *Oxford English Dictionary* notes that "the ulterior relations are uncertain," since scholars are divided over the likely but problematic link with Latin *cunnus,* possibly related to *cuneus,* "a wedge," yielding the Romance relatives *con* (French), recorded from about 1200, and *conno* (Italian). As Eric Partridge noted: "The presence of the *t* in the Germanic has long puzzled the etymologists" (1977).

In the course of Middle English (1150–1500) the term became increasingly taboo. It is a plausible speculation that the French title *count* was replaced by *earl* in English because of its embarrassing phonetic proximity to *cunt*. (Both words would then have had short "u" vowels, as in Modern English "boot" and "put.") In addition to the use in place-names, personal names, and medical texts, there is this remarkable instance from a medieval morality play called *The Castle of Perseverance* (ca. 1425) in which the character Luxuria (Lust) says: "Mankynde, my leue lemman, I[n] my cunte dou shalt crepe" ("Mankind, my dear lover, you shall take refuge in my cunt," 1193). This was a well-known play performed all over England. Yet the form is not found in the works of Chaucer, William Langland, Sir Thomas Malory, or Shakespeare.

From the obscene and taboo senses emerge those of vituperative insult. In this domain it figures in the convention of *flyting,* or ritual insult matches, carried on, curiously, by the Scottish nobility of the early Renaissance. In perhaps the most remarkable of these verbal duels, *The Flyting of Dunbar and Kennedy* (1503), Dunbar refers to his opponent contemptuously as a "cunt-bitten crawdon" (l. 50). This translates into "a pox-smitten coward," a *crawdon* being a cock that will not fight, thus introducing various contemptuous phallic wordplays.

The term's currency naturally declined during the Puritan Commonwealth (1649–1660) but had an extraordinary resurgence during the Restoration in the satirical and bawdy verses of the outrageous violator of taboos, the **Earl of Rochester** (1647–1680), who in "A Ramble in Saint James's Park" wrote scabrously of "your lewd Cunt. . . . Drench't with the seed of half the Town," followed by "your devouring Cunt." His "Satire on Charles II" starts with the outrageous chauvinistic claim that "th' Isle of Britaine" has long been famous "for breeding the best cunts in Christendome" (ll. 1–2). Rochester was not alone: his contemporaries John Oldham, Lord Buckhurst, and George Etherege liberally laced their own verse with extraordinary obscenity. Etherege begins his verse-poem to Buckhurst:

So soft and amorously you write
Of cunt and prick, the prick's delight.

The notorious excesses of Rochester and his set no doubt provoked the ensuing period of restraint. Although the full form was printed in Nathaniel Bailey (*Dictionarium Britannicum,* 1730), it was usually euphemized in forms such as *c**t* (in Francis Grose's *Classical Dictionary of the Vulgar Tongue,* 1785), or plain——in Laurence Sterne's *Sentimental Journey* (1768), or simply passed over, as it was by Dr. Johnson in his *Dictionary* (1755). A letter by John Keats mentions a party during which "there was an enquiry about the derivation of the word C—t" (January 5, 1818).

The term became increasingly taboo, not appearing in any major dictionary for over two centuries, until the publication of the Third Edition of *Webster* (1961) in the United States and the *Penguin English Dictionary* (1965) in the United Kingdom. The most significant omission was from the great *Oxford English Dictionary* (1884–1928). However, it should be borne in mind that at that time the word fell under the legal category of "obscene libel." Even though most standard dictionaries now include the term, a surprising number still do not. These include the *Barnhart Dictionary of Etymology* (1988) and Clarence Major's *Juba to Jive: A Dictionary of African-American Slang* (1994). However, the *Random House Historical Dictionary of American Slang* (1994) offers appropriately wide and detailed coverage.

The use of *cunt* as a term of personal abuse is relatively recent. One of the first, interestingly in an American context, is dated 1860 in Marx E. Neely's, *Lincoln Encyclopedia,* which carries this ribald rhyme:

And when they got to Charleston, they had to, as is wont,
Look round to find a chairman, and so they took a Cu—.

(The rhyme suggests an older pronunciation, closer to "cont," apparent in Rochester, who also rhymed *cunt* with *wont* and the abbreviation *on't.*) While the *OED Supplement* (1972) categorizes the sense as "applied to a person, especially a woman, as a term of vulgar abuse," *Random House* (1994) is more gender-specific: "a despicable, contemptible or foolish man." It has two excellent quotations from the 1960s: "You first-class prick . . . You second-class cunt" (1966) and "Donald, you are a real *card-carrying cunt*" (1968). In the vituperative semantics of the genital area, *cunt* has, of course, far more power than *cock*. Personal insults like the surrealistic *cunt-faced, cunt-pensioner* for "one who lives off the prostitution of a wife, mistress or even daughter," *cunt-struck* for "obsessed with women," and *silly cunt* all became current during the nineteenth century. But the most wounding insult remains the plain form "You cunt!"

Most of these usages were previously more current in British English, since the taboo lasted longer in the American variety. However in the past half-century or so many vulgar or obscene formations have started to surface in American English. These include *cunt cap* for the two-pointed military cap that folds like the labia, *cunt-hound* for a lecher, *cunt-rag* for a sanitary napkin, and *cunt-wagon,* a pimp's car for carrying prostitutes to customers. Most of these are vulgar or jocular male-to-male locutions. More insulting are the self-explanatory *cunt-sucker* and *cunt-lapper.* In other global varieties, *cunt* has not made any special inroads of the kind just mentioned, largely because the traditional taboos governing the word were preserved in the new speech communities in South Africa and Australia.

Variant forms

As is common with taboo words, *cunt* has generated a number of variant forms, some of them euphemistic phonetic disguises. These include *queynte, quim, cunny,* and *coney. Queynte* is found in the bawdy tale of Chaucer's Miller and in the Wife of Bath's risqué memoirs, her *Prologue.* Nicholas, the philandering lodger of the Miller's tale, dispenses with the decencies of foreplay in seizing the moment with Alison with shocking directness:

And privily he caughte her by the queynte
And said 'unless I have my will
For dear love of thee, leman [lover], I spill [I shall die]'
And helde her harde by the haunchbones. . . .
(ll. 3276–79)

This context was sufficiently embarrassing to middle-class sensibilities for Chaucer to apologize in advance. The term appears, however, in the medieval romance *Sir Tristam* (ca. 1320) in this very coarse context: "Hir queynte abouen hir kne / Naked þe kni3tes knewe." ("The knights had carnal knowledge of her cunt"). The much-married Wife of Bath, a liberated woman in every respect, refers to her own genitalia with an exuberant range of register: the directly taboo *queynte,* the coyly euphemistic *thinge,* the stylish French *bele chose,* and the pseudo-scholarly *quoniam* (in Latin meaning "since"). The form *queynte* survived as *quaint,* ingeniously used by Andrew Marvell (1621–1678) in his poem "To His Coy Mistress" in the phrase "quaint honour" and in the North of England until the late nineteenth century.

Quim is recorded from the early seventeenth century to the mid-nineteenth, notably in this bawdy *Broadside Ballad* of ca. 1707: "Tho' her hands they are red and her bubbies are coarse, Her quim, for all that, may be never the worse." In his *Classical Dictionary of the Vulgar Tongue* (1785), Francis Grose defined it as "the private parts of a woman: perhaps from the Spanish *qemar,* 'to burn.'" In 1847, James O. Halliwell noted in his *Dictionary of Archaic and Provincial Words:* "the same as the old word queint, which as I am informed by a correspondent at Newcastle, is still used in the North of England by the colliers and common people." The word was unlisted in the original *OED.* Partridge suggested in his edition of Grose the possibility of "a reference to the Anglo-Saxon verb *cweman,* 'to please,'" adding that "the word was often used in the Army in 1914–18." Although virtually obsolete in British usage now, it is listed in dictionaries of slang on both sides of the Atlantic to mean both the female genitals and women as sexual objects in general. ***Twat*** carried the same meaning, generally in slang and substandard contexts, from 1650 onward.

Some euphemistic forms are surprisingly old. It is astonishing to read in Philip Stubbes's *Anatomie of Abuses* (1583) that "The word pussie is now used of a woman" (97). Although the meaning is uncertain, it is unlikely that Stubbes, a noted Puritan, would have commented on the usage if it were innocent. A clearer source of innuendo dated 1664 is this mock-heroic toast from *Virgil Travestie:* "Æneas, here's a health to thee, / To pusse and to good company." (However, the *OED* questioned this interpretation.) After a long period of limited underground usage, the word has surfaced again, more in American usage than in British. It is especially common in African-American currency meaning variously the vagina, women perceived as a sexual object, and as a term in sexual politics, as in *pussy-whipped,* meaning "henpecked." In this context Germaine Greer coined the ironic term *pussy-power* for female manipulation by "wheedling and caressing, instead of challenging" (*The Female Eunuch* 1970, 126). The global currency is wider than expected: Pidgin English in Melanesia has *pus-pus,* a reduplicative form meaning "to have sexual intercourse," while Afrikaans *poes* (pronounced as "puss") is a highly taboo term for the vagina. In an amusingly reticent caution, Professor Nicolas Mansvelt commented in 1884 in his "Proeve van een Kaapsch-

Hollandsch Idioticon" ("Examples of the Cape-Dutch Dialect") that the new arrival from Holland "takes a risk if he addresses a Cape cat."

Another euphemistic disguise-form is *cunny,* found in Thomas D'Urfey's saucy lyric (1720): "All my Delight is a Cunny in the Night" (*Pills* VI 197). The emergence of this form drove out the old word for a rabbit, namely *cony* or *coney,* which had a similar pronunciation and had been in use since the thirteenth century. Although the *OED* did not include *cunny,* it did comment on *coney:* "It is possible that the desire to avoid certain vulgar association of the word in the *cunny* form may have contributed to a different pronunciation" (as in Coney Island). However, the authority included such punning usages as "They cry like poulterers' wives, 'No money, no coney'" (1622, Philip Massinger, *The Virgin Martyr* II i). A pamphlet in 1652 refers suggestively to "Cupid's Coneyberie or the Park of Pleasure," while in its other form the word yielded *cunny-warren* for "a brothel" and *cunny-hunter* for "a whoremonger," before losing its obscene sense. Shakespeare generally avoided the more direct terms, but exploited suggestive disguise-forms like *cut, constable* (previously and still often pronounced "cunstable"), and *country* (in *Hamlet* III ii 116–22), further discussed in the entries for **William Shakespeare** and **Eric Partridge**. References to the *low countries* are invariably bawdy. The taboo against the use of *cunt* remains strong, but not absolute. However, the older euphemisms *queynte, quim, cunny,* and *coney* have generally become obsolete.

See also: Cock; Genitalia; *Oxford English Dictionary;* Twat.

Bibliography

Ayto, John. *Bloomsbury Dictionary of Word Origins.* London: Bloomsbury, 1991.

Burchfield, Robert. "Four-letter words and the *OED.*" *Times Literary Supplement,* October 13, 1972.

———. "An Outline History of Euphemisms in Old English." In *Fair of Speech,* ed. D.J. Enright. Oxford: Oxford University Press, 1986.

Chapman, Robert L. *New Dictionary of American Slang.* New York: Harper & Row, 1986.

Farmer, J.S., and W.E. Henley. *Slang and Its Analogues.* London: Routledge and Kegan Paul, 1890–1904. Reprint, Oxford: Wordsworth Press, 1987.

Green, Jonathan. *The Slang Thesaurus.* Harmondsworth: Penguin, 1988.

Grose, Francis. *A Classical Dictionary of the Vulgar Tongue.* London: S. Hooper, 1785.

Jay, Timothy. *Cursing in America: A Psycholinguistic Study of Dirty Language in the Courts, in the Movies, in the Schoolyards and on the Streets.* Philadelphia: J. Benjamins, 1992.

Lighter, J.E., ed. *Random House Historical Dictionary of American Slang.* New York: Random House, 1994.

McDonald, James. *Dictionary of Obscenity, Taboo and Euphemism.* London: Sphere Books, 1988.

Maurer, David W. *Language of the Underworld.* Lexington: University Press of Kentucky, 1981.

Partridge, Eric. *Origins.* 3rd ed. London: Routledge & Kegan Paul, 1977.

Sagarin, Edward. *The Anatomy of Dirty Words.* New York: Lyle Stuart, 1962.

Spears, Richard A. *Slang and Euphemism.* New York: Signet, 1991.

CUR. *See:* Dogs

CURSE AND CURSING

The strict and traditional meanings of *curse* are the appeal to a supernatural power to inflict harm or evil on a specific person, the form of words itself, and the sense that a person or place is harmed or blighted by being "under a curse." *Cursing* now has the generalized sense of a profane or obscene expression of disgust, anger, or surprise, especially in American English, where it is commonly used as a synonym for *swearing,* see for example, Timothy Jay's study *Cursing in America* (1992).

The original potency of the term, like that of *charm* and *spell,* derives from belief in **word magic** and the authority behind the words, institutionalized in excommunication and the **anathema**. Over time, with the secularization and enlightenment of society, these beliefs have steadily diminished, so that curses have increasingly come to be regarded as mere forms of words rather than as serious forms of malediction. However, as Montagu shows, there are survivals in various European societies (1973, 35–54). Nevertheless, the recent public curse that a Dutch politician might die of cancer, uttered by an Islamic imam on November 25, 2004, provoked a scandal.

Curse first appears as a noun in late Old English (ca. 1050), but according to the *Oxford English Dictionary* its origins are problematic: "No word of similar form and sense is known in Teutonic, Romanic or Celtic." The original meaning of a prayer or wish that evil or harm befall someone was extended in the course of the Middle English period to include a formal sentence of anathema or excommunication. This is the dominant sense in Chaucer's *Prologue* l. 655: a guilty person should beware "the ercedekenes curse" ("the archdeacon's excommunication").

Shakespeare often interrogates the potency of curses, setting them deliberately against the new skepticism of the Renaissance. The benighted and primitive world of *King Lear* echoes with the verbal power and horror of primal curses invoking sterility (I iv 299–305) and lameness (II iv 165–66). There is grim irony that Lear's specific invocations of sterility conform to the behavior of witches as spelled out in the *Malleus Maleficarum* ("The Hammer of Witchcraft"), the major text of the witch hunts of the Inquisition, first published in 1486. Chapter 6 carries the title: "How witches impede and prevent the power of procreation." *Timon of Athens* is even more vehement, invoking syphilis, sterility, and social chaos.

Since that time *curse* has steadily lost force as a verb, although the noun still has potency. It extended into various forms, now fossilized or lost, such as *curst,* meaning "contrary or perversely cross," much used of Kate in Shakespeare's *The Taming of the Shrew* (1594). Another variant is *cursedly,* defined by Dr. Johnson in 1755 as "miserably, shamefully," but regarded as "a low cant [slang] word." All of these have now become obsolete. In American slang reference works *curse* is now either unlisted or limited to the comparatively trivial sense of "a woman's menstrual period." The main survivor is the colloquial equivalent of *cursed,* namely *cussed,* recorded from about 1848 and still thriving. The general semantic trend of the word is thus **loss of intensity**.

See also: Anathema; Shakespeare, William.

Bibliography

Jay, Timothy. *Cursing in America.* Philadelphia/Amsterdam: Benjamins, 1992.

Montagu, Ashley. *The Anatomy of Swearing.* London and New York: Macmillan and Collier, 1973.

Sprenger, James, and Henry Kramer. *Malleus Maleficarum.* Edited with introduction by Pennethorne Hughes, Rev. Montague Summers, trans. London: Folio Society, 1968 (1486).

D

DAMN

Within the Christian framework, which has been the basis for Western civilization for two millennia, the terrifying notions of eternal punishment, damnation, and hell have naturally become the subjects of a huge eschatological literature and a great tradition of art. Consequently, the term *damn* and its relatives have for centuries been regarded as so potent as to be highly taboo. However, with the secularization of society, the term has become weakened in force to the point of trivialization, in common with many other words with religious significance, such as *hell, the Devil, demon,* as well as the names of God and Christ.

The original sense of *damnare* in Latin was secular and legal, "to condemn, doom to punishment or inflict damage upon," which are the early senses of *damn* in Middle English. In Shakespeare's *Julius Caesar* (1599) Mark Antony says of Publius, a political enemy: "He shall not live; look, with a spot I damn him" (IV i 7). However, the religious senses developed earlier, in the fourteenth century. The first instance cited in the *Oxford English Dictionary* is *goddem,* the common oath of the English soldiers in France during the Hundred Years' War, further discussed in the entry for **goddam**. *Damn* could still be used in a deadly serious way in the late sixteenth century, as in Macbeth's desperate curse: "The devil damn thee black, thou cream-faced loon" (V iii 11), and the denunciation from Queen Elizabeth's Liturgy (1563): "Filthy and dampned Mahomet, deceiver of the world." However, it is often difficult to distinguish between the serious and the fashionable senses, exemplified in this exclamation from 1589: "Hang a spawne? Drowne it; all's one, damne it!" and in Othello's outburst "Death and Damnation!" (III iii 396). Early evidence of *damnable* and *damnably* being used simply as intensives comes from the 1590s, in Falstaff's confession that he has "misused the King's press damnably" (*Henry IV Part I,* IV ii 14). Shortly afterward, in 1619, John Fletcher alludes to the practice of profanity: "Rack a maid's tender ear with dams and Devils" (*Monsieur Thomas,* II ii).

As *damn* became less acceptable in public, so it generated euphemized alliterating variants, such as *deuced* (1774). (This form shows ambiguity, a general feature of swearing, since *deuce* is generally regarded as a euphemism for *devil.*) Tobias Smollett, whose novels contain much racy talk, has a character in *Peregrine Pickle* (1751) say: "I'll be d——d if I ever cross the back of a horse again" (chapter viii). One of the commonest British euphemisms is *dash,* recorded from about 1812, followed by *dashit* some three decades later. In the United

States the process of euphemization was under way contemporaneously, but with different forms, namely *darn* (1770), *tarnation* (1784), *dang* (1790), and the rhyming form *hang it!* (1770). Still later came *durned* (1876).

As with most religious terms, it is difficult to generalize on usage since interpretation varies according to individual sensitivity. Richard Brinsley Sheridan's classic *The Rivals* (1775) contains the mock-serious complaint uttered by Bob Acres, an absurd country squire: "Ay, ay the best terms will grow obsolete. Damns have had their day" (II i), clearly regarding the word as simply a fashionable utterance. On the other hand, Dr. Johnson took the word very seriously, according to this exchange in James Boswell's contemporary biography (1791):

Johnson: I am afraid that I may be one of those who shall be damned (looking dismally).
Dr. Adams: What do you mean by damned?
Johnson: (passionately and loudly) Sent to Hell, Sir, and punished everlastingly. (1893, 640)

In his *Dictionary* (1755) Johnson condemned the uses of *damnable* and *damnably* as mere intensives as "low and ludicrous." However, the Duke of Wellington's assessment of the Battle of Waterloo (1815) was very frank: "It has been a damned serious business—Blücher and I have lost 30,000 men. It has been a damned nice [close] thing—the nearest run thing you ever saw in your life" (*Creevy Papers*, chapter x, 236). When the relevant fascicle of the *OED* came out in 1894, *damn* carried the comment: "Now very often printed 'd——n' or 'd——.'" This practice seems to us now slightly precious, but for the Victorian bourgeoisie, *damn* had a great power to shock. In the comic operetta *H.M.S. Pinafore* (1878), W.S. Gilbert has the Captain declare: "Bad language or abuse, / I never, never use. . . . I never use the big, big D." Anthony Trollope emphasized an episode in his novel *The Prime Minister* (1876) in which the villain Ferdinand Lopez utters the word *damned* in front of his young wife, Emily: "It was to her a terrible outrage. . . . The word had been uttered with all its foulest violence, with virulence and vulgarity. It seemed to the victim to be the sign of a terrible crisis in her young married life. . . . She was frightened as well as horrified and astounded" (chapter xliv).

However, the *Random House Historical Dictionary of American Slang* (1994) comments that usages of *damn* and *goddam* as mere intensifiers are "unquestionably older than the available citations suggest." The same authority notes that the following quotation from 1865–1867 is "the earliest known example of infixing": "'He is, by Jove! A dam incur-dam-able dam coward'" (De Forest, *Miss Ravenel's Conversion*, 272.) Infixing, whereby the term is integrated into another word, with consequent loss of semantic force, is discussed further under **flexibility**. The forms *dammit* (as in "as quick as dammit," recorded from 1908) and *damfool* (used by Mark Twain as *damphool* in a letter of 1881) show the same loss of intensity. At the same period occurs the form *damfino,* abbreviating "damned if I know."

The declining impact of *damn* is largely summed up in the throwaway line in the famous film of *Gone with the Wind* (1939): "Frankly, my dear, I don't give a damn." At the time of the film's release, the offending term was a breach of the Production Code, so that a special exemption had to be negotiated and a $5,000 fine was exacted from the producer, David O. Selznik. Today it is generally regarded as a mild idiomatic oath, still having some force in phrases like "I'll be damned if . . ." and "Damn you!," "Damn your eyes!," but in others like "Well, I'm damned," being an expression of surprise. *Damn* is ranked by the *Longman Dictionary of Contemporary English* (1995) as among the 2,000 most common spoken words. On the rating for "Tabooness" in Jay (1992) it is almost off the scale at 25/28. The term has not developed any particular forms or special currency in other global varieties of English.

See also: Goddam/Goddamn; Religious Oaths; Victorian Age.

Bibliography
Flexner, Stuart Berg. *I Hear America Talking.* New York: Van Nostrand Reinhold, 1976.
Jay, Timothy. *Cursing in America.* Philadelphia/Amsterdam: Benjamins, 1992.

DEFECATION. *See:* Shit Words.

DEVIL, THE

From the earliest times there has been belief in the Devil as a real presence. Dualistic or Manichean systems such as Zoroastrianism and Gnosticism regarded the world as a battleground between the forces of good and evil. In medieval iconography devils were omnipresent in Christian edifices, glaring down on the faithful from gargoyles and grotesque paintings. Although the Renaissance introduced a new spirit of skepticism, it paradoxically generated a revival of the medieval Faust legend, as well as works such as Reginald Scot's *The discoverie of witchcraft* (1584), King James I's *Dæmonologie* (1597), and Samuel Harsnett's *Declaration of Egregious Popishe Impostures* (1603), a treatise on diabolism and an attack on the Jesuits. The Salem witch trials of 1692 were a gruesome continuation of the European Inquisition. Even in 1851, Herman Melville could articulate in *Moby Dick* the deeply disturbing metaphysical and religious view, by then a virtual blasphemy, of "That intangible malignity which has been from the beginning; to whose domination even the modern Christians ascribe one-half of the worlds" (chapter 41).

Consequently, the direct naming of the Devil, as with the deity, has been subject to severe taboos originating in notions of word magic. There has always been respect for diabolical power and a belief that an oath invoking the Devil could be binding if heartfelt. Historically, however, the situation was more complex: the name of the Devil was very current in medieval oaths, then became euphemized, distorted, or "minced" between the Puritan and Victorian periods, and reinstated in the twentieth century. By this time, with the secularization of society, the name had little impact.

Our modern term *devil* derives from Anglo-Saxon *deofol,* which in turn is rooted in Greek διαβολος, "the slanderer, liar or false accuser," the foundation of the notion of the Father of Lies. Although England was technically converted to Christianity in 597, Anglo-Saxon has many compounds, such as *deofol craft* for "witchcraft" or "devil worship," *deofol seocnesse* for "devil sickness" or "possession by the devil," and *deofilisc,* "devilish," all of which seem to be literal. *Fiend* similarly derives from Anglo-Saxon *feond,* which had both the broad sense of "enemy" and the specific sense of *the Fiend,* called by Macbeth "the common enemy of man" (III ii 90), more traditionally, the Arch Enemy, the Evil One, and a host of biblical names, such as Satan, Beelzebub, and Lucifer.

Medieval oaths invoked the devil in specific curses that are very shocking to modern readers. One of the Towneley Plays, in which the devil is frequently invoked, contains the graphic curse: "The dwylle (devil) hang you high to drye" (175). Another typical instance occurs in Chaucer's *Friar's Tale,* a text fundamentally concerned with swearing:

"The feend," quod he, "yow fecche, body and bones."
(He said, "The devil take you, body and bones.")
(l. 1544)

However, within the same period one finds similar oaths less easily understood, as in Chaucer's *Summoner's Tale:*

"Lat him go honge himself a devele way!"
(l. 2242)

The last phrase anticipates a feature common in modern swearing, in that an idiomatic use is taking over from a logical or literal meaning. (Modern equivalents would be *a devil of a mess* and so on, which cannot be explained in terms of traditional grammar.) *Devil,* sometimes reinforced to *twenty devil,* could be used as an intensifier in Middle English of "away": Chaucer has a clearer instance in the oath "A twenty develewey the wynd him drive" (from the *Legend of Good Women,* l. 2177). In this kind of emotive and idiomatic use, the term was to have a large role to play in subsequent centuries.

Devil was used freely in the Elizabethan era in sermons, in folktales, especially in the drama, despite the censorship against the use of the name of God on the stage. Shakespeare uses it in a direct personal fashion of the villainous characters such as Aaron the Moor in *Titus Andronicus* (1592) and Iago in *Othello* (1604), as well as in *Macbeth* and *Hamlet,* which deal with profound spiritual and metaphysical matters. Marlowe's *Dr. Faustus* (ca.1592) contains blasphemously shocking scenes in which the devil Mephostophilis is conjured up on the stage.

However, euphemisms were already starting to appear. The expression "I cannot tell what the dickens his name is," still current in British English, first appears about 1598 in Shakespeare's *The Merry Wives of Windsor* (III ii 19). It thus anticipates the name of Charles Dickens the author by three hundred years, and is still found in many phrases, such as *who the dickens, the dickens of a mess,* and so on. Although not really absorbed into American English, it survives in the Australian variety as plain *dickon,* an expression of disbelief or rejection. Both *Dickens* and *dickon* are abbreviations of Richard, but why this name should have been used as a euphemistic variant has never been explained.

As a result of the Puritan revolution (1644–1660) and the strict censorship it bred, many more euphemisms started to appear. We can gauge the radical change in attitude from this entry in the *Diary* of Samuel Pepys, who moved among a wide range of social circles and was by no means a prude: "My wife . . . used the word 'devil' which vexed me, and among other things I said I would not have her use that word" (May 21, 1663). One of the longest-lived euphemisms was *deuce*, in typical phrases such as *what the deuce!* and *deuce take you!* It became very fashionable in **Restoration** comedy, not as a genuine euphemism, but as a flippant evasion. Although Dr. Johnson condemned it as "a ludicrous word," *deuce* became the standard euphemism through the eighteenth century to Victorian times.

Dr. Johnson's contemporary, the slang lexicographer Francis Grose, recorded many idiomatic uses of *devil,* such as *printer's devil, devil's daughter* (a termagant), *devil's books* (playing cards), and *devilish,* meaning "very," which as he noted ironically "in the English vulgar language is made to agree with every quality of thing; as devilish bad, devilish good, devilish sick, devilish well . . . etc. etc." By the Victorian era, however, the term was certainly becoming taboo in polite society. In R.H. Barham's classic novel *The Ingoldsby Legends* (1837), there is this charming lecture: "Don't use naughty words in the next place, and ne'er in your language adopt a bad habit of swearin'. Never say 'Devil take me,' or 'shake me,' or 'bake me,' or suchlike expressions. Remember Old Nick, to take folks at their word, is remarkably quick." Robert Burns wrote a flippant "Address to the Deil" (1785), including many of the popular names:

O thou! Whatever title suit thee–
Auld Hornie, Stan, Nick or Clootie–

The formal euphemism tactfully introduced by Barham, namely *Old Nick,* is recorded from Restoration times, but is no longer generally current, together with related forms such as *Old One, Old Podger, Old Scratch, Old Toast,* and the more sinister and descriptive *Old Split-Foot.* The grander title of the *Prince of Darkness* dates from 1526.

In American parlance the Devil and his euphemistic variants have not had such a vigorous vituperative life. Despite the opposition of fundamentalists, the word is often used as a name of pride for sporting teams, such as the Red Devils, the Sun Devils, and so on. *Devil* is not current in Australian English as an oath, but the reduplicated form *devil devil* was taken into Aboriginal Pidgin over 150 years ago to mean "an evil spirit."

Although there is a lingering respect for the linguistic power of the Prince of Darkness, the general semantic trend of the word, in common with most emotive religious vocabulary, has been **loss of intensity**. Given the alarming modern manifestations of mass evil in genocide, this is a surprising development. Similarly, *diabolical* has lost its literal force, *demonize* has been used in a secular sense since about 1888, while the cliché "fiendishly clever" means little more than "very cunning." Idioms like "the luck of the devil" or "the devil is in the detail" show the same tendency.

See also: Damn; Malediction.

Bibliography

Garçon, Maurice. *The Devil, an Historical, Critical and Medical Study.* London: Gollancz, 1929.
Grose, Francis. *A Classical Dictionary of the Vulgar Tongue.* London: S. Hooper, 1785.

Charles Dickens—depicted here as an older man before a collection of his characters—generally eschewed swearing and offensive language but made creative use of slang to evoke the everyday reality of Victorian life. However, as the entry for Jews shows, he drew on anti-Semitic stereotypes in the creation of Fagin. *(Library of Congress, LC-USZ62-131744)*

DICKENS, CHARLES

Charles Dickens (1812–1870), famous as the last great popular novelist in English, was also an important journalist and social reformer, arousing the Victorian social conscience through his treatment of a range of social problems and systemic abuses. At the age of twenty he became the Parliamentary reporter, thus acquiring the knowledge of the street life and the underworld that underlies his fiction. Dickens learned shorthand and clearly had a good ear for the idiosyncrasies of actual speech, which he replicated and developed as an aspect of characterization. He greatly developed the notion of the *idiolect,* the technical term for the language unique to an individual or a personal dialect.

However, his attitude toward the lower registers and especially slang showed ambiguity. In the persona of *Vox Populi,* Dickens denounced "the sewerage and verbiage of slang" (*Household Words,* no. 183, September 24, 1853). Yet his creative use of slang is almost unrivaled in English literature. He familiarized the reading public with such Cockney rhyming slang forms as *artful dodger* for "lodger" and *barnaby rudge* for "judge," and much of the argot of lower-class and criminal slang, such as *beak* (magistrate), *crack* (break open, burgle), *do* (swindle), *fence* (receiver of stolen property), *gonoph* (thief, from Yiddish), *lifer* (one sentenced to transportation for life), *nab* (arrest), *peach* (to turn informer), *put-up job* (inside job), *quod* (prison), *shop* (send to prison), *split upon* (to inform against), *stone jug* (prison), and *trap* (a policeman).

Swearing and foul language do not figure largely in Dickens's work, since he was sensitive to accusations of "coarseness" in his novels, preferring the various Victorian euphemisms. Dickens insisted, for example, in the Introduction to *Pickwick Papers* (1838) that "throughout this book no incident or expression occurs which could call a blush into the most delicate cheek or wound the feeling of the most sensitive person." Since the taboo against *damn* and its related forms was still strong, *jiggered* and *drat* are much used in its place. The following exchange from *Nicholas Nickleby* is fairly risqué for 1838:

"What's the dem'd total?" was the first question [Mr. Mantalini] asked.

"Fifteen hundred and twenty-seven pound, four and ninepence ha'penny," replied Mr. Scaley, without moving limb.

"The ha'penny be dem'd," said Mr. Mantalini, impatiently.
(chapter 21)

In *Pickwick Papers* (1836), Sam Weller resorts to this comic circumlocution to avoid *damned:* "[H]e says if he can't see you afore tomorrow night's over, he vishes he may be somethin'— unpleasanted if he don't drown hisself" (chapter 39). Similarly, *Hell* is clearly intended in the following comment: "[he] demanded in a surly tone what the—something beginning with a capital H—he wanted." In giving the clue to the obvious answer, Dickens interposes his authorial voice like a ventriloquist, thus avoiding the offensive word. In this respect he is similar but less sophisticated than **Laurence Sterne**.

Stranger to modern readers is the Victorian taboo against the direct mention of *trousers.* In *Sketches by Boz* (1836), comic negative formations like *inexpressibles, indescribables,* and *inexplicables* are pointedly used. Farmer and Henley commented in their magnum opus, *Slang and Its Analogues* (1890–1904), that many of these precious forms were "invented by Dickens." The taboo is exploited in this farcical passage from *Oliver Twist* (1837) as the butler Giles recounts his reaction to a nocturnal disturbance:

"I tossed off the [bed] clothes," said Giles . . . looking very hard at the cook and the housemaid, "got softly out of bed; drew on a pair of—"

"Ladies present, Mr Giles," murmured the tinker.

"—of *shoes* sir," said Giles, turning on him and laying great emphasis on the word.
(chapter 28)

Yet Dickens could be extremely direct, especially in the sections of *Martin Chuzzlewit* (1843) dealing with America. As the conservative Colonel Driver is expatiating on "the ennobling institutions of our happy country as—," "As nigger slavery itself," comes the shocking suggestion from his associate, Mr. Brick (chapter 16). When another acquaintance uses the phrase "a man of color," Martin responds tartly: "Do you take me for a blind man . . . when his face is the blackest that ever was seen?" (chapter 17). Dickens's interest in and sympathy with the underclass, as well as his gifts for drama and comedy, serve to illuminate many of the taboos and double standards of Victorian society.

See also: Rhyming Slang; Victorian Age.

Bibliography

Brook, G.L. *The Language of Dickens.* London: André Deutsch, 1970.

Dickens, Charles, ed. *Household Words,* no. 183, September 24, 1853.

Farmer, J.S., and W.E. Henley. *Slang and Its Analogues.* 7 volumes. London: Routledge and Kegan Paul, 1890–1904. Reprint, Oxford: Wordsworth Press, 1987.

Phillips, K.C. *Language and Class in Victorian England.* Oxford: Basil Blackwell, 1984.

DICTIONARIES

Crucial to any discussion of the dictionary is the concept of **register**, namely the diction appropriate to a particular literary context or social situation. For, in addition to the common words of the language, there are numerous lexical varieties, including the literary, the foreign, the dialectal, the scientific, the technical, as well as those that are the focus of this work, the "lower" registers, namely the colloquial, the slang, the profane, and the obscene. Historically dictionaries have tended to adopt different policies with regard to usage, namely *prescriptive* (emphasizing correct usage), *proscriptive* (condemning the incorrect), or *descriptive* (reflecting actual usage). The chosen policy will obviously affect the inclusion or exclusion of swearing and foul language.

The history of the English dictionary reflects in a fundamental fashion the familiar division in usage between decent or proper usage and the less acceptable varieties of slang, profanity, and obscenity—that between the language of decorous public discourse and the language of the street. The problem with this distinction is that the "common" words include, to a great extent, the lower registers or **rude words**, making it difficult for a lexicographer to know "where to draw the line." Notions about what is appropriate to appear in print obviously carry weight, as do assumptions that simply by printing an offensive term a dictionary is in some way endorsing it or validating the attitudes it expresses. These may not be valid assumptions, but they are difficult to dismiss. The simple statement that a particular word is or is not "in the dictionary" is often advanced as an argument for acceptability in itself. Until the eighteenth century, dictionaries tended to focus on "hard" or difficult words, and did not claim to be comprehensive, so that words could be omitted at will and without comment. In Victorian times there were legal restraints on the publication of obscene language, so that these issues weighed more heavily with editors and were not simply matters of policy. Today dictionaries generally include all varieties, although the accommodation of swearwords, "four-letter" words, and racist insults is problematic and often incomplete.

Inclusiveness is a fairly recent development. For centuries there have been two lexicographical traditions, the decent and the impolite. The "proper" tradition can be traced from Robert Cawdrey's rudimentary *Table Alphabeticall* (1604), through Nathaniel Bailey's extensive *Dictionarium Britannicum* (1730) and the magisterial *Dictionary* of **Samuel Johnson** (1755), to the monumental **Oxford English Dictionary** (1884–1928). Johnson initiated, and the *OED* virtually perfected, the "historical method," covering the whole span of the English language, separating the word senses, listing them chronologically, and illustrating them with quotations. However, there also is a slang or underworld tradition that is actually older and very extensive. This starts in Elizabethan times with works by Thomas Harman (*A Caveat for Common Cursetors* 1566), Robert Greene (*A Notable Discovery of Coosnage* 1591), and several others, is continued by **Francis Grose** (*A Classical Dictionary of the Vulgar Tongue* 1785), **Farmer and Henley** (*Slang and Its Analogues* 1890–1904), and **Eric Partridge** (*Slang* 1933), continuing in recent times with works appearing virtually on an annual basis.

There is a similar split in the American tradition, with the founder of American lexicography, Noah **Webster**, producing his seminal works in the "decent" tradition, namely *A Compendious Dictionary of the English Language* (1806) and *An American Dictionary of the English Language* (1828), which were the roots of numerous editions carrying his name, notably the Second Edition (1934) and the Third (1961). Despite the vigorous growth of American slang, James Maitland's *An American Slang Dictionary* (1891) was not highly regarded, thus making the first substantial achievement the *Dictionary of American Slang* by Harold Wentworth and **Stuart Berg Flexner** (1960), revised, enlarged, and reissued as *The New Dictionary of American Slang,* by Robert L. Chapman (1986). These have been followed by the superbly comprehensive *Random House Historical Dictionary of American Slang* (ed. Jonathan Lighter 1994 onward, currently in production).

This split in the lexicographical tradition is significant, forming a pair of parameters, implicit or explicit, within which the dictionary should focus. Generally speaking, dictionaries have become more inclusive, less prescriptive, and more descriptive. Dr. Johnson, essentially prescriptive and proscriptive, was very judgmental about what he considered inappropriate for a written standard. Being concerned about the instability of the language, he thus condemned slang as "a fugitive cant [in-group language] . . . unworthy of preservation" (1963, 23). No modern dictionary would adopt his attitudes or use his kind of vocabulary. However, he included *fart, arse, piss,* and other four-letter words without regarding them as taboo, defining them directly, without resorting to odd scientific register, such as "an emission of intestinal gas from the anus" as does the *Collins English Dictionary* (2000).

Although Webster championed American independence, his dictionaries were still bound by the constraints of tradition. He was a considerable bowdlerizer, omitting the bulk of the common sexual and excretory vocabulary. Similarly, he did not copy a single one of Johnson's bawdy quotations, complaining of the inclusion of "ribaldry" in his dictionary. A certain puritanism is apparent in comments appended to definitions, notably under the word *swear,* which Johnson had defined simply as "To obtest [call to witness] some superiour power; to utter an oath." Webster added the moral comment: "For men to *swear* is sinful, disreputable and odious; but for females or ladies to *swear* appears more abominable and scandalous." In his Preface to the *Dictionary for Schools* (1807) he complained with more validity that "Some [dictionaries] contain certain obscene and vulgar terms, improper to be repeated before children."

Inclusiveness has been a continuing problem, canvassed in the section on omission of taboo terms, discussed below. The growth of political correctness in recent decades has of necessity affected dictionaries. Semantic areas of race and disability, previously commented upon without difficulty, have become something of a minefield. Terms like *spastic* and *cripple* are increasingly labeled as "taboo" even though they continue to be in general demotic use. Consequently, unnatural and euphemistic substitutions, such as "physically challenged" or "differently abled" are brought into play. Likewise, the older slighting vocabulary commonly used of "primitive" people is rightly avoided. An instance from the original *OED* is this embarrassing quotation of *canoe:* "used generally of any rude craft in which uncivilized people go upon the water . . . savages generally use paddles instead of oars."

Today "the dictionary" has become something of a genre, with specialist works dealing with the whole gamut of registers mentioned at the outset, as well as many other fields. The "general" dictionary has become more comprehensive and is certainly more inclusive and less judgmental than in the past.

The Lower Registers

The recording of slang, profanity, and obscenity has a surprisingly long and continuous history, actually preceding that of the "proper" dictionary. The practice starts in Elizabethan times with a rich vein of works explicating underground slang or *cant* to an ignorant public, and has continued to the present in related works presented under the general term "slang," with increasing emphasis on obscenity or taboo terms. The earliest works are not dictionaries in format, but are guides to the urban underworld milieu and population, interspersed with glossaries or sections explaining the key terms of the argot known variously as Pedlar's French, Thieves' Latin, and St. Giles's Greek. *Cant* and *slang* are originally code languages developing among particular urban groups, although over time some terms radiate outward into the wider speech community. The original canting works claimed to fulfill a public function by alerting the public to unfamiliar terms used by cheats and confidence-tricksters. The function of the later works is paradoxical: those who do not know vulgar terms or oaths are unlikely to purchase a dictionary to discover their meanings. Those who know the terms do not need such a dictionary.

The first in the field, anonymous and dated 1552, carries the dramatic title *A manifest detection of the moste vyle and detestable use of Diceplay,* describing the cheating practiced in various dens and explaining the unfamiliar terms for false dice. This was followed by a number of works such as John Awdeley's *The Fraternitie of Vagabonds* (1561) and Thomas Harman's *A Caveat or Warening for Common Cursetors* [Tramps] *vulgarly called Vagabones* (1566). Being a magistrate in Kent, Harman was certainly knowledgeable about this underclass and their mores, described by Gamini Salgado as "the unscrupulous activities of this vast army of wandering parasites" (1972, 10). Harman condemned them in some astonishing displays of alliteration:

> Here I set before the good reader the leud [disgusting] lousey language of these lewtering [loitering] lusks [idlers] and lasy lorrels [blackguards] where with they bye and sell [trick] the common people as they pas through the country. Which language they terme Peddelars Frenche, a vnknowen toung onely, but to these bold, bawdy, beastly beggers and vaine vacabondes. (in Salgado, ed., 1972, 146)

Harman introduced a range of minor criminal types, about two dozen, using their underworld jargon, such as a *prigger of prancers,* a horse thief, *Abraham men* "those who feign themselves to be mad," and the ironically termed *upright man* for the highest in the echelons of crime.

In 1591, Robert Greene produced the sensationalist title *A notable Discovery of Coosnage* [Trickery]. *Now daily practised by sundry lewd persons called Connie-catchers* [card-sharpers] *and*

Crosse-biters [Swindlers or Whores]. Greene explains the ironic use of the term "law" in this set, amongst whom *Sacking Law* is "lechery," *Crossbiting Law* is "cosenage by whores," and *Cony-catching Law* is "cozenage by cards." Other specialist uses are *commodity* for a whore, *trugging-place* for a whorehouse, and some oaths, such as "Gerry gan the Ruffian cly thee" interpreted as "A torde in thy mouthe, the deuill take thee."

These Elizabethan canting dictionaries are an important sociolinguistic phenomenon, being the first record of a clearly developed underworld code language or argot. Many of the key terms in these sources are cited as first instances in the *OED*. Foul language also emerges in unexpected places, for instance in the first comprehensive Italian/English dictionary, produced by John Florio under the title of *A Worlde of Wordes* (1598). Among the 46,000 headwords, Florio defined Italian *fottere* with Renaissance exuberance as "to iape, to sard, to fucke, to swive, to occupy." (Interestingly, only one of these is still current in the relevant sense.) Florio added some spicy insults, such as "goodman turd" and "shitten fellow," as well as euphemistic uses such as "Mount Faucon" for the vagina and "gear" for the genitals (both male and female). Likewise, Randle Cotgrave's *Dictionarie of the French and English Tongues* (1611) has an entry on a fish with the unflattering name of *cul de cheval* [horse's arse]: "A small, and ouglie fish, or excrescence of the sea, resembling a mans bung-hole, and called, the red Nettle."

Certainly the most appealing and readable work in the underground tradition is **Francis Grose**'s wonderfully exuberant *A Classical Dictionary of the Vulgar Tongue* (1785). The title is arresting in the contradiction of the key terms *classical* and *vulgar,* the first implying formality and order, the second denoting the more disreputable elements of the language. His work represents a significant shift away from the specialist "canting" guide in the direction of the general slang dictionary. Though full of interesting material, Grose's work did not aim to be comprehensive. That claim could be made for the enormous collaboration of **J.S. Farmer and W.E. Henley**, *Slang and Its Analogues* (issued in seven volumes from 1890 to 1904). Also deserving of his own entry is the major authority on the lower registers in the twentieth century, namely **Eric Partridge**, the first authority to deal with the most notorious of the "four-letter" words in a complete, direct philological fashion.

Curiously the "improper" tradition of lexicography, which Farmer had called "the dark continent," took much longer to establish itself in the United States. This is perhaps because of the lingering influence of Puritanism and also the more immediate authority of Noah **Webster**. The first extensive work, James Maitland's 308-page study, *An American Slang Dictionary* (1891), was severely criticized, not for its immorality, but because, in the view of an anonymous reviewer, most of the words were not American and not slang. The first major achievement in the field came many decades later, in the *Dictionary of American Slang* by Harold Wentworth and **Stuart Berg Flexner** (1960). With some 700 pages, it was fairly comprehensive in its word list and gave citations, but did not list the different meanings or date the quotations. It was revised and reissued as *The New Dictionary of American Slang* by Robert L. Chapman in 1986. A significant volume in the slang tradition, over 400 pages in length, was *A Dictionary of Invective* by Hugh Rawson (1989), which is predominantly American in focus, but includes a considerable amount of British material. The limitations of the previous works are being made good in the *Random House Historical Dictionary of*

American Slang, edited by Jonathan Lighter (1994– currently in production). This work is genuinely comprehensive, follows the historical method thoroughly and has the volume of citation expected by readers of the **Oxford English Dictionary**.

During the last three decades of the twentieth century, slang dictionaries started to appear virtually on an annual basis on both sides of the Atlantic. Although some focused on British and some on American English, an increasing number accommodated both varieties. These were generally small, derivative volumes such as *The Underground Dictionary* by Eugene Landy (1972), *The Dictionary of Contemporary Slang* by Jonathon Green (1984), *The Slang Thesaurus* by Jonathon Green (1986), *The Erotic Tongue* by Lawrence Paros (1988), *A Dictionary of Obscenity, Taboo and Euphemism* by James McDonald (1988), *Lowspeak* by James Morton (1989), and *Forbidden American English* by Richard A. Spears (1991).

Given the dispersal of English, it is natural that slang and foul language should have spread to the four corners of the globe. However, it is surprising to find a glossary of underworld slang appearing under the title of *A New and Comprehensive Vocabulary of the Flash Language,* published as far back as 1819, in Australia. The author was a convict, James Hardy Vaugh, who had been transported three times and escaped twice. "Flash" was a criminal argot used in the underworld in England, defined by Francis Grose as "the canting or slang language." Many of these "flash" terms, such as *grub* ("food"), *mate* ("friend"), and *kid* ("to deceive") have become established in general Australian parlance. Most are general slang terms rather than obscenities, although *bloody,* the staple Australian expletive from the earliest times, was regarded as an obscenity a century ago. Subsequent studies within the Australian provenance are *The Australian Slanguage* by Bill Hornage (1980) and *A Dictionary of Australian Colloquialisms* by G.A. Wilkes (1985).

Generally speaking, other global varieties of English have not attracted such works. This may be because several of them, such as the Canadian, New Zealand, and Indian varieties, do not have thriving underground or obscene vocabularies showing the same efflorescence as the British or American varieties. The main exception in this regard has been the English of **South Africa**, with a wealth of coarse language, much of it borrowed from Afrikaans. Most of the terms were accommodated lexicographically in the various editions of *A Dictionary of South African English* (ed. J. Branford) issued from 1978 onward. However, the major *Dictionary of South African English on Historical Principles* (ed. P. Silva et al. 1996) did not include some of the most egregious. Dictionaries of **pidgin English** have perforce to deal with curious survivals of foul language that have now become destigmatized and established as the common register.

Omission of Taboo Terms

Linguistic taboo can be defined as that which is ineffably sacred or unspeakably vile. This formulation has, of course, a religious overtone, since profanity historically forms the first major area of taboo. It is important to grasp that "obscene," "obscenity," and "profanity" had in earlier times a basic sense of religious violation, and that emphasis on sexual depravity or extreme vulgarity are basically modern interpretations dating back from the eighteenth century. Prior to that period publications were policed by the ecclesiastical courts, which were far more concerned about unorthodox views or heretical statements. However, in the last two centuries, taboos have moved from religious to sexual and racial areas, thus putting different pressures on dictionaries.

Although modern dictionaries are predicated on the assumption that they are *descriptive*—that is, that they should reflect actual usage—there are both lingering and new social pressures about what is appropriate to appear in print. There are also tenacious assumptions that simply by printing an offensive term a dictionary is in some way dignifying the term, relaxing standards, encouraging laxity, or endorsing prejudices. The publication of swear-words, "four-letter" words, and racist insults continues to be a vexatious issue, even though legal restraints are now things of the past. Dictionaries have accordingly used various strategies to accommodate pressures: these vary from omission to the use of mutilated, "minced," or abbreviated forms.

The most drastic strategy is total omission. Thus no major English dictionary included both of the two most egregious of the "four-letter" words, *fuck* and *cunt,* between 1730 and 1965, that is to say between Nathaniel Bailey's *Dictionarium Britannicum* and Eric Partridge's *Dictionary of Slang and Unconventional English.* Between these two points of reference came the major works of **Dr. Samuel Johnson**, who nevertheless included most of the excretory vocabulary in its vulgar forms, and Noah **Webster**, who omitted from both his works, *Compendious Dictionary of the English Language* (1806) and *An American Dictionary of the English Language* (1828) virtually all the common sexual and excretory vocabulary. The puritanical influence of Webster (who subsequently bowdlerized the Bible) was to weigh heavily on subsequent American lexicography.

The monumental **Oxford English Dictionary**, published between 1884 and 1928, was as genuinely comprehensive as it was humanly possible to be, recording with amazing thoroughness in its 414,825 headwords the whole gamut of the lexis, including the lower registers of slang, profanity, and obscenity. Contemporaneously, **John S. Farmer and William E. Henley** were producing, between 1890 and 1904, their vast seven-volume lexicon dedicated to the lower registers, *Slang and Its Analogues.* Yet the *OED* omitted the two ancient taboo terms *fuck* and *cunt,* and *Slang and Its Analogues* the first term, not simply out of editorial squeamishness and in response to Victorian restraints, but because to print them would have put the publishers in breach of the Obscene Publications Act of 1857. Notably, only one contemporary review alluded to the *OED*'s omission. Three decades later the Third Edition of *Webster* (1961), which provoked an uproar because of its avowedly descriptive policy, nevertheless omitted *fuck,* even though the public currency of the word was greatly increasing.

A variation of this strategy is transparent or advertised omission, exemplified by the editor in chief of *Webster's New World Dictionary* (1970), Dr. David B. Guralnik, who pointedly omitted sexual words, since "the terms in question are so well known as to require no explanation" and ethnic slurs such as *dago, kike, wop,* and *wog,* described in the Preface as "those true obscenities, the terms of racial or ethnic opprobrium." This policy was subsequently called "Guralnikism" by Dr. Robert Burchfield. As Dr. Guralnik's manifesto makes clear, in recent decades taboos have moved from sexual to racial terms, so that the accommodation of ethnic slurs has attracted much controversy and occasional legal action. In 1972 a case was brought against the Oxford University Press over the inclusion in the original *OED* of opprobrious senses of the word *jew*. The case was rejected with costs and the meanings stand. However, the second volume of the *Supplement* appended a long note explaining the history and basis of anti-Semitic prejudice.

Another strategy is partial omission or "mincing," exemplified in the forms *a-se, c**t, f—k* and *sh-t*, found in **Francis Grose**'s *Classical Dictionary of the Vulgar Tongue* (1785). These are, of course, simply jocular conniving evasions or overt disguise mechanisms using symbols in the print format to avoid the offending term. They can be read, but are obviously unpronounceable. In the case of extreme mincing (as in the form——), they cannot even be read.

The modern use of corpora, or large bodies of evidence of actual usage, both spoken and written, has enabled lexicographers to make meaningful assessments of word frequency. These show that the notion of "taboo" is a misnomer. Thus the *Longman Dictionary of Contemporary English* (3rd edition, 1995) uses both the Longman Corpus and the British National Corpus to establish the 3,000 most frequently used words in spoken and written English. Although *fuck* is graded as "taboo," it is rated as S3, one of 3,000 most frequently spoken words, while *fucking* as S1, one of the 1,000 most frequently spoken words. *Shit* and *ass* are rated as S2. In the analysis of college student speech in Jay (1992), *fuck* was high in both frequency and tabooness (124 and 143). But the stage has not been reached at which taboos are a matter of history.

See also: Comstockery; Farmer, John S., and William E. Henley; Flexner, Stuart Berg; Grose, Captain Francis; Johnson, Dr. Samuel; *Oxford English Dictionary;* Partridge, Eric; Webster and His Dictionaries.

Bibliography

Bailey, R.W., ed. *Dictionaries of English.* Ann Arbor: University of Michigan Press, 1987.

Burchfield, Robert, ed. *Studies in Lexicography.* Oxford: Oxford University Press, 1986.

Coleman, Julie. *A History of Cant and Slang Dictionaries.* Oxford: Oxford University Press, volume I, 2003; volume II, 2004.

Farmer, J.S., and W.E. Henley. *Slang and Its Analogues.* 7 volumes. London: Routledge and Kegan Paul, 1890–1904. Reprint, Oxford: Wordsworth Press, 1987.

Gotti, Maurizio. *The Language of Thieves and Vagabonds.* Tübingen: Max Niemeyer, 1999.

Green, Jonathon. *Chasing the Sun.* London: Jonathan Cape, 1996.

Jay, Timothy. *Cursing in America.* Philadelphia/Amsterdam: Benjamins, 1992.

McAdam, E.L., and George Milne, eds. *Johnson's Dictionary: A Modern Selection.* London: Gollancz, 1963.

Salgado, Gamini, ed. *Cony-Catchers and Bawdy Baskets.* Harmondsworth: Penguin, 1972.

Starnes, de Witt T., and G. Noyes. *The English Dictionary from Cawdrey to Johnson.* Chapel Hill: University of North Carolina Press, 1946.

Stein, Gabriele. *The English Dictionary before Cawdrey.* Tübingen: Max Niemeyer, 1985.

DISABILITY AND DEFORMITY

Historically, linguistic usage reflects social insensitivity in referring to those now termed "physically disabled" or "handicapped." Words like *cripple* and *spastic* not only had wide currencies, but until recently were also terms of insult, black humor, and belittlement. Political Correctness has heightened awareness and increased sensitivities so that such words have become taboo and been replaced, in official or public discourse at any rate, by terms

Physical disability and deformity have been depicted unflinchingly by major Western artists—such as Pieter Brueghel the Elder in *The Cripples* (1658, also known as *The Beggars*)—but terms reflecting suspicion and hostility rather than sympathy are many centuries old. (The Art Archive/Musée du Louvre, Paris/Dagli Orti)

like *disabled, differently abled*, or *physically challenged*. Most dictionaries now mark terms like *cripple* and *spastic* as "offensive." The extent to which these measures will affect the metaphorical currency, as in "crippling debts" remains to be seen.

In the past the injustices of birth and the accidents of life were depicted unflinchingly by major artists. The teeming canvases of Pieter Brueghel the Elder (?1525–1569) do not exclude the blind, the halt, and the lame. *The Parable of the Blind* (1568) grimly illustrates St. Matthew 15:14: "If the Blind lead the Blind, both shall fall into the ditch," while his huge work *The Fight between Carnival and Lent* (1559) includes a small group of discarded lepers and cripples entertaining themselves with indomitable energy. The same motif fills another small canvas, entitled *The Cripples* (1568), although the virtually legless dwarfs have been identified as lepers, since they are wearing foxes' tails. Diego Velázquez's iconic *Las Meninas* (1656) presents the Spanish royal family and the elegant ladies in waiting of the title, but pointedly includes the female dwarf Maribarbola and Nicolasito Pertusato, a male dwarf and buffoon. They occupy the foreground, virtually obscuring the King and Queen. Velázquez painted at least seven penetrating studies of court dwarfs and jesters, several of them evidently mentally retarded. His official dignified portrait *Don Diego de Acedo* (1644) similarly makes no concessions, since the Don's hands appear minute by being juxtaposed with a huge ledger. Those modern artists who have depicted deformity and disability, like Diane Arbus and Joel-Peter Witkin, tend to treat their subjects as freaks or curiosities.

Dwarfs are historically a complex category, in Teutonic, especially Scandinavian, mythology constituting a special race; in folklore reputed to be endowed with magical powers, especially in the working of metals. In medieval romance they frequently accompany a lady or damsel and often had a position of honor in courts as fools or clowns. Although in modern usage the term is disrespectful rather than insulting, in the *Flyting of Kennedy with Dunbar* (1508), Kennedy uses the old form of the word in mocking his opponent: "Duerch, I sall ding thee" ("Dwarf, I shall smash you," l. 395).

Cripple, related to the verb "to creep," is recorded from Anglo-Saxon times, notably in the place-name Cripplegate in London (about 1000). Gross lack of sympathy is shown in the old saying recorded by Angel Day in 1586: "Of ancient time it hath often been said that it is ill halting before a cripple" (*The English Secretary* II). Among the word's various slang senses were "a damaged coin" and "an awkward oaf; also a dullard." There is even an ironic encouragement, "Go it, you cripples," to a team in William Makepeace Thackeray's *Coz's Diary* (1840). In American English the word has been used in a technical sense in baseball for an easily hit pitch since World War I. Although *disabled* dates from the fifteenth century, its semantic history as a euphemism starts with George Herbert's use in 1633 in a religious poem, *The Temple, Crosse* iii: "I am in all a weak disabled thing." The Earl of Rochester, somewhat typically, wrote a poem "The Disabled Debauchee" (1680), making an elaborate comparison between a retired admiral and a rake for whom "the days of impotence approach" (l. 13).

Studies of the Elizabethan underworld present the disabled as a clearly visible underclass provoking hostility and suspicion rather than sympathy, since there were so many confidence tricksters, bogus cripples, and able-bodied beggars, known at the time as *sturdy beggars.* Works like Thomas Harman's *A Caveat* [Warning] *for Common Cursetors* [Tramps] (1566) and Robert Greene's *A Notable Discovery of Coosnage* [Trickery] (1591) detail what Salgado describes as a "vast army of wandering parasites" (1972, 10), referring to types such as an *Abraham man,* a person feigning madness to seek alms, *Fresh-Water Mariners or Whipjacks,* those "whose ships were drowned in the plain of Salisbury . . . [and] counterfeit great losses on the sea." Harman, a country magistrate in Kent, defines twenty-three of such types, including *Counterfeit Cranks,* "young knaves and young harlots that deeply dissemble the falling sickness [epilepsy]."

Literary depictions show extraordinary historical changes. Shakespeare's pioneering study *Richard III* (1594) is a remarkable example of reverse psychology in the dramatization of a cripple. Richard Crookback (his popular name) is afflicted with a hunchback, a withered arm, and a limp, but he makes embarrassing capital out of his disabilities, harping on his deformity, being consistently aggressive, exhibitionist, and outrageous. "Look how my arm is like a blasted sapling, withered up!" he exclaims, cynically claiming to be the victim of witchcraft (III iv 71). He opportunistically blames his murder of his brother Clarence on "some tardy cripple" (III ii 90). Trading on the traditional physiognomical belief that mind and body reflect each other, Richard gives the proposition a disturbing new twist:

Then since the heavens have shaped my body so,
Let Hell make crooked my mind to answer it.
(*Henry VI, Part III* vi 79–80)

His most vocal enemies are, interestingly, women, who denounce him roundly as "thou lump of foul deformity" (I ii 57), "thou elvish-mark'd abortive rooting hog!" (I iii 228), and "this poisonous bunch-backed toad" (I iii 246). The end of his reign of terror is greeted with the words "the bloody dog is dead." (V iv 15).

Modern studies have been starkly different. Somerset Maugham's major novel, *Of Human Bondage* (1915), seldom discusses the hero's clubfoot directly, and this modern reticence has attracted various psychological interpretations seeing the deformity as a projection of Maugham's homosexuality and even his stammer. Far more direct, even brutal, have been the recent biographical depictions by Peter Nichols, *A Day in the Death of Joe Egg* (1971), about a hopelessly retarded infant; and Christy Brown's *My Left Foot* (1989), about a sufferer from cerebral palsy.

Spastic, originally the adjectival form of *spasm* in the pathological sense, has extended its meaning from "uncoordinated" to more contemptuous senses of "clumsy," "incompetent," or "foolish." In British English it has a wide currency of disparagement, as in "the defense was spastic" and the slang abbreviation *spaz,* recorded from 1965. The original *Oxford English Dictionary* contained only medical and technical senses, but the *Supplement* (1986) added the following usage note: "Although current for some fifteen years or more, it is generally condemned as a tasteless expression, and is not common in print." Virtually all dictionaries now mark it as "offensive."

Basket case has maintained a common currency, now referring to a person, country, or situation so chaotic as to be without hope of resuscitation. The origins, deriving from World War I, are truly horrific, referring with gruesome black humor to a soldier with all limbs amputated who thus had to be carried in a basket. The phrase surfaced in the modern sense several decades later, in the *Saturday Review* (March 25, 1967): "Kwame Nkrumah should not be written off as a political basket case." If the origin were more widely known, the current popularity of the phrase would be severely curtailed.

See also: Political Correctness.

Bibliography

Ingestad, Benedicte, and Susan Whyte, eds. *Disability and Culture.* Berkeley: University of California Press, 1995.
Maugham, Somerset. *Of Human Bondage.* Harmondsworth: Penguin, 1963.
Salgado, Gamini, ed. *Cony-catchers and Bawdy Baskets.* Harmondsworth: Penguin, 1972.

DISEASE

Cursing and imprecation typically call down some catastrophe, such as death or disease upon the object of the curse. *Plague* itself originates in the biblical sense of "a visitation of divine anger or justice," notably the ten plagues inflicted on Egypt in the Book of Exodus.

European society was, of course, greatly afflicted, first by the Plague and then by syphilis, both of which became powerful generators of exclamation and abusive name-calling. Leprosy and smallpox have also disfigured populations at regular intervals, making poignant outcasts of their victims. However, other epidemics like influenza, malaria, and AIDS have had no such semantic extension, possibly because they inflict less disfigurement. Furthermore, disease terms, like many other categories in swearing, follow a pattern of becoming fashionable and then obsolete. In speech communities largely unaffected by these terrible visitations, disease has understandably not really become a linguistic motif.

The principal devastations of the Plague that afflicted England were the pandemic of 1348–1349, in which between a half and a third of the population died, and the attacks of 1360, 1379, and 1664–1666. The disease, now technically termed the bubonic plague (from Latin *bubo,* denoting the symptomatic swellings of the afflicted), was often known simply in the Middle Ages as *the death* and *the great death.* Thus in Chaucer's *Prologue* the Reeve's tenants "were adrad of hym as of the deeth" (l. 605), meaning probably "They feared him like the Plague." Curiously, the popular name *the Black Death* is, in fact, an anachronistic invention, which, according to the *Oxford English Dictionary,* was "introduced into English history by a Mrs. Penrose in 1823." Be that as it may, the name has stuck. **Syphilis**, also called *the pox,* is generally agreed to have been introduced into Europe in 1493 by the crews of Christopher Columbus's ships on their return from the Americas.

Pox is a respelling of Middle English *pockes* and *pokkes,* the plural of *pock,* meaning a pimple, pustule, or pit on the skin, still surviving in *pock-marked.* Although the form *pox* dates from about 1503 the older forms survive, especially as *pocky,* meaning "diseased." There is thus quite a long period when both the *pox* and *pock* forms coexist.

Clearly the terms relating to these infestations had both literal or referential uses ("the pestilence killed many") and emotive or imprecatory uses ("the pestilence on you!"). Generally speaking, in linguistic usage the referential uses come first, as can be seen in the following table:

word	literal use	imprecatory use
pestilence	1303	1386
pocky	1350	1598
pestilential	1398	1531
pestiferous	1542	1458
plague	1548	1566
pox	1550	1588
pest	1568	1570
plaguey	1604	1574
pesky	****	1775

The table shows that the literal uses are spread out over three centuries (from 1303 to 1604) without any special concentration, but there is a large gap between 1398 and 1542. The imprecatory senses, on the other hand, show a considerable clustering between 1531 and 1598. More remarkable are the two cases where the imprecatory sense actually *precedes* the literal: these are *pestiferous* and *plaguey*. These anticipations suggest that the plague had become such a fashionable topic in swearing that the emotive use became dominant. The fact that they are both adjectives is surely no accident, since such forms, like *devilish,* tend to be used very loosely. Dr. Johnson defined *plaguey* in his *Dictionary* (1755) as "vexatious; troublesome," categorizing it as "a low word." Interestingly, most modern dictionaries now record the primary meanings of *pestilent* and *pestiferous* as "annoying or troublesome"—that is, emotive rather than literal. The same is true of *pest,* "a person or thing that annoys," and *pesky,* meaning "troublesome" or "excessively," exclusively American and originally a New England term thought to be a dialectal adjective from *pest + y.* It is found in Harriet Beecher Stowe's reference to "those pesky blackberry-bushes" in *Oldtown Folks* (1869, 119).

Whereas the Plague was an unavoidable catastrophe, especially among the poor, syphilis was a sexually transmitted disease with its attendant stigma and complex of emotions including taboos, coded references, and black humor. Consequently, whereas *pestilence* and *pestilential* appear virtually contemporaneously with the outbreak of the Plague, there is a notable time lag between the arrival of syphilis about 1493 and its overt naming as *the pox* about 1550. The earlier form of the word appears in this scurrilous rhyme of 1528 about Cardinal Wolsey: "He had the Pockes without fayle, / Wherefore people on him did rayle" (Harley Miscellany, ix 32). Even as late as 1631 in Philip Massinger's play *Emperor of the East,* the Surgeon says ironically: "An excellent receipt [prescription]! . . . 'tis good for . . . the gonorrhoea, or, if you will hear it in a plainer phrase, the pox" (IV 4).

The naming of **syphilis**, with its evasions and xenophobic projections, belongs to another entry. However, *pox* itself (once it had broken the taboo) became used in a great range of fashionable exclamations. Some were quite explicit, as in William Congreve's *The Old Batchelour* (1693): "The pox light upon thee for a contemplative pimp!" (III 6). But most were simply ejaculations, such as *a pox on it!, a pox of . . .!, pox take it!, what a pox!,* plain *pox!,* and so on. These show the typical development from a loose grammatical construction to a purely idiomatic use. Of this once-thriving word field, only the related form *pest* still survives.

Scurvy underwent a parallel but later semantic history. The literal sense referring to the disease dates from about 1565, but is preceded by the adjective meaning "covered with scurf" from about 1515. From this derived the common archaic figurative sense of "worthless" or "contemptible," first recorded in 1579 in an Elizabethan guide to the underworld, warning the reader "Looke that thou flee from this scabbed and scurvie company of dauncers" (John Northbrooke, *Dicing,* 64b). Much in use in Elizabethan times, it had petered out by 1900. The related adjective *scrofulous* was used literally from the early seventeenth century, before acquiring the sense of "morally worthless" (often used of literature) from the 1840s. The difference in attitude between modern and previous times is shown in the fact that scrofula was previously called "the King's Evil" or simply "the Evil," the former name deriving from the belief that it could be cured by royalty, a practice followed from Edward the Confessor up to Queen Anne in 1714.

One obvious semantic correlative is *leper,* which has developed a far more powerful sense as a "social outcast" than the literal meaning of one afflicted with physical leprosy. Bishop Hugh Latimer first used the term in the figurative sense in 1552: "We are lepers of our soules." The sense became established in various phrases, notably the alliterating comparison "as lonely as a leper." However, whereas terms relating to the Plague and syphilis have become first fashionable, then weakened, and finally obsolete through overuse, *leper* has been the subject of protests and pressures to limit its currency. "I feel that it is necessary to launch a protest at the continual use of the word 'leper' in medical literature," wrote R. Cochrane in the *Leprosy Review* XIX, 39. This was in 1948, several decades before the advent of Political Correctness, and is one of the first of such semantic interventions. The *OED* now carries a usage note: "The term is often avoided in medical literature because of its connotations."

It is curious that other major diseases like influenza, malaria, and AIDS have generated no semantic extensions. For a brief period AIDS was (erroneously) termed "the gay plague," but in general disease no longer figures as a generator of oaths.

See also: Syphilis.

Bibliography

Clarke, C.H., trans. *The Black Death*. London: Allen & Unwin, 1961.
Kohn, George C. *Encyclopedia of Plague and Pestilence*. New York: Facts on File, 1995.
Ziegler, Philip. *The Black Death*. London: Collins, 1969.

DISGUISE MECHANISMS

Since swearing and foul language are by definition "improper," it is necessary in polite discourse to use various disguise mechanisms to avoid giving offense. These have a long and continuous place in the history of the language, since they provide a useful method of alluding to but not articulating taboo or embarrassing topics. The most common of these are **euphemisms, dysphemisms**, and various distortions or coded forms of the offending word.

Historically, disguise mechanisms are evident from the beginnings of the language. Thus the phrase "to sleep with" was used as a euphemism for sexual intercourse (itself something of a euphemism) in an Anglo-Saxon translation of the Bible by Ælfric (ca. 1000). Some mechanisms are quite explicit, like "the eff word" or *effing*, others less so, like a "four-letter word," since the speaker does not have to be explicit, allowing a choice to the listener. The use of *bleep*, derived from the censorship of radio material, is recorded in American reference works from 1966, and has subsequently expanded to be a euphemistic adjective or verb from 1971; for example: "J.F.K. spent so much time bleeping in the bedrooms of the White House" (*Los Angeles Times Book Review*, March 12, 1978). Some forms are intentionally opaque, like *assault*, which may mean "rape," "a violent attack," or "a beating." The name of God is the prime example of distortions and truncations being used for disguising purposes.

Foreign languages provide a source for disguise mechanisms, since taboos are not usually perceived or felt in other tongues. Some of these are of surprising duration. Two of the most common in medieval times were *pardee* (for *par dieu*, "by God") and *Benedicitee!* ("The Lord Bless you"). One of the earliest recorded allusions to *fuck* occurs in the pseudo-Latin form *fuccant* in a satirical poem composed in Latin and English some time before 1500, alluding to the extra-mural activities of some Carmelite priests in Cambridge. However, in the actual text the word is not used, appearing in the disguised code-form *gxddbov*, in which each letter stands for the previous in the alphabetical sequence of the time, i.e. $g = f$, $x = u$, $d = c$ and so on. In Elizabethan times, when *fuck* was highly taboo, the French term *foutra* was brought into play. Although it has been obsolete for a long time, it has generated cognate, but not obviously related forms, such as *footering* and *footling* and the exclamation *my foot!* This example shows a common feature of the evolution of swearing terms, and language in general, namely that origins become less recognizable with time. The entry for **Shakespeare** discusses a great range of disguise terms used for bawdy subjects.

The famous diarist Samuel Pepys (1633–1703) provides an unusual and revealing instance of a deliberate use of a foreign language as a personal disguise mechanism. When describing adulterous encounters Pepys resorts to slightly unstandard French. Thus on December 20, 1664: "After dinner [lunch] . . . alone avec elle je tentoy à faire ce que je voudrais, et contre sa force je le faisoy, bien que pas à mon contentment [and then alone with her I tried to do what I desired, and had my way with her despite her resistance, to my great pleasure]." A similar entry occurs on April 13, 1668: "She and I drank and yo did tocar her corps all over. . . ." Since Pepys wrote his diary in a coded shorthand, his secret would probably have been safe, but he preferred to use a double disguise. A psychological interpretation suggests that he preferred to describe his unchivalrous deeds in terms that were less direct and embarrassing.

Whole lexical systems operate on the basis of the disguise motive, the most notable being Cockney **rhyming slang**. This scheme refers to taboo subjects by using witty and ingenious coded formulas in which the last term rhymes with the intended word. Thus Bristol City refers to *titty* and Khyber Pass to *arse*. However, in speech only *bristols* and *khyber* are used. Earlier examples of coded lexical systems are cant, originally the slang language of the Elizabethan underworld. Another form is back slang, whereby words are reversed, such as *tenuc* for *cunt* and *yob* for *boy*. These systems have grown up spontaneously in particular speech communities. The noted Welsh poet Dylan Thomas played a sly joke on the B.B.C. in his famous radio play *Under Milk Wood,* broadcast posthumously in 1954, by naming the quintessentially Welsh village of the piece Llareggub, which indeed sounds very Welsh, but takes on a different meaning when it is read backward.

A modern but artificial development is the language of Political Correctness. Formulas like *physically challenged* serve as euphemistic disguises for *disabled* or *crippled,* but are not part of natural language. Various American speech communities use coded references: thus the terms for blacks include *schwartze* (Yiddish), *Blaue* (German), and *melanza* (Italian for "eggplant"). More general manifestations are *HN* in American parlance for "house nigger," *Af* for *African* and *K* for *Kaffir* in South African slang. The latter two have been recently joined by *affirmative,* an ironic derivation from the post-apartheid policy of *affirmative action.*

As these various modes and examples show, the notion of "disguise" varies greatly: in some cases the disguise is obvious; in others the motivation and the logic behind the generation of the form are lost in the past.

See also: Dysphemisms; Euphemisms; Political Correctness; Rhyming Slang; Taboo.

Bibliography

Allen, Keith, and Kate Burridge. *Euphemism and Dysphemism.* New York: Oxford University Press, 1991.
Holder, R.W. *A Dictionary of Euphemisms.* Oxford: Oxford University Press, 1991.
Partridge, Eric. *A Dictionary of Slang and Unconventional English.* London: Routledge, 1970.

DOGS

Opprobrious terms for dogs form the largest category of insults derived from animal terms. Considering the long history of the dog as a domesticated and loyal animal, it is curious that, for example, *cur* and its female equivalent *bitch* should have become terms of such powerful vituperation. *Bitch, son of a bitch* and its variants, *mongrel, cur,* even *dog* itself, have been terms of insult for over five hundred years. Among stereotypical notions drawn on are treachery, cowardice, fawning, and promiscuity, leading to the generation of mongrels. Undoubtedly the class-conscious prestige of purebred stock is a factor. Most of the terms are of British provenance. In modern times only *bitch* has retained some force in a word field of steadily diminishing power.

Bitch has the longest history in the field as a term of abuse, extending from the fourteenth century up to the present. During this long period it has been applied variously to a promiscuous, sensual, mean, or difficult woman, as well as to a man or thing. Its tone ranges from extremely offensive to mildly critical. *Cur* was originally (from the thirteenth century) a general term for a dog, before becoming a deprecatory word. In Middle English the term could be used of a good, vicious, or cowardly dog, and there was even a curious tautological form *curdogge,* meaning "the Devil." The *Book of St. Albans* (ca. 1486), that rich compilation of ingenious collective nouns, includes "a cowardness of curris." However, the significant semantic extension of the word to what the *Oxford English Dictionary* calls "a surly, ill-bred or cowardly fellow" is first recorded in Shakespeare, whose references to dogs are surprisingly extensive, in *A Midsummer Night's Dream* (1590). In his works it is a term of withering scorn, most memorably in *Coriolanus* (1608), when the hero castigates the Roman plebs as "You common cry of curs!" meaning "You pack of mongrels!" (III iii 118). *Cur* continued to be used as a term of invective through to the nineteenth century. Dr. Johnson comprehensively defined the adjective *currish* (also first used by Shakespeare) as "having the qualities of a degenerate dog; brutal; sour; quarrelsome; malignant; churlish; uncivil; untractable." Since that time the term's currency, unlike that of *bitch,* has steadily declined, and it is now obsolete.

Hound, originally the basic term for a dog in the Germanic languages, was also the first to be applied opprobriously to a man: the Anglo-Saxon religious poem *Judith* (ca. 1000), refers to "Done haeþenan hund," that is, "the heathen dog." The application was common in the Middle Ages, the last memorable quotation also being from *Coriolanus* (1608) when the hero, infuriated by being called a "boy," replies to the taunt: "Boy! False hound!" (V vi 113). *Mongrel,* also first recorded in the *Book of St. Albans* (ca. 1486), appears in strange canine company, together with "a Grehownd, a Bastard, a Mengrell, a Mastyfe," thus including breeds now regarded as pure. The original spelling indicates the root *meng,* meaning "to mix." Sir Thomas Overbury, author of some insightful characterizations of men, commented in 1613: "Like a true mongrel, he neither bites nor barks, but when your back is towards him." Interestingly, the first application to a person as a term of abuse occurs in a Scottish flyting-match in 1585, when Montgomerie refers to his opponent Polwart, among other things, as an "auld mangrell." The human application died out in the course of the eighteenth century. *Tyke,* meaning a low-bred cur or mongrel, also carries considerable contempt. Interestingly, the first instance in the *OED* (ca. 1400) has a human application: "Thou false heathen hound, [thou] hast stolen away like a tyke" (*Melayne,* l. 1325). In similar vein the comic boaster Pistol in Shakespeare's *Henry V* (1599) demands "Base tyke, callst thou me Host?" (II i 31). The term is no longer generally applied to people.

Spaniel provides an interesting case. Noted originally for its gentleness, keen scent, and hunting skill, the breed started to gain a reputation for duplicity and sycophancy as the political rivalry and religious antagonism between England and Spain developed. Shakespeare seems to have had a special fixation with this aspect, since there are many contemptuous references to the breed in his work. In *Julius Caesar* (1601), Caesar dismisses flattery as "base spaniel fawning" (III i 42–43), adding arrogantly: "I spurn thee like a cur out of my way" (III i 46). The rare verbal sense *spanielled* is also found in *Antony and Cleopatra* (IV xii 21).

Poodle is a similar example, becoming a term of contempt, predominantly British in currency, meaning a lackey or sidekick, with overtones of French effeteness. David Lloyd George, the prime minister and noted orator, is credited with the first use in a speech to the House of Commons in 1907. Very recently (from about 2002) the term has been widely used in Britain to criticize the subservience of Prime Minister Tony Blair in his political relationship with President George W. Bush. *Poodle-faker* was previously used in services slang for "a man, usually a socialite or newly commissioned officer, who cultivates female society, especially for professional advancement."

The most powerful term from the global varieties of English is the Australian *dingo*, "applied figuratively to a person who displays characteristics popularly attributed to the dingo, especially cowardice, treachery" (*The Australian National Dictionary*). This source records uses from 1869, illustrated by two quotations from 1978: "All politicians are dingos" and "He's not a dinkum [genuine] man, he's just a yellow, gutless dingo cur." Curiously, the term has also had a limited currency in the United States, originally as a tramp or beggar, subsequently as a foolish or crazy person.

It is notable that the field has developed from dogs posing some sort of threat by being violent or treacherous, to those that are harmless and largely ornamental. The major modern exception is *rottweiler,* which is starting to acquire an ugly figurative sense of a thug.

See also: Animal Terms; Bitch; Son of a Bitch.

Bibliography

The Book of St. Albans, 1486. Updated as *An Exaltation of Larks,* ed. James Lipton. New York: Grossmann, 1968.

Leach, Edmund. "Animal Categories and Verbal Abuse." In *New Directions in the Study of Language,* ed. E.H. Lenneberg. Cambridge, MA: MIT Press, 1964.

Partridge, Eric. *A Dictionary of Slang and Unconventional English.* London: Routledge, 1937.

Rawson, Hugh. *A Dictionary of Invective.* London: Hale, 1991.

DOZENS, THE

Forms of verbal dueling recorded among black youths in America have been termed variously "playing the dozens," "playing," and "sounding." There is also a related term, "to signify," meaning more "to insult through pointed insinuations and oblique remarks." The genre, which has been commented on and researched for well over half a century, has clear affinities to flyting, which has a long history in the United Kingdom, extending from Anglo-Saxon times. However, flyting is an individual, extended, and finally written display of verbal skill in the fine art of savage insult (some of the participants having been major poets), whereas sounding is extempore, taking place in the context of rival street gangs and the establishment of dominance.

An article on playing the dozens by John Dollard in 1939 emphasized the aspects of taboo and discipline:

> One asked the other, "Do you want to play the dozens?" The other boy said, "Yes." These reactions of concealment and shame convinced me that playing the Dozens is not an orgy of licentious expression for lower-class Negroes; all know that the themes treated are in general forbidden, some refuse to play the game and still others are very resentful and defensive at the mere thought of it.
> (*American Imago,* November 6, 7)

This sense of the dozens containing taboo topics is corroborated by a citation from the *Random House Historical Dictionary of American Slang* (1994) dated 1928: "It is the gravest of insults this so-called 'slipping in the dozens.' To disparage a man is one thing; to disparage his family is another" (Fisher, *Jericho,* 9). The same source records the significant phrase "the dirty dozens" from 1926, as well as the sociological comment that "'Playing the Dozens' is the most common way a convict has of using profanity" (Clemmer 1940).

Roger D. Abrahams noted in 1962: "The dozens are commonly called 'playing' or 'sounding'" (*Journal of American Folklore* LXXV, 209). The earliest cited reference in *Random House* (1994) is dated 1915, from *American Negro Folk-Songs:* "I don't play the dozen / And don't you ease me in." Erskine Caldwell's classic novel *God's Little Acre* (1933) has the plural form: "If you want to play the dozens, you're at the right homestead" (x, 142). William Labov's substantial article "Rules for Ritual Insults" noted that "the activity is remarkably similar throughout various black communities" (1972, 307), although much of the basic research derived from Philadelphia. "Many sounds," Labov continues, "*are* obscene in the full sense of the word. The speaker uses as many 'bad' words and images as possible—that is, subject to taboo and moral reprimand of middle-class society" (1972, 324).

Abrahams observed in a related article: "Sounding, especially Mother-Sounding, demonstrates the second place given to the mother-son bond in comparison to the primary place assigned to the clique" (*Journal of American Folklore* LXXVIII, 1965, 209). (While flyting matches contained disparaging allusions to the paternity of the opponent, the mother was not a target of insult.) Instances of sounding thus typically involve insults often delivered in couplets directed at the victim's mother, using a concentrated mixture of vigorous metaphor and savagely chauvinistic humor:

I hate to talk about your mother, she's a good old soul
She got a ten ton pussy and a rubber asshole.
(cited in Labov 1972, 307)

Others rely on black humor and punning: "Your mother's like a police station—dicks going in and out all the time" (cited in Labov 1972, 320).

On a wider perspective, David Crystal observes: "Verbal duelling contests between street gangs or individuals, before or instead of violence, are probably universal, and involve a highly inventive figurative language, in which the taunts subject the participants, their close relatives, and selected parts of their bodies to an increasingly bizarre set of unpleasant circumstances" (1995, 401). Although flyting seems to have died out in the United Kingdom, "the dozens" continues to thrive in the United States.

See also: Flyting.

Bibliography

Abrahams, Roger D. "Sounding." *Journal of American Folklore* LXXVIII, 1965.
Clemmer, Donald. *The Prison Community.* New York: Holt, Rinehart, and Winston, 1940.
Crystal, David. *The Cambridge Encyclopedia of the English Language.* Cambridge: Cambridge University Press, 1995.
Dollard, John. "The Dozens: Dialectics of Insult." *American Imago* I (1939): 3–25.
Dundes, Alan. *Mother Wit from the Laughing Barrel.* Englewood Cliffs, NJ: Prentice Hall, 1973.
Fisher, Rudolph. *The Walls of Jericho.* New York: Alfred A. Knopf, 1928.
Labov, William. "Rules for Ritual Insults," in *Language in the Inner City.* Oxford: Basil Blackwell, 1972.

DRAT

Drat is a predominantly British imprecation or expression of annoyance, now fairly dated, commonly applied to things or situations, as in *drat it!*, but occasionally to people, as in *drat the man!* Although it means virtually the same as *damn* or *curse* in their weakened senses, the term is seldom applied personally in the manner of *damn your eyes!* The origin is religious, being an aphetic or shortened version of *od rot!*, itself an abbreviation of *God rot!*, found in forms such as *God rot your bones!* and other such curses. Obviously, with the erosion of both the name of God and the verb, the formula lost force. *Drat* is recorded only from 1815, but became very fashionable, to the point that the Victorian novelist Anthony Trollope, who used the form frequently in his novels, has this ironic instance in *Barchester Towers* (1857): "The quintain [post] was 'dratted' and 'bothered' and very generally anathematised by all the mothers" (326). Dickens has a typical usage in *Bleak House* (1852): "Drat you, Be quiet!" Although the term is still current in British usage and the erstwhile colonies, it is generally confined to older speakers. Although reported in American usage, it is generally unrecorded in slang dictionaries.

See also: Euphemisms; God, Euphemisms for; Victorian Age.

Bibliography

Brook, G.L. *The Language of Dickens.* London: André Deutsch, 1970.
Phillips, K.C. *Language and Class in Victorian England.* Oxford: Basil Blackwell, 1984.

DUNBAR, WILLIAM

William Dunbar (?1456–1513) was a highly versatile Scottish poet whose work incorporated the extremes of diction, namely an ornate, artificial, and highly Latinate vocabulary in his religious poems and the crudest imaginable low-register diction in his satires, most notably in the flyting match with his fellow poet Walter Kennedy. (**Flyting** is a curious genre, an individual and extended display of verbal skill in the fine art of savage insult, which reached its highest point in the Scottish court, several of the participants being aristocrats and major poets.) Dunbar was a Master of Arts, and more surprisingly, a Franciscan preaching friar in the king's service for a number of years and received a royal pension by King James IV. Although not as well known as his famous predecessor **Geoffrey Chaucer**, he shows many of the same qualities.

The *Flyting of Dunbar and Kennedy* (ca. 1503) is over 550 lines long. Kennedy, who was of royal blood, had similar academic qualifications and was greatly admired as a poet. Fairly extensive quotations from this remarkable match are given in the entry for **flyting**. These show that sexual insults figure to a higher degree than would be expected in England. Dunbar also wrote a notable satirical parody of a courtly love debate called "The Two Married Women and the Widow." Dunbar's ladies are very cynical and physical. The Widow (whose sexual values are reminiscent of Chaucer's adventurous and much-married Wife of Bath) shows total contempt for her dominated husband, cuckolding him (l. 380), making him do all the housework (l. 351) and emasculating him:

Quhen I that grom geldit of gudis and of nature
[When I had castrated that fellow of his goods and potency]
(l. 392)

The Widow is sexually opportunistic and crude in her language. Her aggression is also expressed in the demeaning terms used of the husband, such as *wif carll* ("woman-man"), *grom* ("groom"), *schaik* ("fellow"), and *that auld schrew* ("that old bugger"). These are all low-class or insulting terms, and are pointedly juxtaposed by the upper-class company the Widow claims to enjoy, that of *knychtis* ("knights"), *clerkis* ("scholars"), and *cortly persons*. The reader begins to suspect that the Widow is perhaps indulging in a courtly *cum* erotic fantasy with *baronis and knychtis / And othir bachilleris blith* ("jolly young knights") who entertain her in various ways:

Sum rounis and sum ralyeis and sum redis ballatis,
[Some whisper and some jest and some read ballads]
Sum raiffis furgh rudly with riatus speche
[Some rant forth rudely with wanton speech]

Sum stalwartly steppis with a stout corage
[Some step boldly and stout-heartedly into my chamber]
And a stif standard thing staiffis in mi neiff;
[And thrust a stiff rampant penis into my fist]
(ll. 480–86)

The main features of the Widow's outrageous behavior, namely sexual promiscuity, predatoriness, snobbery, and the language of a fishwife, suggest that Dunbar was using certain misogynist stereotypical notions in his poem, rather as Chaucer had in his creation of the Wife of Bath.

See also: Flyting; Women, Stereotypes of; Women, Swearing in.

Bibliography

Kinsley, James, ed. *The Poems of William Dunbar.* Oxford: Oxford University Press, 1979.
Mackenzie, W. Mackay, ed. *The Poems of William Dunbar.* Edinburgh: Porpoise, 1932.

DYSPHEMISMS

Dysphemisms are technically the opposite of **euphemisms**. Whereas euphemisms seek to soften the impact of some horrific event or taboo subject by indirect language and calming metaphors, dysphemisms are starkly direct, macabrely metaphorical, or gruesomely physical. An obvious element of black humor is also apparent, since the bizarre metaphors strip away any notion of human dignity. Instead of the classical lexis generally prevalent in euphemisms, the core vocabulary is highly apparent, often in idiomatic phrases. Although this linguistic mode has been established for centuries and the term *dysphemism* was first recorded in 1884, it has only recently acquired even a specialist currency, being unlisted in many general dictionaries and reference books. The French psychologist Albert J. Carnoy gave an extensive definition in his study *Le Science du Mot,* which in translation runs: "Dysphemism is unpitying, brutal, mocking. It is also a reaction against pedantry, rigidity and pretentiousness, but also against nobility and dignity in the language" (1927, xxii, 351). There is virtually no aspect of human experience free from dysphemism.

Death generates such typical euphemisms as *to pass away, to pass on, to depart this life, go to one's Maker,* and so on. Parallel dysphemisms would be *to snuff it, to croak,* and *to push up daisies,* since these allude graphically and cruelly to the physical aspect of death, down to breathing one's last, the death rattle, and being reincorporated into the cycle of nature. Similar examples drawn from sensitive or embarrassing topics are *to have a bun in the oven* for to be pregnant, to be *pissed* for to be drunk, and *to take a technicolor yawn down the great white telephone* for to vomit. Many of the huge variety of sexual metaphors are dysphemic, such as *bed-pressing, belly-bumping, bum dancing, a squeeze and a squirt, screw,* and *poke.* As these examples show, dysphemisms are offensive and crude without necessarily using "four-letter" words.

In literature dysphemism shows a considerable overlap with bawdy. Shakespeare's *Romeo and Juliet* (1595) is, among other things, a brilliant analysis of the nature of love: Romeo and Juliet embody the idealistic and noble view, while Mercutio and various other characters express a cynical, physical view liberally stocked with dysphemisms. The opening macho exchanges between the servants Gregory and Sampson are in this vein (I i 17–22). Mercutio mocks the great romantic lovers of history in dysphemistic terms: "Laura [the inspiration for Petrarch] was but a kitchen maid; Dido a dowdy; Cleopatra a gipsy; Helen and Hero hildings and harlots" (II iv 48–50). These are all low-register derogatory terms for women: a *dowdy* was ugly or overdressed, a *gipsy* was a loose woman, a *hilding* was a worthless woman, and a *harlot* was a whore. Several of Shakespeare's plays, notably *Antony and Cleopatra* and *Troilus and Cressida,* set dysphemisms against heroic and romantic myths.

Dysphemisms abound in current insults. To take the example of stupidity and incompetence, from a rich field there are such terms as *blockhead, bonehead, dickhead, lamebrain, not have a full deck of cards, not know one's arse* (ass) *from one's elbow,* or *couldn't organize a booze-up in a brewery.* Among terms for ugliness or unattractiveness there is the old euphemism *plain,* the pseudo-euphemism *no oil painting,* or the crudely dysphemistic *a face to shatter glass, to stop a clock,* or *something the cat dragged in.*

See also: Disguise Mechanisms; Euphemisms.

Bibliography

Allen, Keith, and Kate Burridge. *Euphemism and Dysphemism.* Oxford: Oxford University Press, 1991.
Carnoy, Albert J. *Le Science du Mot.* Louvain, 1927.

E

ENGLISH, THE

The sociolinguistic dynamics generating opprobrious terms commonly derive from war, race or color, religion, political rivalry, economic subservience, lack of social prestige, immigration, or sudden demographic changes. Since the English (who are commonly conflated in popular parlance with the British) have been a dominant colonial power and politically influential globally for centuries, opprobrious terms applied to them have not been numerous. Predictably, they have come from enemies, such as the French, and from erstwhile colonies, such as American *limey,* Australian *pom,* and South African *rooinek,* all discussed below. These terms have not really been absorbed into British English.

The stereotypes associated with or personifying the English are complex. John Bull was created by John Arbuthnot in 1712, and this robust, belligerent national figure continued up to the bulldog-like personage of Winston Churchill. Since then the cartoon figure of Andy Capp has come to symbolize the quintessential Englishman, idle, cynical and opportunistic. However, previously the *English malady* was identified as lowness of spirits or melancholy in 1733, the *English disease* described a state of economic ill-health in the last three decades, while *English vice* has alluded euphemistically to both sodomy and flagellation for at least as long. The entry for **French** contains a number of critical views and terms.

Curiously, the first hostile term for the English derives from their habit of swearing. This was *goddem,* applied to them by the French during the Hundred Years' War on account of their copious profanity, discussed in the entry for **goddam**. However, the name did not really stick, apart from a facetious revival in the nineteenth century in contexts like "It seems the 'Goddems' are having some fun" (1830), and is now obsolete. Revealingly, the tradition of swearing has continued in the recent French nickname for the English, namely *les fuckoffs,* recorded by Mort (1986, 77). A term now much associated with the rowdy behavior of English football fans is *hooligan,* which sprang into life from obscure origins in 1898. Together with the antithetical *gentleman,* it has been borrowed in French.

Within the British Isles, *Sassenach* is used of the English by the Gaelic peoples—that is, the Scots and to a lesser extent the Irish. Derived from *Saxon,* it was originally used by the Scottish Highlanders of the Lowlanders, whom they regarded as similar to the English in language and race. Since the nineteenth century it has been generally applied to the English in a slightly provocative but also amiable way. There is also the Welsh form *Seisnig.* The principal American term,

The ever-robust John Bull—an enduring personification of the English character—taunts the figure of Napoleon at a French fortification across the English Channel in an 1803 cartoon. The John Bull character dates to 1712. (Library of Congress, LC-USZ62-112481)

limey, was originally *lime-juicer,* dating from the 1850s, referring to British sailors and their ships on account of the limes issued to prevent scurvy. Occasionally used to express hostility, as in "When we get through with Jerry, we'll clean up the God damned limeys" (O'Brien, *Wine, Women & War* 1918, 210), it has never been a term of major provocation. After considerable currency in World War II, it is becoming obsolete, except in Australian English. By contrast the Australian label **pom** and its adjectival form **pommy** (pommie) continue to thrive.

Gringo, now a common term for an Englishman or an Anglo-American in Latin America, was originally a name of contempt and hatred coined at the time of the Mexican-American War. J.W. Audubon recorded in his *Western Journal* (June 13, 1849): "We were hooted and shouted at . . . and called 'Gringoes'." The term has a linguistic base, *gringo* being American Spanish for *griego,* meaning Greek, that is, one whose language is "Greek to me," although there is a fanciful **folk etymology** deriving it from "Green grow the rushes O." *Anglo,* recorded later from 1941, has never had the same emotional quality. Curiously, neither term is listed in the *Random House Historical Dictionary of American Slang* (1994).

In South African English the principal terms derived from the hostility between the British and the Boers, leading up to the Boer War (1899–1902). The first and most enduring word was Afrikaans *rooinek,* literally "red neck," followed by the more explicit *khaki,* from the color of the British uniforms. In the post-colonial era, *limey, pom,* and *rooinek* have diminished currencies, and their tone is now generally humorous and ironic.

See also: Ethnic Insults; Goddam, Goddamn; Pom and Pommy; South Africa.

Bibliography
Flexner, Stuart Berg. *I Hear America Talking.* New York: Van Nostrand Reinhold, 1976.
Mort, Simon, ed. *Longman Guardian Original Selection of New Words.* Harlow, Essex: Longman, 1986.
Ramson, W.S., ed. The *Australian National Dictionary.* Melbourne: Oxford University Press, 1988.
Silva, P.M., et al., eds. *Dictionary of South African English.* Oxford: Oxford University Press, 1996.

ETHNIC INSULTS

Ethnic insults are the most obvious linguistic manifestation of xenophobia and prejudice against out-groups. They are usually based on malicious, ironic, or humorous distortions of the target group's identity or "otherness." Stereotypes, **blasons populaires,** and nicknames are also major contributing features, used to create and label these identities. The key factor in the development of a term of abuse is not the word itself, but who uses it. As J.L. Dillard points out, "even *nigger* was not offensive to Blacks until whites used it in a derogatory way" (1977, 96). The word field does not grow consistently, but shows periods of comparative stasis and marked expansion. These generally coincide with periods of migration, religious conflict, war, territorial expansion, political and business rivalry, immigration, and colonialism. Distinguishing features like race or color obviously play a major role.

Up to about a half-century ago ethnic insults had a fairly common and undisturbed currency. They were not marked as "offensive" or "taboo" in dictionaries, nor were they stigmatized as were words regarded as profane, obscene, or indecent. It is significant that the first lexicographer to focus on such terms should have been an American: H.L. Mencken included notes on terms of ethnic abuse in the early editions of his great work, *The American Language* (1919–1945). Assessing the growth of such words Irving Lewis Allen observes in his major study, *The Language of Ethnic Conflict,* "Over a thousand usually derogatory terms for more than 50 American groups have been accumulated in scholarly records of slang and of dialectal English" (1983, 7). Eric Partridge, the intrepid researcher of the lexical underworld of British English, recorded many offensive ethnic terms, but did not focus on them especially. Generally speaking, the topic has been accorded a greater degree of academic interest in the United States than in the United Kingdom.

In recent decades the use of ethnic slurs has rightly become an issue of great sensitivity and protests, even leading to court proceedings. (The term *ethnic* itself, currently more favored than *racial* or *racist,* is a virtual euphemism, although it was originally a chauvinistically hostile term: Greek *ethnikos,* meaning "heathen," denoting those nations that were not Christian or Jewish—that is, Gentile, pagan, or heathen.) Despite official dissuasions and prohibitions, ethnic terms continue to maintain currency. A great number of terms in the semantic field have their own entries, as can be seen from the list below as well as the entries for **Blacks, Chinese, English, French, Germans, Irish, Italians, Japanese,** and **Jews.**

The Semantic Field of Xenophobia and Ethnic Insults

Time	General Terms	Specific Terms
Anglo-Saxon	heathen	
1500	infidel, paynim	
1550		bugger, Turk, Greek, coolie
1600	savage, alien, intruder, barbarian, foreigner	blackamoor, ethiop, Jew, tartar
1650		bogtrotter,
1700		vandal, goth, macaroni, dago
1750		hottentot, yankee, cracker, frog
1800	native	kaffir, nigger, coon, Frenchy, wi-wi, sheeny
1850		greaser, gringo, canuck, sambo, Jap, yid, mick, limey
1900		kike, hun, chink, wop, boche, fritz, jerry, kraut, pom, wog, spick, eyetie, ofay, spaghetti, wetback, nip, gook, anglo
1950–present		slant, slope, munt, honkie, Paki

The earliest terms in the word field date from the Middle Ages and have a religious basis: hence *heathen, infidel, paynim* (pagan), and *bugger,* which originally meant "a heretic." This group was later joined by *kaffir,* originally meaning an infidel, from the Islamic point of view. The religious ructions of the Reformation generated many hostile terms for Catholics, such as *papist, Romish,* and *Jesuit.* Several general terms like *savage, alien, barbarian,* and *foreigner* obviously derive from prejudicial notions about the superiority of the "home" culture and the barbarism of outsiders. Some fairly neutral descriptive words have taken on an edge of hostility. The semantic history of *barbarian* shows clearly that the term has been successively applied, by the Greeks, Romans, and Christians, to cultural outsiders. Interestingly, a much older civilization, the Chinese, applied the sense "barbarian" via the character "I" to the English. Some general names for foreigners have acquired connotations of barbarism, the most prominent being *Vandal, Goth,* and *Hottentot.* All these terms were originally ethnographic, *Goth* referring to the ancient Germanic people from about 900 and *Vandal* and *Hottentot* used similarly from the seventeenth century. All were being used in a hostile fashion by the eighteenth century to stigmatize someone devoid of culture or destructive of art. This is still the prime sense of *vandal,* although the meaning has generalized into a barbaric wanton destroyer; the other two terms have become largely historical.

The catalyst of war is very striking in its immediacy and power. In the course of World War I a whole array of nicknames and hostile terms for the Germans emerges: *boche* is first recorded in 1914, *fritz* in 1915, *kraut* in 1918, and *jerry* in 1919. In American English, *Yankee* is a prime example; having been originally applied to the Dutch settlers in the United States, it was then used as a term of contempt for a Union soldier during the Civil

War, but was appropriated for American soldiers generally during World War I. Nevertheless, it still retains a hostile overtone, especially when used by foreigners to signify an American.

Several terms of ethnic insult are unspecific. Thus, although *frog* has been used by the English for the French from the eighteenth century, it was used previously for the Jesuits (1626) and the Dutch (1652). Likewise, in American English *gook* has in a short period performed many xenophobic roles, expressing hostility toward the interloper, the business rival, and the military enemy. References can be found to Haitians from 1920, Filipinos from 1935, Koreans from 1947, the Japanese from 1959, and perhaps most powerfully, to the Viet Cong from 1969. Similarly, *dago* was generally applied in the United States from the 1820s to Spaniards and Mexicans, but from the 1880s it was used more of Italians. However, the first instance in the *Oxford English Dictionary* (dated 1723) is to "a negro Dago." In British English the term is, according to the same source, "used disparagingly of any foreigner." *Wog* was likewise first used in British English as an ethnic insult for blacks in general, especially by colonial whites, but has since come to be used generally of any foreigner. *Sambo* and *coolie* show similar patterns of usage.

Allen's study incorporates a "Historical Lexicon of Ethnic Epithets," reflecting in its makeup areas of conflict and rivalry, since by far the largest categories refer to Afro-Americans, Whites, and Jews. While these semantic categories continue to grow, Allen notes that "no new terms for Yankees have been coined for over a century, which suggests a diminishing image of them as a distinctive ethnic group" (1983, 73). On the other hand, in a new theatre of war, he observes (under the terms for Vietnamese): "All nicknames for Vietnamese originated during the Vietnam War were brought forward from the Korean War and World War II" (1983, 69).

Whereas the ideology of America has been of an egalitarian and unified nation from independence, that of Britain has traditionally been based more on hierarchy and national differences. Thus a number of stereotypical notions and blasons populaires have grown up about the other nations in the United Kingdom, according to which the Scots are mean, the Irish wild, and the Welsh overemotional. The nicknames include *Jock* for a Scotsman, *Mick* for an Irishman, and *Taffy* for a Welshman. In earlier times some had more of an edge: *bogtrotter* was a seventeenth century nickname for an Irishman.

One of the obvious consequences of colonialism has been the denigration of the colonized peoples. This is evidenced in three modes: The first is the use of general categorizing terms such as *native,* which start as labels of inferiority, as opposed to *European.* Equally important since the colonizers were white were notions of color and purity, and the words for the different gradations of color. Captain (Frederick) Marryat illustrated the point in *Peter Simple* in 1834: "A quadroon looks down upon a mulatto, while a mulatto looks down upon a sambo, that is half mulatto and half negro" (chapter xxxi). In the same category are *chi-chi* and *half-breed. Colored,* originally a euphemism for *black* in the United States, and still so used occasionally, was established in South Africa during the period of British rule for the mixed race population during the 1820s. Third, and most obvious, are the more specific labels like *kaffir, boer,* and *hairyback* from South Africa, *coolie* and *pariah* from India, *abo* and *boong* from Australia. As general attitudes of chauvinism and xenophobia grew, so terms like *dago, wop, sambo,* and *wog,* which had been fairly specific in

148

meaning, became applied indiscriminately to foreigners. These have all become impacted both in global English as well as the home variety.

That curious feature of British English, Cockney **rhyming slang**, subsumes ethnic insults into its disguise mechanism by means of irony and humor. Thus *army tanks* is a coded reference to *yanks, bubble and squeak* (a common dish made of cabbage) refers to *Greek, four by two* (a standard size of material) to *Jew, lucozade* (a health drink) to *spade, egg and spoon* to *coon*, and *tiddlywinks* (a common game) to *chinks*. Phonetic similarities in xenophobic nicknames are especially noteworthy, existing in two basic categories. One group consists of short and contemptuous names, found in *pom, yid, frog, boche/bosch, fritz, kraut, jap, gook, wog, hun*, and *coon*. The other contains ironic diminutives, shown in the ending ——y, seen in *limey, sheeny, pommy, frenchie, wi-wi, whitey, honky, jerry, paki, eyetie*, and *yankee*.

An important indicator of the assimilation of an ethnic insult into the language is the degree of grammatical flexibility it develops from its basic noun function. Most terms come to be used as adjectives, an in "a jap car," "a gook grave," "a limey suit," and so on. The further extension as a verb is rarer and significant: thus "they want to frenchify the whole place" or "the West [i.e. Western Australia] is not yet as yankified or pommified to the same extent as is Sydney" (1936, cited in the *Australian National Dictionary*). In this regard the term *jew* is by far the most prolific, showing the depth of the stereotype and labeling as an outsider, evidenced in such forms (*OED* sense 3) as *jew-boy, jew-butcher*, and the verb sense, defined as "to cheat or overreach in the way attributed to Jewish traders or userers," also "to drive a hard bargain, to haggle." These meanings are now marked as "offensive." Equally significant indicators of ethnic hostility are the idiomatic or compounded terms, such as *jew hater, jew baiter*, and *paki-bashing*.

Such ingrained lexical forms suggest that attempts to prohibit or discourage ethnic insults face considerable obstacles. Dictionaries and educational programs are obviously efficacious, to a point. A notable development in the United States is the generation of forms like *Afro-American* and *American Indian*. These contradict Theodore Roosevelt's declaration that "There is no room in this country for hyphenated Americanism" (in a speech on October 12, 1915), but they are an effective way of defining the complexities of identity in a plural society while respecting the dominant fact of nationhood. One problem is that formulations such as *Jewish-American* or *Polish-American* do not really exist in natural language; furthermore, equivalents such as *Jewish-British* or *Pakistani-British* would be even less natural. However, it is certainly clear that the language of ethnic insult has become genuinely taboo, carrying the strongest prohibition, of being "unspeakable," as profanity and obscenity previously were.

See also: Aliens; Barbarian; Blason Populaire; Bugger; Catholics; Coolie; Coon; Gook; Honky; Hottentot; Hun; Jews; Kaffir; Nicknames; Nigger; Pom, Pommy; Rhyming Slang; War; Wog; Xenophobia; Yankee.

Bibliography

Allen, Irving Lewis. *The Language of Ethnic Conflict.* New York: Columbia University Press, 1983.

Aman, Reinhold, ed. *The Best of Maledicta: The International Journal of Verbal Aggression.* Philadelphia: Running Press, 1997.

Dillard J.L. *American Talk.* New York: Vintage Books, 1977.

Flexner, Stuart Berg. *I Hear America Talking*. New York: Van Nostrand Reinhold, 1976.
Green, Jonathan. *The Slang Thesaurus*. Harmondsworth: Penguin, 1988.
Lighter, J.E., ed. *Random House Historical Dictionary of American Slang*. New York: Random House, 1994–.
Mencken, H.L. *The American Language*. New York: Alfred A. Knopf, 1919–1945.
Partridge, Eric. *A Dictionary of Slang and Unconventional English*. London: Macmillan, 1937.

ETYMOLOGIES

Etymology denotes the root or origin of a word, as well as the branch of linguistic study dealing with the subject. The root of *etymology* itself is in Greek *étumos,* meaning "true," but research shows that etymologies are often far more complex than simple dictionary entries indicate. Thus *The Oxford Dictionary of English Etymology* (1966 edition) traces the etymology of the verb *bear* back through Old English to Indo-European **bher-,* but a note explains that the asterisk "indicates a hypothetical etymological form." Etymologies are the ancestors of words, not their living descendants, existing in a different time frame and usually with different meanings.

Furthermore, there are often rival claimants for the status of the ultimate root of a word, and a problem of how far back in time to go. The roots of words are fascinating to anyone interested in language, and can be very illuminating. For instance, the root meaning of Latin *vagina* is "sheath" or "scabbard," which would imply that the male member is a sword or weapon (which was indeed one meaning of Anglo-Saxon *wæpon*), but the meaning of Latin *penis* is "tail." There is little doubt that these etymologies throw up metaphors of violence associated with the sexual act.

The cases of swearing and foul language are interesting because a number of special features and dynamics are at work. First, the etymologies of several of the major terms, notably those of the "four-letter" words, remain problematic and unsolved, probably because of the taboo nature of the words. Second, public curiosity in the origin of such terms has always been highly charged: ordinary people, normally uninterested in the origins of common words like *table* or *tree,* will be almost insatiably curious about the etymologies of *fuck* and *cunt*. Third, various half-truths or popular misinterpretations come into play. One such mistaken notion is that the most egregious of the taboo terms are **Anglo-Saxon** in origin: this is a half-truth at best. Another is the process known as **folk etymology**, meaning the plausible but inaccurate explanation of the origin of a term, often with the aid of a tall story or amusing anecdote. These three features are clearly related, since public curiosity is frustrated by the simple academic category of "origin unknown" and, assuming that all words have detectable origins, shows a collective preference to make one up, or believe a fictitious one, rather than accept a vacuum.

See also: Anglo-Saxon; Folk Etymology.

Bibliography

Onions, C.T., G.W.S. Friedrichsen, and R.W. Burchfield, eds. *The Oxford Dictionary of English Etymology*. Oxford: Oxford University Press, 1966.
Burchfield, Robert. "An Outline History of Euphemisms in English." In *Fair of Speech,* ed. D.J. Enright. Oxford: Oxford University Press, 1985.
Partridge, Eric. *Origins. A Short Etymological Dictionary of Modern English*. London: Routledge & Kegan Paul, 1977.

EUPHEMISMS

Euphemism refers to the use of deliberately indirect, conventionally imprecise, or socially "comfortable" ways of referring to taboo, embarrassing, or unpleasant topics. Although many euphemisms are self-evident, as in formulas like "four-letter word" or "go to the bathroom," a surprisingly large number are unconscious and collective. Euphemism is a continuous process, since it is an essential mode of politeness, although there are periods, such as the Puritan and Victorian eras, when it is more pronounced and evident. All speech communities, from the most "primitive" to the most "advanced," have taboo topics and thus demonstrate euphemism. Observers of linguistic mores generally regard the contemporary period as having such a glut of swearing and foul language that there are few euphemisms left. However, this is not the case, as is shown by the whole development of Political Correctness. Furthermore, the feared or prohibited semantic areas that promote the growth of euphemism vary enormously, and include the following: the names of God and the Devil, references to death, disease, madness, being crippled, being fired, being poor, excretion, copulation, and in some societies such comparatively trivial embarrassments as references to underclothes, being fat, or having a humble occupation. Several cases are discussed under **rude words.** As this list shows, euphemism is difficult to avoid: *excretion, copulation,* and *having a humble occupation* are all euphemisms themselves; some readers will feel that *crippled* should be replaced by *disabled.*

Taboo, a key factor in euphemism, is a surprisingly recent borrowing in the language, having been brought back to England from the Pacific by Captain (James) Cook in 1777. It subsequently came to refer generally to human experiences, words, or deeds that are unmentionable because they are either ineffably sacred or unspeakably vile. **Taboo** is now used loosely of any social indiscretion or word that ought to be avoided, since strictly speaking, a taboo word should never be uttered.

In origin euphemism is profoundly involved with **word magic,** a primitive but enduring superstition that there is a mystical relationship between words and things. The etymology of the word in the Greek roots *eu* ("well") and *pheme* ("to speak") is revealing, since the process is to describe the situation as better than it is, or to avoid a taboo topic, thereby pacifying some dreaded force by not offending it. This verbal dynamic is found across all cultures. In Greek mythology the Furies were termed the *Eumenides,* literally "the friendly ones." In many European languages the weasel, a bloodthirsty and ferocious creature, is called by a variety of pacifying names, such as "little beauty" or "little lady" (Ullmann 1951, 77). Within Christian societies there are similar titles of respect for the Devil, such as *Old Nick, the Prince of Darkness,* and so on.

Absolute taboos are obviously problematic, since they impede communication and cause confusion. They are also impractical, since in modern secular democratic society one cannot prevent people from uttering the offending terms. However, in print culture it is possible to enforce them. Thus no major English dictionary included the most egregious of the "four-letter" words between 1728 and the 1960s. In Victorian times there was a taboo against mentioning terms like *leg* and *breast:* consequently one finds references to "the *limbs* of a piano" and the convention of referring to the *white* meat and the *brown* meat of a chicken.

The continuing use of these terms shows that the euphemism was genuine. On the other hand, the Victorian taboo against mentioning *trousers* generated ironic and humorous forms like *indescribables* and *unmentionables*. A quotation in the *Oxford English Dictionary* dated 1809 illustrates the point starkly: "A fine lady can talk about her lover's inexpressibles, when she would faint to hear of his breeches." (In this period *lover* did not have the modern explicit sense, being closer to "suitor" or "amorous admirer.")

Less drastic is the abbreviation or deformation of the offending word. Articulating the name of God is completely taboo in many religions, such as Islam and Judaism, generating coded forms like JWH. Historically, it provides the longest continuous example of euphemism in English, from forms like *gog* and *cokk* in the fourteenth century, followed by several dozen variants. Around 1600 a number of apostrophized forms like *zounds* for "God's wounds" and *'sblood* for "God's blood" sprang into prominence, as a response to injunctions against the use of the name of God on the stage. These are called **minced oaths**. Secular examples are *blooming* and plain *b* for *bloody,* and the euphemistic variants of *pissed off*—namely, *peed off, teed off,* and *kissed off.*

The most typical device of euphemism is the use of metaphor. Although in modern times sexually explicit language is generally common, the majority of speakers still prefer euphemistic formulas such as to *sleep with, go to bed with, make love, make out, do it, have it away with,* and so on, since these are socially acceptable. Interestingly, we find a similar euphemism in the Anglo-Saxon translation of the Bible by Ælfric (ca. 1000). Rendering the attempted seduction of Joseph by Potiphar's wife in Genesis 39:7, Ælfric has "His hlæfdige lofude hine and cwæð to him Slap mid me" (His lady loved him and said to him 'Sleep with me.') The King James Bible (1611) has another euphemistic idiom: "His master's wife cast her eyes upon Joseph and said, 'Lie with me.'" Equally noteworthy here is the suggestive phrase of "cast her eyes upon Joseph," similar to the modern idiom to "make eyes at." Sexual euphemisms can be absurd, notably in the case of six jazz players in the 1930s who called themselves a *septet.* They can also be frustrating, as when Captain Francis Grose defined *larking* in his slang dictionary of 1785 as "a lascivious practice that will not bear explanation." (He was referring to cunnilingus.) It can even be tragic, as in L.P. Hartley's novel *The Go-Between* (1953) where the sexually innocent young boy referred to in the title is perplexed by the meaning of *spooning,* imagining to be mean merely "kissing" or "flirting."

These euphemistic idioms are made up of common, everyday core words. However much euphemism employs high-register classical terminology or abstraction. As older native words for sexual activity became unacceptable, a great number of classically derived terms were absorbed into the word field. Among them are *rape* (1482), *consummation* (1530), *seduce* (1560), *erection* (1594), *copulation* (1632), *orgasm* (1684), *intercourse* (1798), *climax* (1918), and *ejaculation* (1927). These have to a large extent become standard direct terms, discussed more fully in the entry for **copulation**. Others have faded away: two centuries ago Grose wittily defined *commodity* as "the private parts of a modest woman and the public parts of a prostitute." If there is no socially acceptable native term, a direct classical borrowing is often used, as in the case of *fellatio* and *cunnilingus*. This process was succinctly described by Edward Gibbon in the eighteenth century as a recourse to "the decent obscurity of a learned language" (1854, 212).

The preference for some classically derived abstractions has often come about naturally and spontaneously in the speech community. However, examples can also be seen in *perspiration, urination, micturition, defecation,* and such terms, which make up the vocabulary of medicine. In this case the development is not truly natural. Up to medieval times "four-letter" words could be used in medical contexts; since then the professional language of medicine has separated itself from ordinary, everyday parlance in order to establish distance and status. Still more deliberate is the institutional euphemization of the vocabulary of death, seen in formations like *elimination, extermination, neutralization,* and *liquidation.* These are all modern terms or new senses generated by government propaganda machines. Interestingly, however, the actual terminology used by the armed forces, who deal with the fact of death regularly, is also full of euphemisms, but of a different kind. Prominent along them are *wasted* for "killed," general in American English, matched by strange metaphorical idioms in British English, such as to *go for a burton, have one's chips, buy it,* and *kick the bucket,* most of which have problematic origins.

Politically correct language constitutes a recent development of a whole series of euphemistic formulas. These include *vertically challenged* for "short," *differently abled* for "disabled," *sex worker* for "prostitute," and *substance abuse* for "drug addiction." These are all artificial coinages, not natural developments, to the point that they invite irony, humor, and parody: one cannot envisage the first two formulas being used in conversation or a newspaper report. However, *substance abuse* and *sex worker* are starting to develop a general currency, since they avoid stigmatizing labels. They clearly contain an agenda to use nonjudgmental language, just as *ageism* has been coined to highlight prejudice against the elderly. In the United States matters of race and color are tempered by the avoidance of *black* and *white* through the use of terms like *African-American* and *Caucasian,* which is technically a misnomer. One can see here certain ideological motives coming into play.

Euphemisms are a fundamental aspect of language, being variously spontaneous, unconscious, collective, contrived, and institutional. There is, however, a general tendency, even a continuous process, whereby euphemisms lose their "disguise" capacity and become direct or explicit, and then need to be replaced.

See also: Disguise Mechanisms; Dysphemism; Fuck; God, Euphemisms for; Jesus; Minced Oaths; Political Correctness; Taboo.

Bibliography

Allen, Keith, and Kate Burridge. *Euphemism and Dysphemism.* Oxford: Oxford University Press, 1985.
Burchfield, Robert. "An Outline History of Euphemisms in English." In *Fair of Speech,* ed. D.J. Enright. Oxford: Oxford University Press, 1985.
Gibbon, Edward. *Autobiography.* London, 1854.
Holder, R.W. *The Oxford Dictionary of Euphemisms.* Oxford: Oxford University Press, 1995.
Mencken, H.L. *The American Language.* New York: Alfred A. Knopf, 1919–1945.
Rawson, Hugh. *A Dictionary of Euphemisms and Other Double-Talk.* London: Macdonald, 1981.
Spears, Richard A. *Slang and Euphemism.* New York: Signet, 1991.
Ullmann, Stephen. *Words and Their Use.* London: Frederick Muller, 1951.

EXPLETIVES

The term now refers generally to swearwords, profanity, or foul language, without actually mentioning the terms in question. It thus has the characteristic of a euphemism, as does *ejaculation* in its old nonsexual meaning. The original meaning, dating from the sixteenth century, was a word used simply to make up a sentence or supply a metrical gap in a poem, without adding anything to the sense. (A modern example is the slightly pompous phrase "at this moment in time" used in preference to plain *now.*)

Early in the nineteenth century the term started to acquire its modern sense, defined in the *Oxford English Dictionary* as "applied to a profane oath or other meaningless exclamation." An example from 1891 runs: "'Confound him!' or some stronger expletive exploded from the Earl's lips." The *OED* definition is revealing in its assumption that expletives should not be taken literally, an attitude common now, but unusual at the time of publication, since the literal meaning of most expletives was precisely what caused offense. More obvious examples would be meaningless curiosities such as *pish!, tush!,* and *pshaw!*

Although the term has become formal and obsolescent over recent decades, it was given an unexpected new lease of life in the phrase *expletive deleted,* used in the editing of the sensational White House tapes recording the surprisingly frank language used by President Richard Nixon and his associates at the time of the Watergate scandal in 1972. When the full transcript of the tapes was published, the phrase *expletive deleted* was used to cover up such banal presidential expressions as *asshole, bullshit, crap, I don't give a shit,* and the idiom *it's just a bunch of crap.* The language itself was not especially shocking: Harry S Truman was famous for worse. It was the status of the speaker, his apparent propriety, his furtiveness, and the locale of the utterance that made it so.

See also: Euphemisms; Minced Oaths.

Bibliography
"Transcripts of Eight Recorded Presidential Conversations." Hearings Before the Committee of the Judiciary, House of Representatives, 93rd Congress 2nd Session, May–June 1974.

F

FABLIAU, THE

The term denotes a medieval literary genre: a short, ribald tale in verse with stock characters, realistic details, sexual transgressions, obscenity, scatology, and a clever plot mocking human weaknesses and making cynical fun of conventional notions of morality, authority, and poetic justice. Deriving from the medieval French dialect word *flabel or fablel,* the fabliau forms an original generic combination of the farce and the dirty story. In the fabliau the "givens" are infidelity, opportunism, trickery, and gullibility. Considering their shocking and subversive content, fabliaux were surprisingly popular in medieval France, especially between the mid-twelfth and mid-fourteenth centuries. Most were anonymous, probably composed by wandering minstrels, usually termed *jongleurs.* Of the great number originally current, only about 150 survive. Although the content is obviously low, there is still academic dispute about whether the intended audience was bourgeois (according to Joseph Bedier 1895) or aristocratic (according to Per Nykrog 1957) or popular.

Their influence was naturally strongest in France, but there is an anonymous Middle English fabliau, *Dame Sirith,* written in the late thirteenth century. Furthermore, elements of the fabliau are powerfully apparent in certain works of Chaucer, Boccaccio, Shakespeare, and Ben Jonson. Chaucer's remarkable narrative compendium, the *Canterbury Tales* (1386–1400), contains at least six examples of modified fabliaux, namely the tales of the Miller, Reve, Merchant, Shipman, and Manciple, all showing ingenuity and originality in the use of fabliau elements. Most concern adulterous triangles, usually arising out of doting old husbands who have foolishly acquired sly, materialistic, and sexually adventurous young wives. The specifics of sexual congress and bodily functions are crudely and vigorously described with the whole range of "four-letter" words in their Middle English forms: *ferte, erse, pisse, shiten, queynte* (cunt), *coillons* (testicles), and *swyve,* which thrived in the medieval period prior to the arrival of *fuck* around 1500. In the comic bedroom confusion of the *Reve's Tale,* John the clerk winds up in bed with the carpenter's wife:

So myrie a fit ne hadde she nat ful yoore
[She hadn't had such an orgasm for years]
He priketh harde and deepe as he were mad.
(ll. 4230–31)

The denouement of the *Merchant's Tale* contains, even more improbably, an adulterous coupling up a tree. When January, the blind husband, has his sight miraculously restored and expresses his outrage, his cunning wife explains that according to folk medicine, it was necessary for her to "struggle with a man upon a tree" to cure his blindness. January protests:

"Strugle!" quod he, "ye algates in it wente"
      ["Struggle!" said he, "it was going in all the time"]
(l. 2376)

In the *Miller's Tale,* the most developed and amusing, Nicholas the lodger, dispensing with the refinements of foreplay, makes a direct, passionate approach to Alison, the "wylde and yong" wife of John the carpenter:

And prively he caughte her by the queynte [cunt] . . .
And helde hire harde by the haunchbones,
And seyde, "Lemman, love me al atones,
[And said, "Darling, love me straight away]
Or I wol dyen, also God me save!"
[Or I shall die, so help me God!"]
(ll. 3276–81)

Furthermore, the tale is cynical on a more disturbing scale, being full of prayers, oaths, religious ejaculations, and even blasphemous machinations. Thus Nicholas persuades John the cuckold that the world will be destroyed by a catastrophic flood, for which he, as the new Noah, should prepare by waiting in a wooden tub up into the roof timbers. The lovers then go to bed "there as the carpenter is wont to lye" ("where the carpenter usually lay," ll. 3651). Typical of farce, there follows crude cartoon violence. Nicholas repulses his improbable rival Absolom with "a fart / As greet as it had been a thonder-dent" ("a fart as big as a thunder clap," l. 3806–7), but is branded on his "toute" (backside) with a red-hot iron so that "off goth the skyn an hande breed aboute." When Nicholas screams out "Water! help, for Goddes herte!," the nexus of the plot is ingeniously fulfilled, since John imagines that the flood has come, cuts the ropes, tumbles down and breaks his arm, becoming an object of ridicule for the curious and unsympathetic neighbors. In the end rough justice is handed to the men, but Alison gets away scot-free.

In virtually all respects the fabliau is the polar opposite or obverse of the romance, which is traditionally long, idealistic, courtly, elevated in language, and morally uplifting. In the context of the *Canterbury Tales,* the *Knight's Tale* (which opens the series) is a typical romance, to which the *Miller's Tale* is a mocking response, emphasizing the animal side of human nature and the physical facts of life in direct and crude language. The fabliau has died out, the bedroom farce being its stylized and euphemized descendant.

See also: Chaucer, Geoffrey.

Bibliography

Bedier, Joseph. *Les Fabliaux*. Paris: Champion, 1895.

Benson, Larry D., and Theodore M. Andersson. *The Literary Context of Chaucer's Fabliaux*. Indianapolis: Bobbs-Merrill, 1971.

Hines, John. *The Fabliau in English*. London: Longman, 1993.

Muscatine, Charles. *Chaucer and the French Tradition*. Berkeley: University of California Press, 1957.

Nykrog, Per. *Les Fabliaux*. Copenhagen: Munksgaard, 1957.

FANNY

A number of slang and underground terms relating to sexual matters are ambiguous, or have had unstable meanings in their semantic histories, among them *bugger, frig, merkin, prat, punk,* and *tail.* However, *fanny* is the most prominent example of a common word having quite different meanings in different speech communities. In British English it refers to the female genitalia, while in American English it denotes a woman's buttocks.

Historically the term is quite recent, its first appearance in a reference work being in Farmer and Henley (1890–1904), where it is defined as "the female *pudendum.*" As one would expect, the usage was already thriving in underworld argot, and is recorded in George Speaight's collection, *Bawdy Songs of the Early Music Hall* (1835–1840): "I've got a little Fanny, / That with hair is overspread" (l. 76). Other nineteenth-century variants were *fanny-fair* and *fanny-artful.* Its origins are problematic, though the name Fanny is commonly claimed as the source. Although not recorded in Grose's *Classical Dictionary of the Vulgar Tongue* (1785), the meaning is surely implied in the title of John Cleland's revised pornographic novel *Fanny Hill* (1750), a punning reference to Latin *mons veneris.* This allusion is suggested as a possible etymological source in *Random House* (1994). The sense was not recorded in the original *Oxford English Dictionary,* nor, strangely, in the *Supplement* (1972–1986). Jane Mills observes in her study *Womanwords:* "Fanny is one of the least objectionable UK euphemisms today for *cunt;* it is so mild that many young British girls, if they use any name at all for their genitalia, they are encouraged to use it" (1989, 78). Up to about World War I, Fanny was a fashionable girl's name in Britain, but the genital sense has ended its appeal, although in France it remains common.

The American sense dates from the 1920s, according to both the *OED* and *Random House.* The semantic distinction between the two speech communities is not absolute, however. In *Private Lives* (1930), by the English author Noel Coward, a character says: "You'd fallen on your fanny a few moments before" (Act I). Clearly in this context the American sense is the more plausible anatomically. Similarly, the English dramatist Terence Rattigan's play *French Without Tears* (1937) carries the ironic comment "Progress. Progress my fanny" (II i 44), clearly the equivalent of "Progress my arse!" The "English" sense is recorded from 1879 but is also found in American usage, although instances are rare. In other global varieties the English sense tends to predominate, but the term is not commonly used.

See also: Bugger; Frig, Frigging; Instability of Swearing Terms; Prat; Punk.

Bibliography

Ayto, John, and John Simpson. *The Oxford Dictionary of Modern Slang.* Oxford: Oxford University Press, 1999.

Farmer, J.S., and W.E. Henley. *Slang and Its Analogues.* 7 volumes, London: Routledge and Kegan Paul, 1890–1904. Reprint, Oxford: Wordsworth Press, 1987.

Flexner, Stuart Berg. *I Hear America Talking.* New York: Van Nostrand, 1976.

Lighter, J.E., ed. *Random House Historical Dictionary of American Slang.* New York: Random House, 1994–.

Mills, Jane. *Womanwords.* London: Virago, 1991.

FARMER, JOHN S., AND WILLIAM E. HENLEY

John Stephen Farmer and William Ernest Henley were unusual collaborators in the production of their prodigiously comprehensive and detailed thesaurus of English slang, compiled remarkably, in the last years of the Victorian era. Their vast work *Slang and Its Analogues Past and Present: A Dictionary, Historical and Comparative, of the Heterodox Speech of all Classes of Society for More than Three Hundred Years. With Synonyms in English, French, German, Italian, etc.* appeared in seven volumes from 1890 to 1904. (It has subsequently been reissued as *A Dictionary of Slang.*) J. S. Farmer (1845?–1915?), an independent American scholar, did most of the editorial work, later assisted by W.E. Henley (1849–1903), a noted poet, man of letters, and flamboyant personality, the original of Long John Silver, the pirate of Robert Louis Stevenson's *Treasure Island* (1883).

Although slang dictionaries of various sorts have been published since the 1560s, Farmer and Henley's was of a completely different order of magnitude from anything that preceded it, and has never been surpassed in coverage. It follows the historical method, "taking the whole period of English literature from the earliest down to the present," separating the senses, listing them chronologically and supporting them with quotations, about 100,000 in number. It naturally incorporates most of the material from the previous canting and underground dictionaries, but adds a vast volume of its own, including a substantial amount of American coverage and synonyms from the major European languages.

Such a work obviously faced major difficulties in circumventing the strict Victorian laws against obscene libel, the legal category that the Act of 1857 had introduced. Since the *Oxford English Dictionary* was already in production and facing a similar situation, Farmer wrote to the Editor of the *OED,* James Murray (June 3, 1891) explaining his problems: "I have had no alternative but to bring an action of breach of contract against my first printers, which breach they admit, but plead justification on ground of obscenity of such words as range themselves under 'C' and 'F'." Farmer requested that a letter Murray had written to him on "his own difficulties" might be used in the action, concluding: "I am in a small way fighting your own battle in advance." (The *OED* was then in the process of publishing the letter 'C'.) As he later wrote to Murray (July 23, 1890), his policy was "where the examples are *coarse,* to deal with them decently, and have generally wrapped up my explanation in language 'not understanded' of the people" (i.e., Latin).

As it turned out, the *OED* omitted the most egregious of the "four-letter" words, which left Farmer and Henley with a problem. However, since their work was "printed for subscribers only," it was in a different category of publication. Furthermore, they used an ingenious ploy, exploiting the thesaurus format to their own advantage by choosing unusual and euphemistic headwords, such as *Monosyllable* and *Greens,* instead of the problematic four-letter words. Thus the entry for *Greens* begins: "TO HAVE, GET, or GIVE ONE'S GREENS, *verb phr.* (venery).—to enjoy, procure or confer the sexual favour. Said differently of both sexes." This is an amusing and illuminating juxtaposition of a coarse basic idiom and Victorian euphemism. There follows an astoundingly vigorous collection of more than 600 synonyms for copulation, from the most explicit, such as "up to one's balls," to more humorous metaphors such as "the mattress jig," "beard-splitting," "tail-twitching," and "among the cabbages," followed by a further selection of idioms from Continental languages. That for *Monosyllable* (the vagina) is about twice as extensive. Although *fuck* and *cunt* are listed, they both have quite short entries. The work took slang lexicography into a totally new dimension.

See also: Dictionaries; *Oxford English Dictionary.*

Bibliography

Farmer, J.S., and W.E. Henley. *Slang and Its Analogues.* 7 vols. London: 1890–1904.
Green, Jonathon. *Chasing the Sun.* London: Jonathan Cape, 1996.

FART

As a term of vulgarity or personal abuse, *fart* has never been especially taboo, being quite commonly used in medieval times and up to the eighteenth century. The *Oxford English Dictionary* entry (published in 1895) carried the usage note: "Not now in decent use," which is still generally the case, while a century later *Random House* (1994) concurred: "usually considered vulgar." Reading the citations from Sir James Murray's august work, one clearly detects a sense of spontaneous animal energy running through them.

There is a historical anomaly in that *fart* is regarded as Anglo-Saxon and has many Germanic cognates, but the form *feortan* is hypothetical, there being no instance prior to Middle English. The first quotation in the *OED* is from the charming thirteenth-century lyric "Sumer is icumen in" ("Summer has arrived"). The context runs: "bulluc sterteth, bucke verteth," a line that has caused some academic embarrassment, since the most obvious literal interpretation, namely "the bullock cavorts; the buck farts," is regarded as too crude. Consequently, some scholars have preferred to interpret *verteth* as "to cavort" or "to gamble," even though there is no other contemporary instance of a verb "to vert." Chaucer's foul-mouthed Miller mocks the prissy character Absolon in his bawdy tale by observing that "he was somdeel squaymous of fartyng," that is, "he was rather squeamish about farting" (ll. 3337–38), making fun of this anal retentive behavior. Cruelly, Absolon turns out to be a man more farted against than farting.

Queen Elizabeth, according to an anecdote retailed by John Aubrey, naughtily reminded Edward de Vere of an embarrassing public episode by remarking: "My lord, I had forgot the Fart" (*Brief Lives*). The seventeenth-century clergyman poet Robert Herrick wrote of "the farting tanner" (*Hesperides,* I, 216), while his contemporary Charles Cotton noted in his *Poetical Works*: "He was the loudest of farters" (ca. 1687, 9). Dr. Johnson (1755) included *fart* without special comment, using the old plain definition "to break wind." Francis Grose lists the more

Long a symbolic and idiomatic form of insult, *farting* was a frequently used term and common image from medieval times to the eighteenth century. In this 1798 cartoon, John Bull (representing the English people), expresses his disdain for King George III. William Pitt calls the gesture treason. (Library of Congress, LC-USZC4-8788)

surreptitious *fizzle* and *fice* ("a small windy escape backwards, more obvious to the nose than ears") as well as two racy metaphors, *fart-catcher* for a valet or footman and *fartleberries* for "excrement hanging about the anus" in his slang dictionary (1785). Thereafter the word started to be regarded as indecent, but not heinously so.

Personal insult is more difficult to trace historically, although previously farting was itself a form of symbolic insult. In Ben Jonson's *The Alchemist* (1610), Subtle dismisses Face provocatively, saying: "I fart at thee!" (I i 2). There was also a common medieval idiom that something of little value was "not worth a fart." Yet many of the common modern uses, such as "an old fart" and "farting about" are relatively recent. The *OED Supplement* traces the second to dialect use in the North of England about 1900, while *Random House* (1994) gives a first instance of "old fart" in 1934.

The term is not as common or idiomatically diversified in American English. Although unlisted in the *Australian National Dictionary* (1988), *fart* is fairly common in that variety, while in South African English it is used with the same frequency and application as in British English. However, the Afrikaans equivalent, namely *poep*, is commonly used in colloquial phrases like the dismissive loan translation "he's an old poep." The same term has come from Dutch through to American English, where it has different senses closely related to excrement.

See also: "Four-Letter" Words.

Bibliography

Ayto, John, and John Simpson. *The Oxford Dictionary of Modern Slang.* Oxford: Oxford University Press, 1999.
Farmer, J.S., and W.E. Henley. *Slang and Its Analogues.* London: 1890–1904.
Green, Jonathon. *The Slang Thesaurus.* Harmondsworth: Penguin, 1988.
Hughes, Geoffrey. *Swearing.* Oxford: Blackwell, 1991.
Lighter, J.E., ed. *Random House Historical Dictionary of American Slang.* New York: Random House, 1994–.
"Sumer is icumen in." British Museum, MS Harley 978 fol. 11B.

FASHION IN SWEARING

Generally speaking, the history of swearing shows distinct shifts in mode and in content. These essentially trace a decline from invocation to the gods or some higher force, to various secular modes, such as excretory, copulatory, and racial swearing, the dominant forms of modern times. Fashion implies a self-conscious or collective consciousness in the adoption of certain styles, which Jonathan Swift noted in his *Polite Conversation* (1737), quoting "an ancient poet":

For, now-a-days, men change their oaths
As often as they change their cloaths.
(1963, 30)

Though clothes, apparel and accessories, are the most obvious components of fashion, the notion is also apparent in language, especially in slang.

There is clear evidence from the Renaissance onward of writers being aware of the phenomenon and regarding fashion as an aspect of swearing. One of the first pieces of explicit evidence comes from Queen Elizabeth's godson, Sir John Harrington, in his *Epigrams* (1615), commenting on the debasement of religious swearing:

In elder times an ancient custom was,
To sweare in weighty matters by the Masse.
But when the Masse went down (as old men note)
They sware then by the Crosse of this same grote [value].
And when the Crosse was likewise held in scorne,
Then by their faith, the common oath was sworne.
Last, having sworne away all faith and troth,
Only God damn them is their common oath.
Thus custome kept *decorum* by gradation,
That losing Masse, Crosse, Faith, they find damnation.

Ostensibly offering a witty comment on changing styles in religious oaths, Harrington is making a profound observation on the change of religion in England from Catholicism (symbolized in the Mass) to Protestantism. He is commenting on fashion as superficial (in the reference to *decorum*), but also on debasement, since *gradation* really means "degradation"—that is, going down in steps or stages.

Modes of swearing are often alluded to in **Restoration** comedy (from 1660 to ca. 1700), characterized as generally bawdy and decadent. That entry discusses a remarkably explicit example from *Love in a Bottle* (1698), by George Farquhar, where the pronunciation of *zounds* (with its horrific origin in "God's wounds" in the crucifixion) is trivialized and treated simply as a matter of fashion. Decades later, Richard Brinsley Sheridan's highly popular play *The Rivals* (1775) contains the casual comment "Ay ay, the best terms will grow obsolete. Damns have had their day" (II i). This was not so, historically speaking, as the entry for *damn* shows, but for the high society of the time the word was passé.

As with all matters of fashion, the problem is defining who are the leaders and what is in fashion. In Shakespeare's *Henry V* (1599) Henry says to his bride-to-be: "Dear Kate, you and I cannot be confined to the weak list of a country's fashion: we are the makers of manners, Kate" (V ii 292–93). Today the leaders of fashion are more "celebrities" and entertainers. Context is always vital. As the entries for *Pygmalion* and **Kenneth Tynan** show, a swearword may be common, but a publicized use of it can still provoke outrage.

See also: Class and Swearing; Damn; *Pygmalion;* Tynan, Kenneth.

Bibliography
Hughes, Geoffrey. *Swearing*. Oxford: Blackwell, 1991.
Montagu, Ashley. *The Anatomy of Swearing*. New York: Collier, 1973.

FEMINIZATION OF OPPROBRIOUS TERMS

This formulation refers to the sociolinguistic process whereby opprobrious terms, swearwords, and insults originally referring to creatures, males or both genders have shifted semantically to be applied to women. The terms are very numerous, the shift has taken place over centuries, and there are virtually none that have undergone the reverse process. This suggests a definite sexist dynamic at work. Although men have traditionally been the dominant sex, all speech communities are made up of both men and women, so that these shifts in meaning are in some sense the responsibility of both genders.

The process of feminization is evidenced in the following terms: *bawd, coquette, doll, dragon, hag, harlot, harpy, harridan, minx, scold, shrew, siren, sow, tartar, termagant, witch,* and *wench.* Of these, **scold, shrew,** and **witch** have their own entries. These bring out such interesting points that male *witches* are actually recorded earlier (from about 890) than the female variety and that *shrew* and *scold* were applied to males before being used to stereotype the loud, aggressive, or "difficult" woman. Most of the other terms fall under the entries for **prostitutes** and **women, stereotypes of.**

The semantic histories of *wench, coquette, doll, minx,* and *gypsy* contain many surprises. *Wench* has its origins in Old English *wencel,* a child of either sex, but by the time that William Langland used it (ca. 1377), it was female-specific. He uniquely described the Virgin Mary as "Goddes Wenche" (C Text, Passus xix, l. 134), but also referred to the polar opposite, "a wench of the stews," that is, a woman of the brothel (B Text, Passus xix, l. 433). Thereafter it degenerated to mean a mistress, a wanton woman, or one perceived to be sexually available. Although often preceded by *common* or *wanton,* it could be a term of affection, albeit condescending, as at the end of Shakespeare's *The Taming of the Shrew* (V ii 181).

Coquette is a remarkably simple case of sex change: the original form was male *coquet,* a young cock, notable for what the *OED* rightly calls "its strutting gait and amorous characteristics." The first appearance of the female form *coquette* is in 1669, but the word could be used of both a male flirt and of "a wanton girl that speaks fair to several lovers at once" (Edward Phillips's *Dictionary* of 1706). In *The Beggar's Opera* (1728), John Gay refers to "the coquets of both sexes," while the *Monthly Review* of 1770 commented revealingly on "One of those Narcissus-like, or Lady-like, gentlemen, called a male-coquet." The term maintained its male form for about a century, although contexts and definitions refer to a jilt.

Various terms develop from meaning a pet or a toy to a woman. The primary meanings of *doll,* as given by the *Oxford English Dictionary,* are surprisingly chauvinist: "A pet form of the name Dorothy. Hence given generically to a female pet, a mistress. Also the smallest or pet dog in a litter (dialect)." About a century later, about 1700, came the modern senses of *doll* and *dolly* as a child's plaything, and subsequently, from the mid-nineteenth century, the more damning use of "a pretty, but empty or frivolous woman."

Animal terms form a major category. **Bitch** has developed a range of reference, although its most powerful application is still to a woman. *Minx,* of obscure origin, is used of a pet dog from about 1540, a pert girl or hussy from about 1592, and a whore from about 1598. In the past even *sow* did not have an exclusively female application, being used, in the words of the *OED,* of "a person (male or female) as a term of abuse." As late as 1803 a Scottish song carries the line "You're a sow auld man."

Gypsy combines in its semantic development strains of both xenophobia and misogyny. The term arose in the early sixteenth century with the appearance of the Romanies, a dark-skinned race of Hindu origin assumed to have come from Egypt, the name itself being a corruption of *Egyptian*. A male sense of "a cunning rogue" appears briefly in the early sixteenth century, whereafter feminization and sexual deterioration set in. The sense of "a contemptuous term for a woman as being cunning, fickle, deceitful" is found from Shakespeare until the mid-nineteenth century. A similar pattern can be seen in the semantic development of *tramp* from "a male vagrant," recorded from the seventeenth century, to "a sexually promiscuous woman" from the early twentieth.

The trend of feminization partly overlaps with that of moral deterioration in terms for women, covered in the entry for **women, stereotypes of.**

See also: Bitch; Prostitution; Scold; Shrew; Virago; Witch; Women, Stereotypes of; Women, Swearing in; Xenophobia.

FICO. *See:* Body Language and Gesture.

FILM. *See:* Cinema; Hollywood.

FINES AND PENALTIES

Swearing has traditionally been regarded as an act that is irreligious, antisocial, or personally provocative, and thus deemed worthy of some legal punishment. Punishments are extremely severe in the Hebrew Bible, even including stoning, but the offense is more leniently viewed, as are all human failings, in the New Testament. Within the English tradition, the historical span of fines is enormous, extending from **Anglo-Saxon** times down to the eighteenth century, when the legislation lapsed. In the United States, the First Amendment to the Constitution obviously protects free speech, but it equally makes provision for fining for the broadcasting of obscenities.

In the past, when there were both ecclesiastical and temporal courts, the grounds for penalties were different. The great legal authority Sir William Blackstone, in his *Commentaries on the Laws of England* (1765–1769), makes a series of valuable distinctions on this point:

> Gross impieties and general immoralities are taken note of and punished by our municipal law . . . the spiritual court punishing all sinful enormities for the sake of reforming the sinner, *pro salutate animae* [for the sake of his soul]; while the temporal courts resent the public affront to religion and morality on which all governments must depend for support, and correct more for the sake of example than private amendment.
>
> The fourth species of offences, therefore, more immediately against God and religion, is that of *blasphemy* against the Almighty by denying his being or providence; or by contumelious [contemptuous] reproaches of our Saviour Christ. Whither also may be referred all profane scoffing [ridicule] at the holy scripture, or exposing it to contempt or ridicule. These are offences publishable at common law by fine and imprisonment, or other infamous corporal punishment; for Christianity is part of the laws of England. (Book IV)

Blackstone's incisive analysis makes the important distinction that swearing, under which profanity is generally subsumed, is a common-law offense, whereas blasphemy is a crime. It also underlines the important difference between Britain and the United States: the Christian religion has traditionally been regarded as part of the legal foundation of the British system, whereas the Constitution of the United States specifies that there shall be no state religion, the phrase "under God" being used mainly out of deference to the Almighty. Consequently, offenses such as profanity and blasphemy have always attracted more attention and punishment in Britain than in America.

Blackstone's assumption of a Christian foundation also highlights a major difference between his time and the present. Swearing *per se* is a problematic offense in the modern world, since in a secularized society the justice of punishment is as dubious as its efficacy. (The offense of blasphemy was abolished by the British Parliament in 1989.) Taking into account inflation and the cost of living, fines have become less severe over time. In modern times the offense is usually dealt with under other legal categories, such as libel or the South African category of *crimen injuria,* that is, an act of personal insult so outrageous that it constitutes a legal offense.

The earliest instance of fines occurs in the laws of the **Anglo-Saxon** kings Hlothhere and Eadric (673–685?), no. 11:

> If anyone in another's house calls a man a perjurer, or shamefully accosts him with insulting words, he is to pay a shilling to him who owns the house, and six shillings to him to whom he spoke that word, and to pay twelve shillings to the king.

This law clearly reflects the seriousness with which verbal utterance was regarded in Anglo-Saxon society. Furthermore, the category of "insulting words" is put on a par with perjury. The fines are heavy and on a hierarchical scale: the punishment, incidentally, is the same as that for stealing a cup. A revealing constraint from the Laws of Alfred (900) is contained in the injunction: "Do not ever swear by the heathen gods." This was some three hundred years after Christianity was first brought to England, but certainly implies the existence of pagan swearing. In the North of England and Scotland, the penalties were far more severe, which suggests that the abuse was widespread: under the statutes of Donald VI and Kenneth II (died 995), the punishment for swearers was cutting out the tongue.

William the Conqueror seems not to have introduced any specific penalties for swearing. However, according to Alexander Howell's work *A Sword Against Sinners,* published in 1611, the Conqueror's son Henry I (1068–1135) is said to have instituted the following hierarchical scale of fines for swearing in the precincts of the royal residence: a duke, 40 shillings; a lord, 20 shillings; a squire, 10 shillings; a yeoman, 3s. 4d.; a page, a whipping. In the fourteenth century, when swearing and blasphemy were common, many tracts appeared advocating extreme measures. One of these was the *Summa Praedicantium* (1323–1350) by John Bromyard, an English Dominican who proposed special penalties such as those decreed by St. Louis of France, "who ordered such [offenders] to be branded upon the face with a hot iron for a perpetual memorial of their crime" (in Montagu 1973, 111).

In 1551, in the reign of Queen Mary, the Scottish Parliament enacted a rigorous ordinance:

> In detestatioun of the grevous abominabill aithis [oaths], sweiring, execrationnis and blasphematioun of the name of God [which are then variously listed]. . . . It is statute and ordanit that quhatsumevir [whatever] persoun or persouns sweiris sic [such] abominabill aithis and detestabill execrationnis as is afoir rehersit sall incur the panis [penalties] efter following. . . . That is to say ane Prelate of Kirk [Church], Erle or Lord, for everie fault to be committit for the space of thre monethis nixt tocuni. That is to say unto the first day of Maij exclusive xij.d. [twelve pence or a shilling]. Ane Barrone or benefecit man constitute in dignite ecclesisatick iiij.d. Ane landit man, frehalder, wassal, fewar Burges and small benefecit men .ijd. Ane craftsman, yeoman, a seward man and all uthers .j.d.
> (from The Acts of the Parliament of Scotland, 1442–1567. London, 1814, II, 485.)

Poor people unable to pay such a fine were to be put in the stocks or in prison for four hours. For a repeat offense, the fine was doubled. The system of fining was extended so that heads of families were empowered to levy fines on their servants and relations, and were authorized to keep a collection box. The Act makes a chilling correlation between the excesses of swearing and divine punishment in the form of current famine. It lists

> ugsume aithis [fearful oaths] and execratiounis agains the command of God that the famin is cum in sic ane ungodlie use amangis the pepill of this Realme baith of greit and small Estatis [both high and low] that daylie and hourlie may be hard amangis thame oppin blasphematioun [open blasphemy] of Godis maiestie to the grete contemptioun thairof and bringing of the Ire and wraith [wrath] of God upone the pepill heirfoir.

In England, by contrast, there was greater tolerance for swearing. In 1601 a bill "against usual and common swering" was introduced in the House of Commons, but failed after the first reading. There is some speculation that Queen Elizabeth, a robust swearer herself, would not have signed the bill into law. It was certainly not the kind of constraint that the Elizabethan nobility would have easily accepted. Upon the accession of King James VI of Scotland as James I of England in 1603, no attempt was made to introduce the draconian measures of the Scottish Parliament. However, the Puritans were able to press through a significant piece of legislation, the Act of 1606, making it an offense for any person in an interlude, pageant or stage play to use jestingly or profanely the name "of God, or of Christ Jesus, or the Holy Ghost or of the Trinity" (3 Jac. I. c. 21). The consequence of this legislation was the emergence and rapid growth of **minced oaths**, such as *zounds* for "God's wounds" and *snails* for "God's nails."

The severity of punishment for swearing in Scotland was further increased by the Act of 1609 (103. Parl.7.Jam.6):

> Against Cursing and Swearing, and not delating, or neglect to Prosecute the same, Abominabill Oaths, and detestable Execrations, particularly Swearing in vaine by God's Blood, Body, Pas-

sions and Wounds; saying Devile Stick, Gore, Rost, or Rieve them; and other such Execrations; are punished as in Act 16. Parl. 5 Q. M. [the Act of 1551, previously quoted] which is ratified: The Penalties Augmented: And Censors appointed in the Mercat [market] places of the Burrows [boroughs], and other publick Fairs, with powers to put the delinquents in ward [detention] till Payment, and Surety for abstaining in time coming: And that by Direction and Commission of the Judges Ordinary. And that all House-Holders Delate [report] *Transgressors within their Houses, under pains of being punished as* offenders themselves. And if the Majistrates be remiss [lax], they shall be called before the Council, Committed to ward during pleasure, and fined surety for exact diligence thereafter. [The offending phrases "Devile Stick, Gore, Rost, or Rieve them," which have long passed out of general currency, mean in effect, "May the Devil impale, stab, roast or tear them."]

In England it was only near the end of King James's reign, in 1623, that Parliament passed a significant act against swearing. Although it lacked details of the offense, it was simple, unequivocal and egalitarian:

> For as much as all profane Swearing and Cursing is forbidden by the Word of GOD, be it therefore enacted, by the Authority of the then Parliament, that no Person or Persons should from henceforth profanely Swear and Curse, upon the Penalty of forfeiting one Shilling to the use of the Poor for every Oath or Curse.
>
> If any refuse to pay, upon Conviction, the Money is to be levied by Distress [legal seizure]. And in defeet [failure] of Distress, the Offender is to be set in the Stocks if above twelve years old, if under that Age he is to be whip'd by the Constable, or by the Parent, or Master if present.

The Act was continued and ratified by the succeeding Parliament of Charles I in 1627 (3 Chas. I. c. 4) and again, near the end of his reign in 1640.

As the entry for the **Renaissance** shows, Puritan attacks on the stage became more frequent from the 1580s. One of the most outspoken was William Prynne in his *Histriomastix* (1633), which meant "the beater of actors." When Prynne overstepped the boundaries in criticizing the monarchy, he was sentenced to the gruesome punishment meted out to seditious libelers, to have his ears cut off in the pillory and to be imprisoned for life. Archbishop William Laud continued to prosecute him and had his book burned publicly. While imprisoned in the Tower of London Prynne continued to write and was further mutilated by having the letters S L (for Seditious Libeller) branded on his cheeks. With grim humor Prynne maintained that the letters stood for *Stigmata Laudis,* "the wounds of Laud."

When the Civil War broke out in 1642, the Puritan armies took the field under Oliver Cromwell against the corruptions of religion as they saw them, including "prophaneness." Cromwell claimed: "Not a man swears but pays his twelve pence." There was a notable case of a quartermaster Boutholmey, found guilty by a council of war for uttering impious expressions. He was condemned to have his tongue bored with a red-hot iron and his sword broken over his head, and was ignominiously dismissed from the service. The interpretation of swearing was likewise extremely severe: there were cases of men found guilty for exclamations such as "Upon my life" and "On my troth" (Montagu 1967, 167). On September 2,

1642, the Puritans used an argument similar to that of the Scottish Parliament of 1551, claiming that the parlous state of the nation was the judgment of God. They went further:

> It is therefore thought fit and ordeined by the Lords and Commons in this Parliament Assembled, that while these sad Causes and set times for Humiliation doe continue, publicke Stage-playes shall cease, and be forebourne [forbidden].

This ban or closing of the theaters continued throughout the Puritan Commonwealth, being lifted in 1660 when the monarchy was restored to power in the form of Charles II. In 1694, *An Act for the More Effectual Suppressing of Profane Cursing and Swearing* brought back social gradation in punishment:

> every Servant, Day Labourer, common soldier, and common seaman, is, for every offence, to pay one Shilling. Every other Person to pay two Shillings. And, if after Conviction, such Persons offend a second Time, they are to pay double. And if a third time, treble to what was paid for the first Offence.
>
> The Money to be levied by Distress [legal seizure]. And in defect of Distress, the Offender is to be set in the stocks if above sixteen. If under that Age to be whip'd by the Constable, or by the Parent, Guardian, or Master of such Offender in the presence of the Constable.
>
> Magistrates that wilfully and willingly omit their Duty in the Execution of this Act, are to forfeit five Pounds; the one Moiety [half] to the use of the Informer. . . .
>
> This Act is appointed to be read in Churches four times every Year, immediately after Morning Prayer.
> (Act 6 and 7 William III. c. 2.)

The most stringent of the statutes against "the offence of profane and common *swearing and cursing*" was the Act of 1745 in the reign of George II. In his *Commentaries* Sir William Blackstone rehearsed the law, which basically followed the framework of the Act of 1694, keeping the "base rate" at one shilling for common people but raised the schedule of fines to five shillings for those of superior rank and penalized defaulters with ten days in a house of correction. Magistrates omitting their duty were to be fined £5, as were those responsible for reading out the Act in Church. An interesting resuscitation was the theater statute of 1606, "that if in any stage-play, interlude, or show, the name of the Holy Trinity, or any of the persons therein, be jestingly or profanely used, the offender shall forfeit £10, one moiety [half] to the king, and the other to the informer." Since Blackstone's time most of the legal measures concerning swearing have fallen into abeyance in the United Kingdom, but **obscenity** has become the major focus of penalties.

In the United States under the laws of the Puritan Commonwealths of Colonial America, profanity was punishable as blasphemy. Since then swearing has technically been a legal offense in every state, but in view of the First Amendment of the Constitution, it has been enforced only on special occasions—for instance, against the protesters against the Vietnam War. However, **broadcasting** forms a special case, and under Section 1464 of the U.S. Criminal Code (18 U.S.C. Section 1464) it is determined that "Whoever utters any obscene,

In English tradition, fishwives (merchants) have been known for centuries as unregenerate swearers and incessant users of foul language. Indeed, *fishwife* is synonymous with a vulgar or abusive woman.

indecent or profane language, by means of radio communication shall be fined not more than $10,000, or imprisoned not more than two years, or both." This has been the area of considerable legal dispute.

See also: Bible; Blasphemy.

Bibliography

Blackstone, Sir William. *Commentaries on the Laws of England.* Oxford: Clarendon Press, 1765–1769.
Hughes, Geoffrey. *Swearing.* Oxford: Blackwell, 1991.
Mellinkoff, David. *The Language of the Law.* Boston: Little, Brown, 1963.
Montagu, Ashley. *The Anatomy of Swearing.* New York: Collier, 1973.
Pacifica Foundation v. *Federal Communications Commission,* No. 75–1391.

FISHWIFE

Fishwives, together with tinkers, truckers, and troopers, have been regarded as habitual swearers and prolific users of foul language for several centuries. They form a significant English category, refuting the common perception that swearing is uncommon or unknown in women. However, since fishwives belong to the working class, they reinforce the notion that foul language is more common among the lower orders. No such association of swearing attaches to *fishmonger.*

The term *fishwife* is not generally used outside British English, where it is invariably found in the context of swearing, as in the comment, "They abuse one another like fishwives," recorded in John Davies's translation of *Olearius' Voyage* (1662, 80). The term is closely associated with **Billingsgate**, the name of an ancient London fish market, especially with the strong language of the fishwives there. Today *fishwife* has a declining currency, having moved into the categories of "literary" and "obsolete."

See also: Billingsgate; Bywords of Swearing; Women, Swearing in.

FLEXIBILITY

A fundamental distinction in semantics, or the study of meaning, is that between *referential* and *emotive* use. Referential language is essentially factual, formal, and concerned with conveying reality in a precise neutral fashion, whereas emotive language essentially conveys the speaker's or writer's feelings. Frequently the difference lies as much in the context as in the words themselves. Thus the statement: "William the Conqueror was a stupid bastard" could be entirely referential, but "Albert Einstein was a stupid bastard" is obviously emotive and judgmental. Emotive use of language thus shows greater latitude in meaning, creating problems of interpretation.

By its nature, swearing consists almost exclusively of emotive language. There are three basic modes: the expletive or exclamation (*damn!*), the curse (*damn you!*), and the intensive (a *damn shame!* a *damn good show!*). Although there is no shortage of referential condemning terms, such as *embezzler, pedophile,* and *plagiarist,* great numbers of other words like *little, old, bloody, fool, idiot, freak, shit, bastard,* and *bitch* are freely used in an emotive fashion, although all have referential uses. Some, like *old,* have been used in this fashion since the Middle Ages: Chaucer's Wife of Bath castigates two of her husbands as "sire oulde lecchour" and as an "olde barelful of lies." Others, like *little,* are comparatively recent, being first recorded in Victorian times. Some have quite extraordinary flexibility. The British use of *awful* is a case in point: "There was an *awful* accident"; alternatively, "She's *awfully* nice," and so on. In some cases it is not possible to establish the meaning from the term itself: thus the simple exclamation "Shit!" could express annoyance, surprise, pleasure, contempt, boredom, and a range of other feelings. As can be seen, the more common a word, the wider its range of uses, an axiom that G.K. Zipf has corroborated with the alarming statistic that except for a few core words, "different meanings of a word will tend to be equal to the square root of its relative frequency" (1945, 255).

In concert with this greatly extended range of meaning, emotive terms acquire greater grammatical flexibility. Thus, to take a prime example, *fuck* has extended its grammatical function from being exclusively a verb in late Middle English to virtually every other part of speech. In its most emotive and personal uses the flexibility extends to the incestuous improbability of *motherfucker,* finally attaining such physical impossibilities as "fuck off!" and "go fuck yourself!" Jonathon Green's *Slang Thesaurus* (1999) lists forty-three different forms and idioms. In the past there were, surprisingly, even more forms, such as *fuckster, fuckish,* and *fuckable,* which have passed out of use.

The table "Flexibility in Swearing Terms" illustrates the degrees and patterns of flexibility. The various functions are categorized from 1 to 8. In the table the asterisk * denotes usage, while the symbol ° denotes lack of capacity in a particular category. Clearly, only those terms that can be used as both noun and verb are likely candidates in all the modes: the nouns are by definition eligible for only the first two categories. However, it is surprising that only one term, namely *bugger,* can be used in all modes, and that *piss* can only be used in one. In United States usage, *fuck* has almost attained complete flexibility.

Flexibility in Swearing Terms

Categories
1. Personal: "You——!"
2. Personal by reference: "The——!"
3. Destinational: "——off!"
4. Cursing: "——you!"
5. General expletive of anger, annoyance, frustration: "——!"
6. Explicit expletive of anger, annoyance, frustration: "——it!"
7. Capacity for adjectival extension: "——ing" or "——y"
8. Verbal usage: "to——about"

Term	Category							
	1	2	3	4	5	6	7	8
Damn (vb)	°	°	°	*	*	*	°	°
Fuck (n + vb)	*(US)	°	*	*	*	*	*	*
Cunt (n)	*	*	°	°	°	°	°	°
Shit (n)	*	*	°	°	*	°	*	°
Fart (n + vb)	*	*	°	°	°	°	°	*
Piss (n + vb)	°	°	*	°	°	°	°	*
Bugger (n + vb)	*	*	*	*	*	*	*	*
Bastard (n)	*	*	°	°	°	°	°	°
Arse (n + vb)	*	*	°	°	°	°	°	*
Asshole (n)	*	*	°	°	°	°	°	°

Although the table focuses on modern usage, the historical perspective shows that flexibility is not a new feature. Two centuries ago the following range of idioms using *the devil* or *the deuce* were common: "What *the devil* is going on?"; "Who *the devil* does he think he is?"; "*The devil* he will!" (rebutting some statement); "She's taking *the devil* of a long time!" The entry for **devil** also shows that *devil* was used in a wide range of emotive ways in medieval times.

Infixing

This denotes the process by which an intensive term is integrated into a word or phrase, with consequent loss of semantic force. The previous paragraph carried examples using *the devil.* More typical and topical examples are *absobloodylutely, kangabloodyroo,* and *unfuckingbelievable,* where the intensifying term has become part of the whole verbal unit. H.L. Mencken commented on the infixing of *goddam* in *The American Language* (1936, 315). The process was generally thought by linguists to be a modern phenomenon, but in fact it has been found as far back as the nineteenth century. Thus the phrase "I was so God damned drunk" is recorded in 1847. According to the *Random House Historical Dictionary of American Slang* (1994), the following quotation from 1865–1867 is "the earliest known example of infixing": "'He is, by Jove! A dam incur-dam-able dam coward.' (When Van Sandt was informed next day of this Feat of profanity he seemed quite gratified.)" The quotation is from De Forest, *Miss Ravenel*, 272. This degree of flexibility is a clear sign that the word chosen—for example, *goddam, bloody,* or *fuck* is sufficiently weakened to be used simply as a rhythmic counter. However, an earlier instance is the medieval infixing of *devil* as an intensive in the phrase "a twenty develewey" for "a very long way," discussed under **devil**.

Flexibility also extends to word creation. Forms like *fag-hag, bull-dyke, dumb-ass, stick in the mud,* and *goofball* are original in two senses: although they derive from two recognizable forms, the compounds have unique meanings as insults; furthermore, they do not have referential meanings, as do traditional compounds such as *breakfast* or *cupboard,* which can be explained in terms of their roots. All have developed their own idiomatic meanings, which are quite separate from their root meaning.

Bibliography

Flexner, Stuart Berg. *I Hear America Talking*. New York: Van Nostrand Reinhold, 1976.

Green, Jonathon. *The Slang Thesaurus*. Harmondsworth: Penguin, 1988.

Hughes, Geoffrey. *Swearing*. Oxford: Blackwell, 1991.

Lighter, J.E., ed. *Random House Historical Dictionary of American Slang*. New York: Random House, 1994–.

Mencken, H.L. *The American Language*. New York: Knopf. Four editions: 1919–1936.

Montagu, Ashley. *The Anatomy of Swearing*. London and New York: Macmillan and Collier, 1973.

Ross, Thomas W. "Taboo-Words in Fifteenth-Century English," in *Fifteenth-Century Studies,* ed. Robert F. Yeager, 137–60. Hamden, CT: Archon, 1984.

Spears, Richard A. *Slang and Euphemism*. New York: Signet, 1991.

Zipf, G.K. "The meaning-frequency relationship of words." *Journal of General Psychology* 33: 251–66.

FLEXNER, STUART BERG

A notable scholar of slang and colloquial American English, Stuart Berg Flexner was the major author of the first edition of the *Dictionary of American Slang* (with Harold Wentworth, 1960) and the sole author of the groundbreaking work *I Hear America Talking: An Illustrated Treasury of American Words and Phrases* (1976). The earlier work was fairly comprehensive in its word list, but excluded the more egregious of the "four-letter" words; it gave citations, but did not follow the historical method completely, since it did not list the different meanings nor date the quotations. However, Flexner illuminated the topic by estimating in the *Dictionary of American Slang* (1960) that half the entries in the work "could be traced directly to some forty-five general sub-groups of our culture," from "airplane pilots" to "unskilled factory workers."

As the title *I Hear America Talking* implied, the second volume explored the diversity of American idioms, coinages, and key words as an aspect of the nation's social history, supported by well-chosen illustrations. Words were arranged thematically and alphabetically in 150 entries, from *Abolition* to *Yes and No,* and the work was truly comprehensive. Nothing was excluded, so that a reader could proceed from *Fuck and Screw,* to *Fundamentalism,* to *It Was a Lovely Funeral,* to *The Gay 90s,* to *The Germans,* and so on. First instances of words were dated as far a possible.

Flexner took an unusually liberated view for the lexicography of the period, as is shown in his concluding comments under *Goddamn, Darn and Oh Perdition!:*

> be it mincing expressions, mild oaths, blasphemy, obscenity or scatology, when I hear America talking I hear America cursing—thank God! What a docile unfeeling people we would be if we didn't have strong emotions and beliefs that need strong words. It's good to live in a country where people give a good Goddamn.

Bibliography

Flexner, Stuart Berg. *I Hear America Talking.* New York: Van Nostrand, 1976.
———. *Listening to America.* New York: Simon & Schuster, 1982.
Flexner, Stuart Berg, and Harold Wentworth. *The Dictionary of American Slang.* New York: Harper & Row, 1960.

FLYTING

This unfamiliar term denotes a swearing match or competition in insult, a form with a long tradition, being found in Old Norse and Anglo-Saxon literature, where the participants are both legendary and historical. This development is itself unusual, being the polar opposite of the reticence greatly valued in Germanic society. However, the genre became most highly developed in the Scottish court in the sixteenth century, remarkably among aristocrats and major poets. The most famous examples are *The Flyting of Dunbar and Kennedy* (ca. 1503), *The Flyting of Montgomerie and Polwart* (ca. 1585), and a similar contest between King James V and Sir David Lindsay (ca. 1537). Although forms of verbal dueling like "playing the dozens" and "sounding" among youths in the United States have some similar features, there are no modern equivalents showing the same individual and extended displays of verbal skill in the fine art of savage insult. (All the Scottish flyting matches are carried out in quite complex forms of alliteration.) The key similarity between the genres, however, is that language that would normally be taboo and extremely provocative does not lead to hostilities, but is tolerated in this particular conventional use.

The northern provenance of flyting is apparent in the Norse root *flyta,* which covered a variety of heroic "eggings" (or provocations) and scatological insults apparent in the sagas, notably in the skaldic tirades of the Icelander Egil Skallagrimsson in *Egil's Saga* (ca. 1200). Egil was a historical *skald,* or bard, whose extempore effusions were both verbally complex and savagely satirical. He showed total fearlessness in his flyting verses, to the point of grievously insulting Eric Bloodaxe, king of Norway (946–949) and his queen, Gunnhild. In his *nið* ("curse"), uttered in the king's presence, Egil calls him, "This inheriting traitor [who] disinherits me by betrayal" and later "Lawbreaker not lawmaker . . . brothers' murderer . . . [whose] guilt stems all from Gunnhild" (*Egil's Saga,* chapters 56–57). The king did not retaliate. (Incidentally, English *scold* is cognate with Old Norse *skald.*)

In the Eddic poems there are similar examples of calumny and slander in contests between Odin and Thor, and between Loki and the other gods. In his flyting with the gods (*Lokasenna*), Loki singles each out, stanza by stanza, accusing them of cowardice, adultery, incest, and homosexuality. As Einarsson points out, the most famous heroic instance of *mannjafnaðr,* or "man matching" is the verbal contest between the two royal brothers Sigurðr and Eysteinn, sons of King Magnus berfœttr ("barefooted") in Snorri Sturluson's *Heimskringla* (1957, 38–39). However, the context shows that this match is more of a performance put on by the brothers to entertain their retinues. Eysteinn explains: "It has often been an ale custom to match men against each other" (*Heimskringla* 1932, 624). Elsewhere in the comparatively uncensored provenance of Old Norse, there are far more survivals of set-piece insult than is the case in early English. Among them were the *flim* and the *niðvisur,* which specialized in the foulest infamy.

The cognate Anglo-Saxon term *flītan* had the broader sense of "contend or strive," though the meanings of "chide, wrangle, or scold" were also included. It is possible to see vestiges of flyting in the sharp exchanges in the Anglo-Saxon epic poem *Beowulf* between the hero and the enigmatic, provocative character Unferth, a person of undefined office who sits in a privileged position at the feet of the Scylding king, Hrothgar (ll. 499–661). This curious exchange has attracted a variety of modern interpretations, as a piece of flyting, an exchange of ritual insults between champions, a piece of fooling, or an elaborate exercise in irony. (See Short 1980.) Another instance lies in the insults traded by the Saxons and the Vikings before they join battle in *The Battle of Maldon* (11th century).

More developed examples are the medieval debate poems *The Owl and the Nightingale* (ca. 1250) and Chaucer's *Parlement of Foulys* (ca. 1382). The first is an anonymous text from which the more fulsomely vituperative sections were excised in the early editions. The poem uses two new phrases for "strong language," namely *fule worde* ("foul words") and the coarser *schit worde* ("shit words"), the latter in a context with an interesting class gloss: "So herdsmen offend others with shit words" (l. 286). Although the poem is sophisticated in many ways, dealing with a range of moral and religious issues in the manner of the medieval *débat,* or debate, it has a considerable scatological element.

Chaucer's *Parlement of Foulys* also has clear elements of flyting, although the poem belongs to another medieval genre, the love vision. Set on St. Valentine's Day, the love decision of the tercel eagles, the highest in rank, involves the whole avian parliament, provoking increasingly uncourtly, sharp, and impatient responses as the debate moves down the hierarchical scale. As in his delightful animal fable of Chantecleer and the Fox in the *Nun's Priest's Tale,* Chaucer makes considerable humorous capital by applying human idioms to the fowls:

"Wel bourded [joked]," quod the doke [duck], "by min hat!"
(l. 589)

The goos seyde, "Al this nys nat worth a flye!"
(l. 501)

As the tone descends, the tercelet intervenes to upbraid a low comment in these terms:

"Now fy, cherl!" ["Now shame on you, peasant!"]
"Out of the donghil cam that word ful right!"
["That word came straight out of the gutter!"]
(l. 596–97)

The juxtaposition of animal noises and human conventions is often sharp: "Now parde! fol!" (Now, by God, you idiot!") is followed by "Ye quek!" ("You quack!"). Most of the idiom of abuse is taken from secular references, but a tercel "of lower kynde [rank]" makes his declaration of love "by seint John" (l. 451). These stylistic differences are, assuredly, Chaucer's sociolinguistic observation on the oaths of his time.

In his edition of William Dunbar, W. Mackay Mackenzie included as traditional influences on flyting "the *agon* or 'altercation,' one of the essential elements of the Old Comedy of Greece," as well as parallels in Arabic, Italian, and Celtic (1932, xxxii). There were, however, various Continental antecedents, such as the Provençal *sirvente, tenso,* and *partimen,* as well as a tradition of Latin invective from St. Jerome through some of the fifteenth-century humanists to Erasmus. Mackenzie defined the genre in a vigorous metaphor as a "verbal tournament *a outrance"* [to the bitter end] (1932, xxxii), stressing that the roots of flyting lie in competition and in the demonstration of skill, not solely in personal execration.

Flyting can be called, paradoxically, "the fine art of savage insult," since the Scottish participants were noted authors and their works are neither repetitive, nor extemporaneous, nor crude. Indeed, James Kinsley surmises that the *Flyting* between Dunbar and Kennedy (which is over 550 lines long) "may have developed in a series of attacks and counter-attacks circulated in manuscript at court" (1979, 284). **Dunbar** (who has his own entry) was a Master of Arts, a Franciscan preaching friar, a priest in court service for a number of years, and the recipient of a royal pension from King James IV. Kennedy, who had similar academic qualifications, was greatly admired as a poet and was of the blood royal.

What makes the Scottish flytings the more striking is that they occur in a country with a vehement tradition against profanity. (Documentary evidence is to be found in the entry for **fines and penalties.**) However, these texts demonstrate an astonishing use of language so sophisticated and so foul that it clearly belongs to a convention of linguistic versatility quite unfamiliar to us, having been long obsolete. It was evidently designed as an entertainment for a sophisticated, not a "common" audience, as has also been argued for the *fabliau.* "Montgomerie and Polwart flyted one another in a variety of metres and forms which were designed to demonstrate their versatility to the court audience for whom the whole exercise was presumably staged" (Jack 1988, vol. I, 51).

In the *Flyting of Dunbar and Kennedy,* every conceivable insult is hurled: sexual, religious, natural, social, excretory (and many that baffle the imagination or amaze with their directness). Dunbar opens the altercation with some hyperbolic threats of how the sea would burn, the moon would suffer eclipse, and rocks would shatter, should he choose to "flyte." This provokes from Kennedy the immediate opening riposte "Dirtin [filthy] Dunbar," the first of an astonishing catalog, which includes "fantastick fule" (fool) and "wan fukkit funling" (ill-conceived foundling) (ll. 35–38). Dunbar replies in kind, using equally personal insults, such as:

Cuntbitten crawdon [pox-smitten coward]

Crawdon, an obsolete dialect term, contains a rich resonance of masculine contempt, since the sense of "coward" derives from a cock that will not fight. The remarkable adjective *cuntbitten* intensifies the insult by playing on the various meanings of *cock*. Less subtly, but succinctly, Kennedy calls Dunbar "a shit but wit" (l. 496) who would "like to throw shit by the cartload" (l. 469). (This is one of the earliest uses of *shit* as a personal insult.) He then launches a ferocious alliterative assault, using all the categories of abuse:

Deuill dampnit dog, sodomyte insatiable

. . .

Thy commissar Quintine biddis the cum kis his ers
[Your associate Quintin [a Scots poet] bids you come and kiss his arse]
(ll. 527–35)

This last line shows the astonishing range of register, since *commissar* is an ancient title of rank, implying that Quintin was a superior poet, while the vulgar phrase "to kiss someone's arse" obviously meant, as it still does, to be completely servile. (The Latin phrase *osculum in tergo* was often used of worship of the Devil; today a *kiss-arse* refers to a toadying underling.) The exchanges contain an amazing range of cultural reference and the earliest recorded instances of several current terms of insult, notably the noun *get* (now *git*) in its old, strong sense of "bastard": "Fals tratour, feyndis get" ("False traitor, devil's bastard," 244). In the equally scurrilous *The Flyting of Montgomerie and Polwart* (ca. 1585) there is the invitation to "kis the cunte of ane kow" (l. 817), while the *Answer to [the] King's Flyting* (l. 1535–36) contains the frenzied alliteration: "Ay fukkand [fucking] like ane furious Fornicatour" (l. 49).

In England the tradition of flyting had considerably atrophied by 1600. The most vigorous invective is to be found in the early Elizabethan stage farces, such as *Ralph Roister Doister* (ca. 1552) and *Gammer Gurton's Needle* (acted 1566). In the latter we find such new vituperative idioms as "What the devil," "how a murrain [plague]," "Fie shitten knave and out upon thee," "the pox," "bawdy bitch," "that dirty bastard," "the whoreson dolt [idiot]," "for God's sake," and "that dirty shitten lout."

There are also vestiges of flyting in some of the violent confrontations in Elizabethan tragedy, such as Hamlet's caustic repartee, the furious exchanges between Lear and Kent, and the berating of Oswald by Kent in *King Lear* (II ii 14–22). In all of these there is a savage irony and bitter humor. There are also features of flyting in the comic stichomythia of *The Taming of the Shrew* and *Much Ado About Nothing*. (*Stichomythia* is a highly formalized series of sharp exchanges in which two characters deliver one line at a time, rather like a rally in a tennis match.) The following is from the opening of hostilities between Petruchio and Katharina in *The Taming of the Shrew*:

Katharina: I knew you at the first,
       You were a moveable [piece of furniture]
Petruchio: Why, what's a moveable?
Katharina: A joint-stool.
Petruchio: Thou hast hit it. Come and sit on me.
Katharina: Asses are made to bear, and so are you.
Petruchio: Women are made to bear, and so are you.
(II i 197–201)

However, the great Shakespearean scenes of linguistic confrontation are essentially passionate expressions of character-conflict in which language is taken in deadly earnest, and lives are irrecoverably changed or even destroyed. Flyting, on the other hand, has an essential element of license, of wordplay, since otherwise the grievous insults would lead to duels and other extreme modes of exacting satisfaction. Flyting has died out in the United Kingdom. The main survivors of the genre are those forms of verbal dueling recorded among black youths in America and termed variously, "playing the dozens," "playing," and "sounding."

See also: Dozens, the; Dunbar, William; Lawsuits; Scold.

Bibliography

Chaucer, Geoffrey. *The Works of Chaucer,* ed. Larry D. Benson. Cambridge, MA: Houghton Mifflin, 1987.

Einarsson, Stefan. *The History of Icelandic Literature.* Baltimore: Johns Hopkins Press, 1957.

Jack, R.D.S., ed. *The History of Scottish Literature.* Aberdeen: Aberdeen University Press, 1988.

Kinsley, James, ed. *The Poems of William Dunbar.* Oxford: Oxford University Press, 1979.

Mackenzie, W. Mackay, ed. *The Poems of William Dunbar.* Edinburgh: Porpoise, 1932.

Short, Douglas D., ed. *Beowulf Scholarship: An Annotated Bibliography. Criticism.* New York: Garland, 1980.

Snorri Sturluson. *Heimskringla, or The Lives of the Norse Kings,* ed. E. Monsen. Cambridge, MA: W. Heffer & Sons, 1932.

FOLK ETYMOLOGY

Etymology is the study of the origins of words, a fascinating, complex, but often frustrating discipline. *Folk etymology* is the phenomenon whereby plausible but factually inaccurate explanations develop, often accompanied by a corroborating tall story. These colorful explanations result from various popular notions and expectations, namely that all words have specific origins and that these root meanings are the key to the words in question.

As their name implies, folk etymologies are collective and spontaneous. They commonly involve not only explanations of the origins of words but also alterations in the form of words to suggest their origin. In the process, the actual origin of the word is, ironically, obscured. Thus *cockroach* is a corruption of the original Spanish form *cucaracha,* and the entry for **women, stereotypes of** shows that the base word *woman* has generated several misogynist folk etymologies with word play on "woe." Two prime examples are **bloody,** popularly derived from the archaic phrase "by our lady!," and **crap,** ascribed to Dr. Thomas Crapper. Even lexicographers have occasionally blundered into folk etymology. Both Dr. Johnson (1755) and Francis Grose (1785) erroneously derived *nickname* from French *nom de nique.* Stuart Berg Flexner retails a fanciful derivation explaining the origin of *Honky* from white men honking the horns of their cars when picking up black girlfriends (1980, 58). Antony Burgess likewise ascribes *Old Nick,* the euphemism for the Devil, to Niccolò Machiavelli in a book on Shakespeare, although the title is recorded only from about 1643 (1972, 103).

Most people are especially curious about the origins of the "four-letter" words. Since most have problematic origins, they naturally attract folk etymologies. Two ingenious explanations of the origin of *fuck* claim that the term was originally an acronym, deriving from a royal edict issued during the Plague: "fornicate under command of the King," alternatively from a police formula, "for unlawful carnal knowledge." A moment's reflection will usually question such explanations. Why so natural a process as procreation should require a royal command, and why the injunction should be issued in such an arcane form, are only two of the more obvious objections. The notoriously decadent King Charles II (1661–1685) would more likely have echoed King Lear's lascivious edict: "Let copulation thrive!" (IV vi 117). Nor is there any obvious reason why the police should resort to such a coded reference. More significantly, both explanations come well after the first appearance of the word *fuck* (ca. 1503), and are thus anachronistic.

Wop, discussed under **Italians**, has a well-attested origin, but folk etymologies claim that the word is also an acronym, derived from an immigration category WithOut Passport or WithOut Papers. Irving Lewis Allen has pointed out two obvious logical objections to these etymologies: "First, all immigrants without documentation would have been nicknamed the same, but Italians were the only immigrant group in the 1890s and later who were called *wops.* Secondly, the nickname emerged in American slang . . . before acronyms came into wide use in government bureaucracies" (1983, 119). Nevertheless, such explanations typically retain credibility. In 1977 no fewer than 228 readers sent the "WithOut Papers" explanation to a syndicated columnist, Dr. Max Rafferty (Eisiminger 1978, 582). Clearly these folk etymologies serve to strengthen the negative stereotype of Italians being illegal immigrants, like the explicit term *wetback* for a Mexican.

Folk etymologies are remarkably tenacious and continue to thrive, defying logical or historical refutation. Thus the relationship between etymology and folk etymology is similar to that between astronomy and astrology: the first is a science often yielding complex results unsatisfying to human curiosity; the second is a pseudo-science fed by popular expectations and folklore. Astrology continues to thrive despite being discredited. The continuing phenomenon of folk etymology suggests that the speech community prefers attractive fiction to cold fact in etymology as in other areas.

See also: Bloody; Crap; Folk Etymology; Fuck.

Bibliography

Allen, Irving Lewis. *The Language of Ethnic Conflict*. New York: Columbia University Press, 1983.
Cochrane, James. *Stipple, Wink and Gusset*. London: Century, 1992.
Eisiminger, Sterling. "Acronyms and Folk Etymology." *Journal of American Folklore* 91 (1978).
Flexner, Stuart Berg. *I Hear America Talking*. New York: Van Nostrand Reinhold, 1976.
Quinian, Michael. *Port Out, Starboard Home and Other Language Myths*. London: Penguin, 2004.
Rawson, Hugh. *Devious Derivations*. New York: Crown, 1994.

**FOREIGNERS, *Terms for. See:* Ethnic Insults.

FORMAL OATHS

Today formal swearing is generally required of citizens only on special occasions, such as taking the oath in court or taking an oath of office. The form of words makes the point with simple clarity: "I swear by Almighty God that I shall tell the truth, the whole truth, and nothing but the truth." The tag phrase "So help me God" ("May God help me to do this") is generally optional. Marriage also involves making a formal pledge, although the archaic wording used in some services obscures the point. Thus "I plight thee my troth" means "I pledge my word of honor to you"; the root term of both *wedding* and *wedlock* is Anglo-Saxon *wedd,* meaning "a pledge."

In the past, when European society was more hierarchical, the bonds between master and subject were established by means of personal oaths of *allegiance,* the original meaning being "the tie or obligation of a subject to his lord or sovereign." The liege-lord provided protection, while the bond-man provided service. These oaths were the foundation of the powerful interpersonal relations in Anglo-Saxon society and later in the feudal system. A curious survival of this ritual occurred on July 1, 1969, when Prince Charles was invested with the title of Prince of Wales. During the ceremony he knelt before the queen and made his oath to her in this archaic wording: "I am your liege man in life and limb."

During the political and religious conflicts of the Reformation, all English citizens were required to make public oaths of allegiance to the monarch. However, these oaths were often framed in politico-religious terms deriving from crises of authority. In perhaps the most famous rejection of this requirement, Sir Thomas More, a devout Catholic, refused to take the oath endorsing the Act of Supremacy (1534) whereby Henry VIII proclaimed himself Supreme Head of the Church in England, thus supplanting the Pope. For his continued defiance More was accused of high treason and beheaded in 1535.

Despite increasing religious freedom, positions in the government and the universities in the United Kingdom remained dependent on applicants taking an oath specifying belief in certain tenets of the Christian faith. This requirement, formalized under the Test Act of 1673, effectively excluded Jews, Catholics, Methodists, and others from such positions. It gave a special and enduring meaning to the term *test,* meaning that the test of a person's loyalty or fidelity to the nation's religion lay in the oath. In the past the Oath of Allegiance was as much concerned with refuting the authority of the Pope and preventing assistance to foreign powers as it was with pledging loyalty to the monarch, reflecting the political and religious power struggles stemming from the Reformation.

Furthermore, a member of the British Parliament has traditionally been required to take the oath "on the true faith of a Christian." Members of other faiths in the past found themselves unable to take such an oath and were therefore barred from taking their seats. This led to concessions in the form of the Roman Catholic Relief Act (1829), the Quakers and Moravians Act (1833), the Jews Relief Act (1858), and the Parliamentary Oaths Act (1866), all of which reduced the direct religious content of the oath. Today the standard oath is: "I swear by Almighty God that I will be faithful and bear true allegiance to Her Majesty Queen Elizabeth, her heirs and successors, according to law. So help me God." The alternatives are "I swear that I will be faithful . . ." etc., or "I solemnly, sincerely and truly affirm . . ." etc.

There are still problems for members who question the authority of the monarch. One such, Mr. Tony Benn, prefaced the oath with these remarks "As a committed republican, under protest, I take the oath required of me by law." A deeper and unresolved crisis arose in 1997 when two elected members of Sinn Fein, the political arm of the Irish Republican Army, refused to take the oath and so were not allowed to take their seats. Appeals to higher courts failed.

From the beginning, America set out to be a society free of religious authority. Yet technically the Declaration of Independence (1776) is in the form of an oath by the signatories, since it ends with the words: "And for the support of this Declaration, with a firm reliance on the Protection of Divine Providence, we mutually pledge to each other our lives, our Fortunes and our sacred Honor." Significantly, the Declaration does not use the word "God" in the traditional fashion, preferring "Creator" at the outset and "Divine Providence" at the conclusion, although there is the curious phrase "Nature and Nature's God" near the beginning. Thus in the United States, formal oaths were and are completely secularized, omitting any reference to the Divine, as can be seen from the Presidential Oath of Office: "I do solemnly swear (or affirm) . . . etc." As Harold M. Hyman has observed in an analysis of the Oath of Office:

> Framers of the Federal Constitution of 1787 and members of the first Congress held under its provision decided that officeholders . . . should be bound neither by religious tests nor by elaborate loyalty oaths. Instead they believed that a simple oath of office was adequate.
> This decision ran counter to the practice of almost every other government in the world at the time.
> (1966, 432)

Furthermore, the Constitution of the United States (1789) derives its authority, not from any religious entity, but from the democratic formula "We the People." The First Amendment pointedly stipulates that "Congress shall make no law respecting an establishment of religion, or prohibiting the free exercise thereof," while Article VI specifies: "that the Senators and Representatives . . . shall be bound by an Oath or Affirmation, to support this constitution; but no religious Test shall ever be required as a qualification to any office."

However, as Hyman notes, the critical divisive pressures of the Civil War led to modifications of the wording, producing "the so-called 'iron-clad' test oath" of 1868, referring to "all enemies, foreign and domestic" and specifying that the oath is taken "freely, without any mental reservation or purpose of evasion" (1966, 434). The anxieties and paranoia of the Cold War also led to attempts to modify loyalty oaths in certain states. As Hyman concludes: "Our jurists have not yet found a clear formula by which government may secure itself against disloyalty, through oaths or otherwise, while simultaneously holding to the uncertain but inspiring set in the Bill of Rights" (1966, 436).

The Pledge of Allegiance, originally instituted in 1892, currently runs:

> I pledge allegiance to the Flag of the United States of America, and to the Republic for which it stands, one nation, under God, indivisible, with liberty and justice for all. (36 U.S.C. 172)

Since there is no verb governed by "pledge," as there is in most formal oaths, there is no strict grammatical or syntactical link between the first phrase and the section after "stands," even though it expresses important ideals. The words "under God" (an echo of Lincoln's Gettysburg Address) were not part of the original pledge, being added on June 14, 1954. Their function can be interpreted various ways, but their addition has occasioned a number of legal challenges, most recently *Newdow* v. *United States Congress 2002*.

The problem with any formal oath is the degree to which the oath taker regards it as binding on his or her conscience. In an increasingly secularized society with a generally cynical view of politics and the exercise of power, this "binding" quality is clearly not of the same order. It is further weakened in the case of an oath not taken voluntarily, but as a bureaucratic requirement. As George Washington poignantly asked in his Farewell Address in 1796: "Where is the security for property, for reputation, for life, if the sense of religious obligation *desert* the oaths which are the instruments of investigation in courts of justice?" (1966, 202).

Bibliography

Commager, Henry Steele. "Thomas Jefferson, Declaration of Independence, 1776." In *An American Primer,* ed. Daniel J. Boorstin, 65–75. Chicago: University of Chicago Press, 1966.

Hyman, Harold M. "The Oath of Office, 1868." In *An American Primer,* ed. Daniel J. Boorstin, 432–36. Chicago: University of Chicago Press, 1966.

Mellinkoff, David. *The Language of the Law.* Boston: Little, Brown, 1963.

"The Parliamentary Oath," House of Commons Research Paper 00/17, 14 February 2000.

Washington, George. "Farewell Address, 1796." In *An American Primer,* ed. Daniel J. Boorstin, 192–210. Chicago: University of Chicago Press, 1966.

FORMULAS IN SWEARING

Swearing appears to be fairly random in its makeup, especially in the semantic latitude and anomalous conjunctions of adjectives and nouns. However, there have developed over the centuries certain combinations of highly charged words that have common semantic, alliterative, rhyming, and rhythmic features. They have become established through traditional use as idioms, and are thus not readily accessible to logical explanation.

Some have grown up as units like *son of a bitch,* developing a great range of applications to both persons and situations. They can also be elaborated on, as in "son and heir of a mongrel bitch," by Shakespeare in *King Lear* (II ii 22). Others, like *goddam,* shift from their original semantic function to become general-purpose counters, as in "I don't give a goddam" to "I don't give a good goddam." These are more in the nature of clichés or fixed forms than formulas, which tend to be made up of certain common features and interchangeable elements. One typical arrangement, found in *you bloody bastard!* and *the stupid old fool!* comprises [article + adjective + noun] or [pronoun + adjective + noun]. **Alliteration** is the dominant feature in the first example, as it was in "I don't give a good gooddam." Other features are **rhyme** as in *Hell's bells!* and assonance, as in *Stone the crows!* and the archaic naval oath *Shiver me timbers!*

As is also typical in swearing formulas, there is no obvious semantic relationship between adjective and noun: Thus *bloody, fucking,* and other highly charged adjectives can be combined with a great variety of incongruous nouns, as in *bloody hell!* or with each other, as in *bloody fucking hell!* Although the choice of words appears to be random, the order is certainly not: *bloody* always comes first. Thus *fucking bloody hell!* is not idiomatic, any more than are such arrangements as *old bloody fool!* or *old stupid arsehole!* Furthermore, the use of *old* is typical in formulas, largely for rhythmic purposes, as a make-weight. Historically it first appears in the Wife of Bath castigating one of her husbands as "olde barelful of lyes" (*Prologue,* l. 302), and it continues to thrive in modern parlance in *he's an old rogue,* as opposed to *you old scoundrel,* which does not have to be age-specific. Also used in the same way is *little,* as in *dreadful little man* and *stupid little fool.*

Rhythm is an important aspect of formulas in swearing. There also seems to be an undoubted phonetic preference for words beginning with certain particular consonants, frequently combined by means of **alliteration**. This phonetic preference is in itself an indication that formulas are not random.

See also: Alliteration; Flexibility; Loss of Intensity; Rhyme; Rhythm.

Bibliography
Flexner, Stuart Berg. *I Hear America Talking.* New York: Van Nostrand Reinhold, 1976.
Hughes, Geoffrey. *Swearing.* Oxford: Blackwell, 1991; Harmondsworth: Penguin, 1998.

FORSWEARING

This term, now obsolescent, means variously swearing falsely, breaking one's oath, or going back on one's word, meanings essentially taken over by *perjury.* In earlier times when personal relations often took the form of an oath, to be *forsworn* was a great social stigma. The Laws of the Anglo-Saxon king Ecgbert (ca. 1000) specified that a layman who forswore should be imprisoned for four years (II § 24). A number of proverbs reinforced the ethic: "Forsworn man shal neuer spede!" ("A person who is forsworn will never prosper") from about 1330 and the similar sentiment: "Once forsworne ever forlorne," from 1619.

However, from the eighteenth century onward the term was used in an increasingly trivial fashion, meaning generally to abandon, renounce, or simply give up something. Thus a character in Sheridan's classic play *The Rivals* (1775) announces: "I will forswear your company" (II i), while another in Benjamin Disraeli's novel *Vivian Grey* (1826) is almost ironic: "I forswore, with the most solemn oath, the gaming [gambling] table" (V xiii). The decline in the strength of the meaning is a direct reflection of the diminishing importance attached to oaths.

See also: Abjuration.

FOUL LANGUAGE

"Foul language" is a broad category combining and involving such diverse offensive elements as "dirt," **shit words, obscenity,** and **pornography,** of which the last three have their own entries. The use of terms like *foul, filth, dirt,* and *dirty* to categorize offensive or abusive language is profound and ancient. Anglo-Saxon *ful* ("foul") was used to gloss "obscene" as well as "dirty." "Shit worde," dating from 1250, is historically the earliest categorization of coarse speech, followed by "foul speech," recorded from about 1455. Shakespeare is the first author to use the modern compound *foul mouthed* in 1597 when Mistress Quickly condemns Falstaff for being "a foul mouth'd man as he is" (*Henry IV, Part I,* III iii l.122).

Other meanings attaching to *filthy* were "morally or spiritually unclean" and "lascivious," thus yielding expressions as diverse as the medieval formulation "the foul fiend" for the devil and the modern "filthy book" with its "dirty bits." The puritanical view that sexuality should be regarded as "foul," even evil, is an extreme Manichean idea expressed, for example, by King Lear, albeit in a deranged state:

But to the girdle do the gods inherit,
Beneath is all the fiend's.
(IV vi 129–30)

The discussion of the play in the entry for **Shakespeare** considers these notions in more detail. The same connection appears in foul play, originally meaning a criminal offense before it became merely sporting.

Dirt originally meant "ordure," before acquiring the modern sense of "soil," which also previously had the sense of "ordure," specifically in the euphemistic phrase night soil, for the contents of chamber pots. Much of the legal debate concerning obscenity and pornography has focused on the phrase "dirt for dirt's sake," meaning, in effect, sex for sex's sake. The entry for **Lady Chatterley's Lover** contains a number of prime instances of the marked correlation between explicit sexuality and "filth," both in the American judgment and the original hostile critical dismissals of the work as "the fetid masterpiece of this sex-sodden genius," "the abysm of filth," and "the foulest book in English literature." Many of the problems in defining obscenity and pornography derive from the vagueness of the terms themselves and the breadth of foul and dirty.

See also: Lady Chatterley's Lover; Obscenity; Pornography; Shit Words.

"FOUR-LETTER" WORDS

Obscene or offensive language is usually (but not always) unacceptable in "polite society," and therefore decorum requires some euphemistic manner of referring to obscenities indirectly. The continuing need for such euphemisms is shown in such earlier indirect references to foul language as **cherles termes** from medieval times and **Billingsgate** from the seventeenth century. Since in English it coincidentally happens that virtually all the words in question consist of four letters, the euphemistic phrase "four-letter words" has come into being.

The first instance of the phrase is comparatively recent, in 1934 in Allen Walker Read's pioneering article, "An Obscenity Symbol," in *American Speech:* "The obscene 'four-letter words' of the English language are not cant or slang or dialect, but belong to the oldest and best established element of the English vocabulary" (IX, 264). "For most people," he continued, "the bare word forms of these four-letter words have become sexual fetishes" (IX, 267). However, the phrase curiously escaped capture by the *OED Supplement* of 1972 and, even more remarkably, by the *Random House Historical Dictionary of the American Language* (1994). There is a variant usage whereby one can refer to someone as "a four-letter man," but this is a conflation with *letterman,* originally referring (from the 1920s) to a student who has received a letter of acceptance from a university and is regarded as obnoxious. The alternative explanation is that it comes from one who has earned a varsity "letter" in high school or college athletics. Although the phrase "four-letter words" is often used as an alternative to "**Anglo-**

Saxon," this equivalence is based on a popular misconception, since only about half of the "four-letter" words actually derive from Anglo-Saxon. Other polite but knowing evasions are covered in the entry for **fuck.**

See also: Anglo-Saxon Terms; Billingsgate; Cherles Termes; Euphemisms; French, the; Fuck.

Bibliography
Read, Allen Walker. "An Obscenity Symbol." *American Speech* IX, 1934.

FRENCH, THE

Xenophobic attitudes tend to focus on nations that are military or financial rivals and that have geographical proximity and pose a threat, real or imagined, to the "host" nation. The most typical manifestations are *blasons populaires,* or negative stereotypes, and demeaning nicknames, which commonly turn into ethnic insults over time.

Of England's European neighbors, France has had the longest and most problematic relationship. Although the Norman Conquest united England with the northern French kingdom of Normandy, the prolonged hostilities of the Hundred Years' War (1338–1453) did not lead to a rapprochement. Military rivalry continued in the periods of Louis XIV and the Napoleonic era. On the other hand, the relationship between the United States and France was quite different, both countries sharing the same democratic and libertarian ideals. The French naturally supported the American Revolution and established cordial relations with the new American Republic, which the English government regarded as rebellious.

The *blasons populaires* for the French focus on sordid or dishonest practices, mainly associated with sex. Commenting on the stereotype in 1816, an American writer, James Kirke Paulding, observed: "In plays, poems, romances, the Frenchman was almost always a swindler, a coward, a braggadocio [boaster], or a frog-eater" (I, 183). The standard representation of the Frenchman in British cartoons of the nineteenth century was of an effete but ostentatiously dressed figure, pointedly contrasted with the robust, blunt, and plainly dressed farmerlike figure of John Bull, the stereotype created by John Arbuthnot in 1712.

Earliest in the semantic field are the terms for venereal disease although, as the entry for **syphilis** shows, the disease did not actually start in France. Nevertheless, the stereotypic association generated *French pox* (1503), followed by *French marbles* (1592), *the French disease* (1598), *French measles* (1612), *French aches* (1664), *French goods* (1678), *French complement* (1668), and *French gout* (ca. 1700). Also early was *Pedlars' French* for "cant" or underground criminal slang, recorded from 1566 and widely used for about a century. Later came *French leave,* recorded from 1771, noted by Francis Grose in his *Classical Dictionary of the Vulgar Tongue* (1785) to refer to those escaping from their creditors. It was returned with compliments by the French in the phrase *filer à l'anglaise,* meaning to abandon a project without permission.

All of these instances were included in the *Oxford English Dictionary,* which drew the line at recording what were regarded as the more sordid details of sexual behavior. A private letter to the editor by James Dixon, a voluntary reader (December 6, 1888) generalizes: "Everything obscene comes from France," then discusses the presumed French origins of "an article called a Cundum . . . supposing that it will be too utterly obscene for the Dictionary"

The association of the French people with frogs appears to date to the aftermath of the French Revolution. In this 1799 cartoon by an English artist, Napoleon—depicted as a crocodile after his return from Egypt—dissolves the Council of Frogs in his coup d'etat of that year. (The Art Archive)

(Murray 1977, 195). In *Slang and Its Analogues* (1890–1904) Farmer and Henley defined *French vice* as "A euphemism for all sexual malpractices" but dealt fairly thoroughly with this material. Thus *French letter* is recorded from about 1856 for a condom, but is similarly returned as *capote anglaise*. Similar associations are found in *French prints*, a euphemism for pornographic pictures, recorded from about 1842, and "excuse my French," an ironic exculpation for expressing a vulgar or obscene term or phrase, from about 1865. In American slang many of these idioms are reduced to the simple omnibus term *French*, in forms like "to be *on French* [leave]," "to *speak French*," or to *Frenchy* (to practice oral sex) and *French deck* (erotic playing cards).

Although *frog* is the nickname with the longest association with the French, the earliest meaning, "a vile or contemptible person" is recorded from the fourteenth century, and the first xenophobic references are to the Jesuits ("these infernall frogs") in 1626 and to the Dutch in 1652. Fanny Burney's novel *Evelina* (1778) has the modern use: "Hark you Mrs. Frog . . . you may lie in the mud till some of your Monsieurs come to help you out of it." (Dr. Johnson defined *Monsieur* in 1755 as "a term of reproach for a Frenchman.") Although a number of reference works, such as *Random House* (1994) associate the word with the French habit of eating frogs' legs, the first recorded explicit reference "frog eating sons of Bitches" is in 1809 (W. Wheeler, *Letters,* 31). Crockett's *Almanack* (1838) provides the first American allusion to the Anglo-French rivalry: "Then down comes Mr. Frog again on John Bull" (28). An apposite comment in the *American Journal of Sociology* (1951) notes that in World War II "many Americans formed the habit of calling all British 'goddam Limies' and all French 'dirty Frogs'" (LI, 436). The related term *crapeau,* derived from *crapaud,* the French word for a toad, is recorded from 1803.

Although *frog* continues to be current as the principal nickname for the French in the global varieties of English, it does not have the animus of previous times. In South African English it is comparatively rare, while in Australian English the term shows the sexual association in the sense of a condom, recorded from the 1950s.

See also: Blason Populaire; Ethnic Insults; Syphilis.

Bibliography

Allen, Irving Lewis. *The Language of Ethnic Conflict.* New York: Columbia University Press, 1983.
Lighter, J.S., ed. *Random House Historical Dictionary of American Slang.* New York: Random House, 1994.
Murray, K.M. Elisabeth. *Caught in the Web of Words: James A.H. Murray and the Oxford English Dictionary.* New Haven: Yale University Press, 1977.

FRIG, FRIGGING

Frig is an excellent example of the **instability of swearing terms**, since in the four centuries of its semantic history the verb has meant, variously and simultaneously, to rub or chafe, to masturbate, to copulate, and to waste time in pointless activity. The participial form *frigging* has become a general-purpose adjective expressing annoyance or frustration, often used as a euphemism for *fucking,* since the original sexual sense is now virtually obsolete. There are various reasons for this imprecision. First, the principal original activities, namely masturbation and copulation, have been surrounded by strenuous taboos, which have the effect of drawing quasi-euphemistic terms into the field. Second, the term's original meanings were not directly sexual but acquired by implication. Third, in common with other powerfully taboo terms, *frig* and *frigging* have undergone **loss of intensity** in modern times, as the original sexual meanings have receded.

The first written example, from John Skelton (1529), refers to a boar in the old sense of "to rub": "his rumpe . . . he frygges Agaynst the hye benche" (*E. Rummynge,* l. 178). The entry in John Florio's *Worlde of Words* (1598) is usually taken to be sexual, although his translation of Italian *fricciare* is simply "to frig, to wriggle, to tickle." The explicit sexual sense surfaces in the **Restoration**, especially in the **Earl of Rochester** (1647–1680), who uses it in an ironic prophecy of a Utopian time when

> Cowards shall forget to rant,
> School-Boyes to Frigg, old whores to paint.
> ("A Ramble in Saint James's Parke," ll. 143–44)

More remarkable is the riotous quotation from Ashbee ca. 1684: "All the rest pull out their dildoes and frigg in point of honour" (*Bibliography* II, 333). A presumably ironic *Indictment of J. Marshall for the Public School of Love* (1707) runs: "My lovely Phil. is . . . so well versed in the various manners of fucking and frigging." In his *Classical Dictionary of the Vulgar Tongue* (1796), Grose gave a typically judgmental definition: "To be guilty of the crime of self-pollution." The copulatory sense is first recorded as far back as ca. 1610, thus overlapping with the masturbatory sense for centuries. Although there are written instances up to modern times, *Random House* (1994) notes, "as early as ca.1650 the word seems to have been regarded as coarse and to be avoided." The expletive sense is entirely modern, the first clear instance being in James T. Farrell's novel *Judgment Day* (1935): "Phrigg you, Catherine!" (The classical misspelling suggests that the author had not seen the word.) A pseudonymous "Justinian" in a work called *America Sexualis* (1938) gave both definitions: "to copulate with . . . Often used as a euphemistic expletive for the phrase 'Fuck it!'"

Francis Grose (1785) was the first to record the dominant modern sense, noting that "Frigging is also used figuratively for trifling." The "verbicidal" use, with reduced force as a mere intensifier, is first recorded by Farmer and Henley in their *Slang and Its Analogues* (1890–1893) with the examples "*frigging bad*—'bloody' bad; *a frigging idiot*—an absolute fool." This source suggests that the meaning must have been current for some time. This sense is now largely confined to the United States.

Among the other global varieties of English, *frig* is common in South African English, mainly in the sense of "to frig about." It is uncommon in Australian English: Hornage included the sense "tired, worn out" in his glossary, but it is unrecorded in *The Australian National Dictionary* (1988).

See also: Instability of Swearing Terms.

Bibliography

Hornadge, Bill. *The Australian Slanguage*. North Ryde: Cassell, 1980.
Lighter, J.S., ed. *Random House Historical Dictionary of American Slang*. New York: Random House, 1994.
Rochester, Earl of. *Rochester, Poems*, ed. Keith Walker. Oxford: Blackwell, 1984.

FUCK

The most powerfully taboo term for copulation over several centuries, *fuck* is still regarded as unmentionable by the vast majority of middle-class people. It was unlisted in standard dictionaries from 1728 until 1965, being therefore omitted by Dr. Johnson (1755), by the monumental *Oxford English Dictionary* in 1898, and even by *Webster III* in 1961. The simple appearance of the word was for many decades regarded as grounds for obscenity or pornography, an assumption not properly challenged in the courts until 1959 in the United States and 1960 in Britain. The *Supplement* to the *OED* (1972), it carried the following usage note: "For centuries, and still by the great majority, regarded as a taboo-word; until recent times not often recorded in print but frequent in coarse speech." The *Random House Historical Dictionary of American Slang* (1994) has a broader and more concessive note: "usually considered vulgar," the dictionary's standard designation for a great variety of vulgar, obscene, and profane language. *Fuck* has generated a great number of meanings, compounds, idioms, and tones.

The history of the word is full of surprises. Contrary to popular misconception, *fuck* is not an Anglo-Saxon term, the first recorded instance being only in 1503. This lateness might suggest a lexical gap, but in fact two ancient terms, *sard* and *swive,* now both obsolete, did service in Anglo-Saxon and medieval times. These and other synonyms are covered fully in the entry for **copulation**. However, John Ayto notes that the personal name *John le Fucker* is recorded from 1278 (1991, 242).

The ulterior etymology of the term is uncertain, a surprising fact considering the relative modernity of the word. Etymologists have long puzzled over the relationship between *fuck* and its Continental semantic partners, French *foutre,* recorded from the twelfth century, and German *ficken,* meaning "to strike." There are problems with both phonetic and semantic links. Eric Partridge, in his etymological dictionary *Origins* (1977), stressed the link between Latin *futuere* (the root of French *foutre*) and Latin *battuere,* "to strike." These connections invoke the slang metaphorical terms for sexual intercourse in terms of aggression, namely *knock, bang,* and the recently fashionable British *bonk.* (The relevant metaphors for "penis" are also suggestive: *tool, prick, chopper,* and *weapon,* a basic term in Anglo-Saxon.) Another potentially germane root, not usually canvassed in standard works, lies in Old Norse *fukja,* "to drive," which generates the forms *windfucker* (an alternative to *windhover*) and Scots *fucksail,* "a foresail." According to William Craigie in *A Dictionary of the Older Scottish Tongue* (1931–), *fucksail* acquired the transferred sense of "a woman's skirt" and was also reduced to plain *fuck.* The link between Old Norse *fukja* and the earliest forms such as Scots *fuk* still remains metaphorical. *Random House* (1994) follows this Scandinavian connection very plausibly, categorizing the word as "an English reflex of a widespread Germanic form." It cites as cognates Middle Dutch *fokken,* "to thrust, copulate with," a Norwegian dialect form *fukka,* "to copulate," and Swedish *focka,* "to strike, push, copulate."

More unexpectedly, *fuck* first appears, not as part of the language of the gutter, but in a noble context, in the work of major Scots poets and aristocrats. William Dunbar has the first recorded instance, dated 1503: "he wald have fukkit" (*Poems,* lxxv 13), while the noted Scots satirist Sir David Lindsay commented scathingly in 1535 on the hypocrisy of the clergy: "Bischops . . . may fuck their fill and be vnmarryit" (*Satire of the Three Estates,* l. 1363).

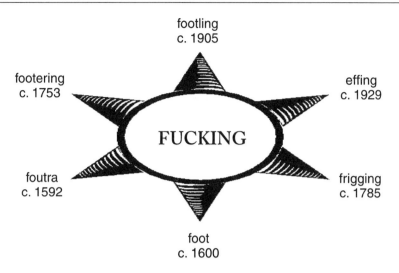

footling
c. 1905

footering
c. 1753

effing
c. 1929

FUCKING

foutra
c. 1592

frigging
c. 1785

foot
c. 1600

The dynamic between a taboo term and related euphemisms

Another early instance is, amazingly, in a swearing match, or *flyting*, in this case Lindsay's *Flyting with King James* (ca. 1540), which contains this piece of riotous alliteration: "Aye fukkand [fucking] lyke ane furious fornicatour." In another flyting match between two major poets, Sir Walter Kennedy dismisses William Dunbar as a "wan fukkit funling" ("an ill-conceived foundling") (l. 39). **Flyting** is an archaic term referring to a verbal contest of insult and obscenity. As these and other instances suggest, the term was initially more widely used in the North, a tradition continued by Robert Burns in his *Merry Muses* (ca. 1800):

When maukin bucks, at early f—ks,
In dewy glens are seen, sir.
(ll. 67–68)

There were in the past a number of cognate terms, such as *fuckable, fuckish,* and *fuckster* (a good performer), in addition to the surviving *fucking* and *fucker.* This proliferation suggests a vigorous, albeit scandalous, currency.

In England, it took some time for *fuck* to be recorded. Unexpectedly, the word did not appear in any of the "canting" dictionaries recording the argot of the underworld from the late sixteenth century, first emerging in John Florio's comprehensive English/Italian dictionary, *A Worlde of Wordes* (1598). Translating the relevant Italian verb, Florio ran through the whole gamut of available English synonyms with Renaissance exuberance:

Fottere: To iape [jape], to sard, to fucke, to swive, to occupy.

We notice that out of this extensive word field, only one term has survived into Modern English in the copulatory sense. There is no usage note suggesting that any of the words

189

was taboo. However *fuck* does not appear in the major literature of the times (see, however, E. Wilson's article, 1993, 29–34). The natural explanation is that bilingual dictionaries had greater freedom than their "native" equivalents. Thus Randle Cotgrave's contemporary *Dictionarie of the French and English Tongues* (1611) uses a fair amount of coarse language. As one might expect of a dramatist subject to certain constraints, **Shakespeare** avoids direct use of the term, preferring euphemistic forms from various other languages, such as *foutra,* a variant of French *foutre* (*Henry IV, Part II,* V ii 98). Likewise in *The Merry Wives of Windsor* (1597), there is a pun about "the focative case" (IV i 53). These would obviously be risqué in-jokes.

During the **Restoration**, a period of decadence reacting to the Puritan Commonwealth, the taboo was jauntily violated by such outrageous poets as the Earl of Rochester (1647–1680), who begins his deceptively titled poem "A Ramble in Saint James's Park" in this fashion:

Much wine had past with grave discourse
Of who fucks who and who does worse.

The Prologue to Rochester's attributed play *Sodom* is spoken by a character called Fuckadilla, who announces that "A little fuck can't stay our appetite" (l. 19). Four-letter words also abounded in contemporary poems by various upper-class figures, partly as displays of aristocratic insouciance. Thus "A Letter from the Lord Buckhurst to Mr. George Etherege" opens an exchange of letter-poems about the various women they had shared:

Dreaming last night on Mrs. Farley [a noted actress]
My prick was up this morning early.

Etherege responds:

For by a gentler way I found
The nymph would fuck under ten pound.
(ll. 43–44)

These were, of course, matters of individual taste as well as class. Whereas Rochester and his set flaunt the word, Samuel Pepys (1633–1703), avoids it, preferring French euphemisms, even in the private record of his *Diary,* written in his own shorthand code.

The taboo became more entrenched in the eighteenth and nineteenth centuries, when dictionary policies were understandably reticent: Nathaniel Bailey (1728) printed the full form, oddly giving a Latin definition, *feminam subagitare*; Dr. Johnson (1755) omitted it; and Francis Grose (1785) minced it to *f—k,* a convention that was to become virtually standard in subsequent centuries as the word went underground. The *OED* also famously omitted the term, and even in a private letter of 1869, Dante Gabriel Rosetti wrote: "If Byron f——d his sister, he f——d his sister and there an end."

Of course, it is extremely unlikely that *fuck* was unheard in the streets, taverns, and brothels from the eighteenth century onward, possibly being used by even the best mannered citizens. But it virtually disappeared from the public page. A typical example of the double standard between the public persona and the private person lies in two anecdotes covered in the entry for **Dr. Samuel Johnson** (1709–1784). These show that Johnson used the word in company, but omitted all vulgar sexual terms in his *Dictionary* (1755), a model of decorum.

From 1857 the word fell under the category of "obscene libel," which meant that a publisher could be prosecuted for printing it. Sir James Murray, the broad-minded editor of the monumental *Oxford English Dictionary* (1884–1928), fastidiously recorded a huge range of the vulgar and obscene terms, but drew the line at *fuck* and *cunt*. These topics are discussed in more detail in the entries for **Oxford English Dictionary** and the major contemporaries, **John S. Farmer and William E. Henley**, who included an astonishing thesaurus of over six hundred synonyms. Their compendium shows that obscenity and profanity were thriving behind the Victorian facade of respectability.

The ensuing spirit of censorship, prudishness, and **Comstockery**, as well as stringent laws against obscenity, ensured that *fuck* remained taboo for decades on both sides of the Atlantic. It first reappeared lexicographically in the United Kingdom in the *Penguin English Dictionary* in 1965. Naturally, the omissions from the original *OED* were made good in the first volume of the *Supplement* (1972). Having understandably been excluded in the earlier American dictionaries, notably those of **Webster** (1806 and 1828), *fuck* remained unlisted in the United States, even being omitted from the Third Edition of *Webster* (1961). This despite the pioneering article, "An Obscenity Symbol" by Allen Walker Read in *American Speech,* December 1934. It was eventually included in Stuart Berg Flexner's *I Hear America Talking* (1976) and *The New Dictionary of American Slang* (1986) but did not find a place in the *Barnhart Dictionary of Etymology* (1988). However, the *Random House Historical Dictionary of American Slang* (ed. Jonathan Lighter, 1994–) provided truly comprehensive treatment.

The wording of the Obscene Publications Act (1857) upheld a traditional notion of obscenity as being "of a nature calculated to shock the common feelings of decency in a well-regulated mind." Although the test for obscenity from 1868 focused on "the tendency of the matter . . . to deprave or corrupt" rather than on the language *per se,* the mere existence of "four-letter" words clearly influenced decisions. The entries for **censorship** and **obscenity** deal more fully with these and the more notable trials on the grounds of obscenity, while that for **Lady Chatterley's Lover** covers the novel and the celebrated lawsuit of 1960 (*Regina* v. *Penguin Books*).

The victory of the publishers in the lawsuit led to a radical increase in publications in the United Kingdom with obviously pornographic titles such as *Screw, Orgy, Pleasure, Suck,* and *Cunts and Grunts.* However, in 1965, **Kenneth Tynan**, the noted theater critic and producer, provoked a scandal through the first broadcast utterance of *fuck* on B.B.C. television. Yet Tynan's comments were tame compared with some of the slogans in violent protests in the United States against the Vietnam War. The most notorious of these were "Fuck the Draft" and "Fuck the Pigs." Commenting on the new vocabulary of protest in an article entitled "The Rhetoric of Violence" in 1970, E. Goodhart observed "The operative words are 'pig,' 'bullshit,' 'motherfucker.' It is the language of left militant students . . . the 'alma-mater fuckers'" (399).

In common with many powerful terms of abuse, *fuck* has developed a great range of grammatical functions and tones. Among them are *fuck all, fuck about, fuck it! fuck off,* and such phrases as *fuck a duck!, fuck you Jack, I'm all right, I'm fucked if I know, fuck that for a lark!,* and *go fuck yourself.* Most of these idioms are comparatively recent in the great time span of the language, although *Fuck you!* is dated ca. 1895, *Fuck you Jack, I'm all right,* ca. 1915, and *fuck a duck!,* ca. 1934. The last expression was possibly more literal: Grose (1785) has the humorous entry: "*Duck f-ck-r,* The man who has care of the poultry upon a ship of war." The surrealistic *flying fuck* dates from James Jones's war classic *From Here to Eternity* (1946). Another typical feature is the infixing of the term into other words like *unfuckingbelievable* and phrases such as *get the fuck out,* a process noted in Sagarin (1962, 148). American usage uniquely includes the insulting use as a noun, as in "You blooming fuck!" recorded from ca. 1927, but current only in recent decades. Jonathon Green's *The Slang Thesaurus* (1999) lists forty-three different forms and idioms. A veritable thesaurus of usage is recorded in Jesse Sheidlower's coyly titled study, *The F-Word* (1995), in which, according to the blurb, "every sense of the word f#@k is examined in detail."

Among the multitudinous euphemisms are French *foutra* (ca. 1592), *fut* (ca. 1605), *foot* (ca. 1735), *footering* (ca. 1735), *frigging* (ca. 1785), *footling* (ca. 1905), *effing* (ca. 1929), and *fugging* (coined by Norman Mailer in *The Naked and the Dead* (1947, 10), still mainly confined to American usage. This historical sequence, set out in the accompanying figure, shows the continuing need for new euphemisms, as the more remote forms are no longer generally recognized as related to the core term. (*Frig* carries in British slang the sense of "masturbate.") Various polite but knowing euphemisms exist in formulas in British English. These include "the f-word," "to eff off," and "effing," first recorded in Robert Graves's reminiscences of World War I, *Goodbye to All That:* "(The bandmaster, who was squeamish, reported it as: 'Sir, he called me a double effing c——)" (1929, 70). This instance provides a clear verification of the time gap between actual and recorded use. Although *eff* is generally regarded as British, Ernest Hemingway is accorded the first use in *Across the River and Into the Trees* (1950): "'Eff Florence,' the colonel said" (98). In the phrase "effing and blinding," *blinding* is a less obvious reference to *bloody,* also found in usages like "He didn't take a blind bit of notice."

Although still widely considered taboo and marked as such in most dictionaries, the actual currency of *fuck* is steadily encroaching on areas of polite discourse. Naturally, there is still a great variation of individual tolerance and diversity of use. Alan Clark, minister of trade in Margaret Thatcher's last cabinet, recorded in his devastatingly frank *Diaries* his final meeting with the prime minister, a highly decorous personage, just prior to her resignation. When Thatcher mentions the possibility of Michael Portillo as her successor, Clark snaps back: "Who the fuck's Michael? No one. Nothing. He won't last six months" (1993, 366). Clark's diaries record many similar idioms and a great variety of coarse language used in the presence of important political figures, without demur or rebuke. The wider aspect is simply shown in the recent French characterization of the English as *les fuckoffs,* on account of their copious use of the phrase. The clothing retailer French Connection gained considerable publicity by styling itself FCUK in Britain about 1994.

The most obvious global influence accelerating the acceptability of the term has been **popular**

culture, especially in film and television. **Hollywood**, initially an influence for restraint, has become one for license. Under the Production Code of 1930, "pointed profanity or vulgar expressions, however used [were] forbidden." The Code was revised in the course of the 1960s, so that a number of Vietnam War films, such as *Apocalypse Now!* (1980), *Platoon* (1987), and *Full Metal Jacket* (1988), subjected the audience to a veritable verbal bombardment of obscenity. Similar in style were such significant works as *The Commitments* (1991), *Trainspotting* (1996), *Kids* (1997), and most of the films of Spike Lee, notably *Do the Right Thing* (1989). Publicity material for Quentin Tarantino's *Pulp Fiction* (1994), winner of the Palme d'Or at the Cannes Film Festival and a Golden Globe Award for the Best Screenplay, claims with a mixture of coyness and pride, that "the f-word is used 271 times." In several of these instances the content and the milieu concern the gangster underworld or the military, both notorious for swearing and profanity. However, some works showing a similar proliferation have quite different content and questionable qualifications for the category of "popular culture." Thus David Mamet's play *Glengarry Glen Ross* (1983), set in a real estate office, was suffused with copulatory idioms, as was Mark Ravenhill's directly titled *Shopping and Fucking* (1996).

Within the realm of poetry, Philip Larkin, a reclusive librarian at Hull University suggested as the successor to Ted Hughes as Poet Laureate, caused a minor sensation with his poems using demotic language, notably "This Be the Verse" (1971), which opens with this "Freudian" insight into family relationships:

They fuck you up, your mum and dad.
They may not mean to, but they do.

Fiona Pitt-Kethley's collections, notably *Sky Ray Lolly* (1986), uses similarly earthy language. Recent fiction has produced many works in the same vein, among them Erica Jong's *Fear of Flying* (1973), Martin Amis's *Success* (1985), and James Kelman's *How Late it Was, How Late* (1994). This book's principal lexical feature is the astonishingly concentrated use of the word *fuck* and other four-letter words (up to a dozen times per page): "Fucking bunk man it was fucking hollow, he was lying on the fucking bare spring and it was killing him man his fucking shoulder, jesus christ; he turned on to his front" (1994, 29). (The "decapitalization" of Jesus Christ is a more provocative eccentricity.) The novel won the prestigious British Booker Prize in 1994, but only after a division in the jury and a critical furor. A less acrimonious controversy surrounded the copious use of *fucken* in the Booker Prize–winner for 2003, D.B.C. Pierre's *Vernon God Little*. Organs of "quality journalism" have not been left behind. The Anniversary Issue of the prestigious *New Yorker* magazine (February 19 and 26, 2001) carried an article "Fast Woman," by Susan Orlean about Jean Jennings, a high-speed driver, who complains about a slow-moving truck: "Un-fucking-believable" (152). Such copy would not have been countenanced in earlier decades, let alone a century ago.

Other global varieties of English have tended to be less persistent and exploratory in their use of the term. In South African English *fuck* is still generally regarded as taboo and is seldom printed, uttered in public, or broadcast. However, it has a fairly vigorous demotic usage, particularly among second-language speakers, for whom the taboo is less real. The phonetic proximity of the Afrikaans cognates *fok, fokken,* and *fok-al* supplies a common euphemistic outlet. Australian English, notable for its colorful and vigorous slang, is oddly reticent over the use of the term, generally preferring the euphemisms, *the naughty* and *to do the naughty*. However, it includes *fuckwit* for an idiot, the ironic *fucktruck* for "a panel van, especially one fitted with a mattress," and the spoonerism "No wucking furries."

The entry for **copulation** deals with the related word field. The use of *fuck* and its variant forms as swearwords and terms of abuse is relatively recent, dating from the early decades of the twentieth century. Overall, the term has developed from being powerfully taboo to a split status, still shocking to many, but nevertheless increasingly current. In its grading of word frequency, the *Longman Dictionary of Contemporary English* (1995) listed *fucking* in the top 1,000 most spoken words and *fuck* in the top 3,000 most spoken. Timothy Jay's studies into the language of college students similarly showed a high level of taboo and of frequency (1992, 143–57). As is typical of swearwords, increased currency has led to the semantic trend of **loss of intensity**.

See also: Comstockery; Copulation; Farmer, John S., and William E. Henley; Johnson, Dr. Samuel; *Lady Chatterley's Lover; Oxford English Dictionary;* Tynan, Kenneth.

Bibliography

Ayto, John. *Bloomsbury Dictionary of Word Origins.* London: Bloomsbury, 1991.
Burchfield, Robert. "Four-Letter Words and the *OED*." *Times Literary Supplement,* October 13, 1972.
———. "An Outline History of Euphemisms in Old English." In *Fair of Speech,* ed. D.J. Enright. Oxford: Oxford University Press, 1986.
Chapman, Robert L. *New Dictionary of American Slang.* New York: Harper & Row, 1986.
Clark, Alan. *Diaries.* London: Phoenix, 1993.
Farmer, J.S., and W.E. Henley. *Slang and Its Analogues.* London: Routledge and Kegan Paul, 1890–1904. Reprint, Oxford: Wordsworth Press, 1987.
Flexner, Stuart Berg. *I Hear America Talking.* New York: Van Nostrand Reinhold, 1976.
Goodhart, E. "The Rhetoric of Violence." *The Nation,* April 6, 1970.
Green, Jonathon. *The Slang Thesaurus.* Harmondsworth: Penguin, 1988.
Grose, Francis. *A Classical Dictionary of the Vulgar Tongue.* London: S. Hooper, 1785.
Hughes, Geoffrey. *Swearing.* Oxford: Blackwell, 1991; Harmondsworth: Penguin, 1998.
Jay, Timothy. *Cursing in America: A Psycholinguistic Study of Dirty Language in the Courts, in the Movies, in the Schoolyards and on the Streets.* Philadelphia: J. Benjamins, 1992.
Kelman, James. *How Late it Was, How Late.* London: Secker & Warburg, 1994.
Lighter, J.E., ed. *Random House Historical Dictionary of American Slang.* New York: Random House, 1994.
McDonald, James. *Dictionary of Obscenity, Taboo and Euphemism.* London: Sphere Books, 1988.
Major, Clarence. *Juba to Jive: A Dictionary of African-American Slang.* Harmondsworth: Penguin, 1994.
Maurer, David W. *Language of the Underworld.* Lexington: University Press of Kentucky, 1981.
Montagu, Ashley. *The Anatomy of Swearing.* London and New York: Macmillan and Collier, 1973.
Partridge, Eric. *Shakespeare's Bawdy.* London: Routledge & Kegan Paul, 1947.
———. *Origins.* 3rd ed. London: Routledge & Kegan Paul, 1977.
Read, Allen Walker. "An Obscenity Symbol." *American Speech,* December 1934.
Sagarin, Edward. *The Anatomy of Dirty Words.* New York: Lyle Stuart, 1962.
Sheidlower, Jesse. *The F-Word.* New York: Random House, 1995.
Spears, Richard A. *Slang and Euphemism.* New York: Signet, 1991.
Wilson , Edward. "A 'damned f——in Abbot' in 1528." *Notes and Queries,* New Series Vol. 40, No. 1, March 1993, 29–34.

G

GENDER IN SWEARING

Gender in swearing covers three basic aspects: the gender of the swearer, that of the terms themselves, and the application or "target." Traditionally it has been assumed, and is commonly evident, that swearing is predominantly a male domain and that even swearing in the presence of women is a severe breach of good manners. As the entry **women, swearing in** shows, this is generally, but not absolutely, true, since notable female swearers have a long tradition in both literature and history. Studies by Timothy Jay into swearing among American college students showed that women were ahead in certain categories, but did lag significantly behind men in using terms for the genitalia, such as *pussy, cunt, tits,* and *cock* (1992, 143–53).

The gender of swearing terms has become part of a wider debate in recent decades centered on the assumption that language is a male-controlled construct exhibiting chauvinist prejudices. The general feminist view argues that since language is generated in a "patriarchal" or "phallocratic" dispensation, there has developed, especially in male swearing, a preponderance of the terms derived from the female anatomy, notably *tit* and *cunt*. This dynamic has been identified as "the semantic derogation of women" (Schultz 1975) and explored by linguists such as Dale Spender, Casey Miller and Kate Swift. There seems definitely to be a *prima facie* case for such a view.

However, some closer examination is needed to analyze the distribution of terms of vehement personal abuse. These should include, not only female terms derived from various fields, anatomical and natural (e.g., *cow* and *bitch*), but also general neutral terms, such as *moron* and *bastard*. Accordingly, a study of the distribution of terms is a useful starting-point for such an investigation. The field is set out below in the table "Gender in Swearing."

The field reveals the interesting and somewhat surprising distributional dynamic in that virtually all the terms, from whatever provenance, are applied exclusively to the male sex. As has been stated, it has been argued that this concentration has arisen because the field of swearing has been dominated by men. This dynamic is, however, particularly paradoxical in the genital area, where the gender of origin and application do not match at all. It emerges that it is only in the animal category that origin and application follow each other logically. It is also notable that the pig is the only animal to feature in all categories, in the forms *pig, sow,* and *swine*. In the "general" category, obviously *bugger, motherfucker,* and *sod*[*omite*] are deter-

Gender in Swearing

Category	Gender of Terms			Application of Terms		
	male	female	indeterminate	used of male	used of female	used of either sex
religion			Devil	X		
genitalia	Prick			X		
		Cunt		X		
		Twat		X		
	Pillock			X		
anatomy		Tit		X		
			Arsehole	X		
excretion			Shit	X		
			Turd	X		
			Fart	X		
stupidity			Idiot	X		
			Imbecile	X		
			Moron	X		
			Cretin	X		
			Prat	X		
animal		Cow			X	
		Bitch			X	
		Sow			X	
			Swine	X		
	Pig			X		
general			Bastard	X		
			Fucker	X		
	Motherfucker			X		
	Bugger			X		
	sod			X		

mined by sexual role, but against this, there is no reason why *devil, bastard,* and *fucker* should be exclusively male in application. The same is true of *idiot, moron,* and *cretin.*

It is also noteworthy that virtually all the terms in the genital, anatomical, and excretory categories have developed the sense of "a worthless person" or "fool." (The British slang term *prat,* which now has the same sense, had older meanings of "buttocks" or "arse.") The other curious feature is that there is no term that can be used freely of both sexes. In recent decades *bitch* has started to be used more of men (though this currency is predominantly among homosexuals) and in the generalized sense of a difficult situation, as in "This is a real bitch."

While the general distribution or application of terms is revealing, it perhaps lacks discrimination, since the **impact** of insults is equally important. This assessment is also problematic, being affected by variables such as context, tone, social codes, and degree of deliberation. While most would regard *cunt, motherfucker,* and *bastard* as deeply wounding, others would claim rightly that these terms are not always powerful and provocative, but can convey, variously, hatred and contempt, but also sympathy and affection. (Incidentally, of these three terms, one is masculine, one is feminine, and one is neutral.)

The issues are complex, since there are conflicting criteria. There is a need to balance intensity of insult against range. Thus the feminine-derived terms *cunt, tit,* and *bitch* are obviously more potent than the male derived *prick* or *pig.* On the other hand, *all* the indeterminate terms, such as *bastard, idiot,* and *shit,* which should logically be "bisexual" in application, are invariably applied only to males. Consequently, the "levels of injury" inflicted or sustained by these words would vary greatly from speaker to speaker and from hearer to hearer. However, the historical perspective shows one significant trend, namely that several of the terms like *bitch* and *sow,* were first used of males (or of both sexes) and only later applied exclusively to women, a point discussed further under **feminization of opprobrious terms**.

See also: Billingsgate; Bywords of Swearing; Feminization of Opprobrious Terms; Impact; Women, Swearing in.

Bibliography

Miller, Casey, and Kate Swift. *Words and Women.* London: Victor Gollancz, 1977.
Mills, Jane. *Womanwords.* London: Virago, 1991.
Schultz, Muriel. "The Semantic Derogation of Women." In *Language and Sex: Differences and Dominance,* ed. B. Thorne and N. Henley, 64–73. Rowley, MA: Newbury House, 1975.
Spender, Dale. *Man Made Language.* London: Routledge & Kegan Paul, 1980.

GENITALIA

In the history of swearing, the general focus has moved from the higher forces controlling human destiny to their polar opposite, the excretory and genital functions. Thus in medieval times religious swearing was dominant, whereas in recent centuries swearwords relating to copulation and excretion have come to the fore. The two principal terms falling under this category, namely *cock* and *cunt,* are interestingly different philologically in their origins, their semantic development, and the taboos that have come to surround them. Both have generated great numbers of synonyms used almost exclusively in male-to-male discourse. *Cunt* has always had a specific meaning, since its origins are not complicated by metaphorical extension, as is the case with *cock.* To simplify the discussion, **cock** and **cunt** have their own entries.

The clear separation of registers that now obtains between "coarse" taboo native terms such as those just mentioned, and "polite" general, anatomical, or technical language made up of classically derived terms like *penis* and *vagina,* did not exist in the past. Many medieval proverbs and plays contained extremely coarse language. More surprisingly, medieval medical texts used the core words now regarded as obscene or grossly impolite as terminology. Even in his translation of the Bible (1385), John Wycliffe uses the graphic term *arse-ropes* for *intestines* and *balloks* for testicles, which were also termed *cods,* now surviving only in *codpiece.* Also now obsolete is medieval *coillons,* surviving as *cullion,* a term of abuse ("that crafty cullion knave") through to the seventeenth century. Its distant relative *cojones* has recently come into American English in the macho sense of English "balls." Two obsolete terms for the penis, namely *tarse* (from Anglo-Saxon *teors*) and *yard* (from Middle English *yerde*), are similarly recorded in medical contexts.

Middle English *taile* denoted both the male and female genitalia, and the verbal noun *tailing* meant "intercourse." Chaucer's Wife of Bath, always frank on venereal matters, says simply, "A likerous [lecherous] mouth moot han [must have] a licorous tayl" (*Prologue* l. 6048), while the Reeve laments that "we olde men" have "an hoor [hoary] head and a grene [vigorous] tayl" (*Prologue*, l. 3878). These senses have continued in underground slang up to the present in phrases such as "a piece of tail" and "get some tail." Less well known is *scut*, meaning as animal's tail, first used (1596) in the bawdy phrase "My doe with the black scut" in the *Merry Wives of Windsor* (V v 20). By about 1705 it was being used of woman's genitalia: "Come in, says he, you silly [simple] slut, I'll lay the itching of your scut" (*Merry Songs and Ballads* I, 177). Although the sexual sense died out in the eighteenth century, it was replaced by that of "a contemptible person" in the nineteenth. *Penis* itself, a Latin term also meaning "a tail," entered the language only in 1693, several decades after the rarer Greek-derived term *phallus*, recorded from 1613. Other old terms for the male genitalia are *purse* for the scrotum, leading to the slang sense of *spend*, meaning "ejaculate," first used in an embarrassing episode in Samuel Pepys's *Diary* (September 7, 1662). *Vagina*, meaning a sheath, was borrowed from Latin in 1682. (*Genitalia* itself is a Victorian formation, dating from the 1870s.) Unlike *cunt*, which has become both an obscenity and a term of serious insult, *cock* is less powerful on both fronts.

See also: Cock; Cunt.

Bibliography

Chapman, Robert L. *New Dictionary of American Slang*. New York: Harper & Row, 1986.
Farmer, J.S., and W.E. Henley. *Slang and Its Analogues*. London: Routledge and Kegan Paul, 1890–1904.
Flexner, Stuart Berg. *I Hear America Talking*. New York: Van Nostrand Reinhold, 1976.
Green, Jonathan. *The Slang Thesaurus*. Harmondsworth: Penguin, 1988.
Grose, Francis. *A Classical Dictionary of the Vulgar Tongue*. London: S. Hooper, 1785.
Hughes, Geoffrey. *Swearing*. Oxford: Blackwell, 1991; Harmondsworth: Penguin, 1998.
Jay, Timothy. *Cursing in America: A Psycholinguistic Study of Dirty Language in the Courts, in the Movies, in the Schoolyards and on the Streets*. Philadelphia: J. Benjamins, 1992.
Lighter, J.E., ed. *Random House Historical Dictionary of American Slang*. New York: Random House, 1994.
McDonald, James. *Dictionary of Obscenity, Taboo and Euphemism*. London: Sphere Books, 1988.
Read, Allen Walker. "An Obscenity Symbol." In *American Speech*, December 1934.
Sagarin, Edward. *The Anatomy of Dirty Words*. New York: Lyle Stuart, 1962.
Spears, Richard A. *Slang and Euphemism*. New York: Signet, 1991.

GERMANS

Historically xenophobic attitudes towards Germany have derived principally from military rivalry or threat. The most typical manifestations have been *blasons populaires*, or negative stereotypes, and demeaning nicknames, which develop into ethnic insults over time. Cartoon representations of a militaristic national type are also significant.

Prior to World War I, relations between Germany and Britain were cordial; indeed, much was made of the common Anglo-Saxon heritage shared by the two nations. The House of Hanover had become the English ruling family in the forms of George I to IV, from the death of Queen Anne in 1714 until 1830. The unexpected marriage of Queen Victoria to Prince Albert of Saxe-Coburg in 1840 occasioned some initial suspicion, but during the latter part of the nineteenth century there developed a powerful fashion for things Germanic, reflected in terms like *Germanism, Germanize, Germanophilist* (1864), and even *Germanomania* (1893). The notions of what was "Germanic" were rooted in idealism and mysticism, embodied in the impressive romantic figures like Goethe, Schiller, and Beethoven. However, contemporaneously, the militaristic culture of Prussia was generating apprehensive terms like *Prussianism* (1856) and *Prussianize* (1861), followed by "the Prussianist goose-step" in 1922.

Surprisingly, the earliest and most hostile term, **hun**, was given great currency as a consequence of a belligerent speech by Kaiser Wilhelm II in 1900, detailed in a separate entry. Immediately upon the commencement of World War I a powerful field of hostile terms for the Germans surfaced. *Bosch,* usually *the bosch,* was the earliest, borrowed from French *boche,* deriving from *tête de boche,* meaning "wooden head" and recorded from 1914, followed by *fritz* from 1915 and *jerry* from 1918. In the context of extreme nationalism and xenophobia that the war engendered, even *German* itself became an inflammatory term, as Eric Partridge records: "In 1915 an indignant defendant in the Middlesex Police Court excused himself by saying "He called me a German and other filthy names" (1933, 7). The date of this provocation was, significantly, 1915: in 1905 or 1925 the provocation would have made no sense. The British Royal Family, seeking to obscure its close relations with Germany, even changed its name: King George V changed his family name from Wetlin to Windsor by royal proclamation in 1917. The Battenbergs became the Mountbattens.

Hostile nicknames were virtually contemporaneous in British and American English, with two exceptions. *Bosch* has never developed a real currency in the United States, while *kraut,* from *sauerkraut,* is recorded from 1918 in British English but was established at least fifty years earlier in America. A powerful instance is recorded from a Civil War context of 1864: "Some puppy finally cried out 'kraut' and another echoed it with 'kraut by the barrel.' [General Osterhaus] wheeled his horse and rode up to us, his face white with passion. 'Vat regiment ish dis?' No one answered. . . . Yelping 'sauer kraut' at a German is a poor way to gain his favour" (C.W. Wills, *Army Life,* 304).

All these terms, with the exception of *bosch,* were taken over into World War II. Even prior to the outbreak, from 1930, *Hitler* was being used as name for a dictatorial type, especially in the formula *a little Hitler.* Another that joined the field was **goon**, a term of largely American provenance with an entry of its own. Since World War II, *fritz* has tended to diminish in currency, but the other terms have flourished. Apart from the conflation of *Hun* and *Hungarian* in American English, the terms have been quite specific in application to Germans, unlike *spik, dago, gook,* and *wog,* which have become general-purpose xenophobic epithets.

German stereotypes and terms are discussed by Stuart Berg Flexner in *I Hear America Talking* (1976), while in *The Language of Ethnic Conflict* (1983), Irving Lewis Allen lists over thirty nicknames and hostile epithets in the United States for Germans, which, apart from those already discussed include *bucket-head, cabbage-head, dummerhead, hans-wurst, heinie, hitlander, johnny-squarehead, kamerad, nazi,* and *pretzel.* These range from comparatively inoffensive stereotyping to the more emotive terms obviously derivative from World War II, namely the militaristic *kamerad* and *nazi.* Curiously, since the war the term *nazi* itself has not become entirely synonymous with the German people generally, any more than *fascist* has become specifically associated with the Italian people. Both words refer more to a dictatorial or militaristic type of personality. This association is also apparent in the general use of the term *neo-nazi*.

See also: Blason Populaires; Ethnic Insults; Goon; Hun.

Bibliography

Allen, Irving Lewis. *The Language of Ethnic Conflict.* New York: Columbia University Press, 1983.
Flexner, Stuart Berg. *I Hear America Talking.* New York: Van Nostrand Reinhold, 1976.
Partridge, Eric. *Words, Words, Words!* London: Methuen, 1933.
Wills, C.W. *Army Life of an Illinois Soldier.* Washington, DC: Globe Printing Co., 1906.

GIT

The term is largely confined to the British Isles, where it has the broad sense of "a worthless person" (always male), commonly preceded by the adjectives "idle" or "stupid." It originates as a variant form of *get,* recorded in Scots from the early sixteenth century in the sense of "bastard." The remarkable swearing match, the *Flyting of Dunbar and Kennedy* (ca. 1503) contains this damning insult:

Fals tratour, feyndis gett
[False traitor, devil's bastard]
(l. 244)

An abbreviation of *beget, get* is through most of its early history a specially northern and Scottish word, also found ca. 1570 in a Scottish poem, "The Treason of Dunbarton":

Ganylon's gets, relics of Sinon's seed.
(I 171)

The references are to two great traitors in world history: Ganylon betrayed the great French hero Roland at the Battle of Roncesvalles in 778; Sinon betrayed Troy. Joseph Wright's voluminous *English Dialect Dictionary* (1898–1905) gives instances in Scottish and northern use in the senses of "a child, especially in contemptuous use, a brat; a bastard," including the harshly punitive "Tak that, thou Deils [Devil's] gaet" from John Mackay Wilson, *Tales* (1836). In a curiously contemporary utterance in a series of songs entitled *The Gentle Shepherdess* (1725), Allan Ramsay alluded to "Whingeing getts about your ingle side [hearth]" (song 5).

As the word filtered southward, it lost both intensity and currency. In his *Classical Dictionary of the Vulgar Tongue* (1785), Captain Francis Grose included it under the phrase "one of his get; one of his offspring or begetting," but did not elaborate. The term revived in modern times in the form *git,* greatly generalized and having entirely lost its denotation of illegitimacy. It is rare in American English, and virtually unknown in Australian and South African English.

See also: Bastard.

GOD, EUPHEMISMS FOR

In many religions, including Judaism, Brahmanism, and Islam, direct reference to the name of God is taboo. Christianity is more concessive in this regard, but the Old Testament injunction against taking the Lord's name in vain (the Third Commandment) has continued to be regarded as a serious religious and moral breach. Since English has developed for most of its history in Christian societies, great numbers of euphemistic variants of this sacred name have grown up over the centuries. The same process has, understandably, occurred in the cases of the names of Jesus, Christ, and Lord, but to a lesser extent.

Historically, the earliest instances date from the fourteenth century, which is seemingly late, given the fact that Christianity was brought to England by Saint Augustine in the year 597. The **Anglo-Saxon** laws allude more to prohibitions against the naming of the pagan gods than to the Christian God. The historical development of the word-field is shown in the accompanying table:

1350s	gog	1706	ounds
1386	cokk	1728	agad
1569	cod	1733	ecod
1570	Jove	1734	goles
1598	'sblood	1743	gosh
1598	'slid (God's eyelid)	1743	golly
1598	'slight	1749	odrabbit it
1599	'snails (God's nails)	1760s	gracious
1600	zounds (God's wounds)	1820s	ye gods!
1601	'sbody (God's body)	1839	begorra
1602	sfoot (God's foot)	1842	by George
1603	gods bodikins	1842	s'elpe me Bob ("so help me, God")
1611	gad	1843	Drat! ("God rot!")
1621	odsbobs	1851	Doggone (God damn)
1650s	gadzooks (God's hooks)	1884	Great Scott
1672	godsookers	1900	Good grief
1673	egad	1909	by Godfrey!
1695	odso		

Although the growth of the field has been continuous, it has not expanded at a constant rate. There is a notable hiatus between the first two instances in the fourteenth century and the plethora recorded nearly two hundred years later, especially the concentration of terms between 1598 and 1602. This group constitutes about a quarter of the whole field. If we regard 597 as the starting point of Christianity in England, we find that only two euphemisms are recorded in the thousand years elapsing between that date and the Elizabethan period. One explanation for this extraordinary gap could be the lack of surviving written documents. The other is somewhat paradoxical: although the Middle Ages can be rightly regarded as an age of faith, a quite astounding volume of religious swearing was uttered in the form of asseverations, ejaculations, blasphemies, and curses, both personal and institutional. Euphemisms were thus not required, until **censorship** was instituted in the sixteenth century. Subsequently there are other growth clusters between 1728 and 1749, as well as in the 1840s. Then there is an apparent hiatus between the appearance of the last term (*by Godfrey!*) and the present. This indicates a diminution of the power of the taboo as the name of God has become more openly used in print and broadcasting.

As with euphemisms in other categories, such as obscenity and scatology, the process may be overt, covert, or unconscious. Thus the peculiarly British ejaculations "by Jove!" or "ye gods!" are fairly obvious overt modes of avoiding the offending name. On the other hand, "by golly!" or "doggone!" are more covert, in that the context clearly indicating a profanity, although the form of words is seemingly innocent. Finally, forms like "strewth!" or "drat!" are more in the category of the unconscious, since the origins ("God's truth!" and "God rot!") are so deeply buried in the past that the original forms have become obscured. There are, however, plenty of marginal cases, such as "so help me" (for "so help me, God").

In all cases the basic process of euphemization is the same: there is a surreptitious erosion of the unacceptable or taboo word, transforming it by means of phonetic disguise into a seemingly innocuous variant. The results are also termed **minced oaths**, since God's name is mangled in some way. Although there are some standard words used as substitutions, such as *cod* (ca. 1569) and *gracious* (ca. 1760s), nearly all the forms so generated are original and odd, including such bizarre formations as *odsbobs, gadzooks, ounds,* and *odrabbit it.* (The *OED* lists other oddities such as *God's pittikins, God's diggers, God's ludd, God's niggs,* and *God's sonties,* not all of which are understood.) Generally speaking, the process is collective and unconscious, the terms developing in waves of fashion and then, in the manner of all euphemisms, becoming unrecognizable and needing to be replaced.

Several major medieval texts were extremely censorious about swearing. These included Dan Michel's *Ayenbite of Inwit* ("The Remorse of Conscience," 1340) and Robert of Brunne's *Handlyng Synne* (ca. 1300). In Chaucer's *Canterbury Tales* (1386–1400) the issue of profanity and its avoidance in public speech is openly dramatized in a number of combative exchanges, notably (*Epilogue of the Man of Law's Tale,* ll.1166–80) discussed further in the entry for **Geoffrey Chaucer**.

With the subsequent development of the theatre and of printing, authors came under pressure to avoid blasphemous or profane terms and thus created new euphemisms. This is especially the case in the Elizabethan period, when censorship became overt and active. Thus it is noteworthy that all the "minced oaths" listed from 1598 to 1602 are first recorded in dramatic contexts, the first instances of *'sblood* and *'slid* occurring in Shakespeare, while those of *'slight* and *'sbody* are found in Ben Jonson. In the decadent drama of the **Restoration** (1660–1700), the appropriateness of particular euphemisms even becomes part of the text.

Naturally, there are variations in the extent to which an individual speaker may be aware of the literal religious origins of the terms in question. However given the vast time scale of the language and the lack of philological awareness of most speakers, the origins of these euphemisms are commonly lost. There is also an element of fashion at work, so that many of these forms pass out of usage in a decade or two. Looking back over the field, it is notable how very few forms have survived longer than a century: among them are *Jove, gosh, golly, by George, drat! Doggone, Great Scott!,* and *Good Grief!*

Reflecting the general secularization of Western society, the taboo against using the name of God in vain has now largely eroded: hence the diminution of euphemisms in recent decades. Whereas Britain has become largely uncritical of profanity and blasphemy, in the United States concentrations of religious and ethnic communities generate correspondingly great variations from state to state on a scale between liberalism and fundamentalism. In the field of broadcasting, some American programs still censor out the name of God (even to the point of leaving a moment of silence on a soundtrack) in contexts where it would stand in the United Kingdom. In Australia and South Africa the comparative acceptance found in the United Kingdom largely applies. However, in the South African context the Afrikaans language provides a whole series of euphemistic outlets, since speakers are less sensitive about using taboo terms in other languages. Thus Afrikaans phrases like *God!* (pronounced with a guttural "g") and the adjective *Godverdomned* ("goddammed") and the like are often heard on the lips of English speakers.

See also: Censorship; Chaucer, Geoffrey; God's Wounds.

Bibliography

Montagu, Ashley. *The Anatomy of Swearing.* London and New York: Macmillan and Collier, 1973.
Ross, Thomas W. "Taboo-Words in Fifteenth-Century English." In *Fifteenth-Century Studies,* ed. Robert F. Yeager, 137–60. Hamden, CT: Archon, 1984.

GODDAM/GODDAMN

Although *goddam* is now regarded as generally, if not exclusively, American in usage, its origins lie in English history. From its imprecatory origins in serious curses like "God damn you!" or, stranger, "God damn me!," it has developed many semantic nuances and grammatical functions, undergoing semantic loss of intensity as its functions have proliferated.

Curiously, it is first found in medieval times as a hostile term used to designate the English. This was in the form *goddem,* applied to them by the French during the Hundred Years' War on account of their copious profanity and use of the word *goddam.* According to Joan of Arc, as quoted in D.A. Barante, *The Kings of Burgundy* (1431), the English used it "a hundred thousand times." The name did not long outlive that period of hostilities, although it had a brief ironic revival in the nineteenth century: J.P. Corbett wrote in *A Tour of Italy* (1830), "It seems the 'Goddems' are having some fun" (8).

In the period of the English Civil War (1642–1649), swearing became a significant discriminator of the opposing sides: the Puritans were severely opposed to taking the Lord's name in vain, while the Cavaliers were very free in their oaths. "The courtiers garnished their mouths with God-dammes, as if they desired Damnation rather than Salvation," wrote

Sir Edward Peyton in his history, *The Catastrophe of the House of Stuarts,* in 1652. The fashion thus attracted the nickname of the *God-damn-me*s, used by the noted controversialist William Prynne, who referred directly to "The God-dam-me Cavaliers" in *The Sovereign Power of Parliament* (1643, 17).

This fashion proved to be very resilient. Daniel Defoe criticized in "A Tilt at Profanity" (1712) the "senseless stuff" spoken by beaux or dandies in fashionable coffee houses: "at play it is G—d damn the cards; a-hunting it is G—d damn the hounds" (1951, 260). In *The Marriage of Figaro* (1784) the French dramatist Pierre-Augustin Caron de Beaumarchais observed ironically, "The English, in truth, do add here and there some other words when speaking; but it is obvious that 'God-damn' is the foundation of their language" (III v). Lord Byron agreed:

'G-d damn!'—those syllables intense, —
Nucleus of England's native eloquence
(*The Island,* 1823, Canto 3, section 5)

There is a revealing and curious anecdote recorded by Captain Basil Hall when he visited the Sandwich Islands in the Pacific. An islander greeted him with this series of salutations: "Very glad to see you! Damn your eyes! Me like English very much. Devilish hot, sir! Goddam!" (1831, 89). The man was simply repeating the more colorful points of communication left by Captain James Cook's expedition in 1778.

During the nineteenth century, as *goddam* tended to peter out in British English, it started to expand into its modern range of uses in the United States. The linking sense of "accursed" is found in a powerful quotation from 1816: "A villain overtook me and said you *God dambd Brasington* and . . . gave me blow . . . on my left cheek" (J.K. Williams, *Vogues in Villainy,* 15). By the 1840s there were instances like "that's a God damned lie," "I'm God damned if I care," and "I was so God damned drunk," showing loss of intensity. Consequently, the superlative form became necessary: "This is the G-d damnedest shot of work I ever saw," wrote J.M. McCaffrey in *Manifest Destiny* (1847, 80). The use as a mere intensive dates from the period of the World War I, well illustrated in Hemingway's comment about *Ulysses* in 1922: "Joyce has a most god-damn wonderful book." (All citations are from the *Random House Historical Dictionary of American Slang.*) Although such usages were originally confined to American English, they are now generally current and banalized.

As the entries for **damn** and **flexibility** show, the use of the word as a mere intensive, infixed into another word, is recorded from the mid-nineteenth century. Infixing, whereby the term is integrated into another word, is otherwise recorded from only the 1920s. Since then the process has developed in forms like "ambigodamdexterous" and "indegoddampendent," showing that the original word is being used simply as a filler without semantic content. Similarly revealing is the emergence of the oxymoron "a good goddam," also recorded from the 1920s, which continues to flourish. Stuart Berg Flexner has pointed out that "the two-syllable *goddamn(ed)* is often merely suggested by the other two-syllable words, such as *consarned, confounded, doggone(d),* and *dad-burn(ed)*" (*dad* perhaps coming from *Gad* or *–d,* earlier euphemisms for *God*) (1976, 171).

In British English, *goddam* now has generally diminished in currency. The same is true of other global varieties, notably South African and Australian English.

See also: Damn; Flexibility.

Bibliography

Defoe, Daniel. "A Tilt at Profanity" (1712). In *The Best of Defoe's REVIEW,* ed. William Payne. New York: Columbia University Press, 1951.
Flexner, Stuart Berg. *I Hear America Talking.* New York: Van Nostrand Reinhold, 1976.
Hall, Basil. *Fragments of Voyages and Travels.* Edinburgh: Robert Cadell, 1831.
Lighter, J.S., ed. *Random House Historical Dictionary of American Slang.* New York: Random House, 1994.

GOD'S WOUNDS

It is a paradox of medieval Christian society that, out of all the mysterious and wonderful properties of the divine, extending from the Creation to the Last Judgment, the central act of the redemption, the sufferings of Christ at the Crucifixion have become the principal focus of religious swearing. There are, admittedly, a few allusions to God's creative power in phrases like "as sure as God made little apples" (really a euphemism) or the ancient asseveration "by God's light," but they are greatly outnumbered by those alluding to the Crucifixion. The gruesome invocations of Christ's wounded body and blood, even the nails of the Crucifixion, seem as grotesque and bizarre to us now as modern genital, copulatory, and excretory swearing would have seemed to medievals.

The traditional medieval condemnation of such swearing was that such blasphemous oaths were regarded as a renewal of the Crucifixion. Nevertheless, the mode thrived throughout the period, being memorably reiterated by John Donne centuries later:

They kill'd once an inglorious man, but I
Crucifie him daily, being now glorified.
(John Donne, *Holy Sonnet XI*)

This motif took various forms. It could be expressed in a quite dignified and classical manner, as in *by Goddes corpus!* (using the Latin *corpus* for "body") or *by Cristes passioun!,* used in the dominant medieval sense of "suffering," still found in forms like "The Passion according to St. Matthew." However, the more common mode was crudely physical. The entry for **Chaucer** discusses various classic and familiar instances in his *Canterbury Tales* (1386–1400), notably those in the *Pardoner's Tale,* reiterating the traditional medieval condemnation, based on taking the gruesome oaths literally:

And many a grisly ooth thanne han they sworne,
And Cristes blessed body al torente—
[And tore Christ's body all to pieces]
(ll. 708–9)

Many contemporary ecclesiastical authorities issued similar condemnations of dismembering oaths, some of them as extreme and hysterical as the swearing itself. Dan Michel, a brother of the Cloister of Saint Austin [Augustine] at Canterbury, wrote about 1340 in his major spiritual text, *The Ayenbite of Inwit* ("The Remorse of Conscience") that in swearing "the Christians are worse than the pagan or infidel. They are worse than the Jews, who crucified Christ, but did not break any of his bones. But these mince him smaller than men do swine in a butchery" (Folio 19a, 64). The same point is made by John Bromyard in his major compilation of sermons, the *Summa Praedicantium* (ca. 1323–1350): "The Jews gave up Christ's body unmaimed, but the Christians cut it up in pieces, limb by limb, with the devile's sword, that is, their tongue" (I, 419).

Rosemary Woolf remarked in her major study, *English Religious Lyric in the Middle Ages*: "The theme of a fresh wounding or crucifying of Christ seems to have occurred very early in a spectacular and popular form, that of the *exemplum* of the Bloody Child" (1968, 396). She traces the first appearance of the motif to another standard medieval spiritual text, the *Handlyng Synne* (ca. 1300) of Robert of Brunne, in which the Christ child is the victim of dismembering oaths. In the parable, the Blessed Virgin Mary shows the sinful swearer her child, hideously deformed. She upbraids the "rich" (powerful) man who, typical of his class, "commonly swears great oaths grisly":

"Thou," she said, "has him so shent [damaged]
And with thy oaths all to-rent [torn to pieces]."

Such severe condemnations, based on the literal interpretation of dismembering oaths, were repeated over the centuries. The same motif is found in the English version of the *Gesta Romanorum* (ca. 1440) where the Virgin dramatically accuses the sinners:

Why come ye hidder? For to shew thee my sone, lo!" she saide, "here is my sone lyeng in my lappe, with his hede, all to-broke, and his eyen drawen oute of his body and layde on his breste, his armes broken a-twoo, his legges and his fete also."
(Woolf 1968, 396–97).

Even more imaginative and powerful is the transference of the speech to the Savior himself, a development found in a collection of homilies under the title of *Festial* by Johannes Mirkus (John Mirk; ca. 1450). Here Christ upbraids callous and insensitive swearers:

and what particularly grieves me is that you care nothing for my passion which I suffered for you, but I am affronted all day by horrible swearers, who swear by my face, by my eyes, by my arms, by my nails, by my heart, by my blood, and so forth, by my whole body.
(author's translation, *Early English Text Society* vol. 96, 113)

Numerous instances of the same motif are to be found in medieval lyrics and the dramatic genre known as the miracle plays discussed in the entry for **medieval period**. Woolf also shows that the power of the metaphor of the dismembered Christ extended even to extraordinary visual analogues, for in some contemporary depictions of the Savior in ecclesiastical stained glass, parts of Christ's body are actually missing, while "Around are a group of fashionably dressed young men, grotesquely holding the missing limbs" (Woolf 1968, 397–98). This class gloss is quite common, being found in the earlier comments cited from Robert of Brunne's *Handlyng Synne*. *An Invective Against Swearing* (1543) by Thomas Becon was one of the last wholesale denunciations of those who swear by "by all the members of [Christ's] glorious body," which are listed in detail and condemned: "The Jews crucified Him but once, and then their fury ceased; but these wicked caitiffs crucify him daily with their unlawful oaths. . . . It is not a rare thing now-a-days to hear boys and mothers tear the most blessed body of Christ with their blasphemous oaths" (cited in Montagu 1973, 129).

Despite these numerous and powerful condemnations, the mode continued to thrive. Although there were some early euphemistic variants, such as the medieval oath "by cokkes bones!" liberally used in Chaucer, the favorite oath of Queen Elizabeth was, allegedly "by God's wound's" (Montagu 1973, 139). However, toward the end of her reign the old gruesome invocations of the Crucifixion started to be supplanted by **minced oaths,** euphemistic and sanitized forms, such as *zounds, 'sblood,* and *'snails,* with the name of **God** truncated. As the forms became less recognizable, so their currency declined: thus the last recorded fragments of these powerful oaths were *gadzooks* (literally "God's hooks") in the 1650s, the variant *godsookers* about 1672, and *ounds* in 1706. The final ironic footnote is a discussion in George Farquhar's Restoration comedy *Love in a Bottle* (1698) on "the most fashionable Oaths in Town," in particular whether *zounds* should be pronounced *zoons* or *zauns* (II i). The answer is *zauns,* showing that the oath is no longer even recognizably derived from "God's wounds."

See also: Censorship; Chaucer, Geoffrey; Class and Swearing; God, Euphemisms for; Zounds.

Bibliography

Becon, Thomas. *An Invective Against Swearing.* London: 1543.
Bromyard, John. *Summa Praedicantium,* 1323–1350.
Brunne, Robert. *Handlyng Synne,* ed. F.J. Furnivall. London: Early English Text Society, 1901.
Michel, Dan. *The Ayenbite of Inwit,* ed. R. Morris. London: Early English Text Society, 1866.
Montagu, Ashley. *The Anatomy of Swearing.* London and New York: Macmillan and Collier, 1973.
Owst, G.R. *Literature and Pulpit in Medieval England.* Cambridge: Cambridge University Press, 1933.
Woolf, Rosemary. *English Religious Lyric in the Middle Ages.* Oxford: Oxford University Press, 1968.

GOOK

Gook, a comparatively modern term and almost exclusively American in usage, is a powerful and revealing expression of xenophobia. Unlike most ethnic insults, it does not have a clear etymology, and its semantic history combines hostility toward outsiders with great flexibility in application. It thus shows the dynamics of linguistic xenophobia, which include race, war, immigration, and business rivalry.

The word is usually derived from two sources, both of them only probabilities. The earlier is *goo-goo,* a contemptuous expression of baby talk, originally applied to Filipinos and similar peoples from about 1900. (Linguistic belittlement is also the root of **Hottentot**.) The later source is *gook,* meaning a fool or a peculiar person, an extension of an older meaning of the word, namely a prostitute, recorded in Farmer and Henley (1890–1904). Both possibilities are suggested by the *Random House Historical Dictionary of American Slang* (1994), which specifies that the term was "originally military," and gives this extensive definition: "a dark- or yellow-skinned foreigner; native; a native of the Philippines, the Southwest Pacific or adjacent areas, Central America, Japan, North Africa, Southern Europe and the Eastern Mediterranean, Korea or Indo-China; (now *esp.*) an East Asian person of any nationality; (*broadly*) any usu. non-European foreigner."

This definition has extraordinary demographic breadth, extending much further than equivalent terms such as *dago, wop,* and *wog.* Quotations date from 1920, the first reference being to Haitians in the U.S. Marines, who were "nicknamed 'Gooks,' and have been treated with every variety of contempt, insult and brutality." Subsequent applications are to the Philippines as "Gook Land" (1921), to the Nicaraguans (1927), to South Sea natives and to Italians (1944), to the Japanese (1945), to Koreans (1947), to Chinese Communists (1951), to Mexicans (1952), to Vietnamese (1967), to Indians (1970), to Lebanese (1970), to Turks (1974), and to Arabs (1988).

These semantic extensions and their chronology clearly indicate two factors. The first is that the term has steadily become a general-purpose expression of xenophobia applied to virtually all the peoples that American troops encountered, as enemies or allies. This is illustrated by dating the entry of American troops into various theaters of war: these include World War II (1941), the Korean War (1950), and the Vietnam War (1965). There are even World War II references to white New Zealanders in American works published much later, in 1958 and 1965. As one author frankly puts it, "A gook in the purest sense is anybody what ain't American" (Karp, *Doobie Doo* 1965, 97). The second is that the term is used with a variety of tones, from the contemptuous to the affectionate. As tends to occur in words with wide semantic applications, the term has various grammatical extensions, such as *Gooksville* (1967, for North Vietnamese airspace) and *gook-legged.*

Although *gook* is largely an exclusively American term, it was borrowed by Australian troops during the Vietnam War. "This is a gook grave" was a comment reported in the *Brisbane Sunday Mail Magazine* (July 6, 1969). However, it is unlisted in the *Australian National Dictionary* (1988). The term has not gained currency in any other variety of English.

See also: Ethnic Insults; Hottentot.

Bibliography

Farmer, J.S., and W.E. Henley. *Slang and Its Analogues.* London: Routledge and Kegan Paul, 1890–1904.
Flexner, Stuart Berg. *I Hear America Talking.* New York: Van Nostrand Reinhold, 1976.
Lighter, J.S., ed. *Random House Historical Dictionary of American Slang.* New York: Random House, 1994.

GOON

This curious word, largely of American provenance, is a unique instance of an invented term becoming popular and developing a wide range of critical senses. It was coined by

Frederick Lewis Allen in 1921 to mean "a stolid, usually unimaginative person, especially a writer or public figure." Allen made up the term in a playful essay in *Harper's Magazine,* "The Goon and his Style": "A goon is a person with a heavy touch, as distinguished from a jigger, who has light touch. While jiggers look on life with a genial view, goons take a stolid and literal view" (121). Since then it has developed a great range of meanings.

Alice the Goon, a dull-witted muscular character in a popular comic strip from 1933 has been regarded as influential on the subsequent development (*Random House Historical Dictionary of American Slang,* 1994). A comment in *Life* (November 14, 1938) showed the extension of the meaning: "The word 'Goon' was first popularized by college students who used it to mean any stupid person." *American Speech* noted two senses: in 1941, *Goon* denoted "a soldier who falls into the lowest [intelligence] category in Army classification," but in the context of labor union parlance the word had a more sinister sense, meaning a "beat-up man" or "a member of the labor-union's beef-squad . . . who can be depended on to cow and frighten recalcitrant union-members" (1938, vol. XIII, 178). The German connection in the sense of "a prison-camp guard" is recorded only from 1945, being also found from the same date in Australian English.

Two related forms are also recorded. The English dialect term *gooney,* recorded from 1872, meaning a stupid or silly person, is found in the same sense in the Maine and Cape Cod dialects from 1896 and 1904, respectively. It subsequently emerged in xenophobic use, similar to *gook,* of "dark- or yellow-skinned natives, especially in military service" in various theaters of war, including the Nicaraguan (1927), the Japanese (1943), and the Korean (1953). In the Vietnam War *gooner* was used of a Communist Vietnamese soldier from 1969. The English radio comedy program called "The Goon Show," which used bizarre humor, absurd plots, and curious voices, dates from 1951, but is an independent usage.

Goon is thus a prime example of a word that, lacking a clear referential sense, has been taken over as a term of abuse with various applications.

See also: Gook.

Bibliography

Allen, Frederick Lewis. "The Goon and His Style." *Harper's Magazine,* December 1921.
Lighter, J.S., ed. *Random House Historical Dictionary of American Slang.* New York: Random House, 1994.

GORBLIMEY

This expression, which is confined to British English, is an interesting instance of two features of swearing, namely the survival of a powerful oath in a euphemized and disguised form, and the genre of the "self-immolating oath." The origin of the expression lies in the bizarre appeal "God blind me!," recorded from about 1896, when J.R. Ware listed it in *Passing English* (1909) as "a gutter phrase" recorded from "about 1875." (Although not exclusively lower-class, the expression is now more commonly encountered in working-class milieus, and especially in Cockney argot.) The genre exists in various expressions of surprise, as in "Well blow me down!" in which the name of the Almighty is excluded, or "Strike me dead!" in which it is implied, and the archaic nautical exclamation "Shiver me timbers!"

Because the phrase was originally oral it has appeared in various forms, such as *gawblimy* and *Cor blimey,* suggesting that its profane origins were not really understood. The form *Gor* does not have an extensive recorded existence, even in dialect dictionaries, although Shakespeare has "By gar!" in *The Merry Wives of Windsor* (I iv 123). It is occasionally encountered as an expression of surprise as *Gor!* and *Cor!* Consequently, the currency of the original phrase has obviously diminished, as the word is not understood. Thus the abbreviated form *blimey,* now the common survivor, is recorded from slightly earlier, in Barrère and Leland's *Dictionary of Slang, Jargon and Cant* (1889).

Blimey has an unusual historical currency in American English, where it was recorded from 1918 as meaning "an English person, especially a Cockney," an identification with the most frequent users of the word, and possibly through proximity to *limey.* References include "the frogs [French] and the blimeys" (1924). The association of a distinctive swearword with a particular people or social group is also found in *goddam* and *fuckoff. Blimey* continues to have a thriving currency in British English, especially in the southern varieties. In Australia and South Africa it is encountered, but principally among expatriate British communities.

See also: Censorship; God, Euphemisms for.

Bibliography

Barrère, Albert, and Charles G. Leland. *Dictionary of Slang, Jargon, & Cant.* Edinburgh: Ballantyne Press, 1889.

Lighter, J.E., ed. *Random House Historical Dictionary of American Slang.* New York: Random House, 1994.

Ware, J. Redding. *Passing English of the Victorian Period: A Dictionary of Heterodox English, Slang, and Phrase.* London: Routledge, 1909. Reprint, Boston: Charles River Books, 1977.

GRAFFITI

Graffiti, the plural form of *graffito,* meaning "a scratch" in Italian, was originally a term in art history describing a method of decoration whereby designs are produced by scratches through a superficial layer of plaster or glazing to reveal a background of a different color. However, the popular modern use of the term is entirely different, denoting unauthorized and anonymous writings, messages, slogans, and symbols, commonly of a provocative, obscene, or taboo nature, scratched or painted on monuments or buildings. Although graffiti is commonly regarded as a particularly modern manifestation of social protest or personal obnoxiousness, the most ancient examples are the scribbles found on the walls of Pompeii and Rome.

In *Up the Nile* (1877), A.B. Edwards noted that certain ancient monuments had been "visited by crowds of early travellers who have as usual left their neatly scribbled graffiti on the walls" (xxi, 653). The phrase "as usual" clearly implies that the practice was familiar to travelers even then, while "neatly scribbled" indicates a discreet and careful superscript or intervention quite at variance with modern graffiti, which is typically brash, crude, and often indecipherable.

Graffiti may be personal, social, political, or arcane in its messages. It covers declarations of love and hate, expressions of prejudice against out-groups, political slogans,

Graffiti (Italian for "scratchings") have been found on houses and monuments in ancient Rome and Pompeii. Inscriptions of an obscene or taboo nature are a more recent phenomenon. (The Art Archive/Bibliothèque des Arts Décoratifs Paris/Dagli Orti) often using party logos or symbols like the hammer and sickle or the dollar sign, and personal symbols used as cryptic autographs. In the course of the twentieth century graffiti has generally become more public, intrusive, and daring. From obscene symbols and dirty jokes in public lavatories, there developed the innocent clichéd designs and slogans such as the popular American figure Kilroy with the standard statement "Kilroy was here" and the British figure called Chad, asking the standard question "Wot, no . . . ?" Both these figures appeared around the time of World War II, and explanations for their origins are legion.

One of the earliest literary references to graffiti occurs at the end of F. Scott Fitzgerald's *The Great Gatsby* (1922) when Nick Carraway observes an unquoted "obscenity" which has been scrawled on the dead Gatsby's mansion. The British poet Tony Harrison's poem "V" (1985) was an expression of outrage at the desecration of his parents' grave, replicating the shocking capitalized forms FUCK, CUNT, SHIT, etc. The broadcast of the poem in 1987 provoked a national controversy.

Especially in its political dimension, graffiti has become a new sociological phenomenon of protest, commonly exploiting forms of linguistic aggression and extreme freedom in swearing. Modern graffiti commonly carries a tinge of the illicit, and can therefore only be used for subversive or hostile messages of an anti-establishment nature. Thus the statement "Property is theft" is ideal as graffiti, whereas "Property is a good investment" would be counterproductive, being inseparable from advertising. Outgroups are also targeted: William Leap's *Word's Out* (1996) contains a chapter illustrating in a frame-by-frame fashion the evolution or degeneration of graffiti about gays.

The spray-paint can is now used with the same purpose that the provocative pamphlet or broadsheet was exploited in earlier times. Previously, the bulk of the population was static, but could be reached by means of movable type. Nowadays, with the bulk of the population commuting, messages are placed in locales where they will perforce be seen by the passing public. Whereas pamphlets were sold, thereby involving the purchaser in a choice, graffiti typically catches the observer's eye unawares. However, the initial message can become a palimpsest, vulnerable to ironic ripostes, since subsequent "authors" can subvert it. Thus during the apartheid regime the following slogan appeared in the London subway: "The ANC [African National Congress] will break the shackles of Apartheid," to which had been added the racist comment: "Kaffirs [blacks] break everything." This is a powerful instance of the "straight" political slogan using conventional metaphors of political struggle, and the rejoinder exploiting taboo language and racist stereotyping. The subversive element can also be reinforced by wit and wordplay, as in the example "Phallic Symbolism is a lot of cock," punning on the British idiom for "a lot of rubbish."

In recent decades graffiti has reached such volumes as to be regarded as a public nuisance, so that in 2002 utilities like British Rail instituted prosecutions and fines for the defacement of public property. Town and city authorities in Britain, the United States, and South Africa have followed the same practice.

See also: Kaffir.

Bibliography

Brassaï. *Graffiti*. London: Thames & Hudson, 2002.
Freeman, Richard. *Graffiti*. London: Hutchinson, 1966.
Leap, William. *Word's Out: Gay Men's English*. Minneapolis: University of Minnesota Press, 1996.
Macdonald, Nancy. *The Graffiti Subculture*. New York: Palgrave, 2001.

GRAMMAR. *See:* Flexibility.

GRAVES, ROBERT

Robert Graves (1895–1985) was a versatile man of letters, a notable poet, novelist, anthropologist, and historian, whose works ranged from *The White Goddess* (1948), a study of mystery rites in ancient times, to *I, Claudius* (1934), a historical dramatization of the deranged Roman emperor. His contribution to the understanding of swearing consists of a small incisive volume originally issued under the title of *Lars Porsena, or The Future of Swearing* (1929), revised as *The Future of Swearing and Improper Language* (1936). In this work he drew partly on his experiences in the army in World War I, memorably documented in *Goodbye to All That* (1929), as well as his extensive knowledge of English literature. (The reference to Lars Porsena alludes to the opening line of Thomas Babington Macaulay's highly popular poem "The Lays of Ancient Rome" (1842): "Lars Porsena of Clusium, by the nine gods he swore.")

The future of swearing and foul language attracts great interest and speculation among the general public. The customary view is that the state of the language is so bad that it is hard to conceive of any further deterioration. Graves, however, advances a completely contrary argument. His basic thesis, relating swearing to social causes, is set out with admirable clarity and a slightly provocative tenor:

> Of recent years in England there has been a noticeable decline of swearing and foul language, and this, except at centres of industrial depression, shows every sign of continuing indefinitely until a new shock to our national nervous system—envisageable as war, pestilence, revolution, fire from Heaven, or whatever you please—may (or may not) revive the habit of swearing, simultaneously with that of praying.
> (1936, 1)

Graves clearly sees swearing, not as a continuous practice but as a verbal response to various crises in social development, contained in his examples of "war, pestilence [and] revolution." This is a persuasive argument, and is supported by the great upsurge of xenophobic and vituperative terms generated in times of hostility and by political upheavals. The entries for **war, disease,** and **ethnic insults** cover these topics. His pointed reference "except at centres of industrial depression" underlines the social context, for both versions of his study appeared during the Depression. He also makes the observation, implied in the last phrases, that "the habit of swearing" and that of praying are related. This draws on the **medieval period**, which juxtaposed religious faith and the most appalling utterances of blasphemy.

However, his thesis obviously ignores at least three salient factors. The great efflorescence of swearing in Elizabethan and Restoration times took place during periods of great national prosperity and optimism, not depression. The terms related to the Plague appear decades, if not centuries, after the cataclysm. Furthermore, swearing of the excretory and genital kind shows a continuous history not dependent on national disasters as catalysts. Nevertheless, Graves has a point in claiming that swearing seems to be more fashionable or *de rigueur* at some periods than at others.

His ending is ironic: "As for *The Future of Swearing*, who is going to write about it? Not I. To begin with, I cannot believe that it has a future, at least, not one worth setting beside its past" (1936, 65). He proceeds to suggest a title (his own), but proposes to leave someone else "to do the dirty work," offering a compendium of themes and causative factors varying in persuasiveness from the cogently plausible to the plainly ridiculous. They include:

> the imaginative decline of popular swearing under industrial standardization and since the popular Education Acts of fifty years ago; the part played in this decline by the rise in the price of liquor and the shortening of drinking hours; following the failure of the Saints and the Prophets, and the breakdown of orthodox Heaven and Hell as supreme swearing stocks; the questionable compensation by such superstitious objects as hammers, sickles, swastikas, and shirts of different single colours, and by Freudian symbolism; the effects on swearing of the spread of spiritistic belief, of golf, of new popular diseases such as botulism and sleepy-sickness, of new forms of scientific warfare . . . of gallantly foul-mouthed feministic encroachment on what has been hitherto regarded as a wholly male province.
> (1936, 65).

This curious list has some successful predictions but, on balance, more failures. Compulsory education has made the young aware of "improper" language, yet school is where most middle-class children learn to swear. The correlation between drunkenness and swearing seems sound, as does the decline in force of religious swearing. Political movements have indeed generated insulting labels, such as *commie* and *fascist*, but "spiritistic" belief (presumably emotive evangelism) has had little effect. Nor have new diseases, nor even scientific warfare, contributed to the word stock of swearing. "Freudian symbolism" seems a bizarre irrelevance, since it is the actual vulgar words for the genitalia and copulation, not the symbols, that were becoming current. Yet if "golf" (an especially frustrating game) is taken to symbolize sport in general, then there is no question that Graves has indeed anticipated a major source of modern profanity, although major golf players, unlike weekend amateurs, are invariably models of decorum.

Behind Graves's pronouncements on the decline of swearing and improper language there lies, one surmises, a biographical factor. For a literary man who had been immersed in the copious profanity of the war, everything subsequent must have seemed very tame. In his memoir, *Goodbye to All That* (1929), he records a number of such episodes:

The greatest number of simultaneous charges that I ever heard brought against a soldier occurred in the case of Boy Jones, at Liverpool in 1917. They accused him, first, of using obscene language to the bandmaster. (The bandmaster, who was squeamish, reported it as: "Sir, he called me a double effing c——.")
(1929, 70)

By the time that Graves died in 1985, there had in fact been a tremendous upsurge of swearing. But it had been brought about by less cataclysmic factors than he envisaged, such as the trial of *Lady Chatterley's Lover* (1960), and Kenneth Tynan's notorious articulation of "fuck" on B.B.C. television, over thirty years after Graves's original publication. They show the difficulty of prediction in this strange linguistic field.

The Future of Swearing and Improper Language is typical of its time, being based on anecdote and literary knowledge rather than hard data and statistics. But Graves manages his material and marshals his arguments in an appealing and thought-provoking fashion, bringing out the paradoxes and inconsistencies of attitudes toward swearing. It was also a brave book to write at the time, as Graves mischievously reminds us at the outset: "It is to be hoped that this essay will steer its difficult course without private offence to the reader and without public offence to the Censor" (1936, 1).

See also: Political Names; War.

Bibliography

Graves, Robert. *The Future of Swearing and Improper Language.* London: Kegan Paul, Trench Trubner, 1936.
———. *Goodbye to All That.* Harmondsworth: Penguin, 1929.
Harris, Roy. "*Lars Porsena* Revisited." In Ricks, Christopher, and Leonard Michaels eds., *The State of the Language 1990s Edition.* London: Faber & Faber, 1990.

GROSE, CAPTAIN FRANCIS

Captain Francis Grose (1731–1791) is a significant but not well-known figure in the history of foul language and obscenity, being the author of the most racy and entertaining work in the field, *A Classical Dictionary of the Vulgar Tongue* (1785). Grose was an antiquary who wrote two substantial works, *Antiquities of England and Wales* (1773–1787) and *A Treatise on Ancient Armour and Weapons* (1785–1789). However, as the robust tone of his *Classical Dictionary* suggests, he was a noted character of the times, having been the paymaster of the Hampshire Militia from 1763 to 1769 and an innkeeper used to the hurly-burly and coarse speech of army and street life. "A veritable Falstaff of lexicographers, Grose was a hugely fat man whose servant allegedly strapped him into bed to prevent the covers slipping from his vast belly; he was well known for his consumption of porter [dark beer] and his telling of stories," recounts Jonathon Green (1996, 232). Like Dr. Johnson, he was a "character," a great bon viveur, humorist, and raconteur, whose personality shines through many of his entries.

The *Classical Dictionary* is an unexpected record of demotic English both in the date of its appearance and the comprehensiveness of its coverage. The eighteenth century was generally a period of semantic conservatism very concerned with imposing order on the language and keeping the unruly and disreputable elements at bay. A number of major authors, including Jonathan Swift, Daniel Defoe, Richard Steele, and Joseph Addison wrote condemnations of the fashionable slang of the times. Defoe underlined the absurdity of such language in his "A Tilt at Profanity" in 1712: "at play it is G-d damn the cards; a-hunting G-d damn the hounds; they call dogs the sons of whores and men sons of bitches" (1951, 260). In his magisterial *Dictionary* of 1755 Dr. Johnson was especially condemning of "cant," the perpetually flourishing but generally unstable language of the underworld, regarding it as "unworthy of preservation" (1963, 23).

Grose's title, *A Classical Dictionary of the Vulgar Tongue,* is arresting in the contradiction of the key terms *classical* and *vulgar,* since the first implies formality and order, while the second now denotes the more disreputable elements of the language. Most works dealing with slang or underworld argot preferred titles that exploited the language itself, such as *A Notable Discovery of Coosnage* [trickery] by Robert Greene (1591). They had thrived in Elizabethan times, but were virtually unknown in the eighteenth century. Grose's title brings out the semantic shift undergone by the term *vulgar,* which in its earlier sense meant simply the "common, ordinary or vernacular language used by the majority." In time there developed more class-bound senses, referring to the language of those "not reckoned as belonging to good society" or "lacking in refinement and good taste, uncultured, ill-bred" (the definitions of the *Oxford English Dictionary*). While the second exclusive sense seems the more fitting, the older meaning reminds us that *vulgar* has clear associations with the majority.

Various entries show that Grose's sense of *vulgar* is close to what we would now call slang. For instance, he points out that *devilish* has virtually no literal force, meaning simply "very: an epithet which in the English vulgar language is made to agree with every quality of thing; as, devilish bad, devilish good; devilish sick, devilish well; devilish sweet, devilish sour; devilish hot, devilish cold, &c. &c." He defines *slang* as "cant language" and *canting* as "a kind of gibberish used by thieves and gypsies, called likewise pedlars' French, the slang, &c. &c." In his Preface, Grose frankly advertises the usefulness of his volume:

> The many vulgar allusions and cant expressions that so frequently occur in our common conversation and periodical publications, make a work of this kind extremely useful, if not absolutely necessary, not only to foreigners, but even to natives resident at a distance from the Metropolis. . . . [since it contains] terms of well-known import at Newmarket [racecourse], Exchange-alley [the Stock Exchange], the City [the mercantile center] . . . and Newgate [the principal jail].

Grose's work is an exuberantly witty thesaurus containing approximately 3,500 entries, many of them concerned with the underworld or the seamy side of life. Seldom judgmental, Grose simply records the terms, adding a dry or humorous definition. Typical examples are *abbess,* "a bawd, the mistress of a brothel"; *academy or pushing school,* "a brothel"; *active citizen,* "a louse"; *covent garden nun,* "a prostitute"; *thingumbobs,* "testicles"; *bumbo,* "brandy, water and sugar; also the negro name for the private parts of a woman"; *scotch warming pan,* "a wench, also a fart"; *scourers,* "riotous bucks [decadent men about town], who amuse themselves with breaking windows, beating the watch [police], and assaulting every person they meet"; *buss beggar,* "an old superannuated fumbler, whom none but beggars will suffer to kiss them"; *rushers,* "thieves who knock at the great houses in London, in summer time, when the families are gone out of town, and on the door being opened by a woman, rush in and rob the house"; *riding St. George,* "the woman uppermost in the amorous congress, that is to say the dragon upon St. George"; *molly: A miss Molly,* "an effeminate fellow, a sodomite."

Grose also records, frequently for the first time, slang words that are still current. These include *to hump,* "once a fashionable word for copulation"; *to screw,* "to copulate"; *to shag,* "to copulate"; a *beak,* "a justice of the peace or magistrate"; *to fence,* "to pawn or sell to a receiver of stolen goods"; *Yankey or Yankey Doodle:* "a booby, or country lout: a name given to the New England men in North America. A general appellation for an American"; *to kick the bucket,* "to die"; *swig,* "a hearty draught of liquor"; *buggy,* "a one-horse chaise"; *brat,* "a child or infant"; *bum,* "the breech, or backside"; *birthday suit,* "stark naked"; *to swing,* "to be hanged"; *to shoot the cat,* "to vomit from excess of liquor"; and *shrimp,* "a little diminutive person."

However, Grose ventures further into the area of obscenity than any of his contemporaries, including the following: *cundum,* "the dried gut of a sheep, worn by men in the act of coition, to prevent venereal infection"; *c**t; duck f-ck-r,* "the man who has the care of the poultry on board a ship of war"; *burning shame,* "a lighted candle stuck into the parts of a woman, certainly not intended by nature for a candlestick"; *buttock ball,* "the amorous congress"; *bob tail,* "a lewd woman, or one that plays with her tail; also an impotent man or a eunuch"; *to blow the grounsils,* "to lie with a woman on the floor"; *bunter,* "a low dirty prostitute, half whore and half beggar"; *bum fodder,* "soft paper for the necessary house"; *to roger,* "to lie with a woman."

Although his entries are usually brief and to the point, Grose often elaborates, as with *bitch:* "a she dog or doggess; the most offensive appellation that can be given to an English woman, even more provoking than that of whore." He also provides interesting etymologies, such as that for *coxcomb:* "Anciently, a fool. Fools, in great families, wore a cap with bells, on the top of which was a piece of red cloth, in the shape of cock's comb. At present, coxcomb signifies a fop, or vain self-conceited fellow." Similar explanations are provided for *to send one to Coventry, covent garden, salmon-gundy* (i.e., *salmagundy*), and *billingsgate language:* "Foul language, or abuse. Billingsgate is the market where the fishwomen assemble to purchase fish; and where, in their dealings and disputes, they are somewhat apt to leave decency and good manners a little on the left hand."

Grose's confidence in his *Dictionary* was well placed: a second edition came out in 1788 and a third in 1796. For decades it was plagiarized, extended, and revised. The most accessible version is the expanded edition by **Eric Partridge** first published in 1931 and since available in various formats.

See also: Dictionaries; Restoration, the.

Bibliography

Defoe, Daniel. "A Tilt at Profanity" (1712). In *The Best of Defoe's REVIEW*, ed. William Payne. New York: Columbia University Press, 1951.

Green, Jonathon. *Chasing the Sun*. London: Jonathan Cape, 1996.

Grose, Francis. *A Classical Dictionary of the Vulgar Tongue*. London: S. Hooper, 1785.

Partridge, Eric, ed. Francis Grose's, *A Classical Dictionary of the Vulgar Tongue*. London: Routledge & Kegan Paul, 1931.

GRUNDY, MRS.

Censorship of language and morality takes both official and unofficial forms. In addition to the **Master of the Revels** and the **Lord Chamberlain**, there have been various significant individuals who have simply taken up the role of self-appointed supervisor of public morals. These included a number of Puritans who attacked the Elizabethan stage, covered in the entry for **Renaissance**, and Jeremy **Collier**, who launched a similar work, *A Short View of the Immorality and Profaneness of the English Stage* in 1698. Though all were regarded as extremists, they had considerable impact on the thought of the time, but none had influence extending beyond their own era.

The figure who acquired genuine institutional force was a curious successor, the mythical Mrs. Grundy, an imaginary character in a long-forgotten play, Thomas Morton's *Speed the Plough* (1798). Though Mrs. Grundy never actually appears on stage, she is still able, *in absentia,* to exercise her influence, particularly over one vulnerable character, Dame Ashfield, who persistently asks the anxious question, "What would Mrs. Grundy say?" A typical exchange in the play (which is written in dialect) is as follows:

Dame Ashfield: If shame should come to the poor child [her daughter]—I say, Tummas, what would Mrs. Grundy say then?

Farmer Ashfield: Dom Mrs. Grundy; what wou'd my poor wold heart zay?
[Damn Mrs. Grundy; what would my poor old heart say?]

The question became proverbial, and Mrs. Grundy came to be what the *Oxford English Dictionary* calls "a personification of the tyranny of social opinion in matters of conventional propriety," or what would now be called the voice of disapproving bourgeois morality. Unlike her predecessors, who founded their arguments on religious objections, Mrs. Grundy was an entirely secular figure of social conformity. Her formidable influence is reflected in the subsequent semantic growth of *Grundyism* (1836), *Grundyites* (1845), and *Grundyist* (1883). Various major authors referred disparagingly to her: Tennyson commented sourly on "the Grundyites" (in his *Memoirs* of 1897, I, 227), while Thomas Hardy was more direct in the *New Review* (January 19, 1890), rejecting a work as "Unreal and meretricious, but dear to the Grundyist and subscriber."

Mrs. Grundy's successors were various influential individuals who were by no means offstage characters. The first was the **Bowdler** family, Elizabeth, Harriet, and Thomas, whose principal enterprise was the expurgated *Family Shakespeare* (1807). In the United States the spirit of Grundyism was personified in the career of Anthony **Comstock**, the campaigner against obscene literature. The most recent and successful has been **Mrs. Mary Whitehouse**, who started a campaign "Clean Up Television" in 1964. Mrs. Grundy is now a largely passé historical figure, but her influence lives on, both in the form of active campaigners and in the more elusive spirit of self-censorship.

See also: Bowdlerization; Collier Controversy; Comstockery; Whitehouse, Mrs. Mary.

Bibliography

Morton, Thomas. *Speed the Plough*. London: 1798.

H

HATE SPEECH

Hate speech is a significant new categorizing term, denoting the deliberate or concerted use of provocative slurs or offensive epithets. First recorded in 1988 in the United States, it obviously reflects awareness of the power of language as the bearer of prejudice. However, the practice of stigmatizing foreigners, believers of "alien" religions, homosexuals, and outsiders in general has been established and *de rigueur* in English-speaking societies for centuries. The entry for **ethnic insults** shows that terms like *infidel, bugger, coolie,* and *Jew* in its various opprobrious senses have been in use for over four hundred years. More significantly, these and other hostile terms like *dago, hottentot, frog, kaffir, nigger,* and *coon,* first recorded in the period 1600–1800, were also included in major dictionaries, such as the *Oxford English Dictionary (OED)* (1884–1928) and *Webster II* (1934), usually without comment. These omissions indicate both a general insensitivity to such words and an assumption that a lexicographer's function did not extend to giving usage labels for racist terms.

There was in the past no generic term to describe or denote this linguistic activity. The earliest word, *nickname,* is now inadequate in that nicknames can be personal or general, affectionate as well as hostile or demeaning. As the entry for **nicknames** shows, the earlier uses were generally hostile, provocative, or contemptuous. Francis Grose, in his *Classical Dictionary of the Vulgar Tongue* (1785), was the first lexicographer to include epithets for ethnic groups, including the Irish, Scots, Welsh, Jews, Catholics, Dutch, blacks, and gypsies. His entry for Jew, for example, runs: "An overreaching dealer, or hard, sharp fellow; an extortioner." He also included *molly,* an early slang term for a homosexual: "an effeminate fellow, a sodomite."

Consequently, perhaps the most significant feature of this phenomenon is the recency of such categorizing descriptions as *hate speech, linguistic xenophobia, ethnophaulism, ethnic insult,* and *homophobia.* All these terms have been generated in recent decades in the United States, reflecting greater sensitivity to this issue and a considerable volume of research devoted to it. In the United Kingdom there has been research, notably by Eric Partridge, from the 1930s, but by contrast, critical categories and usage labels have been far slower to develop. *Hate speech* itself is, of course, a more direct, accessible, and condemning formula than such earlier categories as *linguistic xenophobia, ethnophaulism, ethnic insult,* and *homophobia,* which have the disadvantage of being opaque and not readily comprehensible because of their classical roots.

Ethnophaulism, meaning a nickname used for an ethnic group, is still not recorded in many standard dictionaries, not having developed a general currency outside specialist research. The term was coined by a psychologist, A.A. Roback, who carried out the first research into ethnic slurs in the United States in 1944. In the first quantitative study of nicknames for ethnic groups in a society, Erdman Palmore in 1962 advanced the proposition that "There is a close correlation between the amount of prejudice against an outgroup and the number of ethnophaulisms for it" (442). While this seems plausible, it can also be a circular argument, namely the explanation of a linguistic fact by an assumed psychological process for which the principal evidence is the fact to be explained. Palmore rightly conceded, therefore, that "greater hostility could be expressed and reinforced by the repetitions of a small number of ethnophaulisms or by using stronger ones" (443). In addition, very few members of a speech community will know the whole range of ethnophaulisms available.

In his major study, *The Language of Ethnic Conflict* (1983), Irving Lewis Allen compiled a substantial thesaurus of over 1,000 ethnic insults for more than fifty American groups, analyzing the field rigorously from both a historical and sociological perspective in order to explain the quantitative distribution. He also acknowledged an ideological problem of pursuing such research in the United States. Given the fact that "Many of the slurs are genuinely offensive and will strike some persons of ethnic sensibility as obscene," Allen suggested that "The reluctance of social scientists to deal extensively with abusive words for ethnic groups may stem from an ambivalence about the ancient issue of conflict and consensus in society" (1983, 4). Bringing into play such important factors as immigration and urbanization stressed by H.L. Mencken and Louis Wirth before him, Allen interpreted the diversity of ethnic slurs as being a historical reflection of pluralism and diversity in a multicultural society that values assimilation, but is also based on economic competition. In his preamble he returns to the contrary pressures of assimilation and diversity. "These words also show something of the dynamism of ethnic diversity and document the strains of assimilation. In what seems a paradox, the stereotypes generated by the plural society underscore its diversity" (1983, 7).

British history has followed a different pattern, England having become the dominant nation of the United Kingdom, with the other component nations retaining their ancestral native territories. Religious conflicts, though extremely bitter and violent, were eventually contained by various settlements, with the major exception of Ireland. (Extreme examples of incitement, such as "Kill all Peelers"—"Kill all British policemen"—still occur in Northern Ireland.) Military, mercantile, and political rivalry have been focused outward, continentally and globally. All of these tensions have left semantic markers, which make up the great preponderance of xenophobic terms in English. Although immigration from the Continent has been a perennial social fact, the major influxes of Indians, Pakistanis, West Indians, and others from erstwhile member nations of the Empire is a comparatively recent phenomenon, having started in the 1960s. Yet the volume of sociological and semantic evidence from these latter sources has not yet reached the proportion available in America. The semantic field of British-based xenophobic terms that has evolved in the course of the twentieth century is small, and is mainly focused on Continental nations: *hun, wop, boche, fritz, jerry, kraut, wog, eyetie*, the only new term being *paki*.

Homophobia, meaning hatred or fear of homosexuals and homosexuality, was coined as far back as the late 1960s, the first reference usually being given as 1969 in *Time* magazine. Being an artificial rather than a natural term, it did not develop a very strong currency until the 1990s, when it started to be used quite aggressively as part of gay awareness, a topic covered in the entry for **homosexuals**. It has subsequently generated the noun *homophobe*.

The lexicographical aspect of hate speech is obviously significant. Dr. Johnson was very critical of certain slang words or jargon infiltrating the language, but was unconcerned by obscenity and racist terms. The *OED* famously omitted *fuck* and *cunt*, which were technically illegal as well as powerfully taboo, but included a whole range of racist epithets without comment. Since then opprobrious racist terms have become the new potent area of taboo. This development is illustrated in the entry for the word **nigger**, in which dictionary policy is indicated in the comments, ranging from "colloquial" through "offensive" to "taboo." The trend from acceptance to condemnation is obvious, the turning point clearly occurring in the 1960s. Although much of the criticism leveled at *Webster III* (1961) derived from the dictionary's apparent policy of *laissez faire*, at least one attack focused on the formula "usually taken to be offensive" attached to *kike, dago, nigger*, and *coon* (see Perlmutter in Morton 1994, 238). While the social context and race of the speaker are always important, there was clearly a belief that such words themselves were normally offensive. Such a view manifestly lay behind the determined campaign against Oxford University Press to suppress the opprobrious uses of the word *Jew* in the *OED,* leading up to an unsuccessful prosecution in 1972. In the most extreme response, in 1970 Dr. David B. Guralnik, editor-in-chief of *Webster's New World Dictionary,* 2nd College Edition, omitted what he termed "those true obscenities, the terms of racial and ethnic opprobrium." No other major dictionary has followed this policy. However, Robert L. Chapman, editor of the *New Dictionary of American Slang* (1986), instituted "impact symbols" in the form of solid black triangles (▲) for "taboo" words which "are *never* to be used"; these included "terms of contempt and derision for racial or other groups" (1986, xxxiii).

Hate speech has become part of a currently evolving debate over whether the right to free speech should be curtailed in this special instance. Up to now such an infringement of civil liberties has not been supported. However, in the United Kingdom there have been moves to stamp out a related form of hate speech, namely racist chanting in football matches. Some clubs have put in place disciplinary measures including the ejection of offenders from matches. In South Africa the legal category of **crimen injuria** is significant in this respect.

Historically, it is possible to detect a reversal of standards. In medieval times xenophobia was often virulently expressed, especially against Muslims and Jews, notably by the terms *heathen* and *infidel.* Today such practices are completely unacceptable in tolerant Western societies. However, extremist Muslim leaders, such as Osama bin Laden, regularly use inflammatory and archaic religious terminology by referring to America as "the Antichrist," to Israelis as "Zionists," and to Christians as "Crusaders."

See also: Crimen Injuria; Heathen, Infidel, and Pagan; Jews; Nicknames; Nigger.

Bibliography

Allen, Irving Lewis. *The Language of Ethnic Conflict.* New York: Columbia University Press, 1983.

Morton, Herbert C. *The Story of Webster's Third.* Cambridge: Cambridge University Press, 1994.

Palmore, Erdman B. "Ethnophaulisms and Ethnocentrism." *American Journal of Sociology* 67 (1962).

Roback, A.A. *A Dictionary of International Slurs.* Cambridge: Sci-Art, 1944.

Walker, Samuel. *Hate Speech: The History of An American Controversy.* Lincoln: University of Nebraska Press, 1994.

Whillock, Rita K., and D. Slayden, eds. *Hate Speech.* Thousand Oaks, CA: Sage, 1995.

HEATHEN, INFIDEL, AND PAGAN

Most religions, especially those with proselytizing, recruiting, or militant characteristics, make a sharp distinction between "true believers" or "keepers of the faith" and "unbelievers," namely outsiders, opponents, and holders of rival religions. In the course of the Middle Ages, when Christianity was in the ascendancy in Europe, various terms developed to denote and stigmatize those who were not followers of the Christian faith. These were, in order of historical appearance, *heathen, pagan,* and *infidel.* Although there were originally distinctions between the meanings of these three terms, these have tended to be lost in their somewhat indiscriminate use in subsequent centuries. *Heathen* is first recorded in its Anglo-Saxon form *hæðen,* often denoting the Viking marauders, for example, in the entry for the year 793 in the *Anglo-Saxon Chronicle:* "in the same year the harrying of the heathen destroyed God's church in Lindisfarne." This became quite a common use. However, *hæðen* could be used less emotively to mean "gentile" (as opposed to "Jew") and is applied to the Good Samaritan.

By the early twelfth century it was being used (in the Middle English form *hethen*) to mean "not Christian or Jewish, thus pagan," ignoring other religions. The term is assumed to derive ultimately from Gothic *haithi* meaning "dwelling on the heath," in the translation of the Bible into Gothic by Ulfilas, the Bishop of the Goths in the sixth century (Mark 7:26). Cognate forms of *heathen* are found in all the ancient Germanic languages and are taken to be a translation of Latin *paganus,* a rustic villager, the root of *pagan.* The assumption behind both *heathen* and *pagan* is that the old idolatry lingered longest in rural areas. *Pagan* was taken into English in the late fourteenth century, originally in the sense of "heathen"—that is, one unconverted to the Christian religion. In Middle English it developed two related forms *payens* and *paynim,* both of which were widely used and developed considerable emotive force, especially in the context of religious wars.

The origin of *infidel* lies in Latin *in* (not) and *fidelis* "faithful," the term originally denoting a non-Christian, especially a Muslim. The word is defined with rather dry wit in the *Oxford English Dictionary* as "One who does not believe in (what the speaker holds to be) the true religion; an 'unbeliever.'" In its early stages it denoted "an adherent of a religion opposed to Christianity, especially a Mahommedan," being so used in Sir Thomas Malory's *Morte d'Arthur* (1485) in a reference to "two honderd sarasyns or infydels" (Curiously, *saracen* is actually the older term.) It became common in the Middle Ages to denote these outsiders impersonally as "the infidel" or "the heathen," used of both Muslims and Jews, as if these religions were of no validity, so that the Crusades were commonly styled "the war against the infidel or heathen." In the *Canterbury Tales,* Chaucer's exemplary Knight had "foughten for oure faith" extensively against the "hethen" (ll. 62–66). Yet two of Chaucer's most respectable pilgrims, the Man of Law and the Prioress, tell tales charged with religious animosity, the first against heathens and pagans, the second against "the cursed Jews."

Subsequently *infidel* was applied to followers of other religions in general. In William Tyndale's translation of 2 Corinthians 6:15 (ca. 1526), the term has the stronger sense of a person of no religion, an atheist. In *The Merchant of Venice* (1596), a play dealing directly with anti-Semitic attitudes, Gratiano says in a tense moment of legal tussling to Shylock, "Now, infidel, I have thee on the hip" (IV i 344). However, in the same play the curious character Launcelot Gobbo, "clown and servant to Shylock," says a poignant farewell to Jessica: "Most beautiful pagan, most sweet Jew!" (II iii 11). In the post-Renaissance period, both *pagan* and *heathen* started to be used in a more secular fashion. Shakespeare extended the sense of *pagan* to mean "a prostitute" (*Henry IV Part II,* II ii 68) while Alexander Pope satirized the sexual promiscuity of a society lady styled Narcissa for being "a very heathen in the carnal part" ("Of the Characters of Women," I, l.67).

With the general secularization of Western society and the consequent decline of religion as a social force, all these terms have declined in currency and potency in the West. However, with the rise of militant Muslim sects, such as Al Qaeda, *infidel* is being brought back into currency as a propagandist term against the West, especially America. (Interestingly, similar chauvinist assumptions lie behind the original use of *kaffir,* which is rooted in Arabic *kafir,* an infidel.)

See also: Kaffir; Mahomet/Mohammed.

HELL

The concept of a place of eternal suffering, the obverse of paradise, is one largely derivative of gnostic or Manichean notions, namely that the world is a battleground between the principles of good and evil, and these ultimate states form parts of a system of punishment and reward. Within the Christian framework the idea of the Last Judgment and its extreme consequences have become established, not only as a dominant motif of western literature and religious art, but engrained in the mind-set of the civilization. Since the English language has evolved in this framework of ideas, notions of damnation and the consigning of others to hell have become correspondingly powerful idioms. However, the general semantic development has been from the literal to the metaphorical to the trivial.

Interestingly, the term *Hell* itself is pagan in origin, deriving from Old Norse *Hel,* the goddess of the realm of the dead and the underworld in Scandinavian mythology. However, the word appears (as *helle*) in Old English about 725—that is, after the conversion to Christianity—in Ælfric's version of Genesis 37:35: "ic fare to minum sunu to helle" ("I will go down into the grave unto my son mourning" in the King James version). *Hell* is only used literally in Anglo-Saxon.

According to the Fathers of the Church, the majority of mankind was consigned to hell, and outside of the Catholic Church there was no salvation (*extra ecclesia nulla salus*). Furthermore, cursing someone to Hell was both an ecclesiastical privilege (covered in the entry for **anathema**) and a motif in folklore. Chaucer's *Friar's Tale* explores the motif of the curse "the Devil take you" coming true if it is heartfelt, describing, "The peynes of thilke [that same] cursed hous of helle" (l. 1652), clearly regarding Hell as a place. However, in the *General Prologue* the corrupt Summoner, who accepts payment in lieu of spiritual penance, claims that the guilty will be punished, not in the afterlife, but here and now, in monetary terms:

in his purs he sholde ypunysshed be
"Purs is the ercedekenes helle," seyde he.
["Money is the archdeacon's damnation."]
(l. 658)

Naturally, the traditional physical interpretation continued, becoming a major feature in eschatology, in architecture, literature, and drama. One of the major scenes in the medieval Miracle plays was the Gate of Hell, sometimes depicted as the mouth of a great monster devouring the damned. Shakespeare draws on this symbolism in his great tragedy of damnation, *Macbeth* (1605) when the Porter of Macbeth's castle makes a number of references to "hell gate," "devils," saying finally, "I'll devil-porter it no longer" (II iii 2–22). Macbeth's villainy is marked by two significant terms Shakespeare creates for him, namely *hell-kite* for his massacre of Macduff's children (IV iii 217), and *hell-hound,* when he is finally challenged by Macduff (V vii 32). In Christopher Marlowe's astonishingly daring play *Doctor Faustus* (1592) the great scholar Faustus, epitomizing Renaissance skepticism, utters the bold challenge: "I think hell's a fable," to which the subtle devil Mephistophilis coolly responds, "Ay think so, Faustus, till experience change thy mind" (v 127–28). Although at the end "Hell is discovered" (revealed) in the traditional form of "a vast perpetual torture-house," the play also shows that hell is a state of mind, a modern notion, since Mephistophilis says exasperatedly to Faustus, "Why, this is Hell, nor am I out of it" (iii 78).

A related term thrown up by the violent controversies of the Reformation was *rake hell,* meaning "an utterly immoral or dissolute person; a vile debauchee or rake," which the *Oxford English Dictionary* notes, was "in common use ca. 1550–1725." J. Bell in 1581 attacked the whole ecclesiastical hierarchy with effective alliteration, castigating "momish [mumbling] monckes, flatteryng Friers and other such like religious rakehells" (*Haddon's Answer to Ossory,* 315). The term is largely obsolete now, having been superseded by *hell-raiser.*

Both Shakespeare and Ben Jonson use *hell* as an exclamation in secular contexts in the modern mode. Shylock's daughter complains melodramatically in *The Merchant of Venice,* "Our house is hell" (II iii 2), while Jonson's *Eastward Ho!* (1605) has this infuriated outburst: "What! Landed at Cuckold's Haven! Hell and damnation!" (IV i). Although Shakespeare has the phrase "Let Fortune go to hell for it, not I" in *The Merchant of Venice* (III i), this is not truly the modern idiomatic use, which is recorded from 1788: "The ansare vas (excuse moy, monsieur) 'go to h-ll, if you please'" (S. Low, *Politician Outwitted* I i). Peter Hausted's play *Rivall Friends* (1632), acted before the king and queen, has the exclamation "Fie fie, hell is broke loose upon me." In the conservative period of the eighteenth century, the term became less socially acceptable. Thus a group of dissolute dandies daringly called themselves in 1720 "The Hellfire Club, kept by a Society of Blasphemers," ordering "Holy Ghost pie" at taverns. The hellfire sermon increasingly became a thing of the past. In a neat satirical sally in 1731, Alexander Pope criticized the cowardly politeness of a tame clergyman's sermon in a wealthy establishment:

To rest, the Cushion and soft Dean invite,
Who never mentions Hell to ears polite.
(*Epistle to Burlington, On the Use of Riches,* ll. 149–50)

Considering the antiquity of the term, the loose use of *hell* as an emotive intensifier is a surprisingly modern development. The phrase *What the hell* is first recorded in Captain Frederick Marryat's novel *Frank Mildmay* (1829) in this reticent nineteenth-century form: "What the h—- brought you back again, you d———d young greenhorn?" (22). The response, "Like hell!," used ironically or to express irritation or skepticism is late Victorian, found in Rudyard Kipling, but subsequently highly current in the United States. The idiomatic use of *hell* has proved extremely fruitful. The expansion that began in British English has proceeded apace in the American variety. The table below gives some sense of this development by noting the earliest recorded instances of the phrases and idioms.

	British English	American English
hellcat	1605	
hell and damnation!	1605	
hell of a . . .	1680	
go to hell		1788
raise hell	1796	
hell to pay	1807	
hellhole		1828
what the hell	1829	
hell's bells	1832	
hell's kitchen		1834
hellbent		1835
give—hell		1836
hell on wheels		1843
to hell and gone		1863
hell's half-acre		1864
hope to hell	1891	
hell for leather	1892	
hell and high water		1915
hellacious		1929
till hell freezes over		1931
for the hell of it		1934
. . . from hell		1965

Sources: Oxford English Dictionary (2nd ed., Oxford: Clarendon Press, 1989); *The Random House Historical Dictionary of American Slang* (New York: Random House, 1994–).

The table deals with only the more familiar idioms, but there are many bizarre and picturesque phrases, such as *to lead apes to hell* (to die an old maid), *hell and scissors!* (an American exclamation, reduced in England to plain *scissors!*), *hell is popping* (hell is breaking loose), and *from hell to breakfast* (everywhere). Nevertheless, it is notable that since the 1930s there has been only one significant new entry, "the boss/mother in law/landlady from hell." The fact that *hell* was banned in terms of the Hollywood Production Code of 1930 is significant. In the same year *Hell's Angels* is recorded as a film title, presumably just evading the code. But even in 1954, in the Marlon Brando film *The Wild Ones*, the motorcycle gang was restyled the *Black Rebels*. Even more surprising was the title of the film *Road to Perdition* (2002), an obviously euphemized version of the proverbial saying "The road to hell is paved with good intentions."

As with all profane terms, euphemistic variants abound. These take three forms. The first is the distortion of the offending term, as in *heck*, recorded from about 1887 in British English and 1895 in American English, where it is more common. This variety also has *blazes, Hades, Jesse, Sam Hill,* and *thunder.* The second strategy is the substitution of a high-register classical equivalent, as in *infernal* and *perdition*, already alluded to, and used by Othello (III iii 90–91). Chaucer uses *infernal* literally in *Troylus and Criseyde* (ca. 1386), while his contemporary, John Lydgate uses the phrase "infernal falseness" meaning "diabolical" or "devilish" in his *Fall of Princes* (ca. 1439). The modern colloquial use as an intensive meaning "detestable" occurs as "the infernal bugs" in John Cooke's *How a Man May Choose a Good Wife* (1602, ix 50). This usage, always predominantly British, is found in various trivial phrases like *infernal cheek, infernal nonsense,* and so on. Finally, in print format, there is the use of dashes or asterisks, as found in the quotation from Captain Marryat in 1829 cited above: "What the h— brought you back." H.L. Mencken's remark "American grammar is fast going to hell," made in a lecture on December 1, 1939, was euphemized in the New York *Journal-American* the following day to "h—l." Hugh Rawson notes: "According to a 1983 report by the American Library Association's young-adult services division, the [book] clubs 'may remove four-letter words including 'damn' and 'hell.'" He concludes: "So the Victorian strain is very much alive" (1991, 191).

Although the taboo against the term is clearly receding in contemporary usage, it remains a source of sensitivity to many. However, in African-American slang, *hell* can be used, like *wicked*, in a positive sense to mean "excellent," "good," "an impressive person," while *hellacious* can similarly be used to mean "remarkable or outstanding." In the other global varieties of English, such as the Australian and South African, *hell* is used with the comparative ease and breadth of idiom found in British English. Clearly the diminished force of the term and its increasing idiomatic range reflect the secularization of Western society.

See also: Damn.

Bibliography

Major, Clarence. *Juba to Jive.* New York/London: Viking/Penguin, 1994.
Mencken, H.L. "American Profanity." *American Speech,* December 1944.
Rawson, Hugh. *A Dictionary of Invective.* London: Hale, 1991.

HOLLYWOOD

The awareness of the powerful role of motion pictures in relation to the wider society has created very different expectations and norms surrounding the film industry, both historically and geographically. This entry focuses on Hollywood in the sense that the name *Hollywood* has been used from the 1920s to epitomize the world of American filmmaking, both studio-based and independent. The British industry is covered under the entry for **cinema**. The American film industry has been a model of the struggle between opportunistic capitalism and religious control, having operated under censorship in the sense of interference prior to publication, especially between 1934 and 1968, after which there was a greater degree of free enterprise. The effects of these changes on film language have been dramatic. Timothy Jay quantifies this in "A Study of Cursing in American Films 1939–89" (1992, 222–34), discussed further below.

Even by 1913 there was in existence a National Board of Review for Motion Pictures, which in its "Definition of Censorship" mentioned the medium's potential for "political, social, religious propaganda, for muckraking . . . [and] for revolutionary ideas" (Ross 2002, 4). This educational and didactic assumption has remained ingrained: "Movies do more than simply show us how to dress, how to look, or what to buy," runs the introduction to a recent collection of essays on *Movies and American Society:* "They teach us how to think about race, gender, class, ethnicity and politics" (Ross 2002, 1). No scholar or critic would write in such terms of the British or European cinema. The collection is illuminating in its focus on particular content-themes, such as the Cold War, the Vietnam War, race relations, feminism, and other political issues.

The history of the American film industry is very much bound up with the struggle between freedom of expression and prohibitions over the treatment of most of the topics just listed. In the early years the two principal antagonists, namely the Hollywood producers and their censors and critics, were capitalists and moralists, all unelected. As early as 1909 the mayor of New York, inundated by complaints of "indecency," closed down the movie theatres. In a landmark case in 1915, the year of D.W. Griffith's *The Birth of a Nation,* the Supreme Court ruled that the motion picture industry was "business pure and simple," and therefore not protected by the First Amendment guaranteeing freedom of speech. Clarence Darrow commented: "It is an anomaly in a free country to guarantee freedom to speak, to publish, or to put anything upon the stage, and to single out the moving pictures as subject for censorship" (Darrow and Vittum 1918, 188). (This judgment has since been reversed and reinstated.) A complicating factor in this libertarian argument is that the movies attracted a vast, unselected, and growing audience: in 1922 the average weekly attendance at theaters was 40 million; by 1928 it had risen sharply to 65 million, and by 1930 it had leaped to 90 million.

Between 1915 and 1922 more direct control was passed to the National Board of Censorship, but producers felt sufficiently free to release films with salacious titles like *A Shocking Night, Luring Lips, Virgin Paradise,* and *The Truant Husband,* together with increasingly explicit love scenes. There were calls for tighter controls and for federal intervention to "rescue the motion pictures from the devil and 500 unchristian Jews" (Hamilton 1990, 58). This ugly religious and ethnic edge was given to the conflict since many of the studio owners were Jewish and most of the moralists were Catholic. In 1922, in response to the industry's request for an outsider to head the newly created Motion Picture Producers and Distributors of America (M.P.P.D.A.), President Warren G. Harding appointed Will H. Hays, the former postmaster general, to this position. What became known as the Hays Office issued guidelines, which originally focused on content. With the arrival of sound, these perforce included the matter of "bad language," another area of contention.

The Production Code

In March 1930, in response to waves of protests and threatened boycotts, the Hollywood producers negotiated a new form of censorship with one their most powerful and determined opponents, the Catholic owner and publisher of *Motion Picture Herald,* Martin Quigley. This resulted in a detailed Motion Picture Production Code, first known as the Hays Code, but actually drawn up by Quigley and Daniel J. Lord, S.J. (a St. Louis drama professor). The Code stressed "the MORAL IMPORTANCE of entertainment," its overriding principle was that "Evil must not be presented alluringly," and the section dealing with "Plot Material" spelled out particular stringent prohibitions concerning the handling of "'the triangle,' adultery, seduction and rape, scenes of passion, murder, crime in general, costume, dancing, locations (no brothels or bedrooms)." In addition there were certain banned topics, namely "sex perversion—or any reference to it"; "miscegenation (sex relationships between the black and white races)"; "sex hygiene or venereal diseases"; "scenes of actual childbirth, in fact or in silhouette." Most germane to the present inquiry were the Code's rulings on language in Section V, termed Profanity: "Pointed profanity (this includes the words God, Lord, Jesus, Christ—unless used reverently—Hell, S.O.B., damn, Gawd) or other profane or vulgar expressions, however used, is forbidden." The Code was modified in various ways subsequently to include such restrictions as "Vulgarity: Oaths 'should never be used as a comedy element. The name of Jesus should never be used except in reverence.'"

By all accounts, the films of the next four years blatantly ignored the Code in terms of content. The most notorious instances were Marlene Dietrich in *The Blue Angel* (1930) and *Blonde Venus* (1932), Joan Crawford in *Possessed* (1931), Jean Harlow in *Red Dust* (1930), and Mae West in *She Done Him Wrong* and *I'm No Angel* (both 1933). By 1934 more than 46 million people had seen the last two films. Representing the most insidious and subversive threat to the restrictions of the Code, "Mae West made any attempt at censorship look foolish [since] she could turn the most innocent-sounding dialogue in a script into blatant sexual innuendo" (Ross 2002, 109). Her most famous line is still: "Is that a gun in your pocket or are you just pleased to see me?" (Hamilton 1990, 66–67).

Within Hollywood itself, always both glamorous and suspect, a double standard obtained, as the magazine *Confidential* showed. Yet the film moguls imposed a rigid code of "family decency," summed up in this lecture from Louis B. Mayer to Hedy Lamarr: "We have an obligation to the audience—millions of families. We make clean pictures . . . of course . . . if you like to make love . . . fornicate . . . screw your leading man in the dressing room, that's your business. But in front of the camera, gentility. You hear, gentility." He concluded the conversation on a more personal note: "you have a bigger chest than I thought! You'd be surprised how tits figure in a girl's career" (Latham 1972, 154). Mayer's oscillations of register from the formal *make love* and *fornicate* to the coarse *screw* and *tits* to the absurd euphemism *chest* reveal his essential hypocrisy.

Largely in response to the flaunting of the Code, a group of Catholic bishops formed in April 1934 the League of Decency and organized a nationwide boycott, which at one point obtained eleven million pledges. Faced with already declining audiences as a result of the Depression, the Hollywood producers agreed to a system of "prior restraint" or censorship in advance. The Hays Office appointed Joseph Breen, a Catholic journalist to head the Production Code Office, which would approve every film before distribution. The results were dramatic. Gangster films, which had achieved notable successes with *Little Caesar* (1930), *The Public Enemy* (1931), and *Scarface* (1932), were dropped (at a time when the Mafia was on the rise). There was an increase in musicals, costume dramas, and biographies. Within a few months commentators on the industry noted that "the obscenity that was found in four or five pictures before last June has disappeared." In an unprecedented sign of approval from Rome, Pope Pius XI issued an encyclical in July 1936 congratulating the League of Decency campaign, on "the outstanding success of the crusade" (Hamilton 1990, 68).

From 1934, until its abolition in 1968, the Production Code Office (P.C.O.) influenced the social, political, sexual, racial, and linguistic content of every American film. Furthermore, in response to demands, the industry withdrew from circulation a number of films deemed to be "immoral," including Ernest Hemingway's *A Farewell to Arms* (1932) and the adaptation of William Faulkner's *Sanctuary,* namely *The Story of Temple Drake* (1933).

Up to this point the principal site of struggle had been sex, that is to say, heterosexual sex, since the taboo on "perversion" was maintained. Studies such as *The Lavender Screen* (1993) and *Queer Cinema* (2004) explore what was going on behind the façade. With the outbreak of war, communications between the White House and Hollywood focused on how filmmakers might contribute to the propaganda potential of the war effort. Many films reflected the hysteria at the start of World War II by exploiting xenophobia and negative stereotypes, using such emotive titles as *The Menace of the Rising Sun, Secret Agent of Japan,* and *Little Tokyo, USA.* This last, actually shot in Chinatown in Los Angeles, has a scene with a police detective dragging off a spy suspect, saying "Take that for Pearl Harbor, you slant-eyed." President Franklin D. Roosevelt's representative, Lowell Mellet, had a team of analysts who interpreted the film as "an invitation to a witch-hunt" (Hamilton 1990, 218). In *Objective Burma* (where there were no actual American troops) a soldier surveys the remains of a village overrun by the Japanese and exclaims: "This was done in cold blood by people who claim to be civilized. Civilized! They're degenerate, immoral idiots. Stinking little savages. Wipe them out, I say. Wipe them off the face of the earth" (Hamilton 1990, 229). By 1943 there were over two hundred screenwriters serving in the armed forces.

The involvement of Hollywood in the Vietnam War was, of course, radically different. During the war *The Green Berets* (1968), the result of a proposal by John Wayne to President Lyndon B. Johnson, presented America's role as an idealistic mission. The correspondence is quoted in Ross (ed.) 2002, 303–5. However, after the war ended in 1975, a number of major antiwar films appeared frankly critical of America's role, most notably *Apocalypse Now* (1979), *Platoon* (1986, although Oliver Stone actually wrote the script in 1976), and Stanley Kubrick's *Full Metal Jacket* (1987). All had scabrous scripts.

The erosion of the Production Code was already being initiated by television, which had started transmission in 1939 and was to expand to twelve channels by 1952. Being essentially a family medium, television was subject to even more rigorous prohibitions against nudity, profanity, and immorality than film. With the consequent decline in cinema audiences, producers saw their opportunity to make films that were "alternative," "adult" entertainment. In 1968 this development was formalized: the Production Code Administration became the Code Seal Rating Office, and films were rated G (General), PG (Parental Guidance), R (Restricted), and X (Over 16). However, "When classification started it was quickly found that the most commercially attractive rating was the 'X'" (Trevelyan 1973, 195). In January 1988 the classification of video films included the categories L for "language" and EL for "extreme language."

Among films of the 1960s that marked a shift away from the narrow prescriptions of the Production Code were Arthur Penn's *Bonnie and Clyde* (1967) and Roy Hill's *Butch Cassidy and the Sundance Kid* (1969). Although the first attracted criticisms of excessive violence, both scripts were almost entirely "clean." Edward Albee's devastatingly frank depiction of domestic warfare in *Who's Afraid of Virginia Woolf* (1966) was also free of verbal overkill: a single witheringly contemptuous "screw you!" from the matriarchal Martha carried more weight than a train of four-letter words. Timothy Jay's study *Cursing in America* (1992) contains an Appendix quantifying the "total Number of Bad Words" in films from 1939 to 1989. This endorses the general impression of a dramatic increase, the mean number rising from 1.58 for the period 1939–1960, to 24.8 in the decade of the 1960s, up to 84.1 in the 1970s, and flattening out to 81.03 in the 1980s. Gender stereotypes are also endorsed, since films with male leads show a rise from 1.5 in the first period to over 70 in the 1970s, while those with female leads predictably increase more demurely to a peak of only 19.48 in the 1980s (1992, 231–34).

An obvious, even extreme example of the absolute change in the values depicted in the American cinema lies in the work of Quentin Tarantino, notably *Reservoir Dogs* (1992), his directorial debut, *Natural Born Killers* (1995), and *Pulp Fiction* (1994). All the taboo topics, such as gratuitous violence, gangsterism, the drug culture, sexual promiscuity, sodomy, and racism are paraded without restraint, combined with a large measure of black or sick humor. Obscenity occurs in virtually every piece of dialogue. Sex is crudely chauvinist: "She's getting this serious dick action. . . . Her pussy should be Bubble-Yum by now. But when this cat fucks her, it hurts" (1994, 5). Racism is overt and virulent. One gangster complains about the "inappropriate" allocation of parole officers to criminals: "Fuckin' jungle bunny goes out there, slits some old woman's throat for twenty-five cents. Fuckin' nigger gets Doris Day as a parole officer. But a good fella like you gets stuck with a ball-busting prick" (1994, 48). Another is even more savage: "Now ain't that a sad sight, daddy, walks into a jail a white man, walks out talkin' like a nigger. It's all that black semen been shooting up his butt. It's backed up into his brain and comes out of his mouth" (1994, 51). *Pulp Fiction* won the Palme D'Or at Cannes in 1994 and a Golden Globe for the Best Screenplay. Publicity material for the film noted coyly: "The f-word is used 271 times." Yet curiously, there are vestiges of the old code. For out of this miasma of savagery, a crude rough justice emerges: in the final shoot-out all the gangsters die, having shot each other or been killed by the police. More surprisingly, "pointed profanity" is comparatively limited, with *Jesus, Christ,* and *God* absent, and "Holy shit" or "What the Sam Hill?" making only the occasional appearance.

The American cinema has broken all the previous restraints to which it was subject. Virtually all the modern varieties of swearing now abound, to the point that sensitive audiences routinely face a virtual bombardment of obscenity, often combined with xenophobic, racist, and homophobic comments. Only profanity still carries the weight of a taboo, to the point that sacred names are commonly euphemized, "bleeped," or even erased from the sound track. Rhett Butler's famous violation of the Code in *Gone with the Wind* (1939): "Frankly my dear, I don't give a damn!" is obviously tame alongside contemporary ejaculations. (Incidentally, the remark was not in the original script, was censored, but passed by Joseph Breen only after a personal written intervention by David O. Selznik, and the payment of a $5,000 fine.) The persistent avoidance of profanity in the American cinema is an enigma in a nation without an official religion. It is certainly not a feature of British or European film, which has evolved in avowedly Christian societies.

See also: Censorship; Cinema.

Bibliography

Benshof, Harry, and Sean Griffith, eds. *Queer Cinema: The Film Reader*. London and New York: Routledge, 2004.

Black, Gregory D. *Hollywood Goes to War*. London: I.B. Tauris, 1987.

———. *The Catholic Crusade Against the Movies, 1940–75*. New York: Cambridge University Press, 1998.

Darrow, Clarence, and Harriet Vittum. "Censorship of 'Movies': Clarence Darrow and Harriet Vittum Debate New Ordinance." *City Club Bulletin* 11, 3 June 1918, 187–88.

Hadleigh, Boze. *The Lavender Screen*. New York: Citadel, 1993.

Hamilton, Ian. *Writers in Hollywood*. London: Heinemann, 1990.

Jay, Timothy. *Cursing in America*. Philadelphia: Benjamins, 1992.

Ross, Steven J., ed. *Movies and American Society*. Oxford: Blackwell, 2002.

Tarantino, Quentin. *Reservior Dogs*. London: Faber & Faber, 1994.

Trevelyan, John. *What the Censor Saw*. London: Michael Joseph, 1973.

Walker, Alexander. *Double Takes*. London: Elm Tree Books, 1977.

Wolf, William, and Lilian Kramer Wolf. *Landmark Films*. New York & London: Paddington, 1979.

HOMOSEXUALS

English-speaking societies historically have regarded heterosexuality as the norm and homosexuality as an aberration or deviation to be viewed with hostility and abhorrence, being prosecuted as a crime in the United Kingdom from 1861 until 1967. It was regarded as a *perversion*, a term that originally (in medieval times) meant "a change to error in religious belief," the opposite of *conversion,* before taking on its psychosexual meaning. (The entry for **bugger** shows the same combination of senses.) The Kinsey report on *Sexual Behavior in the Human Male* (1948) offered this illuminating legal insight: "Perversions are defined as unnatural acts contrary to nature, bestial, abominable, and detestable. Such laws are interpretable only in accordance with the ancient tradition of the English common law which . . . is committed to the doctrine that no sexual activity is justifiable unless its objective is procreation" (viii, 264). The report showed that individual sexual behavior did not match the traditional division between a heterosexual "norm" and a homosexual "abnormality." The

The conviction and imprisonment of Irish poet and dramatist Oscar Wilde on homosexuality charges in 1895 left him a ruined man. Common epithets have long reflected the public attitude toward homosexuals as abnormal and morally detestable, if not criminal. (Library of Congress, LC-DIG-ppmsca-07756)

history of the acknowledgment and problematic naming of homosexuals supports Michel Foucault's thesis that sexuality is controlled as much by discourse and narration as by formal repression and legal measures.

Although what is termed "history from below" (the history of the common people) does not cover this intimate aspect of life, traditional English history ("from above," that is, of the ruling class) furnishes a number of spectacular and scandalous examples. The infatuation of Edward II (1284–1327), especially for Piers Gaveston, was regarded by the nobles as so detestable that they first limited the royal privileges and finally put both the favorite and the king to death, the latter in a gruesomely symbolic fashion. The traditional version derives from "an emotional and highly colored account written by the chronicler Geoffrey le Baker some thirty years later, which culminates in the disgusting scene in which Edward was murdered by means of a red-hot plumber's iron thrust up his anus" (Prestwich 1980, 99). However, Christopher Marlowe's play *The troublesome raigne and lamentable death of Edward the Second* (1594) daringly juxtaposes critical words like *minion* with terms of endearment like "lovely boy," "my friend," "my Gaveston," and contains a catalogue of famous classical homosexual lovers (I iv 390–400).

The equally public affair between James I (1566–1625) and his favorite the Duke of Buckingham provoked frank disapproval in the court but no political protest. The king was described by Sir Anthony Weldon as decadent, "his fingers . . . ever fiddling about his cod-piece . . . and not temperate in his drinking" (Goldberg 1983, 55). Francis Osborne was more explicit about James's public demeanor toward his favorites: "the love the King shewed was as amorously convayed as if he had mistaken their sex and thought them ladies; which I have seene Sommerset and Buckingham labour to resemble, in the effeminateness of their dressings . . . kissing them after so lascivious mode in publick" (Goldberg 1983, 143). Intimate letters, in which King James addressed his favorites as "sweete boyes" with responses such as "my dear dad and master" and "your humble slave and dog" were read aloud in court (Goldberg 1983, 143–44). Toward the end of James's reign, on August 29, 1622, Sir Simonds D'Ewes confided to a guest about "the sinne of sodomye, how frequent it was in this wicked cittye" (Goldberg 1983, 143). After the Restoration the noted diarist Samuel Pepys, who was decidedly heterosexual in his tastes and moved in high society circles, wrote in his entry for July 1, 1663: "Buggery is now almost grown as common amongst our gallants [smart society men] as in Italy, and . . . the very pages [personal servants] of the town begin to complain of their masters for it. But blessed be God, I do not to this day know what is the meaning of the sin, nor which is the agent nor which the patient."

The first evidence of homosexuality in English literature is embodied in Chaucer's corrupt Pardoner, placed last in the cavalcade of pilgrims with long, beautifully groomed yellow locks, a thin goatlike voice, and beardless, singing a love song in unison with his "freend and compeer [partner]," the physically revolting, venal, and alcoholic Summoner. Chaucer the pilgrim-narrator slyly uses equine symbolism as innuendo:

I trowe he were a gelding or a mare.
[I imagine he was a eunuch or effeminate.]
(*Prologue* l. 691)

While the portrait invites a variety of sexual interpretations (see Benson 1988, 824), the Pardoner unwittingly reveals his relationship in a hysterical denunciation:

O dronke man, disfigured is thy face,
Sour is thy breeth, foul artow [art thou] to embrace.
(*Pardoner's Tale*, ll. 551–52)

Although the term *sodomite* was available, Chaucer preferred to be less direct. References in Elizabethan times are covered later.

The major turning point in English perceptions was the scandal surrounding the trial of Oscar Wilde, the brilliant playwright, wit, and personality for homosexual practices in 1895. This brought out into the open "the love that dare not speak its name," alluded to in a poem, "The Two Loves," by Wilde's lover, Lord Alfred Douglas, quoted during the proceedings. Wilde had been provoked into bringing an action of libel against Douglas's father, the Marquess of Queensberry, who had left a note at the Albermarle Club addressed to "Oscar Wilde posing somdomite [sic]" (Ellmann 1988, 412). Queensberry subsequently accused Wilde of some fifteen instances of seeking to corrupt young boys. Wilde lost the libel action, was arrested for "committing indecent acts," found guilty, and sentenced to prison with hard labor, left England in disgrace for exile in France, and died there, ruined at the age of forty-six. However, a double standard prevailed: the homosexuality of many nineteenth-century public figures was either covert or undiscussed.

The naming of homosexuals directly reflects public attitudes toward this sexual condition or preference. At the time of the compilation of the *Oxford English Dictionary* (1884–1928), there was no neutral term for what was then regarded as an abnormal, detestable, and criminal activity. The two prime words, *bugger* and *sodomite,* were part of a large, hostile, and expanding semantic field. There was no generic Greek word, presumably because homosexuals were not regarded as a discrete category. There was no Anglo-Saxon word. *Homosexual* itself appears to have been coined in 1869 by a Hungarian physician, K.M. Benkert, but given currency by Richard Krafft-Ebing in his classic on sexual disorders, *Psychopathia Sexualis* in 1886, translated into English by C.G. Chaddock in 1892. Krafft-Ebing deals with "homo-sexuality" as "the demonstration of perverse feeling for the same sex" (188), a deviation he puts on a par with fetishism, masochism, and sadism. In addition to distinguishing between "acquired homo-sexuality" and "congenital homo-sexuality," he devotes a whole section to "Homo-Sexual Individuals or Urnings" (255–79). This curious term, coined in German by Carl Heinrich Ulrich in 1864, is related to *Uranism* and *Uranian,* both deriving from Plato's *Symposium:* "This is noble, the heavenly love, which is associated with the heavenly muse, Urania" (1951, 56). The term, now virtually obsolete, became quite fashionable among the contemporary literati: "What a number of Urnings are being portrayed in novels now!" wrote John Addington Symonds to Edmund Gosse (Pearsall, 1969, 547). Symonds, who was openly homosexual, wishing to promote a more tolerant climate toward homosexuality, collaborated with Havelock Ellis in *Studies in the Psychology of Sex* until his death in 1893. However, when Ellis published the first volume entitled *Sexual Inversion* (his preferred term) in 1897 under their joint names, the Symonds family forced him to withdraw the coauthor's name from the book. In the trial of George Bedborough in 1898 for selling the book, it was labeled a "lewd, wicked bawdy, scandalous libel" and was withdrawn from sale.

Although Krafft-Ebing clearly understood *homosexual* to apply to both sexes, there was a general misinterpretation of the word as deriving from Latin *homo,* "a man," as opposed to Greek *homos,* "the same" (as in *homogeneous*). The ambiguity certainly led to the widespread misconception that the term referred exclusively to males. Indeed, as the word field clearly shows, it is a curious fact that for centuries there were only words for male homosexuals. Not only is the male field far larger, virtually every word in the field is far more virulent and contemptuous than any in the female equivalent. The semantic imbalance no doubt reflects an odd legal double standard. Whereas male homosexuality has been a criminal offense in the United Kingdom for centuries, lesbianism has never had this status. Ronald Pearsall has traced the Victorian roots of this anomaly: "This state of affairs was largely accidental; when the Criminal Law Amendment Act of 1885 was amended to make homosexual acts in private a crime it referred only to men—no one could think of a way to explain to Queen Victoria what homosexual acts between women were" (1969, 576).

Word-Field for Homosexuals

Male		Female	
1300	sodomite	1601	tribade
1542	bardash	1890	lesbian
1552	buggerer	1902	sapphist
1555	bugger	1927	lesbo
1591	ganymede	1931	dyke
1592	ingle/ningle	1931	bulldyke
1593	catamite	1936	butch
1603	pathic	1938	lezzie
1613	pederast		
1694	he-whore		
1708	huffler		
1709	molly		
1818	sod		
1824	miss nancy		
1850	poof		
1869	homosexual		
1888	nancy		
1890s	gay		
1891	cocksucker		
1895	fairy		
1910	poofter		
1914	faggot		
1923	fag		
1922	homo		
1924	queen		
1929	lavender		
1929	pansy		
1932	queer		

Sources: Oxford English Dictionary; Random House Historical Dictionary of American Slang.

The word-field is made up entirely of two distinct kinds of vocabulary: the scholarly items, which are rare and opaque, and the low-register slang terms, which are hostile, demeaning, or ironic. There are no common or neutral terms. The earliest word, *sodomite,* is a biblical toponym deriving from the sexual rapacity of the men of Sodom in Genesis 18–19. Its arrival in the fourteenth century is historically late, indicating the absence of an Anglo-Saxon equivalent, and suggests that the application of *sodomite* to homosexuals is a medieval construction. There is a rapid expansion of the field during the Elizabethan period, then a slowing down, followed by another period of efflorescence from the early decades of the twentieth century. There has been a steady shift in the origins of the terms, in that many of the early words are classical (e.g., *ganymede, catamite, pathic, tribade,* and *pederast*) while nearly all the additions of the past century or so are slang terms or metaphorical extensions of common words (e.g., *fairy, gay, nancy, faggot,* and *queen*). Whereas classical terms are rare, distinctive, precise, high-toned, and obsolete, the slang terms are generally contemptuous or insulting, although like *fairy* and *pansy,* they have quite charming or innocent origins, thus belonging to the category that Stephen Ullmann calls "pseudo-euphemism" (1964, 90–91). Furthermore, it is often difficult to separate the senses in this second category and thus pinpoint the arrival of the new meaning.

Gay is a notable case in point: to many the use became apparent in the 1980s, when it attracted much controversy. However, even the semantic and lexical authorities are not in agreement. John Ayto's study *20th Century Words* dates the new sense to 1933, the earliest reliable printed record, but notes that the homosexual sense can be traced to earlier clues. The most recent comprehensive source, the *Random House Historical Dictionary of American Slang* (1994), gives the first written instance as 1922 (in a quotation by Gertrude Stein). However, the *OED Supplement* (1972) traces the sense back to 1889, to the Cleveland Street Scandal, which concerned a homosexual brothel in London frequented by many respectable society gentlemen. In the court proceedings a policeman explained to the magistrate that the term *Mary Anne* was used of "Men that get a living by bad practices," and a male prostitute, John Saul, referred to his associates as "gay" (Pearsall 1969, 574). He was evidently using the word in the established heterosexual senses of "sexually active" or "promiscuous," found in Chaucer's *Miller's Tale* ("some gay gerl," l. 3769) and of a prostitute, as in "the gay ladies of the beat."

The terms chosen out of preference for "the decent obscurity of a learned language" are *pederast* ("lover of boys"), *ganymede* ("a Trojan youth, whom Zeus made his cup-bearer"), *catamite,* which is, extraordinarily, "a corrupt form of *Ganymede*," and *pathic,* defined much later: "The persons who suffered this abuse were called pathics, and affected the dress and behaviour of women" (1795). These are, of course, their literal meanings, which are far more polite than were their critical uses. Naturally, respectable origins (etymologically speaking) do not ensure high status in subsequent semantic history. In one of the earliest instances, John Florio used *ganymede* to translate Italian *catamito* with characteristic trenchancy: "a ganimed, an ingle, a boie hired to sinne against nature" (*Worlde of Wordes* 1598), while Ben Jonson's friend William Drummond of Hawthornden uttered the prayer (in 1649): "I crave thou wilt be pleased, great God, to save my sov'reign from a Ganymede." A character in Thomas Heywood's play *Captives* (1624) denounces "that ould catamiting cankerworm" (II ii). Yet the comment on Francis Bacon by John Aubrey (1626–1697) in *Brief Lives* is completely frank and non-judgmental: "He was a παιδεραστής [a pederast]. His Ganimeds and Favourites took bribes; but his lordship always gave sound Judgements." Of this classical group, only *catamite* still survives, as a recherché literary term.

Two of the oldest terms in the field, *sodomite* and **bugger,** have lost force over the centuries. This is a consequence of the semantic trend of generalization, and possibly of the growth of greater tolerance for homosexual activity as a result of political correctness. There is also the complicating factor of outsider ignorance about homosexual sex acts, which can lead to ambiguity in the use of the terms. Thus under English law *buggery* can refer to anal intercourse with a person or unnatural intercourse with an animal. The same complication surrounds the early history of *cocksucker.* The earliest instances, in Farmer and Henley's *Slang and Its Analogues* (1890–1904) and in Cary's *Veneris* (1916), define the term as *feliatrix,* denoting a feminine agent, though the latter authority specifies that the term is "said of either sex." Although now seldom used of women, it has become a generalized term of abuse in the United States. The reference to "the cocksucking leisure classes" by E.E. Cummings (in a letter of 1923) could be general or specific. However, Malcolm Cowley's use in a letter of 1946 ("I'm working on Whitman, the old cocksucker") is surely a sly dig at Walt Whitman's sexual preferences (*Burke-Cowley Correspondence,* 273).

The historical disposition of the word-field indicates that homosexual activity was openly acknowledged only around 1600. In his groundbreaking play *Edward II* (1593), Marlowe frequently uses the complex term *minion* ("The King is love-sick for his minion," I iv 87) in the sense defined by the *OED* of "a (usually male) favourite of a sovereign . . . with contemptuous suggestion of homosexual relations." Only used by Edward's enemies, the word is usually preceded by *base*. Shakespeare seems the first user of *favorite* in 1599 in the euphemistic sense of the *OED* definition: "one who stands unduly high in the favour of a prince etc." (*Much Ado About Nothing* III i 9). Antonio's covert homosexuality in *The Merchant of Venice* (1596–1597) is referred to symbolically in his self-identification: "I am the tainted wether of the flock" (IV i 114). His contemporary Ben Jonson is far more outspoken: *The Poetaster* (1601) has the exclamation: "What, shall I have my sonne a stager now? an enghle [ingle] for players?" (I ii). John Minshew in his *Guide to Tongues* (1617) was also very direct: "*ingle*: a boy kept for sodomy," while John Florio defined Italian *cinedo* in 1598 similarly as "a buggring boy, a wanton boy, an ingle." Philemon Holland's *Pliny* (1601) mentions a place "called Cinedopolis, by reasons of certain Catamites and shamefull bagages [rubbish] left there by Alexander the Great" (I, 111). Samuel Purchase's *Pilgrimage* (1613) contains an account, no doubt tinged by xenophobia: "He tells of their Pæderastie, that they buy Boyes at an hundred or two hundred duckats and mew [cage] them vp for their filthie lust" (293).

The modern terms have common phonetic characteristics, being short and laden with hostility or contempt. In this respect they are notably similar to xenophobic terms such as *chink, jap, wog, gook,* and so forth. *Homo* is the abbreviated and critical form of a term that was originally neutral. Some show great semantic flexibility. Thus in British English *sod* has greatly generalized into the exclamations *sod it!* and *sod off!*, the intensive epithet *sodding* and *sod all*, the phrase *not give a sod* and even *sod's law* (similar to Murphy's Law). Likewise *fag*, which in its English Public School sense denotes service by junior boys for seniors, often with the implication of sexual favors, has generated in American English *fag-hag, fag-bash, fag-bait,* and *fag-bag*, all within the semantic parameters of "homosexual" sense.

Reticence over explicit reference to lesbian activity surely explains the remarkable gap in time between the emergence of the male and female categories. The translators of the King James Bible (1611) clearly had a problem with a lexical gap when they came to render Deuteronomy 23:17: "There shall be no whore [marginal note: *sodomitesse*] of the daughters of Israel, nor a sodomite of the sons of Israel." (*Sodomitesse* is thus a genuine "nonce-word" or unique example of a word made up for a specific context.) Ben Jonson is, once again, a prominent contributor with the first, classically derived, term *tribade* (from a Greek root meaning "to rub"): In the Prelude to *The Forest* (1601) he writes suggestively of "Light Venus . . . with thy tribade trine, invent new sports." (*Rub* also has a slang sense of "masturbation" recorded from about 1599.) The seminal figure of the lyric poet Sappho of Lesbos (ca. 630) has generated the two central terms, although *sapphist* (1902) was anticipated by *Sappho-an,* used in the title of an anonymous erotic poem published by the Grub Street printer Edmund Curll in 1749. Although Sappho and her poetry were widely admired in classical times, the first recorded references to *lesbian* are in medical textbooks, including Krafft-Ebing's *Psychopathia Sexualis* (1886). The *OED* cites a letter by Aldous Huxley dismissing Florence as "a third rate provincial Italian town colonized by English sodomites and middle aged Lesbians" (April 21, 1925). Less hostile was Evelyn Waugh's arch inquiry, "I think Swedish Countess was a Sapphist?" in a letter of May 1951, using the term as a pseudo-euphemism. Yet Waugh could be very frank. Commenting on the homosexual revelations in the Kinsey Report, he wrote to Nancy Mitford: "All popular plays in New York are about buggers but they all commit suicide. The idea of a happy pansy is inconceivable to them" (August 18, 1949).

In recent decades homosexuals have "come out of the closet," a phrase recorded from 1971, four years after the British laws were changed to permit sex between consenting adults. Homosexuality is now seen in terms of individual human rights, sexual preference, and lifestyle choice. The simultaneous growth of political correctness with its taboos on stigmatic terms has also had an influence. There has been in concert a considerable program of semantic engineering. This has involved the appropriation of positive terms like *gay* and *queen* as well as neutral terms like *pink,* the reclaiming of the traditionally stigmatic words like *queer,* and the invention of new stigmatizing terms such as *homophobic,* as used by the *Observer* in 1981: "Rat-packs of homophobic punks, white or Latino, prowled gay neighbourhoods." When *homophobic* was first coined in the 1920s, it referred to "fear or hatred of men," but in the 1970s it started to be popularized in the modern sense of "fear or hatred of homosexuals" as part of the Gay Liberation Movement, notably by the American writer George Weinberg.

The reclamation of the stigmatic vocabulary has not been a simple or consistent process, as is shown in a number of studies, such as that of William L. Leap (*Word's Out: Gay Men's English,* 1996), arguing for the existence of "Gay English" as a variety. However, one of the first sociolinguistic studies was Stephen O. Murray's "The Art of Gay Insulting" (1979), an investigation into an interesting variation of "sounding," but played as an in-group game using traditional taunts. Furthermore, as the mainstream culture has become more tolerant of homosexuals, some practitioners of **rap** and reggae have continued to be blatantly homophobic.

An unusual historical and geographical provenance has produced the colloquial South African English noun *moffie*. Its origins are remarkable, though disputed: the word seems clearly linked with *mophy,* seaman's slang for "a delicate and well-groomed youth," used from the nineteenth century. Though *maufee,* "a bad fairy" has been suggested, the more likely derivation is from *mophrodite,* a corruption of *hermaphrodite*. The abbreviated form was current slang in the eighteenth century, appearing in Henry Fielding's novel *Joseph Andrews* (1742) when a society lady is advised that if she continues to fire all her servants: "You must get a set of mophrodites to wait upon you" (I ix). A mixture of affection and contempt surrounds the term, also found in the compound *koffie-moffie* for an airline steward. A recent study of South African gay argot by Ken Cage under the title of *Gayle* (2003) includes a comprehensive dictionary.

A curious bureaucratic intervention in the naming of homosexuals occurred in 2002. The British Department of Trade and Industry, in the process of drafting new anti-discrimination laws, took the view that "*homosexual* is no longer the way forward in defining sexual orientation" and proposed in its stead the form OTPOTSS, an abbreviation for "orientation toward people of the same sex." Clearly the problem of naming is not yet solved.

See also: Bugger; Queer.

239

Bibliography

Benson, Larry D. (ed.). *The Riverside Chaucer*. Oxford: Oxford University Press, 1988.

Boswell, John T. *Christianity, Social Tolerance and Homosexuality*. Chicago: University of Chicago Press, 1980.

Cage, Ken. *Gayle*. Johannesburg: Jacana, 2003.

Chesebro, James. *Gayspeak*. New York: Pilgrim, 1981.

De Jongh, Nicholas. *Not in Front of the Audience: Homosexuality on Stage*. London: Routledge, 1992.

Dynes, Wayne R., ed. *Homosexuality: A Research Guide*. New York: Garland, 1987.

———. *An Encyclopedia of Homosexuality*. New York: Garland, 1990.

Ellmann, Richard. *Oscar Wilde*. Harmondsworth: Penguin, 1988.

Goldberg, Jonathan. *James I and the Politics of Literature*. Baltimore: Johns Hopkins, 1983.

Krafft-Ebing, R. von. *Psychopathia Sexualis*. 7th ed., trans. G.C. Chaddock. Philadelphia: F.A. Davis, 1920.

Leap, William L. *Word's Out: Gay Men's English*. Minneapolis: University of Minnesota Press, 1996.

———, ed. *Beyond the Lavender Lexicon: Authenticity, Imagination and Appropriation in Lesbian and Gay Languages*. Newark, NJ: Gordon and Breach, 1989.

Murray, Stephen O. "The Art of Gay Insulting." *Anthropological Linguistics* 21 (1979): 211–23.

Pearsall, Ronald. *The Worm in the Bud: The World of Victorian Sexuality*. Harmondsworth: Penguin, 1969.

Plato. *The Symposium*. Trans. Walter Hamilton. Harmondsworth: Penguin, 1951.

Prestwich, Michael. *The Three Edwards*. London: Weidenfeld and Nicholson, 1980.

Rodgers, Bruce. *Gay Talk*. New York: Paragon Books, 1972.

Robb, Graham. *Strangers: Homosexual Love in the Nineteenth Century*. New York: Norton, 2003.

Ullmann, Stephen. *Language and Style*. Oxford: Basil Blackwell, 1964.

HONKY

Opprobrious terms for groups tend to reflect, in their vehemence and their number, the social status of the group. As a number of sociolinguists have pointed out, in the United States and in the English-speaking communities in general, opprobrious terms for blacks greatly outnumber those for whites. Of the terms for whites, *honky*, which is exclusive to the United States, has become in a comparatively short time the term expressing the strongest contempt.

The term derives from *Hunky*, and is related *Hun*, diminutive and contemptuous forms of *Hungarian*, both words being originally applied to a person of Eastern European ancestry, especially a Hungarian or Slav, and often a manual laborer. *Honky* is thus typical of terms stigmatizing outsiders, especially workers of low status regarded as interlopers. Generalization is evident in two ways. The first is in the misnomer: the Hungarians are not Slavs but occupy an adjacent area of Europe; the Huns historically were a nomadic Asian race, before Kaiser William II co-opted them propagandistically as Germans. The second is that the term has expanded emotively in meaning, as have *gook* and *wog*.

The *Reports of the Immigration Commission* (1907–1910) noted under *Magyar*: "'Huns' and 'Hunkies' are names given . . . incorrectly to this race and to Slavs indiscriminately in some parts of America" (I, 255). An earlier report in the New York *Daily News* (June 8, 1890) stressed the hostility deriving from labor rivalry: "The Huns who are here [Pennsylvania] are said to be creating a widespread dissatisfaction. They are engaged chiefly as laborers in the mines and ironworks." In the buildup to World War I, there was confusion with *Hun* meaning a German, recorded in this quotation from *Slavic Citizen* (1910): "To be a German is nothing to be ashamed of . . . 'I ain't no Hun, I'm an American,' expresses their reaction to the situation" (414).

Although *Hunky* has continued as a nickname for an East European, references to whites in general date from the early 1950s. A phonetic overlap with *honky,* which has become the dominant term, is apparent in certain records. A revealing report in *Time* magazine (August 4, 1967) explained the term as part of the vocabulary of radical black politics: "Damning Lyndon Johnson for sending 'honky' cracker federal troops into Negro communities to kill black people' Brown called the president 'a wild mad dog, an outlaw from Texas.' Honky, or honkie, is a black-power word for any white man, derived from 'Hunkie'–Hungarian."

Honky has an unusual semantic history in that it is confined to the United States and has greatly broadened in reference, being used successively of Hungarians, Slavs, Germans, and whites in general, but has simultaneously retained its animosity. Other terms that have generalized in application, like *wop, gook,* and *wog,* have lost some of their animus in the process.

See also: Hun.

Bibliography

Allen, Irving Lewis. *The Language of Ethnic Conflict.* New York: Columbia University Press, 1983.
Flexner, Stuart Berg. *I Hear America Talking.* New York: Van Nostrand Reinhold, 1976.
Lighter, J.S., ed. *Random House Historical Dictionary of American Slang.* New York: Random House, 1994–.

HOTTENTOT

The dynamics of colonialism commonly generate a predictable agenda of stereotypes, whereby the colonized or dominated peoples are presented as savages living in a barbaric state of nature without religion, their speech being caricatured as incomprehensible and subhuman gabbling. The term **barbarian** itself is rooted in this agenda. *Hottentot,* used to refer to one of the aboriginal native peoples of South Africa now known as the Khoikhoi or the San, is a classic example of this process. "Hottentot is a word meaning 'stutterer' or 'stammerer,' applied to the people on account of their stuttering speech," according to Olfert Dapper, a Dutch explorer, in his *Beschryvingh der Afrikansche Gewesten (Description of the African Deserts* 1670). To this William Dampier added in his *Voyage Round the World* (1697) this inherently implausible explanation: "Hottantot . . . is the name by which they call to one another . . . as if every one of them had this for his name" (I, 536). The point of incomprehension lay in "the peculiar 'clicks' which gave their speech its distinctive character" (Schapera 1930, 44). These clicks are, of course, alien to the phonetic systems of most other languages. The word itself is derived from Dutch *Huttentut,* "stammerer" or "stutterer" possibly related to German *hotteren-totteren,* meaning "to stutter." Jan van Riebeek, the first Dutch governor of the Cape, used the forms *Ottentot* and *Hottentoo* in his *Journal* (January 1652). The stereotype of cultural difference is encapsulated in the history of the so-called Hottentot Venus, Saartjie Baartman (1789–1816) who was taken to Europe and shown off as a freak, mainly because of what was called the Hottentot *apron* or "enlarged labia pudendi" (*Oxford English Dictionary*).

There subsequently developed the predictable deterioration to mean "a person of inferior intellect or culture." However, this sense is first recorded not in Holland, the original

SARTJEE, THE HOTTENTOT VENUS.

Hottentot, referring to natives of South Africa now known as the Khoikhoi, was derived from the Dutch word for "stammerer" or "stutterer"—alluding to the native language. It survives as a term of insult in South Africa. (© The British Library) colonial power, but in England, before Britain had shown much interest in South Africa. In an unexpected context, Nicholas Amherst's *Terrae filius: or the secret history of the university of Oxford* (1726), the writer was "Surprized to find a place, which he had heard so much renown'd for learning, fill'd with grey-haired novices and reverend hotentots" (xxxv, 190). Even more surprising is the provocative description of Dr. Johnson as "a respectable Hottentot" by Lord Chesterfield in a letter to his son (February 28, 1751).

Long obsolete in this sense in the United Kingdom, *Hottentot* still survives in South Africa as a general term of insult. The *Dictionary of South African English* (1996) carries the following usage note: "The word 'Hottentot' is seen by some as offensive and Khoikhoi is sometimes substituted as a name for the people, particularly in scholarly contexts. However the use of 'Hottentot' does not seem to be avoided in the names of plants, fish, birds, etc." (The dictionary lists about twenty such items.) The term also survives in the abbreviated form *hotnot,* recorded with comparative neutrality from the early nineteenth century, but now regarded as "an offensive mode of address to a coloured person." The *Cape Times* (July 8, 1949) carried a report referring to "His uncouth remarks about 'Hotnots, Coolies and Kaffirs.'"

See also: Barbarian; Kaffir.

Bibliography

Schapera, Isaac. *Khoisan Peoples of South Africa.* London: Routledge & Kegan Paul, 1930.

Silva, P.M., et al., eds. *Dictionary of South African English on Historical Principles.* Cape Town: Oxford University Press, 1996.

HUN

The most hostile term that can be applied to a German. However, the original Huns were not a Germanic people, but a nomadic warlike Asian race that overran Europe in the fifth century under their barbaric warlord Attila, who arrogantly styled himself *Flagellum Dei* (the Scourge of God). Anglo-Saxon references to the Huns list them simply with other peoples like the Franks, but their name became a byword of cruelty during the Renaissance: "Companies or Armies of Huns, wandering up and down with most swift Horses, filled all things with slaughter and terrour" (Edward Topsell, *The historie of four-footed beastes,* London: William Jaggard, 1607, 226). Attila the Hun's legendary reputation continues as a byword of ruthlessness, albeit in the nomenclature of office politics and business hierarchies.

However, the term *Hun* fell out of general use for centuries, except as a historical reference. When revived in the early nineteenth century it meant a reckless and uncultured devastator, as *Vandal* still does. The *Pall Mall Gazette* of 1893 comments on "the marauding Huns, whose delight it is to trample on the flowers, burn the underwood and kill the birds and beasts" (May 3, 2). The specific application to the Germans was given, not by their enemies, as is usual with such hostile terms, but ironically, by Kaiser Wilhelm II himself. In an inflammatory speech given to German troops about to set sail for China on July 27, 1900, the Kaiser appealed to an atavistic, barbarian mythology in a way that now seems shockingly crude:

No quarter will be given, no prisoners will be taken. Let all who fall into your hands be at your mercy. Just as the Huns a thousand years ago, under the leadership of Etzel [Attila], gained a reputation in virtue [strength] of which they still live in historical tradition, so may the name of Germany become known in such a manner in China that no Chinaman will ever again even dare to look askance at a German.
(*The Times,* July 30, 1900, 3)

This extraordinary speech can be seen as the seed of what has become the stereotype of the "ugly" German: brutal, militaristic, jackbooted, and helmeted, upholding in Aryanism and in Nazism a diabolical mixture of warped ideology and gruesome pragmatism.

The troops evidently took the Kaiser's words seriously, so that in November of the same year, in a debate in the Reichstag the Socialist leader August Bebel quoted from "the so-called 'Letters from the Huns' (*Hunnenbriefe*), epistles from German soldiers in China to their relatives at home giving an account of the cruelties which have been perpetrated by the army of occupation" (*The Times,* November 21, 1900, 5). Unsurprisingly, the stereotype started to take hold. Rudyard Kipling wrote as far back as 1902 of "the shameless Hun" (*The Times,* December 22, 9), and instances multiplied thereafter. The use of the definite article naturally has the effect of endorsing a stereotype. On May 21, 1941, *The Times* daringly printed a poem containing the line "I really loathe the bloody Hun," provoking some controversy.

With passing of time and the emotive context of war, the term has lost some of its hostility, being often used in a slightly ironic fashion, as in "He's bought a big solid Hun car." In British English the term has always referred specifically to the Germans, but in the United States, *hun* has erroneously been used to mean a Hungarian and taken to be the root of *hunky,* later **honky.** *Hun* is not generally current in other global varieties of English, except among the diminishing circle of war veterans.

See also: Blason Populaire; Ethnic Insults; Honky.

Bibliography
Allen, Irving Lewis. *The Language of Ethnic Conflict.* New York: Columbia University Press, 1983.
Lighter, J.S., ed. *Random House Historical Dictionary of American Slang.* New York: Random House, 1994–.
Partridge, Eric. *Words, Words, Words!* London: Methuen, 1933.

ILLEGITIMACY. *See:* Bastard

IMPACT

Discussions of swearing and foul language have traditionally assumed that certain of-fending words have in themselves a general or universal impact. Likewise, notions of obscenity and pornography have been predicated on the simple presence of certain offensive words. Thus *The Times* wrote in 1960: "Having regard to the state of current writing, it seems that the prosecution against *Lady Chatterley's Lover* can only have been launched on the ground that the book contained the so-called four-letter words" (No-vember 7). Similarly, *The New Dictionary of American Slang* (1986, ed. Robert L. Chapman) used symbolic triangles as usage indicators for words regarded as "offensive" and as "taboo."

This degree of impact is certainly true of words dealing with universal moral categories, such as *liar* or a *thief,* or conventional insults like *shit* or *cunt.* However, even this moral logic does not always hold, as can be seen in the following exchange:

X: Bastard!
Y: Terrorist!
X: Cretin!
Y: Rapist!
X: Turd!
Y: Pedophile!
X: Son of a bitch!
Y: Swindler!

Clearly, from a logical point of view, *Y* has the more seriously antisocial insults, but they do not have the impact deriving from the weight of tradition behind *X*'s more conven-tional epithets. The entry for **gender in swearing** considers the complexities of gender and impact.

The founding assumption of universal impact also derives from notions of a monolithic culture, which has largely been the case in English-speaking society for most of its history, having been predominantly white, Anglo-Saxon, and in latter centuries Protestant and imperialist. Consequently out-groups like Catholics and foreigners have been stigmatized by terms like *papist, frog,* and *wog.* Alien political systems have likewise introduced *fascist* and *communist* as terms of insult. However, as America and Britain have become more demographically diverse through immigration, so the balance of power between traditional in-groups and out-groups has changed.

Even within the mainstream culture, verbal impact is determined by a complex mixture of contextual social factors, including class, community, and family, as well as personal issues. Thus *cheat* has the greatest impact in the social context of in-groups such as schools and clubs of various kinds, sporting, gambling, and social. Similarly, *coward* has the greatest impact in the army and among the erstwhile aristocracy, where it was an insult certain to provoke a duel. The famous accusation that Oscar Wilde was a sodomite was especially insufferable because the Marquess of Queensberry published it in a note visible to the members of Wilde's London club.

In addition to the social context, the directness of the insult and personal factors form important determiners of the force of a term. Thus in British English to refer to someone as "a real shit" or "an absolute bastard" is generally more condemning than to use some of the more apparently taboo terms. The following views demonstrate the personal aspect: (A) "There is no worse word in the English language." (B) "It's the filthiest, dirtiest, nastiest word in the English language." "A" is Lisa Nemrow, referring to *cunt* in an essay on "Dirty Words" (in Ricks and Michaels 1990, 436). "B" is Christopher Darden, a black lawyer, referring to *nigger* in the O.J. Simpson trial (*New York Times,* January 14, 1998, 7).

There are complications, however, in that some social contexts actually diminish or even neutralize the moral quality concerned. Thus *crook, thief,* and *gangster* are largely meaningless in the underworld of the mafia, but *informer* there takes on the moral aspect of *traitor.* Less predictable have been the vagaries undergone by *bastard* and *bugger,* which have developed very different impacts in British, American, and Australian English.

In modern times, impact has been further complicated by the phenomenon of **reclamation**, whereby a target or out-group community starts to use stigmatic terms such as *nigger, yid,* and *queer* ironically or even affectionately as an in-group term. However, this dynamic only works in one direction. Thus in the South African context, Archbishop Desmond Tutu does call himself, tongue in cheek, "a cheeky kaffir," accommodating the traditional insulting term, but he would be outraged if a white person were to use the phrase. On the other hand, former president Frederik Willem de Klerk cannot call himself "a white baas," even ironically, any more than former U.S. president Bill Clinton can say "I'm a honky cracker."

These complexities of the dynamic make simple assessments of impact very problematic. Thus the Third Edition of *Webster* (1961) was criticized for labeling ethnic slurs like *kike, dago, spick,* and *coon* as "usually taken to be offensive" rather than plain "offensive." One of the few reference works to include a useful contextual guide to offensiveness and impact is Richard A. Spears's *Forbidden American English* (1991).

See also: Gender in Swearing; Reclamation of Opprobrious Terms; Webster and His Dictionaries.

Bibliography

Chapman, Robert L. *New Dictionary of American Slang*. New York: Harper & Row, 1986.
Spears, Richard A. *Forbidden American English*. Lincolnwood, IL: Passport, 1991.

IMPRECATION

The formal and precise meaning is the use of a form of words or an action invoking evil, calamity, or vengeance upon another. Imprecation, being deeply serious and focused, thus has a narrower meaning than swearing or even cursing, which can be indiscriminate. Although the term is rooted in Latin *precare,* meaning "to pray," it has always been used in a negative sense since in the fifteenth century. George Puttenham was one of the first to use the word in his study *English Poesie* (1598), using the synonyms "exclamation, or crying out, imprecation or cursing" (III xix 221). The most famous literary examples are those in *King Lear* (1604–1605) formulated by the King cursing his daughters ("Into her womb convey sterility" I iv 299–313 and "Strike her young bones, you taking airs, with lameness" (II iv, 164–70.) The term is now generally obsolescent.

See also: Blasphemy; Malediction; Profanity.

INDIA, SWEARING IN

India is a culturally and linguistically complex country with many religions and languages. Being one of the earliest colonies in which English became established, since independence in 1947 the English language has become increasingly common as the medium for politics and commerce, although technically it does not have official status. Being predominantly a Third World country with a First World overlay, there is generally less swearing in the Indian countryside than in the cities. There is more swearing in general in the north, possibly as a result of the political tensions and the influence of Islam. Taboos against swearing are more observed in the south. Furthermore, swearing in the north is more sexual and crude, but more benign in the south.

English swearwords such as *bugger* and *bastard* have come into Hindi; there is also a translated or transposed version of *motherfucker* in that language. However, the use of swearwords from the older languages like Urdu and Arabic is more common. Another feature is the creation of words from different sources. One such example is *jungli,* meaning a savage person still living in the jungle. The word is basically English with a Hindi suffix (although *jungle* is borrowed from Hindi *jangal,* ultimately Sanskrit *jangala*). Curiously, this word is probably related to the earlier Gujarati form *junglo,* from the early nineteenth century referring disparagingly to white men as savages.

As tends to happen with an international language, local swearwords often expand their currency into wider usage. The phrase *not to give [or care] a damn* has been derived from *dam,* an Indian coin of very low value, an etymology supported by some authorities, such as

Farmer and Henley, but rejected by others, such as the *Oxford English Dictionary*. **Coolie** is the term of greatest opprobrium to have entered global English from Indian sources. Its original meaning was a hired laborer of very low status. A term from the same provenance is *pariah,* from Tamil, originally meaning a person of a distinct caste in southern India, but subsequently misapplied generally to mean a person of low caste. It has been used in English from 1711 mainly in the sense of a social outcast. The word has become well established as a descriptive term denoting loss of social status or respect, rather than as an emotive or personal usage, as is usual with swearwords.

An interesting social factor in modern times has been the change in the character of the Bollywood hero, who obviously serves as something of a role model in the wider society. Like his Hollywood counterpart, he was previously polite and reticent, but in recent decades has become far more aggressive and foul-mouthed.

Educated Indian English, both written and spoken, tends to be formal and slightly stilted alongside British English. But many authors have produced works of impressive literary quality, recognized in the numerous awards and prizes they have won. Many have become émigrés assimilated in the West but often writing from the point of view of expatriates. A recent collection of such writings comments: "The writers in the diaspora are the product of movement. They embody travel. The kind of language that these writers use . . . conveys the variety of their translated lives" (*Away,* ed. A. Kumar 2004, xvii). Several authors, such as V.S. Naipaul and Salman Rushdie, have moved on to other topics. The Kumar collection contains Hanif Kureishi's aptly named story "Wild Women, Wild Men," set in Southall, a suburb of London, where "arse" and "cunt" are, surprisingly, on show. Yet overall the register remains consistently formal and polite, unlike that of much contemporary literature in Britain and America, even though many of the authors have experienced rudeness and suffered from ethnic insults. In his *Autobiography* (1927) Mahatma Gandhi describes the indignity of being called a *coolie* and a *sami* in South Africa. The unique furor surrounding Salman Rushdie's *The Satanic Verses* (1988) is covered in the entry for **blasphemy**.

See also: Coolie.

Bibliography

Kachru, Braj. *The Indianization of English*. Delhi: Oxford University Press, 1983.

Kumar, Amitava, ed. *Away: The Indian Writer as an Expatriate*. New York: Routledge, 2004.

Yule, H., and A. Burnell. *Hobson Jobson: A Glossary of Colloquial Anglo-Indian Words and Phrases*. London: John Murray, 1903.

INDIANS, NORTH AMERICAN

The history of the aboriginal indigenous population of the Americas has been that of progressive dispossession, most notably of their land, their lives, even of their name. Those of North America called themselves simply "the people" or the *Anasazi,* "the Ancient Ones," as the Navajo termed their ancestors. The first recorded use of *Indian* in relation to America is "Indian tobacco" (1618), deriving from the misnaming of the people and their territories by Amerigo Vespucci, Christopher Columbus, and others, who erroneously believed they

The dramatic portrayal of a native chief stabbing "Custer" in a Wild West Show of 1905 typified and perpetuated the stereotype of the savage, treacherous Indian—itself a misnomer. (Library of Congress, LC-USZ62-112856)

had circumnavigated the globe and reached the Indies. The misnomer remained in general use for centuries up to about 1970 when activists began calling themselves *Native Americans* as a form of historical reclamation of their aboriginal status. This process of renaming, as in *Afro-American,* endorses the bitter observation of Toni Morrison: "In this country American means white. Everybody else has to hyphenate" (*The Guardian,* January 29, 1992).

The earliest records stereotypically describe the native population as savages beneath consideration. Richard Hakluyt's *Divers Voyages Touching the Discoverie of America* (1582) refers to three men "clothed in beasts skins, [who] ate raw flesh, and spake such speech that no man could understand them and in their demeanour were like to brute beasts" (A 3). Although Captain John Smith had a high opinion of the local government of Virginia and the authority of Powhatan, he nevertheless wrote in his *Generall historie of Virginia* (1624) that "The Warres in *Europe, Asia* and *Africa,* taught me how to subdue the wild Salvages [sic] in Virginia" (Utley and Washburn 1977, 15). William Bradford wrote in his *History Of Plimouth Plantation* (ca. 1630, ten years after the Plymouth settlement) of "those vast and unpeopled countries of America . . . where there are only savage and brutish men which range up and down, little different from wild beasts" (Miller 1956, 12). John Winthrop's *Journal* entry for September 22, 1642, similarly records "having come into a wilderness where are nothing but wild beasts and beastlike men" (Miller 1956, 42). In King James I's famous *Counterblaste to Tobacco* (1604), he attributed the origin of smoking to "the barbarous and beastly maners of the wilde, godlesse, and slavish Indians."

The phrase *Indian country* is recorded in *The Dictionary of American English* (1715) in the sense of "enemy or hostile territory," thus reflecting the essentially adversarial relationship between the colonists and the indigenous population. In the period of the great western expansion of the United States, the stereotype of the savage, scalping, and treacherous Indian developed as the people resisted, most spectacularly at the Battle of the Little Big Horn, or "Custer's Last Stand," in 1876. Especially revealing is the aggressive, virtually genocidal slogan, "The only good Indian is a dead Indian" (attributed to Philip Henry Sheridan at Fort Cobb, Oklahoma, January 1869). The abbreviated form *injun* is recorded from 1825, but has since largely passed out of use, being unrecorded in the major recent dictionaries of American slang.

A curious but revealing footnote to the English perception of the American Indian occurred in eighteenth-century London in references to a notorious gang of aristocratic ruffians who styled themselves the Mohocks, after the Mohawks. Dr. Johnson's *Dictionary* (1755) carried the following entry: "The name of a cruel nation of America given to ruffians who infested, or rather who were imagined to infest, the streets of London."

The phrase or characterization "Indian giver" derives from the Colonial period. In Thomas Hutchinson's *History of the Colony of Massachusetts Bay* (1764), "An Indian gift is a proverbial expression, signifying a present for which an equivalent return is expected." However, in his *Dictionary of Americanisms* (1848), John R. Bartlett noted that the phrase was being used by New York schoolchildren in its modern sense, that is, for one who gives a present and then takes it back.

The subsequent policy of separation whereby the Indians were confined to reservations (a term that dates from 1790) obviously had the effect of reducing their social impact on the broader American society. Interestingly and ironically, the phrase *Indian country* resurfaced, not in relation to the people themselves but in the contexts of World War II, recorded from 1945–1948, and the Vietnam War from 1967, referring to the territory outside the Saigon government's control.

Allen (1983) and others have argued that the number of hostile nicknames for a people reflects their perceived threat to the "host" speech community. On this basis it is an ironic reflection of the reduced status of the American Indian that on this basis they rank seventh, behind African-Americans, Jews, Italians, Irish, Chinese, and Germans. The harshest terms are the oldest, namely *savage* and *barbarian,* being generic and part of common colonialist discourse that is now unacceptable. Most of the specific terms were first descriptive, then ironic adoptions from native culture and hierarchy, as in *chief, brave, squaw,* and *papoose.* However, some of these, like *brave,* first used by James Fenimore Cooper in 1837, are positive, emphasizing the idea of the "noble savage." Cooper seems also to have introduced *paleface.* The contrasting color red supplies a range of terms, such as *red-skin* (1699), *red-man* (1725), and *red-devil* (1834), finally generating the most common formation, *red-indian* only in 1878. In comparison with terms for other groups, these have generally less impact. However, as Allen points out, many nicknames for American Indians were used locally (1983, 51). With the increasing sensitivities of political correctness, virtually all the native terminology is viewed critically in some circles.

See also: Blason Populaire.

Bibliography
Allen, Irving Lewis. *The Language of Ethnic Conflict*. New York: Columbia University Press, 1983.
Flexner, Stuart Berg. *I Hear America Talking*. New York: Van Nostrand, 1976.
Lighter, J.S., ed. *Random House Historical Dictionary of American Slang*. New York: Random House, 1994–.
Miller, Perry. *The American Puritans*. New York: Doubleday Anchor, 1956.
Utley, Robert M., and E. Wilcomb Washburn. *Indian Wars*. Boston: Houghton Mifflin, 1977.

INFIDEL. *See:* Heathen

INNOVATION

Swearing by its nature involves traditional forms of expression, reliant on established terms, modes, and idioms, many of them quite bizarre departures from "normal" or "natural" language. As the entry for **impact** makes clear, original insults such as *son of a cow* or *tax dodger* obviously lack the impact of the more traditional *son of a bitch* or *crook*. Historically only a few literary authors, such as **Geoffrey Chaucer**, **François Rabelais**, **William Shakespeare**, **Ben Jonson**, and the **Earl of Rochester** have managed to add to the stock of swearwords, foul language, and insults.

British English historically has formed the major tradition, as is to be expected, but in recent decades American English has manifestly become the major source of innovation. As the entries for **bitch**, **crap**, **hell**, **lousy**, and **punk** make clear, these terms have had long histories in British English, but most of the modern semantic extensions derive from American usage, many of them of surprising duration. Thus, *scum* has developed a thriving currency in the form of the comparatively new American compound *scumbag* (originally meaning a used contraceptive sheath, from ca. 1976). Another indicator is the shift from the use of British *arse* as a term of insult, first to American *arsehole* and then to *asshole* from ca. 1933. The *Random House Historical Dictionary of American Slang* (1994) has over a dozen pages covering the main terms and compounds in American slang, from plain *ass* to *ass-wiper*. Although *fuck* used as a verb is found as far back as the early sixteenth century in British usage, its use as a noun, as in "You lying fuck!," is still exclusively American and recorded from ca. 1927. *Geek* is possibly related to Elizabethan English *geck*, "a fool," but its modern currency, from ca. 1908, is American. *Jerk*, from ca. 1919, is exclusively American; so is the egregious *motherfucker* from ca. 1935. Also American in origin are *fuck-all* from ca. 1918, *fuck around* from ca. 1931, and *fuck over* from ca. 1961. Other original or predominantly American contributions are *bullshit* from ca. 1886, *cocksucker* from ca. 1891 but common from World War I, *beaver* from ca. 1927, *chickenshit* from ca. 1929, and *dickhead* from ca. 1962. *Joint* in the sense of "penis" dates from ca. 1931, and as a marijuana cigarette from ca. 1942. Terms for prostitutes include *hooker* from ca. 1845, *broad* from ca. 1914; *call-girl* and *hustler,* both from ca. 1924; and *tramp* from the same era.

Terms for homosexuals originating in American usage are *fairy, faggot,* and *dyke*. The *American Journal of Psychology* noted in 1895 that "'The Fairies' of New York are said to be a similar secret organisation" (vii, 216); in 1914 Jackson and Hellyer's *Vocabulary of Criminal Slang* explained: "All the faggots (sissies) will be in drag at the ball tonight" (30), while Tamony's *Americanisms* (1931) carries a reference to "pansies and dykes" (8). A fair number of these American innovations have been borrowed into British English and other global varieties.

See also: Bitch; Crap; Hell; Lousy; Punk.

Bibliography

Lighter, J.S., ed. *Random House Historical Dictionary of American Slang*. New York: Random House, 1994–.

INSTABILITY OF SWEARING TERMS

Swearing demonstrates with most force the semantic fact that words do not have stable or fixed meanings, either historically or even within the same basic speech community. To some extent swearing is a special case, since the language is consistently emotive rather than referential, leading to the characteristics discussed in the entry for **flexibility**. Thus the term *shit* has a whole range of expletive meanings and tones, expressing anger, surprise, frustration, even pleasure, whereas the notional synonyms *excrement* and *feces* are simply factual and limited in tone, thus having no swearing potential. This example demonstrates another general truth that native **Anglo-Saxon terms** have greater emotive potential, and classical terms correspondingly less. However, not all of the "four-letter" words are actually of Anglo-Saxon origin. Furthermore, meanings of basic swearwords vary according to speech community. Thus *bastard* has very different senses in American, Australian, and British English, as does *motherfucker* even in America. *Fanny* remains a source of transatlantic anatomical confusion, meaning "vagina" in British English but "the buttocks" in American English. As can be seen below, *tail* had a similarly confusing range of meanings in medieval times.

The historical dimension illuminates the proposition of instability still more dramatically. Thus if one reduces and simplifies the basic meanings of a number of key terms as they have evolved, the results show extraordinary semantic changes.

bugger (noun)
1. heretic 1340
2. sodomite 1555 >
3. practicer of bestiality 1555 >
4. chap, fellow 1719 >

punk
1. whore 1575
2. catamite 1904 >
3. worthless person 1917 >

tramp
1. male vagrant 1664 >
2. sexually promiscuous woman 1922 >

shrew
1. small aggressive mole-like animal 800 >
2. rascal 1250
3. belligerent spiteful woman 1400 >

harlot
1. rogue, vagabond 1225
2. prostitute 1432 >

frig
1. to masturbate 1598 >
2. to copulate 1707 >
3. to fiddle 1785 >

minx
1. pet dog 1542
2. pert girl, hussy 1592 >
3. whore 1594
4. scheming, cunning woman 1812 >

pimp
1. pander, procurer 1607 >
2. minister to evil 1704 >
2. informer (Australian) 1885 >
3. Peeping Tom (Welsh) 1940 >

prat (UK)
1. buttocks 1598

2. female genitals 1800s
3. fool, idiot 1968 >

roger
1. penis 1653
2. to copulate 1709 >
3. to rape (U.S.) 1930s

wench
1. child of either sex (OE *wencel*)
2. girl, maid, female child 1330s >
3. mistress, lover 1380s >
4. wanton woman, 1550s >
5. young woman of lower class 1850s >

faggot
shrewish woman 1591 >
naughty child 1873 >
male homosexual 1914 >

tail
1. backside 1303 >
2. "female pudendum," 1362
3. penis 1386

This list is selective, not comprehensive, and thus does not include the most potent "four-letter" words, which have their own entries. Nor does it contain words like *bitch* and *cow*, which are metaphorical extensions of animal terms. Some of these, like *sow* and *dragon*, have quite complex histories. But it clearly shows remarkable shifts of meaning. As can be seen, many of these terms have changed gender as well as reference: *harlot, shrew, tramp,* and *wench* have all become feminized, while *prat, faggot,* and *punk* have become male terms. Those that come to refer to a woman almost invariably deteriorate to mean one who is sexually promiscuous, while terms that refer to males, like *bugger, punk,* and *prat,* tend to become less condemning. Several, such as *harlot, shrew,* and *wench,* have become either obsolete or obsolescent. Others, like *bugger, frig,* and *tail,* have left their sexual senses behind and become used very commonly, although *bugger* has limited usage in the United States, and *tail* survives in the chauvinist expression "a piece of tail." Some, like *punk, faggot,* and *tramp,* have become more commonly used and more critical in American English. *Tail* is an interesting example since the evidence shows that in the fourteenth century it had three quite different meanings running concurrently. There was also a verbal sense, "to copulate." Furthermore, the sexual senses are found in all the major authors from Geoffrey Chaucer and William Langland in the fourteenth century through to Alexander Pope in the eighteenth, admittedly in "naughty" or risqué contexts.

There are various explanations for this instability. The most plausible is that the terms deal with aspects of life of which many speakers are ignorant or prefer to avoid. A remarkable instance is the term *merkin,* which few modern readers will recognize. No doubt because of this rarity and its predominantly underground usage, the word has had the following senses: "the female *pudendum*" (1535), followed by "counterfeit hair for the privities of women" or a pubic wig (1620), succeeded by "an artificial vagina" found in Richard Burton's translation of the *Arabian Nights Entertainments* (1886, X, 239) and "hair dye" in American thieves' slang. Because of the physical proximity of the items, it is not always possible to determine the exact sense. Many terms of ethnic abuse show a great range of applications. Thus *frog* has been applied to the Dutch and the Jesuits as well as to the French, while *gook* and *wog* have still wider range of insulting targets.

See also: Ethnic Insults; Flexibility.

Bibliography
Lighter, J.S., ed. *The Random House Historical Dictionary of American Slang.* New York: Random House, 1994.

IRISH, THE

The Irish, being physically separated from the rest of the British Isles, remaining predominantly Catholic, and speaking *Erse,* their own variety of Celtic, have consequently been regarded as outsiders and even foreigners by many in the United Kingdom. This separation was accentuated in medieval times by a significant physical and political barrier called the English Pale, a palisade built by the English colonists to demarcate their territory. Those Irish who were outside or "beyond the pale" were termed "the wild Irish" from as far back as William Langland in the fourteenth century. In time this negative characterization was applied stereotypically to the whole people, as in the unflattering comments made by the King in Shakespeare's *Richard II* (II ii 155–58). Ania Loomba makes the point that "Various English administrators such as Edmund Spenser, John Davies, or Fynes Morison describe the Irish as wild, thieving, lawless, blood-drinking, savage, barbarous, naked; these are also the terms routinely used to describe New World Indians" (2002, 41). The subsequent protracted history of colonialism, exploitation, hostility, and violence, leading to the partition of the island under Home Rule in 1922, obviously exacerbated an already bitter situation.

The *blason populaire* or stereotype subsequently applied to the Irish has focused on such negative qualities as backwardness, belligerence, stupidity, idleness, and dirt, mollified by a charming volubility. These perceptions are reinforced by a number of key terms. Although Dr. Johnson defined *bogtrotter* in 1755 simply as "one who lives in boggy country," the term had been applied to the Irish specifically as far back as 1682 in a reference to "an idle flam of shabby Irish Bogtrotters" in the anonymous *Philanax Misopappas,* "Tory Plot" (II, 18). The term implied an Irishman by about 1800, and since then it has come to denote one. (The political label *Tory* originally referred to Irish outlaws, robbers, or bandits.)

The term *blarney,* deriving from Blarney Castle near Cork, has had the negative connotations of "soft, wheedling speeches and flattery to gain some end" since at least its appearance in Francis Grose's *Classical Dictionary of the Vulgar Tongue* (1785). A quotation from

Xenophobic labels and ethnic slurs applied to the Irish have traditionally emphasized the image of a wild, raucous, hard-drinking, earthy people. This illustration, titled "St. Patrick's Day," dates to 1838. (*Graphic Works of George Cruikshank*, Richard A. Vogler, Dover Publications)

Walter Scott in 1796 indicates that the flattery is transparent: "I hold it . . . to be all blarney" (September 26). Authorities such as *Brewer's Dictionary of Phrase and Fable* derive the association of the Castle with flattery and deception from an episode in 1602. In American thieves' slang the verb *blarney* has meant "to pick locks" for over a century. However, the legendary power of the Irish rhymers, attested to in Elizabethan times, was commented on by Owen Connellan in relation to the rural Irish of the 1820s: "Many a man, who would kindle into rage at the sight of an armed foe, will be found to tremble at the thought of offending a rhymer" (1860, xxx).

The slightly provocative nickname *mick* (from *Michael*) is recorded from 1850 in American sources, interestingly contemporary with both *mickey* and *paddy* (from *Padraig*, the Irish version of *Patrick*). Most of the quoted contexts for *mick* are stereotypical: "The Micks got to throwing stones through the Methodis' Sunday School windows" (Mark Twain, *Roughing It* 1871, 253). From about 1924 *mick* could also refer generally to a Catholic. The religious provenance has maintained Catholic oaths such as *Mary and Joseph* and *Mother of God,* which have either died out or never become established in British speech. *Begorrah!*, recorded from the mid-nineteenth century, had become an Irish cliché oath, variant of *by God!*, but is "rarely heard in current speech" (*Oxford English Dictionary*).

The epithet *Irish* is used ironically in many ethnophaulisms or ethnic slurs harping on their alleged backwardness. Some are of surprising antiquity, and include *Irish apricots* for potatoes (1785); *Irish apples,* the same (1890s); *Irish hurricane,* a flat calm sea (1803); *Irish pennant,* a dangling rope (1840); *Irish dividend,* a fictitious profit (1867); *Irish clubhouse,* jail or police station (1904); *Irish confetti* for bricks and stones (1913); and *Irish ambulance* for a wheelbarrow (1931). A great number of these are of American origin, including the use of *Irish* to denote "fighting spirit, especially in an Irish person." "It raised the Irish in me pretty quick . . . , " wrote William Caruthers in *A Kentuckian in New York* in 1834, continuing "for I jumped up and kicked the table over" (I, 63). The phrase "the fighting Irish" is first recorded about 1830. The use of the term *Irishism,* or the comment "*very Irish,*" characterizes a statement that is bizarre, paradoxical, illogical, or a nonsequitur.

Whereas opprobrious comments, ethnic slurs, and xenophobic labels are usually generated by outsiders, the Irish themselves participate enthusiastically in their own denigration. "Ireland is the old sow that eats her farrow," wrote James Joyce in *A Portrait of the Artist as a Young Man* (1916, chapter 5). In the same vein the major contemporary novelist Roddy Doyle writes in *The Commitments* (1987, 13): "The Irish are the niggers of Europe, lads. An' Dubliners are the niggers of Ireland . . . An' the northside Dubliners are the niggers of Dublin—Say it loud. I'm black an' I'm proud" (quoting the song by James Brown in 1968).

In his major study *The Language of Ethnic Conflict* (1983), Irving Lewis Allen lists fifty-five nicknames for the Irish in the United States, placing them fourth in the table, behind Blacks, Whites, and Jews. Generally speaking, the terms are not especially offensive, many of them, such as *emeralder, mulligan, murphy, pat, peat-bogger,* and *red-shanks* even having a tinge of affection. However, *The Random House Historical Dictionary of American Slang* (1997) marked all the ironic uses of *Irish,* such as *Irish wheelbarrow,* as "now usually considered offensive." From a British perspective it is noteworthy that a study of offensive terms in British broadcasting,

A Matter of Manners? (1991), reported the audience view that terms like *taffy, jock, mick,* and *paddy* were regarded as being the least unacceptable, in comparison, that is, to terms for Asian and European groups (1991, 17).

See also: Blason Populaire.

Bibliography

Allen, Irving Lewis. *The Language of Ethnic Conflict.* New York: Columbia University Press, 1983.
Connellan, Owen. *Transactions of the Ossianic Society* 5 (1860).
Hargreave, A.M. *A Matter of Manners? The Limits of Broadcast Language.* London: John Libbey, 1991.
Loomba, Ania. *Shakespeare, Race, and Colonialism.* Oxford: Oxford University Press, 2002.

ITALIANS

English attitudes toward Italy and its peoples have historically been contradictory, a mixture of admiration and repulsion, governed by cultural affiliations and religious divisions. The positive stereotype derives from the status of Italy as the cultural repository of Roman civilization, much emphasized in medieval and Renaissance times, and persisting to this day. The list of major poets who have drawn inspiration from Italy and Italian models is almost endless, including Geoffrey Chaucer, Sir Philip Sidney, Edmund Spenser, Lord Byron, Percy Bysshe Shelley, John Keats, Robert and Elizabeth Browning, and in the modern period, Ezra Pound. (Several of them died there.) Chaucer visited Italy at least twice and was profoundly influenced by Italian models, namely the spirituality of Dante, the idealism of Petrarch, and the realism of Boccaccio. The first two figures served as seminal models to Renaissance poets. Baldassare Castiglione's *The Courtier* (1561) had a profound influence on the English nobility, demonstrating the virtues of an ideal courtly life and offering the model for a perfect gentleman.

However, as a consequence of Henry VIII's break with Rome in 1536 and his declaration of the Church of England, Italy became the home of a hostile religion and a political enemy. Sir Henry Wooton (1568–1639) in his *Letters from Italy,* encapsulated contradictory attitudes in the description that "Italy is a paradise inhabited by devils" (84). "The number of obdurate papists and Italianate atheists is great at this time," wrote Edmund Grindal, Archbishop of Canterbury, to Lord Burleigh in a letter of 1572. On the Elizabethan and Jacobean stage, Italy was depicted as a decadent, corrupt, politically devious society, a hotbed of family betrayal, incest, murder, and treachery of every conceivable form. Cardinals and bishops were frequently the instigators of appalling crimes. A new stage villain emerged, ruthless, demonic, and cynically amused at his treacheries. He was styled the *machiavel,* derived from Niccolò Machiavelli, the Italian statesman and author of *The Prince* (1523), a highly influential work of political philosophy. It was translated into English only in 1640, but the negative stereotype of the *machiavel,* really a travesty of Machiavelli, preceded it. Announcing his program of evil, Shakespeare's Richard III boasts (1590–1591) that he will "set the murderous machiavel to school" (*Henry VI Part 3,* III ii 193). The figure of Machiavel plays the Prologue to Christopher Marlowe's *The Jew of Malta* (1589).

"Unnatural" sexual practices also formed part of negative stereotyping. The phrase "in the Italian fashion" early became established as a euphemism for sodomy. Benvenuto Cellini relates in his *Autobiography* (1558–1566) how his mistress and model Catarina unscrupulously brought a case against him in France, accusing him of using her "in the Italian fashion, that is to say, unnaturally like a sodomite." (In the trial only the phrase "in the Italian way" was used.) Cellini angrily refuted the charge: "To this I answered that such was not the Italian way, and that on the contrary it must be the French way, since she knew all about it and not I" (1956, 249–51). Samuel Pepys noted in his diary entry for July 1, 1663: "Buggery is now almost grown as common amongst our gallants [smart society men] as in Italy."

The arrival of opera on the London stage in the early eighteenth century, more especially the extraordinary vocal artists known as the castrati, of whom Carlo Farinelli was the most brilliant, provoked great controversy and much hostility. The major satirist Alexander Pope castigated the decadent era entertained by "New eunuchs Harlequins and Operas" (*Fourth Satire of John Donne*, l. 125). Henry Carey went further, associating Italy with homosexuality and sodomy in his "Satire on the Luxury [Lust] and Effeminacy of the Age":

Curse on this damn'd Italian pathic mode,
To Sodom and to Hell the ready road.

The reference to Sodom is obvious; *pathic* was an early term for a homosexual.

The earliest specific nickname for Italians is *macaroni,* suggested in the *Spectator* (April 24, 1711) where Joseph Addison made the seminal observation linking diet and national nicknames: "in Holland they are termed Pickled Herrings; in France Jean Pottages; in Italy maccaronies; and in Great Britain Jack Puddings," (no. 47). From the Macaroni Club in London (1760–1775) grew up the associated meaning of a fop, the membership being described by Horace Walpole, the indefatigable letter writer and gossip, as "composed of all the travelled young men who wear long curls and spying glasses" (letter of February 6, 1764). It was used with diminishing frequency through the early part of the twentieth century, and is now obsolete in British English.

Italian immigrants to the United States were initially viewed as aliens and outsiders. Being a large and distinctive population, they attracted many nicknames, according to Irving Lewis Allen (1983) over fifty, of which *dago, eytie, greaseball, guinea, spic,* and *wop* have been the most prominent. Of these *wop,* dating from the 1890s, is the term of greatest impact, possibly because it is Italian in derivation, from Neapolitan and Sicilian *guappo,* meaning a dude, a swell, or a bold showy ruffian. It appeared, significantly, during the peak of Italian immigration to the United States, among a population predominantly from southern Italy, especially from the Naples area. From being used initially by Neapolitans and Sicilians, the term spread outward.

The association with organized crime was made explicit in the first recorded use of *wop,* then spelled as *wap:* "there is a society of criminal young men in New York City . . . known by the euphonious name of 'Waps' or 'Jacks' . . . They form one variety of the many gangs that infest the city." This comes from a detailed description by Arthur Train, a former Manhattan assistant district attorney, in his study, *Courts, Criminals and Camorra* (1912, ix, 232). The Camorra were the Neapolitan version of the *Mafia,* that term being recorded from about 1866, originally referring specifically to a secret criminal organization originating in Sicily. Although the early associations with America were stressed, the term is now generalized, as in "the Nigerian mafia" or "the Eton mafia." Despite the well-attested origin of *wop,* persuasive but fanciful **folk etymologies** have been advanced claiming that *wop* is an acronym derived from the supposed immigration category With Out Passport or With Out Papers, alternatively Working on Pavement. Clearly these etymologies serve to strengthen the negative stereotypes of Italians as being illegal immigrants (as with *wetback* for a Mexican) or menial laborers (as with *cotton-picking* for a Negro).

Harper's Weekly (October 16, 1890) observed: "The lower 'sporting' element in the poorer quarters of New York call them 'Guineas' and 'Dagoes.'" This is the first recorded Italian application of *guinea,* which originally denoted a black person, usually a slave from the Guinea coast. *Dago,* from *Diego,* the equivalent of the name *James,* originally referred to a Spaniard or Portuguese, but started to be used generically of a person from the Mediterranean from the 1860s, a typical generalization to apply to dark-skinned or swarthy foreigners. In similar fashion, *greaseball* was used originally (in the period of World War I) of a person of filthy or greasy appearance, but within a decade was being applied to any white person of Latin-American or Mediterranean descent. A similar pattern of semantic generalization is found in *spic,* dating from 1915 and often presumed to derive from "no spick English."

Various distortions of the name *Italian* have served as nicknames. *Eyetalian* is first recorded in 1840, interestingly prior to major Italian immigration to the United States, but *eyetie* is generally found much later, immediately after World War I. American servicemen clearly imported their own terms, for even in 1943 a writer observed: "We hardly ever heard Italian soldiers referred to as Italians. It was either 'Eyeties' or 'Wops' or 'Guineas'" (Ernie Pyle, *Your War,* 166). The term is generally regarded (by lexicographers) as less offensive than *wop,* being marked as "jocular" by the *Oxford English Dictionary,* of "lesser impact" by the *Dictionary of American Slang* (1986) and "used derisively" by *Random House Historical Dictionary of American Slang* (1994).

Also from World War II came *meatball,* which was already establishing the senses of "a stupid or objectionable person." Other distinctive food metaphors are *spaghetti, spaghetti-bender, spaghetti-head,* and the variants *spigotti* and *spig,* the more plausible origin of *spic.* Swearing, especially blasphemy, is extremely common in Italy (see Averna and Salemi 1977–1987, 42–47), but this aspect is not alluded to in the nicknames. Likewise, although Fascism originated and thrived in Italy for over two decades, the term has retained no semantic link or specific association with Italians, as is the case with the generic use of *nazi* and *Hitler.* The undistinguished Italian war record led to jokes like "How many gears has an Italian tank got?" Answer: "Five. One forward and four reverse." However, World War II also generated the *Italian salute,* a provocative obscene gesture using the bent forearm to signify "up yours."

In general, terms for Italians would seem to fall into the categories of "insulting" or "demeaning," rather than "offensive" or "taboo." However, as always, perceptions vary depending on role and user.

See also: Blason Populaire.

Bibliography

Allen, Irving Lewis. *The Language of Ethnic Conflict.* New York: Columbia University Press, 1983.

Averna, Giuliano, and Joseph Salemi. "Italian Blasphemies." In *The Best of Maledicta,* ed. Reinhold Aman. Philadelphia: Running Press, 1977–1987.

Cellini, Benvenuto. *Autobiography,* trans. George Bull. London: Folio Society, 1956.

Eisiminger, Sterling. "Acronyms and Folk Etymology." *Journal of American Folklore* 91 (1978).

J

JAPANESE, THE

Terms for the Japanese have reflected the catalysts of war and economic competition, both comparatively recent. Prior to the nineteenth century, geographical and cultural distance and the complete lack of contact between Japan and Britain limited lexical borrowings to titles like *shogun, tycoon,* and *mikado.* Japan and its peoples remained shrouded in an Oriental mystique. Very much the same applied to relations between Japan and the United States. However, two radical developments changed perceptions, attitudes, and vocabulary. The first was the importation of indentured Japanese labor into California from the 1840s, a process which accelerated after the Chinese Exclusion Act of 1882. The second was the devastating, unprovoked attack on Pearl Harbor on December 7, 1941.

By 1930 there were 140,000 Japanese in the United States. Prior to World War II, the most common nickname was *skibby,* dating from about 1910 and probably derived from Japanese *sukebei,* meaning lechery or lewdness. Allen suggests that it "might have been heard as a salutation of prostitutes" (1983, 60). The abbreviation *Jap* was common, recorded from the 1850s, but not always offensive: "Ladies' short silk waists, made of plain colored Habutai Jap silk," (*Montgomery Ward Catalog* 1895). According to H.L. Mencken, prior to 1941, American-born Japanese objected vigorously to the designation (1963, 373). From the same era came *brownie* (ca. 1900) and *slant-eye* from the 1930s, neither of them specifically applied to the Japanese, but clearly part of the process of ethnic insults.

After Pearl Harbor, memorably described by President Franklin D. Roosevelt as "a date which will live in infamy," the Japanese population became stereotyped as the treacherous enemy within the gates and were interned in camps for the duration of the war. The word field rapidly expanded with new terms of abuse, notably the verbs *to jap* and *to pull a jap,* meaning "to take by surprise." "The fellows at Pearl Harbor were caught napping by the Japanese japping" was the caustic comment by W.C. Fields in his autobiography, *By Himself,* published the following year (1942, 186). In street slang the verbal senses *to jap,* meaning "to sneak" and "to ambush one's rivals" survived for several decades after the war. The contemptuous abbreviation *Nip* (from *Nippon,* the Japanese name for Japan) seems first recorded in *Time* magazine (January 5, 1942) referring to "three Nip pilots" (20). *Tojo,* the name of the Japanese premier, Hideki Tojo, who ordered the attack on Pearl Harbor, became slang for a Japanese soldier among American and Australian forces.

As the entry for **Hollywood** shows, the film studios entered into the war effort seriously, producing several propagandist films with titles like *Menace of the Rising Sun* and *Secret Agent of Japan,* driven by highly inflammatory scripts. For decades the Hollywood depiction of the Japanese was that of a treacherous, devious, inscrutable alien. Typical of stereotyping, peoples with similar appearance are conflated, in this case the Chinese and others from the Far East, all of whom were labeled as ***gooks.*** From 1942 *chink,* previously used of Chinese, started to be applied contemptuously to any East Asian person. A hostile generalization by Edith Cresson, the French prime minister in 1991, alleged dehumanization in the Japanese corporate structure: "Ants . . . little yellow men who sit up all night thinking how to screw us" (L'Estrange 2002, 313). This remark provoked outrage and protests in Japan.

Two quotations reflect changing attitudes in the United States. General Norman Schwarzkopf recalled: "When I was in elementary school [during World War II] the worst thing you could call anyone was a *Jap*" (CBS, May 8, 1995). Yet in *The Death of Meaning,* George Zito recorded that "the students I interviewed [ca. 1970] could not understand why *Jap* was understood as a term of opprobrium for the Japanese, since it simply abbreviated the name" (1993, 66).

The involvement of British and Australian troops in the war against the Japanese naturally increased the currency of *jap* and *nip.* The dropping of the atom bomb on Hiroshima was reported in the British *Daily Express* with the terse front-page headline "Japs told 'Now quit'" (August 7, 1945). *Nip* also appeared in British armed forces slang: the RAF journal of 1942 referred to "the Nip pilots" and generated various puns on the saying "there's a nip in the air." In Australian English anything completely unacceptable is, in ironic idiom, something "you wouldn't give to a Jap on Anzac Day," that is during the celebrations ending the war. South Africans, having had less direct contact with the Japanese, have no hostile semantic reflectors. In general during the postwar era both names have lost their emotive quality.

See also: Blason Populaire; Gook.

Bibliography

Allen, Irving Lewis. *The Language of Ethnic Conflict.* New York: Columbia University Press, 1983.
L'Estrange, Julian. *The Big Book of National Insults.* London: Cassell, 2002.
Mencken, H.L. *The American Language.* Abridged by Raven I. McDavid Jr. New York: Knopf, 1963.
Peterson, William. *Japanese Americans: Oppression and Success.* New York: Random House, 1971.
Zito, George V. *The Death of Meaning.* Westport, CT: Praeger, 1993.

JESUS

The name of Jesus falls under the basic taboo against "taking the Lord's name in vain" and has therefore generated a considerable number of euphemistic variants, although they are markedly less numerous than those for the name of God and evolve later. As the accompanying table shows, there are approximately a dozen such forms, starting from the early sixteenth century, while the field for the name of God is nearly three times as large and starts two centuries earlier. Significantly, the name of Jesus is not recorded at all in Anglo-Saxon, the standard mode of reference being *se Haeland*, meaning "the Healer," and in Early Middle English the name was rarely written in full, various abbreviations like IHS being preferred. This practice makes the powerful Chaucerian uses below the more striking. Most forms are first recorded in British English, but those with asterisks first appear in American English.

1528	Gis, Jis	1866	Jehosophat*
1660	Geminy	1876	Gee wiz*
1694	Jingo	1892	Jesus H. Christ *
1821	Bejabbers	1905	Gee
1830s	Jiminy	1920s	Jeepers
1830	Jeez*	1922	Jesus wept
1848	Jiminy Crickets	1922	Judas Priest
1849	Jerusalem cricket*	1934	Jeepers Creepers
1851	Gee whillikins*		

Taking the year 597 as the date when Christianity officially came to Britain, this word-field starts very late in the timescale of the language. One can posit a number of reasons for this. Whereas records of the Old English period give little insight into the "street talk," those of Middle English are far more revealing, showing a remarkable profusion of religious exclamations, curses and blasphemy, unexpected in an age of faith. The volume and range in the works of **Geoffrey Chaucer** and William Langland alone are quite astonishing, and include the names of God, Jesus, and Christ, as well as the names of numerous saints, both common and unfamiliar. The irrepressible and much-married Wife of Bath ends her tale with two secular invocations to Jesus, both improper and the second blasphemous:

>   and Jhesu Christ us sende
> Housbondes meeke, yonge and fressh abedde . . .
> [Husbands who are compliant, young and vigorous in bed]
> And eek I praye Jhesu shorte hir [their] lyves
> That wol nat be governed by hire [their] wyves;
> (ll. 1258–62)

This second "death wish" is a specialty of the outrageous Alisoun of Bath, reserved for her old husbands. Showing that blasphemous swearing was by no means a male monopoly in Chaucer, another Alison, the deceiving wife in the *Miller's Tale,* roundly rejects a suitor who has interrupted her adulterous love play:

I love another. . . .
Wel bet than thee, by Jhesu, Absolon.
(ll. 3710–11)

It is a typically Chaucerian irony that one of the most seemingly heartfelt uses of the name of Jesus should come from the spiritual charlatan, the Pardoner, in the "sales spiel" for his pardons and relics:

And Jhesu Crist, that is oure soules leche,
So graunte yow his pardoun to receyve.
[And may Jesus Christ, our soul's doctor,
Allow you to receive his pardon.]
(ll. 916–17)

But he receives a forthright rebuttal from the Host:

"Nay, nay!" quod he, "thanne have I Cristes curs!"
["No way!" he said, "then I would have Christ's damnation!"]
(l. 946)

Euphemisms were thus not really required in late medieval times, since the name of Jesus was so frequently invoked. However, with the coming of printing and its accompanying restraints, as well as the growth of fundamentalist Christian sects, the previous freedom of swearing started to be curtailed. Furthermore, the censorship against using the name of God on the Elizabethan stage obviously had its effects. Nevertheless, the field shows only two terms, *gis* and *jis,* prior to the Elizabethan period, one form, *geminy,* which coincides with the Restoration, followed by a long hiatus until the mid-nineteenth century, after which there is a fairly steady accumulation of terms up to the 1930s. Thereafter, the taboo clearly was no longer respected, and the name of Jesus started to be used with its medieval frequency. *By jingo* has a complicated history, but was used by Motteux in his translation of Rabelais (1694) to render *par Dieu,* and became quite fashionable in the phrase *by the living Jingo* during the eighteenth century.

American English shows respect for the taboo with some picturesque euphemisms, such as *Jerusalem cricket* (1849), *Gee whillikins* (1851), *Jehosophat* (1866), *Gee wiz* (1876), and *Jesus H. Christ* (1892). However, the variety also tends to have more unsympathetic uses of the name in conjunctions like *Jesus freak* (1966), and the ironic name for sandals, namely *Jesus boots.* In the 1930s, H.L. Mencken acerbically commented on the use of the name by Hispanics: "*Jesus* (hay-soos with the accent on the second syllable) often sticks to his name, but is occasionally constrained to change to José or Joe in order to allay the horror or check the ribaldry of 100 percent Americans" (1963, 637).

The potency of the name has not diminished. One of the most powerful instances was the spontaneous exclamation, captured on television, of a woman witnessing the attack on the World Trade Center on September 11, 2001. She screamed out, "Jesus Fucking Christ!"

American lexical authorities generally do not mark the name as taboo, preferring the formula "usually considered offensive."

The British view is hard to determine in a secularized society. A study carried out by the Broadcasting Standards Council in the United Kingdom, *A Matter of Manners?: The Limits of Broadcast Language* (1991), showed that assessments of "the strength of swearwords" varied greatly according to gender and age. Older respondents found all religious swearwords far more shocking than sexual terms; young men found virtually all swearwords weak. In an essay on "Blasphemy" in the symposium, the Reverend Dr. Colin Morris, an experienced administrator and advisor on television, observed:

> Whereas the casual use of "God" might be regarded as poor taste, the insulting employment of "Jesus" or "Christ" would certainly be viewed by most Christians as an affront to conscience and therefore an attack on something very precious to them.
> (1991, 83)

However, the B.B.C. noted that according to a survey carried out in 2005, the majority of young British children thought that "Jesus" was a swearword rather than a person.

See also: Christ; God, Euphemisms for.

Bibliography

Hargreave, Andrea Millwood. *A Matter of Manners?: The Limits of Broadcast Language.* London: John Libbey, 1991.
Mencken, H.L. *The American Language.* Abridged by Raven I. McDavid Jr. New York: Knopf, 1963.

JEWS

Jews have for centuries attracted animus, negative stereotypes, ethnic insults, and persecution from the host populations among whom they have lived. The grounds, so far as they can be rationally explained, have ostensibly derived from their religious difference and their commercial practices. However, the growth of other vicious stereotypes, based on legend, fabrication, and propaganda rather than fact, has led to *pogroms* (a Russian word meaning "destruction") and even genocide. Prejudicial notions have persisted long after rational exposure.

Religious hatred derives from the rejection of Christ as the Messiah and the self-imposed blame for his Crucifixion, according to St. Matthew 27:25: "Then answered all the people and said His blood be on us and on our children." Many medieval Passion plays dramatized this motif powerfully, as did numerous literary authors, so that Jewish blame had doctrinal status until the ruling by Second Vatican Council (1962–1965) exculpating the Jews for the death of Christ. The Hebraic foundation of the Scriptures contained a number of allusions linking Jews to Satan, notably St. John 8:44 and the Book of Revelation 2:9 and 3:9. Furthermore, a number of major medieval ecclesiastical authorities wrote influential works depicting Jews as the enemies of Christians, if not Antichrist himself. Among them were those of Rabanus Maurus in the ninth century and Peter of Blois's *Contra perfidium Judaeorum* ("Against the Treachery of the Jews," ca. 1200). Furthermore, Jews were exempt from the regulations of Canon Law forbidding Christians to charge interest on loans. An explanatory note added

The Nazi propaganda film *Der ewige Jude* ("The Eternal Jew," 1933) played on longstanding anti-Semitic fears by depicting Jews as a corrupt, rat-like, alien people who threaten to take over the world by controlling banking and commerce. (©Topham/The Image Works)

to the *Supplement* of the *Oxford English Dictionary* in 1972 runs: "Thus the name of Jew came to be associated in the popular mind with usury and extortionate practices that might be supposed to accompany it, and gained an opprobrious sense."

In the early Middle Ages there were occasional instances of anti-Jewish riots and persecution in England, the most notable being the massacre of Jews at the coronation of Richard the Lion-Heart on September 3, 1189. An English manuscript shows Jews being attacked in thirteenth-century London: they are identifiable since Jews were legally required to wear two strips of yellow cloth on their garments (British Library, MS Cotton Nero D ii fol. 183v). The motivation for such attacks derived from deeper roots than their religious difference and advantageous commercial situation. "It was in England that the first accusation of ritual murder was formulated against the Jews. In 1144, they were said to have crucified a boy named William in Norwich. Many miracles were reported to have taken place at his grave" (Sinsheimer 1947, 39). A similar legend surrounded the murder of St. Hugh of Lincoln in 1255: the account of Matthew Paris claims that the Jews "disemboweled the corpse, for what end is unknown, but it was said to practice magical arts." There was also the sensational case of the alleged ritual murder of the boy Simon at Trent in 1474.

However, there is an anomaly or disjunction between the growth of this stereotype and historical actuality. There were virtually no Jews in England from 1290, when they were expelled by Edward III, to 1655, when they were readmitted by Oliver Cromwell. (By special permission a few were allowed to remain resident during the interim.) Yet precisely during this period there developed the vicious stereotypes of Jews being child murderers and social saboteurs, one of the most common myths being that they poisoned wells. The typical qualifying adjective in medieval times was *corsed,* "cursed or damned." In numerous texts their role in the Crucifixion is reiterated. From the inhuman or insulting behavior of a single variously named Jew toward Christ at this historic moment, the whole legend of the Wandering Jew takes root. In view of the widespread mocking of Christ at the Crucifixion, this exclusive punishment in itself seems like discrimination. As the entry for **God's wounds** shows, those spiritual authorities who denounced Christians for swearing by God's body and wounds routinely made invidious comparisons with the Jews.

Literary Depictions

References to Jews in Anglo-Saxon literature are limited to Biblical events. Indeed the word *Jew* is first recorded only ca. 1275. However, Chaucer's Prioress, Madame Eglentyne, presented as a demure and dignified nun in the *General Prologue* of the *Canterbury Tales,* tells a melodramatic and savage tale based on the legend of the murder of St. Hugh of Lincoln and driven by virtually all the stereotypes of xenophobia and anti-Semitism. The "cursed Jews," sustained by "foul usure and lucre of vileynye, / Hateful to Crist and to his compaignye (ll. 491–92), are presented as diabolically evil:

Our firste foo [enemy] the serpent Sathanas
That hath in Jues herte his waspes nest.
(ll. 558–59)

The Jews murder a boy chorister, but the corpse miraculously continues to sing, so that the perpetrators are found, pulled apart by wild horses, and hanged. The Prioress also denounces the Jews as "O cursed folk of Herodes al newe" (l. 574), making an explicit comparison with the massacre of the innocents (Matthew 2:16). She ends with a prayer to St. Hugh of Lincoln, "slayn also with cursed Jewes."

This hideous tale, which would now be condemned as hate speech, provokes no response in the pilgrim company beyond sober reflection on the miracle, thus giving a sense of how deeply engrained were anti-Semitic sentiments in medieval times. In his standard edition, F.N. Robinson noted: "The general tradition of the murder of Christian children by Jews is much more ancient than this particular story, beginning at the time of the Church historian Socrates (5th century), and is still alive" (1957, 734). The subsequent edition by Larry D. Benson (1987) deals more directly with the problem of the anti-Semitism of the tale for readers and critics.

Two major character studies of Jews dominated the Elizabethan stage. The most famous is Shylock in Shakespeare's *The Merchant of Venice* (1596–1597), but equally significant is Barabbas in Christopher Marlowe's earlier play, *The Jew of Malta* (1589). Shylock is an original and sympathetic study of the Jew as alien and victim, called impersonally "Jew" or "the Jew" throughout, using language full of Old Testament references to Jewish custom. When Shylock agrees to make the loan, Antonio expresses mock surprise, saying "gentle Jew" (punning on *gentile*), adding (after Shylock has exited) the ironic comment: "This Hebrew will turn Christian: he grows kind" (I iii 178–79). The play juxtaposes the strict punitive code of the Old Testament, symbolized in Shylock's "bond," and the merciful code of the New, which Portia seeks to evoke in her famous speech on "the quality of mercy" (IV i 184). Despite Shylock's intensely moving speech "Hath not a Jew eyes?" (III i 60–75), he remains an alien rejected by Venetian society and in the end is totally ruined.

While Shylock provokes mixed feelings, Barabbas is a melodramatic version of the ruthless Machiavellian intriguer and a continuation of the figure of Herod, presented on the Elizabethan stage as arrogant and bizarre. Marlowe defiantly names his protagonist after one of the thieves crucified with Christ, while the title, *The Jew of Malta,* clearly demarcates him as an outsider in an alien multicultural context. The Prologue is spoken by Machievel, a figure obviously derived from the Italian political philosopher Niccolò Machiavelli (1469–1527), stereotyped in England as an atheistic opportunist. Machiavel announces casually: "I hold religion but a childish toy" (l. 14). Barabbas is openly contemptuous of "these swine-eating Christians, / Unchosen nation, never circumcised" (II iii 7–8), pointedly referring to "our Messias that is yet to come" (II iii 302). In the same scene, the speech beginning "Sometimes I go about and poison wells" is a catalogue of all the anti-Semitic stereotypes. He steadfastly refuses to convert, acknowledging the ruinous financial consequences and asks mockingly of the Christians: "Is theft the ground of your religion?" (II iii 155). He poisons a whole convent of nuns billeted at his house, including his daughter Abigail, and yet is preposterously joyful: "How sweet the bells ring now the nuns are dead" (IV i 2). As his stratagems catch up with him he retains a haughty defiance: "Devils, do your worst! I'll live in spite of you" (V i 38). Seeking to be the ultimate Machievel, ruthless and amoral, he is finally destroyed by treachery and by his own ingenuity. Whereas Shylock leaves the play destroyed, with a bitterly ironic "I am content," Barabbas dies with a final curse: "Damned Christian dogs! and Turkish infidels!" (V vi 88).

Equally significant to the popular conception of the Jew was the controversial figure of Dr. Lopez (1517–1594), a Spanish Jew who in 1581 became Queen Elizabeth's physician and a political adviser. He was accused by the Earl of Essex of conspiracy to murder the queen by poisoning and was denounced by the attorney general Sir Edward Coke: "That . . . murdering traitor and Jewish doctor is worse than Judas himself" (Sinsheimer 1947, 66). At his public hanging at Tyburn on June 7, 1594, the crowd had a simple denunciation: "He is Jew! He is Jew!" The similarities between Barabbas and Lopez, both Jews, Spaniards, poisoners, and traitors, seem not to be coincidental.

The later literary depiction of Jews is more balanced. The evil outsider stereotype is continued most famously in Fagin, the sinister "godfather" of a gang of juvenile thieves in Charles Dickens's *Oliver Twist* (1837–1839). Generally called simply "the Jew," Fagin is introduced in chapter viii as a crude caricature, "a very old shrivelled Jew, whose villainous looking and repulsive face was obscured by a quantity of matted red hair." He is made decidedly alien: "As he glided steadthily along, the hideous old man seemed like some loathsome reptile, engendered in the slime and darkness through which he moved." Similar is Ferdinand Lopez, the villain of Anthony Trollope's *The Prime Minister* (1876), simply and strongly sketched as "without a father, a foreigner, a black Portuguese nameless Jew [with] a bright eye, a hook nose, and a glib tongue" (1983, 146). A new development, that of the positive sympathetic stereotype, is found in Riah in *Our Mutual Friend* (1864–1865), Dickens's last complete novel, and in Daniel Deronda, the eponymous hero of George Eliot's novel (1876). The most famous Jew in Victorian public life, Benjamin Disraeli (1804–1881) was also a notable novelist, creating in his political novel *Coningsby* (1844) an impressive Jewish character, Sidonia.

On the wider political front there emerged a seminal anti-Semitic document, *The Protocols of the Elders of Zion,* privately printed in 1897 and published in various European languages from 1905 with savage propagandist caricatures. It was ostensibly a record of a secret Zionist Congress at Basel to plan world domination. However, after an exposé by the London *Times* in 1921, a judicial inquiry in 1934 revealed that "the supposed minutes were highly sophisticated forgeries made in the Paris office of the Russian Political Police (the Okhrana) probably for use by the Czarist regime against the Russian liberals" (Maser 1970, 165). Bizarrely, sections had been copied from two novels, *Biarritz* (1868), by Hermann Goedsche, and *Dialogues in Hell* (1864), by Maurice Joly. But since the content perfectly fitted the stereotype of a Jewish conspiracy, it was highly effective as propaganda and was widely disseminated, notably by Adolf Hitler and the Nazis, and by Henry Ford in the United States. Its influence is not entirely extinguished.

The Word-Field

The word-field of hostile terms starts relatively late in the Elizabethan period with the senses of the noun *Jew* (ca. 1600), defined by the *Oxford English Dictionary* as "a name of opprobrium or reprobation, *spec.* applied to a grasping or extortionate money-lender or usurer who drives hard bargains or deals craftily." The equally controversial verbal sense, "to bargain sharply with; cheat; beat down the price; haggle" is recorded in American English from about 1818: "A Yankee can Jew a Jew directly," a few decades earlier than in British English. A note by the Reverend R. Manning Chipman in the *Dictionary of American English* in 1870 observes that *to jew* "is used all over the U.S. In [New England] Jews themselves use it in the same way." The literal origin of *jew-boy* is explained in a British Police document of 1796: "Jew Boys . . . go out every morning loaded with counterfeit copper, which they exchange for bad silver, to be afterwards coloured anew, and again put into a circulation." Within a few decades the term was being used offensively of grown-ups. The sense that the Jews were "different" or "alien" is shown in the considerable number of compounds such as *Jew-butcher, Jew-physician, Jew-pedlar,* and *Jew-fencer* (buyer or seller, generally of stolen goods).

More significant witness words were the arrival over a century ago of *Jew-baiting* (ca. 1883) and *Jew-hatred* (ca. 1898). However, it would be naive to see anti-Semitism as being a feature of right-wing organizations alone. The correspondence of Karl Marx, one of the founders of communism and himself a Jew, has some virulently racist comments. In a letter to Friedrich Engels, the coauthor of the *Communist Manifesto* (1848), Marx referred to the German politician and sociologist Ferdinand Lassalle, as "the Jewish Nigger," adding that "It is now quite plain to me—as the shape of his head and the way his hair grows also testify—that he is descended from the negroes who accompanied Moses' flight from Egypt (unless his mother or paternal grandmother interbred with a NIGGER)" (letter dated July 30, 1862). (Marx himself was dark and nicknamed *der Mohr* ["The Moor"] even by his friend Engels.) Anti-Semitic attitudes surface frequently in everyday speech: in Henry Mayhew's *London Underworld* (1862), a "bunter," or low-class prostitute, says that "she never paid any rent, hadn't done it for years, and never meant to. They [the landlords] was mostly Christ-killers, and chousing [cheating] a Jew was no sin" (1983, 53). Even Thomas Carlyle (1795–1881), perhaps the greatest Victorian intellectual, referred to Benjamin Disraeli, anglicized, baptized, and twice Prime Minister, politely as "a superlative Hebrew conjuror" and savagely as a "cursed old Jew not worth his weight in cold bacon" (Sutherland, ed.), 1975, 224).

It is notable that in comparison with the growth of demeaning nicknames for other nationalities, those for Jews are late, the earliest recorded use of *sheeny,* ca. 1810, about a century after *bogtrotter, macaroni,* and *dago.* The most obvious reason is that *Jew* itself was already being used in various opprobrious senses. The broad chronology of the principal nicknames is as follows: *sheeny* (ca. 1810), *ikey* (1864), *yid* (1874), *kike* (1880s), *heeb* or *hebe* (1926), and *hymie* (1973). While all of these have been current in the United States, the first three terms were previously current in the United Kingdom but are now obsolescent. In *The Language of Ethnic Conflict* (1983), Irving Lewis Allen shows that in the United States there are sixty-four nicknames for Jews, more than for any other immigrant group.

Of the most common terms, *sheeny* dates from about 1816 in British usage, possibly deriving, according to Eric Partridge, "from the Yiddish pronunciation of German *schön,* 'beautiful,' used in praising wares" (1972, 825). William Makepeace Thackeray uses it as a nickname in *Snobs* (1847): "Sheeny and Moses are . . . smoking their pipes before their lazy shutters in Seven Dials" (xiv). The definition in the *Dictionary of American Slang* (1986) is tactlessly specific: "a pawnbroker, tailor, junkman or other traditionally Jewish occupation." *Ikey,* derived from *Isaac,* is first recorded in John Camden Hotten's *Slang Dictionary* (1864) and defined as "a Jew fence," that is, receiver of stolen property. *Yid* seems to be the first term coined by the Jews themselves, according to the 1874 edition of Hotten's dictionary: "The Jews use these terms [*yid, yit, yidden*] very frequently." It derives from German *Jude,* a Jew, an abbreviation of *Yehuda,* the name of the Jewish Commonwealth. American usage dates from about 1915. As with many terms of ethnic insult, the degree of offensiveness depends on who uses it: Hugh Rawson retails the anecdotal point that "Chaim Weizmann, the first president of Israel, would describe himself appealingly as just 'A Yid from Pinsk'" (*New York Times Book Review,* June 30, 1985). A less expected cross-cultural manifestation was Richard "Kinky" Friedman's country and western band, founded in the early 1970s and styled "The Texas Jewboys."

The earliest term to develop in America was *kike,* recorded in the 1880s. As Allen explains, the etymology is much disputed (1983, 121–23), but the picturesque explanation advanced by Leo Rosten in *The Joys of Yiddish* (1968) seems to be the most plausible. According to Rosten, the root is *kikel,* the Yiddish word for a circle, the symbol used by Jewish immigrants, many of whom were illiterate, when signing their papers at Ellis Island, instead of the usual X, a Christian symbol. Consequently, immigration officers began to refer to such a person as a *kikel,* later abbreviated to *kike.* Rosten's authority is Philip Cowen, whom he styles "the dean of immigration inspectors" (180). Significantly, the term was first used by assimilated American German Jews to disparage "uncouth Jewish immigrants from Russia or Eastern Europe" (*The Random House Historical Dictionary of American Slang* 1997). R. Glanz in his study *The Jew in Folklore* (1904–1905) noted that "No longer is it limited to the Russian Jew. Noble Bavarian hurled the epithet at equally noble Prussian and Swabian . . . and we have heard of 'kike' goyim too" (205). Now used disparagingly of Jews in general, the term has remained largely confined to American usage.

During the first half of the twentieth century, prior to the growth of political correctness and the general sensitivity to opprobrious ethnic labels, there developed in the United States a campaign against the insulting uses of the word *Jew,* especially as a verb. H.L. Mencken, who was not very sympathetic to this development, observed: "Certain American Jews carry on a continuous campaign against the use of *Jew,* and American newspapers, in order to get rid of their clamor, often use *Hebrew* instead. Thus one encounters such forms as *Hebrew comedian, Hebrew holidays* and even *Hebrew rabbi*" (1936, 297). (See also Hugh Rawson 1983, 133, and 1991, 189). However, the offensive abbreviation *heeb* (or *hebe*) started to emerge about 1926 (first recorded in Ring Lardner) and has maintained a slang or underground currency ever since. More recent forms have been *hymie* (from Hyman) and *Hymietown* (for New York). Recorded ca. 1973, the terms gained notoriety in 1984 when the Reverend Jesse Jackson, an African-American spokesman, admitted using them in private conversations (*New York Times,* February 27, 1984). Though he apologized, he insisted that he had been using "noninsulting colloquial language" (*Newsweek,* April 1, 1984).

Despite these stigmatic terms, Jewish humor contains a rich store of jokes based on anti-Semitic stereotypes. Leo Rosten's exuberant collection, *The Joys of Yiddish* (1968), illustrates this point on virtually every page, often in the witty definitions of the disparaging terms for social types like *schmuck, schlemiel, schmegegge, yenta,* and so on. In British English some references for Jews are disguised by the mode of **rhyming slang**, in which the last term in the phrase rhymes with the unstated word. Among the codes for *Jew* are *four by two, five by two, half-past two,* and *kangaroo.* Similar forms for *yid* are *front-wheel skid* and *saucepan lid.* Not all rhyming slang is exclusively British: *box of glue* originated on the Pacific coast of America.

Other coded terms in the United States are *goldberg,* limited to Black English, and JAP, an abbreviation pronounced "jap" for *Jewish American Princess,* dating from the late 1960s. According to Hugh Rawson, "Always portrayed as rich, spoiled and straitlaced" (1991, 217), the type became the subject of many jokes, such as "What does a good JAP make for dinner? Reservations" (B. Raskin 1987, 287). The issue led to a Conference on Current Stereotypes of Jewish Women, sponsored by the American Jewish Committee in 1987. However, in his study *The Death of Meaning,* George Zito noted: "Most Jewish students I have interviewed do not . . . understand why some ultra-sensitive Jews find the JAP term so objectionable" (1993, 67).

South African English provides an almost identical stereotype in the term *kugel,* current from the 1970s, defined in the *Dictionary of South African English* (1991) as: "*Jewish.* A young woman of the wealthier class, whose interests are men, money and fashion, speaking in a recognizable drawling dialect developed within the group." Although *kugel* describes a social type rather than strictly denoting a Jewish woman, this identity is implied in the derivation, from the Yiddish name of a pudding. *Smous,* amazingly recorded in Grose (1785) for a German Jew, migrated to South Africa, where it formerly denoted "an itinerant pedlar, often Jewish, who made a living hawking goods from farm to farm." In 1797, Le Vaillant noted that these hawkers had "obtained the name Capse-Smouse, or Cape Jews" (I, 55). It is also an American slang term for a Jew.

The strangest South African term is *peruvian,* which has followed the same sociolinguistic pattern as *kike.* Almost certainly originating in an acronym derived from P.R.U., standing for "Polish and Russian Union," yielding a pronounceable form "peru," it first denoted an Eastern European Jewish immigrant to South Africa. In 1899 there is a reference to "Peruvian Jews . . . compelled to contribute to the Pretorian war-chest" (Froes 1899, 14). As with *kike,* the term was first used by South African Jews to stigmatize those new arrivals who still retained their characteristic foreign accents, customs, and eating habits, before becoming a derogatory term for an unacceptable, crude, or dishonest person in the community. Finally it developed a general anti-Semitic sense. The term is now virtually obsolete.

The long history of anti-Semitism, the growth of political correctness, and increased sensitivity to opprobrious categorizing labels have all combined to diminish the currency of ethnic insults. In some cases traditional names have been altered. Thus in 2001 the committee of names of fishes of the American Fisheries Society ruled that the name *jewfish* was offensive, and the fish was renamed as the *Goliath grouper.* While official alteration of names obviously has impact, prejudice and underground slang cannot be so easily controlled. Thus a *jew canoe* has been a satirical term for an expensive automobile in both American slang and the upper-class British argot of the Sloane Rangers for at least three decades. The surfacing of such terms expressive of envy and contempt shows that the impulse toward denigration continues. As has been noted, a number of originally stigmatic or critical terms, like *kike* and *yid,* have been through the same socio-semantic cycle of being used first to mark Jews as outsiders, then by insider Jews to discriminate against other Jews, finally returning to the original dynamic. The same pattern can be seen in *nigger.*

See also: Blason Populaire; God's Wounds.

Bibliography

Allen, Irving Lewis. *The Language of Ethnic Conflict.* New York: Columbia University Press, 1983.

Almog, S., ed. *Antisemitism Through the Ages.* Oxford: Pergamon, 1988.

Benson, Larry D., ed. *The Riverside Chaucer.* Oxford: Oxford University Press, 1988.

Cohn, Norman. *Warrant for Genocide.* New York: Serif, 1996.

Dimock, I.F. "The Conspiracy of Dr. Lopez." *English Historical Review,* 1894.

Froes, T. *Expelled from the Randt.* Cape Town: William Taylor, 1899.

Le Vaillant, M. *My Travels into the Interior Part of Africa.* London: Robinson, 1797.

Lighter, J.L., ed. *The Random House Historical Dictionary of American Slang.* New York: Random House, 1997.

Maser, Werner. *Hitler's Mein Kampf.* London: Faber, 1970.

Mayhew, Henry. *London's Underworld* (1862). London: Bracken Books, 1983.

Mencken, H.L. *The American Language.* New York: Knopf, 1936.

Rawson, Hugh. *A Dictionary of Invective.* London: Robert Hale, 1991.

Robinson, F.N., ed. *The Works of Geoffrey Chaucer.* London: Oxford University Press, 1947.

Rosten, Leo. *The Joys of Yiddish.* New York: McGraw-Hill, 1968.

Sinsheimer, Hermann. *Shylock.* London: Gollancz, 1947.

Sutherland, James, ed. *Oxford Book of Literary Anecdotes.* Oxford: Oxford University Press, 1975.

Trachtenberg, Joshua. *The Devil and the Jews: The Medieval Conception of the Jew and Its Relation to Modern Anti-Semitism.* New Haven: Yale University Press, 1943.

Zito, George V. *The Death of Meaning.* Westport, CT: Praeger, 1993.

JOHNSON, DR. SAMUEL

Samuel Johnson (1709–1784) is still the most famous lexicographer of the English language, and his magisterial *Dictionary of the English Language* (1755) remains a major monument in the history of the English dictionary, to the point that many of its definitions were carried over into the authoritative *Oxford English Dictionary* and acknowledged by a simple bracketed capital "J." As Robert Burchfield, the editor of the *OED Supplement,* has pointed out, Johnson's is the only English dictionary compiled by a writer of the first rank (1985, 87). The most remarkable Renaissance man of letters in his own time, he made significant contributions to all the major literary genres. Amazingly, he completed the huge work in nine years virtually single-handed, with only the assistance of six amanuenses whose sole functions were to copy out quotations, sort, and file them as part of the onerous historical method. To illustrate 40,000 headwords he amassed 116,000 citations or illustrative quotations, tending to favor the usage of the previous century and what he called, significantly, "the wells of English undefiled" (McAdam 1963, 18).

"Dictionary Johnson," as he was called, lived through the Enlightenment, or the Age of Reason, when the virtues of rationality, order, and decorum were especially stressed.

These mental and social qualities were in clear contrast with the decadence of the **Restoration** preceding it, and the emotional and political liberation of the succeeding Romantic era. Many of the major literary minds of the period saw the English language as being in a state of confusion and decay. These included the great satirists **Jonathan Swift** and Alexander Pope, as well as the influential essayists Joseph Addison and Richard Steele. Swift had written as early as 1712 *A Proposal for Correcting, Improving and Ascertaining the English Tongue.* Daniel Defoe underlined the absurdity of the fashionable slang of the times in his essay "A Tilt at Profanity" in 1712: "at play it is G-d damn the cards; a-hunting G-d damn the hounds; they call dogs the sons of whores and men sons of bitches" (1951, 260).

In the remarkable Preface to his great work, Johnson initially saw himself as a linguistic Newton come to impose order on unruly philology: "Every language has . . . its improprieties and absurdities, which it is the duty of the lexicographer to correct or proscribe" (McAdam 1963, 4). But by the time he had completed his task he recognized that the language was subject to "causes of change, which, though slow in their operation and invisible in their progress, are perhaps as much superiour to human resistance, as the revolutions of the sky and the intumescence of the tide" (McAdam 1963, 25).

Johnson was a formidable personality, who was trenchant, pompous, witty, and dogmatic, qualities apparent in many of his definitions. This was a period, furthermore, in which the preferred diction was not direct and rude, but in the words of Edward Gibbon, favored "the decent obscurity of a learned language" (1854, 212). However, Johnson was by no means prudish: various anecdotes reveal that he rather relished coarse speech. When the famous actor David Garrick asked what was the greatest pleasure in life, Johnson "answered fucking and second was drinking. And therefore he wondered why there were not more drunkards, for all could drink though all could not fuck" (Hibbert 1971, 68). (Significantly, his famous biographer James Boswell noted but did not record these remarks.) After a performance of Johnson's tragedy *Irene,* Garrick invited him backstage, but when invited a second time he demurred: "No, David, I will never come back. For the white bubbies and the silk stockings of your actresses excite my genitals" (Hibbert 1971, 74). He defined *bubby* simply as "a woman's breast" without further comment, although it was a colloquialism.

Johnson especially condemned "cant," the perpetually flourishing but generally unstable language of the underworld, regarding it as "unworthy of preservation" (McAdam 1963, 23). He himself defined *cant* as both "(1) a corrupt dialect used by beggars and vagabonds" and "(2) a particular form of speaking peculiar to some certain class or body of men." The first is the historical sense, while the second conforms more to modern "jargon" or "in-group vocabulary" and fashionable nonsensical exaggeration. He simply omitted a number of words in the first category, like *cove* for a man, *beak* for a judge, and *fence* for a receiver of stolen property, even though they had been in the language for centuries and survive to this day. In the second category he noted that *frightful* was "a cant word among women for anything unpleasing," that *horrid* was similarly so used to mean "shocking; offensive; unpleasing," that *monstrous* was a "a cant term" for "exceedingly" or "very much," and that *Billingsgate* was "a cant word." Another of his usage markers was the phrase "a low word": among terms so categorized are *cajole, fuss, job, sham, plaguy, plaguily, mishmash, swop, tiff, touchy,* and *uppish,* which are really "colloquial" rather than "low." His hostility was thus more toward the imprecise or affected use of words than simply to their low class or to foul language.

In keeping with the sense of decorum of the time, Johnson did not include the grossest of the "four-letter" words (although his contemporary Nathaniel Bailey had). This omission is ironically acknowledged in the contemporary anecdote of two society ladies who "very much commended the omission of all naughty words. 'What! my dears!' Johnson mischievously enquired, 'then you have been looking for them?'" (Beste, *Memorials,* cited in Sutherland 1975, 84). Although he excluded *shit, cundum, frig, swive,* and *bugger,* he included and had direct definitions of *fart* ("wind from behind"), *piss* ("to make water"), *bum* and *arse,* simply defined as "the buttocks; the part on which we sit." None carried any usage label such as "vulgar" or "low." He likewise defined *piddle* unexpectedly in the context of eating as "to pick at table; to feed squeamishly and without appetite" and defined *job* as "petty, piddling work." *Lousy* was given an interesting class gloss: "mean; low born; bred on the dunghill," while *bitch* was simply "a name of reproach for a woman."

Concerning swearing *per se,* Johnson was clearly hostile to the fashionable but loose use of serious terms. He thus defined *damn* literally as "to doom to eternal torments in a future state," castigating the contemporary colloquial use of *damnable* and *damnably* for "odious" or "pernicious" or "odiously" or "hatefully" as "a low and ludicrous sense." He likewise criticized *whoreson* for being "generally used in a ludicrous dislike" and similarly rejected *deuce* in the sense of "the devil" as "a ludicrous word." As can be seen, *ludicrous* is another of Johnson's armory of condemning epithets, well exemplified in his comment on *abominable:* "In low and ludicrous language, it is a word of loose and indeterminate censure." His hostile instinct was frequently right, since many of these words continued to show the semantic trend of **loss of intensity.** However, exclamations which had no literal meaning, like *foh!, fy!, pish!,* and *pshaw!,* were included without comment. Likewise, *foutra,* borrowed from French *foutre,* meaning "to fuck," is defined in its euphemistic English sense: "a fig; a scoff; an act of contempt." The definition is elucidated by the entries under *to fig* and *fico,* "an act of contempt done with the fingers, expressing a *fig for you.*" The gesture is explained more fully in the entry for **body language**.

Modern assessments of Johnson generally emphasize his shortcomings, partly by invidious comparisons with later lexicographical standards, pointing out his deficiencies in etymology, especially his ignorance of "Teutonick" or the Germanic roots of English. Criticism is leveled at his judgmental, proscriptive stance, clearly at variance with modern linguistic notions that "usage" is the dominant criterion of validity. Thus W.K. Wimsatt Jr. commented dryly: "His attempts to discourage some words by applying a kind of linguistic weed-killer, or notation of censure, were not very successful" (1959, 66). However, Robert Burchfield noted the work's longevity and endorsed "its steady belief in the superiority of the vocabulary of the best writers, its rejection of foreign expressions and dialectal words . . . and its rejection of illiterate or modish vocabulary," stressing that Johnson "set a standard of lexicography" surpassed only much later (1979, iii). It is certainly notable that Johnson's sense of what was proper to include or exclude from his dictionary on the grounds of decency was virtually identical to that of his great successor James Murray, the editor of the *Oxford English Dictionary,* a century and a half later.

See also: Dictionaries.

Bibliography

Bate, Walter Jackson. *The Life of Samuel Johnson.* New York: Harcourt Brace Jovanovich, 1975.
Boswell, James. *The Life of Johnson.* 1791. London: Macmillan, 1893.
Burchfield, Robert. Preface to *Facsimile of Johnson's Dictionary.* London: Times Books, 1979.
Defoe, Daniel. "A Tilt at Profanity" (1712). In *The Best of Defoe's REVIEW,* ed. William L. Payne. New York: Columbia University Press, 1951.
Gibbon, Edward. *Autobiography.* London: 1854.
Hibbert, Christopher. *The Personal Life of Samuel Johnson.* London: Longman, 1971.
Johnson, Samuel. *A Dictionary of the English Language.* London: W. Strachan, 1755.
McAdam, E.L., and George Milne, eds. *Johnson's Dictionary: A Modern Selection.* London: Gollancz, 1963.
Sutherland, James, ed. *The Oxford Book of Literary Anecdotes.* Oxford: Oxford University Press, 1975.
Wimsatt, W.K. "Johnson's Dictionary." In *New Light on Dr. Johnson: Essays on the Occasion of His 250th Birthday.* New Haven: Yale University Press, 1959.

JONSON, BEN

The notable playwright, collaborator, actor, and friend of William Shakespeare, Ben Jonson (1572–1637) was a cantankerous man who lived adventurously, killing a fellow actor in a duel, converting to Catholicism while in prison, leaving and reconsorting with his wife, and having an indeterminate number of children, not all of them legitimate. Consistently in trouble with the authorities for his daring theatrical satires, he was imprisoned several times. Yet he was made Poet Laureate, enjoyed royal favor and a pension, was awarded an honorary degree from Oxford University, and finally laid to rest in Poets' Corner in Westminster Abbey. None of these honors was accorded to Shakespeare, in comparison with whom Jonson is in general more savagely satirical and disturbing.

Jonson's work varied greatly: he could write in a severe classical style, create exquisite lyrics, or use the coarsest imaginable register. He created realistic and cynical urban comedies often set in London and coarse-veined satires using the idioms and language of the street to great effect. Many authorities have commented on "the vigour and flamboyance of popular speech" in his finest plays (Thomson and Salgado 1985, 244). Jonson himself insisted, in the Prologue to his comedy *Everyman in His Humour* (performed 1598, with Shakespeare in the cast) on exploiting "deeds and language such as men do use" (l. 21), rather than rarefied, poetic, and polysyllabic diction.

Swearing and foul language form overt features of several of his plays. A considerable proportion of *Everyman in His Humour* focuses on the contemporary incidence of swearing by means of ironic exposés and disapproving commentaries. Thus the elder Kno'well observes ironically that the education of infants is marked, not by repression of swearing, but by encouragement:

Their first words
We form their tongues with, are licentious jests.
Can it call whore? Cry bastard? Oh then kiss it,
A witty child! Can't swear? The father's darling!
Give it two plums.
(II iii 19–23)

When Cob, a water bearer, utters the blasphemous expletive "for God's sake," Clement, the major authority-figure in the play, corrects him soberly with the reproof, "Nay, God's precious" (III iii 103–4). Bobadill, cast in the stereotype of the *miles gloriosus,* or boasting soldier, is predictably given the most exuberant swearing role in the play, using such original expletives are *base cullion* [testicle], *whoreson filthy slave,* and *a dungworm, an excrement!* Though Jonson had more of a classical education than Shakespeare, he enjoyed dropping classical names into coarse speech and juxtaposing Christian and pagan elements, as in *Body o' Caesar!* and the absurd oath *by the foot of Pharaoh.* In *Bartholomew Fair* (1614), containing an Epilogue addressed to King James on the subject of profanity and license, Wasp comes out with such earthy vituperation as *Turd I' your teeth!* and *Shit o' your head!*

The *Alchemist* (1610) is, according to the introductory Argument, about "A cheater and his punk," that is, a confidence trickster and his prostitute. The play opens in the middle of a furious row between Face and Subtle, who crudely dismisses his opponent with the insult "I fart at thee" (l. 2). They continue to trade insults vehemently:

				Cheater!	
Subtle:					
Face: Bawd!					
Subtle:	Cowherd!				
Face:		Conjurer!			
Subtle:			Cutpurse!		
Face:					Witch!

Eventually the prostitute Doll Common separates the combatants, berating them savagely:

'Sdeath, you abominable pair of stinkards,
Leave off your barking (I i 105–18)

Jonson fell foul of the stringent dramatic censorship of the times on two occasions. He and his coauthors were imprisoned in 1605 for libelous and satirical references to Scotland in *Eastward Ho!* Much later a performance of *The Magnetic Lady* (1632) led to a charge of blasphemy. Since the text had been approved by the Master of the Revels, Sir Henry Herbert (brother of the poet George Herbert), Jonson was mystified. In the court proceedings (from which he was excused, since he had suffered a stroke), the actors eventually confessed that they had found the dialogue insufficiently racy and had larded it with their own interpolations. Whether these were "excessive use of oaths" or for "uttering some profane speeches in abuse of the Scriptures" is still in dispute (Happé 2000, 25). The Archbishop of Canterbury finally attributed all blame to them (Gildersleeve 1908, 79, 126). This episode explains part of Hamlet's famous advice to the Players: "And let those who play your clowns speak no more than is set down for them" (III ii 42–43). However, the pressure told, and when Jonson prepared his plays for the press he toned down many oaths. Thus "by Jesu" became "believe me," "by heaven" is changed to "by these hilts," and "faith" is replaced by "marry" or "indeed"; even the pagan gods are banished, so that "by the gods" is watered down to "by my sword" or "by my life" (Gildersleeve 1908, 128–29).

Several four-letter words are found in Jonson's savage satires, castigating the activities of "the servants of the groin" of his materialistic and hypocritical times. In "An Epistle to a Friend," sexual congress is consistently presented in crude animalistic images. Thus there are references to "pound a prick," to "a saut [randy] Lady Bitch" and to "Stallion [Sir Stud] who has spent so much for his Court-bred filly" that she must "fall upon her back in admiration" and

> must lie down: Nay more,
> 'Tis there civilitie to be a whore.
> (ll. 47–54)

The epigram *On Sir Voluptuous Beast* is amazingly open in its exposé of cruel sexual games:

> While Beast instructs his fair and innocent wife
> In the past pleasures of his sensual life,
> Telling the motions of each petticoat,
> And how his Ganymede moved and how his goat,
> And now her, hourly, her own cuckquean makes
> In varied shapes, which for his lust she takes.
> (ll. 1–6)

Jonson is the first major author to introduce "alternative" sexual vocabulary. *Ganymede* is a classically derived word for a catamite or male concubine, while *cuckquean* is an even rarer term for a female cuckold. To satisfy her husband's fantasies, the innocent wife is forced to impersonate other lovers, thereby cuckolding herself. (*Quean* is an old term for a prostitute.) The term *tribade,* the earliest word for a lesbian, was also first introduced by Jonson in 1601.

His scatological poem written under the ironic title "The Famous Voyage" (1614) mentions "the grave fart, late let in Parliament" and the discharging into a London sewer of a "merdurinous load" (l. 65), a curious lexical combination of French *merde* ("shit") and Latin *urine.* Unsurprisingly, this is a nonce-word or unique formation. It is typical of Jonson's capacity to scrape the bottom of the lexical barrel in an original fashion.

See also: Censorship; Homosexuals; Quean and Queen; Shakespeare, William.

Bibliography

Bawcutt, N. *The Control and Censorship of Caroline Drama*. Oxford: Oxford University Press, 1996.

Donaldson, Ian, ed. *Ben Jonson*. Oxford: Oxford University Press, 1985.

Gildersleeve, Virginia Cocheron. *Government Regulation of the Elizabethan Drama*. New York: Columbia University Press, 1908.

Happé, P., ed. *The Magnetic Lady*. Manchester: Manchester University Press, 2000.

Jonson, Ben. *Discoveries* [1641]. London: Bodley Head, 1923.

Thomson, Peter, and Gamini Salgado. *The Everyman Companion to the Theatre*. London: Dent, 1985.

JOURNALISM. *See:* Press, the

K

KAFFIR

The most offensive word that can be used of a black person in South Africa, where its use is actionable and constitutes **crimen injuria**. The semantic history of the term, like that of *infidel* and *heathen,* reveals the cultural ironies and arrogance attaching to claims of exclusive belief in the "one true God." Like the compared terms, *kaffir* has at its root the notion of the infidel, being derived from Arabic *kafir* meaning an unbeliever, from the Muslim point of view. A letter written in 1799 noted that Tipoo Sultan "wished to drive the English Caffers out of India" (Sir T. Munro, *Life* 1799, I, 221). In view of the subsequent history of the term, this is a most ironic application. The original religious sense still surfaces occasionally in English. In V.S. Naipaul's novel *The Suffrage of Elvira,* set in Trinidad, the old sense is apparent in this sharp exchange between two men of Indian descent: "He lifted his arm and pinched the loose skin. . . . 'This is pure blood. Every Hindu blood is pure Aryan blood.' Baksh [a Muslim] snorted: 'All-you is just a pack of kaffir'" (1958, 129–30).

As Arab traders moved down the east coast of Africa they converted many of the peoples along the coastline to Islam, applying the term *kafir* to the black peoples of the interior. The term was subsequently adopted by the Portuguese navigators, the Dutch and the British colonists, so that whole area of the eastern part of Cape Colony in South Africa came to be named as *Cafir-land* or *Cafraria* from as early as 1599 in the writings of Richard Hakluyt. (This was prior to the Dutch settlement in the Cape in 1652.) *Kaffir* subsequently became a common regional term applied to the Xhosa-speaking peoples of the Eastern Cape Colony and was extended to dozens of names of places (*Kaffirstad*), flora (*kaffirboom*), fauna (*Kaffir finch*), and food (*Kaffir corn, Kaffir beer*). In the 1890s the term started to become current in the parlance of the London Stock Exchange to refer to South African mining shares, the sector being termed, not very complimentarily, "the Kaffir Circus."

Because the term was not used by the peoples themselves, but applied to them by foreigners, it acquired a derogatory sense. (The same dynamic is found in *hottentot* and *nigger.*) The Reverend William Shaw observed in his *Diary:* "'Kaffir' is not a term used by the natives to designate either themselves or any other tribe. . . . The Border Kaffirs know that the white nations apply the terms to them, and many of them regard it as a term of contempt" (December 28, 1847).

The Border in question represented the frontier between the native people and the English settlers who had been encouraged to take up land there from 1820. The consequence was a protracted series of Kaffir Wars. Reporting on a punitive expedition in 1812, Lieutenant-General Sir John Cradock wrote the following arrogant remarks: "I am happy to add that there has not been shed more Kaffir blood than would seem necessary to impress on the minds of these savages a proper degree of terror and respect" (cited in Thompson 1990, 55).

From the earliest accounts, the stereotype of the savage predominated, especially in the categorization of the "red" or "raw" kaffir, so called because of the red ochre that they smeared on their bodies. An early *Geographical Dictionary* (1691) by Edmund Bohun shows typical ignorance and prejudice: "The inhabitants [of *Cafraria*] are so barbarous that they are called by this name [*Kaffir*] which signifies the lawless people; they were all heretofore man-eaters and many of them continue such to this day" (cited in Pettman 1913, 244). The noted novelist R.M. Ballantyne opined that "The *Red Kaffir* is in truth a savage" in his study with the revealing title *Six Months at the Cape* (1879, 44). However, not everyone saw the people in the same way: the liberal journalist Thomas Pringle observed in 1834 that "the Kaffers are a tall, athletic handsome race." Lady Anne Barnard, the first lady of the Cape, gave an artist's impression in a letter of July 10, 1797: "I had a visit at the castle from one of the caffre chiefs with his train of wives and dogs; he was as fine a morsel of bronze as ever I saw" [receiving gifts] with "gallantry of nature" (Robinson 1973, p. 56).

In their *Zulu Dictionary* (1948), C.M. Doke and B.W. Vilikazi included the following usage note: "Term of contempt for a person (black or white) of uncivilized manners (a swearword if used direct to a person)." In general usage and in literature *kaffir* has steadily disappeared, except in the mouths of characters, usually Afrikaners, marking them as conservative racists. Yet some authors, notably Herman Charles Bosman (1905–1951) used the term with sophisticated and disturbing irony, notably in *Mafeking Road* (1947), a story set at a critical point in the Boer War (1899–1902). Bosman, like Mark Twain, uses a naive persona or narrative voice, one with paternalistic views and uncomfortably racist vocabulary, thereby inviting the more perceptive reader to put a different interpretation on the narrative. Bosman's usage is unusual and daring, to the point that his readership has declined and most universities avoid teaching him in post-apartheid South Africa. Virtually no modern or contemporary author uses the term, in any context. The parallel with Twain's use of *nigger* and its repercussions is notable.

As *kaffir* became increasingly taboo, it was both replaced by synonyms or abbreviations. Thus the *kaffirboom* (*Erythrina caffra*) was renamed the "coral tree," *kaffir beer* was retermed *sorghum beer* or *KB*. Following the latter practice the initial "k" was brought into play in euphemistic forms like *k-sheeting* (from 1981) for a thick soft cotton material traditionally known as *kaffir sheeting*. A contemporary coinage is *the k-factor,* meaning "an expected degree of abuse in machinery requiring built-in self-protective devices."

The insulting personal use of the term has increasingly led to civil proceedings. The *Eastern Province Herald* newspaper reported on April 4, 1976: "The Supreme Court ruled yesterday that the word 'Kaffir' was an insult and awarded an African damages of R150 (about $225)." Today such usage falls under the South African legal category termed **crimen injuria,** defined as insulting behavior, linguistic and other, that is a deliberate affront to a person's dignity. In his discussion of the category, Professor Jonathan Burchell, a legal authority, comments: "The epithet 'kafir' [sic] has become to be regarded as self-evidently an *injuria*" (1997, 752). Partly because of these legal actions, the word has become genuinely taboo. There is no reclamation of the term, as there has been with *nigger*.

See also: Blacks; Crimen Injuria; Hottentot.

Bibliography

Ballantyne, R.M. *Six Months at the Cape.* London: James Nisbet, 1879.
Bosman, Herman Charles. *Mafeking Road.* Johannesburg: C.N.A., 1947.
Burchell, Jonathan. *Principles of Criminal Law.* Kenwyn: Juta, 1997.
Le Vaillant, M. *My Travels into the Interior Part of Africa.* London: Robinson, 1797.
Pettman, the Reverend Charles. *Africanderisms.* London: Longmans Green, 1913.
Pringle, Thomas. *African Sketches.* London: E. Moxon, 1834.
Robinson, A.M.L., ed. *The Letters of Lady Anne Barnard.* Cape Town: Balkema, 1973.
Thompson, Leonard. *A History of South Africa.* New Haven: Yale University Press, 1990.

KNAVE

The term is exclusive to British English, with a strange semantic history, having been originally a common neutral word meaning simply "boy," before deteriorating to mean a rogue or a rascal, finally becoming virtually obsolete. The development is not entirely unique, since *churl, wretch,* and *villain* have followed this pattern, defined by C.S. Lewis as "the **moralization of status words**" (1960, 7).

Knave originates in Anglo-Saxon *cnafa,* meaning "a boy," and maintained this neutral sense for centuries: thus a male child was termed a *knave child* up to the fifteenth century. The lower status of the term becomes apparent from the subsequent senses of "servant," "peasant," or "page." The use of *knavish* to mean "dishonest" is first found in Chaucer, ca. 1390, while *knavery* is recorded much later, ca. 1528. The term was clearly an insult by 1480, when the records of the English Guilds list it as actionable: "If any Brother despise another, calling him knave, horson" (Early English Text Society 1870, 315). By Shakespeare's time semantic deterioration had become completely established, since the basic meaning is "a villain," with the implication of "lower-class" still apparent. In *King Lear* (1604–1605), Oswald, a supercilious steward who has given cheek to the King, receives a vituperative reprimand from the Duke of Kent: "A knave, a rascal . . . a base, proud, shallow, beggarly . . . knave, a lily-livered [cowardly] action-taking [legalistic] knave . . . the son and heir of a mongrel bitch" (II ii 15–24).

Thereafter *knave* started to lose moral force, becoming more of a loose insult, before steadily declining in currency. It is now a generally passé upper-class British usage, also found in cards to refer to the jack. It has made no impact on the other global varieties of English.

See also: Moralization of Status Words; Rogue; Villain.

Bibliography

Lewis, C.S. *Studies in Words.* Cambridge: Cambridge University Press, 1960.

L

LADY CHATTERLEY'S LOVER

When David Herbert Lawrence died at the age of forty-four he had written over twenty novels, three plays, ten collections of poetry, and a large body of nonfiction, including a number of translations. The son of a coal miner, his scandalous elopement in 1912 with a German aristocrat, Frieda von Richthofen, the wife of his English professor Ernest Weekley, altered the path of their lives irretrievably, making them suspect in England and subsequently exiles. Although ill with tuberculosis for much of his short life (1885–1930), Lawrence was an insatiable traveler, responding with great empathy to the different values and mores of mainly pre-industrialized societies. Perceiving the life of modern man as one of alienation and conformity in a mechanized environment, Lawrence developed a profound, almost religious belief in the importance of spontaneous and natural feelings, especially the sex drive. Strongly influenced by Sigmund Freud, he came to regard the phallus as having an iconic, almost mystical force. These ideas were to become dominant themes in his major early novels, *The Rainbow* (1915) and *Women in Love* (1921). The first was declared obscene, the publisher Methuen was fined, and all existing copies were ordered to be destroyed. Undeterred, Lawrence continued to create fictions challenging prevailing norms, most famously in his last major novel, *Lady Chatterley's Lover* (1928).

The notoriety surrounding this one book has distorted Lawrence's reputation, but also served to subject the literary use of "foul language" to legal scrutiny. It has a unique history, being published privately, suppressed, pirated, expurgated, republished, the issue of a groundbreaking trial, and finally rehabilitated. It was adjudged "obscene" under the broad definition applying at the time: "obscenity" (technically "obscene libel" or "matter tending to deprave or corrupt") was usually interpreted as the explicit depiction of sex and the use of "dirty" or taboo words. In the decades after Lawrence's death it became the principal text around which the legal definition of obscenity was challenged. Its critical history shows remarkable oscillations in interpretation and evaluation.

Despite the setbacks of *The Rainbow* (1915), Lawrence remained undeterred in his role as sexual evangelist: "I feel that one has to fight for the phallic reality, as against the non-phallic cerebration unrealities," he wrote in a letter to Witter Bynner (March 13, 1928) in the year of the genesis of the novel. "So I wrote my novel, which I want to call *John Thomas and Lady Jane,*" he continued, somewhat naively (*John Thomas* being a British slang euphemism for "penis"). "But that I have to submerge into a subtitle, and call it *Lady Chatterley's Lover.*" He

The unexpurgated edition of D.H. Lawrence's novel *Lady Chatterley's Lover* (1928) was prosecuted for obscenity and banned in the United States and Great Britain until 1959 and 1960, respectively. When it finally appeared, buyers came out in droves. (©Topham/The Image Works)

described the half-written work to Samuel Kotelianski as "the most improper novel ever written" (*Collected Letters*, 1028), but he always denied that it was pornography. Subsequently, in *A Propos of Lady Chatterley's Lover* (1930) he used the tone of a manifesto: "If I use the taboo words, there is a reason. We shall never free the phallic reality from the 'uplift' taint till we give it its own phallic language, and use the obscene words" (Moore 1955, 267).

The book was printed and published privately in Florence in July 1928, and by April of the following year five pirated editions had appeared all over the Continent and in America. The initial critical responses were universally hostile, as can be assessed from *D.H. Lawrence: The Critical Heritage* (ed. R.P. Draper 1970). Under the headline "Famous Author's Shameful Book," an unsigned review in the patriotic magazine *John Bull* (October 20, 1928) denounced the work in extraordinarily vituperative terms as "the most evil outpouring that has ever besmirched the literature of our country. The sewers of French pornography would be dragged in vain to find a parallel in beastliness. The creations of muddy-minded perverts, peddled in back-street book-stalls in Paris, are prudish by comparison" (cited in Draper 1970, 278). The marked correlation between explicit sexuality and "filth" is shown in the dismissals of the work as "the fetid master-piece of this sex-sodden genius," "the abysm of filth," and "the foulest book in English litera-ture," culminating in the call that "The circulation in this country of *Lady Chatterley's Lover* must be stopped" (cited in Draper 1970, 280). The book was suppressed for immorality. Copies imported into England were regularly seized and destroyed by order of the Home Secretary. Uncharacteristically, Lawrence attempted an expurgated version, which he found almost impos-sible, observing: "I might as well as try to clip my own nose into shape with scissors. The book bleeds" (cited in Draper 1970, 21). Nevertheless, the expurgated version appeared, also in 1928.

Some thirty years later in 1959, Grove Press of New York published an unexpurgated edition in the United States. The ensuing action eventually generated the celebrated judg-ment by Judge Frederick van Pelt Bryan in favor of the publishers, conceding that "Four-letter Anglo-Saxon words are used with some frequency," but insisting that "The book is not 'dirt for dirt's sake'" (in Craig 1962, 158). In the same year the Obscenity Act was revised in important ways in the United Kingdom. These revisions set new ground rules for a pivotal trial in 1960 at the Old Bailey in London in which *Lady Chatterley's Lover* became a test case (*Regina* v. *Penguin Books*), the proceedings of which are described in detail in C.H. Rolph's study *The Trial of Lady Chatterley* (1961). The new act required that the book had to be "regarded as a whole" and that the courts had to listen to evidence from experts who could be called to justify the work as being "for the public good on the ground that it is in the interests of science, literature, art or learning." However, the old core was retained, since a book could be "deemed to be obscene if its effect . . . [is] such as to tend to deprave and corrupt persons who are likely to read it" (cited in Rolph 1961, 10).

As expected, much discussion in the trial focused on the artistic suitability of the most notorious "four-letter" words. In the novel these are copiously used by the gamekeeper Mellors in dialect, as in this dialogue with Connie Chatterley:

> "Th'art good cunt, though, aren't ter? Best bit o' cunt left on earth. When ter likes! When th'art willin'!'"
>
> "What is cunt?" she said.
>
> "An' doesn't ter know? Cunt! It's thee down theer; an' what I get when I'm i'side thee, and what tha gets when I'm i'side thee; it's a' as it is, all on't."
>
> "All on't," she teased. "Cunt! It's like fuck then."
>
> "Nay nay! Fuck's only what you do. Animals fuck. But cunt's a lot more than that. It's thee, dost see: an' th'art a lot besides an animal, aren't ter—even ter fuck? Cunt! Eh, that's the beauty o' thee, lass!"
>
> (1960, 185)

Today this reads like an unconvincing lesson in sex education with some unintentional comedy as Mellors, close to the earth and nature, "initiates" Connie into sexual mysteries which her upper-class breeding has supposedly denied her. Aldous Huxley shrewdly reflected in *The Genius and the Goddess* on the problematic relationship between "four-letter words" and "four-letter acts": "In silence, an act is an act is an act. Verbalized and discussed, it becomes an ethical problem, a *casus belli* [grounds for war]" (1955, 103).

In the trial some thirty-five defense witnesses were called, including major authors and academics, such as E.M. Forster, Richard Hoggart, Helen Gardner, Raymond Williams, Graham Hough, Kenneth Muir, and the Bishop of Woolwich. There was something slightly ironic in the spectacle of these fine minds and subtle sensibilities opining on the coarsest and most taboo words in the language. The prosecution avoided articulating the words by asking the witnesses for their assessment of the literary merits of the book. Virtually all took the view that it undoubtedly had literary merit, but was not Lawrence's best work. Likewise, they supported the coarse language on artistic grounds, though in considering the passage just quoted, Dr. Graham Hough a respected Cambridge academic and authority on Lawrence, dissented: "I don't think that this passage comes off at all. I see what he has tried to do, but I think he has failed" (cited in Rolph 1961, 49). Professor F.R. Leavis, also a great champion of Lawrence, was far more critical. He wrote after the trial about "turning on the dialect," that is, using it as "a way of putting over 'the four-letter words'—of trying to make the idea of their being redeemed for non-obscene and undefiant, or 'normal,' use look less desperate." He concluded trenchantly: "I find these performances on Mellors's part insufferable" (Coombs 1973, 416–17).

The issue of "redeeming" fallen words loomed large in the trial. Dr. Helen Gardner of Oxford took the view that "by the end Lawrence has gone very far within the context of this book to redeem this word from low and vulgar associations" (cited in Rolph 1961, 60). Dr. Richard Hoggart agreed, saying: "They [the words] were being progressively purified as they were used" (cited in Rolph 1961, 99). Significantly, he was the only witness to use the word *"fuck"* personally, pointing out: "Fifty yards from this Court I heard a man say the word 'fuck' three times as he passed me" (cited in Rolph 1961, 99). A profound comment by William Butler Yeats was invoked more than once, from a letter to Olivia Shakespear in 1933: "The coarse language of the one, accepted by both, becomes a forlorn poetry uniting their solitudes, something ancient, humble and terrible" (cited in Draper 1970, 298).

Several witnesses justified Lawrence's treatment of sex as having a religious quality. A distinguished lawyer, Norman St. John-Stevas, author of a standard work, *Obscenity and the Law* (1956), took the view that Lawrence is "essentially a writer in the Catholic tradition" (cited in Rolph 1961, 136). Dylis Powell, a noted film and book reviewer, asserted: "I regard it as an extremely moral book," before making this powerful distinction: "a great deal of the contemporary cinema seems to degrade the whole sanctity of sex, treating it as something trivial. But in Lawrence's book, which has great elements of sacredness, sex is taken as something to be taken seriously and as a basis for a holy life" (cited in Rolph 1961, 150).

On November 2, 1960, the jury took less than three hours to reach its decision that Penguin Books was not guilty of publishing an obscene article. In retrospect the trial has been shown to have focused too much on certain areas of sexuality and to have ignored others. The prosecuting counsel, Mervyn Griffith-Jones, used the phrase "putting adultery on a pedestal" some thirty-two times. However, it appears that despite Lawrence's almost obsessive "positive belief that the phallus is a great sacred image" (*Collected Letters,* 967) and his daring use of "the obscene words," he was not entirely candid in his description of the crucial union between the lovers late in the book, in chapter xvi. Here he writes symbolically of "Burning out the shames, the deepest oldest shames, in the most secret places," of "the sensual flame [that] pressed through her bowels and breast" to "the core of the physical jungle, the last and deepest recess of organic shame. The phallos alone could explore it." More disturbingly, "She had to be a passive, consenting thing, like a slave." Lawrence only hints that this is intercourse of a different kind: "It was not really love. It was not voluptuousness. It was sensuality sharp and searing as fire, burning the soul to tinder." He uses strange metaphors, such as "to burn out false shames and smelt out the heaviest ore of the body into purity" and shows Connie Chatterley's ambivalent response to the act: "And how, in fear, she had hated it. But how she had really wanted it!" (1960, 258–59).

A little over a year after the trial, John Sparrow, the Warden of All Souls College at Oxford, caused a furor in an article in the intellectual review *Encounter* 101 (February 1962). Analyzing the passages just quoted, he questioned the acuteness of interpretation of some of the "expert" witnesses, and even accused Lawrence of "this failure of integrity, this fundamental dishonesty" (41). Sparrow argued cogently that "The practice approved by Lawrence is that known in English law as buggery. . . . [of which] the 'full offence' involves *penetratio per anum* [i.e. sodomy]" (36). In an earlier article in *Encounter* 96 (September 1961), Andrew Schonfield had argued that such an interpretation seemed "a reasonable guess" (64). Much later Professor Frank Kermode of London University concurred in his standard study of Lawrence, even implying that there had been a conspiracy of silence on this embarrassing point: "The fact that it describes anal intercourse was long ignored; nobody mentioned it in the 1960 trial. . . . As in *Women in Love,* the climactic sexual act is buggery, conceived as a burning out of shame" (1973, 130).

J.M. Coetzee, the noted South African Nobel Laureate, later cast some useful light on the taboos broken in the novel in his curiously titled article "The Taint of the Pornographic: Defending (against) *Lady Chatterley*." Coetzee argues, unexpectedly for a writer of modern fiction, that the book "offends against *decorum* on a fairly gross scale," continuing: "The intercourse of Lady Chatterley with the gamekeeper transgresses at least three rules: it is adulterous; it crosses caste boundaries; and it is sometimes 'unnatural,' that is anal" (1988, 304).

Arguing that in the Edwardian period in which the novel is set, *caste* is a more appropriate term than *class,* Coetzee continues: "Lady Chatterley not only has a passionate affair across caste boundaries with her husband's servant, she falls pregnant and decides to elope with him. More seriously, Mellors sodomizes the Lady of the Manor just as, according to his ex-wife, he had sodomized her" (1988, 305–6). In addition, Coetzee demonstrates, there is a fourth transgression: "Mellors *pollutes Connie's mind* (I use the language of the time) by instructing her in the use of taboo words" (1988, 306). According to the prevailing double standards, bad language was harmless among men, but taboo in women, unless they were "fallen." This throws light on the passage quoted previously and several others: "his fingertips touched the two secret openings to her body, time after time, with a soft little brush of fire. 'an if tha shits and an if tha pisses, I'm glad. I don't want a woman as couldna shit and piss.' Connie could not help a sudden snort of astonished laughter, but he went on unmoved" (1960, 232). An important supporting point for Coetzee's argument is that Mellors's uses the notorious "four-letter" words only when he speaks in dialect. At the same point in the novel, Lawrence in the authorial voice adopts a very different style: "With quiet fingers he threaded a few forget-me-not flowers in the fine brown fleece of the mound of Venus." More pointedly, when the lovers talk of the future:

"You do as you wish," he said.
And he spoke in good English. (1960, 232)

Although, as F.R. Leavis objected earlier in the discussion, Lawrence seems to be "turning on the dialect," Lawrence himself clearly felt that only among the lower orders and in regional speech could the words still be used in an innocent fashion.

Another aspect was ignored in the trial. Considering that Lawrence wrote like an evangelist for sexuality, and was more concerned with the woman's orgasmic response than the man's, there is a surprising hostility toward lesbianism expressed by Mellors:

"It's astonishing how Lesbian women are, consciously or unconsciously. Seems to me that they're nearly all Lesbian."
    "And you don't mind?" asked Connie.
"I could kill them. When I'm with a woman who's really Lesbian, I could fairly howl in my soul, wanting to kill her."
(1960, 212)

In retrospect, it is interesting to speculate how this watershed trial would have developed had the defense raised these contentious issues.

The verdict seemed to usher in what was termed in the journalistic cliché of the times, "the permissive society." The poet Philip Larkin paid ironic homage to this change in mores in his little ditty "Annus Mirabilis" (1967):

Sexual intercourse began
In nineteen sixty-three
(Which was rather late for me)
Between the end of the *Chatterley* ban
And the Beatles' first L.P.

As it was, the verdict made *Lady Chatterley's Lover* a *succès de scandale* and a fortune for the publishers. It also served to rehabilitate Lawrence from the status of disgrace in which he had died. Five years after the trial *The Rainbow* was prescribed for school study.

When Lawrence died in 1930, he was still a deeply controversial figure. The previous year an exhibition of his nude paintings at Dorothy Warren's gallery in London was closed and the works were confiscated by the police. This had a wider literary repercussion, since his publisher omitted fourteen poems from his forthcoming collection *Pansies* out of fear of prosecution. In the title poem Lawrence daringly articulated some unorthodox sexual ideas, clearly using *pansy* as a *double-entendre:*

Ronald, you know, is like most Englishmen,
by instinct he's a sodomist
but he's frightened to know it
so he takes it out on women.

This is one of the earliest uses of *pansy* to mean "a male homosexual." In his remarkable essay, "Introduction to his Paintings" (also 1929), Lawrence attempted to identify the roots of the puritanical attitude toward sex that he found to be a major feature of English society. He detected the cause in syphilis, which, he argued, had caused a fundamental rupture in the emotional life of Renaissance England.

Although Lawrence's influence as a pioneer in breaking the taboos against explicit sexuality in modern fiction is clear, the degree to which his championship of the "four-letter" words has redeemed them is questionable. Frank Kermode concluded that "They can hardly be said to have acquired a tender, let alone a numinous quality" (1973, 123). Lawrence has also drawn some severe criticism in modern times for his frequently chauvinist attitude toward women, his hostility to lesbianism, and for the general political implications of his ideas.

See also: Censorship; Cunt; Fuck; Taboo.

Bibliography

Carey, John. "D.H. Lawrence's Doctrine." In *D.H. Lawrence: Novelist, Poet, Prophet,* ed. S. Spender. London: Weidenfeld and Nicolson, 1973.

Coetzee, J.M. "The Taint of the Pornographic: Defending (against) *Lady Chatterley*" (1988). In *Doubling the Point: Essays and Interviews,* ed. D. Attwell. Cambridge, MA: Harvard University Press, 1992.

Coombes, H., ed. *D.H. Lawrence: A Critical Anthology.* Harmondsworth: Penguin, 1973.

Craig, Alec. *The Banned Books of England.* London: Allen & Unwin, 1962.

Draper, R.P. *D.H. Lawrence: The Critical Heritage.* London: Routledge & Kegan Paul, 1970.

Hardy, Barbara. "Women in D.H. Lawrence's Works." In *D.H. Lawrence: Novelist, Poet, Prophet,* ed. S. Spender. London: Weidenfeld and Nicolson, 1973.

Huxley, Aldous. *The Genius and the Goddess.* London: Chatto & Windus, 1955.

Kermode, Frank. *Lawrence.* London: Fontana Collins, 1973.

Lawrence, D.H. *A Propos of Lady Chatterley's Lover* (1930), ed. Michael Squires. Cambridge: Cambridge University Press, 1993.

———. *Lady Chatterley's Lover.* Harmondsworth: Penguin, 1960.

———. "Introduction to His Paintings" (1929). In *Selected Essays.* Harmondsworth: Penguin, 1950.

Millett, Kate. *Sexual Politics.* New York: Avon Books, 1971.

Moore, Harry T., ed. *Sex, Literature and Censorship: Essays by D.H. Lawrence.* London: Heinemann, 1955.

Myers, Jeffrey. "D.H. Lawrence and Homosexuality." In *D.H. Lawrence: Novelist, Poet, Prophet,* ed. S. Spender. London: Weidenfeld and Nicolson, 1973.

Rolph, C.H. *The Trial of Lady Chatterley.* Harmondsworth: Penguin, 1961.

St. John-Stevas, Norman. *Obscenity and the Law.* London: Secker and Warburg, 1956.

LARKIN, PHILIP

Few English poets after the **Earl of Rochester** in the seventeenth century dared to use the "four-letter" words or the crude argot of the street. D.H. Lawrence, who was so daring in his novels, was less adventurous in his poetry. Even in the postwar period, when frankness and directness were very much the supposed hallmarks of the new British literature of John Osborne, John Braine, Alan Sillitoe, Sylvia Plath, and Ted Hughes, most poets actually shied away from what William Wordsworth had called "the language of ordinary men."

The major exception was Philip Larkin (1922–1985), an enigmatic, shy, reclusive academic librarian who passed most of his life at Hull University in the north of England. He became a major voice in English poetry from the 1960s, articulating the frustrations and dreary lives of ordinary people in a modern welfare state—anonymous, secularized, and banal—at the end of an era. His early poems were low-key, subtle, and profound. In "Church Going" (1954) he reflects the passing of the church as a dynamic force in the land, the ignorant persona of his poem having only a limited physical sense of "some brass and stuff up at the holy end." Yet even he is also sensitive to "a tense, musty unignorable silence / Brewed God knows how long." The ironic significance of the casual blasphemy is typical.

Larkin is very much the poet of the little conforming man, a cog in the machine of a grinding urban existence, wishing to protest but lacking the necessary courage. In "Toads" (1955) his would-be rebel laments: "Ah, were I courageous enough / To shout *stuff your pension!*" According to the *Oxford English Dictionary* this is the first recorded instance of the common idiomatic use of *stuff*. Later demotic idioms burst out startlingly, in this comment on "the sexual revolution" of the 1960s:

When I see a couple of kids
And guess he's fucking her and she's
Taking pills or wearing a diaphragm
I know this is paradise.
("High Windows" 1967)

However, this supposed permissive "paradise" comes with knowledge, in the form of this ironic and twisted version of Freudian psychology:

They fuck you up your mum and dad.
They may not mean to, but they do.
("This Be The Verse" 1971)

Alone of his contemporaries, Larkin also admitted into his poems a subject still largely taboo, what Lawrence had called "the dirty little secret" of masturbation: "Love again: wanking at ten past three" ("Love Again" 1979). (*Wank,* a peculiarly British word, is a colloquialism recorded from the late nineteenth century.) These fairly shocking instances caused little comment, since they were largely contemporary idioms.

In 1984 Larkin turned down an offer of the prestigious position of Poet Laureate. Although he wished his papers to be burned after his death, only his diaries were destroyed. The publication of his *Selected Letters* in 1992 revealed an author who was not only surprisingly active sexually, but very outspoken and cantankerous. When he was nineteen he commented on a poem of his own: "I think that this is really bloody cunting fucking good," regarding another as "buggering fine" (1992, 12). He complained to his lifelong (and equally conservative) friend Kingsley Amis about the steadily lengthening of the Christmas holidays: "Eventually the whole bloody fucking arseholing country will be on its back from Guy Fawkes's night [November 5] to St. Valentine's Day" (1992, 635). However the furor provoked by the *Selected Letters* arose from other revelations, that Larkin was politically reactionary and frankly racist. References to "la divine Thatcher" and to "the successive gangs of socialist robbers who have ruled us since the last war" (1992, 635) did not go down well, although such views were not uncommon when the letters were actually written. Far more provocative were his racist comments, such as "we don't go to [cricket] Test matches now, too many fucking niggers about" (1992, 584) and "Thanks for the card from Coonland" [Morocco] (1992, 690).

As a consequence of these comments, the associations of Larkin's work rapidly changed from being "melancholy, cynical, reflective of *fin de siècle* Britain" to "bigoted, racist, reactionary." The fact that these were private letters unintended for publication and written to like-minded correspondents was largely ignored. One professor of English in Britain, Lisa Jardine, wrote publicly of her experiences when she and her department at the University of London consequently devised a course to "recontextualise" Larkin and so "edged Larkin from the center to the margins" (in Dunant, ed., 1994, 111). In many ways the private Larkin of the letters was expressing the kind of racism that could be heard in pubs, clubs, football stadiums, and canteens. But in print it was unacceptable.

See also: Political Correctness.

Bibliography

Jardine, Lisa. "Canon to the Left of Them, Canon to the Right of Them." In *The War of Words,* ed. Sarah Dunant. London: Virago, 1994.

Thwaite, A., ed. *Philip Larkin: Collected Poems.* London: Faber, 1988.

———. *Philip Larkin: Selected Letters.* London: Faber, 1992.

LAWRENCE, D.H. *See: Lady Chatterley's Lover*

LAWSUITS

Laws are revealing evidence of social mores, since they focus on those breaches of conventional behavior that a society regards as unacceptable and punishable. The legal consequences of swearing naturally have a long history, stretching from the earliest times to the present. The entry for **Fines and Penalties** sets out the punishments for such infractions. However, the typical grounds for bringing lawsuits have varied greatly as social norms and sensitivities have changed, especially toward the use of profanity, obscenities, or ethnic slurs. Comments or accusations impugning a person's honor, which in medieval times implied cowardice or treachery, have been replaced by provocations relating to race or sexual preference. Furthermore, the notion that a particular book, poem, play, or film can be sufficiently offensive to public morals to be prosecuted has continued through to modern times. The situation in America is, of course, grounded in the First Amendment guaranteeing freedom of speech and of the press. British law underwrites no such freedoms, regarding the courts as the protector of public morals and decorum. The development of **broadcasting** has obviously introduced new complexities.

As the entry for the **Anglo-Saxon Period** shows, the laws were punitive on what would now be called slander, or spoken insult, as opposed to libel, which is in written or printed form. This is to be expected in an oral culture. The laws also included the interesting prohibition "Do not ever swear by the pagan gods." The historical records of the period, now greatly diminished, do not indicate how often these revealing laws were invoked.

In the medieval period, the relationship between language and honor was no less intense. However, different notions of trial applied—namely, trial by ordeal and trial by combat. Charges of treason, more common than today, were usually decided by duel than by process of law. In late medieval and Renaissance times elaborate schedules of fines were established for blasphemy and profanity. The vigilance of the **Master of the Revels** over the content and the language of plays from Elizabethan times led to a number of proceedings. **Ben Jonson** became embroiled in two cases, the first concerning libel in *Eastward Ho!* (1605), which led to him and the co-authors being imprisoned. The second involved the religious language of *The Magnetic Lady* (1632), over which he was exonerated. The subsequent censorship of the stage is covered in the entry for **Lord Chamberlain**.

Two major lawsuits that scandalized Victorian respectability were precipitated by insulting or incriminating language. The famous trials of Oscar Wilde in 1895 are covered in the entry for **homosexuals.** Less well known was The Cleveland Street Scandal, which arose in 1889 when Lord Euston sued *The North London Press* for libel when it claimed that he and other high-society gentlemen frequented a homosexual brothel in Cleveland Street in London. Although the evidence supporting the newspaper's reports was very strong, the editor was found guilty of libel and sentenced to a year's imprisonment. The trial is covered in Pearsall (1969).

The bulk of lawsuits in modern times have arisen from charges of **obscenity,** in itself a comparatively recent term in the language, dating from around 1600 and continuously problematic in its definition. The Obscene Publications Act of 1857, originally designed to counter the flow of pornography in Victorian times, also led to many successful prosecutions against major or significant literary works. The definition of obscenity, deriving from a later key judgment of Lord Chief Justice Alexander Cockburn in 1868, was so broad that, as George Bernard Shaw wrote in 1928, "There is not a work of literature which Counsel would defend as being outside that all-embracing definition" (Moore 1955, 47). This proved to be largely true, the principal cases being covered in the entry for **censorship**. A highly significant prosecution was launched in 1928 against Radclyffe Hall's *The Well of Loneliness*, which dealt frankly with lesbianism, although in the proceedings the preferred terms were "inversion", "perversion" and "unnatural practices." The Chief Magistrate, Sir Chartres Biron, would not admit the evidence of forty distinguished authors called as expert witnesses for the defense. (Unlike D.H. Lawrence's *Lady Chatterley's Lover*, the work had been well received initially.) The court order was that the book should be destroyed as "an offence against public decency." The conduct of the subsequent appeal was even more outrageous, since the presiding Judge, Sir Robert Wallace, would not even permit the jury of twelve magistrates to read the book. He dismissed the appeal with the words: "This is a disgusting book. It is an obscene book prejudicial to the morals of the community."

A similar pattern of prosecutions occurred in America under the provisions of the so-called **Comstock** Act of 1873, designed to suppress "obscene and indecent matter." Section 1461 of the Criminal Code (18 U.S. Constitution Section 1461) prohibits the mailing of material that is "obscene, lewd, lascivious, indecent, filthy or vile." The act led to the suppression of works as diverse as *From Man to Man* by Olive Schreiner (1926), *The Sun Also Rises* by Ernest Hemingway (1926), *Elmer Gantry* by Sinclair Lewis (1927), and *What I Believe* by Bertrand Russell (1929). (Hemingway's novel was subsequently published, without harassment, in the United Kingdom under the title of *Fiesta*.) More significant, however, were the failed prosecutions against *The Well of Loneliness* (1929), *Ulysses* (1933), and a great number of other significant works. In the *Ulysses* case Judge John M. Woolsey's "considered opinion" was acerbic but sensible: "Whilst in many places the effect of *Ulysses* on the reader is undoubtedly somewhat emetic, nowhere does it tend to be an aphrodisiac. *Ulysses* may, therefore, be admitted to the United States" (Phelps and Deane 1968, 146).

The entry for **Lady Chatterley's Lover** deals with the suppression and prosecution of D.H. Lawrence's most controversial novel from its first publication in 1928 through its suppression, to its eventual vindication in 1959 in the United States and 1960 in the United Kingdom. Thereafter the number of prosecutions for obscenity declined greatly. However, even after the milestone *Chatterley* case, there was an attempt by the Commonwealth of Massachusetts to censor **John Cleland**'s notable pornographic classic *Memoirs of a Woman of Pleasure*, first published in 1749. The Supreme Court overturned the ban in *Memoirs of a Woman of Pleasure* v. *Attorney General of Massachusetts* (1966).

The monumental **Oxford English Dictionary**, published between 1884 and 1928, became a revealing indicator of the taboos that could lead to lawsuits. Largely owing to the pressure of the Obscene Publications Act of 1857, the taboo words *fuck* and *cunt* were omitted, without contemporary comment. However, a great deal of profanity, obscenity, and ethnic insults were included. The only case brought against the publishers (*Shloimowitz* v. *Clarendon Press,* 1972) was on the grounds that the work included insulting uses of the word *jew*. The case was dismissed with costs on July 5, 1973.

The widespread protests in the United States against the Vietnam War involved the politicization of foul language, notably by radical students at Berkeley, California. What started out as the Free Speech Movement was stigmatized as the so-called Filthy Speech Movement as a consequence of mobilizing the use of obscenities in slogans as a form of protest. The two most favored were "Fuck the Pigs!" and "Fuck the Draft." One of the consequent landmark cases was that of *Cohen* v. *California* 403 US. 15 (1971), arising out of Cohen wearing a jacket bearing the words "Fuck the Draft" in a Los Angeles courthouse corridor. The state's decision to convict Cohen was reversed on appeal by the Supreme Court, which ruled in a comprehensive judgment that "Words are often chosen as much for their emotive as their cognitive force." Following other rulings rejecting the banning of specific words, it continued: "We cannot indulge the facile assumption that one can forbid particular words without also running a substantial risk of suppressing ideas in the process." It concluded: "The state may not, consistently with the First Amendment and the Fourteenth Amendment, make the simple public display here involved of this single four-letter expletive a criminal offence." It also noted wryly: "While the particular four-letter word being litigated here is perhaps more distasteful than most others of its genre, it is nevertheless often true that one man's vulgarity is another's lyric" (25–26).

In the field of broadcasting, complaints commonly derive from the special relationship of the medium with the audience, especially such notions as the privacy of the home, the protection of unconsenting adults, and the presence of children. Complaints have increased in recent decades, but proceedings have been comparatively rare. A Citizen's Complaint was mounted in 1973 against the Pacifica Foundation Radio Station WBAI, New York, over the broadcast in the early afternoon of a twelve-minute comedy routine called "Filthy Words," a record of a live show, a monologue by "George Carlin, Occupation Foole." After the introductory remarks, the monologue consisted of a discourse on the words *shit, piss, fuck, cunt, cocksucker, mother-fucker, fart, turd, twat,* and *tits,* making fun of the inconsistencies between acceptable idiom and taboo usage. The complaint was upheld by the Federal Communications Commission. Pacifica Foundation appealed against the decision in 1975 (*Pacifica Foundation* v. *Federal Communications Commission,* case no. 75–1391). The U.S. Supreme Court upheld the F.C.C. "Declaratory Order" against the radio station, arguing that the standard for obscenity was appropriate for Carlin's words, which were therefore not constitutionally protected.

In another high-profile case, the Communications Decency Act was introduced in 1995 in response to increasing pornography on the internet and passed the following year. However, on June 26, 1997, the Supreme Court struck down the Act (*Reno v. American Civil Liberties Union*), upholding the decision of a court in Philadelphia, on the grounds that a portion of the Act was an unconstitutional abridgement of the First Amendment guaranteeing freedom of speech.

Even after the revision of the Obscene Publications Act in the United Kingdom in 1959 and the revisions to film classification, prosecutions were still brought. That against Bernado Bertolucci's film *Last Tango in Paris* in 1974 led to the noted British film critic Alexander Walker commenting appositely on "the futility of trying to pass moral judgements on aesthetic works, particularly when the visual image was bound to be judged by words on the printed page" (1977, 239).

The entry for **blasphemy** covers two unusual, highly publicized cases in the United Kingdom. The first was the successful private prosecution for blasphemous libel brought by **Mrs. Mary Whitehouse** against the magazine *Gay News* in 1977 for publishing a poem by James Kirkup under the title of "The Love That Dares to Speak Its Name." The title is a direct riposte to that of a poem by Oscar Wilde's lover Lord Alfred Douglas, namely "The Love That Dares Not Speak Its Name." However the poem is the homosexual fantasy of a Roman centurion for the crucified Christ, who is depicted on the Cross in the style of Aubrey Beardsley, complete with a large penis. This is referred to as "that great cock, the instrument of our salvation" (quoted in Travis, 2001, 259). The second case was the failed attempt in 1989 to invoke the law against Salman Rushdie's controversial novel *The Satanic Verses*.

A special category in South African law is that of **crimen injuria**. This is defined as an unlawful action intentionally injuring the dignity of another person, and is most commonly invoked for cases of swearing, especially for using highly offensive ethnic slurs such as *kaffir* and *coolie*. On this issue the United States Supreme Court rejected as "plainly untenable" the theory that the use of a particular word could be proscribed because of the likelihood that its utterance would provoke a violent reaction.

See also: Blasphemy; Broadcasting; Censorship; Comstockery; Crimen Injuria; Fines and Penalties; Homosexuals; Jews; *Lady Chatterley's Lover;* Mrs. Mary Whitehouse.

Bibliography

Craig, Alec. *The Banned Books of England.* London: Allen & Unwin, 1962.

Hasse, Liz. "Violent Acts and Prurient Thoughts." In Ricks, Christopher, and Leonard Michaels, eds., *The State of the Language.* London: Faber & Faber, 1990.

Mellinkoff, David. *The Language of the Law.* Boston: Little, Brown, 1963.

Moore, Harry T., ed. *Sex, Literature and Censorship: Essays by D.H. Lawrence.* London: Heinemann, 1955.

Pacifica Foundation v. *Federal Communications Commission,* U.S. Court of Appeals, District of Columbia, case no. 75–1391.

Pearsall, Ronald. *The Worm in the Bud: The World of Victorian Sexuality.* Harmondsworth: Penguin, 1969.

Phelps, Robert, and Peter Deane. *The Literary Life.* New York: Farrar, Straus and Giroux, 1968.

Rolph, C.H., ed. *The Trial of Lady Chatterley.* Harmondsworth: Penguin, 1961.

Souhami, Diana. *The Trials of Radclyffe Hall.* London: Virago, 1999.

Travis, Alan. *Bound and Gagged: A Secret History of Obscenity in Britain.* London: Profile Books, 2001.

Walker, Alexander. *Double Takes.* London: Hamish Hamilton, 1977.

LEGAL RESTRAINTS. *See* Censorship

LESBIANS. *See* Homosexuals

LITERATURE

In the Preface to the great *Oxford English Dictionary,* Sir James Murray set out in a famous diagram illustrating **register**, a hierarchy of linguistic usage ranging from "literary" down through "common" and "colloquial" to "slang." The placing of "literary" above "common" reflected the prevailing sense of literary decorum in the late nineteenth century, evidenced in the great Victorian novelists and poets and their predecessors. Today it is questionable whether there is such a category as "literary" language at all, since it incorporates all the other categories, as well as two unmentioned by Murray, namely "obscenity" and "taboo."

This entry is not designed to be comprehensive, but to give an overview of the topic, the names and categories in boldface highlighting entries containing more detailed treatment. The literary use of swearing and foul language is discontinuous, being largely absent in **Anglo-Saxon** literature, surprisingly prevalent in the Middle English period, especially in the work of

Geoffrey Chaucer, William Langland, and much medieval drama, but erratic thereafter, when notions of decorum and the active intervention of **censorship** began to influence many authors and inhibit literary output. However, even these generalizations are problematic, since there are egregious examples of authors who remain impervious to such controls. These include the exponents of the extraordinary Scots tradition of **flyting**, including significant authors like **William Dunbar** and Walter Kennedy, the astonishing displays of obscenity by the **Earl of Rochester** and the robust translation of **François Rabelais** by Thomas Urquhart and Peter Anthony Motteux. Within the Elizabethan period, **William Shakespeare** erred creatively on the side of caution, while his contemporaries Christopher Marlowe and **Ben Jonson** were far more daring in testing the boundaries. Likewise, **Jonathan Swift** and **Laurence Sterne** were often outrageous, while their contemporaries Alexander Pope and **Dr. Samuel Johnson** stayed within the bounds of decency. Only in the **Victorian Age** could it be said that all the major authors subscribed to the same notions of propriety, possibly encouraging the growth of a thriving underground industry in pornography.

In American literature there are the same divergences. The general tenor up to the nineteenth century is polite and decorous, but Herman Melville's *Moby Dick* (1851) is metaphysically and religiously a deeply disturbing book. However, since the ostensible narrative is about the monomaniac Ahab's feud with the White Whale, it was not a socially threatening text. **Mark Twain**'s *Huckleberry Finn* (1884), on the other hand, became the target of protests both upon publication for being "trash," and in recent decades on account of the racist attitudes evident in the copious use of the word *nigger*. However, Jane Mills reminds her readers that "No pornography was produced in the USA until the middle of the nineteenth century" (1993, 218).

Even in the modern era, the generalization that swearing and foul language have become more frequent in literature, while sound in the main, is not absolute. There are the conspicuous exponents like D.H. Lawrence and Henry Miller, but they are counterbalanced by major authors like Henry James, Thomas Hardy, George Bernard Shaw, E.M. Forster, Virginia Woolf, Joseph Conrad, T.S. Eliot, Somerset Maugham, Graham Greene, Evelyn Waugh, Samuel Beckett, F. Scott Fitzgerald, Tennessee Williams, and William Faulkner, all of whose work is linguistically chaste. Shaw archly observed: "I could not write the words Mr Joyce uses: my prudish hand would refuse to form the letters" (*Table Talk* 1925). The same division is found in contemporary writers: coarse language is a major feature of the novelists Philip Roth, Martin Amis, and Jeanette Winterson, the dramatist **David Mamet**, and the poet **Philip Larkin**. Yet it is virtually absent from significant authors like Iris Murdoch, Arthur Miller, John Barth, A.S. Byatt, and the Nobel laureates Harold Pinter, J.M. Coetzee, V.S. Naipaul, Seamus Heaney, and Derek Walcott. Xenophobia and anti-Semitism feature strongly in the popular novels of John Buchan and occasionally in the poetry of Ezra Pound and T.S. Eliot, but less so in their contemporaries. The British poet Tony Harrison is virtually unique in juxtaposing the classic styles of the English tradition and earthy demotic speech. W.H. Auden is a special case, most of his work being highly erudite and refined, but his astonishing pornographic and slightly comic poem "The Platonic Blow" appeared in an American magazine *Fuck You*, published by the Fuck You Press (1965).

In recent years issues of obscenity have often become sticking points in the award of literary prizes, no less than in the other arts. Thus James Kelman's novel, *How Late It Was,*

How Late won the prestigious British Booker Prize in 1994, but only after a division in the jury and a critical furor over the multitudinous repetitions of *fuck* and its derivatives. A similar controversy surrounded the copious use of *fucken* in the Booker Prize–winner for 2003, D.B.C. Pierre's *Vernon God Little*. A reaction to these developments, essentially a protest against a perceived decline in literary standards, has been the institution of unofficial posthumous "Booker" awards for books published a century ago. The judges' award for 1894 was George Moore's *Esther Waters*.

See also: Anglo-Saxon Period; Medieval Period.

Bibliography

Mills, Jane, ed. *The Bloomsbury Guide to Erotic Literature*. London: Bloomsbury, 1993.

LORD

The term is unusual in that its religious significance is not original, but a metaphorical extension of the Anglo-Saxon secular status term, *hlaford*. Most religious swearing terms derive from the name of the deity, Christ, or the saints. *Lord* derives from the root form *hlafweard*, meaning literally "the guardian of the loaf," referring to the social role of the lord as provider for his followers. The Old English vocabulary had several terms denoting "the person in power," which after the conversion to Christianity started to be used as titles of God. Among them were *Liffrea* ("Lord of Life"), *Metod* and *Wealdend* ("Ruler"), and *Frea* ("Lord"). *Hlaford* was used in this fashion somewhat later, ca. 1000, toward the end of the Anglo-Saxon period, by Ælfric, in the phrase "Sy lof þam Hlaforde" ("Praise be to the Lord").

In Middle English the term started to be used more freely. Chaucer's irrepressible Wife of Bath, who uses a great range of exclamations, refers to "Lord Jhesu" (*Prologue* l. 146), and uses the exclamation "Lord Crist!" (l. 469), while the author himself in his Retractions at the end of the great work, thanks "Lord Jhesu Crist" (l. 1,088). The independent use "O Lord" began around 1400 and was general up to the seventeenth century. Interestingly, it was not included in the list of forbidden sacred names detailed in the legislation of the fifteenth and sixteenth centuries, which focused mainly on the names of God, Jesus, Christ, and the Devil. Although *lord* was never a seriously profane term, euphemistic or "minced" forms develop in the eighteenth century, generating a variety of idiomatic formulas, most of which thrived in the Victorian era:

1725	Lud
1765	Lawks
1835	Lor
1844	Law sakes!
1861	Law
1865	Law a mussy (Lord have mercy)
1870s	Lawdy!
1898	Lumme! (Lord love me)

These are largely British, since in American parlance, *Lord* has generally had less profane resonance. However, H.L. Mencken, following an unpublished source, gives *laud, law, lawks, lawdy,* and *lawsy* (1963, 395). Generally speaking, *lumme!* is today the sole survivor of this now obsolete field, since "Oh Lord!" has become an acceptably mild exclamation.

See also: God; Jesus; Minced Oaths.

Bibliography

Chaucer, Geoffrey. *The Works of Geoffrey, Chaucer*, ed. F.N. Robertson. Boston: Houghton Mifflin, 1957.
Mencken, H.L. *The American Language*. Abridged, ed. Raven I. McDavid. New York: Knopf, 1963.

LORD CHAMBERLAIN

The Lord Chamberlain historically has been one of the most powerful positions in England, since as the chief official of the Royal Household he often embodied or expressed the wishes of the monarch. In Elizabethan times, when companies of actors needed patronage to obtain a license for their productions, the Lord Chamberlain became one such benefactor. Shakespeare's own company were the Lord Chamberlain's Men prior to becoming the King's Men upon the accession of James I in 1603. However, the Lord Chamberlain also had indirect power of censorship over the stage and public entertainments via the **Master of the Revels**, a court officer in his service who was increasingly given the preemptive right to censor plays.

The critical legislation was the Stage Licensing Act of 1737 (10 Geo II, c 2) granting virtually absolute powers to the Lord Chamberlain via the office of "the Examiner of the Stage." This Act was the legal consequence of satirical attacks on various politicians, especially the prime minister, Robert Walpole, in plays by Henry Fielding (1707–1754), the noted novelist, and staged at the Haymarket Theatre. These included *Don Quixote in England* (1734), *Pasquin* (1736), and *The Historical Register of the Year 1736* (1737), an outspoken exposure of Walpole's corrupt administration.

Although the Licensing Act was in reality a form of private political revenge by Walpole, effectively silencing Fielding and bringing his career as a dramatist to an end, the powers of the Lord Chamberlain remained in place, astonishingly, for over two centuries. As with the procedure used by his predecessor, the Master of the Revels, plays had to be approved and receive a license prior to performance. Powerful initiatives to limit censorship were made as far back as 1832 and 1843, resulting in the directive that the Lord Chamberlain was forbidden to withhold his license unless on the grounds of "the preservation of good manners, decorum or the public peace." While this concession limited refusals on the grounds of content, the Lord Chamberlain could still ban or edit plays on the original grounds of political scandal or controversy, and the representation of the Royal Family or living politicians as characters. Petitions by public authors of note made in 1865 and 1907 resulted in greater flexibility, but the responsibilities of the Lord Chamberlain for theatrical censorship were abolished only in the Theatres Act of 1968.

Grounds for the refusing of a license varied greatly and included obscenity, profanity, blasphemy, immorality, and indecency. The assessment of these problematic qualities was left to men appointed by the Chamberlain, the Examiners or Comptrollers, "mostly upper-middle-class, retired senior officers from the armed services. In the twentieth century they tended to be intelligent and diplomatic, but were also often philistine, with little knowledge of serious drama and it traditions" (de Jongh 2000, xi). In his study *The Censorship of English Drama 1824–1901,* John Russell Stephens researches the activities of the six Examiners of Plays. The first, George Colman, told the Select Committee on Dramatic Literature in 1832: "Nothing on the stage is to be uttered without licence" and was especially severe on all uses of *heaven, God, Lord,* and even *angels* (Stephens 1980, 93). Among the major suppressions were Ibsen's *Ghosts* (1891) and George Bernard Shaw's *Mrs. Warren's Profession* (1894). Oscar Wilde's *Salome* (1892) was described by the Examiner Smyth Pigott as "written in French—half Biblical, half pornographic," but was allowed (Stephens 1980, 112). *King Lear* was prohibited during the madness of George III (Stephens 1980, 162).

If an author or manager refused to comply with the editing prescribed by Examiner, the matter would be handed over to the Director of Public Prosecutions to proceed with a case against the theatre. The files of the Lord Chamberlain and his staff from 1901 to 1968 were withheld from the public domain until 1991. On the basis of access to them and to other correspondence, Nicholas de Jongh's study *Politics, Prudery and Perversion* (2000) surveys the historical evolution of this cultural struggle and delineates the various stratagems employed by authors and managers. As is usually the consequence of censorship, much ingenuity was employed in circumventing the Lord Chamberlain's rulings. The formal device was to have a select club performance, but many anecdotes attest to the effectiveness of irony. Thus the highly successful satirical show *Beyond the Fringe* (1961) contained a sketch for "Bollard, the man's cigarette" and the stage direction "Enter two dreadful queens." Their risqué line "Hello darlings!" provoked an objection from the Lord Chamberlain's office. The producers kept the scenario the same but simply changed the line to "Hello men!" Over the years a great deal of verbal sanitation was carried out, much of it trivial: after the sensational use of *bloody* in Shaw's *Pygmalion* (1912), the expletive was not heard again on the stage until Noel Coward's *Red Peppers* in 1936 (de Jongh 2000, 185). There was some comic confusion among examiners over the meaning of *punk* and *screw* in American plays, and some absurd suggestions, such as "Omit 'shit' and substitute 'educated man'" (de Jongh 2000, 174). But serious plays dealing with war situations, like *US* (1966) faced many deletions, including this horrifying image: "I see his great black cock sizzling and spitting like a cabab [sic] on a skewer" (de Jongh 2000, 154). Samuel Beckett's *Endgame* was acceptable in French (*Fin de Partie*) in 1957, but ran into problems when presented in English. The crux was Hamm's bizarre expletive about God after trying to pray: "The Bastard! He doesn't exist!" Although in the play Clov answers "Not yet," The Lord Chamberlain would not permit the blasphemy until Beckett substituted "swine" for "bastard."

Theatrical managements still had to negotiate with the Lord Chamberlain's officers on a number of grounds. The previously neglected and highly contested terrain of homosexuality on stage is covered in de Jongh's earlier study, *Not in Front of the Audience* (1992), which points out that J.R. Ackerley's *Prisoners of War* (1925) was the first modern British play to deal openly with homosexual desire. Simulated sodomy on stage became a recurring problem, in such different treatments as Tony Kushner's *Angels in America* (National Theatre 1992) and Mark Ravenhill's *Shopping and Fucking* (New Ambassadors Theatre 1996).

Although the 1960s are stereotyped as "permissive," the ending of the *Chatterley* ban (1960) did not immediately extend to the stage. A parliamentary bill introduced in 1962 to abolish stage censorship was rejected by 134 votes to 77. In common with many managers, Kenneth Tynan's tenure as artistic director at the British National Theatre (1963–1969) was typical, marked by much frustration, by minor victories (restorations of text), and by defeats. From *Dingo,* an antiwar play by Charles Wood proposed for 1963, "the Lord Chamberlain wanted the deletion of all four-letter words, all blasphemy . . . and impersonation of living persons. The play was not done" (Tynan 1988, 228). Tynan's most scandalous production, his own nude sex revue *Oh! Calcutta!* appeared the year after the end of the Lord Chamberlain's reign. Nicholas de Jongh has summed up the last decades of that reign: "Relatively speaking, the twentieth century English stage was subject to more censorship than in the reigns of Elizabeth I, James I and Charles I" (2000, xv).

See also: Censorship; Tynan, Kenneth.

Bibliography

De Jongh, Nicholas. *Not in Front of the Audience: Homosexuality on Stage.* London: Routledge, 1992.
———. *Politics, Prudery and Perversion: The Censoring of the English Stage 1901–68.* London: Methuen, 2000.
Stephens, John Russell. *The Censorship of English Drama 1824–1901.* Cambridge: Cambridge University Press, 1980.
Tynan, Kathleen. *The Life of Kenneth Tynan.* London: Methuen, 1988.

LOSS OF INTENSITY, WEAKENING, OR VERBICIDE

This formulation describes a semantic trend, widely apparent in the history of swearing, whereby words that originally had great emotive force and impact have their power eroded through constant repetition and indiscriminate use. As Samuel Beckett wrote in *Waiting for Godot,* "The air is full of our cries, but habit is a great deadener" (1959, 91). H.L. Mencken put it characteristically: "All expletives tend to be dephlogisticated by over-use" (1963, 399). *Verbicide* was coined by the Boston Brahmin Oliver Wendell Holmes in 1858, though C.S. Lewis gave the word a later currency in his work on semantic change, *Studies in Words* (1960, 7). The trend applies to virtually all categories of swearing, religious, genital, copulatory, and excretory. Examples abound, not just in swearing, but in words which previously had some powerful religious sense, such as *awful, ghastly, hellish,* or *dismal,* as well as positives such as *divine, heavenly, paradise,* and *miracle.* George Santayana's succinct observation "Oaths are the fossils of piety" (1900, 148) sums up the history of this semantic area.

Religious oaths and ejaculations provide clear cases of both generalization and weakening or loss of intensity. In the medieval period they had obvious potency and wide currency, but from the Renaissance onward this power was steadily eroded to the point that they became simply fashionable. As the dramatist Richard Brinsley Sheridan wrote in *The Rivals* (1775): "Damns have had their day." Although in the Victorian era invoking the names of God, Christ, the Devil, and topics like damnation in oaths became taboo, their power has since eroded once again in general discourse. A century ago expletives like *damn* and *for God's sake* were unmentionable in polite society, while *cunt, fuck,* and *shit* were completely taboo. In essence the great range of euphemistic variants of the sacred names and obscene terms (such as *Jove, golly, Jiminy, Cripes, Lor!,* and *effing*) are tributes to the power that the core original words had in the past. Today these euphemisms seem very dated and precious, mainly because the originals have again become so common.

Over the centuries animal terms like *pig, swine, sow, shrew,* and *bitch* have become words of powerful insult, but then generalized and weakened. In more recent decades terms derived from genital and excretory functions have become toned down to mean nothing more offensive than "a worthless person" or "a fool." This trend can also be seen in the terms *arse, arsehole, asshole, fart, shit, cunt,* and *prick*. Weakening is apparent both in the more specifically British English swearwords *twat, berk,* and *prat,* as well as those of a more American provenance, such as *cocksucker, motherfucker,* and plain *fuck* used as a noun. The trend also incorporates general terms like British English *bastard, sod,* and *git,* as well as American English *punk* and *son of a bitch*. It is also apparent in the grammatical extensions to the verbal formulas *fuck off* and *piss off,* as well as the adjectives *fucking* and *sodding*. Obviously context, the directness of the insult, and social and personal factors are important determiners of the force of a term. In an amusing comment in *Class,* the British author Jilly Cooper, recalls "I once heard my son regaling his friends: 'Mummy says that *pardon* is a much worse word than *fuck*'" (1981, 39). This is an essentially upper-class attitude.

An alternative method of assessing the diminishing impact of abusive terms is to consider them in the categories of the following format of usages, namely "taboo," "offensive," "slang," and "jocular/familiar." Fifty years ago all the words cited below were taboo, with the exception of *bastard* and *nigger*. Today the situation is less clear-cut. In the table an asterisk (*) means that the term belongs in the category, while an "x" indicates that it generally cannot be used, except in certain contexts within the speech community shown in parentheses:

Word	Taboo	Offensive	Slang	Jocular/Familiar
fuck	*	*	*	*
cunt	*	*	*	x (U.K.)
motherfucker	*	*	*	x (U.S.)
bastard	*	*	*	x (U.K., etc.)
nigger	*	*	*	x (U.S.)

The general point, that previously powerful and taboo terms can now be used in less emotive and even jocular modes, is valid but has to be modified to allow for particular contexts. Thus *cunt* can be used in the *jocular/familiar* mode only in certain contexts and idioms, such as "You silly cunt!," while *motherfucker* and *nigger* can be used in this mode, but only among blacks in the United States. Similarly, *bastard* can be used in these modes in British and Australian English, but not in other varieties.

The principal exceptions to the general trend are the areas of race and disability. Up to half a century ago terms like *nigger, wog, coolie, spastic,* and *cripple* were in fairly common currency: Joseph Conrad's novel, *The Nigger of the Narcissus,* published in 1897, would certainly have had its title changed a century later. Likewise, Victor Hugo's famous work, translated as *The Hunchback of Notre Dame* (1832). With the rise of political correctness, ethnic insults and demeaning terms for disability have become genuinely taboo, requiring new euphemisms. With these exceptions in mind, verbicide, weakening or loss of intensity, remains the dominant trend in the history of swearing.

Agglomeration

Agglomeration is a major consequence of loss of intensity. Since swearing consists of language used in its most emotive mode, that is, with the most concentrated personal feeling, words are often used not in a literal fashion but as mere counters of insult without logical organization, as agglomerations thrown together. Thus the plain insult "You bastard!" can become elaborated emotively into "You bloody bastard!" then "You bloody little bastard!" and even "You bloody fucking little bastard!" Similarly, the exclamation "Jesus!" is often developed, first and logically to "Jesus Christ!" and then bizarrely into "Jesus fucking Christ!," which was actually uttered by a horrified woman watching the terrorist attacks on the World Trade Center on September 11, 2001.

There would seem to be a limit of tolerance on the number of semantically unrelated adjectives that can be strung together. However, an extreme and remarkable example from Australia is cited by Bill Hornadge: "You rotten, bloody, poofter, commo, mongrel bastard!" (1980, 136). Although apparently random, this "shotgun" range concentrates in an astonishing fashion many of the prime categories of insult: personal dishonesty, illegitimacy, and aspects of the sexual, the political, and the animal. It should be noted that in the context of Australian speech, *bloody* and *bastard* carry little weight. While conceding that semantic impact may seem to be reduced by verbicide, it is important to realize that swearing has a function, not simply of logical condemnation but of emotional release. The entry for **impact** discusses these aspects further. Although it might appear that this is a modern trend, powerful instances of agglomeration from several centuries ago can be found in the entry for **William Shakespeare**, notably in the passages in *King Lear* (II ii 12–22) and *Hamlet* (II ii 568–70) and in the entry for **François Rabelais**.

See also: Flexibility; Impact; Minced Oaths; Rabelais, François; Shakespeare, William.

Bibliography

Beckett, Samuel. *Waiting for Godot.* London: Faber, 1959.
Cooper, Jilly. *Class.* New York: Knopf, 1981.
Hornadge, Bill. *The Australian Slanguage.* North Ryde, New South Wales: Cassell Australia, 1980.
Lewis, C.S. *Studies in Words.* Cambridge: Cambridge University Press, 1960.
Mencken, H.L. *The American Language.* Abridged, ed. Raven I. McDavid. New York: Knopf, 1963.
Santayana, George. *Interpretations of Poetry and Religion.* New York: Scribners, 1900.

LOUSY

Lousy, like *filthy, dirty,* and *flea-pit,* originally had a literal significance, meaning "infested with lice," exemplified in the medieval author William Langland's reference to "a lousi hatte" in

Piers Plowman (B v 195). A number of idiomatic phrases confirm the presence of lice in previous times: Francis Grose's *Classical Dictionary of the Vulgar Tongue* (1785) has *louse-bag,* "a black bag worn to the hair or wig"; *louse-house* for a prison cell; *louse-ladder,* "a stitch fallen in a stocking"; and *louse land,* a prejudicial name for Scotland.

However, the modern figurative use of *lousy,* meaning "worthless," "inferior," or "contemptible" is of surprising antiquity, being first recorded in Chaucer's *Friar's Tale,* when the sinister devil-figure says "A lowsy jogelour kan deceyve thee," meaning "a second-rate juggler can trick you" (l. 1467). In Shakespeare's *Henry V* (1599) the excitable Welshman Fluellen condemns a supposed traitor profusely: "What an arrant, rascally, beggarly, lousy knave it is" (IV viii 35). Since then the word has greatly generalized to apply to anything unpleasant or disliked, to the point that it has driven the literal meaning out of currency. For instance, the phrase "a lousy paltry, sum of money" sounds modern, but is found in 1663 in John Dryden's play *The Wild Gallant* (I i). In the same period *louse* was already in use as a term of personal contempt.

In American English the phrase *lousy with* meaning "having a great deal of" has become extremely common, on the analogy of *crawling with.* It is not only used of undesirable things: "He was lousy with money" is recorded in 1843 in *The Spirit of the Times* (March 4), and Sacramento was described at the time of the Gold Rush as being "lousy with gold." Indeed, the use became so common in the Gold Rush that Andy Gordon complained in his diary (July 12, 1849) that he wished never to hear the word again. The American variety has also regenerated *louse* as a term of personal contempt. All these senses are found in South African English, while Australian usage includes the different meaning of "mean or tight-fisted." The journal *American Speech* asked the question: "How long will the vogue for this unpleasant adjective continue? It is applied indiscriminately and means nothing in particular except that it is always a term of disparagement." That was in 1928 (Vol. III, 345).

M

MAHOMET/MOHAMMED

Military or cultural invasions commonly generate *blasons populaires,* or popular stereotypes, and semantic derogation in the form of nicknames or distortions of proper names. The Moorish expansion and conquest of parts of Europe from the eighth century generated xenophobic animus against Muslims, especially in two ways. The first was the predictable application of such terms as *heathen, pagan,* and *infidel* to these peoples. Less expected were the various corruptions of the name of the prophet Mahomet that came to be used throughout the Middle Ages.

From the Christian perspective Mahomet was a false prophet, who in the words of the *Oxford English Dictionary* was "in the Middle Ages often vaguely imagined to be worshipped as a god." The name Mahomet in the sense of "an idol" is recorded from about 1205. Furthermore, the name itself is used as a plain insult by Walter Kennedy in *The Flyting of Dunbar and Kennedy* (1553): "Sarazyne, symonyte, . . . Mahomete, mansuorne" ("Saracen, simonite [trafficker in relics], . . . Mahomet, oath-breaker") (l. 526). Most common among the corruptions of the name was the form *Mahounde,* used in an abusive fashion to mean variously, "a devil," "a false prophet," or "a monster." Swearing by Mahounde became a specialty of the evil or benighted characters in the medieval mystery plays. In the Coventry Play *Herod the Great,* the infanticide Herod enjoys the "report-back" from the soldiers sent to massacre the innocents, saying: "Be gracious Mahound more myrth never I had" ("By gracious Mahound I never had so much joy," l. 209). Mahounde is sometimes transformed into a dramatic figure, often related to and confused with Termagant, defined by the *OED* as "a violent and overbearing personage representing a deity supposedly worshipped by Muslims." In his satire "Why come ye not to Court?" directed at Cardinal Thomas Wolsey, John Skelton wrote in 1522: "Like Mahound in a play, / No man dare him withsay" (ll. 594–95). Mahound survived the Middle Ages, appearing in Alexander Pope, Sir Walter Scott, and other literary contexts up to the mid-nineteenth century.

An earlier form is *mawmet,* meaning "a false god" or "idol," recorded from about 1205, and its related variant *mawmetrie,* "the worship of false gods," "idolatry." Sir Thomas More wrote in his *Dialoge* (1529) of "the idolles and mamettes of the pagans." However, the iconoclastic impulses generated by the Reformation, leading to the mass destruction of religious images, resulted in the term being used by extremist Protestants to stigmatize the images of Christ and the saints. In his work *Reliques of Rome* (1553) Thomas Becon even used the proper name in this Christian context, referring to "Idols and mahomets" (88). In due time these originally xenophobic senses were applied to Catholic ritual and lasted for centuries, especially in the demeaning sense of a doll or puppet. The *OED* has a reference to a "Guy Fawkes momet" (an effigy of the Pope) dated as late as 1892. All these terms are now obsolete, also showing the semantic trend of generalization, a common feature of xenophobic terms.

See also: Heathen.

MALEDICTA

Generally speaking, American linguistic scholarship has put considerable focus on oral, as opposed to written, usage. There is thus no real equivalent in Britain of the journal *American Speech,* founded in 1925. *Maledicta: The International Journal of Verbal Aggression,* edited by Reinhold Aman, who founded it in 1965, has followed the example of such pioneering figures as H.L Mencken and Stuart Berg Flexner, but has gone to the true limits of the oral spectrum by printing articles dealing with every conceivable taboo or embarrassing topic, including pieces on other languages, mainly European. While not always strictly scholarly, in that references are often minimal, the journal fearlessly illuminates the vibrant qualities of scatological and bawdy speech, as well as breaking many of the taboos that have grown up around the attitudes broadly assumed under the heading of political correctness. Unlike most publications, the journal does not "draw the line" anywhere, and includes, for example, pieces on AIDS jokes, Ethiopian jokes, and a huge variety of obscene swearing and ethnic humor. From 1977 to 1989 it published annual collections, followed by three between 1995 and 2004. Its appearance is thus contemporary with a growing interest in profanity and obscenity, evidenced in increasing numbers of dictionaries published in this field in the past two decades.

As Aman wrote in the Introduction to the collection *The Best of Maledicta* (1997), "Thus, 22 years ago, I decided to dedicate my life to the collection and analysis of all those words and expressions shunned by academia and to publish the results in our annual journal *Maledicta*, with the motto: 'They say it—we print it.'" However, Aman is very aware of the serious side of the topic, writing at the outset: "Every day around the world, tens of thousands of people are humiliated, demoted, fired, fined, jailed, injured, killed or even driven to suicide because of *maledicta:* insults, slurs, curses, threats, blasphemies, vulgarities and other offensive words and expressions."

Precisely because of its unconventional stance, the journal has printed many valuable contributions to obscenity and profanity actually in use, such as Stephen O. Murray's "Ritual and Personal Insults in Stigmatized Subcultures" and Leonard R.N. Ashley's study of the sexual side of **Rhyming Slang,** "The Cockney's Horn Book." Volume XIII (2004) contains an article on "The Foul-Mouthed and Lying Clintons."

See also: Dictionaries.

Bibliography

Aman, Reinhold, ed. *The Best of Maledicta: The International Journal of Verbal Aggression.* Philadelphia: Running, 1997.

MALEDICTION

The term, which is now obsolescent and mainly historical in usage, has two related meanings as entered in the *Oxford English Dictionary:* "the utterance of a curse," the familiar sense, and "the condition of being under a ban or a curse," the less common. The first instance, dated 1447, refers to a person being absolved of "this legal maledyccyoun." Shakespeare refers in *King Lear* (1605) to "menaces and maledictions against King and nobles" (I ii 160), while the novelist Sir Walter Scott notes that in 1661 "the malediction of a parent was made a capital offence in Scotland." Henry Wadsworth Longfellow's usage in 1851 strikes most modern readers as dated in sentiment and style: "The malediction of my affliction is taken from me."

See also: Curse and Cursing; Damn; Word Magic.

MAMET, DAVID

A noted American playwright, screenplay writer, and film director also credited under the name Richard Weisz (1947–), Mamet uses powerful language to a far greater extent than most of his contemporaries. His plays generally concentrate on male-centered situations in which swearing and foul language form an essential aspect in macho posturing and the establishment of dominance. Christopher Bigsby, in his perceptive study on Mamet in *Modern American Drama* (1992), comments that "the past does not inform the present except as the origin of a now degraded language or as the source of a set of decayed and disregarded values" (1992, 200).

Glengarry Glen Ross (1983), which won a Pulitzer Prize for Drama, was inspired by Mamet's own experience in a Chicago real estate agency where, as he confesses, "I sold worthless land in Arizona to elderly people" (in Bigsby 1992, 214). The play contains many exchanges like the following, in which a newcomer to the sales force is introduced to the office argot:

Williamson: . . . my job is to marshall the leads.
Levine: Marshall the leads . . . marshall the leads? What the fuck, what bus did *you* get off, we're here to fucking *sell. Fuck* marshalling the leads. What the fuck talk is that? Where did you learn that? In school . . . ? (Scene i, ll, 95–100)

Curiously, Bigsby gives only a passing reference to the foul language: "Shelley Levine's speeches are sprinkled with italicized or capitalized words and with obscenities" (1992, 216).

American Buffalo (1976), set in a junk store in Chicago, concerns the inept scheme of some minor crooks to rob a man who has purchased a buffalo-headed nickel. The dialogue of the all-male cast is laden with profanity. Mamet has commented, however: "I don't think it's a naturalistic play at all . . . The language is very stylized . . . the fact that it has a lot of four-letter words might make it difficult to see that it's written in free verse" (quoted in Bigsby 1992, 209). Yet the Introduction to the printed text of the film, starring Dustin Hoffman, recalls the problems Hoffman had in recalling the rhythm while checking his work at the video replay station: "Wait, stop the tape a second. I *had* this. Christine, is it 'Fuck you. Pause. Fuck. Pause. Fuck you'? or 'Fuck you. Fuck. Pause. Fuck . . . '? Aaagh fuck *me*, what's the line?" (1996, x).

Oleanna (1992) dealing with an accusation of rape against a member of a university faculty by a student, created the most furious controversy although the language was comparatively mild. There were three provocative factors: the accuser is a manipulative female student who is persuaded to make the charge by some feminist supporters, the victim is male, and the audience knows the accusation to be false. The play enraged feminists and scandalized audiences, responses that clearly suggested Mamet had touched a nerve or breached some taboo. In an article ("Why Can't I Show a Woman telling Lies?" in *The Guardian,* April 8, 2004), Mamet claimed sexist prejudice against himself as a male, saying, "The sex of an author is nobody's business."

Christopher Bigsby has written eloquently of the debased language of Mamet's plays: "a language evacuated of meaning and principles, distorted and deformed by greed and suspicion" (1992, 211). Thus in *American Buffalo,* Teach defines free enterprise crassly as "The freedom . . . of the individual . . . To Embark on any Fucking course that he thinks fit . . . in order to secure his honest chance to make a profit" (1978, 35). In *Edmond* (1982) set in a prison cell, the aftermath of a homosexual rape contains this exchange, an ironic distorted homage to *Hamlet* V ii 10 : *Edmond:* "There is a destiny that shapes our ends . . ." *Prisoner:* "Uh huh." *Edmond:* "Rough-hew it how we may." *Prisoner:* "How'er we motherfucking may" (p. 100).

See also: Literature.

Bibliography

Bigsby, C.W.E. *Modern American Drama.* Cambridge: Cambridge University Press, 1992.
———, ed. *The Cambridge Companion to David Mamet.* Cambridge: Cambridge University Press, 1994.
Mamet, David. *American Buffalo.* New York: Grove, 1996.

MASTER OF THE REVELS

The title of this official was originally literal, referring to the person appointed to organize and lead revels in the Royal Household or the Inns of Court prior to the construction of the early theaters. The first recorded reference to the Master of the Revels is in 1495, and his office was initially concerned with building and painting spectacular scenery. However, during the reign of Queen Elizabeth (1558–1603), the function of the Master changed from being that of a Minister of Entertainment, as the name suggests, to a licenser and censor of plays and stage performances. This occurred, significantly, several years before James Burbage even built the first theater in London in 1576. Since all companies of actors had to have a license to perform, they needed either patronage or to be attached to the royal household, leading to an informal arrangement of control. As a Court officer in the service of the Lord Chamberlain, the Master of the Revels was increasingly given the preemptive right to censor plays, which the actors were required to recite and present to him prior to public performance. The final irony was that the players had to pay him a fee: up to 1633 the theatrical company known as the King's Men gave the Master a day's takings from the Globe and the Blackfriars theaters.

The most important early incumbents of the post were Edmund Tilney (1579–1610), Sir George Buc (1610–1622), Sir John Astley (briefly in 1622), and Sir Henry Herbert (1623–1642). In 1581 Queen Elizabeth commanded players and playwrights to recite their shows, interludes and plays before Tilney, who was authorized "to order and reforme, auctorise [approve] and put down [suppress]" them as he thought fit (Chambers, 1923, IV, 285–87). If he approved a play, he signed the text, which became the only "allowed copy" for performance. In the early period the grounds for censorship usually derived from matters of doctrine and politics, since the drama was becoming secularized, politically "relevant" and satirical of contemporary issues and personages. In 1559, the second year of her reign, Elizabeth commanded that no plays were to be performed "wherein either matters of religion or the governaunce of the estate or the commonweale shalbe handled or treated" (Chambers 1923, IV, 263–64). Accordingly, in Shakespeare's *Richard II* (1597), the scene depicting the abdication of the king was cut. In the same year a lost play, *The Isle of Dogs,* was suppressed, and in 1605 Ben Jonson and George Chapman were imprisoned for *Eastward Ho.* Yet Marlowe's *Edward II* (1594), in which the homosexual monarch is deposed and fatally sodomized, seems to have incurred no censorship. Putting the interventions in perspective, some thirty instances of censorship are recorded out of about 2,000 plays written between 1590 and 1642, when the theaters were closed (Lambert 1992, 3).

Profanity also became grounds after legislation against it in "An Act to Restrain the Abuses of Players" in 1606 and a more general prohibition in 1623. In subsequent decades there were increasing Puritan pressures against the use of profanity and sacred language on the stage. The interventions of the Master, as well as some self-censorship, resulted in the toning down of oaths in the plays of Shakespeare (1564–1616) and Ben Jonson (1572–1637) and to the growth of **minced oaths.** However, the Master did not always get his way. King Charles I took issue with the current and the most eager incumbent, Sir Henry Herbert, over his proposed deletions in the case of Sir William Davenant's play *The Wits* (1634). In Herbert's papers, which give a detailed day-to-day record of his activities, there is his version of a meeting:

> This morning, being the 9th of January, 1633 [i.e., 1634] the kinge was pleasd to call mee into his withdrawinge chamber to the windowe, wher he went over all that I had croste in Davenant's playe-booke and allowing of *faith* and *slight* to bee asseverations only, and no oathes, markt them to stande, and some other few things, but in the greater part allowed of my reformations.

Clearly piqued, Herbert then added his own dissenting view:

The kinge is pleasd to take *faith, death* and *slight* to bee asseverations only, and no oathes, to which I doe humbly submit as my masters judgment; but under favour, conceive them to be oaths, and enter them here, to declare my opinion and submission. (cited in Gurr 1980, 54)

This disagreement lies at the heart of most interpretations of swearing: whether to regard an instance as "light" swearing or as a serious oath.

After the Restoration of the theaters in 1660 (following their closure in 1642 during the Puritan Commonwealth) the function and title of the Master were revived. In 1737, following repressive legislation by Sir Robert Walpole, the role was taken over by the Examiner of the Stage, an official of the **Lord Chamberlain**, and was abolished only in 1968.

See also: Censorship; Lord Chamberlain; Minced Oaths.

Bibliography

Chambers, E.K. *The Elizabethan Stage.* 4 vols. Oxford: Oxford University Press, 1923.

Dutton, Richard. "Jurisdiction of Theater and Censorship." In *A Companion to Renaissance Drama*, ed. Arthur F. Kinney. Oxford: Blackwell, 2002.

Gildersleeve, Virginia Cocheron. *Government Regulation of the Elizabethan Drama.* New York: Columbia University Press, 1908.

Gurr, Andrew. *The Shakespearean Stage.* Cambridge: Cambridge University Press, 1980.

Lambert, Sheila. "State Control of the Press in Theory and Practice." In Myers, Robin, and Michael Harris, *Censorship and the Control of Print.* Winchester: St. Paul's Bibliographies, 1992.

MASTURBATION

Attitudes toward masturbation have generally changed historically from revulsion to acceptance. The severity of the older taboo was such that the early words were strongly condemning, such as *pollution* or *self-abuse,* or religious in origin, notably in the case of *Onanism.* These have generally given way to comic or ironic metaphors like *jerk,* which have in some cases become terms of personal denigration.

Engrained myths about masturbation causing insanity, blindness, and deafness, are articulated in the early recorded uses of the term, such as *Onania, or the Heinous Sin of Self Pollution and all its Frightful Consequences, in both SEXES,* the title of a highly successful anonymous collection of salacious case histories published in 1712, after which were added numerous supplements. In the same vein was A. Hume's study *Onanism, or a Treatise upon the Disorders produced by Masturbation* (1766). Chambers *Cyclopaedia* of 1727–1741 referred to Onanism more severely as "the crime of self-pollution," yet Jonathan Swift makes obvious jokes in the first chapter of *Gulliver's Travels* (begun in 1719): "Mr. Bates my master" and "my good master Bates." The word seems first to have been used in 1708 (Laqueur 2003, 29). A scientific study in 1874 maintained that "Onanism is a frequent accompaniment of insanity and sometimes causes it." Walt Whitman referred to "The sick-gray faces of the Onanists" in *Leaves of Grass* (1855, v. 70), and D.H. Lawrence, who broke the modern taboo by referring to "the dirty little secret," declared in *Pornography and Obscenity* that "the masturbation self-enclosure produces idiots," asserting that "This is perhaps the deepest and most dangerous cancer of our civilization" (1929, 316).

In earlier centuries it was generally assumed that masturbation was an exclusively male practice: the choice of the term *Onanism* clearly reinforced this myth (just the derivation of *hysteria* from Greek *hysteros,* "the womb," served to create the false notion that hysteria was an exclusively female complaint). In the Book of Genesis 38: 8–10, Onan broke the Levirate law by refusing Judah's command to marry his brother's widow, and in the King James version, "spilt his seed upon the ground," which "displeased the Lord: wherefore he slew him." The offense thus lay more in the violation of the law than in the act itself. The earliest term for a lesbian, namely a *tribade,* recorded from 1601, is derived from a Greek verb meaning "to rub," which itself had a slang sense of "masturbation" recorded from about 1599.

However, some underground literature, such as Thomas Stretzer's *New Description of Merryland* (1741), described the female genitalia in coded allegory: "Near these forts is the metropolis, called CLTRS . . . the chief palace or rather pleasure seat of the Queens of Merryland." Others were more open, writing of "the uncommon Exercise of the clitoris" (cited in Laqueur, 2003, 28). Indeed, the theme of female masturbation became a staple of Grub street in the eighteenth century and even of increasingly explicit cartoons by French artists, as well as by Isaac Cruikshank ("Luxury" 1801) and Thomas Rowlandson ("Lonesome Pleasures" 1812). Because of its biblical origin and condemnatory overtones, *Onanism* is becoming obsolescent, although George Steiner revived it in his provocative essay "Night Words," referring to "the recent university experiment in which faculty wives agreed to practice onanism in front of researchers' cameras " (1967, 98). There is, however, no exclusively feminine term.

A turning point in attitudes was Philip Roth's scandalously successful novel *Portnoy's Complaint* (1967) with its comedy, detailed treatment, and varied metaphors. In recent decades, as permissiveness and the pursuit of sexual pleasure have become social imperatives, a newer vocabulary of acceptance has appeared, including neutral terms such as *self-stimulation, self-arousal,* and positives like *self-pleasuring.* Upscale Sunday newspapers in the United Kingdom now regularly carry book-club advertisements with titles like *Sex for One.* Thomas Szasz commented wryly in *The Second Sin:* "In the nineteenth century [masturbation] was a disease; in the twentieth it's a cure." The assumption that masturbation is a solitary activity is still dominant.

The principal slang terms in British English are surprisingly old. Recorded from the Restoration is **frig**, which has its own entry. Similarly, *toss off* is listed in Francis Grose's *Classical Dictionary of the Vulgar Tongue* (1785) and defined as "manual pollution," but seems to have become obsolete until it made a surprise reappearance in the Victorian pornographic magazine *The Pearl* in this awkward rhyme: "I don't like to see, though at me you might scoff, / An old woman trying to toss herself off" (1879–1880, 280). As these words have lost specificity and faded away, a new term, *wank* has come into play, recorded only from about 1950. It generated *wanker,* a term of unknown origin that was originally specific, but has taken the common semantic route of generalization, now meaning "an objectionable or stupid person." The agent noun *tosser* has shown the same development. All these words are exclusively male in application.

In American English, the principal slang terms have been *jack off* and *jerk off,* the latter being first listed in Farmer and Henley's compendious British dictionary *Slang and Its Analogues* (1890–1896). Both terms are used, occasionally, of women. *Jerk* itself has an early verbal sense of "to masturbate" recorded from 1888, some three decades before the common noun sense of "an offensive or worthless person." It has become widely used as a noun of general contempt. Similarly, the noun *jerk-off* in the sense of an "act of masturbation" also precedes that of a "dolt or worthless person."

Among the more picturesque and humorous British metaphors are "to beat the bishop" and the earlier "box the Jesuit," the latter recorded, surprisingly, in Grose (1785) with the gloss "A crime that is said much practiced by the reverend fathers of that society." This is an interesting instance of mild xenophobic malice. In South African slang the Afrikaans idiom meaning "pulling the wire" is often used, while the Australian terms are more jocular, notably "jerkin the gerkin."

However, the word itself seems to be what Frank Rich called "The Last Taboo" in a column commenting on President Clinton's firing of the Surgeon General Jocelyn Elders for articulating views on masturbation (*New York Times,* December 18, 1994). Laqueur concludes that "masturbation is that rare thing in modern talk about sexuality: something best left unspoken and so discomforting that it can only be broached under the protection of a joke. If there is a taboo topic in our culture, this may be it" (2003, 496).

See also: Frig, Frigging.

Bibliography

Lawrence, D.H. "Pornography and Obscenity" (1929). In *A Selection from Phoenix,* ed. A.A.H. Inglis. Harmondsworth: Penguin, 1971.

Steiner, George. "Night Words." In *Language and Silence.* Harmondsworth: Penguin, 1967.

Laqueur, Thomas W. *Solitary Sex: A Cultural History of Masturbation.* New York: Zone Books, 2003.

MEDIEVAL PERIOD

The medieval period was paradoxical and inconsistent from the point of view of swearing and profanity, but more predictable in its obscenity and xenophobia. An age of faith, its intense spirituality and great religious energies were manifest in the building of cathedrals and monasteries, the founding of idealistic orders, the pursuit of arduous pilgrimages, and the military exploits of the Crusades, whose original intentions were to find the True Cross and liberate the Holy Land from the heathen. But in time these institutions became venal and corrupted. The fixations with death in the form of the *memento mori* and the horrors of the Last Judgment were profound and ubiquitous.

Yet verbally there was an astounding volume of religious asseveration, ejaculation, profanity, blasphemy, anathema, and cursing, both personal and institutional, both fraudulent and genuine. The word of God, so signally absent from the older Anglo-Saxon oaths and asseverations, was used and abused, elevated, debased, cynically exploited, and distorted as never before. Furthermore, whereas at the beginning of the medieval period the Church was united, by the end it was bitterly divided by reformist impulses and sectarian strife. These divisive forces were to intensify during the Reformation. Consequently the monolithic and unifying ecclesiastical vocabulary turned into labels of vilification.

Most medieval oaths were naturally generated from a religious dynamic. However, many are now hardly recognizable as such because they have been "minced" into innocent forms

311

or lost their original intensity. Thus *by my faith!* eroded into plain *faith; by Mary* similarly became commonplace *marry;* and *I pray thee* continued as simple *prithee.* In time all became moribund and then obsolete. Extraordinarily, the central act of sacrifice in the Christian religion, the Crucifixion, became the generator of numerous grisly oaths in which Christ's wounded and bloody body, even the very nails of the Cross, were callously and often profanely exploited. Oaths like *by Goddes armes, for Cristes peyne, by the blood of Crist,* and *by nayles and by blood,* now seem as grotesque and bizarre to modern readers as modern genital, copulatory, and sexual swearing would have seemed to medievals. Indeed, sexual swearing, now *de rigueur,* is hardly apparent, according to Ralph Elliott "non-existent in Chaucer" (1974, 241). Equally strange were the conventions of courtly love whereby the object of desire, the Lady, was placed on a pedestal, deified, and worshiped in the Petrarchan convention to a degree that strikes modern readers as profane. As the sacred was downgraded, so the amorous and secular were spiritualized. The polar opposite was the convention of the adulterous and opportunistic wife-figure in the genre of the **fabliau**, a mixture of the farce and the dirty story with liberal use of obscenity.

Most strangely, there were no official restraints imposed on such utterances and activities, authors enjoying almost complete artistic freedom. This was a reflection of the manuscript culture. All the forms of censorship with which the modern world is familiar were instituted after the Middle Ages. (As the entry for *censorship* shows, the Index was instituted by the Vatican in 1546.) Language now regarded as coarse and obscene thrived in common words, sayings, and even names. Two London streets were called, astonishingly, *Gropecuntlane* and *Shitteborrowlane,* and there were numerous *Pissing Alleys.* The *dandelion* flower, with its heraldic name rooted in French *dent du lion,* was commonly known by the grosser name of *pissabed,* on account of its diuretic properties. As the entry for **Geoffrey Chaucer** makes clear, the diversity of the Middle Ages, both literary and linguistic, is encapsulated in his *magnum opus,* his *Canterbury Tales* (1386–1400). Chaucer and his contemporaries, indeed most medieval writers, could exploit a whole range of vituperation and obscenity in which no word was taboo. He himself used the whole range of "four-letter" words, and introduced a range of new secular terms of personal disparagement like *foul, lousy, old, shrew, swine,* and *idiot.* His contemporary William Langland, author of *Piers Plowman,* uses such daring juxtapositions of register as "He pissed in a potel [bottle] a pater noster while" (Passus B V l. 348). (By Elizabethan times a short interval was called "a pissing while.") This juxtaposition of the religious and the grossly physical is captured in some religious paintings, notably Pieter Brueghel the Younger's canvas, *The Kermesse [Feast] of St. George* (1628), showing drunken villagers drinking, fighting, kissing, urinating, dancing, vomiting, and defecating with compete abandon.

Many of the personal exchanges in Chaucer, both between pilgrims and between characters in the tales, are still astonishing in their robustness, cruelty, and profanity. To take a single example, the sense of outrage felt by the Host of the Tabard Inn at the cynical charlatanism of the Pardoner's hawking of bogus relics leads to this damning response, the first line intensely spiritual, the second grossly physical:

"By the cros which that Seint Eleyne fond,
I wolde that I hadd thy coillons [testicles] in my hond."
(*Pardoner's Tale,* l. 952)

Obviously these authors were socially aware and spiritually sensitive people. Chaucer apologizes in advance for the "cherle's tale" (ill-bred story) of the Miller, and in the very last words of his great narrative compendium, the Retractions to the *Canterbury Tales,* he disavows the racy tales of sin and smut and devoutly prays that at the Day of Judgment he will be one of those who will be saved.

Equally surprising was the development in the medieval period of the strange convention known as **flyting**, namely exchanges of ritual insults and swearing matches. As the relevant entry shows, the genre has its origins in Norse literature, with both the anonymous work *The Owl and the Nightingale* (ca. 1250) and Chaucer's poem *The Parlement of Foulys* (ca. 1382) being significant early English contributions. Both show a range of swearing, from the religious mode to the scatological, thus making sociolinguistic observations on the hierarchical distribution of oaths.

The dramatic impulse in these debate poems was more fully developed in the dramatic pieces known as the Mystery plays, celebrating the Christian story from the Fall of Lucifer to the Day of Judgment and dramatizing the life and miracles of Christ. Coarse language is surprisingly abundant, especially in the speech of the lower-class and bad characters, such as Cain and an invented figure, Mak the sheep-stealer, in the *Second Shepherds' Play.* (According to one of the quaint traditions of the Middle Ages, the churls of the world were descended from Cain.) In the Towneley plays attributed to the Wakefield Master (ca. 1554–1576), the *Mactatio Abel* ("The Killing of Abel"), the servant boy of Cain called Pickharness, opens the play summarily telling the audience to be quiet, threatening those who do not with the punishment of "blowing my black hollow arse" (l. 7). When Abel wishes Cain "God speed," he gets the rude response "Com kys mine ars!," alternatively "kys the dwillis toute" ("kiss the devil's arse," ll. 59, 63). Whereas Abel invokes God, Cain consistently refers to the Devil, and when God from on high chides him for quarreling with his brother, Cain answers impudently in mock surprise: "Who is that hob [hobgoblin] over the wall?" After his terrible crime, he shouts out contemptuously: "ly ther old shrewe, ly ther, ly," obviously using *old* and *shrew* ("rogue") in an emotive and contemptuous sense. Being a thoroughly medieval rather than strictly biblical character, Cain uses contemporary idioms such as "for Godys pain!" and "by him that me deere boght!" anachronistically referring to the future Crucifixion. One of his last antisocial comments is "Bi all men set I not a fart."

The spectacular ranting of Herod the Great in the *Towneley Play* similarly exploits blasphemous utterance, oscillating between Christian and pagan referents. In the course of a mere twenty lines Herod swears "by Gottys dere naylys," "the dewill [devil] me hang and drawe!," "by God that syttys in trone," and bizarrely "by Mahounde [Mahomet] in heuen" (ll. 116–38). The character of Mak the sheep-stealer, used to introduce low-life and light relief in the context of the Nativity, shows similar comic religious confusion: pretending to go to sleep, he utters the odd prayer: *"Manus tuas commendo, / Poncio Pilato"* ("Into your hands I commend myself, Pontius Pilate"), following it up with the more conventional "Cryst crosse me spede!" ("May Christ's cross protect me!" ll. 266–68).

On a wider front, there were xenophobic semantic growths deriving from martial competition with other religions, especially Islam. As the Church militant mobilized against the expansionism of Islam, so terms like *heathen, pagan,* and *infidel* took on narrower senses. The xenophobic animus against Muslims has its memorial in various corruptions of the name of the prophet Mahomet used throughout the Middle Ages. First among these is the form *Mahounde,* used in an abusive fashion to mean variously, "a devil," "a false prophet," or "a monster." An earlier form is *mawmet,* meaning "a false god" or "idol," and its related variant *mawmetrie,* "the worship of false gods," "idolatry." In due time these originally xenophobic senses relating to heathen practices came to be exploited by rival Christian sects in the bitter exchanges of the Reformation.

See also: Chaucer, Geoffrey; Cherles Termes; Class and Swearing; Fabliau, the; Flyting; God's Wounds; Heathen, Infidel, and Pagan; Mahomet / Mohammed.

Bibliography

Benson, Larry D., and Theodore M. Andersson. *The Literary Context of Chaucer's Fabliaux.* Indianapolis, IN: Bobbs-Merrill, 1971.

Elliott, Ralph. *Chaucer's English.* London: André Deutsch, 1974.

Happé, Peter, ed. *English Mystery Plays.* Harmondsworth: Penguin, 1975.

Ross, Thomas W. *Chaucer's Bawdy.* New York: E.P. Dutton, 1972.

MENCKEN, H.L.

Henry Louis Mencken (1880–1956) is, after Noah Webster, the most significant observer and authority in the study of American English. Since he was essentially a maverick, this status would probably surprise and even annoy him. Mencken did not regard himself as a scholar, but his lifetime in journalism in Baltimore, especially as a court reporter, and his omnivorous philological interest put him in touch with the language actually in use. Consequently, his *magnum opus, The American Language: An Enquiry into the Development of English in the United States,* is a treasure-house of observation and fact, revealing the distinctive qualities of American English, especially its resiliently informal character. This great work, with its pointedly independent title derived from Webster, went through four editions, revisions, and enlargements from 1919 to 1936, by which time it had expanded to 800 pages. To this he added two huge Supplements, in 1945 and 1948. His industry stimulated the founding of the important journal *American Speech* in 1925. Eight months after the appearance of Supplement Two, Mencken had his first stroke and never wrote again, although various "Postscripts to the American Language" appeared subsequently in *The New Yorker.*

In the main work Mencken traced the growth of the new variety and its struggles to gain its independence from the mother tongue. He wrote in an incisive fashion laced with broad humor and an acerbic wit:

> The hardest thing for these peewee pedants to understand is that language is never uniform— that different classes and even different ages speak it differently. The American of a Harvard professor speaking *ex cathedra* is seldom the same as the American of a Boston bartender or a Mississippi evangelist. Let the daughter of a hogsticker in the Omaha stockyards go home talking like a book and her ma will fan her fanny.
> (1963, 517–18)

He labeled the early stages of American English with typical irony "The Earliest Alarms," "The English Attack," "American 'Barbarisms,'" and so on. He was frequently intemperate in his judgments, dismissing Samuel Johnson as "the grand master of all pedantic quacks of his time. No eminent lexicographer was ever more ignorant of speechways than he was" (1963, 100). James Murray and the *OED* are largely ignored. Yet he was by no means a simple chauvinist, as his even-handed treatment of Noah Webster shows: he reveres him as the first champion of American English, but is contemptuous of his attempts to bowdlerize the Bible (1963, 357–58). As Raven I. McDavid, editor of the Abridged edition rightly asserts, "In short, *The American Language,* uniquely Mencken's, is . . . a work of serious scholarship" (1963, ix).

Unlike most scholars of the American variety, Mencken gave space to the less reputable aspects of the language, with sections on "Euphemisms," "Forbidden Words," "Terms of Abuse," and "Expletives." One natural target in the first category is the extensive vocabulary generated by the death industry "whereby they have sought to bedizen their hocus pocus with mellifluous euphemisms," words such as *casket, mortician, parlor, memorial park, slumber robe,* and so on (1963, 341–43). His hatred of cant and pomposity led him to identify a particularly American form of euphemism, the inflated title for a menial position, such as *rodent operative* for rat-catcher and *termite engineer.*

"Forbidden Words" begins with the observation that "The American people, once the most prudish on earth, took to a certain defiant looseness of speech in World War I and Prohibition. Today after a second world war, words and phrases are encountered everywhere—on the air, on the screen, in the theaters, in the comic papers, in the newspapers, on the floor of Congress and even at the domestic hearth—that were reserved for use in saloons and bagnios a generation ago" (1963, 355). However, he notes that a Scottish visitor, "James Flint, in his 'Letters from America,' reported that *rooster* had been substituted for *cock* (the latter having acquired an indelicate anatomical significance) by 1821" (1963, 356–57). "The palmy days of euphemism ran from the 1820s to the 1880s. Bulls became *male cows . . .* the breast became the *bosom,* cockroaches became *roaches,* trousers became *inexpressibles . . .* the biblical *ass* homonymous with *arse,* was displaced by *jackass, jack* or *donkey*" (1963, 357). The discussion is wide-ranging, including references to the "four-letter words," notably in quoting Allen Walker Read's important article, "An Obscenity Symbol" (1934): "surely a student of the language is even less warranted in refusing to consider certain four-letter words because they are too 'nasty' or too 'dirty.'" Nevertheless, Mencken, like Read, avoids mentioning the grossest himself.

"The American language boasts a large stock of terms of opprobrium, chiefly directed at aliens," Mencken rightly observes at the beginning of his twenty-page discussion of "Terms of Abuse" (1963, 367). Less inhibited in this area, Mencken traverses the field with flair and unusual detail. Names for syphilis, he notes, are foreign, as in *French pox;* likewise lice, fleas, and cockroaches, he notes, are often given national names (*espagnol,* "Spanish") or regional (*Preussen,* "Prussian"). "*Woppage* appeared in England as a designation for the retreating Italian Army in North Africa, but it did not survive" (1963, 372).

Mencken showed some regrettable signs of race prejudice, and his discussion of *Jew* (partly covered in the relevant entry) is frank, often verging on the tactless: "In 1936 a vigilant male Jew from Chicago undertook a jehad [sic] against the publishers of Roget's Thesaurus because it listed *Jew* as a synonym for lender." He continued: "Certainly the sort of Jew who devotes himself to visiting editors seems to prefer *Hebrew*" (1963, 376). In similar tone he observes that "*Nigger* is so bitterly resented by the more elegant blackamoors that they object to it even in quotations, and not a few of their papers spell it *n——r*" (1963, 383). Today Mencken is undoubtedly classified as "politically incorrect," but his discussions are revealing on a number of grounds, beyond simply showing the comparative lack of sensitivity in the handling of ethnic terms in the 1920s and 1930s. He brings out strict semantic and historical distinctions, as between *Hebrew* and *Jew,* and between *Negro* and *nigger;* he also reminds readers of the special use of *Creole* in Louisiana. But above all he records and resents the attempts of pressure groups to suppress particular usages.

The discussion of "Expletives" starts, curiously, with a whole rehearsal of the English history of *bloody, God's wounds,* and *hell* before the more specifically American *darn, tarnation, goddam,* and *son of a bitch,* "the hardest worked by far" (1963, 399). However, he brings out the useful distinction that *bloody* "is entirely without improper significance in America, but in England it is regarded as indecent, with overtones of the blasphemous" (1963, 389) and that *bugger* "is not generally considered obscene in the United States" (1963, 398). He quotes extensively from a pioneering article, "*Hell* in American Speech," published in 1931 by L.W. Merryweather. This distinguished fourteen different functions of the word (1963, 393). Even more valuably he unearths "the only comprehensive collection of American swear words," namely "A Dictionary of Profanity and its Substitutes," by M.R. Walter of Dalton, Pennsylvania, noting wryly: "It has not been published, but a typescript is in the Princeton University Library and may be consulted there by learned men of reasonable respectability" (1986, 398). Mencken produces a fairly lengthy list of euphemisms, from Walter and other sources (1963, 394–95). A selection of them shows the creativity of American expletives:

For *damn: drat, bang, blame, blast, bother, darn, cuss, dang, ding, bean.*
For *goddam: goldarn, doggone, consarn, goldast, goshdarn,* and various terms in *dad-,* e.g., *dad-blame, dad-blast dad-burn,* etc.
For *Jesus: Jemima, Jerusalem, Jehosaphat, jiminy whiz, gee-whittaker.*

His generalized view is typically Menckenian: "All expletives tend to be dephlogisticated by over-use" (1963, 399).

Bibliography

Mencken, H.L. *The American Language.* New York: Knopf, 1919–1936.
———. *The American Language.* Abridged, ed. Raven I. McDavid. New York: Knopf, 1963.
Merryweather, L.W. "*Hell* in American Speech." *American Speech* VI (August 1931): 433–35.
Read, Allen Walker. "An Obscenity Symbol." *American Speech* IX (December 1934): 264–78.

MINCED OATHS

This designation refers to a specific kind of euphemism or disguise mechanism, whereby an offending term or taboo phrase is distorted or "minced" so that it no longer offends. (We still have the idiom "not to mince one's words" meaning to speak frankly.) The first specific reference is in Jonathan Swift's "A Letter of Advice for a Young Poet" (1720): "My young Master, who at first minced an Oath, is taught there to mouth it gracefully and to swear, as he reads French, *Ore rotundo* [in a declamatory style]." The classic early examples are found in oaths like *God's wounds!* becoming plain *zounds!*, *God's truth* becoming *strewth!*, *by God!* becoming *egad* or plain *Gad!*, and *by Mary* becoming *marry*. In similar fashion we find *Jee whiz* for *Jesus*, *Crickey* for *Christ*, *Lummey!* for *Lord love me!*, *tarnation* for *damnation*, *heck* for *Hell*, *Deuce* for *the Devil*, *shoot!* for *shit!*, and *eff off!* for *fuck off!*

As can be seen, minced oaths cover the full range available topics, from religion (which historically supplies the greatest variety) to excretion and copulation. Some terms are so thoroughly minced that they are no longer recognizable: thus *Gor blimey!* (often reduced to plain *blimey!*) is a minced form of *God blind me!* Others are fairly obvious: as H.L. Mencken observed, *bullshit* is often partially minced to *bullsh* or *bull* (1963, 364). Furthermore, minced oaths are found over a great historical range, mainly from the sixteenth century to the present, although *gog* and *cokk* are recorded as euphemisms for *God* two centuries earlier. By contrast, minced forms of *Jesus, Christ, Lord,* and *shit* show no such concentrations.

As with evolution of euphemisms, the seminal question is whether the generation of minced oaths occurs spontaneously out of a sense of decorum, or in response to some threat. When Chaucer used the phrase *by cokkes bones!* (instead of *by Godes bones!*) in his *Canterbury Tales,* he was probably doing so for various motives: out of politeness, out of respect for the moral character of the teller, or in deference to the notional audience, since there were no official pressures. In his text Chaucer exploited the whole range of sacred names, both seriously and sacrilegiously. However, as the entry for **Renaissance** shows, in the late sixteenth century there were increasing Puritan injunctions against the use of profanity on the stage, so that there is no doubt that the response was the great number of minced oaths. Consequently, the name of God was either distorted to *gad* or abbreviated to *od,* producing curious forms like *'od's my will* for "as God is my will" and *'od's me* for "God save me." Similarly, older euphemistic forms like *cock* and *gog* were resuscitated, and foreign forms like *perdy* (from French *par Dieu*) were introduced. Alternatively, the name of God was omitted. About a dozen of these forms sprang up within a few years, between 1598 and 1602, all of them significantly first recorded in dramatic contexts:

Oath	Date	Author and play
'sblood	1598	Shakespeare, *Henry IV, Part I,* I ii 82
'slid [eyelid]	1598	Shakespeare, *Merry Wives,* III iv 24
'slight	1598	Jonson, *Everyman Out of His Humour,* II ii
'snails	1599	Hayward, *Henry IV,* I 19
zounds	1600	Rowlands, *The Letting of Humours,* V 72
'sbody	1601	Jonson, *The Poetaster,* II i
'sfoot	1602	Marston, *Antonio's Revenge,* IV iii

These technical evasions of sacred names may seem strange now, but would have had fairly obvious meanings for the contemporary audience. The fact that they anticipated the legislation of 1606 suggests that active policing was already being carried out. The plays of both the major dramatists, William Shakespeare and Ben Jonson, were revised for publication several years after their first stage performances, and both texts show widespread expurgation of religious oaths.

The new **Restoration** drama was both a rebellion against Puritanism and a mirror of the decadence and open sexuality of the Court. Thomas Otway's play *The Soldier's Fortune* (1679) opens with a curse, "A pox o' Fortune!" and keeps up a steady stream of minced forms, such as *Igad, 'sdeath, Odd, Odd's life, Odd's fish, Odd's so,* and two euphemisms for *Jesus,* namely *Criminy* and *Gemini,* a variant of *Jiminy,* first recorded about 1660. The second part of the play (1684) shows more daring in the title, *The Atheist,* and in its oaths, which include *Ah dear damnation!* and *Hell and the devil!* It also makes swearing part of its content, and contains a scene where a character called Daredevil casually dismisses the oath *Dam'me* as "mere Words of course."

See also: Disguise Mechanisms; Euphemisms; God, Euphemisms for; God's Wounds; Religious Oaths; Restoration, the.

Bibliography
Gurr, Andrew. *The Shakespearean Stage.* Cambridge: Cambridge University Press, 1980.
Mencken, H.L. *The American Language.* New York: Knopf, 1919–1936.

MOHAMMED. *See:* Mahomet / Mohammed.

MORALIZATION OF STATUS WORDS

This significant formulation describes the semantic change whereby words that previously denoted rank acquire connotations of moral conduct. Thus terms like **knave** and **villain**, which previously denoted people of low social status, undergo semantic deterioration, describing people of low morals, while on the other hand, those that previously denoted people of high social status, like *noble* and *gentle,* undergo the opposite semantic trend of amelioration, describing people with good qualities. The process of moralization seems initially to have reflected the difference in status between Norman overlords and Saxon underlings, the assumption being that the ruling class was not only "gentle" or "noble" by birth, but by nature, just as the lower orders were "base" by both criteria. (The criterion of birth is obviously the key to the deterioration of **bastard.**) Moralization has now ramified in many social directions. Although many semanticists have sought to establish "laws" of semantic change, they have generally not succeeded. This seminal formulation was set out by the great medievalist and renaissance scholar C.S. Lewis in *Studies in Words* (1960, 7).

Obviously within the context of swearing, the negative aspect of moralization is most significant. These instances are more numerous than the positive examples and include, in addition to *knave* and *villain,* the terms *blackguard,* **rascal,** **wretch,** *slave, churl,* and the adjectives *lewd* and *uncouth,* all of which initially described people of low status. Of these terms only *wretch* originally carried negative moral implications, since Anglo-Saxon *wræcca* meant an exile or outcast. However, the ancestor of *knave,* namely Anglo-Saxon *cnafa,* meant simply "a male child," while that of *churl* (Anglo-Saxon *ceorl*) was a general term for a man with a great variety of meanings. *Villain,* originally a servant at a villa, became in medieval times "a low-born, base-minded rustic" (the definition of the *Oxford English Dictionary*), but is now free of class associations; in fact "the villain" in modern times is frequently a personage of wealth or status. *Blackguard,* a later term historically, originally meant (from the sixteenth century) "one of the lowest menials of the household who had charge of the pots and pans." A parallel status term, *scullion,* now obsolete, meant "a domestic servant of the lowest rank" and developed an abusive currency in the late sixteenth century: Hamlet berates himself for cursing "like a scullion" (II ii 616). Other terms originally denoting low status are **beggar** and **rascal**, defined by the *Oxford English Dictionary* in its earliest sense as "the rabble of an army; common soldiers or camp-followers; persons of the lowest class."

The low status accorded to being a captive is shown in the deterioration of *vassal* and *slave,* from Latin *Sclavus,* a *Slav.* Similarly Latin *captivus,* a captive, has generated French *chetif,* meaning "poor, weak, miserable," and English *caitiff,* now obsolete, but which since the Middle English period developed the sense of "a base, mean, despicable wretch, a villain" (Ullmann 1962, 232). Revealingly, all the terms in Ullmann's own characterization are status words, with the exception of *despicable.* These lead us back to the fundamental semantic link between status and morality, found in *low, base,* and *mean,* contrasted with *high* and *generous.*

Less obvious notions of status have come to be attached to the urban environment, originally conceived as "civilized" and "urbane," as opposed to the country, which was backward. Thus *peasant, rustic* (noun), *bumpkin,* and *boor* are rather old-fashioned prejudicial terms that acquired their negative senses in the sixteenth century. Even *clown* and *lout* originally referred to rustics, as did the more obviously condemning *dunghill,* meaning a grossly immoral person. They have been joined by *backwoods, hick, peckerwood,* and *clodhopper.*

Another area of low status derives from lack of education. The prime historical example is *lewd,* which originally in its Anglo-Saxon form *læwed* meant "lay," that is, not of the church, and by Middle English meant simply "uneducated." In John Wycliffe's translation of the Bible (1382) St. Peter and St. John are "men unlettrid, and lewid men" (Acts 4:13). Clearly no stigma attaches to the word in this context. The term then deteriorated to mean "ignorant," "stupid," "foolish," and "worthless" before shifting to the modern senses of "lascivious," "indecent," and "vulgarly sexual." More recent examples can be seen in the condemning overtones of *ignorant* and *illiterate,* as against the laudatory overtones of *educated* and *knowledgeable,* and so on, which should logically be simply descriptive terms. Perhaps the most interesting term is *ignoramus,* deriving from the name of the main character and a popular play by Stephen Ruggle and acted in 1615 before the King at Cambridge "to expose the ignorance and arrogance of the common lawyers." A related semantic field concerns terms for intelligence: thus *dumb, stupid, moron, imbecile,* and *cretin* have come to carry powerfully negative overtones, whereas *brilliant* has become a general term of praise.

The process of moralization is thus not confined to the distant past, as the examples from feudal times might suggest. The process continues in a whole variety of semantic fields, even in modern supposedly egalitarian and democratic societies. Terms originally denoting low status, which have come to label people as immoral or the undesirable products of low-class locales, are *street urchin, guttersnipe, scum, trailer trash,* and the less condemning status marker *the wrong side of the tracks.* The complex term *ghetto,* rooted in religious persecution and poverty, has now acquired associations of criminality.

See also: Beggar; Knave; Rascal; Rogue; Villain; Wretch.

Bibliography
Hughes, Geoffrey. *Words in Time.* Oxford: Blackwell, 1988.
Lewis, C.S. *Studies in Words.* Cambridge: Cambridge University Press, 1960.
Ullmann, Stephen. *Semantics: An Introduction to the Science of Meaning.* Oxford: Blackwell, 1962.

MOTHERFUCKER

Clearly this term represents in its literal sense the violation of the most extreme sexual taboo, that of incest, and has thus been long regarded as a heinous term unmatched in impact. It essentially encapsulates the potent Oedipal archetype identified by Sigmund Freud as a form of illicit subconscious desire. (There is, curiously, no corresponding expression of the Electra complex, that is, no *fatherfucker.*) However, the articulation of the desire in such gross terms represents in an intensified form a violation of both cultural and verbal taboos.

The literal Freudian emphasis suggests that the taboo and its violation are a European fixation, since the insulting injunction "Go and have intercourse with your mother!" is highly dispersed among European languages (some of which extend the invitation to one's sister). Ernest Hemingway remarked in a letter from Spain in 1929: "In a purely conversational way in a Latin language in an argument one man says to another *'Cogar su madre!'*" Malinowski covered incestuous swearing in a number of cultures, commenting that it was a specialty of the Slavic peoples (1927, 106–7). Similar idioms have been recorded among the Cape York aborigines of Australia, according to Ashley Montagu (1973, 17), and in Cameroon pidgin in the form "Chak yu mami!" (Todd 1984, 104). The Vietnamese *du-ma* is recorded from 1983 in the *Random House Historical Dictionary of American Slang* (1997).

The term and its currency are paradoxical on a number of grounds. In the first place, unlike *bastard* and *bugger,* the word is hardly ever used literally. *Random House* describes the literal use as *"rare,"* but gives no clear examples, carrying the concessive usage note: "usu. considered vulgar," rather than "taboo." The *Oxford English Dictionary* (1989) classifies it as "coarse slang." The *Random House Dictionary* has many examples of the general meaning, "a despicable or contemptuous [sic] man or woman." First instances have been steadily backdated as dictionaries have become bolder, and currently date from 1928, although some authorities claim uses as early as about 1900. Several quotations are highly emotive, such as this from 1935: "Motherfucker, I'll slice off your prick" (Logsdon, *Whorehouse Bells,* 95) and the threat in the radical newspaper *Black Panther* in 1973: "We will kill any motherfucker that stands in the way of our freedom" (16).

Historically the word was originally exclusive to the provenance of Black American English, and it is a possible speculation that it was carried over from a pidgin or creole form of the kind cited earlier. Its expansion into general American parlance started at the time when this variety was starting to show a resurgence of obscenity after a long period of puritanical restraint. (A similar development surrounded the earlier emergence of *cocksucker*.) The reasons for the more generalized usage are usually given as the integration of the American army in the late 1940s and the spread of the term with the demobilized troops returning from wars in Europe, Korea, and Vietnam. An article on "Army Speech and the Future of American English" in 1956 offered the following explanation: "This linguistic vacuum [created by the overuse and resulting enfeeblement of *fuck*] is being filled by a new obscenity symbol, *motherfucker,* which goes beyond simple obscenity itself by outraging the most engrained of human sensibilities" (*American Speech* XXXI, May 1956, 111). Certainly one early source for the euphemistic variant *motherfugger* was Norman Mailer's war novel *The Naked and the Dead* (1947).

The *Random House Historical Dictionary of American Slang* separates a sense (b), designated as *Black English & Military* and defined as "(with reduced force) fellow; person; (*hence*) a close friend or admirable person," with quotations from 1958, including the definition in *Dictionary of American Speech* (1967): "A familiar, jocular even affectionate term of address between males." Clarence Major's lexicon of African-American slang, *Juba to Jive* (1994), claims a greater historical time span (1790s–1990s) and even wider application: "profane form of address; a white man; any man; anybody; of black origin; sometimes derogatory, sometimes used affectionately; other times used playfully." A further sense is that of "a difficult or infuriating situation" recorded from 1947.

As is typical with such powerful terms, a great number of euphemisms proliferate in the semantic field, including *motherfuyer* (1935), *motherfeyer* (1946), *mothersucker* (1946), *motherfouler* (1947), *motherjumper* (1949), *motherlover* (1950), *motherhubba* (1959), *mother-raper* (1959), *motherhumper* (1963), and *mothergrabber* (1963). The plain euphemistic form *mother* is recorded form 1935 and has become extremely common. (The dates are sourced from the *Random House Historical Dictionary of American Slang*.)

Clearly, context is vital in determining the degree of insult. Yet there has obviously been surprising relaxation in usage over recent decades. Lenny Bruce's complaint about the lighting of a show in 1967 ("Where is that dwarf motherfucker?") in part led to his arrest for violating Penal Code Section 311.6—that is, uttering obscene words in a public place (Rawson 1991, 258). However, a "poetic" usage by Sonia Sanchez in "TCB" (Broadside Press, 1970) provoked no such response. The work consisted of three-line "verses" arranged in "incremental repetition" along the following scheme:

wite/motha/fucka
wite/motha/fucka
wite/motha/fucka
    whitey

The burden is repeated six times, the only significant variation being the following ethnic insults that are substituted for *whitey:* namely *ofay, devil, pig, cracker,* and *honky.* The work ends with a call for collaboration: "now. That it's all sed / let's get to work." The term has become common in films dealing with African Americans (such as those by Spike Lee) and the underworld.

The term has been exclusively confined to American usage. Norman Moss made the observation in his *British/American Dictionary* (1984) that *motherfucker* is a term "so obscene as to be beyond the bounds of native British speech." That observation still holds, in spite of the infiltration of much American slang into British English. It surfaces only occasionally in Britain. When the pop star Madonna presented the Turner Prize awards in London in 2002, she created a mediated furor with her egalitarian exclamation: "Right on, motherfuckers—everyone is a winner!" While the popular press was outraged, a spokesman for Tate Britain described the remarks as "vintage Madonna. It is the sort of thing people expect her to say." The term is not current in Australian or South African English.

Although context is vital, the term clearly shows the familiar semantic process of loss of intensity. Rating the term in 1991, Hugh Rawson commented that it "now has about as much punch as much *bastard* and *bitch*." But, he continues, "the effective lives of the latter words were measured in centuries, while *motherfucker* was a force to be reckoned with for only a few decades" (1991, 258).

See also: Loss of Intensity, Weakening, or Verbicide.

Bibliography

Aman, Reinhold, ed. *The Best of Maledicta: The International Journal of Verbal Aggression.* Philadelphia: Running Press, 1997.

Major, Clarence. *Juba to Jive: A Dictionary of African-American Slang.* London: Penguin, 1994.

Malinowski, Bronislav. *Sex and Repression.* London: Kegan Paul, Trench & Trubner, 1927.

Montagu, Ashley. *An Anatomy of Swearing.* London and New York: Macmillan and Collier, 1973.

Norman, Arthur M.Z. "Army Speech and the Future of American English." *American Speech* XXXI (May 1956): 107–12.

Rawson, Hugh. *A Dictionary of Invective.* London: Hale, 1991.

Todd, Loreto. *Modern Englishes: Pidgins and Creoles.* Oxford: Basil Blackwell, 1984.

N

NICKNAMES

Naming, a crucial aspect of identity, is an important aspect of the exercise of dominance, notably evident in the naming of conquered territories by colonial powers. It is also significant that nations that undergo colonization generally acquire a great number of nicknames for their indigenous populations. The giving of nicknames to individuals, groups, and nations springs from mixed motives. Although the *Oxford English Dictionary* entry notes that nicknames are "usually given in ridicule or pleasantry," modern sociolinguistic research indicates that the attribution of group nicknames derives more from ridicule, belittlement, and prejudicial motives. They are commonly manifestations of martial and religious rivalry, competition in business or employment, or generalized xenophobia. Many of the terms in the discussion have their own entries. Because *nickname* is not a precise critical word, some scholars have taken up the term *ethnophaulism* for "ethnic slur," coined by A.A. Roback in 1944. However, because of its opaqueness, it has not achieved general currency.

Nickname itself has an interesting etymology, being originally in Middle English *an eke name,* meaning "an extra name." Through the process known as misdivision, the form was misunderstood as *a neke name* (understandable in an oral situation when the bulk of the population was illiterate) before becoming the modern form *nickname.* In one of the earliest uses of the old form, Robert Brunne wrote in his moralistic text *Handlyng Synne* (1303): "he is to blame þat ʒeveþ a man an yvle ekename" ("the person who gives someone a bad nickname is to blame"). This anticipates the general modern critical attitude, especially in the regime of political correctness. The English essayist William Hazlitt commented that "A nickname is the heaviest stone the Devil can throw at a man" ("On Nicknames," *Sketches and Essays,* 1839). Dr. Johnson (1755) erroneously but understandably derived the word from French *nom de nique,* meaning "a name of contempt," so that his definition matches that meaning: "A name given in scoff or contempt; a term of derision; an opprobrious or contemptuous appellation." His contemporary Francis Grose, in his *Classical Dictionary of the Vulgar Tongue* (1785) accepted the etymology, explaining that "Nique is a movement of the head to mark contempt for any person or thing." However, this attribution is erroneous, a notable example of **folk etymology**.

Historically, nicknames were given to distinguished individuals long before the actual term *nickname* became current. Thus Ethelred the Unready (died 1016) was styled in Anglo-Saxon Æthelred Unræd, properly meaning "ill-advised," while William II (1087–1100) was known as Rufus, that is, "red-complexioned" and Edward I (1272–1307) was termed Longshanks, that is "tall." These might be called *soubriquets,* the term for neutral or favorable nicknames, such as Edward the Confessor. However, in the course of the Hundred Years' War the English troops were so notorious for their profanity that they were nicknamed *les goddems* by their French opponents. This is seemingly the first instance of a national nickname given on the basis of unpleasant behavior.

The nicknaming of religious out-groups is a major feature of English ecclesiastical history from the Reformation onward. However, even prior to the break with Rome the followers of the reformer John Wycliffe (ca. 1330–1380) were called *Lolleres* or *Lollards,* from Middle Dutch *lollaerd,* meaning a "mumbler" or "stutterer." In a spirited exchange in Chaucer's *Canterbury Tales* (1386–1400), the Host of the Tabard Inn says of the Parson, who clearly has Wycliffite tendencies, "I smell a Lollere in the wind" (Epilogue to the *Man of Law's Tale,* l. 1171). Hostile nicknames for **Catholics** became so numerous that they have their own entry.

As sectarian strife intensified, so did the volume of derisive nicknames. Thomas Hall wrote in *The Pulpit Guarded* (1651): "We have many Sects now abroad, Ranters, Seekers, Shakers, Quakers, and now Creepers" (15). **Quaker** (ca. 1647) and **Shaker** (ca. 1648) have their own entries. In the comparative religious tolerance of the United States, especially in Maryland, founded by the Catholic Lord Baltimore as a refuge for persecuted English Catholics, a blasphemy law was passed in 1649. This was directed against "persons reproaching any other by the name or denomination of Heretic, Schismatic, Idolator, Puritan, Independent, Presbyterian, Popish priest, Lutheran, Calvinist, Anabaptist, Brownist, Antinomian, Round-Head, Separatist, or by any other name or term, in a reproachful manner relating to the subject of religion." It ordered fining, whipping, or imprisonment for offenders who did not publicly supplicate for forgiveness (Myers 1943, 46).

There are two striking features in this list of offending terms. First, it is an indiscriminate mixture of general condemnatory terms like *heretic, schismatic,* and *idolater* and names of particular sects, such as *Puritan, Lutheran,* and *Calvinist.* Second, with the passage of time, many of the names have become neutral or obsolete. *Presbyterian* and *Lutheran* are now simply denotative terms, whereas labels like *Anabaptist, Brownist, Antinomian, Roundhead,* and *Separatist* are either historical or obsolete. Only *Puritan* and *Calvinist* have retained the critical senses of being "unreasonably austere" or "extremely strict in morality and religious observance" to the point that they can still be used in an insulting fashion.

Extremists generally attract the greatest number of nicknames. In the religious fanaticism of the sixteenth and seventeenth centuries, even the term *enthusiasm,* and especially the adjective *enthusiastic,* underwent marked semantic deterioration, so that *enthusiast* came to mean a religious maniac or, in the wry definition of the *OED,* "one who believes himself to be the recipient of special divine communication." Zealotry generated ironic forms like *Bible-bigot,* used by John Wesley of himself in 1766, followed by *bible-moth* (1789) and *craw-thumpers* (defined by Grose in 1785 as "Roman Catholics, so called from their beating their breasts in the confession of their sins"). The Bible proved a potent symbol of stigmatization, found in *bible-banger* (1885), *bible-pounder*, found in both slang dictionaries of Barrère & Leland (1889) and Farmer & Henley (1890), and many variations, such as *Bible-bashing* and *bible-thumper*. *The Bible Belt*, coined about 1926, was greatly popularized by H.L. Mencken. An early reference in *The American Mercury* located Jackson, Mississippi, at "the Heart of the Bible and Lynching Belt" (February 1926, 141–42).

Political crises have the semantic effect of generating labels, and the entry for **war** shows how martial conflicts expand and accelerate the process. The origins of *Cavalier*, *Roundhead*, *Whig*, and *Tory* are covered under the entry for **political names**. Nicknames for those in power range from the serious, such as *Bloody Mary* (Mary Tudor) and *The Iron Lady* (Margaret Thatcher) to the comic and ironic, such as *Slick Willy* (Bill Clinton), *Phony Tony* (Tony Blair), and *Dubya* (George W. Bush). *Roundhead* and *Tory* were listed by Grose in 1785, as were *Taffy* for a Welshman, *Paddy* for an Irishman, and *Froglander* for a Dutchman. He defined *shit sack* as "dastardly fellow; also a non-conformist" and *Yankey, or Yankey Doodle*, as "A booby, or country lout: a name given to the New England men in North America." Dr. Johnson, whose *Dictionary* (1755) was generally more concerned with polite or "proper" use, was understandably less inclusive. The major subsequent lexicographers of slang and the underworld, namely Farmer and Henley (1890–1904) and Eric Partridge, notably in his *Slang* (1933), included a great number of terms, as have all subsequent slang dictionaries. Although many nicknames for foreigners have developed, such as *chink, coolie, coon, dago, wog,* and *wop*, there have generally been little research and specialized interest in the topic in Britain until recently.

As has partly been shown, in the United States there is far greater sensitivity to and awareness of nicknames. Furthermore, the notion of national identity is complicated by the facts of diversity, economic competition, multiculturalism, and numerous minorities. For these and other reasons an astonishing number of nicknames have evolved, both regional and ethnic, leading to comment, research, and analysis by many scholars, including H.L. Mencken, A.A. Roback, Stuart Berg Flexner, and Irving Lewis Allen. In his study *The Language of Ethnic Conflict* (1983), Allen accumulates 1,078 nicknames for more than 50 specific ethnic groups and analyzes them as markers of inter-group conflict, as part of ethnic and urban folklore, stereotyping of stigmatized subcultures and marginalized groups. He notes that they focus on group features like appearance, as in *darky* and *thicklips*; diet, as in *frog* and *sauerkraut*; occupation, such as *cotton-picking* and *grape-stomper*; negative stereotyping, such as *wetback* and *mafia*; and mispronunciation of group names, such as *eyetie* and *ayrab*. Furthermore, names of groups change into derisive adjectives, such as *russki*, or verbs, such as *to dutch*; also into stereotypes, like *pole* for a stupid person, or metaphors, like *Irish spoon* for shovel, often extended to proverbs or ethnic jokes. Allen concludes: "All ethnic name-calling is at bottom, status-disparagement" (1983, 113).

Regional nicknames abound: among them are *Dixielander*, for a Southerner generally; *Arky* for a person from Arkansas; *Okie* for one from Oklahoma, particularly a migrant worker during the Great Depression. This period of economic hardship had the semantic consequence of generating great numbers of terms for poor whites and rustics in the South. **Yankee** has a complex history, expanding from a derogatory term referring to Hollanders, then to the Dutch of New York, then to all New Englanders, then to Northerners in the Civil War. Allen (1983) shows that by far the greatest number of nicknames focus on African-Americans (233), Jews (64), Irish (55), Italians (45), and Mexicans (42). However, in the category of names used by Blacks for Whites, Allen finds no less than 111 terms, although many are regional, mild, or jocular, such as *ghost, marshmallow, thin people,* and *eel.* A possible problem with Allen's methodology is that it emphasizes volume of names rather than intensity. Obviously *gook* and *nigger* have greater individual impact that a whole range of *honky, cracker, ofay,* and so on.

In the other global varieties of English, ethnic nicknames are very common and have generally been used with colonial insensitivity and local xenophobia. Thus Australian English has *chows, chinks, slit-eyes, quangs, slants,* and *yellow bastards* for the Chinese and Asians generally, *abos* and *boongs* for the indigenous population, while *pom* has become the enduring term for the English. In South African English, the English were termed *rooineks* (red necks) and *khakis* from the period of the Boer War (1899–1902), the Indians were called *coolies* and *curry-munchers,* the Africans *kaffirs* and *munts,* and the Afrikaners *jaaps, hairy-backs,* and *rock-spiders.* These tended to thrive during the era of apartheid (1948–1994), when race and group differences were greatly emphasized, but have steadily lost currency during the period of democracy.

See also: Blason Populaire; Catholics; Coolie; Coon; Ethnic Slurs; Gook; Mencken, H.L.; Nigger; Partridge, Eric; Quakers and Shakers; Wog; Yankee.

Bibliography

Allen, Irving Lewis. *The Language of Ethnic Conflict.* Columbia: Columbia University Press, 1983.
Flexner, Stuart Berg. *A Dictionary of Nicknames.* New York: British Book Centre, 1963.
———. *I Hear America Talking.* New York: Van Nostrand–Reinhold, 1976.
Mencken, H.L. *The American Language.* New York: Knopf, 1936.
Myers, Gustavus. *History of Bigotry in the United States.* New York: Random House, 1943.
Partridge, Eric. *Slang.* London: Routledge, 1933.
Roback, A.A. *A Dictionary of International Slurs.* Cambridge, MA: Sci-Art Publishers, 1944. Reprint, Waukesha, WI: Maledicta, 1979.

NIGGER

The history of the term is largely, but not exclusively, confined to American English and to insulting references to blacks. In detail it is more complex, as are the semantic nuances, which in American English vary from extreme offensiveness when used of blacks by whites, to affectionate expressions of solidarity when used in black English. The history of the term shows three basic stages. The first is as a descriptive term not always intended to offend, recorded from ca. 1574 to 1840. However, many of the early instances derive from the practice of slavery: "One niggor Boy" comes from an inventory of slaves dated 1689, while John Anderson styled himself as "Governor over the niegors in Connecticut" in

"THE NIGGER" IN THE WOODPILE.

By the mid-1800s, *nigger* was one of the most offensive racial insults in American English—at least in some circles. In this racist parody of Republican efforts to play down the antislavery plank in their 1860 platform, candidate Abe Lincoln sits atop a construction made of rails that imprisons a black man. (Library of Congress, LC-USZ62-8898)

1766. This primal link with slavery is obviously vital, since it embodies in an intensified fashion the demeaning roles of servitude and of being an outsider that have characterized the early roles of black people in Western society. In his *Classical Dictionary of the Vulgar Tongue* (1785), Francis Grose noted that the basic term *negro* carried the sense of "slave" in uses like "I'm no man's Negro." The history of the term in the southern United States is obviously colored by the slave relationship.

The second and dominant sense is that of the contemptuous and highly offensive racial insult (ca. 1800 to the present), recorded in a dismissive comment of the poet Lord Byron to "The rest of the world—Niggers and what not" in 1811, and the comment in 1860 that "A Southern gentleman rarely, if ever, says *nigger*" (in Hundley, *Southern States,* 170). The key factor in the dynamic of insult, as with most ethnic terms, is who uses the term and the context. Thus a problematic instance is Mark Twain's comment in a letter of 1853: "I reckon I had better black my face, for in these Eastern states niggers are considerably better than white people" (*Twain's Letters,* vol. I, 4). In one of many such discriminating comments, John Dollard observed in *Caste and Class in a Southern Town* (1927): "Evidently Southern white men say nigger as standard practice, "nigruh," a slightly more respectful form, when talking to northerner (from whom they expect criticism on the score of treatment of Negroes), but never Negro; that is the hall-mark of a northerner and caste-enemy" (47).

A third usage, strictly dependent on context, is a reclaimed currency of the term by those previously insulted but used exclusively among themselves, as an affectionate, ironic, or jocular epithet. This usage is comparatively recent, with quotations dating only from the 1950s, especially in contexts expressing solidarity, such as "You know you're my nigger, man" (in J.A. Williams, *The Angry Ones* 1956–1960, chapter xxi). However, the usage was commented on in 1925 by Carl Van Vechten in *Nigger Heaven*: "While this informal epithet is freely used by Negroes among themselves, not only as a term of opprobrium, but actually as a term of endearment, its employment by a white person is always fiercely resented" (26). The term can be used as an honorific title "for a nonblack person behaving in an admirable manner associated with African-Americans" (*Random House Historical Dictionary of American Slang*, 1997). The authority's first instance is from Claude Brown's *Manchild in the Promised Land*, referring to the early 1950s: "that paddy boy is twice the nigger of any of you cats might think you are" (1965, 137). In popular culture, especially in rap, the term has been reclaimed, as is shown in groups with provocative names like *Niggaz with Attitude*. (Alternative spelling, usually of an illiterate kind, is also a way of establishing identity: it is also found in the British alternative form *wimmin,* coined in 1983.) A similarly provocative title is *Capitalist Nigger* (2003) by a Nigerian author, Chika Onyeani. The films of Spike Lee, notably *Do the Right Thing* (1989) and *Get on the Bus* (1996), which focus frankly on the Black community, use the term profusely, often in an ironic and self-mocking stereotypical fashion.

To these may be added a fourth sense, recorded for about half a century, which is not confined to Blacks or Americans, referring to any victim of racial or other prejudice, a person who is disenfranchised economically, politically, or socially. Thus *Atlantic* magazine for December 1972 observed: "The Jewish, the Italian and the Irish people were the niggers of the white world" (91). The major Irish novelist Roddy Doyle concurred in *The Commitments*: "The Irish are the niggers of Europe, lads" (1987, 13).

The extensive treatments in the *Dictionary of American Regional English* and in the *Random House Historical Dictionary of American Slang* (1997) bring out both the complexity of usage and the term's problematic origins. The second source argues that *nigger* is not, as is commonly claimed, "originally a mispronunciation of *Negro,*" but an independent early modern English term derived from Latin *niger,* "black." It also observes: "The historical record epitomized here . . . suggests that the high degree of offensiveness attached to the term *per se,* particularly in the discourse of whites, has increased markedly over time, perhaps especially during the 20th century." Of many instances, James Agate's comment "This was nigger Shakespeare" in his review of Paul Robeson's role as Othello in 1930 is especially notorious (1943, 287). The contemptuous quality of the term is reflected not simply in the main word but in the great number of compounds and idioms, such as *nigger gin* (ca. 1890>), *niggerhead* (tobacco, ca. 1809>), *nigger heaven* (the topmost balcony in a theater (ca. 1866>), and *nigger lover* (ca. 1856>). All such uses, many of them in currency for a century and a half, are marked "usually considered offensive" in *Random House*.

The high degree of offensiveness of the term has not always been registered in dictionary usage labels, as is shown in the following table:

Dictionary	Comment
OED (ca. 1900)	"colloquial"
Farmer & Henley, *Slang and Its Analogues* (1900)	no comment
Webster II (1934)	"often used familiarly; now chiefly contemptuously"
Partridge (1937)	"colloquial, often pejorative"
Mencken, *Supplement One* (1945)	"hated," "abhorred," "bitterly resented"
Webster III (1961)	"usually taken to be offensive"
Webster New World College (1970)	omitted as an "obscenity"
Concise Oxford (1986)	"offensive"
New Dictionary American Slang (1986)	symbolically marked as taboo
Juba to Jive (1994)	"usually offensive and disparaging"
Longman Dictionary of Contemporary English (1995)	"taboo"
Random House Historical Dictionary of American Slang (1997)	"usually considered offensive"
Collins (2003)	"offensive"

The trend from acceptance to condemnation is obvious, especially in the American dictionaries. The turning point clearly occurred in the 1960s, a time of increased racial sensitivity and the Civil Rights Movement. In the racially charged atmosphere of the trial of O.J. Simpson, the *New York Times* reported that Mr. Darden, a black member of the prosecution team, "his voice trembling, added that the 'N – word' was so vile that he would not utter it. It's the filthiest, dirtiest, nastiest word in the English language." (January 14, 1995, 7).

Although *nigger* is still found in British English, it has diminished in currency in the face of an increasing taboo. H.W. Fowler's *Modern English Usage* (1926) clearly regarded the term as being insulting, not *per se,* but when used of other races: "applied to others than full or partial negroes, is felt as an insult by the person described." Eric Partridge showed a mixture of accuracy and insensitivity in *Usage and Abusage* (first published in 1947 and revised up to 1980): "*Nigger* belongs only, and then in contempt or fun, to the dark-skinned African races and their descendants in America and the West Indies. Its application to the native people of India is ignorant and offensive."

There is a different dynamic in Caribbean usage, as Frederic Cassidy, the noted authority on Jamaican English, has observed: "The feeling of the Jamaican Negro that he was far above the African is reflected still in many expressions. The word *niega,* which the *OED* enters under *neger,* but which is usually spelled *nayga* or *naygur* in the dialect literature, is used by black people to condemn those of their own colour. . . . *Naygur* is often tantamount to 'good for nothing' and *neegrish* is 'mean and dispicable'" (1961, 156–57).

Although the word no longer features in other global varieties, it was previously a basic term used to demean black people in the colonial era. Thus the first white settlers to Australia (from 1788) used *nigger* of the aborigine population in the nineteenth century, but this usage has since steadily declined, having been replaced by *abo* and *boong.* Surprisingly, the *Australian National Dictionary* (1988) carries no usage label, although the early quotations are openly racist and hostile. Thus G.C. Lefroy wrote in 1845: "It is shocking . . . to see a fine young fellow cut off by the odious detestable niggers" (in C.T. Stannage, ed., *The New History of Western Australia* 1981, 95). There are also references from 1901 to "nigger hunts" (originally used in America from the mid-nineteenth century to refer to hunts for escaped slaves).

The same pattern occurred in South Africa. In his major collection *Africandersims* (1913) the Rev. Charles Pettman noted that the word was "a term of contempt widely applied to people of coloured blood, and as a rule vigorously resented by them." He carried a quotation from Olive Schreiner's powerful anticolonialist visionary novel *Trooper Peter Halkett* (1897), in which British soldiers "talk of the *niggers* they had shot, or the kraals [villages] they had destroyed" (20). Since then *nigger* has steadily declined in usage, the dominant insulting terms for black people having become *munt,* and the highly offensive *kaffir.*

See also: Blacks.

Bibliography

Agate, James. *Brief Chronicles.* London: Cape, 1943.

Cassidy, Frederic G. *Jamaica Talk.* London: Macmillan, 1961.

Dollard, John. *Caste and Class in a Southern Town.* New York: Doubleday, 1937. Reprint, Madison: University of Wisconsin Press, 1988.

Doyle, Roddy. *The Commitments.* London: Secker & Warburg, 1987.

Hundley, Daniel R. *Social Relations in Our Southern States.* New York: Henry B. Price, 1860. Reprint, Baton Rouge: Louisiana State University Press, 1979.

Lighter, J.E., ed. *Random House Historical Dictionary of American English.* Vol. II. New York: Random House, 1997.

McDavid, Raven I., Jr. "A Study in Ethnolinguistics." *The Southern Speech Journal* 25 (Summer 1960): 247–54.

Pettman, Rev. Charles. *Africanderisms.* London: Longmans Green, 1913.

Ramson, W.S., ed. *The Australian National Dictionary.* Melbourne: Oxford University Press, 1988.

Stannage, C.T., ed. *The New History of Western Australia.* Perth: University of Western Australia Press, 1981.

NON-JURORS

A historical term denoting those who in earlier times refused to swear an oath of allegiance to the English monarch. Since English law has the notion of an established church of which the monarch is the titular head, the necessity or willingness of the clergy to swear allegiance to the monarch has been a requirement since 1534, when Henry VIII proclaimed himself Supreme Head of the Church of England. The subsequent arrival of Catholic claimants to the English throne consequently created crises of conscience and constitutionality. The term *non-juror* was coined to denote those of the beneficed clergy and officers who refused to take the oath of allegiance to the Protestants William and Mary in 1689. However, the term came to be used in a hostile and emotive fashion to imply that a non-juror was a rebel and a traitor. Thus the diarist John Evelyn has an entry for February 26, 1696, describing "a conspiracy of about 30 Knights . . . many of the Irish and English Papists and Non-jurors or Jacobites (so call'd), to murder K[ing] William." The great legal authority William Blackstone ruled in 1796: "Every person properly called a non-juror, shall be adjudged a popish recusant convict." (*A recusant* was a Catholic who refused to accept Protestant authority.) The term is now historical, although members of the British Parliament are still required to make an oath of allegiance to the monarch.

See also: Formal Oaths.

Bibliography

Blackstone, William. *Commentaries.* London, 1796.

O

OATHS OF OFFICE. *See:* Formal Oaths.

OBSCENITY

Since obscenity can manifest itself in various ways, this entry focuses on the semantic changes of the terms *obscene* and *obscenity*. These changes have been curiously haphazard as different interest groups in English cultural history have sought to define the terms. In earlier times both words had a basic sense of religious violation. The emphases on sexual depravity or extreme vulgarity are basically modern interpretations dating from only the eighteenth century. Prior to that period publications were policed by the ecclesiastical courts, which were far more concerned about unorthodox views and heretical statements. However, in the last two centuries, taboos have moved from religious to sexual and racial areas. Considering the powerful impact that the concept of "obscenity" and the categorization of "obscene" have had on modern culture, especially in relation to **pornography**, the terms are comparatively recent in the history of the language and still surprisingly vague in their definitions.

The obvious problem is that what is "obscene" depends on many variables relating to age, culture, personal preferences, and notions of taboo. D.H. Lawrence rightly observed in the second paragraph of *Pornography and Obscenity* (1929): "What is obscene to Tom is not obscene Lucy or Joe, and really, the meaning of a word has to wait for majorities to decide it." Bertrand Russell had a more pragmatic view: "It is obvious that 'obscenity' is not a term capable of exact legal definition; in the practice of the courts, it means 'anything that shocks the magistrate'" (1928, 124) *Obscene* and *obscenity* do not originally have as strong a semantic overlap as might be expected. Nevertheless, both have become key terms in assessing the public acceptability of books, films, and stage performances

The basic definition of *obscenity* as given by the *Oxford English Dictionary* is "impurity, indecency, lewdness," which is broad but not entirely condemning. The first instance has a sexual emphasis, being Thomas Nashe's comment in 1589 on "Virgil's unchast Priapus and Ovid's obscenity" (*The Anatomie of Absurditie*, chapter 3). Yet John Milton provides a powerful religious use in his tract on *Divorce* (1643): "Worse than the worst obscenities of heathen superstition" (II iv). The sense of unseemly eroticism is clearly exemplified in a much later quotation from the *Christian Times* (October 6, 1893) referring to "Pictures of foul obscenity not to be surpassed in Pompeii" (995).

As the entry for **pornography** shows, prior to 1857 the application of *obscenity* to literature was problematic, since the relevant offence was termed *obscene libel.* The use of *obscenity*
to refer to "an instance of foul language" is not treated separately in the *OED* entry, but the
first recorded instance appears to be in 1768: "Whenever he [the Earl of Moreland] heard
any Profaneness or Obscenity in the Streets, he would stop to reprove and expostulate with
the Offender" (Henry Brooke, *The Fool of Quality*, III, xvi, 343). In recent decades a very
broad condemnatory sense has developed, evidenced in "The obscenity of racial hatred" in
The Times of March 21, 1970, and the comment by Robert Fisk in the *Independent* newspaper
on the Iraq war: "It was an outrage, an obscenity" (March 27, 2003).

Obscene is designated as "of doubtful etymology" by the *OED,* which nevertheless derives
it from Latin *obscenus*, which had a strong religious sense of "inauspicious, ill-omened, abominable, disgusting, filthy, lewd." Shakespeare is accorded the first quotation, in 1597, from
Richard II when the Bishop of Carlisle condemns the usurping of the throne as "So heinous,
black and obscene a deed" (IV i 122). The earlier meanings are clearly intended, in view of
the disastrous consequences of the action. However, the term possibly derives from Latin
caenum, "filth," and there are Elizabethan quotations referring to "obscene ballads" and to
"obscene and filthy communications." Robert Graves in his illuminating essay "Poetry and
Obscenity" stresses a theatrical context, deriving the second element from Latin *scænus,* and
Greek *skene*, "scene." He argues that the secondary sense of "depraved" or "indecent" developed when "plays, originally performed in honour of deities and heroes under the protection of Dionysus, god of the Mysteries, came to include scenes of indecent buffoonery
offensive to the gods themselves . . . [especially] when public sexual handling of one another
by Roman actors—the 'actresses' being boys—became fashionable" (1972, 63).

The term started to develop a sexual specialization during the seventeenth century, mainly
through the use of the phrase *obscene parts* for "private parts," from Latin *partes obscenae*
meaning the genitals. Both John Dryden in his translation (1697) of Vergil's *Æneid* (III, l.
545) and Alexander Pope in his translation (1725) of Homer's *Odyssey* use the phrase: "Her
[Scylla's] parts obscene the raging billows hide" (*Odyssey,* Book xii, l. 115). Clearly this sexual
connection lay behind the definitions of *obscene* and *obscenity* which were to become crucial in
the assessment of literature and the arts.

In 1857 the Obscene Publications Act was passed, but "only after intense opposition in both
Houses [Commons and Lords], and on the assurance of the Lord Chief Justice John Campbell
that it was to apply 'exclusively to works written with the single purpose of corrupting the morals
of youth and of an nature calculated to shock the common feelings of decency in any well-
regulated mind'" (Taylor 1954, 204–5). However, the "Campbell" Act of 1857 became modified
by some later comments made by Lord Chief Justice Alexander Cockburn in a case in 1868 (*Rex
v. Hicklin*, LR 3 QB 360 1868). Although strictly uttered *obiter dicta* and not a true definition, they
nevertheless became the standard criterion for obscenity for nearly a century:

> I think the test of obscenity is this, whether the tendency of the matter charged as obscenity is
> to deprave and corrupt those whose minds are open to such immoral influences and into
> whose hands a publication of this sort may fall.
> (cited in Craig 1962, 44)

Because this "test" did not allude to content, intention, or shock-value, it became an effective legal instrument allowing only sections of a work to be assessed. The results, in the form of numerous successful prosecutions, are discussed in the entries on **censorship** and **lawsuits**. The high profile cases naturally became a part of the public record, but in the early 1950s the number of "novels in respect of which orders for destruction have been made by various Magistrates Courts" was approximately 4,000. "The titles were all listed in a secret Blue Book that was issued to chief constables by the Home Office" and its existence was kept secret from MPs (Travis 2001, 98–99). In the Blue Book for 1954 were Daniel Defoe's *Moll Flanders* and Gustave Flaubert's *Madame Bovary*.

The eventual revision of the Obscene Publications Act in 1959 (Acts 7 & 8 Elizabeth II c. 66 § 1) resulted in the following similar definition:

> An article shall be deemed to be obscene if its effect is, taken as a whole, such as to tend to deprave and corrupt persons who are likely to read, see or hear the matter contained and embodied in it.

The phrases "into whose hands a publication of this sort may fall" and "persons who are likely to read" admitted a double standard in format and publication, whereby an edition of Boccaccio leather-bound was "literature" but in paperback became "pornography." Elements of class and gender also became explicit in the famous trial concerning D.H. Lawrence's **Lady Chatterley's Lover** in 1960 when the counsel for the prosecution asked frequently: "Is it a book that you would even wish your wife or servants to read?" However, in addition to the important qualification "taken as a whole," the new Act allowed for expert witnesses to be called by the defense. This factor more than any other produced a landmark verdict in favor of the publishers.

The United States Supreme Court has ruled that the constitutional protection of freedom of speech (which it upheld notably in *Cohen* v. *California* [1973], a case of an obscenity on a jacket) does not extend to obscenity in literature, which it defined in *Miller* v. *California* (1973) in terms of a three-part test, often referred to as "the Miller test":

(a) whether the average person, applying contemporary community standards, would find that the work, taken as a whole, appeals to the prurient interest;

(b) whether the work depicts or describes, in a patently offensive way, sexual conduct specifically defined by the applicable state law; and

(c) whether the work, taken as a whole, lacks serious literary, artistic, political, or scientific value.

Other important rulings concerning obscenity are *Roth* v. *United States* 354 U.S. 476 (1957) and *Jacobellis* v. *Ohio* 378 U.S. 184 (1964).

It is significant and anomalous that in relation to literature, stage, and film, the notions of both "obscene" and "obscenity" are still geared almost exclusively to material regarded as prurient or sexually corrupting. The modern generalized senses of "horrific," "disgusting," or "revolting" still have little significance. Thus in Shakespeare's savage tragedy *Titus Andronicus* (1590), "obscenity" in the sexual sense is not especially prominent, but unimaginably hideous crimes are staged, including rape followed by mutilation, the victim's tongue being cut out, and even cannibalism. Yet the play has never been banned or even condemned as "obscene." In recent times war has been legitimately described as "the ultimate obscenity," but films such as *Apocalypse Now!* (1979), *Platoon* (1987), and *Full Metal Jacket* (1988) containing the most gruesome depictions of war, still do not fall under the category.

See also: Censorship; *Lady Chatterley's Lover;* Lawsuits; Pornography; Victorian Period.

Bibliography

Craig, Alec. *The Banned Books of England.* London: Allen & Unwin, 1962.
DuBois, Thomas A. "Obscenity." In *Folklore: An Encyclopedia,* ed. Thomas A. Green. Santa Barbara, CA: ABC-CLIO, 1997.
Graves, Robert. "Poetry and Obscenity." In *Difficult Questions, Easy Answers.* London: Cassell, 1972.
Lawrence, D.H. *Pornography and Obscenity.* London, Faber, 1936.
Perrin, Noel. *Dr. Bowdler's Legacy.* London: Macmillan, 1969.
Robertson, Geoffrey. *Obscenity.* London: Weidenfeld and Nicolson, 1979.
Russell, Bertrand. "The Recrudescence of Puritanism." *Sceptical Essays.* London: George Allen & Unwin, 1928.
St. John-Stevas, Norman. *Obscenity and the Law.* New York: DaCapo, 1974.
Taylor, Gordon Rattray. *Sex in History.* New York: Ballantyne, 1954.
Travis, Alan. *Bound and Gagged: A Secret History of Obscenity in Britain.* London: Profile Books, 2001.
Trevelyan, John. "Obscenity and the Law." In *What the Censor Saw.* London: Michael Joseph, 1973.

OLD ENGLISH. *See:* Anglo-Saxon Period; Anglo-Saxon Terms.

OXFORD ENGLISH DICTIONARY

The latter part of the nineteenth century was a period of enormous lexicographical productivity, generating such diverse works as Roget's *Thesaurus* in 1852, Joseph Wright's *English Dialect Dictionary* (six volumes, 1898–1905), John S. Farmer and W.E. Henley's *Slang and Its Analogues, Past and Present* (seven volumes, 1890–1904), and Joseph Bosworth and T.N. Toller's *Anglo-Saxon Dictionary* (1898). The *Oxford English Dictionary,* or *A New English Dictionary on Historical Principles* or *NED* as it was originally titled, is rightly regarded as the ultimate monumental lexicographical achievement in semantic comprehensiveness and the historical reconstruction of the English language. The finished work, originally published in fascicles, or small volumes, from 1884 and 1928, comprised 414,825 headwords, about ten times the number in Dr. Johnson's dictionary of 1755.

The enterprise started in 1842 under the aegis of the Philological Society, comprising such major talents as the first appointed editor, Herbert Coleridge, who died tragically at the age of 31, and his successor, Frederick Furnivall, who supervised the editing of early texts but resigned for reasons of ill health in 1878, having taken no part in the actual editing. However, the scholar who was the dominant force in the dictionary's production was James Murray (1837–1915), so that for many years it was called "Murray's dictionary." Although he did not live to see the end of the alphabet in print, by the time he died (having reached *turn-down*) he had written almost half of the 15,487 pages, a truly astonishing achievement.

Murray's appointment as editor in 1879 might appear an unexpected choice, since he was an autodidact experienced at secondary school level, with only a conventional B.A. Pass degree from London University. However, he was awarded an Honorary LL.D. degree by St. Andrews University in 1874 for a number of advanced research projects. Long before the end of his life (in 1903) this modest and devout man wrote in terms typical of the faith and sense of duty of Victorian times: "I think it was God's will. In times of faith, I am sure of it" (Murray 1977, 341). Murray was a genuine polymath, phenomenally learned in many fields apart from the obviously relevant areas of phonetics, dialects, etymology, semantics, grammar, and comparative philology. He had acquired a working knowledge of the main Indo-European languages and many others and was, above all, extraordinarily industrious and disciplined.

Important contributions to the early planning were two papers read to the Philological Society in November 1857 by Dean Richard Chenevix Trench on "Some Deficiencies of English Dictionaries." In a major policy statement, Trench defined "the true idea of a dictionary" as being "an inventory of the language . . . all the words good or bad." The lexicographer was "an historian, not a critic" (cited in Morton 1994, 7). Considering the timing of Trench's papers in the mid-Victorian era with its great emphasis on decency and decorum, this was a bold blow for inclusiveness. The original aim was to show the life history of every word, its origin, and any changes of form and meaning. Murray wrote in 1883: "The Dictionary aims at being *exhaustive*" (Mugglestone 2000, 10). But total inclusiveness proved difficult to achieve, both historically and in terms of lexical range.

Like Dr. Johnson before him, Murray wrote a magnificent Preface setting out with great clarity the huge problem of classification that lay ahead. Following Trench's policy, Murray had to be "descriptive," accepting what he called "that vast aggregate of words and phrases which constitutes the Vocabulary of English-speaking men," an entity he compared to a huge nebula of stars with a brilliant core surrounded by zones of decreasing brightness:

> So the English Vocabulary contains a nucleus or central mass of many thousand words whose "Anglicity" is unquestioned; some of them only literary, some of them only colloquial, the great majority at once literary and colloquial—they are the *Common Words* of the language. . . . And there is absolutely no defining line in any direction: the circle of the English language has a well-defined centre but no discernible circumference.
> (*OED,* Vol. I, xvii)

Murray illustrated his model by means of a diagram to be found in the entry for **register**— that is, the diction appropriate for particular social situations or written contexts. In common with general perceptions of the structure of the vocabulary, the categories are arranged in vertical and horizontal axes. The vertical axis, which primarily concerns this study, shows the hierarchical arrangement of the categories of Literary > Common > Colloquial > Slang. The axis is a symbolic representation of the range from "proper" to "improper," from "acceptable" to "problematic." Naturally, Murray placed the category "Literary" above "Common"; today the status of "Literary" language is more problematic.

The enormous work was the collaboration of Murray preeminently, and three other major editors, Henry Bradley, William Craigie, and Charles Talbut Onions, "together with the assistance of many scholars and men of science." (These four were extraordinarily learned, but in terms of modern notions of scholarship and qualifications, only Craigie would qualify.) In addition to the etymological data and the complexity of definition, the historical method required separating the senses and illustrating them, ideally by means of one quotation per century.

The progress through what Dr. Johnson had called "the treadmill of the alphabet" proved to be enormously arduous. When Murray was appointed editor he took over two tons of accumulated material. It took six years to produce the first fascicle, or part-volume, covering *A—Ant*. This appeared in 1884, twenty-six years after the initial proposal. So painfully slow was the delivery of copy that Murray became involved in many confrontations and much acrimonious correspondence with the Delegates of the Clarendon Press, he threatening to resign and they threatening to cease publication. Murray did not have the aggression of his predecessor Furnivall, who in an earlier dispute over money had challenged the delegates in un-Victorian language: "Why do you deal thus with us? . . . Why, because you have the capital or the command of it, why screw us?" (Murray 1977, 162). When Murray died in 1915, he had written the letters A–D, H–K, O, P, and T. Only Onions and Craigie survived to the end, in 1928, by which time the total number of head-words was 414,825. In terms of the original agreement with Oxford University Press, the dictionary was to take ten years and would consist of 6,400 pages in four volumes. In fact, it took forty-five years and needed twelve volumes to accommodate its 15,487 pages.

Generally speaking, the great work was remarkably thorough in including "all the words good or bad," a quintessentially Victorian distinction unacceptable in modern descriptive linguistics. The usage note for *bloody* shows the strong contemporary awareness of decorum and class attitudes: "In general colloquial use from the Restoration [1660] to c. 1750; now constantly in the mouths of the lowest classes, but by respectable people considered 'a horrid word', on a par with obscene and profane language." (This entry was published in March 1887.)

When it came to the grossest "four-letter" words, there was the obstacle posed by the possibility of an action for "obscene libel." As the entry for **Farmer and Henley** shows, Murray was not alone in the problematic area of what Dr. J.S. Farmer called "the Dark Continent of the World of Words." The upshot was that Farmer, after having to sue his printers for breach of contract, included *fuck, cunt,* and *condom,* as well as an astonishing variety of compounds, but Murray did not. One voluntary reader, James Dixon, wrote a private letter to Murray saying that *condom* was "too utterly obscene" for inclusion (Murray 1977, 195). All these terms, however, had appeared in earlier dictionaries, such as Francis Grose's *Classical Dictionary of the Vulgar Tongue* (1785), and had vigorous histories. In her biography of her grandfather, Elisabeth K.M. Murray claims that "James had really no choice but to leave them out of the Dictionary" (1977, 195). However, the Murray correspondence shows that his contemporaries were neither unanimous nor prudish: Robinson Ellis of Trinity College, Oxford took the view (shared by three colleagues) that "'cunt' also must in *any* case be inserted, as it is a thoroughly old word with a very ancient history" (undated letter in Elisabeth Murray's possession). (Ellis was a noted classical scholar and editor of the Roman love poet Catullus.) Linda Mugglestone quotes a coy letter to Murray from one John

Hamilton in 1899 (six years after the relevant fascicle had been published). It begins cautiously: "I venture to send you a word that is not found [in the dictionary]"and without ever using the word, alludes to it as having "the same syllable as a contraction of *Contra*." Murray conceded in a reply a few days later: "It was not without regret that any word of historical standing was omitted" (2000, 10–11).

Only one contemporary review (in the *National Observer,* December 30, 1893) alluded to these omissions, accusing Murray of squeamishness and lack of courage, but the issue was not really raised until A.S.C. Ross reviewed the first *Supplement* in 1933: "it certainly seems regrettable that the perpetuation of a Victorian prudishness (inacceptable in philology beyond all other subjects) should have led to the omission of some of the commonest words in the English language: for example, *cunt,* 'female sexual organs'; *the curse,* 'menstrual period'; *to fuck,* 'to have sexual intercourse with'; *roger* = fuck" (1934, Nr ¾, 9). However, no standard modern English dictionary included the words prior to the *Penguin English Dictionary* in 1965. When Volume I of the *Supplement* appeared in 1972, the editor, Robert Burchfield, commented archly in the Preface that "two ancient terms" had been restored, with full supporting evidence.

Although the *OED* may be criticized for these omissions, it nevertheless included an extraordinary range of coarse slang, including *bugger, dildo, fart-catcher, licktwat, piss, shitsack, twat, windfucker,* and many others of similar register, reflecting the robust quality of English over the centuries. The editors obtained examples of speech indirectly, scouring all manner of written sources with indefatigable industry, including letters, journals, and notebooks in their historical reconstruction of the lower registers. Often foreign dictionaries, such as John Florio's Italian-English lexicon, *A World of Words* (1598), and Randle Cotgrave's French-English dictionary (1611), proved to be surprisingly rich sources, being less governed by decorum.

Modern readers might find that the dictionary is Victorian or dated in its lack of sensitivity to racist or demeaning terms, whether general, like *savage,* or specific, like *hottentot, nigger, coon,* and *wog.* John Willinsky's *The Empire of Words* (1994) has criticized the work, in the words of Jonathon Green, as being "overly middle-class, masculinist, chauvinist, imperialist and insulting to minority groups" (1996, 373). But these were times when Britain obviously had imperialist and colonialist attitudes toward other nations and races, when Joseph Conrad could publish *The Nigger of the Narcissus* (1897) in a major literary journal without embarrassment or comment. Furthermore, it has become common to criticize dictionaries for recording the prejudices reflected in the speech community in words like *Jew.* In defining the terminology of many vexed political and religious issues the *OED* managed to steer a course remarkably free of bias.

When Murray died in 1915, the *New English Dictionary* was already something of a misnomer, yet still thirteen years from completion. But its reputation as the ultimate authority on the English language, renowned for meticulous scholarship, was secure. He had been accorded a knighthood in 1908, as well as some twenty honorary degrees and academic awards. The consolidated work in twelve volumes was styled *The Oxford English Dictionary.* An initial one-volume *Supplement* was published in 1933, followed by a substantial four-volume *Supplement* (1972–1986) edited by Dr. Robert Burchfield and his team, bringing the work as up to date as a historical dictionary can be. Since then the two corpuses have been integrated into the Second Edition (1989), and the consolidated work is available on CD-ROM. Oxford University Press issues regular Additional Volumes.

See also: Dictionaries; Farmer, John S., and William E. Henley; Jews; Register.

Bibliography

Burchfield, Robert. "Four Letter Words and the *OED.*" *Times Literary Supplement,* October 13, 1972, 1233.
————. *Unlocking the English Language.* London: Faber, 1989.
————, ed. *A Supplement to The Oxford English Dictionary.* Oxford: Oxford University Press, 1972–1986.
Green, Jonathon. *Chasing the Sun: Dictionary Makers and the Dictionaries They Made.* London: Jonathan Cape, 1996.
Morton, Herbert C. *The Story of Webster's Third.* Cambridge: Cambridge University Press, 1994.
Mugglestone, Lynda, ed. *Lexicography and the OED.* Oxford: Oxford University Press, 2000.
Murray, Elisabeth K.M. *Caught in the Web of Words: James A.H. Murray and the Oxford English Dictionary.* New Haven: Yale University Press, 1977.
Murray, Dr. James, ed. *The Oxford English Dictionary.* Oxford: Oxford University Press, 1884–1928.
Ross, A.S.C. Review of 1933 *Supplement* to the *OED. Neuphilologische Mitteilungen* XXXV, 1934, Nr ¾.
Willinsky, John. *Empire of Words: The Reign of the OED.* London and Princeton: Princeton University Press, 1994.
Winchester, Simon. *The Meaning of Everything.* Oxford: Oxford University Press, 2000.

OZ MAGAZINE

Oz was a short-lived, highly controversial underground magazine that sprang up in the post *Chatterley* period in the United Kingdom and was the subject of a notable trial. It derived its name from the fact that most of the editors came from Australia, where an initial period of publication (1963–1969) was marked by a prosecution for obscenity in 1964. Between February 1967 and the winter of 1973 forty-eight numbers were produced in the U.K. More than simply "permissive," *Oz* was openly "alternative" in advocating sex and drugs as forms of liberation, as well as being satirical and subversive in its campaigns against the police, the judiciary, and the establishment in general. Using the same tactic as radical movements in the United States, *Oz* used four-letter words in a provocative fashion. Some prime examples are to be found in the quotations from Germaine Greer in the entry for **Swearing in Women** and in her collection *The Madwoman's Underclothes* (1986).

"The statement of our values is 'dope, rock'n'roll and fucking in the streets'. We know what we mean by this even if straights don't," wrote Warren Hague in *Oz 42,* 54. In an article entitled "Here Come De Judge" in *Oz 38* by one "Ned Ludd," the writer attacked the supposed injustice of "the system": "Such, however, is the skill of legal brains that 90 percent of the actions of the ruling bastards to steal the wealth from the workers is law" (22). Also alleged is complicity between the judiciary and the police, between "his lordship mafia in ermine" and the "piggies": "pigs are sexually repressed, politically ignorant, psychologically stunted persons who do a very good job of being automations [sic] of state repression" (23). Numbers of the magazine had such thematic titles as *Acid Oz, Gay Oz,* and *Cunt-power Oz,* edited by Germaine Greer.

A prosecution for "conspiring to corrupt public morals" was brought against a particularly outrageous number of the magazine, *Oz 28,* the "Schoolkids Issue," published in May

1970. Ironically the number had been largely edited by invited younger readers between the ages of fifteen and eighteen. In an article on the case, Keith Botsford summarized some of the contents:

> *pp. 8–9,* continued guerrilla action [against the schools] with cartoons whose balloons include "cunt" and "bollocks" [balls]. *pp. 10–11,* school atrocities including schoolmaster and schoolboy post fella-tio (?) . . . *pp. 14–15,* exams, sex freedom and Rupert Bear in congress with Gypsy Granny. (1971, 68)

The last reference would be the British equivalent of, say, "Charlie Brown in congress with Marge Simpson." It was a collage or montage juxtaposing Rupert the Bear, a British cartoon symbol of innocence and Gypsy Granny, the creation of Robert Crumb, the American underground cartoonist.

The verdict of the jury on the main charge was not guilty, but they found the defendants guilty of publishing an obscene magazine and of sending indecent articles through the post. More surprising was the severity of the sentences, in which Judge Michael Argyle, Q.C., meted out a prison term of fifteen months for the editor, Richard Neville (and twelve months and nine months respectively for his associates), provoking outrage from many quarters, including several authors and commentators not sympathetic with *Oz* itself. **Mrs. Mary Whitehouse**, the moral crusader, took the view that "it is a very good thing that the line has been drawn," but Kenneth Tynan, the notable drama critic, producer, and literary head of the National Theatre, used a different metaphor: "The battle has been joined between Judge Argyle's England and a free England." (Both views were quoted on the front page of *Oz 42*.) The sentences were, however, revoked by the Court of Appeal. Although many saw the trial's significance as being political rather than linguistic, Botsford argued that "The real martyrs" were not the editors, but "the words we use, which in the Ozzian mouth become meaningless" (1972, 72). *Oz* ceased publication not long after the trial.

See also: Press, the; Women, Swearing in.

Bibliography

Botsford, Keith. "The Innocence of *Oz.*" *Encounter,* November 1971.
Greer, Germaine. *The Madwoman's Underclothes.* London: Picador, 1986.
Palmer, Tony. *The Trials of Oz.* London: Blond and Briggs, 1971.

P

PAGAN. *See:* Heathen.

PARTRIDGE, ERIC

Eric Partridge (1894–1979) was an intrepid explorer of the lexical underworld, a highly industrious and productive lexicographer in the slang tradition of Francis Grose in the eighteenth century and Farmer and Henley in the nineteenth. Born in New Zealand, he studied in Australia and fought with the ANZACs (Australian and New Zealand forces) in World War I in Egypt and Gallipoli before being injured at the Battle of the Somme in 1915. He resumed his studies in Australia, continued at Oxford, and lectured briefly at the universities of Manchester and London. These experiences put him in touch with many varieties of English, both geographically and in terms of register, on which he was to produce a number of major contributions. In 1927 he abandoned academe, becoming an almost permanent feature in the Reading Room of the British Museum, where he worked for fifty years. He also founded the Scholartis Press, which became the vehicle for several of his early lexicographical and philological productions, prior to a long a fruitful association with the publishers Routledge.

His expanded edition of **Francis Grose**'s *Classical Dictionary of the Vulgar Tongue* (1931) was his major early work. To Grose's usually sharp, succinct definitions and comments, Partridge added his considerable knowledge. Thus Grose's rather evasive entry "C**t. The *konnos* of the Greek and the *cunnus* of the Latin dictionaries; a nasty name for a nasty thing" is amplified by two pages of lexicographical, etymological, and sociolinguistic information. His substantial study *Slang Today and Yesterday* (1933) was structured on both regional and historical bases, and contained in its 470 pages some twenty-five different kinds of specialist slang, ranging from Cockney, the Law, the Church, the Theatre, Sailors, Soldiers, and Yiddish, as well as the American and various colonial varieties. This was followed by *A Dictionary of Slang and Unconventional English* (1937) and *A Dictionary of the Underworld* (1949), dealing with both English and American varieties.

Perhaps his most illuminating and original work was *Shakespeare's Bawdy* (1947), which carried the trenchant remark in the Preface: "If Shakespearean criticism had not so largely been in the hands of academics and cranks, a study of Shakespeare's attitude towards sex and his use of the broad jest might have appeared at any time since 1918" (vii). Partridge elucidated the surprising, even shocking, volume of *double-entendres* and bawdy jests beneath the apparently bland and innocent surface of the Shakespearean text, produced under circumstances of fairly stringent censorship. The aim was not simply to be salacious, but to illuminate the extraordinary ironies and overtones that can reverberate from a simple exchange. Thus Hamlet's farewell to Ophelia: "Get thee to a nunnery," seemingly poignant, becomes a bitter, double-edged rejection when it is explained that in Elizabethan slang *nunnery* had the ironic sense of "brothel." Similarly, the coded slang usage of *nothing* to mean "an 'o' thing," that is, the vagina, adds spice to the title of *Much Ado About Nothing,* and is clearly so used by Hamlet in his riposte to Ophelia's comment "I think nothing my lord," namely, "That's a fair thought to lie between maid's legs" (III iv 111–12). Partridge is direct in exploring what he calls "the fertility and ingenuity of Shakespeare's amative fancy" by listing dozens of terms he categorizes as "the pudend-synonymy" (1947, 24). He was also the first scholar to bring out the important and complex aspects of class and gender in bawdy:

> Sexual dialogue between men is, no less in Shakespeare than in the smoking-room or compartment, frank and often coarse; between members of the lower classes, both coarse and, often, brutal; between members of the middle class—well we hear very little of that!; between aristocrats and other members of the upper and leisured class, it is still frank—it is frequently very frank indeed—but is also witty.
> (1947, 34)

Partridge's etymological dictionary *Origins* followed in 1958. It was original in that entries started with remote roots, not with the conventional headwords, making the search more interesting and surprising. In addition he wrote a number of works more in the prescriptive tradition, such as *Usage and Abusage* (1942); *Chamber of Horrors,* "a Glossary of Official Jargon" (1952); and *You Have Point There* (1953), on punctuation. In all he wrote some thirty-five works, many of which went through several editions. Unlike most modern lexicographers who operate in teams, Partridge worked alone, chiefly in difficult and little-charted territory. This quality gives his works the freedom, personality, and character of his great predecessors, Francis Grose and Samuel Johnson, although it also exposes him to the risk of error. Some have pointed out questionable etymologies in his work, but the *Oxford English Dictionary* cites him more than 770 times, since frequently the first recorded instance of some idiomatic phrase is found in one his voluminous collections.

See also: Dictionaries; Grose, Captain Francis.

Bibliography

Green, Jonathon. *Chasing the Sun: Dictionary Makers and the Dictionaries They Made.* London: Jonathan Cape, 1996.

Partridge, Eric. *A Dictionary of Slang and Unconventional English.* London: Routledge, 1937.

———. *Usage and Abusage.* London: Routledge, 1942.

———. *A Dictionary of the Underworld.* London: Routledge, 1949.

———. *Shakespeare's Bawdy.* London: Routledge, 1947.

———. *Origins.* London: Routledge, 1958.

———. *Slang Today and Yesterday.* London: Routledge, 1960.

Partridge, Eric, ed. *A Classical Dictionary of the Vulgar Tongue by Captain Francis Grose.* London: Scholartis, 1931.

Among the most notorious cases of perjury in English history is that of Titus Oates, who in 1678 made a deposition alleging a Catholic conspiracy to kill King Charles II. When the so-called Popish Plot was later exposed as a fabrication, Oates was publicly disgraced. (©AAAC/Topham/The Image Works)

PENIS. *See:* Genitalia

PERJURY

Perjury is the most extreme violation of verbal trust, more severe than lying in that it involves either breaking or abusing a formal oath in a matter of great personal or even national importance. Whereas lying may not lead to any serious consequences, the punishments for perjury are severe and public. However, not all cases are discovered.

English history has witnessed some sensational examples, two of the most notable concerning Catholic conspiracies, with different outcomes. The notorious equivocation of the Jesuit Father Garnet over his involvement in the Gunpowder Plot (1605, covered in the entry for **William Shakespeare**) was discovered almost immediately, was widely publicized, exacerbated already powerful anti-Catholic feelings, and permanently tarnished the name of *Jesuit.* By contrast the Popish Plot (1678) came to light when Titus Oates and a collaborator, Israel Tonge, both fervent anti-papists obsessed by the Jesuit menace, made a deposition to a magistrate claiming to have uncovered a conspiracy to kill King Charles II and the Duke of York, a Catholic. Such was the vehemence of anti-Catholic feeling that the conspiracy was widely believed, Oates becoming a national hero and being awarded a pension for several years. However, when the conspiracy was exposed as a cunning fabrication, Oates was publicly disgraced, placed in the pillory, pelted with eggs and rubbish, and publicly whipped through the streets of London. The initial success of the Popish Plot shows the efficacy of Adolf Hitler's observation: "The broad mass of a nation will more easily fall victim to a big lie than to a small one" (*Mein Kampf,* 1925, vol. I). As the entry for **Jews** shows, he himself and the Nazis fell victim to the anti-Semitic propaganda of *Protocols of the Elders of Zion,* also a fabrication.

PHONETIC PATTERNS

The relationship between sound and sense in swearing is predicated on the notion of "sound symbolism," which is necessarily complex, relative, and partly a matter of personal preference. Yet particular patterns of concentration can be detected, suggesting a general or fashionable predilection for particular sounds. On the one hand there is the obvious fact that many of the most potent swearing terms in English begin with the consonant *b,* as in *bastard, bitch, blasted, bloody,* and *bugger;* with *d,* as in *damn, darn, devil,* and *drat;* and with *f,* as in *footling, frigging,* and *fucking.*

Two other factors of relativity are those of time and geographical location. Thus from a historical perspective, only *bitch, bugger,* and *devil* of the listed terms were current in the Middle Ages. Furthermore, *blasted, bloody, bugger, drat,* and *footling* are not really current in the United States. These differences in currency obviously limit the notion of universality, necessary to validating any generalization of sound symbolism. Ethnic insults, on the other hand, seem clearly to fall into two distinct patterns, that of shortness and that of the diminutive. In the first category are *frog, coon, jap, yid, mick, kike, hun, chink, wop, wog, kraut, spic, nip,* and *gook.* In the second are *coolie, yankee, frenchy, wiwi, sheeny, limey, jerry, eyetie, honkie,* and *paki.* Both categories extend back over two and a half centuries.

Discussing the vocabulary of love in *A Word in Your Ear* (1942), Ivor Brown commented: "The strange thing about the vocabulary of passion is the inadequacy of words for love's fulfilling. The commonest in use is a mean and ugly monosyllable which is not fit even to be an oath, while the correct and printable are heavy and dull" (89). It is left to the reader to deduce the words implied. At the other extreme was the British grandmother who wrote to Kenneth Tynan in 1965 congratulating him for having articulated what she called "the sweet word *fuck*" on television (1988, 238).

In *The Cambridge Encyclopedia of the English Language,* David Crystal gives emphasis to both initial and final consonants, for example final *k* as in *bohunk, chink, dork, dyke, fuck, lunk, mick, prick, punk, schmuck,* and *spick* (1995, 251). While the individual terms are the "building blocks" of swearing, other phonetic factors come into play, such as **alliteration** (*bloody bastard*) and **rhythm** (*absobloodylutely*). These are often more important shaping forces than semantic content of the words in question.

See also: Alliteration; Rhyme; Rhythm.

Bibliography

Brown, Ivor. *Ivor Brown's Book of Words.* London: Jonathan Cape, 1944.
Crystal, David, ed. *The Cambridge Encyclopedia of the English Language.* Cambridge: Cambridge University Press, 1995.
Tynan, Kathleen. *The Life of Kenneth Tynan.* London: Methuen, 1988.

PIDGIN ENGLISH

A linguistic consequence of empire has been the growth of pidgins throughout those parts of the world colonized by the British. Pidgins are rudimentary communication systems that grow up spontaneously in the contexts of colonialism or business between groups who do not share a common language. They are not fully developed languages, but the makeshift simplified nucleus of a contact language in which most of the vocabulary is, expectedly, drawn from the dominant group. Research into pidgins has burgeoned recently and shown them to be very diverse and flexible. In her study *Modern Englishes: Pidgins and Creoles* (1984), Loreto Todd distinguished no less than thirty-one varieties of English pidgins and creoles, principally located in West Africa, the West Indies, and the Pacific. The curious name *pidgin* derives from a Chinese corruption of English *business*. In the first recorded reference, Captain Basil Hall noted in his *Account of a Voyage to Corea* (1826): "I afterwards learned that 'pigeon,' in that strange jargon spoken in Canton by way of English, means 'business'" (vi, 288). ("Pigeon" is thus an incorrect correction of "pidgin," but did become established for decades.) Originally the term was limited to the China and the Straits settlements.

Since pidgins are essentially oral, male-centered in origin, and direct in their transmission, notions of taboo and decency are largely absent. The point was made when Captain Hall visited the Sandwich Islands in 1820, and an islander greeted him with an odd series of salutations: "Very glad to see you! Damn your eyes! Me like English very much. Devilish hot, sir! Goddam!" (1831, 89). The man was merely repeating the emphatic points of communication left by Captain James Cook's expedition in 1778.

In a number of pidgins, terms regarded as swearwords or indecent in "Standard English" are used as inoffensive general terms. The most prevalent in Papua New Guinea Tok Pisin (Talk Pidgin) is *baga,* from *bugger,* meaning simply and generally "a man." This has generated *lesbaga* ("lazy bugger") and the intransitive verb form *bagarap* ("bugger up"), defined broadly as "to break, become impaired, have an accident happen to, become exhausted or injured, disintegrate," while the form *bagarapim* covers the transitive senses of "to destroy, break etc., rape, render useless." In the *Nupela* [New] *Testament* God's destruction of Sodom and Gomorrah is rendered by the same term. In the *Liklik Katolik Baibel,* Lazarus is characterized as a *rabish man,* derived from "rubbish," but meaning in Neo Melanesian "without wealth or standing in the community" (Hall 1966, 92). Other central terms are *bulsitim* (from "bullshit") meaning "to deceive or cheat," and *sit* ("shit") meaning "residue," as in *sit bilong faia* ("shit from the fire" for "ashes"). *As* (from "arse") is even more highly generalized, meaning "buttocks, bottom, stump, underlying cause, place of origin, underside, rear." Curiously *baksait* means only "back" or "rear," but not "buttocks." Robert A. Hall Jr. notes that English-speaking missionaries, naturally concerned about these taboo connotations, overcorrected *as* to *has* and *sit* to *chit* (1966, 91–92).

The centrality of these derogatory terms indicates, Loreto Todd argues, that "the local people were disparaged by their overseers" (1984, 253). Other scholars, such as Robert A. Hall Jr., surmise that although "many of these words were taken over unsuspectingly by natives who heard coarse-mouthed sailors and traders use them in every-day speech; others may possibly have been foisted on the natives by Europeans who thought that they would have a bit of fun thereby" (1966, 91–92).

The general point is that these pidgin speakers acquired their speech in contexts where the formal separation of registers is not observed: taboo, slang, polite, and formal words all jostle together. Thus in Cameroon Pidgin, the basic vocabulary of the body consists of *anus,* which is technical, *bɛlɛ* ("belly") and *bobi* ("bubby," "breast"), which are informal, and *pis* and *shit,* which are vulgar. The form *piccanin* and variants, derived from Portuguese *pequenino,* meaning "very little" has become widely used in pidgins to mean "small." *Pickaninny* is defined in Grose (1785) as "a young child, an infant" and marked as a *"Negro term."* In this sense it is generally now regarded as offensive in South Africa and the United States.

Bibliography

Hall, Captain Basil. *Fragments of Voyages and Travels.* Edinburgh, 1831.
Hall, Robert A., Jr. *Pidgin and Creole Languages.* Ithaca: Cornell University Press, 1966.
Romaine, Suzanne. *Pidgins and Creoles.* London, New York: Longman, 1988.
Todd, Loreto. *Modern Englishes: Pidgins and Creoles.* Oxford: Basil Blackwell, 1984.

PISS

As is common with excretory and copulatory terms, *piss* has acquired many idiomatic slang usages in modern varieties of English, although it is generally eschewed in formal print. The usage note in the *Oxford English Dictionary,* "not now in polite use," reminds us that it previously had a wide general currency. It is recorded in Scripture in both the Wycliffe and King James versions of the Bible, 1388 and 1611 respectively: "men that sit in the wall, that they may eat their own dung and drink their own piss" (II Kings 18:27 in the King James Bible, 1611). It was also used in medieval medical texts, such as Lanfranc's *Cirugerie* ("Surgery," ca. 1400): "til that he pisse blood" (62). The old word for the dandelion was *pissabed* on account of its diuretic properties, and the general French term is still the related *pissenlit.* With the subsequent separation of registers in English, the word has become inappropriate in professional discourse. Despite being a coarse four-letter word, *piss* is not Anglo-Saxon, the earliest recorded instance being 1290, well into the Middle English period. It is derived from French *pissier* but has no ulterior Romance root, and is often explained as being "echoic" or "onomatopoetic." The word was also borrowed into German, Swedish, and other Germanic languages, originally as a euphemism.

Chaucer uses the term, but chiefly in the tales of the less respectable characters, such as the Miller and Reve. However, the water conduit near the Royal Exchange in London set up by John Wels, the lord mayor, in 1430 was graphically termed the Pissing Conduit because of its thin stream. In an expansive gesture in Shakespeare's *Henry VI, Part 2* the King announces: "I charge and command that of the City's cost / The Pissing Conduit run nothing but claret" (IV vi 4–5). A *pissing* while was a common demotic phrase for a small interval of time in Elizabethan times (also found in **Shakespeare**), and in Restoration drama *piss!* was a vulgar expletive. Eric Partridge's *Dictionary of Historical Slang* (1937) lists no less than forty entries for the term, most of them idioms. Proverbial usages include "Everything helps, quoth the wren, when she pissed into the sea" (1623, quoted in the *Oxford Dictionary of Proverbs*).

Francis Grose included in his *Classical Dictionary of the Vulgar Tongue* (1785) such graphic idioms as *pissing pins and needles* for "to have a gonorrhea," *piss-burned* for "discoloured," and *piss-proud* for "to have a false erection." Other major authors of the eighteenth century using the term were **Jonathan Swift**, **Samuel Johnson**, and Lady Mary Wortley Montagu, while Lord Byron dismissed what he called "Johnny Keats' piss-a-bed poetry" (Rawson 1991, 301). Thereafter, in common with other coarse terms, the word's currency diminished in the face of Victorian censoriousness. Thus the euphemistic form *pee,* recorded from about 1788, began as nursery talk, also being used of animals, and has since developed a wide currency, despite its origins being transparent. The same pattern is found in *piddle,* described by Grose (1785) as "a childish expression; as 'Mammy I want to piddle.'" He also notes that *piddling* means trifling.

Most of the current idiomatic uses, such as the variations of *piss off* meaning "to annoy, to be annoyed, to leave unceremoniously, or to be told to go away," date only from World War II. However, T.E. Lawrence antedates these with the abrupt direction "You piss off, Pissquick" in *The Mint* (1922, 186). From the 1950s and later come the phrases *to piss about, to piss away* money or profits, and odd British formations such as *pisser* (a bar), *pissily* (feebly), *piss artist* (a drunken incompetent), and *to take the piss* (tease, pull someone's leg). Hugh Rawson includes a considerable volume of recent American usage in his *Dictionary of Invective* (1991), while Timothy Jay's analyses of student speech showed that the word did not have a high taboo rating and its frequency was virtually identical for male and female students (1992, 143–51). Alice Walker created a remarkable instance in *The Color Purple* when Shug Avery comments: "I think it pisses God off if you walk by the color purple in a field somewhere and don't notice it" (1983, 167). Generally speaking, there is currently little difference between American and British English in terms of degree of taboo and breadth of currency. However, although both varieties have the euphemistic form *peed off,* only the American has the "double" euphemisms *teed off* and *kissed off.* In other global varieties, both Australian and South African English tend to follow the British pattern, with few original inventions: thus only Australian English has the picturesque phrase *to piss in [someone's] pocket* for "to try to ingratiate oneself." This is probably a survival of *to piss down one's back,* recorded by Grose in 1785 in the sense of "to flatter." Nevertheless, the word has not recovered its general use in formal print.

See also: "Four-Letter" Words.

Bibliography

Jay, Timothy. *Cursing in America.* Philadelphia: J. Benjamins, 1992.
Partridge, Eric. *Dictionary of Slang and Unconventional English.* London: Routledge, 1937.
Rawson, Hugh. *Dictionary of Invective.* London: Hale, 1991.
Walker, Alice. *The Color Purple.* London: The Women's Press, 1983.
Wilkes, George. *A Dictionary of Australian Colloquialisms.* 2nd ed. Sydney: Sydney University Press, 1990.

POLICE

Until the comparatively recent past, there were no formal police. Cities were walled for their own protection; by order the gates were closed and a curfew was maintained all night. Rudimentary protection was supplied by *the Watch,* a term dating from the fourteenth century.

Even in eighteenth-century London there were savage gangs like the Mohocks roaming the streets and burglary was rife. Highwaymen presented a continuing threat in fact and in literature. Consequently, ordinary law-abiding citizens welcomed the passing of the New Metropolitan Police Act in 1828. From the name of its prime mover, Mr. (later Sir) Robert Peel came the affectionate names *peeler* (1817) and *bobby* (1851). However, since *peeler* originally referred to the Irish Constabulary, the name was less popular: the slogan "Kill all Peelers" is still current in Northern Ireland. In general the informal terms for the Police, such as *copper* (1846), were in the past neutral, polite, or affectionate. However, underground slang was not complimentary: *Pig* is defined as "a police officer" in the anonymous *Lexicon Balatronicum* (1811), a recycling of Francis Grose's *Classical Dictionary of the Vulgar Tongue* (1785) with an illustrating quotation: "Floor the pig and bolt" for "knock down the officer and run away." Amazingly, the term seems to have lain dormant for nearly two centuries until its resuscitation in the social and political upheavals in America during the 1960s, although Stuart Berg Flexner gives 1848 as the date of the first American instance.

"Kill the Pigs!" became an inflammatory slogan in the United States, first of the Civil Rights Movement and then of radical students. The rioting surrounding the Democratic Convention in Chicago in 1968 was reported by the *New York Times* in these terms: "Chants of '——the pigs' and 'dirty pigs' drowned out exhortations from the speaker's stand to 'sit down.'" (The U.S. Government Printing Office refused to print the Walker Report *Rights in Conflict* (1968) covering these events because of the Chairman's insistence on faithfully transcribing the terminology verbatim.) Norman Mailer's "informal history" of the two conventions, *Miami and the Siege of Chicago* traces the development of *pig* as a term of political insult with slogans like "VOTE PIG IN 1968" (1969, 133).

As with many terms of insult, the word has become used loosely of any authority figure. In the buildup to the tragic shootings at Kent State University on May 4, 1970, according to James A. Michener, "Girls were particularly abusive, using the foulest language and taunting the Guardsmen [the Ohio National Guard] with being 'shit-heels, motherfuckers, and half-ass pigs'" (cited in Rawson 1991, 2). In the United Kingdom the radical alternative magazine *Oz* carried an article on the administration of justice by one "Ned Ludd" defining "piggies": "pigs are sexually repressed, politically ignorant, psychologically stunted persons who do a very good job of being automations [*sic*] of state repression" (*Oz* 38, 23). In general the term has become less current in Britain in recent decades.

Also predominantly American in usage is the less provocative term *fuzz*, which the *Random House Historical Dictionary of American Slang* marks as "origin unknown," but recorded from 1929 in Irwin, *Tramp and Underground Slang* (1931): "a detective, prison guard or turnkey." There are, of course, many slang terms for the police: Jonathon Green gives over sixty in his *Slang Thesaurus* (1986). But most of them are underground argot or code words used by particular groups, rather than terms of insult.

Bibliography

Green, Jonathon. *The Slang Thesaurus*. New York: Penguin, 1986.
Mailer, Norman. *Miami and the Siege of Chicago*. New York: Penguin, 1969.
Rawson, Hugh. *A Dictionary of Invective*. London: Hale, 1991.

POLITICAL CORRECTNESS

Political correctness is a curious sociolinguistic phenomenon, being a form of self-censorship and conformity that has grown up, paradoxically, in free Western societies, especially in America in the last two decades. Generated by attitudes reflecting social sensitivity rather than frankness, it essentially seeks to eliminate prejudicial language and alter attitudes in addressing a whole range of social and political issues, including culture, education, curricula, gender, disability, and ethnicity. Language is naturally crucial to this dynamic of change, since political correctness involves a whole series of redefinitions of conditions, roles, attitudes, and programs. The axiomatic assumption is that to change language is to change social attitudes. Whereas euphemism and other forms of verbal sanitization have grown up spontaneously in the speech community, political correctness derives from less easily defined origins and pressures.

The formula "politically correct" has been traced back to the American New Left in the 1960s, and the terminology itself probably originated from an English translation of Chairman Mao's *Little Red Book*. (See Cameron in Dunant, ed., 1994, 18–19.) Although the Maoist sense was "conforming to the party line or expectations," the formula came to be used in an ironic or self-deprecating sense in the early years of its currency. However, by the late 1980s political correctness had assumed a whole range of agendas and become a major area of debate, notably in America. On certain campuses attitudes of conformity hardened into programmatic requirements in codes of speech and behavior, often on issues unconcerned with politics *per se*. These were widely criticized (and in some cases legally overthrown) as violating the First Amendment of the Constitution. The irony that institutions that had traditionally upheld free speech and open debate were becoming centers of illiberal censorship and conformity was not lost on critics and opponents. They stigmatized the movement as both an attempt at "Orwellian" thought control achieved by language manipulation and a new "McCarthyite" witch hunt.

Curiously, the most common sources historically of complaint against abusive language, namely religious oaths and sexual insults, have not been the major focus of the debate. Instead, the concentration has been on terms for ethnic groups, disabilities, material deprivations, and criminal behavior, generating new areas of taboo and new euphemisms. Some of these were traditional, such as *financially underprivileged* instead of *poor*. But *Black*, previously euphemized by such terms as *colored* and *darky*, was now avoided as far as possible, even in traditional formations such as *blackboard* and the *black* pieces in chess. In parallel *white* was increasingly replaced by the curious misnomer *Caucasian*. In addition, new areas of prejudice were highlighted by the suffix *-ism* and *-ist*. While this suffix is established in modern forms like *racism* from the 1930s, new forms appeared simultaneously in *sexism* (1968), *ageism* (1969), *ableism* (1981), and *lookism* (1978). *Classism* has been recycled, having been first recorded in 1842 as "the curse of England and Englishmen" in Samuel Bamford's *Passages in the Life of a Radical* (II, xviii, 89).

Portentous pseudo-classical labels like *phallocentric, gynophobic,* and *logocentric* use an arcane register to suggest an agenda. In one of the movement's most publicized ideological categorizations, "the canon of traditional western culture" sketched by Professor John Searle as existing "from, say, Socrates to Wittgenstein in philosophy, and from Homer to James Joyce in literature" (*New York Review of Books,* December 6, 1990, 34), was dismissed and trivialized by extreme political correctionists as being the provenance of "dead white males," often abbreviated to *d.w.m.,* later extended and capitalized to "Dead White European Males" (DWEMs). This offensive formulation exploited precisely the racist and sexist categorizations that the propagandists claim to condemn. John Anette's essay "The Culture Wars on the American Campus" (in Dunant, ed., 1994) recounts some of the more violent episodes in the campaign against "Eurocentric culture."

Politically correct language typically avoids traditionally judgmental terms, preferring an artificial currency of polysyllabic abstract euphemistic substitutions. Thus *drug addiction* is avoided, the preferred formula being "substance dependence," "visually impaired" is preferred to *blind,* while "sex worker" is the politically correct term for *prostitute.* Although *cripple* and *spastic* have become taboo, some formulas, such as "differently abled" for *disabled,* have proved too artificial to gain real currency.

Such substitutions, though apparently trivial, have provoked some scathing ripostes. Barbara Ehrenreich has questioned the efficacy of cosmetic linguistic changes upon underlying attitudes: "If you outlaw the term 'girl' instead of 'woman' you're not going to do a thing about the sexist attitudes underneath . . . there is a tendency to confuse verbal purification with real social change. . . . Now I'm all for verbal uplift . . . [but] verbal uplift is not the revolution" (in Dunant, ed., 1994, 23–24).

In a devastating rejection of the strategy of "verbal uplift" and a radical questioning of its motives, Robert Hughes commented in his polemical commentary on America, *Culture of Complaint* (1993):

> We want to create a sort of linguistic Lourdes, where evil and misfortune are dispelled by a dip in the waters of euphemism. Does the cripple rise from his wheelchair, or feel better about being stuck in it, because someone . . . decided that, for official purposes, he was "physically challenged"?
> (18–19)

These objections go to the heart of the matter, questioning the assumption that changing the language truly solves social and political problems. Clearly George Orwell's artificial "Newspeak" in *1984* was designed to make "thought crime" impossible by eliminating certain crucial concept-words like "free," which Big Brother considered undesirable or subversive (1972, 299). It is a different matter to assume that verbal substitutions will alter mental and political attitudes in a free society. They may, however, serve the role of "raising consciousness." Some critics have gone further, finding bowdlerism, intellectual intimidation, and a degree of pharisaic hypocrisy: "It seems to me that the main purpose of today's bowdlerism is less to protect the ostensible targets of prejudice—black people, women or whomever—than to demonstrate the moral purity of the expurgators, their sensitivity to the evils of prejudice and discrimination" (Melanie Phillips, in Dunant, ed., 1994, 47).

Furthermore, politically correct language is the formulation of a militant minority; it is not the spontaneous creation of the speech community, least of all any particular deprived sector of it. The curious history of *African-American* is germane in this respect. It was first formulated in the 1850s in the United States by black social leaders who wished to avoid the stigmatic overtones of *Black* and *Negro*. It then diminished in currency before being revived from the 1960s as the politically correct term. In Deborah Cameron's terms: "Is not precisely the point of the linguistic intervention to challenge the kind of discourse that defines people by skin colour?" (in Dunant, ed., 1994, 28). While this sounds plausible, the attitudes of those affected by prejudice, when they are consulted, turn out to be quite different. David Crystal points out: "In one 1991 survey of black Americans, carried out in the USA by the black-oriented Joint Center for Political and Economic Studies, over 70 percent of blacks said that they preferred to be called *black*, notwithstanding the supposed contemporary vogue for the politically correct *African-American*" (1995, 177).

A parallel case emerges from the Cape Province of South Africa. From the 1830s the people of mixed race were referred to as *Coloured*, a term that carried increasingly stigmatic overtones in the racial categorization of the apartheid system. With the coming of the new democratic and egalitarian dispensation after the watershed election in 1994, various pressure groups started to campaign for the substitution of "mixed race." However, a survey of the people themselves carried out by the Johannesburg *Star* newspaper in 1994 found that 75 per cent of those polled "did not mind being referred to as Coloured" (October 15–16, 9). Today *Coloured* is their preferred term.

The debate over the efficacy of politically correct language remains unresolved. Although there seem to be more critics than advocates, this mode of language, at once "raising consciousness" and camouflaging social problems, maintains its curious semiofficial status.

See also: Disability and Deformity; Euphemisms; South Africa.

Bibliography

Crystal, David. *The Cambridge Encyclopaedia of the English Language.* Cambridge: Cambridge University Press, 1995.

Dunant, Sarah, ed. *The War of Words: The Political Correctness Debate.* London: Virago, 1994.

Erkens, Rainer, and John Kane-Berman, eds. *Political Correctness in South Africa.* Braamfontein: South African Institute of Race Relations, 2000.

Friedman, Marylin, and Jan Narveson. *Political Correctness: For and Against.* Lanham, MD: Rowman and Littlefield, 1995.

Hughes, Robert. *Culture of Complaint.* New York: Oxford University Press, 1993.

Orwell, George. *Nineteen Eighty-Four.* Harmondsworth: Penguin, 1972.

POLITICAL NAMES

Political names commonly reflect the *status quo* and its assumptions, labels being frequently given to extremists for or against the established order. Their emotive quality depends on the degree of perceived threat that the party constitutes. Thus *communist* was, and continues to be, a political swearword in the United States, just as *capitalist* previously had the same emotive function in communist rhetoric, together with *bourgeois* and *proletariat*. In European political discourse, by contrast, all these terms are less contentious. Furthermore, crises have the semantic effect of generating labels for the contestants. These are often inflammatory and commonly follow one of two semantic routes: that of weakening and loss of intensity, alternatively that of obsolescence.

At the time of the English Civil War (1641–1642), the Royalists were termed the Cavaliers, while those opposing the king were called Roundheads. Although *cavalier* had been in the language since about 1470 in the sense of a horseman, the application to the supporters of Charles I arose promptly at the beginning of the war in 1641. (The term was later charmingly defined by Dr. Johnson [1755] as "a gay sprightly military man.") *Roundhead,* on the other hand, was a new term, also coined in 1641, alluding ironically to the small and limited compass of their minds. This stereotype of attributing a lack of intelligence to supporters of "the other side" is typical. (Francis Grose suggested in his slang dictionary [1785] that the name mocked the Puritan hairstyle, since they were said "the make use of a bowl as a guide to trim their hair," whereas the Royalists typically wore long hair.) Both names are now historical and obsolete.

Similarly, *Whig* and *Tory* sprang into being as political labels during the constitutional crisis in 1679–1680 over whether James Duke of York, a Roman Catholic, should be allowed to ascend the throne of Protestant England. Both were denigrating nicknames, *Tories* (ca. 1646) originally referring to dispossessed Irish outlaws, robbers, or bandits, and *Whigs* (ca. 1646) to Scottish yokels. They remained the nicknames of the two major English political parties for centuries, the *Tories* being the party supporting the traditional balance of authority between Crown and the Church, the *Whigs* being more in favor of reforming the established order. *Whig* has now been obsolete for over a century, having been superseded by *Labour* in 1900; *Tory* is still in use, but as a stigmatic term meaning an ultra Conservative. (*Conservative* itself was coined ca. 1835.) The political use of *Right* and *Left* derives from the disposition of the parties in the French National Assembly about 1789. *Radical,* now an acceptable term in most circles, was a highly emotive label, almost an insult two centuries ago, when the idea of a major change in the political dispensation was unpopular. Sir Walter Scott wrote in a letter of October 16, 1819: "Radical is a word in very bad odour here, being used to denote a set of blackguards." The term became so inflammatory that it was euphemized to *r-d-c-l.*

With the political upheavals in Europe in the nineteenth century, the term *revolutionary* became a powerful political label, but the Reign of Terror in France (1789–1794) gave rise to a far more terrible coinage. Edmund Burke wrote memorably in 1795: "Thousands of those Hell-hounds called Terrorists . . . are let loose on the people" (*Letters on Proposals for Peace with the Regicides of France* iv, Works IX, 75). Since that time both *terrorist* and *terrorism* (coined in the same year) have become regrettably commonplace. The power of the terms is attested to by such euphemisms as *freedom fighter* (from 1942). More surprising is the stigmatic use of the same term from differing standpoints as the political status quo changes. Thus in apartheid South Africa *liberal* was used by the ruling conservatives to mean "radical" and "revolutionary"; in the more socialist ambiance since 1994, *liberal* has become equated with "conservative."

Many political names are eponymous—that is, derived from individuals—usually of an extremist kind, and flagged by the suffixes *–ist* or *–ite.* Probably the earliest is found in the condemning phrase "pestilent *Machiavellian* policie," used by Robert Greene in *A Groatsworth of Wit* (1592) to mean "cynical, agnostic and opportunist." Although this is a travesty of

Machiavelli's philosophy, the derogatory associations have remained. (*Politician* was itself originally a highly critical term, meaning an unprincipled schemer: in Shakespeare the two most common adjectives qualifying it are *vile* and *scurvy*.) Less well known is *Chauvinist,* from Nicolas Chauvin, whose idolatory of Napoleon and French military glory was caricatured in a play in 1831. *Chauvinist* is recorded ca. 1870 in the general sense of an extreme patriot, then fell into disuse before being revived in feminist rhetoric in the emotive slogan *male chauvinist pig* ca. 1970, which has driven out the original political sense. Most eponymous labels have simpler histories, such as *Marxist* (1889>), *Trotskyite* (1919>), *Stalinist* (1928>), *McCarthyism* (1950>), *Maoist* (1964>), and *Thatcherite* (1979>). Many are used in a highly emotive and imprecise fashion: *anarchist* is recorded from the seventeenth century before becoming a political catchword from the 1860s. A recent revival has been *fascist,* originally borrowed into English about 1921 in relation to Benito Mussolini's movement in Italy, but increasingly used to mean rigid, authoritarian, or doctrinaire. Similar formations stigmatizing politically abhorrent attitudes are *racist* (from ca. 1932) and *sexist* (from ca. 1965). We tend to regard such labels as modern, but one writer known as "Hercalio Democritus" anticipated such uses with sophisticated irony in 1680, the year of the Exclusion Crisis in England: "He was the great Hieroglyphic of Jesuitism, Puritanism, Quaqersism [sic], and of the Isms from Schism" (*The Vision of Purgatory,* 46).

While most swearing and foul language are spontaneous, in recent decades political pressure groups have realized the value of both modes as a highly effective method of expressing outrage and as a shock tactic to attract publicity. One consequence of the protests in the United States against the Vietnam War was the politicization of foul language, notably by radical students at Berkeley, California. What started out as the Free Speech Movement was stigmatized as the so-called Filthy Speech Movement as a consequence of mobilizing the use of obscenities in slogans as a form of protest. The two most favored were "FUCK THE DRAFT" and "KILL THE PIGS." The first led to a significant trial, *Cohen* v. *California* (403 US. 15, 25, 1971), while the second was used against both the police and political opponents: the "alternative" newspaper *The Black Panther* of November 14, 1970, carried the galvanizing front-page headline: "DEATH TO THE FASCIST PIGS/SHOOT TO KILL." Radical feminist groups similarly chose provocative acronyms such as SCUM (Society for Cutting up Men), founded 1967 by Valerie Solanis, and WITCH (Women's International Terrorist Conspiracy from Hell), which, according to its manifesto, "was born on Halloween 1968." The founding documents of both groups are to be found in the collection *Sisterhood is Powerful,* edited by Robin Morgan (1970).

One of the unexpected provocations leading to the tragic shootings at Kent State University on May 4, 1970, was the filth of the personal abuse inflicted on the National Guard by young women students. Even more radical is the poem "TCB" (1970) by Sonia Sanchez consisting of three-line verses using "incremental repetition":

wite/motha/fucka
wite/motha/fucka
wite/motha/fucka
   whitey

The burden is repeated six times, the only significant variation being in the sequence of insults, *whitey* being replaced by other terms of demotic insult—namely *ofay, devil, cracker,* and *honky.* The catalogue of abuse ends with an apparent call for collaboration: "Now. That it's all sed / let's get to work."

The loose emotive exploitation of political labels is sharply shown in a report in the *Guardian* (April 26, 2004) covering the visit of the right-wing French politician Jean-Marie Le Pen, leader of the Front National, to a British sister organization, the British National Party (B.N.P.). Mr. Alex Jones of the Merseyside Coalition Against Racism and Fascism reportedly referred to the B.N.P. as "Nazi scum" and shouted "Fascist!" "Communist!" retorted the B.N.P. "In a flurry of 'screw-you' gestures, everyone fled to their cars."

See also: Communism; Nicknames; Red; War.

Bibliography

Hunt, R.N. Carew. *A Guide to Communist Jargon.* London: Bles, 1957.

Morgan, Robin, ed. *Sisterhood is Powerful: An Anthology of Writings from the Women's Liberation Movement.* New York: Random House, 1970.

Ruffner, James A., ed. *Eponyms Dictionaries Index.* Detroit: Gale Research, 1977.

Von Altendorf, Alan, and Theresa Von Altendorf. *Isms.* Memphis: Mustang, 1991.

POM, POMMY

Pom and *pommy* are exclusive to Australian and New Zealand slang as disparaging terms for British immigrants, subsequently settlers. Various journalistic references show both forms suddenly springing into wide currency in 1912. The Sydney *Truth* of December 22 that year carried an explanatory report: "Now they call 'em 'Pomegranates' and the Jimmygrants don't like it." Xavier Herbert's memoir of the period, *Disturbing Element* (1963), is one of several sources confirming this origin: "we kids . . . would yell at them 'Jimmygrants, Pommygranates, Pommies'" (vi, 91). (*Jimmygrant* is recorded much earlier, from ca. 1845 and the abbreviation *Jimmy* from ca. 1859.) Many British immigrants arrived after World War I, and the "pomegranate" reference could allude to their rosy cheeks, also found in Afrikaans *rooinek* ("red neck") referring to British soldiers. There is an alternative convict explanation deriving the term from POME, an acronym for Prisoner of Mother England, a quasi-ironic title of some of the original convicts, found carved on the stone walls of the Port Arthur jail in Sydney from the 1830s. However, the semantic transfer whereby the term shifted from the convicts to the English colonists is obviously problematic.

Pom and *pommy* have maintained a thriving currency, being used with a mixture of hostility and affection, no doubt reflecting the ambivalent attitudes of the Australian settlers toward continuing immigration from Britain. The *Australian National Dictionary* (1988) notes that the word is often preceded by *whingeing* (complaining) and followed by *bastard.* It cites quotations from 1962 and 1954, respectively: "He would refer to him to his face as the 'Pommy,' once going so far as to call him a 'Pommy Bastard.'" However, *bastard* also has an ambivalent quality in Australian English, shown in this quotation from 1957: "When I call *you* a Pommy bastard, sir, that's meant to be friendly. But a Pommy bloody officer is different." When the English moral crusader **Mrs. Mary Whitehouse** visited Australia in 1978, the attorney general of South Australia referred to her as "a notorious pom," provoking the response in an editorial in *The Australian* newspaper that this was "A Stinkardly Insult." In recent decades *pom* and *pommy* have started to develop currencies in South African English.

See also: Australia.

Bibliography

Hornage, Bill. *The Australian Slanguage.* North Ryde: Cassell, 1980.
Ramson, W.S., ed. *The Australian National Dictionary.* Oxford University Press, 1988.
Wilkes, George. *A Dictionary of Australian Colloquialisms.* 2nd ed. Sydney: Sydney University Press, 1990.

POPULAR CULTURE

Although a loose category, *popular culture* essentially prioritizes entertainment and comedy above education, cerebration, and serious issues. The category also implies in earlier times works of anonymous rather than specific authorship, apparent in diverse historical genres, such as the medieval drama, the **fabliaux**, and the broadside ballads, which became popular from the Elizabethan period. The modern forms are most obviously the farce, the cartoon, the **comic**, the soap opera, the sitcom, and **rap**. The earlier forms, especially the fabliaux, tend to be surprisingly immoral in content and coarse in language. The entry for the **medieval period** discusses religious drama, which is often shocking in its blasphemy and crudity. The broadside ballads (popular printed ballads on various topical subjects: political, religious, criminal, amatory, and scandalous) included much racy language and slang terms like *horning* for "cuckolding," *humpers* for "copulators," and *pip* for "syphilis." Obscenities which were sung aloud appeared in print as "I won't F—k for a shilling," and "F—g," rhyming with "plucking." Other uses were simply direct: "Her mamma called her whore and sorry dirty quean" and "the tailors all pist" (nos. 99, 58, and 39 in Holloway, ed., 1975). The popular verse form of the limerick has thrived, especially from the nineteenth century, being practiced by major, minor, and anonymous poets, using witty word-play and registers which vary, being by turns original, decent, and obscene.

The modern forms of the cartoon and the comic originally created safe, sanitized juvenile fantasy worlds, whereas the "alternative" comics of recent decades are crude in every respect. Similarly, the sitcom essentially endorses "family values" by showing that families and relationships survive stress, but the soap opera threatens them through seduction, adultery, and even violent crime. The sitcom is formulaic, with each episode reaching the obligatory happy ending, while the action of the soap opera is notoriously protracted, each episode typically ending in crisis or suspense. By convention, the sitcom permits risqué language, but the soap opera does not. More original and daring are the recent female comedies such as "Sex and the City" (Michael Patrick Long and other writers), depicting differing degrees of women's liberation, both sexual and verbal, with the character of Samantha leading the field in both departments, and the British series "Absolutely Fabulous" (Dawn French and Jennifer Saunders), satirizing upper-class idleness, sponging, heavy drinking, and political correctness.

In recent years there has emerged a new cynical genre, exemplified by "The Sopranos" (David Chase) and "Six Feet Under" (Allan Ball). The former is set in the mafia underworld, the latter in the undertaking business, but both dramatize dysfunctional families, riven by hostility, tension, and guilt, all members, even the matriarchal, using idioms of powerful and relentless obscenity. This last feature suffuses even "Deadwood" (David Milch), a re-creation of the Wild West set in the 1870s. An English reviewer, Simon Hoggart in *The Spectator,* commented coyly that "everyone swears, all the time. I cannot duplicate this in a conservatively inclined magazine, but here is a bowdlerised version of some typical dialogue: 'What you [making love] doing, you [to make love]?' 'Be careful, you [rooster-licker], you and all the other [rooster lickers].' 'You know what, your mouth looks like a [female genitalia].' John Wayne would have been appalled, and as for Roy Rogers, I do not dare to think" (October 9, 2004, 73). The more serious objection is that such language is opportunistically sensational and anachronistic. No doubt the Old West echoed with oaths, but none of these obscenities was then current.

See also: Comics; Fabliau, the; Medieval Period.

Bibliography

Holloway, John, and Joan Black, eds. *Later English Broadside Ballads.* London: Routledge, 1975.
Miller, Toby. *Popular Culture and Everyday Life.* London: Sage, 1998.
Pinto, V. de Sola, and Allan Rodway, eds. *The Common Muse.* London: Chatto & Windus, 1957.
Waites, Bernard, ed. *Popular Culture: Past and Present.* London: Routledge, 1993.

PORNOGRAPHY

As the related entries for **censorship** and **obscenity** show, fundamental problems of definition have not really been resolved. The same is true of *pornography.* Explicit descriptions of nudity, sexuality, and erotic behavior continue to be cultural areas of considerable dispute, repression, and legal action involving complex criteria of authorial intention, likely audience, and in recent decades, choice of vocabulary. The controversy attracts conflicting views and counterclaims of decadence, liberation, Puritanism, and repression. The Judeo-Christian view of sex as a taboo subject in literature and art largely prevented the public depiction of frankly erotic subjects until the twentieth century. Comparisons with the literature and artifacts of other cultures show the diversity and relativity of norms and standards. These include the obscene farces of Plautus and the ancient Greeks, Priapic cults, nudes on Greek vases, the erotic mosaics at Pompeii, similar statues in India, and the naked giant with rampant penis depicted on the hillside at Cerne Abbas in Dorset.

Prior to the nineteenth century there was neither a specific legal category of pornography nor a statute against obscenity. In 1708, when James Read, a printer, was brought to court for having published the anonymous *Fifteen Plagues of a Maidenhead,* Lord Justice Powell dismissed the indictment of obscene libel, ruling strictly on the grounds of libel *per se*:

> This is for printing bawdy stuff but reflects on no person, and a libel must be against some particular person or persons, or against the Government. It is not stuff to be mentioned pub-

licly; [but] if there should be no remedy in the Spiritual Court, it does not follow that there must be a remedy here. There is no law to punish it, I wish there was, but we cannot make law; it indeed tends to the corruption of good manners, but that is not sufficient for us to punish. (cited in Rawson 1991, 7)

This judgment perhaps explains the efflorescence of similar works (at least fifteen between 1700 and 1710, according to *Eighteenth Century British Erotica* (2002). However, Edmund Curll was the first person convicted of corrupting public morals by publishing *Venus in the Cloister, or the Nun in her Smock* in 1727, and John Wilkes similarly went to jail for publishing *An Essay on Women* (1763), a bawdy poem with many four-letter words, the most memorable lines being "just a few fucks and then we die" (l. 4) and "Prick, cunt and bollocks in convulsions hurl'd" (l. 41). But both prosecutions were probably more politically motivated than for obscenity *per se.* These factors perhaps explain why **John Cleland** received merely a fine and a reprimand from the Privy Council for his notorious but highly popular *Memoirs of a Woman of Pleasure* (1749).

The strength of the Puritan influence in America probably explains the curious absence of pornography in the United States until the mid-nineteenth century (see Mills 1993, 218). Yet as the entries for **censorship** and **lawsuits** show, the judgments on *Ulysses* (1933), *The Well of Loneliness* (1929), and *Lady Chatterley's Lover* (1959) in the American courts were more liberal than those in Britain. The climactic line in Radclyffe Hall's landmark novel on lesbianism, *The Well of Loneliness,* is "and that night they were not divided," which as Jane Mills rightly observes, "today seems more romantic than erotic" (281).

Pornography, a comparatively recent coinage dating from the 1850s, derives from Greek *porne* meaning a "harlot." The first meaning in the *Oxford English Dictionary* is thus literal: "description of the life, manners etc., of prostitutes and their patrons," a topic regarded as potentially prurient and thus suspect. It is significant that the term should have arisen in the Victorian era, when prostitution was rampant. (The euphemism *French prints* for pornographic images dates from ca. 1850.) However, even in the nineteenth century, the extended meaning of *pornography* included topics with no clear connection with prostitution, and modes that were not explicit: "the expression or suggestion of obscene or unchaste subjects in literature or art." This was to become the core of the dominant, but highly disputed meaning for decades. The first instance cited in the *OED* is pictorial, from Webster's *Dictionary* of 1864: "licentious paintings employed to decorate the walls of rooms sacred to bacchanalian orgies, examples of which exist in Pompeii." Indeed, the pictorial or descriptive element is still often primary, even in discussions of literature.

Most modern definitions dispense with moralistic terms such as *obscene, unchaste,* and *licentious,* in the manner of *Collins Concise Dictionary* (2000): "writings, pictures, films, etc., designed to stimulate sexual excitement." This behaviorist core has led to considerable debates about the varieties of stimulation and the assumptions that pornography demeans women by depicting them as promiscuous and available sexual objects for male gratification and sexual violence. This presupposes that men are the principal readers of pornography, a traditional assumption slightly weakened by the views of such modern feminists as Germaine Greer and Angela Carter. Furthermore, as Thomas W. Laqueur shows in his monumental study, *Solitary Sex: A Cultural History of Masturbation*, in the eighteenth century the artistic tradition of women reading "is translated into explicit pornography of women rapturously masturbating while reading" (2003, 343). The images, French and English, become increasingly explicit, as do the titles, one of which is *The Dangerous Novel* (1781). However, these are still fantasized erotic images of women by men, constituting a male projection, a "double pornography."

Given the problems of definition inherent in the issues of authorial intention and likely audience, let alone those in defining "obscenity," many legal actions sought to focus on the choice of vocabulary. This verbal emphasis can be futile, as is shown in **John Cleland**'s *Memoirs of a Woman of Pleasure* (1749), now widely regarded as a pornographic "classic," but containing none of the traditionally taboo terms, only picturesque and ingenious metaphors couched in classical vocabulary. The same point could be made about Vladimir Nabokov's highly literary *Lolita* (1955). In the Postscript "On a Book Entitled *Lolita*" Nabokov discourses amusingly on the formulaic expectations of the genre: "in modern times 'pornography' connotes mediocrity, commercialism and certain strict rules of narration. Obscenity must be mated with banality . . . action has to be limited to the copulation of clichés" (1997, 311). Nevertheless, in many of the earlier trials, the mere existence of a sexual theme or of sexual terminology was sufficient to secure a conviction. Gore Vidal was ironically dismissive on this point: "Because of [Henry] Miller's hydraulic approach to sex and his dogged use of four-letter words, *Sexus* could not be published in the United States for twenty-four years" (1974, 198). As the entry on **Lady Chatterley's Lover** shows, the proceedings of this landmark case of 1960 were largely taken up with the question of whether D.H. Lawrence was attempting to "redeem" the notorious "four-letter words."

The *Chatterley* verdict encouraged the growth of a huge pornographic industry, blatantly advertising itself in titles such as *Screw, Ban, Orgy, Pleasure, Suck, Cunts and Grunts, The Whipping Post*, and *Kinky Komics*. This outpouring provoked in the United States the Presidential Commission on Pornography (1970), followed in the United Kingdom by the Longford Report (1972) and the Williams Report (1979). The U.S. report recommended abolition of censorship, but was rejected by President Nixon as "morally bankrupt." The Longford Report proposed a new standard of "outraging contemporary standards of decency." The Williams Report recommended that "the written word should be neither restricted nor prohibited" (1979, 102), but proposed a more specific definition of obscenity in visual material "offensive to reasonable people by reason of the way it portrays or deals with violence, cruelty or horror, or sexual, faecal or urinary functions or genital organs" (1979, 124). Neither report was transmuted into law.

The pornography industry is now commonly quantified as larger than the film and record industries combined. Although even prior to the *Chatterley* judgment the now-familiar abbreviations *porno* and *porn* were in currency, the expansion of the market was reflected in the emergence of such terms as *pornobiography, pornocrat, porno-film, porno-magazine, pornomania,* and *pornophile* in the course of the 1960s. (The upscale term *erotica* dates from 1854, and is steadily increasing in currency.) The further expansion of the category is shown in the distinction between "soft" and "hard" pornography, the latter having come to include perversions such as sadism, masochism, child pornography, and bestiality, which have no explicit vocabulary.

See also: Censorship; Cleland, John; *Lady Chatterley's Lover;* Obscenity.

Bibliography

Carter, Angela. *The Sadeian Woman and the Ideology of Pornography.* New York: Pantheon Books, 1979.
Copp, David, and Susan Wendell. *Pornography and Censorship.* New York: Prometheus, 1983.
Greer, Germaine. *The Madwoman's Underclothes.* London: Picador, 1986.
Lawrence, D.H. *Pornography and Obscenity.* London: Faber, 1936.
Nabokov, Vladimir. *Lolita.* London: Penguin, 1997.
Pettit, Alexander, and Patrick Spedding, eds. *Eighteenth Century British Erotica.* London: Pickering and Chatto, 2002.
Rawson, Hugh. *A Dictionary of Invective.* London: Hale, 1991.
Simpson, A.W.B. *Pornography and Politics.* London: Waterlow, 1983.
Taylor, Gordon Rattray. *Sex in History.* New York: Ballantyne, 1954.
Vidal, Gore. *Collected Essays.* London: Heinemann, 1974.
Williams Report: *Report of the Committee on Obscenity and Film Censorship.* London: HMSO, 1979.

POVERTY

Although the condition of poverty is now generally regarded with sympathy, this has not always been the case, as is partly seen in the entry for **beggar.** In John Skelton's satire "Why come ye not to Court?" (1522), the figure of Cardinal Wolsey actually mocks rascals "not worth two plums" and "rain-beaten beggars" (601–2). Yet in Shakespeare the poor are always treated with dignity: King Lear's moment of illumination and empathy occurs in the storm scene: "Poor naked wretches . . . / That bide the pelting of this pitiless storm" (III iv 28–29). The same attitude informs literature up to recent times. In the semantics of the word-field there is a similar division: the compound *poverty-stricken* shows sympathy, but the adjective *poor* has developed senses of scorn and belittlement similar to *little* and *old* in many phrases and idioms unrelated to poverty *per se.* These include "the poor fool" and "in poor health." In other contexts the term is definitely critical, as in "a poor showing" and "a poor excuse," as opposed to the more literal usages "poor as a church mouse" and "poor relation."

Dr. Johnson (1755) listed the following range of such meanings for *poor:* "paltry, mean, contemptible"; "unimportant"; "unhappy, uneasy"; "mean, depressed, low, rejected"; "wretched." As can be inferred, a fair number of these senses reflect notions of class that have continued and even been accentuated in supposedly egalitarian but actually capitalist societies such as modern Britain and the United States. Although Shakespeare was the first to use *trash* of a person in 1604 (in *Othello* V i 85), the sense has developed in invidious demographic phrases like "poor white trash" and "trailer trash" (from about 1943). *Poor white trash* has a long history and a surprising origin as a term of disparagement for Southern whites by black slaves before the Civil War. In her *Journal* entry for June 1, 1833, the visiting English actress Fanny Kemble noted: "The slaves themselves entertain the very highest contempt for white servants, whom they designate as 'poor white trash.'"

Other terms from the same provenance are *buckra, peckerwood,* and *redneck.* Of these, *buckra* is the most interesting, deriving from an African language, probably Ibo or Efik in Nigeria, in which *mbakara* means "he who surrounds or governs." Clearly imported by African slaves, *buckra* was originally a term of respect both in Caribbean English and in the southern United States, where it was used by slaves to refer to and address their masters. It then was generalized to mean "a white man," losing status in American English (especially after the abolition of slavery by acquiring the association of poverty) but retaining it in the Caribbean.

A similar semantic relationship exists historically between the different senses of *wretched* and *miserable. Wretched* derives from Anglo-Saxon *wræcca,* meaning an "exile," and has continued to combine the senses of "poverty" and "unhappiness," just as *miserable,* from Latin *miser,* "poor," combines the original sense with that of "unhappy," as in the religious phrase "miserable sinner" (ca. 1536) and "idle beggars and miserable persons," used in the minutes of the Privy Council of Scotland in 1585. Both can be used unsympathetically, as in "that wretched builder has let us down again" or "yet another miserable performance from the Minister."

See also: Beggar.

PRAT

An almost exclusively British word, *prat* has in the course of its long history undergone the common semantic shift from being a specific underground term to a general slang word. Its etymology is uncertain, but its earliest sense, in criminal slang, is "the buttocks," shown in a virtually continuous history from Thomas Harman's early underground glossary *A Caveat for Commen Cursetors* (1567) up to the present, in phrases like "I fell on my prat." In his *Classical Dictionary of the Vulgar Tongue* (1785) Francis Grose includes the term under the spelling *pratts.* In the United States a possibly related sense of "a hip-pocket" is recorded from about 1915, while Partridge claims that it carried the meaning of "the female pudend" in the nineteenth and twentieth centuries. (This would give it a similar anatomical ambiguity to *fanny.)* A curious survival in American English is *pratfall,* meaning "a fall on the buttocks," especially in comedy. It seems first to have been used in 1939 by Noel Coward in *Parade.* However, from the 1960s there started to emerge the general sense of "a fool, worthless person or 'jerk,'" now widely current in British English. This shift is paralleled by *arse* and *arsehole* in British English and *asshole* in the American variety.

See also: "Four-Letter" Words; Instability of Swearing Terms.

PRESS, THE

Traditionally the press in English-speaking countries has maintained a standard of usage complying with what is considered "decent" and "polite," since historically "quality" newspapers in the United Kingdom like *The Times* (founded 1785) catered to the establishment and the ruling classes, while the *New York Times* (founded 1851) was similarly written for a cultured, educated readership. However, Montagu cites two outrageous pieces of sabotage perpetrated in 1882 when the word *fucking* was interpolated into formal reports in *The Times* (1973, 308–9). In modern times, there have developed the differing categories of the "popular" and the "tabloid" press, competing with the original "quality" press and with each other. The first popular daily, the *Daily Telegraph* (founded 1855), encouraged the more downscale *Daily Mail* (founded 1896) and the first tabloid, the *Daily Mirror* (founded 1903), followed by the *Sun* (relaunched 1969). In the past hundred years the overall number of newspaper titles has declined, as the "popular" and "tabloid" press have steadily taken over a market formerly monopolized by "quality" journalism. (The phrase *tabloid journalism* is recorded as far back as 1901.) A more sensationalist downscale news style, especially that of the tabloids, has frankly and increasingly exploited the lower registers and demotic idioms.

Idiomatic exclamations and coarse expressions that would not have been granted the dignity of print before World War II have become common in the tabloid press in the United Kingdom. Thus the *Daily Mirror* reprimanded the Soviet premier Nikita Khrushchev for his boorish behavior at the United Nations with the headlined exhortation: "DON'T BE SO BLOODY RUDE!" (May 17, 1960). Similarly, in the midst of one of Britain's financial crises in 1974 the same paper asked despairingly on its front page: "IS EVERY-ONE GOING BLOODY MAD?" The assassination of Lord Louis Mountbatten by the IRA in 1979 was denounced with the headline "MURDERING BASTARDS!" By contrast, "Up yours, Delors," was the neat, rude rejection by the *Sun* (November 1, 1990) of political proposals by Jacques Delors, President of the European Commission.

Although the distinction drawn between the registers [N.B. used in the technical sense] of "quality" and "tabloid" journalism is still generally valid, there have been increasing instances of "leveling down." Even three decades ago a British athlete was described under the headline of "Cool, Real Cool, this Young Man in a Hell of Hurry to Win Gold" in *The Times* (July 16, 1971), while President Ronald Reagan was written off by *The Observer* (a quality Sunday paper) as "The Zombie President" (March 1, 1987). On the same day the tabloid *Sunday Today* informed the health minister: "Here's young Britain's verdict on your AIDS campaign: WE DON'T GIVE A DAMN." In an extraordinary letter to the editor of the respected literary journal, *The London Review of Books* (November 21, 1985, 4), Professor Terence Hawkes summarily wrote: "tell him [Professor Graham Hough] to piss off," an outrage that aroused no controversy whatsoever. Recently the *Times Literary Supplement* noted: "More reflective of our era was the *Evening Standard*'s comment on *A Million Little Pieces* by James Frey: 'Frey can really write. Brilliantly. And if you don't think so, f*** you'" (May 7, 2004, 16). A political commentary in *The Times* observed: "The myth-makers are Mr. Blair's allies . . . who tend to see conspiracy in every cock-up" (September 8, 2004, 19). An article in the up-market *Sunday Times* on the holiday behavior of British youth noted: "On any cut-rate beach . . . young Britons are to be seen in their seething thousands, night and day, pissing, posturing and puking, swearing and shrieking, and ceaselessly and senselessly 'shagging', to use their own nasty expression" (August 24, 2003, 17). The same article complained about visitors to the Notting Hill Carnival (in London) "defecating in our front gardens." Twenty years ago all the behavioral language would have been euphemistic.

There is still some self-imposed censorship. An article on Erica Jong (*Sunday Times,* July 6, 2003, 3) started with a quotation from her *succès de scandale The Fear of Flying:* "Even if you loved your husband there came that inevitable year when f****** him turned as bland as Velveeta cheese." In the original edition, published thirty years previously, the full form of the word was used. Only the "alternative" press has absolutely no taboos. "Cunt Power Trials" was an exhibitionist headline in *Oz* magazine (no. 33, February 1971), which also referred to pornographic films unsqueamishly as "fuck films." In similar register the *International Times* asked the provocative rhetorical question: "Isn't Quintin Hogg an unremitting shit?" (October 27, 1967).

Generally speaking, the register employed in journalism in the United States is of a more uniform and polite order. However the "scandal" magazines like *Confidential* (1952>), *The New York Daily Graphic,* and *Variety* exploited salacious or coarse language in stories like "Lavender Skeletons in TV's Closet," "Call Boys of Manhattan" (Kashner and MacNair 2002, 17). The *New Yorker* (established 1925) has set a benchmark for quality journalism, but it occasionally uses low-register terms. Thus Quentin Tarantino's *Kill Bill Volume I* was assessed in two registers: "The movie is what's formally known as decadence and commonly known as crap" (*Film Notes,* October 20, 2003). The same number ran an interview with Tarantino using uncensored obscenity-laden speech. An acrimonious exchange on the floor of the Senate between Dick Cheney and Senator Patrick Leahy was initially covered by *The Washington Times,* euphemistically reporting that the Vice President "urged Mr. Leahy to perform an anatomical sexual impossibility" (June 25, 2004). The actual words, "Go fuck yourself," were soon widely publicized by other newspapers.

In general, newspapers are becoming bolder in printing offensive remarks verbatim. Thus Ron Atkinson, a former British football manager and commentator, reportedly referred to a Black player in an off-air conversation: "He's what is known in some schools as a fucking lazy thick nigger" (*Guardian,* April 22, 2004). (When it became apparent that his remarks had been aired by some channels, Atkinson resigned immediately.) In this case several British newspapers euphemized the offensive terms. The same newspaper quoted Gary Taylor, the noted Shakespeare scholar commenting: "Even if you don't give a flying fuck for theatrical traditions" (July 28, 2005). Commenting on these issues, Susie Dent observed: "For a serious broadsheet to opt for the full obscenity rather than a sanitized version is not surprising. *The Guardian's* profile is of a radical free-thinking newspaper uninhibited by bourgeois shibboleths" (2005, 84-85).

In the other principal English-speaking countries like India, Australia, Canada, and South Africa, newspapers will normally use foul language only when quoting verbatim, and then often in asterisked forms. A strange case occurred in South Africa in February 1997, when a taped telephone conversation was leaked to the press in which the Springbok rugby coach, André Markgraaf, referred repeatedly to "fokken [fucking] kaffirs." Markgraaf resigned immediately, but the press universally printed the offensive terms as "f****n kaffirs," even though *kaffir* is the more offensive term and grounds for **crimen injuria**.

See also: Oz Magazine.

Bibliography

Dent, Susie. *Fanboys and Overdogs: The Language Report.* Oxford: Oxford University Press, 2005.
Hughes, Geoffrey. *Words in Time.* Oxford: Blackwell, 1988.
Kashner, Sam, and Jennifer MacNair. *The Bad and the Beautiful.* New York: TimeWarner, 2002.
Montagu, Ashley. *The Anatomy of Swearing.* London and New York: Macmillan and Collier, 1973.

PROFANITY

All the principal synonyms for swearing, notably *profanity, blasphemy,* and *obscenity,* originally had strong religious denotations. This is now generally only true of *blasphemy,* although *profanity* in British English still commonly implies language that is irreverent or blasphemous, rather than simply shocking. The roots of *profanity* and *profane* lie in Latin *fanum,* meaning "a temple," and when the words were taken into Middle English they carried this etymological sense of "to desecrate or violate a temple," before being applied to more secular objects. Even John Donne, dean of St. Paul's, could use *profanation* (coined in *The Book of Common Prayer* of 1552) in the private context of love, about 1610:

'T were profanation of our joyes
To tell the layetie our love.
("A Valediction: Forbidding Mourning," ll. 7–8)

Yet in his Devotion on "The Language of God," Donne wrote that "all profane authors seem of the seed of the serpent that creeps" (*Devotions Upon Emergent Occasions,* Expostulation, 19).

The Motion Picture Production Code of 1930 negotiated by the Hollywood producers and their opponents contained among its prohibitions the category of "pointed profanity (this includes the words God, Lord, Jesus, Christ—unless used reverently—Hell, S.O.B., damn, Gawd)." However, in modern English usage *profanity* has steadily lost its specifically religious association in favor of the extended meaning of "vulgar or irreverent action, speech, etc." (from *Collins Concise Dictionary,* 1999). In British usage *profanity* is encountered with diminishing frequency, while in American usage the term generally falls under broad category of "swearing."

The more specific British offense usually termed Profanity on the Stage, which provoked quite stringent policing from Elizabethan times onward, is covered in the entry for **censorship**. Generally speaking, with the secularization of Western society and as the focus of swearing has shifted from the religious mode to the excretory, genital, and copulatory, so profanity in its strict sense has become regarded as less offensive than previously. However, as the entry for **broadcasting** shows, responses to profanity vary greatly according to the age and culture of the audience. Furthermore, out of respect for the religious sensibilities of others, a number of the terms listed under "pointed profanity" above are still avoided in scripts or deleted from sound tracks.

See also: Blasphemy; Broadcasting; Censorship; Obscenity.

PROMISCUITY

Sexual promiscuity, implied or actual, has generated one of the most extensive and powerful word-fields in the vocabulary of swearing and insult. However, as has been noted by many observers, feminist and others, there is an obvious imbalance between the great number and force of terms categorizing women as sexually promiscuous and those applied to men. Furthermore, there is the semantic fact that unfavorable terms for women outnumber positive terms by a proportion of about five to one (see Hughes 1991, 225). This disparity has become part of a broader debate in recent decades in which feminists have argued that language has been and continues to be generated in a "patriarchal" or "phallocratic" dispensation, and is thus the product of male prejudices. See, in this respect, Muriel Schultz (1975), Dale Spender (1980), and Jane Mills (1991). In this entry the sexes are treated separately.

The huge word-field for promiscuity includes the "formal" category of prostitution, which has its own entry, as well as the "casual" and less easily defined class of women who "sleep around." In the first category are such ancient terms as *whore* and the obsolete *quean*, from Anglo-Saxon times, as well as *harlot, strumpet, concubine, call girl, hooker, tart, tramp, moll, hustler, streetwalker, pickup, scarlet woman, fallen woman, woman of the streets, woman of easy virtue, lady of the night,* and *escort.* Although the line between the two categories is not always clear, the second includes *fast woman, hussy, doll, inamorata, siren, gypsy, minx, vamp, wench, trollop, coquette, bint, crumpet, floozy, scrubber, slag, groupie, nympho,* and *slut.*

Imprecision and instability of meaning are common in the semantic field. Previously, *whore,* for instance, had more the sense of an adulteress or promiscuous woman. Furthermore, in gossip or discussion of the sexual reputations of others, ambiguity, innuendo, and implication are important qualities. Thus *piece* is defined by Grose (1785) as "a wench; a girl who is more or less active and skilful in the amorous congress." *Moll* had the sense of "prostitute" in Elizabethan times, but by 1800 had acquired the meaning of the mistress or female accomplice of a criminal. Likewise, in the provenance of American English *hustler* has three meanings: a positive male sense of an energetic person, a negative male sense of a confidence trickster at pool, and the sense of a prostitute.

In addition there are in both categories many archaic and obsolete terms, including *jade, baggage, bawd, drab, trull, doxy, fireship, lemman, slattern, hoyden, bobtail, traipse, biddy, jilt,* and *punk* in its old British sense. While *Jezebel* and *Delilah* are stereotypical names derived from biblical sources, *Lolita* is virtually unique, deriving from Vladimir Nabokov's scandalous novel of 1955. The same source generated *nymphet,* epitomising the supposed seductiveness and desirability of youth, also shown in the recent term *sex-kitten.* Finally there is the paradoxical category of the mistress, at once socially disreputable but recognized as having a certain dubious status. Here the terms are *mistress, paramour, courtesan,* and *kept woman.*

The comparatively small field devoted to male promiscuity reinforces the notion of the double standard alluded to previously. The tenor of the terms is also entirely different: *Casanova, Romeo, Lothario,* and *Don Juan* derive status from their literary and historical pedigrees, while *ladies' man, lady-killer, gigolo, stud,* and *sugar daddy* obviously do not have the same condemnatory overtones as most of the female terms. They embody *machismo* notions of power and conquest. The sole exception is *roué.* The invocation of great lovers of the past, real and fictional, serves to provide role models suggesting respectability.

See also: Gender in Swearing; Prostitutes; Punk; Women, Stereotypes of.

Bibliography

Hughes, Geoffrey. *Swearing*. Oxford: Blackwell, 1991.

Miller, Casey, and Kate Swift. *Words and Women*. London: Victor Gollancz, 1977.

Mills, Jane. *Womanwords*. London: Virago, 1991.

Schultz, Muriel. "The Semantic Derogation of Women." In *Language and Sex: Differences and Dominance*, ed. B. Thorne and N. Henley, 64–73. Rowley, MA: Newbury House, 1975.

Spender, Dale. *Man Made Language*. London: Routledge & Kegan Paul, 1980.

PROSTITUTES

Terms for prostitutes form perhaps the most powerful and extensive word-field for abuse and swearing in the language, emerging consistently throughout its history. Several terms have their own entries, some being discussed in the overlapping category of **promiscuity**. Although prostitution has evidently been practiced throughout history, a history of prostitution is more difficult to construct, and is obviously beyond the range of this work. However, literature gives us a number of sharp vignettes and telling insights. Chaucer's fragmentary *Cook's Tale* briefly describes the underworld of fourteenth-century London, in which the figure of Perkyn Revlour ("Reveller") lives a fast life of "dys, riot and paramour" ("gambling, parties and lovers") (ll. 4392). He takes up with a friend who

hadde a wyf that heeld for contenance
A shoppe, and swyved for hir sustenance.
[had a wife who kept a shop as a front
and fucked for her living.] (ll. 4421–22)

At this point the tale comes to an abrupt and unexplained halt. Another glimpse into the low life of the times comes in the *Miller's Tale* when the unfortunate suitor Absolom, encountering a blacksmith very early in the morning, is playfully asked if some "gay gerl" has kept him up (l. 3769). The euphemism was to have a long currency. Chaucer's contemporary William Langland, the presumed author of *Piers Plowman*, refers bitterly to the institutional corruption of his times, when "rascals become lords, ignorant men teachers and Holy Church helps whores" (C Text, Passus XV, ll. 20–21).

Public baths, one of the unexpected cultural introductions of the Crusades, became places of sexual assignation known as *stews*, generating *women of the stews*, an early name for a prostitute. Langland has two characters called "Jack the Jester and Janet of the Stews" (A Text, Passus VII, l. 65). Because of their evil reputation, *stews* were later renamed *bagnios*, which originally (ca. 1615) signified a Turkish bath before rapidly degenerating into the sense of "brothel." As Dr. Johnson noted: "probably *stew* like *bagnio*, took a bad signification from bad use." Interestingly, *brothel* itself first meant a "rascal" or "lewd person" in the fourteenth century, a *brothel house* being originally a place frequented by such types, before acquiring its independent form and modern meaning about 1593.

The major Elizabethan theaters were all built in an area of London noted for its brothels. Part of Shakespeare's *Measure for Measure* (ca. 1604) is set in a brothel run by the graphically-named Mistress Overdone. The odd underground phrase *Winchester goose*, meaning a prosti-

The Harlots Nurfe, or Modern Procurefs.

Behold the practis'd Baud explore, | Whose lot when she begins to fail
The Nymph from head to foot all O'er, | Is Want Diseases and a Jail
For Cspers whom shes drefs'd w:th Care | While it diverts thus Pufsy play,
(A bait to Catch some Money'd Heir) | With yonder Mouse, then on it Prey.

Printed for & Sold by the Proprietor John Ryall at Hogarths Head in Fleet Street London.

A British engraving of 1750 depicts a tightly corseted courtesan, attended by her maid, or procuress. Terms for and about prostitutes make up one of the most abundant word-fields for abuse and swearing in the English language. *(Library of Congress, LC-USZ62-132015)* tute, found in *Henry VI, Part I* (I ii 53) and *Troilus and Cressida* (V x 53–54), is explained thus by Hesketh Pearson:

> The Bishop of Winchester had his Palace between London Bridge and the Globe Theatre and owned most of the land in that district, fattening himself on the rent of sin; for it was the region of brothels, the women of which were known as Winchester geese.
> (1942, 94)

Ben Jonson also has a reference to "the Winchestrian Goose" in his contemporary satire "An Execration upon Vulcan." But more pointed are the punning jibes in the opening broadside of 1588 by the popular pseudonymous pamphleteer "Martin Marprelate," who attacked the Bishops of London and Winchester as "The right puissant and terrible priests, my clergy-masters of the Confocation-house, whether fickers general, or worshipful paltripolitan" (cited in Colman, 1974, 49). (Shakespeare was to pun on "focative" and *fuck* in *Henry V*, IV i 53–55, while *fickers*, ostensibly a version of *vicars*, certainly echoes "fuckers.")

An unexpectedly thorough source of evidence on prostitution is the great Victorian researcher into London's low life, Henry Mayhew. In 1862, eleven years after the publication of the first three volumes of his gigantic survey, *London Labour and the London Poor*, Mayhew issued *London's Underworld*, containing about a hundred pages on prostitution and its social structure. Working on a current estimate of 80,000 prostitutes out of a population of one million, he distinguished about twenty different categories, such as "Seclusives," "Board Lodgers," "Sailors', Soldiers,' and Thieves' Women," as well as "Clandestine Prostitutes," such as "Female Operatives," "Maid-Servants" and "Ladies of Intrigue." However, Mayhew's criteria and assumptions are strictly Victorian in both his sense of hierarchy and his double standards. He arranges the categories in terms of a class structure, regarding the "Seclusives"— for example, "those women who are kept by men of independent means" as living in a state that is "the nearest approximation to the holy state of marriage" (1983, 34) down to the occasional "base coloured woman" described in horrific detail with "sable black skin, leering countenance and obscene disgusting tongue, resembling a lewd spirit of darkness from the nether world" (1983, 43). However, for Mayhew, "Literally every woman who yields to her passions and loses her virtue is a prostitute" (1983, 34). Furthermore, nowhere does he even hint at the male industry, which surfaced in the Cleveland Street Scandal of 1889. His vocabulary is a mixture of direct terms like *prostitute, brothel,* and *loose women,* and euphemisms like *chère amie* and *prima donna.*

The terminology is mainly native and, as the accompanying word-field shows, the American contribution has been considerable. Only what might be called the globally comprehensible terms have been included, since there are many slang terms from other varieties, such as U.S. Black *ho* (from *whore*), as well as Australian *chromo, grunter,* and *prosso.* Of the core terms, some, like *whore*, are found from the earliest stages of the language and have retained their condemnatory sense; others, like *quean* and *strumpet*, have become obsolete. Still others, like *hussy, trollop,* and *broad*, have moved into a rather ambiguous semantic area between the category of "prostitute" and "loose woman" or "sexually available woman." *Bunter,* for example, was defined by Francis Grose in his *Classical Dictionary of the Vulgar Tongue* (1785) as "a low dirty prostitute, half whore and half beggar." It was still in use in Victorian times. Several have erratic semantic histories: thus *harlot* was originally a male term meaning "a rascal" before becoming feminized, a semantic change that *slag* and *tramp* have followed. *Punk,* on the other hand, has moved in the opposite direction in terms of both meaning and gender, from "prostitute" to "worthless person."

Harlot, a remarkable term, was previously derived from Arlette, the mother of the illegitimate William the Conqueror; however, this etymology is now dismissed as "a random conjecture of the sixteenth century." From about 1225 the word carries the male senses of "vagabond, beggar, rogue, rascal," one of the most memorably scathing uses being the description of Chaucer's sexually ambivalent Summoner: "He was a gentil [noble] harlot and a kynde" (*General Prologue,* l. 647). However, by 1432–1450, when Ranulph Higden used the term in his *Polychronicon,* it clearly had the modern sense, since he recounts this amusing euphemism: "The harlottes at Rome were called the *nonariae* [the nuns]." (*Nunnery* subsequently acquired the sense in Elizabethan underworld slang of a brothel, famously used by Hamlet of Ophelia in *Hamlet* III i 135).

A related term from the sex industry also showing feminization is *bawd.* Of uncertain origin, it is first used in Langland's *Piers Plowman* (ca. 1380) to mean a procurer or a procuress. Although the majority of early applications are masculine, by 1700 it has become exclusively feminized. More on the fringe is *harridan,* which has previous French associations of "an old jade" or worn-out horse, but in English these are sharpened into "a haggard old woman; a vixen," and in Dr. Johnson's *Dictionary* (1755) more classically "a decayed strumpet." More recent is *slag,* amazingly first found in Grose (1785) with the quite different sense of "a slack-mettled fellow" or coward, before appearing in the 1930s onward in various disreputable roles, such as "a vagrant or petty criminal," "a contemptible person." The earliest record of the modern female sense is 1958.

The field has many euphemisms such as *lady of the night,* which are really more in the category of ironic or pseudo-euphemisms. In recent decades, partly through the initiatives of political correctness, there has been an attempt to rehabilitate "the oldest profession" by a species of semantic "make-over," substituting the more industrial term "sex-worker" (ca. 1982) and the superficially more respectable "escort." Like most artificially created euphemisms, they cannot be used as swearwords. *Whore* itself has a long history as a term of abuse, as would be expected, but its earlier applications are sometimes surprising: in the Elizabethan comedy *Gammer Gurton's Needle* (ca. 1575), a character spots a cat sipping milk out of a pan and shouts "Ah hore! Out thefe!" (I iii).

Male prostitution has been acknowledged for centuries, but seldom openly discussed in Anglo-Saxon culture. However, a number of terms for male prostitutes or kept male lovers like *catamite* and *ingle* date from the late sixteenth century and are discussed under the entry for **homosexuals**. In Shakespeare's *Troilus and Cressida* (1606) the candid Fool Thersites provokes Patroclus: "Thou art thought to be Achilles male Varlot," perhaps punning on *harlot,* inducing this exchange:

Patroclus: Why, what's that?
Thersites: Why, his masculine whore.
(V i 20)

Many of the synonyms have become obsolete, but the modern term *rent boy* (ca. 1975) is the most explicit. It is an interesting curiosity to find that *call girl* (ca. 1922), is matched by *call boy* (ca. 1924). In his *Slang Thesaurus* (1988) Jonathon Green lists over thirty such terms, virtually as many as for the female variety, including *ass peddler, cocksman, commercial queer, fag boy, foot soldier,* and the ironic *working girl.* Finally, *whore* is increasingly used in a generalized way of males who prostitute their principles in business or politics.

1100	whore
1200	
1300	strumpet, concubine, quean, common woman
1400	harlot, slut, filth, mistress
1500	drab, trull, mutton, cat, doxy
1600	prostitute, moll, punk, doll, jade, hussy, trollop, gypsy, slattern
1700	biddy, conveniency, bunter
1800	fallen woman, hooker, blowen, streetwalker
1900	broad, call girl, call boy, tramp, tart, lady of the night, hustler, slag
2000	escort, sex worker

The association between prostitutes and swearing is striking in its persistence, being alluded to in *Hamlet* (II ii 568–75). While terms like *slut, slattern, hussy,* and *moll* obviously imply slovenly or crude behavior, the modern term *slag* also has the verbal senses *to slag* or *to slag off,* meaning "to vilify or denigrate," dating from about 1971.

See also: Feminization of Opprobrious Terms; Gender in Swearing; Promiscuity; Punk; Whore and Whoreson; Women, Stereotypes of.

Bibliography
Colman, E.A.M. *The Dramatic Use of Bawdy in Shakespeare.* London: Longman, 1974.
Green, Jonathon. *The Slang Thesaurus.* New York: Penguin, 1986.
Mayhew, Henry. *London's Underworld* (1862), ed. Peter Quennell. London: Bracken Books, 1983.
Mills, Jane. *Womanwords.* London: Virago, 1991.
Pearson, Hesketh. *A Life of Shakespeare.* London: Carroll and Nicholson, 1942.
Prestage, E., ed. *Chivalry.* London: Kegan Paul, 1928.
Schultz, Muriel. "The Semantic Derogation of Women." In *Language and Sex: Differences and Dominance,* ed. B. Thorne and N. Henley, 64–73. Rowley, MA: Newbury House, 1975.

PSYCHOLOGY OF SWEARING AND FOUL LANGUAGE

The traditional psychological commonplace is that swearing releases tension. The Restoration dramatist George Farquhar (1678–1707) is but one author to articulate this point in a melodramatic fashion: "Grant me some wild expressions, Heavens, or I shall burst . . . Words, words or I shall burst" (*The Constant Couple,* V iii). The entry for **Laurence Sterne** deals with various humorous treatments of the theme, more especially the imbalance between the triviality of a provoking situation and the gravity of the resulting oath. Also revealing on the point is the semantic history of the term *ejaculation:* the original sense was the hurling of missiles (Latin *jaculum* meaning "a javelin"), followed by "the emission of sperm" and "a short hasty prayer or utterance." Thus the physical and emotional senses were originally intertwined, although only the sexual sense is still current. While some forms of swearing, like cursing or malediction, are clearly directed at others, some are paradoxically self-directed.

The influence of Sigmund Freud (1856–1939) on modern views has been profound, providing valuable insights into swearing and foul language, the most general being that swearing is an expression of unconscious wishes, a form of aggression in which words are used as weapons. The verbal use of *tirade, broadside,* and *volley* are revealing here. Swearing also expresses certain antisocial, suppressed, and taboo wishes in words like *motherfucker* or veiled death threats or the less obvious verbal "Freudian slip," word-plays which may be hostile, obscene, or revealing. A humorous collection of literary examples is Peter Hainings *A Slip of the Pen.* From his wide literary and cultural knowledge Freud focused on certain seminal sites of unconscious energy. Shakespeare's *Hamlet,* a major source-text of Freudian insights, contains many instances, such as Hamlet's furious execration of the villain Claudius as "Bloody, bawdy villain! / Remorseless, treacherous, lecherous, kindless villain!" (II ii 568–69). This outpouring, revealing in its sexual emphasis, is the more poignant for being uttered, not to the villain's face but in soliloquy. Hamlet similarly says that he will "speak daggers" to his mother but use none (III ii 421), and cruelly dismisses Ophelia to a "nunnery," which in Elizabethan English could mean a brothel as well as place of religious sanctuary (III i 145).

In *Civilization and Its Discontents* (1930), Freud makes an explicit link between antisocial behavior and terms of abuse. He comments on "The man that is not clean, i.e. does not eliminate his excretions, therefore offends others, shows no considerations for them—a fact which is exemplified in the commonest and most forcible terms of abuse" (1930, 67 note). This insight formulates a specific link with historically the earliest category of insults, namely **shit words**, recorded from the thirteenth century. One can also posit a link with the insulting idioms *kiss my arse, kiss the devil's arse,* and its variations, recorded from medieval drama onward.

Freud's explicit perception that sexual shame derives for "all neurotics and many others too" from "the fact that 'inter urinas et faeces nascimur' ('we are born between urine and feces')" (1930, 78 note) leads in many directions. The principal route is to puritanical "sexual repression" and to the disgust articulated in the semantic complex of terms covered in the entry for **foul language**, including a key quotation from *King Lear* (IV vi 129–35). William Butler Yeats's more polite version, "Love has pitched his mansion in the place of excrement" occurs in "Crazy Jane Talks to the Bishop."

Freud's famous insights into the Oedipus Complex (1930, 118) have clear semantic correlatives in the savage insult *motherfucker* and its synonyms in other cultures. His study *Totem and Taboo* (originally 1912–1913) opens with an anthropological chapter on "The Savage's Dread of Incest," but interprets "the incestuous fixations of the libido" as being a key source of neurosis (1950, 17). His linking of Eros and Death or *Thanatos* (1930, 136) is supported semantically by the Elizabethan sense of *die* for "to experience orgasm" and similar metaphors of death, including the later Victorian sense of *go* for modern *come.* The complex of Eros and Death informs the more sinister impulses of murder and suicide by betrayed lovers, dramatized in *Othello, Cavalleria Rusticana,* and *I Pagliacci.* However, his emphasis on the phallus, which profoundly influenced D.H. Lawrence and many others, has since generated the feminist counter-reaction terminology of *phallocentric, phallogocentric,* etc. His almost casual comment "Man too is an animal with an unmistakably bisexual disposition" (1930, 77 note) clearly anticipates, not only the researches of Kinsey et al., but more modern insights and tolerance into homosexual and "alternative" sexual preferences.

Freud took the deeply pessimistic view that "Civilized society is perpetually menaced with disintegration through this primary hostility of men towards one another" (1930, 86). He also retained an unflinching memory of the history of persecution: "Anyone who calls to mind the atrocities of the early migrations, of the invasion by the Huns or by the so-called Mongols under Jenghiz Khan and Tamurlane, the sack of Jerusalem by the pious Crusaders, even the horrors of the last world-war, will have to bow his head humbly before this view of man" (1930, 86). These various forms of hostility underlie the abundance of xenophobic stereotyping and ethnic abuse.

Jacques Lacan's re-reading of Freud, especially his proposition that "the unconscious is structured like a language" (1998, 48) invites insights into the relationship between Manichean polarities of the psyche and those in the binary opposition between sacred and profane language discussed in the Introduction.

See also: Ethnic Insults; Motherfucker; Shit Words.

Bibliography

Brown, Norman O. *Life Against Death.* London: Routledge & Kegan Paul, 1959.
Freud, Sigmund. *Civilization and Its Discontents,* trans. Joan Riviere. London: Hogarth, 1930.
————, *Totem and Taboo,* trans. James Strachey. London: Routledge & Kegan Paul, 1950.
Haining, Peter. *A Slip of the Pen.* London: Robson Books, 2004.
Lacan, Jacques. *On Feminine Sexuality: The Limits of Love and Knowledge,* trans. Bruce Fink. New York: W.W. Norton, 1988.

PUNK

Like many swearwords or terms of insult, *punk* has undergone the semantic trends of generalization and weakening. It is also part of a fairly large group of words, including *harlot, tramp, slag,* and *hustler* showing change of gender over time. In its earliest sense, in Elizabethan times, *punk* meant a prostitute, subsequently the mistress of a soldier or criminal, then the male concubine of a tramp, finally a worthless male person. In the course of this strange eventful history, it has moved from a British to an America provenance, but has retained the original elements of underground sexuality.

The word is of unknown origin, although Eric Partridge suggested ingeniously that "It may be a piece of erudite slang: Latin *punctum,* a small hole" (1947, 170). Nevertheless, it had a clear underground Elizabethan sense, shown when the Duke in *Measure for Measure* (1604) says of Mariana: "She may be a punk, for many of them are neither Maid [virgin], Widow or Wife" (V i 179). Thomas Middleton was more explicit in his *Michaelmas Term* (1607): "I may grace her with the name of a Curtizan, a Backslider, a Prostitution, or such a Toy, but when all comes to all 'tis but a plaine Pung [sic]" (III i). In his *Classical Dictionary of the Vulgar Tongue* (1785) Francis Grose defined the term as "a whore; also a soldier's trull," that is, a female companion.

The word is found in these senses in British contexts up to about 1928, but even by the turn of the century it was being used to mean a passive male homosexual or catamite in American contexts concerning hoboes, sailors, and prison inmates. (The *Oxford English Dictionary Supplement* has quotations dating from 1904.) There is, however, a remarkable antedating recorded in 1761, in *The Genuine Memoirs... of J. D****s,* (possibly John Dennis) wherein the readers are informed that "Augustus Caesar owed his first preferment to having been p—k to Histius in his youth" (23). *The New Yorker* explained in 1977: "The involuntary homosexuals tend to be good-looking young men ... forced into becoming jailhouse 'punks' by older men serving long sentences" (October 24, 64). This is the emphasis in Clarence Major's *Juba to Jive* (1994): "a weak man; any youth who gives in to anal intercourse in prison." Hugh Rawson quotes interesting evidence for the phrase "punk in a bunk," referring to prison sex relationships (1991, 313). There is also a slang verbal sense of "to sodomize."

By the 1920s *punk* was appearing in criminal contexts, suggesting both incompetence and male concubinage. Dashiell Hammett was an early user of the term in *The Maltese Falcon* in both the text (1930) and the filmscript (1939), mischievously adding the related term *gunsel* (meaning a catamite) in a context which suggested a gunman, but then sufficiently new and unfamiliar to evade censorship by the Production Code censors. The sense of a young petty criminal became established for decades in American English, steadily acquiring the sense of "hooligan" or "obnoxious macho type," finally becoming a highly generalized as "a person of no account; a worthless fellow." The term is now almost exclusively American, being no longer common in British slang and virtually unknown in Australian and South African English.

See also: Prostitutes.

Bibliography

Major, Clarence. *Juba to Jive.* New York/London: Viking/Penguin, 1994.
Partridge, Eric. *Shakespeare's Bawdy.* London: Routledge & Kegan Paul, 1947.
Rawson, Hugh. *A Dictionary of Invective.* London: Hale, 1991.

PYGMALION

The first night of George Bernard Shaw's comedy *Pygmalion* in 1914 became a cultural milestone in the history of swearing in England entirely through the use of *bloody.* Shaw (1856–1950) modified the original classical legend of Pygmalion to show how class notions in the United Kingdom were dominated by criteria of accent and propriety in speech. In his play a professorial phonetician, Henry Higgins (based on Henry Sweet), decides to transform a London Cockney flower girl, Eliza Doolittle, into a lady by giving her an upper-class accent as well as appropriate clothes and manners. The experiment succeeds, until Eliza reverts shockingly to her natural low-class speech, a dramatic moment that Shaw exploits through an incongruous juxtaposition of style and content:

LIZA [with perfectly elegant diction]: Walk! Not bloody likely! [Sensation]
I am going in a taxi. (Act III)

In a way that now seems entirely absurd, the popular press sensationalized the whole episode, the *Daily Sketch* giving it this buildup:

One word in Shaw's new play will cause sensation.
Mr. Shaw introduces a certain forbidden word.
WILL MRS. PATRICK CAMPBELL SPEAK IT?
(cited in Huggett 1969, 127–28)

Almost a whole page was devoted to the future utterance, which did indeed cause a scandal. What was alluded to by the press as "SHAW'S BOLD BAD WORD," "the unprintable Swearword," "THE 'LANGWIDGE' OF THE FLOWER GIRL," "the Word," and numerous other evasions, provoked in the first night audience "a few seconds of stunned disbelieving silence" and then hysterical laughter for at least a minute and a quarter (Huggett 1969, 136–37). Yet the performance provoked headlined responses: "THREATS BY DECENCY LEAGUE," "THEATRE TO BE BOYCOTTED," and "I SEE NO OBJECTION SAYS PRIME MINISTER" (Huggett 1969, 141). Although the Bishop of Woolwich insisted that "The Word should be banned," *bloody* became the catchword of the season. So did *pygmalion,* in the ironic use "not pygmalion likely!" Shaw, who had rightly intuited that the censor would not interfere (having passed *bloody* twice before), commented a week later in a statement in the *Daily News:*

> I have nothing particular to say about Eliza Doolittle's language. . . . I do not know anything more ridiculous than the refusal of some newspapers (at several pages' length) to print the word "bloody," which is in common use as an expletive by four-fifths of the British nation, including many highly-educated persons.

By contrast, in the New York performance the word "failed to cause any stir" (Mencken 1936, 311). Richard Huggett comments that "the Americans . . . were not in the least shocked by the Word, regarding it as a charming and delightful piece of English slang" (1969, 171). The *Random House Historical Dictionary of American Slang* (1994) notes that *bloody* is still "considered uncommon and widely regarded as a typical Briticism."

The play was a *succès de scandale* and subsequently reached a global audience as the musical *My Fair Lady* (1956), filmed in 1964. It is ironic that Shaw, a serious dramatist who developed the genre of "the play of ideas" in over forty plays, should have become associated in the public mind principally with one swearword in this comparatively slight piece. Yet after this sensational use, *bloody* was not heard again on the stage until Noel Coward's *Red Peppers* in 1936 (de Jongh, 2000, 185). The episode showed the inherent double standard and hypocrisy surrounding the use of coarse language.

See also: Bloody; "U" and "Non-U."

Bibliography

de Jongh, Nicholas. *Politics, Prudery and Perversion.* London: Methuen, 2000.
Huggett, Richard. *The Truth About "Pygmalion."* London: Heinemann, 1969.
Mencken, H.L. *The American Language.* New York: Knopf, 1936.

Q

QUAKERS AND SHAKERS

The Quakers have never accepted this name, calling themselves The Society of Friends. The name shows, like many others given to religious sects, the strength of stereotypes of irrationality, hysteria, and diabolical possession, often with the innuendo of sexual perversion of various kinds. Two other key terms showing this complex are *bugger,* which has its own entry, and *enthusiasm,* an extremely negative term in the seventeen century, rooted in the sense "inspired by God." *Quaker* (ca. 1647) and *Shaker* (ca. 1648) first carried many of these notions, being derived, according to one observer, "from the Trembling and Quaking, caused in them by Vapours in their Ecstatick Fits" (Edward Chamberlayne, *The Present State of England* 1694, III i 378). (*Vapours* was the old term for hysteria, while in its origins *ecstatick* meant "standing outside oneself," in modern parlance "beside oneself.") One of the first references to the sect comes in a letter written in London in 1647:

> I heare of a Sect of woemen . . . come from beyond the Sea, called Quakers, and these swell, shiver and shake, and when they come to themselves (for in all this fitt Mahomett's holy-ghost hath bin conversing with them) they begin to preache what hath bin delivered to them by the Spirit. (Clarendon mss, no. 2624)

The underlying stereotypical idea is that of demoniality, or indecent intercourse, with an incubus or succubus, alluded to in the pointed reference to "Mahomett's holy-ghost hath bin conversing with them." The original sense of *converse* was "to have sexual intercourse," of which the first recorded instance (in 1536) refers, fascinatingly, to demoniality in a nunnery: "This Albyne, with her fiftie sisters. . . . Conversit with devilis in forme of men, and concsavit [conceived] childrin" (John Bellenden, *Chronicle of Scotland* I, xix).

However, George Fox, the founder of the Quakers, said that the name was given to himself and his followers by Justice Bennet at Derby in 1650 "because I bid them Tremble at the name of the Lord" (Hodgkin 1896, 54). The noted diarist John Evelyn recorded visiting some Quakers in prison in Ipswich on July 9, 1656, referring to them as "a new fanatic sect, of dangerous principles, who shew no respect to any man, magistrate or other." Evelyn was obviously alluding to their refusal on principle to take any oath, nor to remove their large wide-brimmed hats, and to their quaint use of the forms *thou* and *thee.*

Fox and his followers took Christ's injunction in the Sermon of the Mount, "Do not swear at all" (St. Matthew 5:31), literally and seriously, regarding judicial and profane swearing as forbidden. This led to their imprisonment for contempt of court. Keeping their hats on was an acknowledgment of the higher authority of God, while the use of the familiar forms *thou* and *thee* was intended to put everyone on the same basis of brotherhood and friendship. It was unfortunately often taken as an insult. As Fox observed in his *Journal* in 1660: "We were often beaten and abused for using those words to some proud men, who would say, "What you ill-bred clown, do you thou me?" (Mencken 1936, 450). The entry for **thou** records some insulting uses. Ironic comments such as "He . . . Quaker-like, thou'd and thee'd Oliver" are recorded through the seventeenth century, during which various derisive formations had sprung up, including *Quakerism, Quakerish, Quakeristical,* and *Quakerly.*

A quite different and more tolerant view comes from the French philosopher Voltaire (François-Marie Arouet) who spent the years 1726–1729 in forced exile in England, recording his experiences in his *Lettres Anglaises* (1734), of which the first four are on the Quakers. Voltaire presents them as a sober, decent, spiritual brotherhood that would have been "respected in Europe if men could respect virtue beneath ridiculous appearances" (1980, 32). Furthermore, commenting on the agreement that William Penn subsequently reached with the local Indians in Pennsylvania, he noted pointedly: "It is the only treaty between these people and Christians which has never been sworn to and never broken" (1980, 34).

The Shakers were subject to similar hostile stereotyping in England, prior to the founding of the American sect in 1774, even though it was based on different ideals, of mixed communities of men and women living in celibacy.

See also: Nicknames; Thou.

Bibliography

Hodgkin, Thomas. *George Fox.* Boston: Houghton Mifflin, 1896.
Mencken, H.L. *The American Language.* New York: Knopf, 1936.
Voltaire. *Letters on England.* Trans. Leonard Tancock. Harmondsworth: Penguin, 1980.

QUEAN AND QUEEN

These two terms have a complex and interwoven history encapsulating the binary image of woman as contemptible whore and admired regent. *Quean* (pronounced "quayne") always denoted a woman of low class and has become an obsolete term for a prostitute, while *queen* has an ambivalent status, having maintained its royal meaning from Anglo-Saxon up to modern times, but also acquiring associations of prostitution and homosexuality. The confusion between the terms no doubt started with the evident similarity of origin (*quean* from Anglo-Saxon *cwene,* and *queen* from Anglo-Saxon *cwen*) and was aggravated by the basic instability of spelling in Middle English.

From this period *quean,* which originally meant simply "a woman," became in the words of the *Oxford English Dictionary,* "a term of disparagement and abuse," illustrated in a quotation from ca. 1290: "An olde quene ther was biside, strong hore and baudestrote [bawd]." A century later in *Piers Plowman,* William Langland plays on the similarity and difference of the terms, noting wryly that "in the charnel [crypt] it is difficult to tell "a queyne fro a queene" (C Text ix, 46). Lord Byron is one of the last to play on the two terms in *Don Juan* (1811) in this chauvinist tirade: "This martial scold, / This modern Amazon, and queen of queans" (VI, xcvi). However, in Scots *quean* has retained its innocence and means simply "a lass or robust girl." As the term became obsolete in English, so people started to confuse it with *queen* and pronounce it similarly.

According to Jane Mills in *Womanwords,* "the sexual derogation of *queen* began in the reign of Queen Victoria, when the word was used for an attractive woman, a 'girlfriend' or sexual partner" (1989, 203). The *OED* gives instances up to 1975, but most are not derogatory. The homosexual sense has been traced to a quotation in the Australian paper, the Sydney *Truth* in 1924: "*Queen,* effeminate person," (6), implying "the effeminate partner in a homosexual relationship" *(OED).* However Eric Partridge in his *Dictionary of Historical Slang* (1937) has the entry: "*Quean;* incorrectly *queen,* a homosexual, esp. one with girlish manners and carriage; obsolete except in Australia." J.R. Ackerley's posthumously published autobiography *My Father and Myself* (1968) has this personal comment: "I did want him to think me 'queer' and himself part of homosexuality, a term I disliked because it included prostitutes, pansies, pouffs and queans" (xii, 127). However, the *Australian National Dictionary* (1988) does not acknowledge either form. *Queen* has since become the established form in most global varieties of English, both as an independent form and in less critical compounds such as *drag queen,* recorded in 1959 in William Burroughs's *Naked Lunch* (6).

See also: Bugger; Homosexuals.

Bibliography
Mills, Jane. *Womanwords.* London: Virago, 1989.
Partridge, Eric. *Dictionary of Historical Slang.* London: Routledge & Kegan Paul, 1937.
Rogers, Bruce. *The Queen's Vernacular—A Gay Lexicon.* San Francisco: Straight Arrow, 1972.
Sontag, Susan. "Notes on Camp" (1964). In *A Susan Sontag Reader.* New York: Vintage, 1983.

QUEER

The modern denotation of "homosexual" is virtually the last stage in the complex and unstable semantic history of this word of uncertain origin, which first appeared in Scots about five hundred years ago. It then had two basic senses, namely "strange, odd, peculiar in appearance or character," and "questionable, suspicious, dubious." Both of these semantic cores were applied to criminals. Francis Audelay included in his early vocabulary of thieves' cant in 1561 *quire bird* for "one that is come lately out of prison," and by the late eighteenth century *queer* clearly had a thriving underground currency, illustrated by no less than twenty-one entries in Francis Grose's *Classical Dictionary of the Vulgar Tongue* (1796). From the base sense of the adjective, defined as "base, roguish, bad, naught or worthless," Grose has *queer bitch,* "an odd out-of-the way fellow," a seeming anticipation of modern usage, and *queer street* "wrong; improper; contrary to one's wish." The association with criminality and prison (also known as *queer ken*) appears repeatedly, in *queer birds,* defined as "rogues relieved from prison and returning to their old trade," and *queer bit-makers* for "coiners." Most of the references are to males, notably a *queer fellow*, but a *queer mort* is "a diseased strumpet," linked to the modern colloquial phrase "to feel queer," that is, "ill" or "out of sorts."

Although *queer* included the senses of "odd," "abnormal," and "improper," the specific meaning of "homosexual" is apparently American in its early currency. The first instance in the *Oxford English Dictionary* is from the U.S. Department of Labor's *Scientific Study of Juvenile Delinquents* (1922), referring to a young man who is "probably 'queer' in sex tendency" (8). The *Journal of Social History* (vol. xix, 1985) retails a quotation from 1919 referring to "Queers ... fairies ... cocksuckers" (192). Godfrey Irwin's study *American Tramp and Underworld Slang* (1931) gives both the old senses of "crooked, criminal," adding: "also applied to effeminate or degenerate men or boys," as was *punk*. (All of these are, of course, secondary sources.) However, in Cockney rhyming slang, *ginger beer* was the code for *queer*, often reduced to plain *ginger* and recorded from the 1920s, according to Julian Franklyn (1961). This indicates that the term was familiar in the London speech community, but not used openly. The first recorded noun sense is attributed to W.H. Auden in 1932 in a reference to "an underground cottage frequented by the queer." This is also the first recorded use of *cottage* in the sense of "a haunt for homosexuals," long before the term became generally current. An ominous "witness word" for the persecution of homosexuals is *queer-bashing*, recorded in legal proceedings in 1970.

Most of the dictionary citations express criticism, hostility, or embarrassment. However, from about 1960 the process of "reclamation" started, with some newspapers using the term in a neutral way, such as the comment on a play dealing with "simple non-tragic aspects of queerness" (London *Observer*, May 4, 1958). Subsequently the homosexual community and gay pressure groups began to use the word openly in public discourse and to give it respectability in academic contexts. Thus university programs and articles started to appear under titles like "Queer Theory" (ed. Teresa de Lauretis, 1991), "Queer Culture," "Queer Studies," and more recently *The Queer God* (Marcella Althaus-Reid 2003), which includes topics like "Queering the Bible and queering the patriarchs," showing increasing grammatical flexibility. A usage note in the *Collins Concise Dictionary* (2000) explains the new complexities: "Although the term *queer* is still considered derogatory when used by nonhomosexuals, it is now used by homosexuals of themselves as a positive term." The growth of political correctness has obviously reduced the currency of the hostile homosexual senses, while the popular American reality television program "Queer Eye for the Straight Guy" (2003) has publicized the term.

In terms of global usage, *queer* in the sense under discussion is not especially current outside the United Kingdom and the United States, but is found in colloquial Australian and South African English.

See also: Bugger; Homosexuals.

Bibliography

Althause-Reid, Marcella. *The Queer God*. London: Routledge, 2003.
Benshoff, Harry, and Sean Griffin. *Queer Cinema*. London: Routledge, 2004.
Dyer, Richard. *The Culture of Queers*. London: Routledge, 2002.
Franklyn, Julian. *A Dictionary of Rhyming Slang*. London: Routledge & Kegan Paul, 1961.
Grose, Francis. *A Classical Dictionary of the Vulgar Tongue*. London: C. Chappel, 1796.

RABELAIS, FRANÇOIS

François Rabelais (1494–1553) was a remarkable French satirist who had a variegated career, studying at a Benedictine abbey, joining the Franciscan order, continuing at another Benedictine house and various universities, including Montpellier and Paris, finally becoming a notable physician at Lyon. His two highly successful satirical masterpieces, *Pantagruel* (1533) and *Gargantua* (1535), were published under the pseudonym of Alcofribas Nasier (an anagram of his own name). They form an entirely original work combining fantasy and satire, folly and wisdom, coarse physicality and abstruse learning, humanistic values and superstition, all generated by an extraordinary imagination and prodigious verbal creation. The works were highly popular with King Francis I, but condemned by the Church for their unorthodox ideas and mockery of religious practices. For instance Gargantua's father criticizes "idle and lazy monks, [who] doth not labour and work, as doth the peasant and artificer; doth not ward and defend the country, as doth the man of war; cureth not the sick and the diseased, as the physician doth" (Book I, chapter 40). Three other books followed, under his own name.

Rabelais became known and his influence on English literature initiated through the remarkable translation by Sir Thomas Urquhart (Books I and II) and Peter Anthony Motteux (Books III–V) between 1653 and 1694. The epithet *Rabelaisian* (which the *Oxford English Dictionary* dates from 1857) means essentially "characterised by exuberance of imagination and language, combined with extravagance and coarseness of humour and satire." Thus the gigantic infant Gargantua shows his prodigious intelligence in a poetic celebration of an unusual topic, his performance on the chamber pot. Obscene or vulgar topics are often presented frankly with encyclopedic learning, language reaching beyond French, and marked by vivid metaphors. Rabelais's intention, like that of Jonathan Swift in the English tradition, is to bring out the absurdity of certain social taboos and practices, as well as the odd euphemistic language that becomes conventional. Thus Gargantua's governesses, more concerned with his physical prowess than his mental development "very pleasantly would pass the time in taking you know what between their fingers, and dandling it":

> One of them would call it her littel dille, her staff of love, her quillety, her faucetin, her dandilolly. Another her peen, her jolly kyle, her blaberet, her membretoon, her quickset imp: another again

François Rabelais's satirical masterpiece *Gargantua* (1535), about a giant—depicted as an infant in this nineteenth-century book illustration by Gustave Doré—contributed to its author's reputation for ribaldry and coarse humor. (The Art Archive/Collection Claude Germain, Paris/Dagli Orti)

her branch of coral, her female adamant, her placket-racket, her Cyprian sceptre, her jewel for ladies. And some of the other women would give it these names—my bunguetee, my stopple too, my bush-rusher, my gallant wimble, my pretty borer, my coney-burrow ferret, my little piercer, my augretine, my dangling hangers, down right to it, stiff and stout, in and to, my pusher, dresser, pouting stick, my honey pipe, my pretty pillicock, linky pinky, futilletie, my lusty andouille, and crimson chitterling, my littel couille bredouille, my pretty rogue, and so forth.
(Book I, chapter xi)

The passage is full of what would now be called "phallic symbols" (*andouille* and *chitterling* being kinds of sausage). *Coney* is an old euphemism for "cunt," while *pillicock* (also used in *King Lear* III iv 78) is the ancestor of modern slang *pillock,* meaning "prick" in both senses. Another *tour de force* from this bizarre encyclopedia of humorous obscenity is found in the tirade when some cake-bakers insult some grape-pickers:

The bun-sellers or cake-makers did injure them most outrageously, calling them prattling gabblers, lickorous gluttons, freckled bittors, mangy rascals, shite-a-bed scoundrels, drunken roysters, sly knaves, drowsy loiterers, slapsauce fellows, slabberdegullion druggels, lubberly louts, cozening foxes, ruffian rogues, paltry customers, sycophant-varlets, drawlatch hoydens, flouting milk-sops, jeering companions, staring clowns, forlorn snakes, ninny loblocks, scurvy sneaksbies, fondling fops, base loons, saucy coxcombs, idle lusks, scoffing braggarts, noddy meacocks, blockish grutnols, dollipol-joltheads, jobbernol goosecaps, foolish loggerheads, flutch calf-lollies, grouthead gnat-snappers, lob-dotterels, gaping changelings, codshead loobies, woodcock slangams, ninnyhammer flycatchers, noddypeak simpletons, turdy-gut, shitten shepherds, and other suchlike defamatory epithets.
(Book I chapter xxv)

We notice than *injure* is here used in the old sense of "to insult" and that the invective includes many words which have long passed away. It is curious to reflect on Sir Thomas Urquhart, a widely traveled Scot of noble standing, knighted by King Charles I, scouring the lower registers to render Rabelais's extraordinary range of vituperation. His translation of the first two books appeared in 1653, ironically the year of Cromwell's Puritan Common-wealth. Peter Anthony Motteux, a French refugee, completed the work nearly forty years later. They used the contemporary idiom, which must have had considerable impact at the time, but is obviously dated now. They often had to anglicize words fabricated by Rabelais, but their translation has retained its classic status.

Bibliography

Brown, Huntington. *Rabelais in English Literature.* London: Cassell, 1967.
Rabelais, François. *The Five Books of the Lives, Heroic Deeds and Sayings of Gargantua and his son Pantagruel,* trans. Sir Thomas Urquhart and Peter Anthony Motteux. London: A.H. Bullen, 1904.

RACIAL INSULTS. *See:* Ethnic Insults

RADIO. *See:* Broadcasting

RAP

The term is used in popular culture to describe a musical genre that has grown up in the United States in recent decades, a predominantly Black form of social and political commentary that is rhythmically accentuated and uses provocative language. *Rap* became part of Black slang around 1900, meaning "to chat freely," subsequently acquiring the sense of "to talk rapidly, rhythmically, vividly, and boastfully," a style much associated with the braggadocio utterances of the boxer Muhammad Ali (formerly Cassius Clay). It also has the sense of ritualized repartee associated with sounding and playing **the dozens**.

Curiously these modern meanings are an extension of *rap* in the old British English sense of "to utter sharp words or an oath," recorded from the sixteenth century: "I am wont sometime to rap out an oath," confessed Sir Thomas Wyatt in 1541. By the eighteenth century a related sense of "to swear" was in vogue: "I scorn to rap against a lady" says a character in Henry Fielding's novel *Amelia* (1752, II x 1). Francis Grose defined "to rap" in his slang dictionary (1785) as "to take a false oath; also to curse. He rapped out a volley; i.e. he swore a whole volley of oaths." According to the *English Dialect Dictionary* (ca. 1900) *rap* developed related northern dialect senses including "to speak angrily and quickly; to use bad language."

The contemporary usage gained recognition in 1983 when some inner-city high-school students from the borough of Queens in New York styled themselves "Run DMC" and produced "It's Like That," which sold 500,000 copies. Initially rap involved improvising rhymes chanted over a playing record. It has since become recognized as a major independent and lucrative genre. Artists and practitioners who can be included in this category are "Ice T," "easy E," "LL cool J," and "Eminem" in the United States and "Beeny Man," "Bounty Killer," and "Elephant Man" in Jamaica. As with most cultural forms, success creates a double standard: the prestige of recognition is counterbalanced by increasing outrageousness. The British rap artist and poet Benjamin Zephania rejected the award of the O.B.E. (Order of the British Empire) in 2003 with the words "Stick it, Mrs. Queen." The language of the lyrics initially went unnoticed until increasingly flagrant chauvinism, advocacy of drug use, and hostility to authority provoked controversy, especially at the time of awards. A sample from "easy E" runs:

I said "Fuck it, I know what should be done.
Just pull down your panties and I'll fuck the biggest one.
And then I'll get the other pussy and put it in the freezer
So I can always have my own hostesser."

In June 1990 the rap group "2 Live Crew" were arrested by a Florida sheriff on charges of obscenity. Their album, *As Nasty as They Wanna Be,* carried the warning "Explicit Language Contained" and included numbers with titles such as "Bad Ass Bitch" and "Get The Fuck Out of My House (Bitch)." Other groups, by choosing names like "Niggaz with Attitude," show a new kind of Black Pride. In recent years some rap artists have provoked further controversy by explicitly homophobic material. "Eminem" (Marshall Bruce Mathers III), the winner of several awards including an Emmy, was the first of these. He has been the object of a number of complaints and lawsuits by GLAAD (the Gay and Lesbian Alliance Against Discrimination). In 2003 the British Attorney General Lord Goldsmith and the former Solicitor General Lord Falconer took the view that it was feasible to prosecute singers who incite homophobic violence.

See also: Dozens, the.

Bibliography

Krims, Adam. *Rap Music and the Poetics of Identity.* Cambridge: Cambridge University Press, 2000.

RASCAL

The term has undergone considerable semantic change, having originally been a class-term and a collective noun meaning "the rabble or camp followers of an army, or generally people of the lowest class." These meanings remained attached to the French word *rascaille* when it was borrowed into English in the fourteenth century. The modern meaning, defined by the *Oxford English Dictionary* as "a low, mean, unprincipled or dishonest fellow," is recorded in 1586 and has remained current in general English to the present. However, as with *rogue,* the term can be used in a sense of mild reproof, a weakening recorded from the early seventeenth century. Alexander Cooke's surprisingly titled work, *Pope Joane: A Dialogue between a Protestant and a Papist* (1610) catches the ambiguity: "Sweete Rascal! If your love be as earnest as your protestation, you will meet me this night at supper" (3).

See also: Moralization of Status Words.

RECANTATION

The formal withdrawal or renunciation of a statement or article of faith, being therefore similar to abjuration, renunciation, or disavowal. Historically the term was used most frequently to mean a public confession of error in religious matters, a sense recorded from the sixteenth century. Although not technically an oath, the publicity surrounding recantation gave it personal endorsement. At the time of the constitutional and religious crisis during the reign of Henry VIII, recantation of Catholicism became a requirement endorsing his authority. Alternatively, in terms of the legislation, "Such offendour . . . shall be for the firste time admitted to recant and renounce his said errours" (1542–1543, *Act 34 and 35 Henry VIII, c. 1*). The term became particularly associated in the public mind with Thomas Cranmer, the Archbishop of Canterbury, the third and last of the Oxford martyrs, who was burned at the stake on March 21, 1555. There he recanted his previous oaths of conformity to the Catholic Church issued under duress, stretching out his right hand into the fire, saying "forasmuch as my hand offended, writing contrary to my heart, my hand shall be punished therefore"(MacCulloch 1996, 603). As Isaac Disraeli shrewdly observed in 1814: "Recantations usually prove the force of authority rather than the force of conviction" (*Quarrels of Authors* 1867, 453). The term has become used generally in many contexts, not all of them serious.

See also: Abjuration.

Bibliography
MacCulloch, Diarmaid. *Thomas Cranmer.* New Haven: Yale University Press, 1996.

RECLAMATION OF OPPROBRIOUS TERMS

As numerous entries in this work show, particular outgroups become the object of insults and slurs. These groups are regarded with hostility and stigmatized on the basis of various criteria, such as religion (e.g., *papist* and *bible-basher*), nationality (e.g., *frog* and *wop*), race (e.g., *coolie* and *nigger*), and sexual preferences (e.g., *queer* and *dyke*). Until comparatively recent times the dynamic of stigmatization continued virtually unopposed, and opposition usually had the effect of driving the opprobrious terms underground rather than diminishing their currency. In the case of ethnic slurs there has commonly been a double standard in currency for insiders and outsiders: for instance, Jews will refer to themselves as *yids,* and American blacks will use the term *nigger* among themselves, but are offended if an outsider were to take such a liberty.

However, in the past two decades the process of reclamation has begun, by which the stigmatized communities have started to use the terms themselves in public as a form of self-identification and even pride. This has been notably apparent in the use of *queer* in formulations like *Queer Studies, Queer Theory,* and so on. Gloria Steinem noted in 1979: "The Feminist spirit has reclaimed some words with defiance and humor. *Witch, bitch, dyke,* and other formerly pejorative epithets turned up in the brave names of small feminist groups" ("Words and Change"). Jane Mills observed in her study *Womanwords:* "By the 1980s many lesbians, refusing to accept the myth that they are either *butch* or *femme,* began to use *dyke,* without any negative connotations, to refer to all lesbians" (1989, 71). This process, which is an attempt to disarm prejudice, is unlikely to be extended to terms for religion and nationality. Salman Rushdie's provocative novel *The Satanic Verses* (1988) contains the comment: "To turn insults into strengths, Whigs, Tories, Blacks all chose to wear with pride the names they were given in scorn." Rushdie then proceeds to give "our mountain-climbing, prophet-motivated solitary . . . the Devil's synonym: Mahound" (93). This was a xenophobic medieval name for **Mahomet.**

See also: Mahomet / Mohammed; Nigger; Queer; Women, Swearing in.

Bibliography
Steinem, Gloria. "Words and Change." In *Outrageous Acts and Everyday Rebellions.* London: Flamingo, 1984.
Mills, Jane. *Womanwords.* London: Virago, 1989.
Rushdie, Salman. *The Satanic Verses.* London: Penguin/Viking, 1988.

RED

The particular association of the color red with Communism can be dated to 1848, often called the Year of Revolutions. Describing these momentous and violent events, the *Illustrated London News* commented: "The 'Red Republicans' have justified their name; they have filled the streets of Paris with blood. . . . The Working classes or 'Red Republicans' were imbued with the doctrine of Communism" (January 7, 1848). Because communism has never posed a serious political threat in Britain, the term has never gained major currency in English political parlance, certainly not as a term of abuse. However, both *red* and *pink* in the symbolic sense of *radical* have often surfaced in political discussion, as is seen in this ironic passage by Thomas de Quincey a decade prior to 1848: "Amusing it is to look back on any political work of Mr. Shepherd's . . . and to know that the pale pink of his radicalism was then accounted deep, deep scarlet" (*Tait's Magazine,* July 2, 1837). The political definition of *red* in the *Oxford English Dictionary* is extremely broad: "a radical, republican or anarchist," but is supported by very few quotations, the first from Alfred Lord Tennyson in 1864: "Blues and Reds they talk'd of" (*Blue* being the symbolic color of the English Conservative Party). A character in Mrs. Humphry Ward's novel *David Grieve* (1894) explains: "My father was a Red—an anarchist" (II, 349). After the Russian Revolution (often referred to as "Red October") the term tended to be used in Britain of the militant Bolshevik party, and subsequently of an extreme socialist, usually with a sense of irony.

However, in the United States, during the period of the Cold War, the anti-Communist witch-hunt aggravated by McCarthyism became so intense that the term acquired its greatest force in formulations like the "red scare," "reds under the bed," and the nuclear disarmament slogan "Better Red than Dead." Hugh Rawson notes that in this paranoid period "the associations of *red* in the United States were so pejorative that some people strove to avoid it even in nonpolitical contexts" (1991, 325). Unlike *communist,* which has retained a hostile but generalized currency, *red* is becoming obsolete.

See also: Communism.

Bibliography
Rawson, Hugh. *A Dictionary of Invective.* London: Robert Hale, 1991.

REFORMATION, THE

The Reformation involved, not simply the reforming of the Church, more especially the Church of Rome, but a radical redefinition of its authority as a spiritual, political, and economic force. The challenges to existing ecclesiastical authority, which ended the supremacy of the Pope in most of Western Europe, and the subsequent controversies were carried on in a highly public fashion, and the tone and register used became increasingly emotive. Initially, the principal participants were Martin Luther, John Calvin, Henry VIII, and John Knox on the one hand, and various Popes on the other, but as the decades passed, affiliations changed and great numbers of polemicists became involved. What had previ-

The association of red with Communism, dating to the revolutions of 1848, continued with the "Red Republic" of the Paris Commune in 1871. The leadership of that short-lived proletarian government are demonized in this period cartoon. (*Graphic Works of George Cruikshank*, Richard A. Vogler, Dover Publications)

ously been a vocabulary of solidarity split into labels of vilification. Thus terms like *abuse, superstition, heresy, idolatry,* and *abomination,* previously the prerogative of the Church, were used indiscriminately by various sects of each other. The entry for **Catholics** shows how that term itself, the title *Pope,* and even the name of Rome came to be used in a hostile and abusive fashion. By contrast *Protestant,* originally used (from 1539) in a limited sense of the German princes and free cities that supported the Reformation, was rapidly espoused by the English campaigners against the Papacy and used in a generally favorable fashion. Initially the language was fairly neutral, but within a few years as the sectarian strife intensified it became so intemperate as to be virtually insane.

Luther's publication of his Ninety-Five Theses in Wittenberg in 1517 provoked a bitter controversy over indulgences. The Pope's response referred to Luther as "a certain son of iniquity," "a son of perdition" and—after declaring him a heretic—"a roaring sow of the woods [which] has undertaken to destroy this vineyard, a wild beast [which] wants to devour it" (Hillerbrand 1964, 56, 60, and 80). The powerful imagery is effective in presenting Luther as a destructive lunatic or wild animal. Luther had referred to Henry VIII as "a pig, an ass, a dunghill, the spawn of an adder, a lying buffoon, and fool with a frothing mouth" (Rawson 1991, 298). Another potent metaphor is that of the Plague. When Henry VIII entered the fray in 1521 (prior to his break with Rome) with his treatise *Assertio Septem Sacramentum,* he denounced "the pest of Martin Luther's heresy [which] had appeared in Germany and was raging everywhere" (Hillerbrand 1964, 47).

When the Pope would not accede to Henry's request to divorce Catherine of Aragon, Henry proclaimed the Church of England in 1542 with himself as its head, and demoted the Pope to the status of mere "Bishop of Rome," an ironic and demeaning title still used in some quarters. The perennial, centuries-old complaint about the Church exporting the money from tithes to Rome led to hostile terms like *Rome-runner, Rome-raiker,* and Henry Brinklow's ironic gloss (in 1542) on the Latin form of the Pope's name: "Papa means pay pay" (1874, 39). The famous Calvinist John Knox was not alone in referring to the Church of Rome as "the Roman harlot" in his *History of the Reformation,* 1586–1587. In time the vocabulary of prostitution became widely exploited in terms like *harlotry, carnality,* and *fornication.* "The Presbyterians called the Independent churches whore," observed William Erbury, "and the Independents called them whore again; and I say they are all whores together" (Chandos 1971, xxiv). George Buchanan even-handedly condemned "Godles papists, harlat protestantis" in his polemic *Chamæleon* (1570, 24). More remarkably, in the first recorded use of *sodomite* two centuries earlier, John Wycliffe applied the term to spiritual corruption: "þat prelatys . . . ben [are] gostly [spiritual] sodomytis wors þan bodily sodomytis of sodom and gomor" (*Works* 1880, 55).

A tone of hysterical detestation becomes increasingly obvious in some of the belligerents. Thomas Harding in his *Confutation of Jewel* (1565) condemned Luther for bringing to Germany "the poisoned cuppe of his heresies, blasphemies and sathanismes" (II ii 42), using the last word for the first time, to mean "diabolical doctrine." The extreme controversialist John Bale, Bishop of Ossory in Ireland, went so far in his pamphlet *Yet a course at the Romyshe foxe* (1543) as to refer to his Catholic opponents as "fylthye whoremongers, murtherers, thieves, raveners, idolatours, lyars, dogges, swyne . . . and very devyls incarnate" (Bennett 1952, 73). As the schism increased, so new sects multiplied, invariably given demeaning names. In his polemic *The Pulpit Guarded* (1651) Thomas Hall listed the more important: "We have many sects now abroad [around]: Ranters, Seekers, Shakers, Quakers and now Creepers" (15).

However, the Reformation also inspired a new rigor in the use of language, especially in relation to the taking of oaths. When Luther was summoned before the Diet of Worms in 1521 and asked to recant, he refused on the grounds of conscience and scriptural authority. Sir Thomas More likewise refused to take the oath recognizing Henry VIII as the Head of the Church of England, for which defiance he was imprisoned and beheaded. At the same time, reformist programs showed an incipient puritanism. In Geneva, Calvin enforced discipline and morals by forbidding dancing, games of cards and dice, as well as severely punishing blasphemy and ribaldry.

See also: Catholics; Quakers and Shakers.

Bibliography

Bennett, H.S. *English Books and Readers, 1475 to 1557.* Cambridge: Cambridge University Press, 1952.
Brinklow, Henry. *The Complaynt of Roderyck Mors* [ca. 1542]. London: Early English Text Society, 1874.
Chandos, John, ed. *In God's Name.* London: Hutchinson, 1971.
Hillerbrand, H.J., ed. *The Reformation in Its Own Words.* London: S.C.M., 1964.

REGISTER

The term is used in semantics and stylistics to denote a particular choice of diction or vocabulary regarded as appropriate for a certain topic or social situation. The English vocabulary consists of three basic sources: the Germanic base deriving from the original Anglo-Saxon settlers, the French element brought with the Norman conquerors, and the classical element deriving from Latin and Greek that became more prominent from the Middle English period through to the Renaissance. English usage is strongly marked by separation of registers. Thus formal utterances, professional language, and serious literary forms like the epic and the romance use consistently high register, with a large proportion of terms derived from French and classical sources. Ordinary conversation, sitcoms, the **fabliau**, the farce, or the dirty story, on the other hand, use a consistently lower register with a greater Anglo-Saxon element. Consequently, a change of register, especially downward, often constitutes a breach of decorum. On a more mundane level, the topic of sex is marked by a clear separation of registers trenchantly articulated by C.S. Lewis: "As soon as you deal with [sex] explicitly, you have to choose between the language of the nursery, the gutter and the anatomy class" (Tynan 1975, 154).

The classic description and illustration of register is that given by Sir James Murray in his Preface to the great **Oxford English Dictionary** (ca. 1884). It divides the vocabulary on a hierarchical basis from formal to informal, using the central categories of "Literary," "Common," "Colloquial," and "Slang" in descending order, designating the less common as "Scientific," "Technical," "Foreign," and "Dialectal." Being a Victorian, Murray did not include the category of "Obscene."

Murray's digrammatic representation of register

Formal oaths naturally employ elevated diction, being one pole of a binary opposition, whereas the vocabulary of swearing is largely made up of native common words drawn from the categories of colloquial and **slang**, and also illustrated in the entry for **rude words**, Thus *shit* and *turd* are ancient native terms that have retained their insulting capacity up to the present. By contrast, the more formal terms *ordure* and *defecation,* which are classically derived, do not have this ability, although *excrement* was so used in earlier times, for instance, by the dramatist Ben Jonson (1572–1637). The same is obviously true of *fuck* as against *copulate, bum* as against *posterior, cunt* as against *vagina,* and *cock* as against *penis.* In each case the first term of the pair can be used with great insulting diversity, whereas the second has a narrow and fairly precise meaning. Context is always an important factor. Thus in Shakespeare's *Macbeth* (1605) the play's opening question, "What bloody man is that?" (I ii 1) leaves a modern audience in momentary uncertainty about the tone. However, Eliza Doolittle's famous lapse from formal dignity into the demotic exclamation "Not bloody likely!" in George Bernard Shaw's **Pygmalion** provoked a scandal in 1914.

Naturally for a Victorian, Murray placed the category "Literary" above "Common." He would have had in mind the great novels, plays, and poems of English literature up to his day, in which the register is generally elevated. But there are problematic major authors like **Geoffrey Chaucer**, **William Shakespeare**, **Ben Jonson**, and **Charles Dickens**, whose diction includes all the categories down to the most obscene. Today, with "four-letter" words much more common in print, the status and definition of a "literary" register is even more problematic.

Although scientific and technical terms are not naturally qualified to be used in oaths, high-register terms can be used as a form of swearing, for example, *infernal, confounded,* and *perdition.* Similarly, foreign terms have occasionally found a place in the arsenal of English oaths. Thus *foutra* from French *foutre,* meaning "fuck," became fashionable for several decades from about 1592 and is used by Shakespeare. Similar in meaning, currency, and period is Italian or Spanish *figo!* (also *fico!*), which was emphasized by a rude gesture explained in **body language**. Dialect terms, being native and regional, tend to be limited in use to their place of origin, only occasionally gaining wider currency. There was, however, a rare instance when Margaret Thatcher, the British prime minister, in a heated debate in the House of Commons, accused an opposition member of being "frit," which in the dialect of Lincolnshire, her native county, means "cowardly."

See also: Pygmalion; Rude Words, Semantic Field of.

Bibliography
Hughes, Geoffrey. *A History of English Words.* Oxford: Blackwell, 2000.
Tynan, Kenneth. *The Sound of Two Hands Clapping.* London: Jonathan Cape, 1975.

RELIGIOUS OATHS

Historically, religious oaths form the vast majority of terms and phrases making up the variegated vocabulary of swearing in English. This is understandable, given that the normal dynamic of swearing is to invoke some force superior to oneself. However there is always a tension between the necessity of validating an oath and breaking the taboos deriving from biblical authority traditionally surrounding the use of sacred names. George Santayana made the incisive historical observation that "Oaths are the fossils of piety" (1900, 148).

In Anglo-Saxon times the pagan gods, goddesses, and other vital forces played a role, to the point that one of the Anglo-Saxon laws specified "never swear by the pagan gods." William the Conquerer's favorite oath was *By the Splendor of God,* while his son William Rufus preferred *By the Holy Face of Lucca,* alluding to "the wonder-working crucifix of that City" (Montagu 1973, 108). Despite the commandment that "thou shalt not take the name of the Lord thy God in vain," the profusion of explicit Christian oaths in the **medieval period** and in the work of **Geoffrey Chaucer** is so astonishing as to defy belief. The agencies include not just the panoply of the names for God, the Lord, Christ, the Virgin Mary, but the saints, the Fathers of the Church, the Pope, the rituals such as the Mass, the faith, and so on. Many of these were invoked in the bitter polemical controversies of the Reformation. Some unusual oaths, like *by Goddes dignitee!* have faded away, just as *by my faith!* eroded into plain *faith* and *I pray thee* continued as commonplace *prithee.* All are now obsolete.

The central act of Christian sacrifice, the Crucifixion, also yielded many swearing terms, such as the Cross, the nails, and the wounds of Christ, in a way that is shocking and bizarre to modern sensibilities. Oaths like *by **God's wounds*** (reputedly a favorite of Queen Elizabeth I), *by God's nails,* and the like provoked sustained criticism from many religious texts and sermons: "Christ's blood, these days, is reckoned of little price amongst the greater part of the people," complained Friar John Waldeby (in Owst 1933, 417). Censorship and statutory fines in the Renaissance period generated euphemistic or **minced oaths** like *zounds* and *snails.* Steadily the literal senses were eroded, to the point that their origins ceased be recognizable: thus *blimey!* is an abbreviated form of *gor blimey!,* originally *God blind me!* Eventually they became simply fashionable forms of words for the majority of the speech community, such as *strewth!* or *Holy cow!* An alternative mode of euphemism was the use of pagan substitutes, such as *Jove, Jupiter, Mahounde,* and so forth. An illuminating and ironic insight into the change of mode in religious swearing is provided by Sir John Harrington, Queen Elizabeth's godson, in a poem quoted in the entry for **fashion in swearing**, which traces the shift in fashion whereby the Mass was replaced by the cross, then by the faith, so that finally "God damn them is their common oath." The break with Rome also meant that *Mary* declined in force from being the sacred name of the Virgin Mary to the trivialized form *marry,* used simply as a reinforcer, meaning "why, to be sure."

Given the crucial Christian emphasis on salvation and damnation, a less expected religious source is the copious use of the names *Devil* and *Hell,* their derivatives *devilish* and *hellish,* and their euphemistic variations, such as *deuce, dickens, heck, infernal, perdition,* and so forth. Equally strange is the use of *bless* and *blessed* in an ironic or euphemistic fashion to mean the opposite, namely *cursed,* as in the phrase "the blessed thing won't work," uses dating from the early nineteenth century. Summing up his studies into American student speech, Timothy Jay wrote: "God is Dead: Have Religious Terms Lost Their Clout?" In his brief analysis the answer was simple: "College students judge them [religious terms] to be mild" (1992, 167).

Although the force of the traditional taboos against using religious oaths has generally diminished in modern times with the secularization of Western society, they still govern formal public utterances. In the United States the main exception is the use of **goddam** and its various mutations, which have been used by more than one president. In the United Kingdom probably the only religious oaths acceptable in public is "for God's sake" or its variants. It is unimaginable that any modern public figure would use the phraseology "I beseech you, in the bowels of Christ, think it possible you may be mistaken" (Oliver Cromwell, in his *Letter to the General Assembly of the Church of Scotland,* August 3, 1650).

Religious oaths do not truly feature in such contexts in Australia, and only to a limited extent in South Africa, where the distinguishing feature is the use of Afrikaans equivalents, such *Here!* for *Lord!* and *jissus!* For *Jesus!*

See also: Chaucer, Geoffrey; Christ; Devil, the; God, Euphemisms for; God's Wounds; Hell; Minced Oaths.

Bibliography

Elliott, Ralph W.V. *Chaucer's English.* London: André Deutsch, 1974.
Jay, Timothy. *Cursing in America.* Philadelphia: Benjamins, 1992.
Montagu, Ashley, *The Anatomy of Swearing.* London and New York: Macmillan and Collier, 1973.
Owst, G.R. *Literature and Pulpit in Medieval England.* London: Cambridge University Press, 1933.
Santayana, George. *Interpretations of Poetry and Religion.* New York: Scribners, 1900.

RENAISSANCE, THE

Swearing in England during the Renaissance (a period of disputed length, but here taken to extend approximately from 1400 to 1600) showed two radically contrary tendencies, toward efflorescence and censorship. The extraordinary exuberance of the religious oaths of the Middle Ages continued and was enriched by a great variety of new secular modes. The practice of **flyting**, or set-piece tirades of astonishing personal abuse, reached its highest point of development in Scotland in the early sixteenth century. Henry VIII (1509–1547) swore freely and his daughter Queen Elizabeth (1558–1603) reputedly "swore like a man" (Shirley 1979, 10). **Shakespeare** (1564–1616) and **Ben Jonson** (1572–1637) indulged in scurrilous personal "conflicts of wit," and both playwrights included in their plays many passages of personal execration, cursing, and desperate exclamation of such power that they are still painful to read and hear.

The Renaissance essentially embodied a new skeptical and empiricist attitude, a radical contrast with the more credulous medieval mind-set. As John Donne (?1571–1631) acutely observed: "the new Philosophy sets all in doubt" ("Anatomy of the World"; "First Anniversary," l. 205). This included the "nominalist" view of language, holding that the meanings of words were essentially conventional and not based on ultimate realities. Thus in Christopher Marlowe's *Dr. Faustus* (1592) the hero ritualistically calls up the Devil in the form of Mephistophilis, but then expresses the heretical view "I think hell's a fable" (Scene 5, l. 127). Even though the play shows that hell does indeed exist, in both a physical and mental sense, this staging violated the most powerful taboos. Indeed, all of Marlowe's extraordinary heroes test conventional boundaries with deeply subversive views. The insatiable world-conqueror Tamburlaine argues sophistically that "Nature . . . doth teach us all to have aspiring minds," Edward II is tragically obsessed with his homosexual lover Gaveston, while Barabas, the savage Jew of Malta, mocks "swine-eating Christians, never circumcised," cursing them as "infidels."

Consequently, the period also saw the beginnings of severe restraints against swearing, framed in various pieces of legislation. Strict punishments were proposed in Scotland in 1551 and in England in 1606 and 1623. One of the great cultural glories of the Elizabethan Age was the flowering of the drama, highly popular with both the nobility and the groundlings. However, formal censorship of plays was embodied in the figure of the Master of the Revels, a position initiated in 1574, two years before James Burbage had even built the first theater in London.

Furthermore, as John Dover Wilson has stressed, "From the erection of the theatres in 1576 to their suppression at the outbreak of the Civil War [1641], the Puritan party waged an unceasing warfare against the stage" (1944, 227). The Puritans were fundamentally opposed to fiction, regarded the theaters as dens of iniquity, and took literally the injunction in the book of Deuteronomy 22:5 that "The woman shall not wear that which pertaineth unto a man, neither shall a man put on a woman's garment; for all that do so are abomination unto the Lord thy God." The latter practice was, of course, a staple convention of Elizabethan productions. Dover Wilson cites a number of polemical attacks condemning "Italian bawdry [lasciviousness]" and "beastly and filthy matters" (1944, 206, 228). Philip Stubbes questioned the moral function of plays: "Do they not maintain bawdry, insinuate foolery and renew the remembrance of heathen idolatory?" He also condemned the lascivious behavior of the audience and, by insinuation, that of the actors, who "in their secret conclaves (covertly) play the sodomite or worse" (1944, 229). The anonymous "T.G." in "The Rich Cabinet" (1616) denounced "execrable oaths, artificial [ingenious] lies, discoveries of cozenage [deception], scurrilous words, obscene discourses, corrupt courtings, licentious motions, lascivious actions, and lewd gestures" (1944, 224).

These Puritan tendencies took completely new and thorough forms of policing the theater and dramatic language, gaining force as the decades passed and staying on the statute books for centuries. As a court officer in the service of the **Lord Chamberlain**, the **Master of the Revels** during the reign of Queen Elizabeth was increasingly given the preemptive right to censor plays, which the actors were required to recite and present to him prior to public performance. The grounds for not granting the players a license to perform could be political or doctrinal, a reinforcement of previous orders against "players and pipers strolling through the kingdom disseminating heresy and seditions" in "naughty [wicked] plays" (Gildersleeve 1908, 12). The staging of two satirical plays, *The Isle of Dogs* (1597 but now lost) and *Eastward Ho!* (1605), led to the jailing of the actors and the author Ben Jonson. A performance of his play *The Magnetic Lady* (1632) led to a charge of blasphemy.

Following An Act to Restrain Abuses of Players (1606), profanity became a major consideration. Frances Shirley has speculated that the legislation was delayed until after Elizabeth's death, since the queen, a copious swearer herself, would have been unsympathetic to it (1979, 10). According to this Act:

> If . . . any person or persons doe or shall in any Stage play, Interlude, Shewe, Maygame or Pageant jestingly or prophanely speake or use the holy name of God or of Christ Jesus, or of the Holy Ghoste or of the Trinitie . . . [they] shall forfeite for every such Offence by him or them committed Tenne pounds.
>
> (3 Jac. I. c. 21)

Had this legislation been strictly enforced it would have ruined any company putting on the highly popular religious plays known as Wakefield Pageants in the Towneley Cycle, acted all over the realm from about 1554 to 1576. As the entry for the **medieval period** makes clear, the Wakefield Master's language at sacred moments is surprisingly coarse and blasphemous. The spectacular ranting of Herod the Great in one these plays is memorialized in Shakespeare's famous phrase condemning the "ham" actor who "out-Herods Herod" (*Hamlet,* III ii 15).

The immediate effect of this censorship was that profane terms were euphemized into **minced oaths**. The name of God was either distorted to *gad* or abbreviated to *od,* older euphemistic forms like *cock* and *gog* were resuscitated, and foreign forms like *perdy* (from French *par Dieu*) introduced. Alternatively, it was omitted, so that *God's wounds!* became "minced" into *zounds!* and *God's blood!* likewise euphemized into *'sblood!* These technical evasions of sacred names seem strange now, but would have had fairly obvious meanings for the audience.

Another stratagem was to substitute pagan deities like Jove or Jupiter, which are still current. Shakespeare used a wide variety of such names, including Apollo, Hercules, Mars, Pluto, and Venus, especially, but not exclusively, in the Roman plays. In his comedy *Everyman in His Humour* (1598), Ben Jonson created amusing and absurd oaths like *Body o' Caesar!* and *by the foot of Pharaoh!* However, in *King Lear* (ca. 1605), set in pagan times, characters appeal in curses to "Nature" as a goddess and to primitive natural forces, as in "By the sacred radiance of the sun" (I i 111). Both polytheistic forms like "the gods" and the monotheistic "God" are appealed to. Nevertheless, the name of God still flourished in many contexts.

With signs of a decline in the efficacy of religious oaths, secular modes of swearing, which had already been flourishing since the time of Chaucer, developed new varieties. Among the new referents were animal terms such as *cur* and *viper;* genital and excretory modes, such as *base cullion* [testicle], *dungworm,* and *excrement;* vituperative words for women such as *drab, harlot, filth, slut,* and *trull,* as well as combinations such as *whoreson filthy slave.* In addition there are powerfully imaginative epithets like "toad-spotted traitor!" and "abortive rooting hog." In addition, new modes of racist insult emerged, discussed in the entries for **Blacks** and **Jews**. There were even new specialists in verbal aggression, like the **roarers** and the **rufflers**, who have their own entries. In all, the limitations of censorship were matched by new forms of creativity.

See also: Blacks; Fines and Penalties; Flyting; Jews; Jonson, Ben; Lord Chamberlain; Master of the Revels; Minced Oaths; Shakespeare, William.

Bibliography
Gildersleeve, Virginia Cocheron. *Government Regulation of the Elizabethan Drama.* New York: Columbia University Press, 1908.
Shirley, Frances A. *Swearing and Perjury in Shakespeare's Plays.* London: Allen & Unwin, 1979.
Wilson, John Dover, ed. *Life in Shakespeare's England.* Harmondsworth: Penguin, 1944.

RENEGADE

Although *renegade* derives from *renege,* meaning "to renounce," both terms originate in Latin *negare,* "to deny." From their earliest usage in the sixteenth century they denoted betrayal or abandonment of previous loyalties to a cause. *Renegade,* dating from about 1583, is the anglicized form of *renegado,* and was the more critical term, originally meaning "an apostate from any religion, especially a Christian who becomes a Mohammedan." "He was a renegado," wrote Richard Hakluyt in 1599, "which is one that first was a Christian, and afterward becommeth a Turke" (*Voiages and Discoueries of the English Nation,* II i, 186). This gives a clue to the origin of the phrase "to turn Turk." About a century later the word was being used of a traitor or turncoat generally, one who deserts a person, party, or principle. The related term *runagate* is an anglicization meaning "vagabond, fugitive, or renegade." The verb *renege* originally covered most of the same serious meanings, but has since acquired the comparatively trivial sense of not following suit in cards, also known, interestingly, as *renouncing* or *revoking,* condemned by *The Complete Gamester* (1680) as "very foul play" (x, 82).

RESTORATION, THE

The restoration of the monarchy in 1660 in the form of Charles II ushered in a regime as extreme in its licentiousness as the puritanism it replaced. Charles had thirteen known mistresses and many illegitimate children, one authority on genealogy noting: "Of twenty-six dukes in England today, five are direct descendants on the wrong side of the blanket of Charles II" (Delderfield 1986, 90). The king surrounded himself with like-minded nobles, including the brilliant wit, accomplished rake and notorious poet of obscenity, the **Earl of Rochester,** who complimented the king's endowments thus: "Nor are his high desires above his strength, / His sceptre and his prick are of a length." According to Samuel Pepys's account of a particularly scandalous episode in 1663, Sir Charles Sedley, one of the king's boon companions, "coming in open day into the balcony [of Covent Garden] and showed his nakedness—acting all the postures of lust and buggery that could be imagined and abusing of scripture. . . . And that being done, he took a glass of wine and washed his prick in it and then drank it off; and then took another and drank the King's health" (July 1, 1663). For this and other outrageous behavior Sedley was fined £500 (Craig 1962, 23).

The theaters, closed by the Puritans in 1642, were reopened and enjoyed royal patronage. Charles II once even lent his coronation suit to the actor Thomas Betterton for a part in one of William Davenant's plays (Bruce 1974, 17). Although highly fashionable among the elite (Samuel Pepys once went to "the play" twice in one day), the theater ceased to be the truly popular form it had previously been. It now offered alluringly decadent fare in the form of risqué sexual intrigue, outrageous compromising situations, adultery, fashionable swearing, knowing innuendo, outright ribaldry, and seductive actresses. These became a new and upwardly nubile class, of whom the most famous was Nell Gwyn, who rose from being an orange vendor to become a royal mistress, and "retired from the stage at the age of nineteen to pursue a more lucrative career among her erstwhile audience" (Thompson and Salgado 1985, 223). The king's best-known deathbed sentiments, "Let not poor Nelly starve," are recorded by Bishop Gilbert Burnet (*History of My Own Time,* Vol. I, Book II, chapter 17). Nell Gwyn's linguistic abilities are further covered in **swearing in women.**

The great tragedies of passion of the Elizabethan Age died out and were replaced by a new form, the comedy of manners, written by the elite for the elite, of which the hallmarks were artificiality, triviality, and contrived wit. The terrible suffering at the end of *King Lear* (1605) as the King agonizes over the death of Cordelia can be juxtaposed with these flippant lines from one of the most brilliant exponents of the new form, William Congreve (1670–1729):

> Is he then dead?
> What, dead at last, quite, quite for ever dead!
> (*The Mourning Bride* V xi)

Contrived artificiality is well expressed in these sentiments: "There's nothing more unbecoming a man of quality than to laugh; Jesu, 'tis such a vulgar expression of the passion!" (Congreve's *The Double Dealer* IV). George Farquhar (1678–1707) makes comedy out of the inarticulate expression of passion: "Grant me some wild expressions, Heavens, or I shall burst . . . Words, words or I shall burst" (*The Constant Couple* V iii). William Wycherley (1640–1716) alludes to the less reputable expression of emotion:

Quaint: With sharp invectives–
Widow: Alias, Billingsgate
(*The Plain Dealer,* III)

The Concordance to Congreve's plays (five in all) reveals the thematic and verbal emphases. The most common exclamation is *devil!* (72), followed by *pox!* (51), and there are plenty of references to *cuckold* (18), *wittol* (9), *pimp* (10), and *whore* (15). (A *wittol* is a conniving cuckold.)

While there were oaths in profusion, in general they were either minced or secular. Thomas Killigrew's *The Parson's Wedding* (1663) has *Faith!, by this hand!, Cud's body,* and *God's nigs,* the direct form *Jesus,* as well as such unusual exclamations as *Thou son of a thousand fathers!* and *Son of a batchelour!* both meaning *bastard.* Serious oaths are explained away. The character of Daredevil in Thomas Otway's *The Atheist* (1684) casually dismisses his use of *Dam'me*: "Mere words of course. We use a hundred of 'em in conversation, which are indeed but in the nature of Expletives, and signifie nothing." (II ii). It is Farquhar, however, who gives the clearest exposé of the demotion of oaths to the status of mere words of fashion in a scene from *Love in a Bottle* (1698). A character suitably called Mockmore, a "rake" or decadent upper-class idler, newly arrived in London from Oxford, asks his "tutor" Rigadoon:

> Pray what are the most fashionable Oaths in Town? *Zoons,* I take it, is a very becoming one.
>
> *Rigadoon:* Zoons is only used by the disbanded [fired] Officers and Bullies [prostitute's "protectors"]; but Zauns is the Beaux' pronunciation.
>
> *Mockmore:* Zauns—
>
> *Rigadoon:* Yes, Sir, we swear as we Dance: smooth, and with a Cadence. Zauns! 'Tis harmonious, and pleases the Ladies, because 'tis soft—Zauns madam—is the only Compliment our great Beaux pass on a Lady.
>
> (II ii)

Farquhar is certainly being ironic, commenting on a sophisticated, superficial society in which sacred names are used freely, now so emptied of meaning that their pronunciation is merely a point of fashion. (*Zounds* has, of course, a horrific origin in "God's wounds" alluding to the Crucifixion, but is trivialized, since the old pronunciation has become déclassé and the new nonsensical form *zauns* is now "in.") The final irony is that "Zauns madam" is now regarded as a "compliment."

The excesses and absurdities of the Restoration theater provoked a significant reaction in the form of **Jeremy Collier**'s broadside *A Short View of the Profaneness and Immorality of the English Stage* (1698, the same year as Farquhar's play). As the relevant entry shows, the controversy involved several major authors and led to the genre becoming unfashionable.

See also: Collier Controversy; Rochester, Earl of.

Bibliography

Bowle, John, ed. *The Diary of John Evelyn.* Oxford: Oxford University Press, 1983.

Collier, Jeremy. *A Short View of the Profaneness and Immorality of the English Stage.* London, 1698. Reprint, facsimile edition, New York: Garland Publishing, 1972.

Craig, Alec. *The Banned Books of England.* London: Allen & Unwin, 1962.

Delderfield, Eric, ed. *Kings and Queens of England and Great Britain.* London: David and Charles, 1986.

Thompson, Peter, and Gamini Salgado. *The Everyman Companion to the Theatre.* London: Dent, 1985.

RHYME

Swearing and vituperation, being powerfully emotive modes of expression, employ various poetic devices of emphasis, including **alliteration, rhythm,** and **rhyme.** Historically, alliteration was the older mode, being the staple metrical device in Anglo-Saxon poetry, but from the Middle English period (ca. 1150–1500) onward rhyme became the dominant poetic mode. Rhyme can be used in two ways, most commonly as a disguise mechanism creating a euphemistic allusion, such as *ruddy* for *bloody,* or *teed off* for *peed off.* This mode can be developed into forms such as *cunning stunts* or the Australian phrase *no wucking furries,* involving a witty transposition of the initial consonants, technically called a Spoonerism. The rhyming device has been expanded into the ingenious and surprisingly comprehensive code language of **rhyming slang,** which has its own entry, producing such forms as *cobbler's awls* for *balls.* The other mode is internal rhyme, found in formulas such as *hell's bells!, fuck a duck!* and imperfect or partial rhymes such as *shit a brick!, stone the crows!,* and *reds under the bed.* Some of these are of surprising duration: *duck-fucker* is listed in Francis Grose's slang dictionary (1785) for "the man who has care of the poultry on board a ship of war." The generation of new "reduplicating" forms as they are called seems to be accelerating, with *gang-bang* dating from the 1940s, *fag-hag* from the late 1960s, and dozens more arriving on an annual basis. Assonance is also effective in formulations like *yellow peril* (incidentally dating from ca. 1900) and *gay plague.*

See also: Alliteration; Rhyming Slang; Rhythm.

RHYMING SLANG

Rhyming slang is a remarkable, virtually unique example of a highly developed set of codes used by a particular speech community, the Cockneys, devised on the basis of **disguise mechanisms.** It uses witty and ingenious coded formulas to refer to objects of affection and hostility as well as taboo topics. Familiar examples are *trouble and strife* for "wife," *pork pie* for "lie," and *cobbler's awls* for "balls." The basic principle, as the reader can perceive, is that the last word or syllable of the formula supplies the rhyme for the coded word. There is often no logical connection between the formula and the coded term, although irony is often apparent.

The Cockneys are a community traditionally identified as inhabiting the East End of London, one of the poorer working-class districts of the metropolis. They developed this particular set of speech codes at least a century and a half ago. According to Eric Partridge, "The beginnings of rhyming slang are obscure. In colloquialism and slang cant [underground criminal argot] there were scattered traces of it in the seventeenth and eighteenth centuries, but there existed no body of rhyming slang before about 1840" (1960, 273). The first reference is in John Camden Hotten's *The Slang Dictionary* (1859): "This cant . . . is known in Seven Dials [a disreputable part of London] as the Rhyming Slang, or the substitution of words and sentences which rhyme with other words intended to be kept secret. . . . I learn that the rhyming slang was introduced about twelve or fifteen years ago." Henry Mayhew, in his classic study *London Labour and the London Poor* (1851), noted: "The new style of cadgers' [street sellers'] cant is all done on the rhyming principle" (both cited in Ayto 2002, vii–viii). It may have originated, like cant, as a coded criminal language: hence forms like *Barnaby Rudge* for "judge" and *Artful Dodger* for "lodger." But some forms have now become current in British

English and various global varieties. Thus *loaf of bread* is originally rhyming slang for "head," but as often happens, only the first term becomes current, generating the common phrase "use your loaf" for "use your head."

In taboo areas several rhyming slang terms have become generally current in British English, clearly because their origins are no longer widely understood. Thus, *Hampton Wick* originally stands for *prick*, though it is most commonly encountered in such phrases as *flashing his hampton* for public indecency, which in turn gave rise to *flasher* for exhibitionist, as well as *to dip one's wick* for coitus, and less obviously *to get on one's wick* meaning "to annoy." Likewise *Berkeley* (or *Berkshire*) *Hunt* stands for *cunt*, although it is most frequently found in the abbreviated form *berk*, now meaning only a fool or contemptible male person; the origins no longer being generally understood, it is now a common word, pronounced "burk." Also common is *bristols*, derived from *Bristol city,* for *titty*. Similarly, from the example given earlier, *cobblers* is now in general use, meaning "balls" in the sense of "rubbish."

Terms for homosexuals form an area of dispute among the authorities. Barltrop and Wolveridge assert that "There is no Cockney word for homosexuality," pointing out that *"queer* has always meant ill" (1980, 81). However, Franklyn (1961) cites *ginger beer* (= *queer*) often reduced to plain *ginger* and recorded from the 1920s. Furthermore, all authorities agree on *iron hoof* (= *poof,* a term recorded as far back as ca. 1850–1860). *Iron hoof* itself is recorded from the 1930s, but *iron* went on to become a general slang term for "homosexual."

Many of the categories and the concentrations of terms suggest a male chauvinist provenance with paternalistic attitudes toward women and xenophobia. Coded rhymes for foreigners are very common, with the Jews being the community most rhymed against, followed by Blacks. Although few of them are strictly xenophobic in their categorization or metaphorical assumptions, the terms form a fund of covert insider references to outsiders. Some sense of the range and ingenuity of rhyming slang terms can be gauged from the table opposite, which combines sexual, excretory, and xenophobic terms.

Points frequently raised concern the general currency, comprehension, and function of rhyming slang. As has been shown, a number of terms have now passed into general usage, so that their coded function is now lost. Furthermore, as recent studies, such as that by John Ayto (2002), have demonstrated, rhyming slang continues to grow, and is now found in most global varieties of English, having generated new forms, most of them amusing and innocent, such as *Britney Spears* for "beers," Melvyn Bragg for "shag," Sigourney Weaver for "beaver," *Brad Pitt* for "shit," *Swiss Banker* for "wanker" was used in a headline in the British tabloid *The Sun* (July 5, 2004). In many ways it is now a general form of wordplay.

See also: Disguise Mechanisms.

Bibliography

Ayto, John. *The Oxford Dictionary of Rhyming Slang.* Oxford: Oxford University Press, 2002.
Barltrop, Robert, and Jim Wolveridge. *The Muvver Tongue.* London and West Nyack, NY: Journeyman, 1980.
Franklyn, Julian. *A Dictionary of Rhyming Slang.* London: Routledge & Kegan Paul, 1961.
Partridge, Eric. *Slang.* 3rd ed. London: Routledge & Kegan Paul, 1960.

Rhyming Slang Terms for Sexual, Excretory, and Xenophobic Categories

Long Version	Short/Common Version	Disguised Term
Almond rock	almond	cock
Alphonse	Alphonse	ponce
Army tanks		Yanks
Berkeley/Berkshire hunt	berk	cunt
Bolt the door	bolt	whore
Bottle and glass	bottle	arse
Brighton pier	pier	queer
Bristol cities	bristols	titties
Bubble and squeak	bubble	Greek
Cattle truck	cattle	fuck
Charley Ronce	charley	ponce
Cobbler's awls	cobblers	balls
Cuddled and kissed	cuddled	pissed
Early morn	early	horn
Egg and spoon		coon
Elephant and Castle	elephant	arsehole
Feather/peasant plucker		fucker
Fife and drum	fife	bum
Fish and shrimp	fish	pimp
Five to two	five	Jew
Flour mixer		shikse
Four by two		Jew
Friar Tuck		fuck
Front wheel skid		yid
Ginger beer	ginger	queer
Goose and duck	goose	fuck
Grumble and grunt	grumble	cunt
Ham shank		Yank
Hampton Wick	hampton	prick
Harvest moon		coon
Hit and miss	hit	piss
Iron hoof	iron	poof
Kangaroo		Jew
Khyber Pass	khyber	arse
Lucozade		spade
Orchestra stalls	orchestras	balls
Pony and trap	pony	crap
Razor blade	razo	spade
Richard the Third	richard	turd
Sausage roll		Pole
Septic tank	septic	Yank
Tickle your fancy		nancy
Tiddlywink		Chink
Tom tit	tom	shit
Uncle Dick		prick

RHYTHM

Rhythm is an important aspect in swearing, as it is of any kind of emotive language, such as expressions of lamentation, anger, or lyrical praise. Very often the rhythm of a formula will dominate the sense to the point that the word choice is not entirely logical. Thus, in the common arrangements *the silly old fool!, you fucking bastard!, you blithering idiot!, the complete asshole!,* the final nouns carry the weight of the invective, the adjectives *silly, old, little, blithering,* and *complete* becoming mere makeweights with virtually no literal sense or semantic force. (In fact, *blithering,* now a largely meaningless word confined to this formula, is originally derived from *blether,* meaning "to talk nonsense.") The structure of the type is significant, since the rhythm of the preceding adjectives, which is of a rising and falling variety, leads up to the major stress on the final noun.

The first example (*the silly old fool!*) demonstrates a common type, namely [–/–¨/–/=], where the dash (–) signifies a plain stressed syllable, the umlaut (¨) an unstressed syllable, and the equal sign (=) a major stress. The type is found, interestingly, centuries ago in Chaucer's Wife of Bath's castigating one of her old husbands as an "olde barrelful of lyes" (*Prologue,* l. 302). She also has insults made up of ironic deference and contempt, like "O leeve sire shrewe" ("O dear master rascal"), which follows similar rhythmic pattern [–/–¨/ –/=] (l. 365). A similar example is "Sire olde lecchour" (l. 242) ("old master lecher"), which has a similar semantic structure but a different rhythmic pattern [–/–¨/=¨], also found in modern types like *you fucking bastard!* Shakespeare's extremely articulate hero Hamlet, in one of his hysterical bouts, goes to rhythmic and semantic extremes in castigating the regicide Claudius as "Remorseless, treacherous, lecherous, kindless villain!" (II ii 592), finally despatching him with similar polysyllabic invective as: "incestuous, murderous damnèd Dane" (V ii 326).

Such baroque elaboration would not have much impact now. But similar powerful effects can be achieved by juxtaposing a long adjective and a short noun, as in *You unconscionable liar!, What an absolute fool!,* and the actual description of a notable politician as *an unremitting shit.* These examples also show a striking contrast in register, playing off a high-register classical term against lower word of common invective. The strongest instances of rhythm overpowering sense lie in the feature known as "infixing," found in recent forms like *absobloodylutely* and *unfuckingbelievable,* discussed in the entry for **flexibility**.

See also: Flexibility.

RIDDLES

Riddles form an intriguing verbal genre in which ambiguity and innuendo compete to suggest, confirm, or refute solutions, which may be obscene, scatological, or innocent. Although now only marginally current and usually literary, riddles have a long history in English, the first collection being found in the Anglo-Saxon poems of the Exeter Book. Some are simply enigmatic; others finish with the formulaic question: "Ask what I am." While most are amusing and ingenious exercises in wordplay, several are clearly bawdy, since they deal with suggestive topics such as a poker, a knife and its sheath, and with dough, which the woman makes rise and thrusts into her oven. Several knowingly invite an obscene solution but offer an innocent one, a convention which has continued to modern times. However, since the solutions were not given, this can only be a teasing but likely speculation, on which

Anglo-Saxon scholarship has generally been reticent. Consider the following passages, in the translation of Michael Alexander (1966):

(*a-44*)   Swings by his thigh a thing most magical!
Below the belt, beneath the folds
Of his clothes it hangs, a hole in its front end,
Stiff-set and stout, it swivels about.
Leveling the head of this hanging instrument,
Its wielder hoists his hem above the knee:
It is his will to fill a well-known hole
That it fills fully when at full length.
He has often filled it before. Now he fills it again.

(*b-12*)   a dark-headed girl grabs and squeezes me,
silly with drink, and in the dark night
wets me with water, or warms me up
before the fire. Fetched between breasts
by her hot hand, while she heaves about
I must stroke her swart part.

The sexual innuendoes can hardly be disputed, which makes the conventional solutions the more knowing and suggestive, since (a) is a key and (b) is an oxhide.

Medieval lyrics have a fair number of obviously risqué riddle-poems, such as "I have a new garden" (early fifteenth century: British Museum Sloane 2593), in which a pear tree, the centerpiece of the garden, attracts unusual interest:

The fairest maid of this town
Prayed me
To graft her a graft
Of my perry tree

The metaphor of grafting then becomes clearly phallic:

And I grafted her
Right up in her home:
And twenty weeks from that day
It was alive in her womb.

A contemporary mock-riddle with an obviously phallic symbol is "I have a noble cock," covered in the entry for **cock**, a richly ambiguous term in English. The Sloane manuscript has another simple riddling reference to the male genitalia:

I have a pocket for the nonce;
Therein be twain precious stones. . . .
Withouten feet it can stand.

(*Stone* in Middle English also carried the meaning of "testicle," as it still does in agricultural parlance. The riddling paradox of the penis, which can stand without feet, is fairly common in the period.)

The genre was sufficiently popular for William Caxton's successor, Wynkyn de Worde, to publish a collection in 1525 called *The Demaundes Joyous* ("The Merry Riddles"), largely derived from a French collection with a similar title. A number of the riddles are obscene or scatological, making the book a pioneer in English publishing. Typical examples are the following: "What beast is it that hath her tail between her eyes? It is a cat when she licketh her arse"; "Which is the cleanliest occupation that is? That is a dauber [plasterer], for he may neither shite nor eat till he hath washed his hands"; "What time in the yeare beareth a goose most feathers? When the gander is upon her back."

However, a comparison with the French source shows that in borrowing twenty-nine of the eighty-seven French originals, the English compiler rejected a great number of the rudest and most explicit. They include (in translation): "Which are the two best and most necessary things in a household? The prick and the cunt, for without the prick and the cunt you would never have any marriages." "What is the most artful butcher there is? That is a cunt, for it extracts the marrow from bones without breaking them." "How can you divide a fart into two? Put your nose in my arse; Your nostrils will divide it exactly" (Wardroper, ed., 1976, 4–5). (This last motif is developed in Chaucer's *Summoner's Tale*.)

Riddles are thus a form of popular wordplay revealing a continuing interest in bawdy and obscene topics.

Bibliography
Alexander, Michael. *The Earliest English Poems.* Harmondsworth: Penguin, 1966.
Tupper, F. *The Riddles of the Exeter Book.* New York: Ginn, 1910.
Wardroper, John, ed. *The Demaundes Joyous.* London: Gordon Fraser, 1976.

ROARER

The term gives an insight into the surprising decadence, riotous behavior, and vocal force used in earlier times. The earliest sense (recorded ca. 1586) is of "a noisy riotous bully [aggressive type]; a wild roisterer." In *A Fair Quarrell* (1617), a play by Thomas Middleton and William Rowley, there are several "roaring" scenes; in one, Chough and Trimtram agree: "We'll roar the rusty rascal out of his tobacco" (Act IV scene ii). Middleton also wrote *The Roaring Girl* (1606), based on the life of a well-known female criminal, Moll Cutpurse. The aggressively verbose characters of Bobadill in Ben Jonson's *Everyman in His Humour* (1598) and Pistol in Shakespeare's *Henry V* (1599) clearly owe something to the "roaring type." However, Sir Richard Steele observed in the *Tatler* in 1715 that "All your Top-Wits were Scourers [violent ruffians], Rakes [decadent types], Roarers and Demolishers of Windows" (No. 40, 3). Furthermore, the term could also be used of a professional shouter for or against a cause, one who in Dr. Johnson's observation "has no qualification for a champion of controversy than a hardened front or a strong voice" (*The Rambler,* no. 144 § 8). A contemporary publication records their employment: "For roarers of the word 'Church' £40" and "For a set of 'No Roundhead' roarers £40" (*Flying Post,* January 27, 1715). This practice was clearly the beginning of the *claque,* or group of hired supporters or booers, who were to figure substantially in the "opera wars" of the eighteenth century.

See also: Rufflers.

ROCHESTER, EARL OF

John Wilmot, the second Earl Rochester (1647–1680), remains unsurpassed in the history of English poetry and drama for his astonishingly explicit use of obscenity and his unflinching depiction of an ambience of riotous decadence. Having spent part of his childhood in Paris, where his father had been exiled as a Royalist general, he was sufficiently precocious to enter Wadham College, Oxford, at the age of twelve. Rochester epitomized the licentiousness of the **Restoration**, which was as extreme as the Puritanism to which it was a reaction (Walker 1984, ix–x). Briefly imprisoned for kidnapping his intended wife, the heiress Elizabeth Malet, he nevertheless remained a royal favorite. Described as "tall, thin and beautiful," qualities that are endorsed by the portrait in the National Portrait Gallery in London, he was regarded as the most brilliant wit and the most accomplished "rake" or decadent roué in the court of Charles II. The portrait shows Rochester ironically crowning a monkey, a traditional symbol of lust, with a laurel wreath, the symbol of poetic excellence, while the animal tears out pages from his book of poems.

Rochester follows Ben Jonson (1572–1637) in having extremely cynical assumptions about human behavior and sexuality, showing decadence stripped of pretense. However, he goes even further, since this world is seen almost entirely from crotch level and its multifarious participants are reduced to and dominated solely by frantic sexual energy. In "A Ramble in St James's Park" he juxtaposes sacred, profane, animalistic, and taboo language with a casual insouciance:

Much wine had past in grave discourse
Of who Fucks who and who does worse. . . .

But though St. James has the Honor on't
'Tis consecrate to Prick and Cunt.

And nightly now beneath their shade
Are Buggeries, Rapes and Incests made;
Unto this all-sin-sheltering Grove
Whores of the Bulk [shop window] and Alcove [fashionable brothel]
Great Ladies, Chamber Mayds, and Drudges,
The Ragg picker, and Heiress Trudges

Carrmen [carriage drivers], Divines, Great Lords and Taylors,
Prentices, Poets, Pimps and Gaolers,
Footmen, Fine Fopps, doe here arrive,
And here promiscuously they swive [fuck].
(ll. 1–2; 9–10; 23–32)

In this sexual circus he caustically juxtaposes "Some stiff-prickt Clown and well-hung Parson." No one escapes Rochester's biting wit. His "Satire on Charles II" begins with an odd chauvinist compliment:

I' th' Isle of Britaine long since famous growne
For breeding the best cunts in Christendome

ruled over by "A merry Monarch, scandalous and poor," so virile that "His Scepter and his Prick are of a Length." Nevertheless he needs "poor laborious Nelly" (Nell Gwyn, one of the royal mistresses) who "employes hands, fingers, mouth, and thighs / E're she can raise the member she enjoys" (ll. 15; 11; 29–31). In "On Mistress Willis," a whore loosely connected with Court, Rochester wryly admits that "our Ballox [testicles] can make a Man a slave / To such a Bitch as Willis," who is

Bawdy in thoughts, precise in Words,
Ill natur'd though a Whore
Her Belly is a Bagg of Turds
And her Cunt a Common shore [sewer].
(ll. 17–20)

Rochester never excludes himself from his satirical barbs. "The Imperfect Enjoyment" is a comic, poignant, but frank account of premature ejaculation: the poet launches his epic "All-dissolving Thunderbolt" but has the mortification of leaving his unsatisfied lover crying "Is there then no more?" (ll. 10, 22). "Regime d'viver" presents his life as a rake as a horrific cycle of unfulfilled hedonism:

I rise at Eleven, I Dine about Two
I get drunk before Seven, and the next thing I do,
I send for my *Whore,* when for fear of a *Clap* [syphilis],
I spend [come] in her hand, and I spew in her lap . . .
(ll. 1–4)

So the sad roundelay proceeds, until

And in Bed I lye Yawning, till Eleven again.
(l. 14)

A sense of energetic sexual comedy abounds. Thus the arrival of a "Noble Italian call'd Signior Dildo" brings both joy and consternation to the sexual scene as he is vigorously embraced but also mercilessly hunted down. Like Horner in William Wycherley's *The Country Wife* (1675), Rochester knowingly adopts the role of a sexual therapist to the ladies:

This Signior is sound, safe, ready and Dumb,
As ever was Candel, Carret, or Thumb;
Then away with these nasty devices, and Show
How you rate the just merits of Signior Dildo.
(ll. 73–76)

Rochester reputedly took the role further, setting up as a quack doctor specializing in problems of fertility, apparently with some success. Always involved in the theater, he very possibly collaborated in the obscene farce *Sodom, or the Quintessence of Debauchery* (1668), with *dramatic personæ* uniquely named Prince Buggeranthus, Bolloxinian, Cuntigratia, Prickett, Fuckadilla, Cunticula, Clytoris, and Virtuose, the maker of merkins (pubic wigs) and dildos for the royal court. But his involvement remains an area of critical dispute, as does the question of his deathbed repentance. In his funeral address Robert Parsons announced that Rochester had "ordered all his profane and lewd Writings . . . and all his filthy Pictures to be burned" (28–29). The vocabulary is interestingly modern.

Rochester's reputation has oscillated considerably since his demise at the age of thirty-four, probably accelerated by syphilis. His poems, which still have power to shock jaded modern sensibilities, were published in pirated and inadequate texts "merely for lucre's sake" when he died in 1680 (Walker 1984, xii). Contemporary assessments tended to criticize his life more severely than his vocabulary. Andrew Marvell, according to John Aubrey's *Brief Lives,* "was wont to say that he was the best English satirist and had the right veyne" (Farley-Hills 1972, 178). By 1703 the comment could be made that "One man reads *Milton,* forty *Rochester,*" a clear indication of a change of taste (Walker 1984, xi). Voltaire, the rationalist philosopher who detected melodramatic excesses in Shakespeare, commented in his *Lettres Philosophiques* (1729): "I would willingly describe in him the man of genius, the great poet" (Farley-Hills 1972, 194). Recent critics have claimed that Rochester's "obscenities are no worse than those of his court-satirist colleagues" (Thormählen 1993, 286). Perhaps so, but "Signior Dildo" is nearly one hundred lines long, and actually names many society ladies who "fart," "belch," and "swallow pricks." The collection *Rochester: The Critical Heritage* (ed. D. Farley-Hills 1972) charts the ebb and flow of the tide of critical opinion.

See also: Restoration, the.

Bibliography

De Sola Pinto, Vivian, ed. *Rochester: Portrait of a Restoration Poet.* London: Lane, 1935.
Farley-Hills, David, ed. *Rochester: The Critical Heritage.* London: Routledge, 1972.
Love, Harold. *The Poems of John Wilmot, Earl of Rochester.* Oxford: Oxford University Press, 1999.
Thormählen, Marianne. *Rochester: The Poems in Context.* Cambridge: Cambridge University Press, 1993.
Walker, Keith. *The Poems of John Wilmot, Earl of Rochester.* Oxford: Basil Blackwell, 1984.

ROGUE

Originally meaning an idle vagrant or vagabond, *rogue* first appears in mid-sixteenth-century guides to underground or criminal slang. These included John Awdelay's *Fraternitye of Vacabondes* (1561) and Thomas Harman's *Caueat or Warening for Commen Cursetors Vulgarely Called Vagabones* (1567). *Rogue* is possibly related to *roger*, recorded from 1540, meaning "a begging vagrant claiming to be a poor scholar." The early emphasis on being a vagrant yielded the verb *to rogue*, meaning to wander about idly, and the compound *wild rogue* for someone with no fixed abode. The general sense of an unprincipled person or rascal was soon established, and has remained ever since. Although the term is obviously critical, it was also used as a term of endearment by Shakespeare and subsequent dramatists, the earliest instance being "Ah, you sweet little rogue you!" (1597, *Henry IV Part II,* II iv 233). This weakened sense is still current in phrases like "a likeable rogue" or "you old rogue!" suggesting grudging acceptance or even approval.

See also: Moralization of Status Words.

RUDE WORDS, SEMANTIC FIELD OF

Modern English has the peculiar feature in its semantic structure whereby certain intimate physical actions such as defecation, urination, and copulation and their related organs cannot be referred to politely by their native equivalents, that is, shitting, pissing, and fucking, since these are regarded as obscene or taboo. In each case, in formal, especially in professional discourse, the classical Latin or Greek term is preferred. This division of such terms into "polite" and "impolite" is not a feature of all languages. In French, for example, coarse terms like *merde* ("shit"), *con* ("cunt"), and *foutu* ("fucked up") are used in public discourse. Nor has it always been a practice in English.

The problem caused by this separation of registers is that there are no common or neutral terms to refer to these basic "bodily functions" or organs, only the extremes of the rude or demotic and the formal and polite. C.S. Lewis put it incisively: "As soon as you deal with [sex] explicitly, you have to choose between the language of the nursery, the gutter and the anatomy class" (Tynan 1975, 154). Furthermore, while the native terms are "transparent," that is to say their meaning is obvious, the classical terms are generally "opaque" to the bulk of native speakers, since their roots are understood only by those with some classical education. Most readers coming across *excrement, micturate,* and *copulate* for the first time would not immediately understand their meanings. This opaque quality makes these terms ideal for euphemisms, and therefore suitable for polite general discourse. Several, like *fundament, posterior,* and *pudendum* are in reality exclusively written terms. However, opaqueness can be carried too far: under *micturate* the *Oxford English Dictionary* has the curiously ironic note: "The sense is incorrect as well as the form." In the layout of the semantic field, the classical terms are set in bold type, to distinguish them from native terms, which are set in standard type, while those with an asterisk are of uncertain etymology.

The Semantic Field of Rude Words and Their Principal Synonyms

Anglo-Saxon	Middle English	1500–1650	1650–1800	1800–1900	1900–Present
shit (n.) turd	**ordure**	**excrement**	crap*	**defecation**	
	piss (v.)	**urinate**	**micturate**	pee	
sleep with	swive	fuck*	**copulate** screw shag*	make love	bonk
	pollution	frig self-abuse	onanism **masturbation digitation**		wank
arse	bum* buttocks **fundament**	**anus**	bottom posterior(s)		
	cunt* thing	**coney pudendum**	twat* vagina	quim*	
weapon	cock yard	tool prick	penis **(privy) member**		

*Origin uncertain.
Classical terms in bold type.

The historical arrangement of the field illuminates a number of significant points. First is that the commonly retailed generalization that the rude words are "Anglo-Saxon" is only partially true, since *fuck, cunt,* and *piss* are all recorded after the Anglo-Saxon period and the first two are of uncertain origin. Second, the bulk of the classically derived terms are found in the Renaissance period, when such terms began to be borrowed in great numbers, and in the Augustan period, when they became very fashionable. Third, some Anglo-Saxon terms, like *weapon* and *sleep with,* have always had a neutral or euphemistic sense. Thus *thing* has been used of both the male and female genitalia since Middle English. More surprising, up to the Middle Ages medical terminology included obscene and taboo terms like *shit, cunt,* and *piss,* all used in the translation of Lanfrank's *Cirurgery* ("Surgery," ca. 1400) and *The Cyrurgie of Guy de Chauliac* (ca. 1425). Conversely there is the curious obsolescence and disappearance of *swive,* the principal medieval term for "copulate," and the comparatively late appearance of the staple term *fuck.* The scheme necessarily involves some crudification: for instance, *make love,* originally *make love to,* was used from Renaissance times in a Platonic or nonsexual sense, slowly becoming more explicit in referring to romantic or amorous relationships during the eighteenth and nineteenth centuries, before the meaning of coitus is attained.

Turning to the classical element, the opaque and euphemistic senses clearly predominate. However, in some cases the action itself is so suffused with emotion and shame that its articulation is in itself an embarrassment: thus former president Bill Clinton reportedly fired his surgeon-general for using the term *masturbation* in a press conference (Laqueur 2003, 416). More "exotic" sexual practices are termed *fellatio* and *cunnilingus,* resorting totally to what Edmund Burke called the "the decent obscurity of a learned language." This element cannot, in general, be used in swearing: *copulating pandemonium!* makes no sense and carries no impact, even in a community of classical scholars, alongside *fucking hell!* In swearing and vituperation it is commonly the juxtaposition of registers, setting native and classical elements alongside each other, which creates the most potent effects: for example, *you obsequi-*

ous little turd! or *the conceited old fart!* In conclusion, all the polite or standard terms are Renaissance or Augustan in origin.

See also: Cleland, John; Register.

Bibliography

Laqueur, Thomas. *Solitary Sex: A Cultural History of Masturbation.* New York: Zone Books, 2003.
Partridge, Eric. *Origins.* London: Routledge, 1958.
Tynan, Kenneth. *The Sound of Two Hands Clapping.* London: Jonathan Cape, 1975.

RUFFLERS

This sixteenth-century term describes a type of vagabond, or parasite of a military, or more often pseudo-military kind, who made a living out of verbal aggression, extorting money, food, goods, or debts by practiced cursing and threats. The term *ruffler* makes its first appearance in 1535 in legislation from the reign of Henry VIII (Act 27, c. 25) being applied there to "Idell persons . . . calling them selues saruing [serving] men." They were aggressive beggars who fraudulently claimed military injury, and are mentioned caustically by the writers of early guides to underground slang, such as Robert Copland (1535–1536), John Awdelay (1561), Thomas Harman (1567), and Thomas Dekker (1608). The type clearly survived, since Francis Grose defined them as "notorious rogues often pretending to be maimed soldiers or sailors" in his *Classical Dictionary of the Vulgar Tongue* (1785). The term then took on the sense of a proud arrogant aggressive fellow, surviving to late Victorian times, but is now obsolete.

See also: Roarers.

SAINTS' NAMES

Reflecting the potency of the medieval church, the names of saints were invoked in all manner of contexts, such as asseveration, exasperation, and even cursing. The saints vary from the most familiar and expected to some virtually unknown now, like St. Thomas of India. Today these names generally no longer carry such power, being represented by plain names as in "by George!" or "by Godfrey!," which are really euphemistic forms of the name of God. In the same way "by Saint Mary!" was first abbreviated to plain "Mary!," then eroded to *marry!* before becoming obsolete. The practice of abbreviation was found even in medieval literature: the central figure of William Langland's great spiritual poem, *Piers Plowman* (ca. 1360 >) erupts into the action with an irritated oath: "'Peter!' quod [said] a plowman, and put forth his hede" (C Text, passus VIII, l. 182).

In Chaucer's narrative *magnum opus*, the *Canterbury Tales* (1386–1400), as well as in his minor poems, saints' names invoked vary greatly, but are often chosen with insight and discrimination. Thus the "greatest oath" of the prim but expensively and improperly adorned Prioress was "only by St. Loy" (*General Prologue*, l. 120), appropriately the patron saint of jewelers. Similarly, when the Host of the Tabard Inn swears by "St. Ronyan!" in the Introduction to the *Pardoner's Tale* (l. 310), Ralph Elliott has suggested that this unfamiliar name might be a mischievous pun on *ronyon*, "kidney," from French *rognon* and English *runnion*, "the male organ" (1974, 258). This could be a sly allusion to the Pardoner's charlatanism and evident effeminacy. Geographical appropriateness is also a feature: the clerk John in the *Reeve's Tale* (l. 4127) swears by St. Cuthbert, who has northern associations; the carpenter in the *Miller's Tale* invokes St. Frideswide (l. 3449), a local Oxford saint; while Dan John in the *Shipman's Tale*, set in France, invokes "Seint Denys of Fraunce" (l. 151). Yet some of the "saints" invoked are pointedly outrageous. The sexually adventurous Wife of Bath claims to have the sign of a pagan "seinte Venus" (*Prologue*, l. 604), and the sexual vengeance she takes upon her fourth husband is accompanied by the exclamation "by God and Seint Joce" (*Tale*, l. 483), which could also be a phallic allusion (Elliott 1974, 280).

Other names seem to be indiscriminate, such as the Host and the Pardoner appealing "For the love of God and seinte John" (*Wife of Bath's Tale*, l. 164). But these couplings were actually quite common, shown in "by God and seinte Martyn" (*Shipman's Tale*, l. 164). St. John and St. James are the saints most frequently invoked in the *Canterbury Tales*. There are only four references to "Seint Thomas of Kente," that is, Thomas à Becket, the "hooly blissful martyr" of the *Prologue* (l. 17), whose shrine at Canterbury is the focal point and destination of the pilgrimage.

The sanctions against swearing formulated in 1551, 1606, and 1623 specified the names of God, Christ, the Holy Spirit, and the Devil, but not the names of saints, effectively reflecting a demotion of status, which has continued. Thus, the variety of saints appealed to in Shakespeare is greatly reduced in comparison with Chaucer. (In the lifetime of Shakespeare, Catholicism, which was already unpopular, came to be regarded as unpatriotic.) Consequently, the names of saints are more numerous in the early plays, such as *Richard III* (1592), with three references to St. Paul and one to St. John. *Hamlet* (1601) is the only late play with such references, one to St. Patrick and the other to "Saint Charity," not truly a saint. Similarly, the Virgin Mary has some dozen references, all in early plays, and mainly through indirect allusions, such *by our Lady* and *by my holidame*. The two most explicit are *by holy Mary* (*Henry VI, Part III,* III ii 103) and *by the holy Mother of our Lord* (*Richard III,* III, vii, 2). As Catholicism lost power and influence in England, so logically did the potency and currency of saints' names, leaving only a few survivals like the exclamation "My sainted aunt!" and trivialized uses dating from the mid-nineteenth century.

See also: Chaucer, Geoffrey; Medieval Period; Religious Oaths.

Bibliography
Elliott Ralph. *Chaucer's English.* London: André Deutsch, 1974.

SAMBO

Sambo reveals in its various tones the power of cultural and racial stereotyping. It is commonly derived from *zambo,* a Latin American term for a person of mixed Negro and Indian parentage. As with all similar words, such as *half-breed, half-caste, chichi,* and so on, what was originally a racial designation has become a term of insult. Commenting on the gradations of color and their parallel status, Captain Frederick Marryat observed in 1833: "A quadroon looks down on a mulatto, while a mulatto looks down on a sambo, that is, half mulatto and half negro" (*Peter Simple,* chapter xxxi). (These gradations are also covered in the entry for **Caribbean**.) In Spanish the word also referred to a yellow monkey.

In the United States, *sambo* became "known to most colonists as a common Black male name by 1700" (Flexner 1976, 33). The first instance in the *Oxford English Dictionary* is from the *Boston News Letter:* "There is a Negro man . . . calls himself Sambo" (2 October, 1704, 2). This popularity led to the hypothesis that the word may be African in origin, possibly from a Hausa word meaning "second son" or "name of the spirit," alternatively from Foulah, meaning "uncle." The inferiority of status was obviously reinforced during the period of slavery, generating some sociological controversy about "The 'Sambo' stereotype of the loyal, lazy, affectionate and child-like slave" (*Times Literary Supplement,* March 2, 1973, 230–32). Similar stereotypical discussion concerns "the development of a 'Sambo' response of the Negro slave to his environment, which may help explain the paucity of slave revolts in America" (*New York Review of Books,* March 13, 1969). Stanley Elkins has asked the key question: "What then of the

LINCOLN—"*I'm sorry to have to drop you, Sambo, but this concern won't carry us both!*"

Sambo, originally referring to persons of mixed Black and Indian parentage, came to refer to the African American slave stereotype—as in this 1861 political cartoon about President Lincoln's opposition to John Fremont's emancipation proclamation in Missouri. (Library of Congress, LC-USZ62-133077)

'reality' of Sambo? Did the Sambo role really become part of the slave's 'true' personality?" (1959, 227).

In the course of the twentieth century, as racial sensitivities sharpened, the term acquired more of an insulting edge. As Hugh Rawson observed, "A notable casualty of this period [post World War II] was the much loved folk tale *The Story of Little Black Sambo* (Helen Bannerman, 1923, about an East Indian child actually), which is now difficult to find on library shelves" (1991, 334). The demise of the title was no doubt accelerated by the use of "little black sambo" as a paternalistic, colonialist stereotype in British English.

Like *wog*, it was used of any foreigner of color, and in the words of the *Oxford English Dictionary Supplement* (1982), "Now only used as a term of abuse." It is now largely extinct, and was never borrowed into the other global varieties of English, such as South African or Australian English.

Revealingly, in Japan the term is quite neutral, probably because it arrived there before the end of the nineteenth century from the Philippines, then a Spanish possession. The feminine form *zamba* is also applied to a popular ethnic dance, now anglicized to *samba*.

See also: Caribbean.

Bibliography

Elkins, Stanley. *Slavery*. Chicago: Chicago University Press, 1959.
Flexner, Stuart Berg. *I Hear America Talking*. New York: Van Nostrand Reinhold, 1976.
Major, Clarence. *Juba to Jive*. Harmondsworth: Penguin, 1994.
Rawson, Hugh. *A Dictionary of Invective*. London: Hale, 1991.

SCATOLOGY

Derived from a Greek word meaning "dung," the term and its adjectival form, *scatological,* are now purely pejorative, referring euphemistically to language or literature that is "filthy" or unwholesomely concerned with feces. However, the original sense was literal, referring to "that branch of science which deals with diagnosis by means of the faeces" (*Oxford English Dictionary*), a sense that continues in paleontology. The term serves the typical purpose of the classical register by referring to a taboo subject in an abstract or opaque fashion. When the noted Oxford scholar George Saintsbury, in his *History of Elizabethan Literature* (1897), dismissed "large quantity of mere scatology and doggerel" (x, 307), his was the first recorded use applying the term to low-grade literary work, rather than to its content.

The *OED* added a meaning defined simply as "filthy literature," which it described as "rare" but did not illustrate. This sense has become relatively common, in relation to certain authors, notably Jonathan Swift, as in Norman O. Brown's reference: "The most scandalous pieces of Swiftian scatology are . . . *The Lady's Dressing Room, Strephon and Chloe* and *Cassinus and Peter*" (1959, xiii, 179).

Bibliography

Brown, Norman O. *Life Against Death*. London: Routledge & Kegan Paul, 1959.

SCOLD

The word has a strange history, having originally been a noun and male in application, then throughout most of its life exclusively female, but recently generalized as a verb. Its origins are in Old Norse *skald,* the word for a poet, with associations of a lampooner, which possibly derive from the practice of **flyting**. The major skalds in Old Norse literature were devastatingly satirical and fearlessly outspoken. Thus the great Egil Skallagrimsson grievously insulted Erik Bloodaxe, king of Norway, and his queen, Gunnhildr, in their presence

(*Egil's Saga,* chapters 56–57). Although all the skalds in the saga tradition were men, the saga women were extremely outspoken and often egged their men on.

The English form *scold,* recorded ca. 1300, has always had a predominantly feminine application. The *Oxford English Dictionary* notes: "In early use a person (especially a woman) of ribald speech; later a woman (rarely a man) addicted to abusive language." The legal phrase *a common scold* always denoted a woman who was a public nuisance: it is first recorded in 1476, when the Court Rolls announced that "Eadem Katerina est communis scolde" ("the formentioned Katherine is a common scold"). The great juridical authority Sir William Blackstone commented in 1769: "Our law Latin confines it to the feminine gender" (*Commentaries* IV, xiii, 169). Scolds were obviously regarded as a serious menace, and could be punished with a muzzle, the *scold's bridle,* also called a *branks,* recorded from 1595. In his study *Obsolete Punishments* (1858), T.N. Brushfield gives the various names "a Scolds Bridle, a Scolds Bit, the Gossips Bridle," also [in 1623] "a brydle for a curste queane" (an abusive prostitute), adding that "Branks were in active use in Scotland many years before their introduction into England" (6). This consisted of "a kind of iron framework to enclose the head, having a sharp metal gag or bit which entered the mouth and restrained the tongue." The *scold's cart* was also recorded as in use up to the sixteenth century for their public exposure. Dr. Johnson (1755) has a severe definition: "a clamourous [sic], rude, mean, low, foulmouthed woman," but Francis Grose in his *Classical Dictionary of the Vulgar Tongue* (1785) has a more ironic entry under *scold's cure:* "a coffin." The legal category faded away in the course of the nineteenth century. Although the stereotype of the female scold is still found, the term has lost its previous emotive force as it has become generalized.

See also: Flyting.

Bibliography

Jones, Gwyn (trans.). *Egil's Saga.* Syracuse, NY: American Scandinavian Foundation and Syracuse University Press, 1960.

SCOTS

Of the various nationalities that make up the United Kingdom, the Scots have been stereotyped as backward, mean, and tightfisted. This characterization is fairly recent, dating back about two centuries. Dr. Johnson was noted for his prejudices against the people, some of which were enshrined in the most quoted definition in his famous *Dictionary* (1755), that for *oats:* "a grain, which in England is generally given to horses, but in Scotland supports the people." Various English authors, including Horace Walpole, Lord Byron, Charles Lamb, and Sydney Smith contributed their critical comments. In addition, a number of humorous, ironic, and demeaning idioms using the epithet *Scotch* were recorded by Captain Francis Grose in his *Classical Dictionary of the Vulgar Tongue* (1785). Grose (who knew Scotland well and was a friend of Robert Burns) records such ironic uses as *Scotch chocolate* for "brimstone and milk," *Scotch mist* for "sober soaking rain," *Scotch warming pan* for "a wench; also a fart," *Scotch greys* for "lice," and the related *Scotch fiddle* for "the itch," (also a euphemism for venereal disease). The association is further reinforced by *Itchland* and *Scratchland* being given as ironic entries for Scotland.

Many of these have survived, but below the level of standard usage. A number of similar derisive uses, such as *Scotch coffee* for imitation coffee, are recorded in Australian English from 1836. Irving Lewis Allen, in "Lexicon of Ethnic Epithets" (1983, 66), has a few mild generic terms like *kiltie, mack,* and *sandy,* of which only *pinchpenny* could be regarded as offensive. Hugh Rawson's *Dictionary of Invective* (1991) has considerably more. *Jock* is defined by Grose as "a jeering appellation for a north-country seaman," the first explicit association with a Scot being recorded in 1865. The term is also found in a slang sense in J.H. Vaux's *Flash Dictionary* of 1812: "a person of an irritable temper, easily put in a passion." As the entry for **Australia** shows, the flash or criminal slang language spread to Australia with the convicts, and the term *scotty,* meaning "irritable or bad-tempered" has become established. However, as generic names *Scotty* and *Jock* have now lost their negative overtones.

Bibliography

Allen, Irving Lewis. *The Language of Ethnic Conflict.* New York: Columbia University Press, 1983.
Grose, Francis. *A Classical Dictionary of the Vulgar Tongue.* London: S. Hooper, 1785.
L'Estrange, Julian, ed. *The Big Book of National Insults.* London: Cassell, 2002.
Partridge, Eric. "Offensive Nationality," in *Words, Words, Words!* London: Methuen, 1933.
Ramson, W.S., ed. *The Australian National Dictionary.* Melbourne: Oxford University Press, 1988.

SEMANTIC CHANGES AND TRENDS

Semantic changes, or the changes of meaning undergone by words over time, are a fairly obvious linguistic fact. Many of them seem random and difficult to explain: for instance, how does one relate the modern sense of *gossip* to its origins in Anglo-Saxon *godsib* meaning "godparent"? Similarly, why should *bloody,* with its gory origin, have become such a general-purpose intensifier? Semantic trends describe similar changes of meaning shown by groups of related words as their meanings become narrower or wider, stronger or weaker, better or worse, and so on. These changes, commonly apparent to individuals in the course of a single lifetime, become very pronounced as the centuries pass. As Samuel Beckett wrote more specifically on emotive language, "The air is full of our cries. But habit is a great deadener" (*Waiting for Godot* 1959, 91). Beckett was using layman's language to describe what semanticists call the trends of generalization, whereby emotive words become used with less specificity, and especially that of loss of **impact** also covered in the entry for **loss of intensity, weakening, or verbicide.** These trends apply clearly to many categories of swearing and foul language. The entries for **bastard, bitch, bugger, cunt, fuck, God,** and **hell** detail this development. Furthermore, adjectives of such differing literal meanings as *bloody, damned, fucking,* and *awful* can now qualify almost any other quality, such as, *good, bad, stupid, clever,* and so on. *Devilish* was used with similar breadth in the eighteenth century. The more common the word, the wider its range of uses, an axiom that G.K. Zipf corroborated with the alarming statistic that, apart from a few core words, "different meanings of a word will tend to be equal to the square root of its relative frequency" (1945, 255). General works on semantic change by Michel Bréal (1900), Hans Sperber (1922), and Gustav Stern (1931), discussed in Stephen Ullmann (1957, 254–55) and Hughes (1988), sought to formulate certain "laws" of semantic development.

From the start of semantics as a serious discipline over a century ago, a number of scholars noted the trend of deterioration or pejoration in terms relating to women, some attributing it to malicious innuendo, possibly misogynistic in origin, others to false delicacy or tactful vagueness. This aspect is covered in the entry for **stereotypes of women**. **Religious oaths** and ejaculations provide clear cases of both generalization and loss of intensity. Over the centuries animal terms like *pig, swine, sow, shrew,* and *bitch* have become powerful insults, but then generalized and weakened. Obviously context, including the directness of the insult, and social and personal factors form important determiners of the force of a term. These issues are discussed further in the entry for **impact**. But the general semantic trend of weakening undergone by the terms in question can hardly be disputed. Few have remained genuinely taboo as modern speech communities have become desensitized to the impact of religious, genital, and excretory terms. The principal exceptions to the trend are terms of ethnic and racial abuse, although the taboo is relaxed in certain contexts within the speech community, becoming "jocular" or "familiar." The table below shows certain patterns in semantic development, from the specific to the general, and from particular categories such as the genital and the excretory. The black squares indicate current meaning.

Semantic Changes in the Categories of the Genitalia, Excreta, and Race

SPECIFIC	>	>	>	>	>	>	GENERAL
		Worthless/Despicable Person					Rubbish
Genitalia							
prick	>	>	>	>	>■		
cunt	>	>	>	>	>■		
cock	>	>	>	>	>	>	>	>■ (U.K.)
balls	>	>	>	>	>	>	>	>■ (U.K.)
Excreta							
shit	>	>	>	>	>■	>	>	>■
turd	>	>	>	>	>■		
crap	>	>	>	>	>	>	>	■
Race							
coolie	>	>	>	>	>■		
nigger	>	>	>	>	>■		
kaffir	>	>	>	>	>■		

While four of the seven terms in the first two categories listed (*prick, cunt, shit,* and *turd*) can now mean a worthless person, the semantic changes are not entirely predictable, in that *shit, cock, balls,* and *crap* have developed the sense of "rubbish," the first two being more prevalent in British English. Uniquely, *shit* has developed both senses. All the racial terms have generalized, but have intensified in taboo quality, which is against the general trend of loss of intensity. The labels have become insulting since they dehumanize individuals and imply that the person described is inferior or worthless.

Although the dominant semantic trends in swearing are deterioration and loss of intensity, the countertrend of amelioration can be seen in the development of *bastard* and *bugger,* which used to be entirely critical, but can now be used in British and Australian English with a sense of sympathy and even affection—for example, "He's really a good bastard" and "He's a nice old bugger." More striking examples are *bad, bitching, hell,* and *wicked,* all of

413

which are used as positive terms in Black English in the United States. Clarence Major's *Juba to Jive* (1994) defines *bad* as "positive to the extreme," *bitching* as "anything good or wonderful," *hell* as "excellent; good; an impressive person," and *wicked* as "superb; wonderful; intense."

See also: Bastard; Cunt; Gender in Swearing; Instability of Terms; Loss of Intensity, Weakening, or Verbicide; Mother-Fucker; Nigger.

Bibliography
Beckett, Samuel. *Waiting for Godot.* London: Faber, 1955.
Bréal, Michel. *La Semantique,* trans. Mrs. Henry Cust: *Semantics: Studies in the Science of Meaning.* London: Heinemann, 1900. Reprint, New York: Dover, 1964.
Hughes, Geoffrey. *Words in Time.* Oxford: Blackwell, 1988.
Major, Clarence. *Juba to Jive.* Harmondsworth: Penguin, 1994.
Stern, Gustav. *Meaning and Change of Meaning.* Göteborg: Elandors, 1931.
Ullmann, Stephen. *Language and Style.* Oxford: Blackwell, 1964.
Zipf, George K. "The Meaning-Frequency Relationship of Words." *Journal of General Psychology,* xxxiii (1945): 251–66.

SEXUAL SWEARING. *See:* Gender in Swearing

SHAKESPEARE, WILLIAM

William Shakespeare (1564–1616) was "not for an age, but for all time," wrote his great friend and fellow dramatist Ben Jonson (1572–1637), a cantankerous and difficult man not given to idle praise, but a contemporary of unique authority. Virtually every major critic and author in world literature has agreed. For, unlike his contemporaries, who tended to focus on particular themes, locales, characters, and styles, Shakespeare's imaginative creations are astonishing for their cultural diversity. Renowned for his psychological insights, subtle characterization, and capacity to coin original expressions, Shakespeare would not at first sight seem to have much to contribute to the topics of swearing, profanity, foul language, obscenity, and ethnic slurs. But even though his plays are in a highly popular and public form of entertainment, they explore the polar opposites of man's angelic and diabolical potential, and daringly test the conventional limits permitted in these dangerous and taboo verbal areas.

It has taken some time for these aspects to attract scholarship. Earlier linguistic studies either treated the plays generically, as did I for Evans (1959), or in terms of language varieties, as did Hilda Hulme (1962), or individually, as did Frank Kermode (2000). The major exception was Eric Partridge's groundbreaking study, *Shakespeare's Bawdy* (1947), explicating numerous sexual *double-entendres* masking crude insult and bawdy humor to a degree not generally appreciated, clearly ingenious responses to censorship. E.A.M. Colman (1974) developed the theme of dramatic bawdy, while the major glossarial studies of Gordon Williams (1994 and 1997), elucidated multitudes of sexual innuendoes. Shakespeare's creativity, even in this linguistic area where idiom usually reigns supreme, was remarkable.

He was also fascinated by outsiders and foreigners, especially those who had status in the social hierarchy but were nevertheless regarded as aliens and subject to all manner of insults. Elizabethan England was not really multicultural, so that foreigners such as Jews, blackamoors, Italians, and Spaniards stood out. The entries for **Jews** and **Blacks** focus on the stereotypes and prejudices surrounding them, while that for **disability and deformity** considers his treatment of an outsider of another kind, the deformed Richard III. The traditional sanitized view of "sweetest Shakespeare" derives to some extent from censorship and bowdlerized versions of his texts, especially in school editions. In fact some plays articulate an alarmingly pessimistic, even misanthropic, ferocity. His status as the national literary figure and the attitude of "bardolatry," or worship of Shakespeare, have brought with them a reluctance to recognize these disturbing negative qualities.

As the entry for **Renaissance** makes clear, the period was a complex mixture of freedom and restraint, creativity and censorship. Although Shakespeare is rightly regarded as "a Renaissance man," he had, ironically, less artistic freedom than his great medieval predecessor **Geoffrey Chaucer**, whose work is both subtly and overtly critical of many professions and institutions, most of all the Church. Chaucer is also full of an exuberant abundance of savage religious oaths and wicked words. The semantic link between word and religious referent was then still vital, whereas Renaissance attitudes toward language and oaths were more skeptical. Furthermore, the Elizabethan theater, a new, thriving public activity, was regarded with suspicion as being a potentially subversive medium, both politically and spiritually, and was subject to censorship by the official known as the **Master of the Revels**. Following An Act to Restrain Abuses of Players in 1606, profanity became a major consideration, leading to various disguise-mechanisms, such as the use of **minced oaths**, which have their own entry.

Amazingly little is known with certainty about the man who became the most famous and popular playwright in English. The bare familiar facts of his personal life leave a surprising number of gaps, into which legends and hypotheses have been fitted. Although Ben Jonson commented that Shakespeare "had small Latine and less Greeke," he was certainly able to harness all the resources of the rapidly expanding vocabulary with extraordinary facility. His capacity to coin *neologisms* or new words extends to over 600 Latinate terms, some of them rare, like *exsufflicate, assubjugate, multipotent,* and *oppugnancy,* but many of them now common words, like *accommodation, assassination, compulsive,* and *sanctimonious.* There are also hundreds of original demotic terms and phrases, such as *foul-mouthed, leak* (urinate), *do it* (copulate), *make the beast with two backs, seamy side, puke, blinking idiot, boggler, cur, tyke, foppish, fob off, good riddance, what the dickens,* and even *O hell!* Many of his greatest lines have a terrifying power, in which the simplest, plainest words still burn on the page.

When Shakespeare appeared in London in 1592 on the fringe of the new theatrical companies as an obscure actor and aspiring playwright, the theater was not a respectable occupation. Actors were regarded as little better than vagrants, and the new playhouses were sited in a seedy quarter of London surrounded by "stews" (brothels) and other dens of vice. For some twenty years he lived and worked in London, only visiting his family occasionally. His marital relations are a matter of speculation, but he suffered the tragedy of his only son's death at the age of eleven. When he retired in 1612, having made a considerable fortune, largely through his excellence the theater had been transformed from a dubious marginal enterprise into a great national institution appealing to all classes. It has been calculated that by 1600, the London theaters sold between 18,000 to 20,000 seats per week (Loomba 2002, 8).

What is known least of all is where Shakespeare stood in relation to the major contemporary issues of politics and religion. He has been seen, variously, as a royalist, a "church papist" or closet Catholic, a conservative, a radical, and a subversive. He remains a mysterious figure, managing to dramatize these profound and controversial topics without getting into trouble or being imprisoned, punishments meted out to several of his contemporaries. Although England was officially Protestant and there had been a religious settlement, there were still many Catholic sympathizers, possibly including Shakespeare's own father, John. Extreme caution was thus necessary in the treatment of religious topics. The devil was then a disturbing real presence, provoking a revival of the Faust legend in Christopher Marlowe's *Doctor Faustus* (ca. 1592) and studies as diverse as Reginald Scot's *The Discoverie of Witchcraft* (1584), King James I's *Dæmonologie* (1597), and Samuel Harsnett's *Declaration of Egregious Popishe Impostures* (1603), a treatise on diabolism and an attack on the Jesuits. All these texts were known to Shakespeare, whose reading was extraordinarily diverse, and who exploited them judiciously. For those of his tragic figures who are ostensibly Christian, dying in a state of grace is crucial.

A century ago Otto Jespersen noted, very pertinently, that "such words as *Bible, Holy Ghost* and *Trinity* do not occur at all in his writings, while *Jesu, Christ* and *Christmas* are found only in some his earliest plays" (1962, 203). The names of saints are also greatly reduced. Friar Lawrence in *Romeo and Juliet* is a rare exception, appealing to "Holy Saint Francis" (Francis of Assisi) and "Jesu Maria" (II iii 65). Such obvious omissions are very significant, and can be set against the concentrations of other lexical uses, which modern concordances, such as that compiled by Marvin Spevack (1968), set out in detail, both under play and individual character.

Forms of Swearing

In presenting characters in extreme situations of love, passion, vengeance, and suffering, Shakespeare explored the complexities of swearing and exclamation from both individual and cultural perspectives. His plays show the whole gamut of swearing, namely asseveration, invocation, malediction, blasphemy, profanity, and obscenity, ranging from the most solemn oaths and deadly curses to the most absurd and trivial exclamations. Other forms of provocation, such as the insulting gestures used in the opening scene of *Romeo and Juliet* are discussed in the entry for **body language**.

In terms of content, the name of God is often abbreviated to *Od*, euphemized as *gar*, and omitted completely as in *'sdeath*. The names of Christ and Mary are also commonly euphemized to *Jesu* and *marry*, while the names of saints are greatly reduced in comparison with medieval times. *By the Mass, by my faith, upon my soul*, and many such Christian notions also feature numerously, as do forms such as *in good troth* and *upon my honour*. In *Twelfth Night*, when Feste the Fool appears disguised in a priest's habit, Sir Toby Belch greets him with the stagey euphemism "Jove bless thee, master Parson" (IV ii 10). On the other hand, the King of

Navarre in *Love's Labour's Lost* says playfully "Saint Cupid, then!" (IV iii 366). There were, thus, clear signs of self-censorship and evasion even prior to the Act to Restrain Abuses of Players (1606). On occasion, characters swear by less obvious items like their head, hands, gloves, and hats, even the day, the elements, and the clouds. The plays set in classical and pagan periods have an appropriate range of foreign deities.

There is an equal range of attitudes toward and credibility in swearing. As A.P. Rossiter has shown, in the History plays, especially in *Richard III,* curses come true with an alarming precision (1961, 1–23). Yet in a powerful scene in *Henry VI, Part II,* Queen Margaret and the Earl of Suffolk oscillate between violent curses on their enemies and an awareness of their inefficacy. Suffolk's speech, "Would curse kill, as doth the mandrake's groan," admits the element of folklore, while Margaret's response is more pragmatic:

Enough sweet Suffolk, thou torment's thyself
And these dread curses, like the sun 'gainst glass [a mirror]
Or like an overchargèd gun, recoil,
And turn the force of them upon thyself.
(III ii 328–31)

Modern psychological insights abound: in some cases, oaths are substitutes for action, in others they disappear into the "empty, vast and wandering air." Furthermore, Shakespeare's creation of character was so sophisticated that the great tragic heroes have individuated oaths, as well as diction and imagery.

Considering the convention of "swearing as commitment," there are a number of variations. One is this touching but ironic exchange from *Romeo and Juliet* (1595):

Romeo: Lady, by yonder blessed moon I swear,
        That tips with silver all these fruit-tree tops,—
Juliet: O! swear not by the moon, the inconstant moon,
        That monthly changes in her circled orb,
        Lest that thy love prove likewise variable.
Romeo: What shall I swear by?
Juliet: Do not swear at all;
        Or if thou wilt, swear by thy gracious self,
        Which is the god of my idolatry,
        And I'll believe thee.
(II ii 107–16)

Beneath the surface of these expressions of juvenile passion, Shakespeare is exploring the twofold problems of amorous commitment faced by his characters, and his own artistic expression of some notion of the divine, without using the name of God. Juliet's simple injunction is, significantly, taken straight from Christ's Sermon on the Mount: "But I say unto you, Swear not at all" (St. Matthew, 5:34).

By contrast, when the duty of vengeance falls upon the hero in *Hamlet* (1601), he is extremely insistent that all the witnesses, even his personal friends, should swear formally upon a sword that they have not seen his father's Ghost. In this strange ritual, which is really a form of perjury, even the Ghost participates:

Marcellus: We have sworn, my lord, already.
Hamlet: Indeed, upon my sword, indeed.
Ghost: [beneath] Swear.
(I v 155–57)

In a play fundamentally concerned with Heaven and Earth, Purgatory, and the Last Judgment, Hamlet is spiritually sensitive to an unusual degree. At the first appearance of the Ghost, he is clearly fearful that the spirit may be a devil: "Angels and ministers of grace, defend us!" (I v 18). This diabolical possibility is never entirely removed, so that when the Ghost reappears in Act III scene iv, he again cries out "Save me and hover o'er me / You heavenly guards!" After the Ghost's first hideous revelations of murder, adultery, and "damned incest," the most articulate of Shakespeare's characters is simply overwhelmed, not knowing what superhuman force to appeal to:

O all you host of heaven! O earth! What else?
And shall I couple hell? O fie!
(I v 92–93)

Juxtaposing the extremes of swearing, Hamlet is outraged at "marriage vows as false as dicers' oaths" (III iv 45). He himself utters a great variety of oaths, also providing insights into the practice and validity of "swearing at" or vituperation. After the Ghost's revelations he swears "by St. Patrick" (I v 141) appropriately choosing the saint who is the keeper of purgatory. (**Saints' names**, so profusely used in the Middle Ages, were becoming politically incorrect in the new religious climate of Protestantism.)

The Oedipus Complex which Freud and his disciple Ernest Jones saw embodied in Hamlet's situation manifests itself in his schizophrenic language. Hamlet is unable to articulate his detestation of the murderer-usurper Claudius directly, using irony and bitter puns. Instead he turns his verbal aggression against himself, his mother, and Ophelia. His almost hysterical reiteration of the key terms "lecherous" and "incestuous" is as obvious a symptom as his lecture to his mother not to succumb to her husband's amorous advances with his "reechy [filthy] kisses" and his "damned fingers" (III iv 184–85). In the great soliloquy ending Act II, he gives us insights into his self-hatred and into other contemporary provocations:

Who calls me villain, breaks my pate [skull] across,
Plucks off my beard and blows it in my face,
Tweaks me by the nose, and gives me the lie in the throat [accuses me of lying] . . . Ha? [Hey?]
'Swounds [God's wounds], I should take it.
(II ii 560–64)

He first succumbs to a frenzy of execration, then berates himself for descending to the verbal level of a whore or kitchen servant:

Bloody, bawdy villain!
Remorseless, treacherous, lecherous, kindless villain!
O, vengeance!
Why, what an ass am I! Ay sure. This is most brave [fine],
That I . . .
Must, like a whore, unpack my heart with words,
And fall a-cursing like a very drab [prostitute]
A scullion!
(II ii 568–75)

(Scullions were the lowest of kitchen servants, notorious for their foul language. The association of cursing with whores was also commonly stressed.)

Throughout the tragedy the tone of Hamlet's public speech oscillates between low abuse and the dignified utterance of a prince and scholar. Obsessed by his own misogynist generalization, "Frailty, thy name is woman" (I ii 146), he unleashes volleys of savage bawdy against Ophelia. His cruel rejection, "Go thy ways to a nunnery" (III i 131) is a *double entendre*, since *nunnery* in Elizabethan underground slang meant "a brothel," in addition to the conventional sense. (It still had the sense, according to Francis Grose, in 1785.) An extended series of public insults lies in this exchange with Ophelia:

Hamlet: Lady, shall I lie in your lap?
Ophelia: No, my lord.
Hamlet: I mean, my head upon your lap?
Ophelia: Aye, my lord.
Hamlet: Do you think I meant country matters?
Ophelia: I think nothing my lord.
Hamlet: That's a fair thought to lie between maids' legs.
Ophelia: What is, my lord.
Hamlet: Nothing.
(III ii 120–28)

The key puns, which an Elizabethan audience would understand, are the sexual senses attaching to *lap, nothing,* and *country.* The first could mean the female sexual organs, especially in the phrase "in your lap," also so used in *Henry VI, Part II* (III ii 390) and *Much Ado About Nothing* (V ii 99). The title of the latter play naughtily puns on the old slang sense of *nothing* in the sense of "cunt" through the symbolism of "an O thing." Clearly Hamlet intends this sense by his reference to *country matters,* explained by G.R. Hibbard in the *Oxford Shakespeare* edition: "sexual intercourse, quibbling indecently on the first syllable of *country,*" (1987, 254). Dr. Johnson in his edition of 1765 proposed *country manners,* which even the contemporary scholar Edmond Malone summarily rejected in 1793: "What

Shakespeare meant to allude to, must be too obvious to every reader to require any explanation" (cited in Hulme 1977, 92).

The degree to which Hamlet is assuming the "antic disposition" of madness remains an insoluble critical problem. No such doubt exists in the case of the traumatized Ophelia, who in her mad scene recalls her seduction and poignantly resuscitates strange oaths:

(She sings) By Gis and by Saint Charity,
    Alack and fie for shame!
Young men will do 't, if they come to 't,
    By Cock, they are to blame;

Quoth she "Before you tumbled me,
    You promised me to wed."
(IV v 56–62)

Gis, often spelt *jis,* is an old "minced" form of *Jesus. Cock* is a similar form of *God,* dating from the fourteenth century. The context, the revelation of a "buried" sexual experience, clearly invites a Freudian interpretation, since "cock" had been used metaphorically for "penis" for some two centuries, and is used punningly in several contexts.

The uncensored and disturbing sexuality in the speeches of Hamlet and Ophelia derive from the contemporary stereotypical notion that the insane suffered from a sexual fixation. The same condition surfaces in Edgar in *King Lear* when he assumes the role of the lunatic Poor Tom, uttering such odd riddles as "Pillicock sat on Pillicock Hill" (III iv 76). Here *Pillicock* is "a term of endearment for the phallus," the ancestor of modern British English *pillock,* while *Pillicock Hill* corresponds to the Mons Veneris. Edgar continues in this bawdy vein for several lines (III iv 76–92). When Lear descends into true madness, the sexual obsession is unambiguous, expressed in steadily descending register and disintegrating control, starting with the absurd edict, "Let copulation thrive!" proceeding through alarming Manichaeism or extreme dualism, to ultimate horror and disgust at the female sexual appetite, likened to the mouth of hell:

Down from the waist they are Centaurs,
Though women all above:
But to the girdle do the gods inherit,
Beneath is all the fiend's.
There's hell, there's darkness, there is the sulphurous pit,
Burning, scalding, stench, consumption; fie, fie, fie! pah, pah!
(IV vi 127–33).

Another aspect of Edgar's assumed lunacy is diabolical possession, shown in his repeated references to "the foul fiend" and his ironic disclosure that "the Prince of Darkness is a gentleman" (III iv 146). Both aspects derive from Samuel Harsnett's *Declaration of Egregious Popishe Impostures* (1603).

Damnation

Although *Othello* is essentially a secular tragedy, the hero's language and world-view consistently juxtapose heaven and hell, the inspiring and the degrading impulses in man. Unlike Hamlet, Othello lacks the skepticism to examine the evidence against Desdemona and the spiritual reluctance to use violence. Initially he certainly shows heroic status, maintained up to his great vow of vengeance, beginning "Like to the Pontic sea" and ending

> Now by yond marble heaven,
> In the due reverence of a sacred vow,
> I here engage my words.
> (III iii 467–69)

Thereafter he declines remorselessly, cursing Desdemona furiously ("Damn her, lewd mix, O damn her!" III iii 475), becoming so tormented by the poison of jealousy that he descends into a nadir of subhuman and incoherent ravings littered with oaths:

> Lie with her, zounds, that fulsome! Handkerchief—confessions—
> Handkerchief! . . . Pish! Noses, ears and lips. Is't possible? Confess?–
> Handkerchief ?—O devil! [*falls into a trance.*]
> (IV i 35–43)

Othello never completely recovers his heroic status nor his wits, greeting his Venetian in-law Lodovico distractedly: "You are welcome, sir, to Cyprus . . . Goats and monkeys!" (IV i 259). (Goats and monkeys were traditional symbols of lust.) His most reiterated oath is simply "Devil!," together with many others with diabolical associations, such as "Fire and brimstone!" (IV i 229) and the final characterization of Iago as a "demi-devil" (V ii 301). His increasing abuse of Desdemona in outbursts such as "Impudent strumpet!" (IV ii 82) is matched by her increasing dignity. In death he addresses her alternately as "O ill-starred wench!" and "Cold, cold my girl! / Even like thy chastity." Eventually he recognizes the terrible spiritual consequences of his act, damnation gruesomely depicted in apocalyptic medieval terms ("Whip me ye devils . . . roast me in sulphur!" V ii 273–78). The stereotypes surrounding Othello are also discussed in the entry for **Blacks**.

Macbeth (1605) alone of the tragedies has little focus on swearing or oaths *per se*. It is also a strange religious anomaly, being nominally set within the Christian era (the real Macbeth having been king of Scotland from 1040 to 1057) but having remarkably few explicit Christian references. In the moral structure of the play the Witches are clearly the agents of chaos and evil, yet their diabolical status is problematic. Shakespeare was evidently pandering to two of the new king's passionate concerns, namely witchcraft, on which James I had written *Dæmonologie, in forme of a dialogue* (1597), and the political/religious notion of the Divine Right of Kings. Banquo and Macduff alone use religious language, but of an unconventional kind, shown in the arcane symbolism of Macduff's reaction to the "sacrilegious murder" of the King (II iii 64–69). His direct spiritual condemnations of Macbeth are "devilish" (IV iii 117), "hell-kite" (IV iii 217), "this fiend of Scotland" (IV iii 233), and finally "hell-hound" (V vii 32). Despite the increasing horror of Macbeth's tyranny, there are few appeals to the Almighty and no miraculous interventions. When told of the massacre of his entire family, Macduff asks incredulously: "Did heaven look on, / And would not take their part?" (IV iii 223–24).

Macbeth and his wife technically invoke only the powers of darkness ("Stars, hide your fires"; "Come, thick night, and pall thee in the dunnest smoke of Hell"), but they do not conjure up the Devil specifically, as Marlowe's Faustus does. Though he alludes once to having given "mine eternal jewel" to "the common Enemy of man" (III i 68), Macbeth still invokes "Fate [to] champion me to the utterance" (III i 72), as if Fate were partial. Yet he invokes the Witches to create chaos:

I conjure you . . .
Though you untie the winds, and let them fight
Against the Churches.
(IV i 50–53)

Macbeth's invocation is on a cosmic plane, fundamentally destroying "the treasure of Nature's germens" (IV i 59). Alongside this, his curse "The Devil damn thee black, thou cream-faced loon" (V iii 11) is fairly trivial. His final soliloquy, "Tomorrow, and tomorrow, and tomorrow" (V v 19–28) is not an expression of spiritual horror like that of Othello at facing the Last Judgment, but a remarkable articulation of meaninglessness, seeing life as a brief charade. Though the final judgments of Malcolm on "this dead butcher and his fiend-like Queen" (V vii 98) are simplistic and harsh, perhaps the Devil has indeed entered into them, as perhaps it does into Othello.

The most explicit and daring references to swearing and the Devil occur in the least expected scene, that of the Porter, who in his apparently drunken farrago expands on two major themes relating to false swearing, namely equivocation (the deliberate use of ambiguity to deceive) and treachery: "Faith, here's an equivocator, that could swear in both scales against either scale; who committed treason enough for God's sake, yet could not equivocate to heaven" (II iii 9–11). A contemporary audience would immediately recognize a topical reference to the Gunpowder Plot, the unsuccessful conspiracy by Catholic dissidents in the same year (1605) to kill King James and blow up the Houses of Parliament. At his trial, the Jesuit conspirator Father Garnet (who assumed the name of Farmer, used by Shakespeare in this scene) finally confessed to having sworn falsely. When accused of perjury, he explained "that so long as he thought that they had no Proof he was not bound to accuse himself: but when he saw they had Proof, he stood not long in it" (from a contemporary letter by John Chamberlaine dated April 5, 1606, quoted by Muir, 1962, xviii). King James himself commented: "for the Jesuits are the worst and most seditious fellows in the world. They are slaves and spies, as you know" (Muir 1962, xxi). The stereotype is discussed further under **Catholics**.

Cursing

Several of Shakespeare's tragedies are set in pagan times. Although not entirely consistent in his religious references, he often exploits an alien religious setting to explore the psychology and rituals of belief. His first exploration of the ancient world, *Titus Andronicus* (1590), contains this penetrating exchange between the cynical villain Aaron the Moor (also discussed in the entry for **Blacks**) and Lucius, one of the sons of Titus:

Lucius: Who should I swear by? Thou believ'st no god:
       That granted, how cans't thou believe an oath?
Aaron: What if I do not? As indeed, I do not;
       Yet, for I know thou art religious
       And hast a thing within thee called conscience,
       With twenty popish tricks and ceremonies,
       Which I have seen thee careful to observe,
       Therefore I urge thy oath; for that I know
       An idiot holds his bauble for his god,
       And keeps the oath which by that god he swears.
(V i 71–80)

The unique reference to "popish tricks and ceremonies" is obviously anachronistic and one of the very few instances of Shakespeare making risqué contemporary reference to controversial religious matters. There are similar anachronisms in the Roman plays in Cassius's reference to "th' eternal devil" (*Julius Caesar* I ii 160) and in Antony's oath "gods and devils" (*Antony and Cleopatra* III xiii 89).

Shakespeare was to return to the ancient world repeatedly: in *Julius Caesar* (1599), *Troilus and Cressida* (1602), *Antony and Cleopatra* (1606), *Timon of Athens* (1607), and *Coriolanus* (1608). He depicts Rome as a secular society deeply riven by class differences expressed very crudely, the most powerful animus appearing in savage invectives directed at the plebs or lower classes. Thus the tribune Marullus in *Julius Caesar* berates the plebs as "You blocks, you stones, you worse than senseless things" (I i 40). The class hatred of Coriolanus, the patrician war hero, is visceral and unrelenting, right from his first entrance when he confronts the starving "company of mutinous citizens" with "What's the matter, you dissentious rogues?" (I i 170). When he is later labeled "an enemy to the people and his country," he is justifiably provoked by the political insult, but he welcomes exile and arrogantly rejects the plebs:

You common cry of curs! whose breath I hate
As reek o' the rotten fens, whose loves I prize
As the dead carcasses of unburied men
That do corrupt my air, I banish you.
(III iii 118–21)

As the entry for **dogs** makes clear, Shakespeare's use of *cur* as a term of insult is original.

Coriolanus's catalogue of caustic physical abuse, dismissing the plebs as "garlic eaters" and "the mutable, rank-scented meiny" ("the changeable, evil-smelling mob") is compounded with social labels like "apron men" for artisans. His devastating frankness reflects an ugly intolerance of human physicality, pyorrhoea, and body odor. However, he is not alone in his class attitude, articulating in public what most of his class dare say only in private. Thus the more benign patrician Menenius makes a similar observation in IV vi 130–33, while in *Julius Caesar*, Casca is cruelly ironic about the Roman crowd's miasmic hysteria, which, he suggests, might have brought on Caesar's epileptic fit: "the rabblement shouted . . . and uttered such a deal of stinking breath because Caesar refused the crown, that it had almost choked Caesar; for he swooned and fell down at it" (I ii 242–46). Shakespeare seems to have been the first author to depict such class hatred based on stereotypes of physical repulsiveness (attributed solely to the lower orders). Significantly, no such class antipathy is expressed in his English plays.

In addition to the class aspects of the vituperation in *Coriolanus*, Shakespeare explores less predictable features of personal insult. Coriolanus the fearless national war hero is, by a Freudian irony, mother-bound. When his rival and enemy Aufidius mocks him with the schoolboy insult "thou boy of tears," alluding to his tearful reconciliation with his mother at the gates of Rome, the insult drives Coriolanus berserk, into a tirade of frenzy and despair (V v 101–17).

Troilus and Cressida (1602) gives a jaundiced subversive view of the Trojan War, chiefly from the perspective of Thersites, "a deformed and scurrilous Greek," who trivializes the theme immortalized by Homer, claiming that "all the argument is a cuckold [Menelaus] and a whore [Helen]" (II iii 78). What Othello memorably called "the pomp and circumstance of glorious war" is degraded by sordid infighting in both camps and degrading insults, such as those traded by Ajax and Thersites:

Ajax: Thou bitch-wolf's son, canst thou not hear? Feel then. [*Strikes him*]
Thersites: The plague of Greece upon thee, thou mongrel beef-witted lord!

The exchange continues in this vein, Ajax scoring points with such unsubtle barbs as "Cobloaf!" (a small rounded loaf), "You whoreson cur!," and "You dog!," but relying more on his fists, while Thersites replies with "Thou sodden-witted lord!," "thou scurvy valiant ass!," and so on (II i 5–25). This trading of insults is a low-grade example of **flyting**, which has a rich but discontinuous history in English, as the relevant entry shows. *Julius Caesar* also contains an example in V i 27–66, prior to the crucial battle at Phillipi, an exchange not found in the major source for the play, Plutarch's *Lives*.

Thersites is a devastating truth teller, referring to Patroclus as Achilles' "masculine whore" and cursing him with a catalogue of diseases (V i 20–27). This theme, especially that of syphilis, culminates in the Epilogue of Pandarus, diseased himself, addressing his fellow pimps, their prostitutes, and the audience: "Good traders of the flesh . . . Brethren and sisters of the hold-door trade . . . [I] bequeath you my diseases." His allusion to "some gallèd goose of Winchester" (V xi 55) is a topical reference to London whores under the jurisdiction of the Bishop of Winchester, discussed further under **prostitutes**.

Timon of Athens (1607) is the most extreme expression of detestation and rejection of humankind, although "Most critics accept that it is either unfinished or the product of a collaboration, or both" (Kermode 2000, 231). Like Lear, Timon becomes obsessed with ingratitude, of those who parasitically enjoyed his prodigal displays of hospitality but then abandoned him. "I am *misanthropos*," he announces (IV iii 53), unleashing alarming curses upon the citizenry. His imprecations, unlike Lear's, are all-encompassing, willing upon Athens a regime of chaos, savagery, and disease. More bizarrely, they are directed, not at divine or supernatural agencies, but at inanimate objects:

O thou wall
That girdlest in those wolves, dive in the earth,
And fence not Athens!
(IV i 1–3)

This insane address to the wall is a reminder of its comic counterpart, the hilarious scene in *A Midsummer Night's Dream* (V ii 178):

Thou wall, O wall, O sweet and lovely wall,
Show me thy chink to blink through with mine eyne [eyes]!
[*Wall holds up his fingers*]

Timon wishes to destroy wholesale all social and familial cohesion: ("Obedience fail in children!"; "Do't in your parents' eyes!") urging antisocial and criminal imperatives ("Bankrupts, hold fast!"; "bound servants, steal!"; "Maid, to thy master's bed, thy mistress is o' the brothel"). These come from the initially terrifying but increasingly absurd tirade in Act IV scene i, quoted in the entry for **Dr. Thomas Bowdler**, since it expurgated in from *The Family Shakespeare* (1818). As with Lear, a sexual obsession takes hold of Timon, and when he encounters the whores Phrynia and Timandra he urges them in a horrific invocation to spread venereal disease, even specifying its gruesome symptoms:

Consumptions sow
In hollow bones of man . . .
          Down with the nose,
Down with it flat, take the bridge quite away . . .
          Make curled-pate ruffians bald . . .
                              Plague all,
That your activity may defeat and quell
The source of all erection.
(IV iii 152–65)

Timon's final misanthropic words on his gravestone are entirely typical:

Here lie I, Timon, who, alive, all living men did hate
Pass by, and curse thy fill, but pass, and stay not here thy gait.
(V iv 72–73)

In *King Lear* (ca. 1605), the benighted paganism of ancient Britain is sharply evoked from the first act, when the headstrong King invokes against his daughter Cordelia primitive natural forces: "By the sacred radiance of the sun" (I i 111). Protests by the honest Earl of Kent provoke this furious but absurd exchange:

Lear:　Now by Apollo—
Kent:　　　　　　　　　Now by Apollo, King,
　　　Thou swear'st thy gods in vain.
Lear:　　　　　　　　　O vassal! Miscreant!
(I i 162–65)

In this context *miscreant* is a highly ironic term, since it means "a heretic or unbeliever," rather than "rascal or villain," as used in Bolingbroke's insult to Mowbray in *Richard II:* "Thou art a traitor and a miscreant" (I i 39).

　In a profound sense *King Lear* depicts a return to nature. In this dark world of primitive mind-sets and the law of the jungle, the attractive villain Edmund the Bastard announces that "Thou, Nature, art my goddess" (I ii 1), dismissing the whole establishment belief in "legitimacy" and finishing with the bawdy appeal, "Now, gods, stand up for bastards!" (I ii 22). When the King is crossed by Goneril, he exclaims "Darkness and devils!" and denounces her as a "degenerate bastard" (I iv 258–60), uttering the terrifyingly unnatural curse:

Hear, Nature, hear!; dear Goddess hear! . . .
Into her womb convey sterility,
Dry up in her the organs of increase
(I iv 282–86)

He persists in the following act:

All the stored vengeances of heaven fall
On her ungrateful top! [head] Strike her young bones,
You taking airs, with lameness.
(II iv 161–63)

Take, meaning to exert a malign influence, is laden with primitive beliefs in the evil powers of nature which witchcraft or cursing could unlock. It is also used in *Hamlet* (I i 144–45): "then no planets strike, / No fairy takes." In the great mad scene beginning "Blow winds and crack your cheeks. Rage, blow," Lear invokes all the forces of natural disorder, winds, cataracts, hurricanes, lightning, and "all shaking thunder" to

Crack Nature's molds, all germans spill at once
That make ingrateful man.
(III ii 8–9)

The last two lines have an alarmingly modern resonance, meaning "destroy the templates of creation and the basic seeds of life."

The tragedy is a great chorus of such invocations, curses, and desperate appeals, including Regan's "O the blest gods!" and Cordelia's later prayer "O you kind gods!," when she uses spells and charms to heal Lear. Both polytheistic forms like "the gods" and the monotheistic "God" are appealed to. But in the end the gods appear to be silent and indifferent. For the cruelest irony in all Shakespeare is surely the moment when Albany utters the prayer for Cordelia, "The gods defend her!," only to be answered by the stage direction *Enter Lear with Cordelia dead in his arms* and the excruciating line

Howl, howl, howl, howl! O you are men of stones.
(V iii 259)

Bawdy and Obscenity

On a totally different secular level, *King Lear* has many racy insults. Those of the Fool tend be subtle and oblique, but the remarkable tirade with which the Duke of Kent berates Oswald, Goneril's effete steward, seeking to provoke him to a duel, is cruelly direct:

> A knave, a rascal, eater of broken meats [scraps]; a base, proud, shallow, beggarly three-suited, hundred-pound, filthy, worsted-stocking knave, a lily-livered, action-taking [legalistic] knave; a whoreson, glass-gazing, superserviceable, finical [overfastidious] rogue; one-trunk-inheriting slave; one that would be a bawd [pimp] in way of service, and art nothing but the composition of a knave, beggar, coward, pander, and the son and heir of a mongrel bitch.
> (II ii 14–22)

The passage is a rich compendium of established insults, such as **knave, rascal, whoreson, bawd,** and **son of a bitch**, all of which have their own entries, as well as sharper barbs, alluding to Oswald's limited wardrobe, wealth, courage, and capacities as a pander or pimp. Kent's next speech ends: "You whoreson cullionly barbermonger, draw!" (II ii 34). Here *barbermonger* would mean "a patron of hairdressers," implying narcissism. *Cullion,* from Old French *coillon, couillon,* meaning a "testicle," is used literally in Chaucer, but by Elizabethan times it had become a coarse term of abuse, meaning "rascal," found in other dramatists and elsewhere in Shakespeare (*Henry VI, Part II* I iii 38; *Henry V* III ii 22; and *The Taming of the Shrew* IV ii 20). Shakespeare's formation *cullionly* is original.

Similar tirades occur in the bantering scenes between Prince Hal and Falstaff in *Henry IV, Part I*. Falstaff mocks the Prince's thinness with increasingly provocative obscenities: "'Sblood, you starveling, you eelskin, you dried neat's-tongue [ox's tongue], you bull's pizzle, you stock-fish—" (II iv 274–75). Falstaff's bawdy metaphors overstep the boundaries of decorum, since a bull's *pizzle* is its penis, dried and often used as a whip, while *stock-fish,* a long dried-up piece of cod, had similar phallic connotations, often implying impotence. However, the context of comic role-playing both encourages exaggeration and defuses provocation.

Bawdy is more obviously apparent in the comedies, but is found in virtually all

Shakespeare's plays. In characters like Mercutio and Edmund it seems intended to give a nonchalant, macho appeal. Hamlet's bawdy, on the other hand, conforms to the Freudian analysis of being both obscene and bitter. Elsewhere it surfaces in some unexpected contexts. A classic instance occurs in *Twelfth Night,* a comparatively "clean" play, when the professedly puritanical Malvolio publicly deciphers the forged and planted letter apparently written by the lady Olivia: "By my life, this is my lady's hand: these be her very c's, her u's, and her t's, and thus she makes her great P's" (II v 72). Malvolio has unwittingly spelt out what a recent editor has termed "a slang reference to the female pudenda" (Donno, ed., 1985, 90). As if to rub in the bawdy point, Shakespeare has the aristocratic idiot Sir Andrew Aguecheek ask the naive question: "Her very c's, her u's, and her t's: why that?" (II v 75). Elsewhere Sir Toby Belch also uses the term in a proverbial phrase of abuse, assuring Sir Andrew "if thou hast her [Olivia] not i' th' end, call me cut" (II iii 156).

Whereas obscenity is the direct and undisguised use of taboo language, the vital ingredient of bawdy is the stage dynamic, since it becomes a game whereby the author chooses terms that are sufficiently suggestive in their innuendoes to amuse the audience, but superficially innocent or disguised to avoid censorship. It is essentially a form of humorous dramatic irony in which certain motifs become familiar, even standing jokes with the audience. The difference can be illustrated in the treatment of **cuckoldry**, a major theme in Shakespeare. Real or imagined, it is seminal to the plots of *Othello, Hamlet, The Merry Wives of Windsor, Troilus and Cressida,* and *The Winter's Tale,* where it surfaces alarmingly in Leontes's tormented and embarrassing aside to the audience: "There have been . . . cuckolds ere now," including many a husband in the audience unaware that his wife, whose arms he now holds, has "been sluic'd [seduced] in his absence . . . by Sir Smile, his neighbour" (I ii 194–200). Bawdy, alternatively, defuses the horror and violence of sexual jealousy by indirect allusions to infidelity through the key word *horns,* the traditional emblem mocking the cuckold, who becomes a comic scapegoat. Variations are found in *horn* used as a verb: *horned, horner, horn-mad, horn-maker,* and even the Italian term *cornuto.* As the studies of Partridge (1947), Colman (1974), and Williams (1997) show, bawdy was a highly developed code language.

Shakespeare's actual use of taboo terms is not as daring as his contemporary Ben Jonson. Starting with the excretory category, *piss* occurs in a few contexts, notably in the phrase *a pissing while* in *Two Gentlemen of Verona* (IV iv 21) and *horse-piss* in *The Tempest* (IV i 199). *Shit,* on the other hand, never appears; nor does *arse,* but the slang equivalent *bum* is used three times. *Fart* occurs only in the euphemistic form *fartuous,* a comic version of *vertuous* used by Mistress Quickly in *The Merry Wives of Windsor* (II ii 100). *Fuck* is similarly avoided, being amusingly euphemized in the seemingly dry grammar lesson in the same play via the technical term *vocative,* which when put into the mouth of the Welshman Sir Hugh Evans, comes out as the obviously suggestive *focative* (IV i 53):

Sir Hugh Evans: . . . what is the focative case, William?
William: O vocativo, O.
Sir Hugh Evans: Remember, William, focative is *caret* [it is missing].

Mistress Quickly: And that's a good root.
Sir Hugh Evans: 'Oman, forbear [be quiet].
(*Merry Wives of Windsor* II ii 53–57)

Root is a fairly obvious phallic symbol, the symbolic meaning of "O" has been discussed, and *case* could mean "genitals." Elsewhere he uses some of the standard terms and euphemisms for "penis," namely *prick* (*Romeo and Juliet* II iv 121) and *yard* (*Love's Labour's Lost* V ii 676). Perhaps most surprising is the frank expression of xenophobic penis-envy in *Henry VIII*: "Have we some strange Indian with the great tool come to court, the women so besiege us? What a fry of fornication is at the door!" (II ii 115–16).

The other major pseudo-euphemism for *fuck* is *foot,* from French *foutre,* although the French form is also flamboyantly used by the outrageously uncensored fire-breathing braggart Pistol in absurd oaths such as "A foutra for the world and worldlings base!" and "a foutra for thine office!" (*Henry IV, Part II* V ii 98, 120). Although several of his contemporaries (Ben Jonson, George Chapman, and Francis Beaumont and John Fletcher) used *windfucker,* originally a name for the kestrel, as a personal insult, Shakespeare was more cautious. His euphemistic allusions to *cunt* via "country matters" in *Hamlet* (III ii 124) and "cut" in *Twelfth Night* (II v 72) have already been discussed. He clearly relished contriving scenes in which the most obscene terms were put into the most polite mouths. Thus the English lesson given to the French princess in *Henry V* turns out to be a parody of the "facts of life" routine, full of earnest delicacy:

Katharine: Comment appellez-vous le pied et la robe.
Alice: De foot, *madame; et* le coun.
Katharine: De foot, *et* le coun? *O Seigneur Dieu! Ces sont mots de son mauvais, corruptible, gros, et impudique, et non pour les dames d'honneur d'user.*
(III iv 55–58)

By emphasizing the French terms for fuck (*foot*) and cunt (*con* and *coun*), which are innocent or meaningless in English, Shakespeare is making the nominalist point that words are simply sounds and their meanings merely cultural and conventional. The princess puts it simply: "Ces sont mots de son mauvais." ("These are words with a bad sound.")

The notion of "feminine delicacy" is further enhanced by the dramatic irony of the staging. The parts of Mistress Quickly, who enters eagerly into bawdy, and Katharine and Alice, who are embarrassed by it, were, of course, played by men or boys. So were the roles of Mistress Overdone ("a Bawd") in *Measure for Measure,* the Nurse in *Romeo and Juliet,* and Kate the Shrew. Several Shakespearean heroines indulge enthusiastically in bawdy, parrying the puns with men. Beatrice in the bawdily titled *Much Ado About Nothing,* discussing "the man of parts" with her uncle, the Governor of Messina, comments: "With a good leg and a good foot, uncle, and money enough in his purse, such a man would win any woman in the world, if 'a [he] could get her good will" (II i 15–18). Here the *double entendres* are *leg* (= "penis"), *foot* (= "fuck"), and *will* (= "sexual appetite"). Her uncle responds that she will never get a husband if she is "so shrewd of tongue." Cleopatra herself, who utters such extraordinary romantic sentiments and a yearning for eternity, also uses a multitude of frank sexual images, allusions, and innuendoes. "I take no pleasure in aught an eunuch has" is followed by the envious fantasy "O happy horse to bear the weight of Antony!" and reminiscing of her great lovers, when she was

A morsel for a monarch [Caesar]: and great Pompey
Would stand and make his eyes grow in my brow . . . and die
With looking on his life.
(I v 30–34)

In sexual contexts (which *stand* obviously suggests here), *die* meant "to experience orgasm," a sense not even recorded in the original *Oxford English Dictionary,* being first elucidated by Eric Partridge in *Shakespeare's Bawdy* (1947) with the supporting quotation from *Much Ado About Nothing* where Benedick says to Beatrice: "I will live in thy heart, die in thy lap, and be buried in thine eyes" (V ii 99–101). When Antony tells Cleopatra of the death of his wife, Fulvia, she responds with mocking incredulity: "Can Fulvia die?" (I iii 58). Shakespeare's bawdy clearly has no class or sexual barriers, being uttered and relished by servants and noblemen, heroes and villains, kings and queens alike. The same range is only partly apparent in oaths, which are covered more fully in the entry for **swearing in women**.

As this overview has sought to show, Shakespeare was both subtle and daring in his use of oaths, invocations, foul language, ethnic slurs, and vituperation. He went to the very limits, and sometimes beyond, in his expression of souls in terrible anguish, fury, and despair, as well as in scenes of the most uproarious and lewd comedy. In his own lifetime, belief in magic, the spell, and the curse were still genuine, despite Renaissance skepticism, and many of his plays deal openly with their potency. *The Tempest* (1611) is commonly interpreted as Shakespeare's farewell to the stage ("Our revels now are ended") and to his art, especially in his alter-ego Prospero's renunciation of magic in the last act. His wonderful abilities obviously stand at the furthest remove from those of the debased slave Caliban who complains:

You taught me language; and my profit on 't
Is, I know how to curse. The red plague rid [destroy] you
For learning [teaching] me your language!
(I ii 363–65)

Prospero's speech begins with fanciful invocations to the "Ye elves of hills, brooks, standing lakes and groves." But he claims magical powers over the elements and even over the dead. To the accompaniment of "solemn music," he undertakes to break his staff, bury it,

And, deeper than did ever plummet sound,
I'll drown my book.
(V i 57–58)

Prospero thus abandons magic willingly, an action that Faustus finally offers to do out of desperation ("I'll burn my book!") in his final futile plea to avoid damnation. Like Chaucer before him in his Retractions, Shakespeare ends the Epilogue to *The Tempest* with a Christian awareness of the power of prayer and of mercy:

As you from crimes would pardoned be
Let your indulgence set me free.

A curious anonymous footnote lies in the inscription beneath Shakespeare's bust in Holy Trinity Church, Stratford. It is a vehement, almost profane, wish to be left in peace:

Good friend for Jesus sake forbear,
To digg the dust enclosed heare.
Blest be the man that spares these stones,
And curst be he that moves my bones.

After Shakespeare's death his texts were toned down, notably in the First Folio (1623), edited by his friends John Heming and Henry Condell. These alterations were, however, confined to religious oaths, as can be seen in these instances from *Hamlet: O God > Heaven* I ii 150, 195; *O God Horatio > O good Horatio* V ii 297; *Swounds > Why* II ii 564 > *Come* V i 264; *'Sblood > Why* III ii 352; *Do you see this, O God > you Gods* IV v 201. The language of a liberal swearer like Falstaff was similarly edited: *'Sblood > Why* III ii 352; *i'faith* (II iv 438) was simply expunged; *God help the wicked* was altered to *Heaven help the wicked* II iv 464. A recent editor of *Othello* has counted fifty cases where profanities in the earlier Quarto text are deleted or modified in the Folio (Honigmann 1997, 352).

These were symptoms of the Puritanism which was becoming a major force in the land, eventually closing the theaters in 1642. Nor did the passing of Puritanism guarantee a return to the purity of the source. As the entries for **Dr. Thomas Bowdler** and **Bowdlerization** make clear, the expurgation of sexual references continued, and the inroads made into the Shakespeare text in the Victorian era were drastic. Thomas Bowdler's sanitized and enormously popular *Family Shakespeare* did not originally even include *Romeo and Juliet* in the anonymous first edition of 1807, and by 1894 there were some forty expurgated editions of Shakespeare on the market. Even in modern times few school editions are completely unexpurgated.

See also: Bowdler, Dr. Thomas; Bowdlerization; Class and Swearing; Master of the Revels; Minced Oaths; Renaissance, the.

Bibliography

Colman, E.A.M. *The Dramatic Use of Bawdy in Shakespeare.* London: Longman, 1974.
Craig, W.J., ed. *The Complete Works of William Shakespeare.* Oxford: Oxford University Press, 1928.
Donno, E.S., ed. *Twelfth Night.* Cambridge: Cambridge University Press, 1985.
Dutton, Richard. "Jurisdiction of Theatre and Censorship." In *A Companion to Renaissance Drama,* ed. Arthur F. Kinney. Oxford: Blackwell, 2002.
Evans, Ifor B. *The Language of Shakespeare's Plays.* London: Methuen, 1947.
Fabricius, Johannes. *Syphilis in Shakespeare's England.* London: Jessica Kingsley, 1994.
Gildersleeve, Virginia Cocheron. *Government Regulation of the Elizabethan Drama.* New York: Columbia University Press, 1908.

Honigmann, E.A.J., ed. *Othello.* Arden edition. London: Thomson Learning, 1997.

Hulme, Hilda. *Explorations in Shakespeare's Language.* London: Longmans, 1962.

Jespersen, Otto. *Growth and Structure of the English Language* [1905]. Oxford: Basil Blackwell, 1962.

Kermode, Frank. *Shakespeare's Language.* London: Penguin, 2000.

Loomba, Ania. *Shakesepeare, Race, and Colonialism.* Oxford: Oxford University Press, 2002.

Muir, Kenneth, ed. *Macbeth.* Arden edition: London: Methuen, 1962.

Partridge, Eric. *Shakespeare's Bawdy.* London: Routledge & Kegan Paul, 1947.

Rossiter, A.P. *Angel with Horns.* London: Longman, 1961.

Shirley, Frances A. *Swearing and Perjury in Shakespeare's Plays.* London: Allen & Unwin, 1979.

Spevack, Marvin, ed. *A Complete and Systematic Concordance to the Works of Shakespeare.* Hildesheim: George Olms, 1968.

Williams, Gordon. *A Glossary of Shakespeare's Sexual Language.* London: Athlone Press, 1997.

SHIT WORDS

It is a general feature in swearing that terms for excretion come to be used to express insult, annoyance, and contempt. The entry for **psychology of swearing** records some of Sigmund Freud's insights into this correlation. Evidence abounds from other languages, in the form of French *merde,* German *scheiss,* and Italian *stronzo.* As a term of insult, both as a simple noun and in various compounded forms, *shit* has an extended and picturesque history from the medieval period, always male in reference. The likely explanation is that in earlier times *shit* was not an especially taboo term, nor was the verb to *shite.* In fact *shit* was a common term in Anglo-Saxon for diarrhea, as it still is in rural dialects, and in the vulgar expression "to have the shits." In common with other "four-letter" words, *shit* was used in medieval medical texts, such as the *Cirurgerie* of Lanfrank (1363) and Guy de Chauliac (1425). Two common rural names for varieties of the heron are still the *shitepoke* and the *shiterow.*

However, from the medieval period onward it started to gain emotive force. As the accompanying semantic field shows, *shit-breech* is recorded as a personal nickname of a distinguished personage in the early thirteenth century; it was still flourishing as a term of abuse in a reference to "a scurvy, shit-breech lad" in 1675. In the *Flyting of Dunbar and Kennedy* (1503), Kennedy calls Dunbar "A shit but wit" (496) using the term in the modern direct style for the first time. However, the citations in the *Oxford English Dictionary* show a hiatus between the sixteenth and the nineteenth centuries in the general and the personal uses. It is significant that even **Rochester** (1647–1680), whose poems spectacularly flaunt all taboo sexual language, will use *excrement* and *turd* but writes that "My squeamish stomach . . . made me Purge and Spew" ("Tunbridge Wells: A Satyr," 6–10).

Reflecting the word's increasingly taboo quality, Dr. Johnson (1755) likewise included *turd* but excluded *shit,* as did Noah Webster after him (1828), while Jonathan Swift's use of it in various satires, notably in the famous line concluding *Cassinus and Peter* (1731–1734): "Oh Celia, Celia, Celia, sh—" was clearly considered outrageous. The major contemporary novelists, even those like Daniel Defoe and Henry Fielding who wrote in a realistic style, tended to avoid the word. However, Captain Francis Grose has *shitsack* in his *Classical Dictionary of the Vulgar Tongue* (1785) as an epithet for "a dastardly fellow: also a non-conformist." The early field is set out below. Except when attributed otherwise, the quotations are from the *Oxford English Dictionary.*

The Early Semantic Field of Shit Words

Date	Word	Quotation
ca. 1202	*shit-breech*	"Randulphus Bla de Scitebroc"
ca. 1250	*shit word*	"So herdes [herdsmen] doþ oþer mid schit worde"
ca. 1386	*shitten*	"A shitten shepherd and a clene sheepe" (Chaucer)
ca. 1508	*shit* (personal epithet)	"[Thou art] a schit but wit" (Dunbar)
ca. 1598	*shit-fire*	"A hot, violent fellow, a shite-fire" (Florio)
ca. 1690	*shitabed*	"[They] gave them ill language, calling them Tooth-gapers, Sherks, Shittabeds, Slubber-degullions"
ca. 1785	*shit-sack*	"A dastardly fellow" (Grose)
ca. 1795	*shit house*	"For the honour of the Scots, we have his [Wallace's] effigy in the shite houses to this very day."

The references to *shit word* and *shitten* carry significant sociolinguistic implications. The link between herdsmen and *shit word* (in the poem *The Owl and the Nightingale,* ca. 1250) clearly implies that such terms are low class, a point further discussed in **cherles termes**. The Chaucer reference *(General Prologue,* l. 504) is the only use of a four-letter word in that text, clearly as a condemnation of corrupt and venal clergy. The Chester Play, *The Innocents* (ca. 1500) has a similarly contemptuous reference to "a shitten-arsed shrew" (157). *Gammer Gurton's Needle* (acted 1566) includes such new vituperative idioms as "Fie shitten knave" and "that dirty shitten lout." Samuel Pepys records Edward Montagu, the Earl of Sandwich, recounting a current idiom but an old saying of his father's, "that he that do get a wench with child and marry her afterwards is as if a man should shit in his hat and then clap it on his head" (October 7, 1660). Pepys also noted on April 6, 1665: "Sir G. Carteret . . . called Sir W. Batten in his discourse at the table . . . shitten foole, which vexed me." *Shitten* continued to be used in English dialect to mean "paltry, mean, contemptible," but has virtually died out. Of the rest, *shit-sack* still survives in the British variety, as *shit house* does in global English. However, the quotation from 1795 gives historical depth to the symbolic proximity between excretion and insult.

The major modern expansion of the term started in American English. Stuart Berg Flexner notes: "Also in wide use between the 1870s and 1890s were such seemingly modern terms as *shit* and *bullshit* meaning 'nonsense, rubbish, lies' *(chickenshit* and *horseshit* were first recorded in the 1930s)" (1976, 315). The *Random House Historical Dictionary of American Slang* (1994–1997) anticipates these dates by a few years, citing a variety of quotations in letters by major authors such as Ezra Pound, Ernest Hemingway, E.E. Cummings, and others. *Bullshit* has recently (2005) become the topic of a monograph. Part of the legacy of World War II were *shit list* for a blacklist of targeted or disliked people, and *shit on a shingle* for creamed chipped beef on toast. Hugh Rawson's *Dictionary of Invective* (1991) lists some forty picturesque and amusing idioms, most of them of American provenance. The principal exclamation in the field is *holy shit,* recorded from the 1930s, while the more damning personal insults are the compounds *shithead, shitface, shitheel,* and *dipshit.*

As is common when particular terms start to become taboo, less specific relatives are drawn into the field. Shakespeare never uses *shit,* but has "Out! Dunghill! Darest thou brave a nobleman?" in *King John* IV iii 87, while a seventeenth-century commentator dismissed Paracelsus, the sixteenth-century Swiss physician, as "a walking dunghill (so corrupt and offensive his life)." From the late eighteenth century **crap** shifted from its earlier senses of "waste, rubbish, or residue" and started to mean excrement as well as "nonsense, lies, or rubbish" generally. One of the more amusing euphemisms, recorded ca. 1592, is *Sir Reverence,* allowing writers deliberately to confuse the title of respect with the excremental sense.

Usage varies widely in global varieties. The *Australian National Dictionary* lists *shit-kicker* (also found in American English) as an ironic term for an unskilled worker, recorded from 1969, and *shit-catcher* for knickerbockers. South African English has not made much of a contribution, since the Afrikaans equivalent *kak* is widely used, especially in the metaphorical sense of "rubbish." Interestingly, in several varieties of **pidgin English** *shit* is so generalized that it has lost its taboo quality entirely. Usually spelled *sit,* it is widely used as a simple form to mean "residue," so that *sit belong faia* (literally "shit from the fire") is used for "ashes," while the verb *bulsitim* (from "bullshit") is used generally to mean "deceive." It thus has no emotive quality in Pidgin. In all other varieties *shit* continues to thrive as a personal insult, and in contemporary usage it has greatly generalized to express exasperation, anger, surprise, frustration, disgust, and astonishment. According to the frequency rating of the *Longman Dictionary of Contemporary English* (2nd edition, 1995) it is one of the 2,000 most spoken words. Timothy Jay's study *Cursing in America* showed a similarly high frequency among college students (1992, 143–51).

The *OED* entry for *shit* carried the usage label: "Not now in decent use." This is still true, inasmuch as it would be offensive in public, professional, or political discourse. However, the term and its affiliates have shaken off the taboos of previous centuries and are now common in global English in general speech, in literature, film, and television.

See also: Crap; Pidgin English; Swift, Jonathan; Turd.

Bibliography

Flexner, Stuart Berg. *I Hear America Talking.* New York: Van Nostrand Reinhold, 1976.
Frankfurt, Harry G. *On Bullshit.* Princeton: Princeton University Press, 2005.
Grose, Francis. *A Classical Dictionary of the Vulgar Tongue.* London: S. Hooper, 1785.
Jay, Timothy. *Cursing in America.* Philadelphia: Benjamins, 1992.
Maurer, David W. *Language of the Underworld.* Lexington: University Press of Kentucky, 1981.
Montagu, Ashley. *The Anatomy of Swearing.* London and New York: Macmillan and Collier, 1973.
Rawson, Hugh. *A Dictionary of Invective.* London: Hale, 1991.
Rogers, Pat, ed. *Jonathan Swift: The Complete Poems.* New Haven and London: Yale University Press, 1983.

"SHOCK JOCKS"

Broadcasting, traditionally a purveyor of family entertainment, has been governed by norms and regulations concerning decency. However, in recent decades, there has been a divergence between British and American linguistic culture, especially in radio. In Britain the traditional decencies of "family values" are generally maintained, not only by the B.B.C., but by independent stations. However, in America a number of "talk radio" hosts have acquired enormous listenerships by becoming "shock jocks" using cultivated outrageousness and explicitly prurient or shocking verbal content, practices that have also been exploited on television. Controversy and fines have served mainly to increase audience ratings. The emergence of the "shock jock" seems clearly to be a reaction against political correctness, since many of the targets are precisely in areas newly regarded as taboo.

The phenomenon started with outspoken comedians, notably Lenny Bruce (1925–1966), who satirized issues like abortion, drugs, the Ku Klux Klan, and the Roman Catholic Church. Bruce was arrested in 1964 for using various obscenities and sentenced to four months in the workhouse. However, "shock jocks" proper started to emerge on the American radio scene in the 1970s and have become steadily more outrageous, violating taboos over sex, scatology, racism, homophobia, and ridicule of the disabled. The Federal Communications Commission, charged with preserving standards of decency on the airwaves, has fined several channels sums of over half a million dollars, without stemming the tide. Perhaps the most successful American "shock jock" is Howard Stern, self-described as "the ribald radio star" whose programs focus on scandal, and whose Web site announces, for instance: "Howard reveals his long-anticipated top 10 A-holes of 2004" of whom the no. 1 was a personality who "hit his piece-of-ass wife." Among the television competitors are the Osbournes, promoted as "TV's foulest mouthed family."

A similar category is that of the "alternative comedian," exemplified by Andrew Dice Clay, described in a work on British broadcasting as "sexist, racist, profane and very popular. . . . Clay violates every linguistic taboo you can think of. He attacks 'urine-coloured Pakis' for 'that smell.' The audience roars. He invites women in the audience to 'suck my dick.' The woman in question just giggles" (Graef, in Hargreave, ed., 1991, 76). The reduplicating term *shock jock* is American, deriving from *jock* as an abbreviation of *jockey,* recorded from 1947 as an independent form of *disk jockey,* underscoring the origins in radio. The full form seems to be first recorded in 1986.

See also: Broadcasting.

Bibliography

Hargreave, Andrea Millwood, ed. *A Matter of Manners? The Limits of Broadcasting Language.* London: John Libbey, 1991.

SHREW

The word has a curious semantic history, being originally a plain animal term, then in medieval times commonly applied to wicked males, before acquiring the modern feminine specialization denoting an aggressive and mean-spirited woman. Anglo-Saxon *scream,* the root of the word, referred simply to the small, mouselike animal with no metaphorical human extension. However, as with the weasel, various superstitions grew up about the malignant influence of the animal. Some of these were evidently carried over when about 1250 the term started to be used of "a wicked, evil-disposed or malignant man, rascal or villain, specifically the Devil." The adjectives *curst* and *false* often reinforced the sense of evil.

The feminine application starts to emerge in the lifetime of Geoffrey Chaucer, memorably used by the Merchant of the *Canterbury Tales* when he ruefully describes his newly mar-

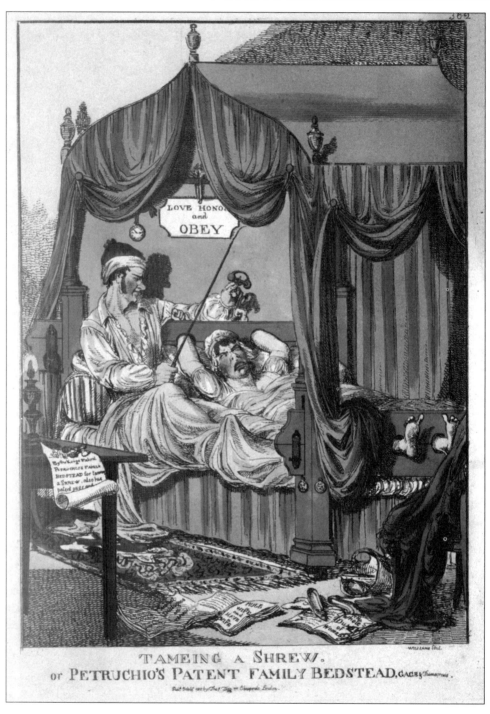

By the late sixteenth century, the time of Shakespeare's comedy, *The Taming of the Shrew*—depicted here in an 1815 engraving—*shrew* referred to a loud, ill-tempered high-spirited woman. Shakespeare's heroine, Katharina, is not born a shrew but made one by male injustice. (Library of Congress, LC-USZC2-3804)

ried wife: "She is a shrewe at al" (*Prologue* l. 1222), which would translate into modern idiom as "She is an absolute bitch." By the end of the sixteenth century it was invariably used of a loud, aggressive, or perverse woman, the stereotypical example being Katharina in Shakespeare's *The Taming of the Shrew* (ca. 1596). Despite its title, the play shows that the heroine is not born a shrew but made one by male injustice, prejudice, macho, and chauvinist attitudes, epitomized in the final comments of Hortensio: "thou hast tamed a curst shrew" (V ii 193). Dr. Johnson's definition (1755) is a *tour de force:* "a peevish, malignant, clamorous, spiteful, vexatious, turbulent woman." The sense survived several centuries, before petering out as a common word around 1850.

Discussing the stereotype of the shrew, Jane Mills observes: "Like the witch and the wanton, the shrew contradicted the patriarchal concept of the submissive, biddable woman" (1991, 218). According to Lucy de Bruyn (1979), the shrew, in association with the witch and the wanton, form stereotypes of the unnatural woman in the sixteenth century. Unlike *scold, shrew* is still current as a term of abuse, and is frequently used by women of other women, as is *witch*.

See also: Scold; Women, Stereotypes of.

Bibliography

de Bruyn, Lucy. *Women and the Devil in the Sixteenth Century.* Tisbury, Wiltshire: The Compton Press, 1979.
Mills, Jane. *Womanwords.* London: Virago, 1991.

SLANG

There is general agreement among authorities that slang is, in the definition of the *Oxford English Dictionary,* "Language of a highly colloquial type, considered as below the level of standard educated speech, consisting either of new words or of current words employed in some special sense." However, there is also an accepted difficulty, acknowledged by lexicographers, over which words should be allocated as "slang," given the overlap with the related categories of "colloquial," "informal," "jargon," and "cant." In the 1930s the American lexicographer Clarence L. Barnhart invited a number of major authorities, American and British, to mark a dictionary manuscript for levels of usage, "but there was little agreement among them" (in Morton 1994, 251). James Murray himself suffered a prolonged indecision over whether to include *bounder* in the *OED*, an anxiety which now seems trivial. The Preface to the major recent contribution to the field, the *Random House Historical Dictionary of American Slang,* concedes that "no commonly accepted definition of slang has won much favor among linguists, who mostly regard the boundaries between slang and other levels of discourse as too insubstantial for analysis" (1994, xi).

Considering the importance of the category, the term *slang* itself is a surprisingly recent coinage, dating from the mid-eighteenth century, when the primary sense overlapped with *cant,* a much older word meaning "the special vocabulary used by a set of persons of a low or disreputable character," thus "language of a low and vulgar type." The word was not in Dr.

Johnson's *Dictionary* (1755), but Francis Grose in his *Classical Dictionary of the Vulgar Tongue* (1785) simply defined *slang* as "cant language." Grose's Preface (quoted in his entry) makes it clear that slang consists of the in-group code-words of urban sets, many of them criminal. These disreputable origins clearly colored subsequent definitions, such as that by Greenhough and Kittredge in 1902, that slang is "A peculiar kind of vagabond language, always hanging on the outskirts of legitimate speech, but continually straying or forcing its way into the most respectable company" (55). The origin is also disputed, but probably comes from canting usage.

However, the hierarchical model which places slang down the sociolinguistic ladder only offers one perspective. In the magisterial Preface to the *OED,* Sir James Murray wrote of "the slang and cant of various 'sets' and classes," such as "nautical slang," "public school slang," and "the slang of the Stock Exchange" (xvii). Eric Partridge's excellent study *Slang* (1933) similarly has twenty-five categories, including overseas varieties such as Australian, Indian, and American English. Robert L. Chapman's *New Dictionary of American Slang* (1986) gives a kaleidoscopic image of about a dozen sources of varieties of slang that make up the whole field (xviii). These include the different branches of the armed forces, hobos and tramps, the underworld, narcotics, jazz, finance, immigrants, baseball, show business, finance, and college students. They thus range from respectable professions to the criminal underworld.

The common factor in these categories is that slang terms form a sociolinguistic barrier within which insiders identify themselves through passwords that are initially unfamiliar and thus disturbing to outsiders. This has generally been truer of British than American and Australian usage, which are more accepting of the lower registers. In the Introduction to his *Slang Thesaurus,* Jonathon Green quotes the dictum of Dr. J.Y.T. Greig in 1938: "The chief stimuli of slang are sex, money and intoxicating liquor," adding his own comment: "Bowing to current events one must add drugs to the list" (1986, xiii). Although slang is now more acceptable than the previous definitions suggest, the most important point is the awareness that in the past the use of slang formed an affront or insult of some kind. The verbal sense of *slang,* "to rail in abusive or vulgar language" is recorded from 1828. This practice is encapsulated in the *slanging match,* an exchange of abuse or a vituperative argument, recorded from 1896, with evident affinities to **flyting**. It is anticipated by the much earlier American term *slangwhang,* found as a noun from 1834 in the sense of "violent or abusive language," as well as in the form *slangwhanging* from 1809, and as a verb from 1880.

A number of points need to be made concerning the antiquity of slang and its survival. As the entry for **dictionaries** shows, the earliest vestigial glossaries of the language explicated not proper usage but cant or underground language. It is also often maintained that slang is ephemeral, in the words of Dr. Johnson, a "fugitive cant unworthy of preservation." While this is largely true, slang continues to flourish: indeed a century ago G.K. Chesterton asserted that "the one stream of poetry which is constantly flowing is slang" (in Partridge 1933, 24). Furthermore, there are some remarkable instances of slang terms which have survived for centuries, despite sometimes disappearing from the written record for decades. Among slang terms which are over two centuries old are *hump* and *shag* for "copulate," *leak* for "urinate," *tool* for "penis," *twat* for "vagina," *frig* for "masturbate," *crap* for "defecate," *cove* for "man," *beak* for "judge," *pig* for "policeman," and *freak-out* for "orgasm." Finally, dictionaries of slang continue to proliferate.

See also: Dictionaries; Flyting; Grose, Captain Francis; Partridge, Eric.

Bibliography
Chapman, Robert L., ed. *New Dictionary of American Slang*. New York: Harper & Row, 1986.
Coleman, Julie. *A History of Cant and Slang Dictionaries*. 2 vols. Oxford: Oxford University Press, 2004.
Green, Jonathon, *The Slang Thesaurus*. London: Penguin, 1986.
Greenhough, James Bradstreet, and George Lyman Kittredge. *Words and Their Way in English Speech*. London: Macmillan, 1902.
Klaeber, F. "Concerning the Etymology of Slang." *American Speech,* April 1926.
Lighter, J.E., ed. *Random House Historical Dictionary of American Slang*. New York: Random House, 1994–1997.
Morton, Herbert C. *The Story of Webster's Third*. Cambridge: Cambridge University Press, 1994.
Partridge, Eric. *Slang*. London: Routledge & Kegan Paul, 1933.

SODOMY. *See:* Bugger; Homosexuals

SOLDIERS AND SAILORS

Sociolinguistic studies consistently show that swearing and foul language are manifestations of "macho" behavior, which becomes intensified in all-male verbal contexts such as the armed forces, the police, the factory floor, locker rooms for athletes, street gangs, and the Mafia. The entries on **the dozens** and for **flyting** endorse the point, as do the observations in Lakoff (1975). In 1795, Joseph Moser noted in his tract *Reflections on Profane and Judicial Swearing,* that there were "two bodies of men . . . more addicted to a wanton profanation of God's holy Name; to swearing for amusement, and blaspheming: I mean our *Soldiers* and *Sailors* " (in Montagu 1973, 223). Conscription introduced most males to concentrated swearing, dominance being established from call-up by foul language as much as by drilling and other routines. Swearing seems generated more readily in the format of group combat of the army and navy than in the air force, where pilots operate more on an individual basis and communicate publicly by radio. As Stuart Berg Flexner noted: "There was such a fantastic increase in the use of *fuck, screw,* and *shit* during World War II that it almost seemed that no serviceman could complete a sentence without using one of them" (1976, 158). The general consequence was that swearwords were brought back into the wider society by demobilized civilians. This point is often made in relation to the spread of *motherfucker* from the 1950s onward.

Historically, the first explicit link between swearing and soldiers appears in the fifteenth century when the English soldiers in the Hundred Years' War were routinely called the *goddems* by their French opponents, a point developed in the entry for **goddam**. There are earlier signs of strong soldierly language in the insults traded by the Saxons and the Vikings before they join battle in the Anglo-Saxon heroic poem *The Battle of Maldon* (11th century), celebrating English defiance at a battle fought in 991. However, these exchanges are dignified in comparison with what was to come later. In the famous speech on "The Seven Ages of Man" in Shakespeare's *As You Like It* (1599), the young man, previously a passionate lover, is now a soldier, "full of strange oaths and bearded like the pard [leopard]" (II vii 139–66). On the Elizabethan stage there emerged the ironic type of the *miles gloriosus,* derived from the Roman comedian Plautus, full of bluster and often incoherent oaths, typified by Pistol in Shakespeare's *Henry V* (1599) and Bobadill in Ben Jonson's *Everyman in His Humour* (1598). Pistol comes out with such contrived vituperation as "thou prick-eared cur of Iceland!," "O viper vile!," and "O braggart vile, and damned furious wight!," the last seeming to be an subconscious self-description. Bobadill is more original and bizarre, with creations like "base cullion [testicle]," "a dungworm, an excrement!" and "by the foot of Pharaoh."

To some extent these figures also derived from the sixteenth-century social type termed the **ruffler,** a vagabond, or a parasite of a military or more often pseudo-military kind, who made a living out of verbal aggression. Tobias Smollett's notable novels *Roderick Random* (1748) and *Peregrine Pickle* (1751) both contain considerable salvos of nautical swearing. The phrase "to swear like a trooper" first emerges in a most ironic context, Samuel Richardson's epistolary novel *Pamela* (1739–1740): "She curses and storms at me like a trooper" (I, 239). It is precisely recorded by Samuel Foote in *The Englishman Returned from Paris* in 1756, according to Farmer and Henley (1890–1904), although Flexner (1976) gives a later date of 1839, perhaps relating to the American context. The saying has an obvious class gloss, although officers presumably swore as well. George Washington's General Order to the Continental Army in 1776 gives an American perspective:

> The general is sorry to be informed that the foolish and wicked practice of profane cursing and swearing, a vice hitherto little known in an American army, is growing into fashion. He hopes the officers will, by example as well as influence, endeavor to check it, and that both they and the men will reflect that we can have little hope of the blessing of Heaven on our arms if we insult it by our impiety and folly.
> (cited in Rawson 1991, 5–6)

A frequently cited modern source for obscene language is Frederic Manning's fictional memoir drawn from his experiences in World War I, *The Middle Parts of Fortune,* originally published anonymously in a limited edition in 1929. An expurgated edition appeared the following year under the title of *Her Privates We* under the *nom de plume* of "Private 19022." (Both titles come from a bawdy exchange between Hamlet and Rosencrantz and Guildernstern in *Hamlet* II ii 240–43). In the following exchange Martlow is complaining to Bourne, the central character, about a pair of binoculars an officer has taken from him:

> "And now the bastard's wearin' the bes' pair slung round 'is own bloody neck. Wouldn't you've thought the cunt would 'a' give me vingt frong [twenty francs] for 'em anyway?"
>
> "Your language is deplorable, Martlow," said Bourne in ironical reproof; "quite apart from the fact that you're speaking of your commanding officer. Did you learn all these choice phrases in the army?"

440

"Not much," said little Martlow derisively; "all I learnt in the army was drill an' care o' bloody arms. I knew all the fuckin' patter [speech] before I joined."
(Manning 1977, 37–38).

Manning's work avoided prosecution for obscenity by being published anonymously in a limited edition. Brophy and Partridge, in their collection, *Songs and Slang of the British Soldier, 1914–1918,* commented that *fuck* was

> so common indeed in its adjectival form that after a short time the ear refused to acknowledge it and took in only the noun to which it is attached. . . . By adding –*ing* and –*ing well* an adjective and an adverb were formed and thrown into every sentence. Thus if a sergeant said, "Get your —ing rifles!" it was understood as a matter of routine. But if he said, "Get your rifles!" there was an immediate implication of urgency and danger. (1931, 17)

In comparison, Robert Graves in his *Goodbye to All That* (1929) and even Norman Mailer in *The Naked and the Dead* (1948) are not as frank in their recording of coarse speech. Both use a fair number of euphemisms, such as Graves's "double effing c—" (1929, 70) and Mailer's continual use of "fugging." Subsequent works, notably Joseph Heller's *Catch 22* (1961) are less coarse.

Swearing has in recent decades become an essential part of the characterization of the military in film. Whereas earlier depictions tended to be unrealistically polite, the more recent have become relentlessly crude. A revealing but simple contrast lies between Stanley Kubrick's *Paths of Glory* (1957) and his *Full Metal Jacket* (1987). Also in the earlier restrained style are Jean Renoir's *Regles du Jeu* ("The Rules of the Game" 1939), Erich Maria Remarque's *All Quiet on the Western Front* (1930), and David Lean's *The Bridge on the River Kwai* (1957), while typical examples of the later obscenity-laden mode are Francis Ford Coppola's *Apocalypse Now* (1979) and Oliver Stone's *Platoon* (1986).

See also: Bywords of Swearing; Dozens, the; Goddam / Goddamn; Ruffler.

Bibliography

Brophy, John, and Eric Partridge, eds. *Songs and Slang of the British Soldier, 1914–1918.* London: Partridge, 1931.
Flexner, Stuart Berg. *I Hear America Talking.* New York: Van Nostrand Reinhold, 1976.
Graves, Robert. *Goodbye to All That.* Harmondsworth: Penguin, 1929.
Lakoff, Robin. *Language and Woman's Place.* New York: Harper and Row, 1975.
Mailer, Norman. *The Naked and the Dead.* New York: Alan Wingate, 1948.
Manning, Frederic. *The Middle Parts of Fortune.* London: Peter Davies, 1977.
Rawson, Hugh. *A Dictionary of Invective.* London: Hale, 1991.
Smith, Philip M. *Language, the Sexes and Society.* Oxford: Blackwell, 1985.

SON OF A BITCH

In common with many insults, this has steadily lost impact over the centuries through indiscriminate use. Originally used only of despicable males, it is now highly generalized. Although this epithet is, in the words of the *Oxford English Dictionary,* "more common in the U.S. than else-where," it is recorded from as early as ca. 1330 in the variant form *biche-sone* in an angry context: "Abide þou þef malicious! Biche-sone þou drawest amis!" ("Stop you wicked thief! You son of a bitch, you draw wrongly!") (*Of Arthour and of Merlin,* l. 333). Thereafter it was used freely for some five centuries by a number of major British authors, invariably in provocative fashion, including Shakespeare: "son and heir of a mongrel bitch" (1605, in *King Lear* II ii 22); Laurence Sterne: "Phelps is a son of a Bitch for saying" (1762, in a private letter of April 8); and finally by Lord Byron in a typical line: "Like lap-dogs, the least civil sons of b——s" (1823, from *Don Juan* XI xli 123). As the entry for **bitch** shows, and as the censored forms show, that term was generally regarded as highly offensive by the late eighteenth century. This no doubt led to the decline of the compound in Britain and its omission from the *OED.*

One the earliest instances of American usage occurs in the diary of a Scottish traveler in New Jersey in 1744: "I was waked this morning before sunrise with a strange bawling and hollowing without doors. It was the landlord ordering his Negroes, with an imperious and exalted voice. In his orders the known term or epithet *son-of- a-bitch* was often repeated" (Mencken 1936, 313). Mencken noted that the term "rose to popularity in the United States during the decade before the Civil War, and at the start was considered extremely offensive" (1936, 313). But by the mid-twentieth century it was showing the familiar signs of weaken-ing and generalization. Like *bastard,* it was being used in a familiar or even sympathetic fashion: "He was a drinking, whoring, kindly savage son of a bitch" (J. Carew, *Wild Coast* 1958, ix, 124). As far back as 1933 John Dos Passos wrote of "Every sonofabitchin yellerleg [cavalryman] in the State of Nevada" (*42nd Parallel,* I, 101), while in 1936, Henry Miller even referred to a woman as "a frigid son of a bitch" (*Black Spring,* 250). Commenting that "All expletives tend to be similarly dephlogisticated by over-use," Mencken continued:

> Our maid-of-all work in that department [profanity] is *son of a bitch,* which seems as pale and ineffectual to a Slav or a Latin as *fudge* does to us . . . when uttered with a wink or a dig in the ribs, it is actually a term of endearment. . . . Worse, it is frequently toned down to *s.o.b.* or transmogrified into childish *son of a gun.*
> (1936, 317)

The old force is not entirely lost, but usually needs reinforcement from some adjective like *miserable* or *insufferable.* A notable instance came from the plain-speaking President Harry S Truman, who said of General Douglas MacArthur: "I didn't fire him because he was a dumb son of a bitch, although he was" (cited in Merle Miller's aptly titled biography *Plain Speaking* 1974, 287). Because of its current range from offensive to trivial, some authorities like Spears (1990) list it as "provocative to some extent." In Timothy Jay's study of student speech, it ranked ninth out of twenty-eight items (1992, 143).

The epithet is now almost exclusive to American and Canadian English, having died out in British usage and being hardly ever encountered in other global varieties such as Austra-lian, South African, and Indian English.

See also: Bitch.

Bibliography

Jay, Timothy. *Cursing in America.* Philadelphia: Benjamins, 1992.
Mencken, H.L. *The American Language.* New York: Knopf, 1936.
Miller, Merle. *Plain Speaking.* London: Gollancz, 1974.
Spears, Richard A. *Forbidden American English.* Lincolnwood, IL: Passport Books, 1990.

SOUNDING. *See:* Dozens, the

SOUTH AFRICA

South African English is a robust, distinctive variety of global English with a marked range of registers and idioms. Its unique feature is that the strongest terms of swearing, racist insult, and foul language are borrowed from other local languages, principally Afrikaans. This is not the case in other global varieties of English. Furthermore, given the country's history of conflict and racial separation, formalized in the policy of apartheid officially implemented from 1948 to about 1990, it is natural that the variety should have a regrettably large stock of terms of ethnic insult. Of these, the native terms **kaffir** and **hottentot** and the borrowed terms **coolie** and **coon** have their own entries.

The founding population of English-speaking immigrants, still known as the 1820 Settlers, were selected by the British government and encouraged to settle in an area of the Eastern Cape Province, then known as Caffraria. (Most of the Western Cape Province had been in the hands of the Dutch colonists from 1652.) The four thousand settlers who landed at Algoa Bay from April 10, 1820, were people of education and some means: farmers, bourgeois artisans, traders, and businessmen from various parts of the British Isles. There was a considerable Methodist element among them: by 1844 five of the ten churches built in the area called Albany were of that sober denomination. They were thus very different in character and motivation from both the Pilgrim Fathers of Plymouth Rock in Massachusetts and the Founding Convicts of Botany Bay in Australia. These various factors perhaps explain why the early records of the settlers show no signs of the swearing and foul language that were the hallmark of Australian English from the arrival of the first convicts in 1788.

However, modern South African English has acquired a wealth of excretory, genital, and racial epithets, many of them confined to oral usage and derived from Afrikaans. Originating in the language of the Dutch colonists, Afrikaans is now more widely used as a home language than English, and has a wide social stratification. There is also a corresponding range of acceptability, from generally used slang terms to the most seriously taboo. As V. de Klerk notes, "SAE [South African English] slang is largely from Afrikaans; sometimes the meanings are borrowed in full, sometimes they shift" (in Mesthrie, ed., 1995, 271). In his fictional memoir *Boyhood*, the Nobel laureate J.M. Coetzee, brought up in an English speaking family, observes: "The language of the Afrikaans boys was filthy beyond belief" (1997, 57).

Among the more common slang terms, that for "shit," namely *kak,* is widely used in both its literal senses and the metaphorical extensions of "rubbish," "nonsense," and "worthless," largely corresponding to American English *crap* or *crappy.* (Incidentally, *poppycock* is actually derived from the related Dutch word *pappakak,* literally "soft shit.") Other fairly mild personal insults are *drol,* meaning "turd," *poep* meaning "fart," and its compound variant *poephol,* meaning "arsehole." Marginally less common is *gat* in the sense of "arsehole" and its various picturesque compounds, namely *gat-kruiper,* "arsecreeper" or "brown-nose" (also found in the bilingual form *gat-creeper*), and *gatvol,* meaning "fed up," "disgusted."

At the taboo end of the scale are two terms for "cunt," namely *poes* and *doos.* The first term is anatomical, the equivalent and relative of "pussy," alluded to in 1884 by a visiting Dutch professor, Nicolaas Mansvelt, who noted amusingly that "the new arrival from Holland takes a risk if he addresses a cat." The second meaning, literally a "box" or "chest," has the parallel metaphor in French *boîte* and is highly insulting. *Fokken* ("fucking") has also been borrowed, but lacks the broad currency of the English equivalent, although it features in the grievous insult *dubbel fokken poes!*

Certainly the most powerful, complex, and protean term is *moer,* meaning variously "mother" or "womb." Its most concentrated form *jou moer* is explained by the *Dictionary of South African English (DSAE,* 1996) as "an obscene and abusive mode of address, equivalent to 'stuff you'; an expletive expressing rage, disappointment, or contradiction." The dramatist Athol Fugard, in the glossary to *Boesman and Lena* (1973), designated the phrase as "the ultimate obscenity; contraction of *You ma se moer,* Your mother's womb." Interestingly, it was an outsider, Eric Partridge, who first recorded the use in his *Dictionary of the Underworld* (1950), noting that *moer* is "a word used only in the worst of company." It is also used as a plain intensive, in *the moer in* "the hell in" and *a moer of a . . .*" a hell of a ". . ."

In the religious domain there are common Afrikaans equivalents for "Lord!," namely *Here!,* and for "Jesus!," namely *Jissus!* or *Yissus!* or *jislaik!,* as well as for "damned," namely *verdomde.* The curious asseveration *'struesgod* and its euphemized version *'struesbob,* derive from "as true as God." The exclamation *God!* is also common, pronounced in its guttural Afrikaans fashion. *Bliksem,* meaning "lightning," can be used as a straight expletive of annoyance or frustration as *bliksem!,* as an emotive epithet as in "the bliksem car!," or as a term of personal abuse, equivalent of "bastard" or "swine": "I'm sure that bliksem stole the money."

A common personal expletive is *voetsak!* also spelt *voetsek!* a highly contemptuous equivalent of "get lost!," traditionally used only of inferiors or dogs, as seen in this early instance from 1837: "Dogs attacked us as we approached; but on the cry of 'voortzuk' from the master, followed by a stone, they left us" (Sir James Edward Alexander, *Narrative of a Campaign in Kaffir-land* [1837]). The Afrikaans term is *voertsek,* derived from the Dutch *voort seg ik,* "away say I." It is now assimilated as a verb: "I told the beggar to voetsek." Powerful expressions of disgust are found in *sies!* and *siestog!*

Most of these terms are commonly used informally by English-speaking South Africans, few of whom would use all the English equivalents. By contrast, there is a comparative paucity of English swearwords borrowed into Afrikaans. The major instance are *blerrie* (from "bloody") and *boggerall* (a loan-translation of *bugger-all*), but significantly, none of the major four-letter words have crossed the linguistic barrier as they have in Pidgin English. This dependence on Afrikaans perhaps explains why there is no recognized "great South African swearword" that has passed into the mainstream of world English.

Among South African writers the noted dramatist Athol Fugard employs highly demotic language in his plays, exemplifying the typical use of Afrikaans equivalents of taboo English terms. In *Boesman and Lena* (1969), depicting the miserable life of two Coloured vagrants, the dialogue is in broad South African English, and is a virtual compendium of integrated Afrikaans swearwords and expletives. Although *bloody* and *bastard* are used frequently, they are outnumbered by some twenty Afrikaans terms of various force, which are set in italics and provide numerous first printed instances. Interestingly, Fugard found it necessary to add a glossary of over 160 items to the 1973 edition, since the play had reached audiences unfamiliar with its dialect.

The traditional animosity between the British and the Boers, deriving from colonialism, competition for resources, and bitter warfare, has its semantic correlatives in many insulting terms. Among these are *hairyback, rockspider, crunchie, soutpiel* ("salt penis"), and plain *Dutchman,* which can be humorous or laden with contempt. All of these are recent coinages, recorded only as far back as 1973, although the *Oxford English Dictionary* records *Dutchy* from 1837. Among terms borrowed from Afrikaans are *jaap* or *japie* (derived from the name Jacob), *plaasjaap* and *gawie* ("bumpkin"), and *takhaar* ("unkempt," "disheveled"). All denote or imply a boorish or backwoodsman stereotype, distortions of the traditional role of the Boer as farmer and trekker into the wilderness. Among Afrikaners it is a severe insult to call someone "a real jaap."

Boer, originally a historical term denoting the early Dutch colonists at the Cape, broadened to mean an Afrikaner, but with an emotive overtones, positive during the period of the struggle for survival against the British in the Boer War (1899–1902), but negative during the phase of Afrikaner political dominance after 1948. As the policy of apartheid was enforced, the derogatory use became particularly prominent among the Black population. Ezekiel Mphahlele recalls in his memoir, *Down Second Avenue* (1959): "Two Whites on a motorcycle . . . came straight at us and we jumped on the pavement. 'Voetsek, you Boers!' I shouted impulsively. They turned back" (127). It is still used generally of those in institutions of power, such as policemen and prison warders, who under apartheid were predominantly Afrikaners.

The principal terms for the British were born out of the hostilities resulting in the Boer War. The first and most enduring word was *rooinek,* literally a "red neck," meaning one sunburnt from the unfamiliar hot climate, recorded from 1891; it did not imply a lack of culture as *redneck* does in American English. With increasing rapprochement the term has lost much of its original animosity, and though still current, often has a tinge of irony. More explicit was *khaki,* from the color of the British uniforms, achieving wide currency from 1900 in quotations like "It was a happy time-away from the khaki, far from the roar of the cannon" (1902, cited in *DSAE* 1996).

Three terms describing minor criminals or villains are *skelm, skolly,* and *tsotsi.* The first entered Afrikaans from Dutch *schelm,* "a rogue," also borrowed into British English and Scots as *skellum,* which renders the current pronunciation. The second comes from Dutch *scholje,* "a rascal," now more a street hoodlum. *Tsotsi* denotes a black street thug, invariably flashily dressed, from Nguni *tsotsa,* to dress in an exaggerated style. In common with underground gangs, they have their own argot, called *tsotsi-taal,* "gangster speech."

The racial divisions of apartheid left obvious semantic correlatives. Insults across the color line are very numerous, ranging from the most notorious and wounding, like **kaffir** and **hottentot** (which have their own entries), *munt* (from *umuntu,* the Bantu word for a person), *houtkop* (Afrikaans for "wooden head") to the comparatively mild and humorous, such as *darky.* This was first used to refer to a black in a patronizing fashion in the southern United States before being taken into British English. In recent decades it has been appropriated or reclaimed by South African blacks, often used ironically, as in: "We darkies are proud of our tribal heritage." There is even a football team called Dangerous Darkies.

Other insulting terms for "non-white" peoples as they were classified under apartheid have higher currency in Afrikaans, including *bruinmens* ("brown people"), *klonkie,* and *kleurling* for a Coloured person. Also current in both Afrikaans and English is **coolie** for an Indian, initially borrowed to denote a porter or bearer—for example, a *wharf coolie* or *fish coolie,* a generic use recorded from about 1827. This highly derogatory term has its own entry.

A paradoxical survival in this racially charged atmosphere is **coon**, which has its own entry. Although occasionally used in the insulting American English fashion of a black person, *coon* has been reclaimed to refer to the *Coon Carnival,* a New Year celebration held in Cape Town by choirs and bands of Coloured people, "so named from the black and white raccoon-style make-up [worn by the participants] similar to that of Negro Christie Minstrels" (Branford, ed., 1978). A similar survival is *nigger-ball,* a sweet, which until recently had a general currency; it was not regarded as offensive, since *nigger* was not commonly used in South Africa.

The term *Coloured* has also changed in semantic force. It was used as a plain descriptive term from the 1830s, becoming an official category in the Population Registration Act of 1950 designating "a person who is not a white person or a native." Often regarded as an embarrassment, it was replaced by "of mixed race," similar to the euphemistic use of *colored* for *black* in American English. However, it is also increasingly reclaimed by the population itself: A survey carried out by the Johannesburg newspaper *The Star* in 1994 found that 75 percent of those polled "did not mind being referred to as Coloured" (October 15–16, 9). It is once more the standard term.

Descriptions of South African English have shown increasing sensitivity to ethnic insults. The earliest glossary, the Reverend Charles Pettman's comprehensive *Afrikanderisms: A Glossary of South African Words and Phrases* (1913), covered terms like *kaffir* with great precision, but focused on the historical uses and ignored slang. Most of the terms discussed above were accommodated lexicographically in the various editions of *A Dictionary of South African English* (ed. J. Branford) issued from 1978 onward. However, the major *Dictionary of South African English on Historical Principles* (ed. P. Silva et al. 1996) did not include several. Recognition of the power of these terms of ethnic insult is reflected in the legal category in South African law of **crimen injuria**, which has its own entry.

See also: Coolie; Coon; Crimen Injuria; Hottentot; Kaffir.

Bibliography

Branford, J., ed. *A Dictionary of South African English.* Cape Town: Oxford University Press. Four editions, 1978–1991.

Coetzee, J.M. *Boyhood.* London: Secker and Warburg, 1997.

Fugard, Athol. *Boesman and Lena.* Cape Town: Oxford University Press, 1973.

Mesthrie, R., ed. *Language and Social History: Studies in South African Sociolinguistics.* Cape Town and Johannesburg: David Philip, 1995.

Mphahlehle, Ezekiel. *Down Second Avenue.* London: Faber, 1959.

Pettman, Rev. Charles. *Afrikanderisms: A Glossary of South African Words and Phrases.* London: Longmans Green, 1913.

Silva, P., et al., eds. *A Dictionary of South African English on Historical Principles.* Oxford: Oxford University Press, 1996.

SPELLS

Spells, charms, and curses all derive from belief in **word magic**, the notion that words, particularly in some complex or incantatory form or ritualistic context, can unlock mysterious and invisible natural and supernatural forces, both malign and beneficent. The belief is profound and survives in societies both primitive and modern. *Spell* itself is an ancient word, of Anglo-Saxon origin, but like *charm,* started to take on its magical senses only in medieval times. However the practice of putting a malign spell on an object is found in Anglo-Saxon literature, albeit in different terms. In *Beowulf* the monster Grendel, described as one of the evil tribe of Cain and an enemy of the Lord, puts a spell on the weapons of his Danish victims the Scyldings, rendering them useless (ll. 801–5). Fascinatingly, the key verb in the text is *forsworen,* literally "forsworn," since the verb *forswerian* could then mean "to hinder by swearing; to render powerless by incantation; to make useless by magic."

The earliest meanings of *spell* were mundane, namely those of "speech, discourse, narration," the first references to the modern meaning surfacing only by 1579: "Spell is a kind of verse or charme, that in elder tymes they used often say over every thing, that they would have preserved" (*Glossary to [Edmund] Spenser's Shepheards Calendar*). The same entry speculates that *gospel* is named "as it were Gods spell or worde." All these early references are, of course, positive.

From the Renaissance *spell* started to acquire its modern exclusively malignant senses, often involving sorcery, occult, and taboo practices, such as George Sandys's record in 1615 that "the spirits of the deceased, by certain spels . . . were customed to be raised" (*Travels,* 28). Many instances are found in the plays of William Shakespeare, Ben Jonson, and other Renaissance dramatists. Apart from expected references in *The Tempest* and *A Midsummer Night's Dream,* there are serious instances such as these from *Othello:* "corrupted by spells and medicines" (I iii 61) and *Coriolanus:* "a spell of much power" (V ii 96). The sense remains reinforced by idiomatic phrases such as *to put a spell on, to weave/cast a spell, to be under a spell,* and the compound *spellbound,* recorded from 1799.

Modern attitudes toward spells are largely skeptical, their potency being rejected by the premises of scientific empiricism. However, the ancient literary traditions that endorse the magical powers of wizards, warlocks, witches, and spells still thrive, being most notably manifest in two enormously successful modern works of fiction, namely J.R.R. Tolkien's trilogy *The Lord of the Rings* (1954–1955) and J.K. Rowling's series of *Harry Potter* books (1997–). The latter have attracted opposition, boycotts, and even book burnings by fundamentalist religious groups in the United States on the grounds of blasphemy. According to the American Civil Liberties Union, Rowling's books acquired the status of the "Most Challenged" works of fiction for 1999–2002.

See also: Charms; Curses; Word Magic.

Bibliography
Kiekhefer, Richard. *Magic in the Middle Ages.* New York: Cambridge University Press, 1989.

SPORTS

Certain sports, such as golf, tennis, and cricket, have traditionally been governed by strict codes of decorum and silence, the only acceptable comments being compliments. Others, such as football, soccer, rugby, and baseball are more robust: trading of insults and stand-up fights are quite common. Polo, one of the most exclusive sports, is marked by copious swearing. Whatever its provenance, sport has not always been gentlemanly. The Puritan Philip Stubbes, in his *Anatomie of Abuses* (1583) wrote: "I protest unto you it may rather be called a friendly kind of fight, than a play or recreation; a bloody or murdering practice, than a fellowly sport or pastime." He was describing football, "whereof groweth envy, malice, rancour, choler, hatred, displeasure, enmity and what not else" (in Dover Wilson, ed., 1944, 38–39).

It is generally conceded that in modern times traditional sporting codes have eroded as competition has become more intense and prize money more lucrative. Golf alone has remained free of the taint of the audible obscenities that have come to disgrace both tennis and cricket in recent decades. John McEnroe's notoriously long and shameful record of public obscenity on the tennis court culminated in ejection from the Australian Open Championship in 1990 for telling the umpire, amongst other things, to "fuck off!" A similar outburst at Wimbledon led to banning from the All England Tennis Club for several years. McEnroe was an extreme example, and it would appear that these strong disciplinary measures did have the effect of reducing instances of public obscenity in tennis.

"It's not cricket," first recorded around 1851, has become a quintessentially English ethical saying applied to any situation, originally endorsing fairness by condemning any infringement of the spirit of the game. However, an ugly modern development has been the growth of "sledging," the deliberate use of provocative, abusive, personal, and intimidatory language directed at a batsman by close fielders and bowlers to distract him or undermine his confidence. The word is first recorded in Australia, according to a report in *The Sydney Morning Herald* (November 4, 1982): "The court has been told by Ian Chappell [the Australian cricket captain] that the expression 'sledging' had come into vogue among cricketers in 1963–64. It came from the expression 'subtle as a sledgehammer' derived from a popular song." The practice has now spread throughout the modern game, being especially prevalent in one-day cricket, the highly lucrative "limited-overs" or abbreviated version initiated in 1975. Umpires no longer make any attempt to limit this use of foul language as a weapon, even though comments have become generally audible through microphones installed near the wickets.

An extreme instance of a different kind led to the cricket Test Match between England

and Pakistan in Faisalabad being halted on December 8, 1987, as a consequence of the English captain Mike Gatting referring to the umpire Shakoor Rana as a "bastard." The umpire regarded the insult as being of such gravity that he refused to continue, reportedly explaining: "Calling me a bastard may be excusable in England, but here people murder someone who calls another man a bastard" (*The Star,* Johannesburg, December 11, 1987, 20). The following day's play was abandoned while a written apology was sought from Gatting, and continued only after it had been forthcoming. However, the other side of the verbal engagement emerged only in the British newspaper, the *Independent,* which reported that "the umpire had allegedly called the England captain a 'fucking cheating cunt'" (Harris, 1990, 417).

Certainly the greatest public outrage of recent decades was provoked during the Soccer World Cup of 1986 when Diego Maradona scored for Argentina against England by means of a blatant foul, using his hand to palm the ball into the goal. When asked after the match about the incident, Maradona said that the goal had been scored by the "hand of Diego," using a basphemous pun, since "Diego" means "God." Maradona eventually confessed to the foul on his chat show on August 24, 2005.

As in other social areas, ethnic slurs continue to surface in sport. In an ugly new development, Australia's spectators abused South African players in cricket test matches, calling them *kaffirs* and *kaffir-boetics* ("nigger-lovers") (*Cape Times,* December 1, 2005, 1). As a penalty, Lehmann was suspended for four matches. Racist abuse has also become an increasingly serious issue in football, notably in the United Kingdom. The report by Lord Justice Taylor into the state of English soccer in 1990 recommended the banning or suppression of "obscene or racist chanting" by football spectators. However, in a match against Spain in Barcelona in 2004, a black English player "was subjected to a barrage of monkey chants and booing whenever he got the ball" (*Independent,* November 18, 2004). A number of leading clubs have started to enforce measures to eliminate the practice, under the aegis of the antiracism campaign Kick It Out. In 2004, FIFA, the Federation of International Football, started to publicize the slogan "Say No to Racism."

See also: Journalism.

Bibliography

Harris, Roy. "*Lars Porsena* Revisited." In Ricks, Christopher, and Leonard Michaels, eds., *The State of the Language 1990s Edition.* London: Faber & Faber, 1990.

Wilson, John Dover, ed. *Life in Shakespeare's England.* Harmondsworth: Penguin, 1944.

STEREOTYPES. *See:* Blason Populaire

STERNE, LAURENCE

Laurence Sterne (1713–1768) was an eccentric clergyman whose fictions were almost entirely atypical of the Age of Reason in which he wrote. Having lived in relative obscurity,

Sterne became a celebrity upon the protracted publication of his magnum opus, *The Life and Opinions of Tristram Shandy* (nine volumes, 1760–1767). Although written at a time when the novel was a comparatively new genre, the work anticipates many recent developments and is now regarded as the first antinovel, violating all the accepted narrative modes, notions of logic, form, and, above all, decorum.

Capitalizing on the fact that the novel is experienced by the reader as a printed artifact, Sterne played all manner of formal and typographical jokes with his readers, even including blank chapters, misplaced prefaces, nonsensical squiggles, and doodles. He particularly relished using puns and suggesting taboo words, with mock politeness disguising them with obvious euphemistic devices like dashes and asterisks, or substituting their equivalents in a foreign language, especially French. Thus in *Tristram Shandy* (Book VII, chapters 20–25) he contrives a hilariously improper situation where two French nuns have to utter the taboo words *bouger* (bugger) and *fouter* (fuck). The ingenious way that they (and Sterne) solve this problem of decorum is covered in the entry for **abbreviations**.

Sterne also creates various confusions arising from bawdy or naughty puns. One such pair surrounds the senses of *mount* and *ass,* which are jumbled up in Book VIII, chapters 31–32, leading to this exchange: "Well! Dear brother Toby, said my father. . . . And how goes it with your Asse?" "My A——e, quoth my uncle Toby, is much better." At the time there was an embarrassing phonetic proximity between the words *ass* and *arse,* since both the **Earl of Rochester** and **Jonathan Swift** had already rhymed *asses* with *passes.* Sterne underscores the semantic difference by the use of dashes.

Swearing becomes a major theme, spectacularly when Dr. Slop cannot undo his medicine bag and starts to curse the man who tied the knots too well, becoming more frenzied as his frustration mounts: "The duce [devil] take it!," "Pox take the fellow!," "Psha!, I wish the scoundrel hang'd—I wish he was shot—I wish all the devils in hell had him for blockhead——." Tristram's father then gives a pious lecture:

> Small curses, Dr. Slop, upon great occasions, quoth my father (condoling with him first upon the accident) are but so much waste of our strength and soul's health to no manner of purpose. . . . For this reason, continued my father, with the most Cervantic gravity, I have the greatest veneration in the world for that gentleman, who, in distrust of his own discretion in this point, sat down and composed (that is, at his leisure) fit forms of swearing suitable to all cases, from the lowest to the highest provocations which could possibly happen to him—which forms . . . he kept ever by him on the chimney piece, within his reach, ready for use.
> (Volume III, chapter 10)

Superficially Sterne is making the commonplace point that trivial frustrations provoke immoderately serious oaths. But he develops the absurd proposal of graded oaths in a bizarre and virtually blasphemous fashion by modifying "a form of excommunication of the church of Rome," complete with the original Latin formula on the left-hand page and English translation on the right. Although the situation is clearly farcical, the vehement comprehensiveness of the ecclesiastical malediction ("from the top of his head to the sole of his foot") is terrifying:

May he be cursed in his reins [kidneys], and his groin ("God in heaven forbid!" quoth my Uncle Toby) in his thighs, in his genitals (my father shook his head), and in his hips, and in his knees, his legs and feet and toenails!
(Volume III, chapter 10)

The introduction of this actual religious text, especially the invocation to "the Son of the Living God, with all the glory of his majesty," goes far beyond the immediate trivial context, interrogating the whole value of mercy in the Church. The reader is left awkwardly poised between the sacred and the profane, the farcical and the serious.

Curiously, the novel was enormously successful, but contemporary authorities were sharply divided in their estimates. Dr. Johnson condemned it in 1776 as eccentric and shallow, prophesying that "nothing odd will do long. *Tristram Shandy* did not last" (in conversation with James Boswell, in Howes, ed., 219). Yet the great French encyclopedist Diderot relished the work's paradoxical qualities: "This book so mad, so wise, so gay, is the English Rabelais; . . . it is a universal satire" (Howes, ed., 385). After a lull, Sterne's popularity has undergone a major resurgence in recent decades, especially after the great Russian formalist critic Viktor Shlovsky argued in 1921 that "*Tristram Shandy* is the most typical novel of world literature" (in Traugott, ed., 1968, 89).

Sterne's other major work, *A Sentimental Journey Through France and Italy,* with similar eccentricities, followed in 1768, the last year of his life. When La Fleur, a Frenchman, is thrown from his horse, the narrator comments that although he

availed himself but of two different terms of exclamation in this encounter—namely *Diable!* ["Devil!"] and *Peste!* ["Plague!"], there are nevertheless three, in the French language; like the positive, comparative and superlative, one or other of which will serve for every unexpected throw of the dice in life. ("The Bidet")

Sterne teases the reader by not revealing the third word, saying: "you may imagine, if you please with what word he closed the whole affair." Later, riding in the coach of Madame de Rambouilet, "the most correct of women . . . desired me to pull the cord. I asked her if she wanted anything—*Rien que pisser* ['Just to piss'] she said." With mock politeness, Sterne comments: "Grieve not, gentle traveller, to let Madame de Rambouilet p-ss on" ("The Rose"). Like *Tristram Shandy,* the novel ends abruptly, in a compromising bedroom situation at night with a tantalizing, probably euphemized obscenity: "so that when I stretched out my hand, I caught hold of the fille-de-chambre's———." Everyone is left in the dark.

Sterne's playing with the taboos of his age, when full printed forms were impolite, has caused endless controversy. He flirted with the taboos, as he reputedly did with many women, but he never broke them, as **Jonathan Swift** did. Nevertheless, as the anthology *Sterne: The Critical Heritage* shows, he was consistently criticized in his own time and later for writing "bawdy compositions . . . to inflame with lust, and debauch and corrupt our youth of both sexes" (in Howes, ed., 183). Modern scholars remain unresolved over the question of whether, like **François Rabelais** before him, Sterne was mocking bourgeois hypocrisy in a robust and healthy fashion, or was more psychologically involved and guilty of using exhibitionism and innuendo to take "malicious joy in throwing back upon the reader's dirty mind and lubricious imagination the responsibility for the smuttiness" (Mayoux, in Traugott, ed., 108–9).

See also: Abbreviations; Ass/Arse; Swift, Jonathan.

Bibliography

Berthoud, Jacques. "Shandeism and Sexuality." In *Laurence Sterne: Riddles and Mysteries,* ed. Valerie Grosvenor Myer. London and Totowa: Vision and Barnes & Noble, 1984.

Howes, A.B., ed. *Sterne: The Critical Heritage.* London: Routledge & Kegan Paul, 1974.

Mayoux, Jean Jacques. "Laurence Sterne." In *Laurence Sterne: Twentieth Century Views,* ed. John Traugott. Englewood Cliffs, NJ: Prentice Hall, Traugott, 1968.

Myer, Valerie Grosvenor, ed. *Laurence Sterne: Riddles and Mysteries.* London and Totowa: Vision and Barnes & Noble, 1984.

Sterne, Laurence. *The Life and Opinions of Tristram Shandy, Gentleman.* 3 vols. Oxford: Basil Blackwell, 1926.

Traugott, John, ed. *Laurence Sterne: Twentieth Century Views.* Englewood Cliffs, NJ: Prentice Hall, 1968.

STUPIDITY

This category is perhaps the richest source of terms of personal insult and abuse, both historically and geographically through its incorporation of numerous terms from the global varieties of English. The field indeed is so vast and unmanageable that this entry can be only a brief discussion of the salient points. The first of these is that a lack of intelligence is invariably and unfairly regarded as a lack of worth, thus adding a sense of contempt. However, the long history of terms like *fool* and the category of the "holy fool" show that people with unconventional intelligence were valued in the past. Furthermore, court fools have a long history as figures of special status in Europe, often developing close relationships with monarchs, as Richard Tarleton did with Queen Elizabeth I. The *Oxford English Dictionary* also notes that *fool* "has in Modern English a much stronger sense than it had in an earlier period," when it could be used as a term of endearment and of sympathy. Finally, the root of *fool,* in French *fol,* "a mad person" is significant, since many terms show an overlap between stupidity and madness. Two further points of usage are notable. First, the vast majority of terms are habitually applied only to men. Second, while Political Correctness has reduced the currency of unsympathetic technical terms like *feeble-minded, brain-damaged,* and *spastic,* the field continues to grow.

Words are drawn in from many categories. There are multitudinous odd and colorful metaphors, such as *cement head* and *lunchbox.* Some predictably come from animals of proverbial stupidity, such as *donkey* and *ass;* others are less obviously derived from birds, such as *coot, loon, drongo,* and *cuckoo,* also found in regional English *gowk,* "a fool," from Anglo-Saxon *geac,* "cuckoo." Many, like *bozo, dork, dweeb,* and *gink* have no proper referential meaning, but are sustained by an apparently appealing phonetic structure. Many compounds show a preference for *dumb-* in the first element and *-head* in the second.

As with psychological terms like *maniac, psychotic, psychopath,* and *pervert,* words like *moron* and *cretin,* originally intended to be specific neutral technical terms for low intelligence have become insults. Although *moron* is derived from an ancient Greek word meaning "foolish" or "stupid," it was coined by the American researcher H.H. Goddard in 1910 and adopted in the same year by the American Association for the Study of the Feeble-Minded. It referred to a person with mild mental retardation, specifically with an IQ (Intelligence Quotient) of 50–70. However, it was almost immediately taken up in the modern contemptuous sense of a fool or idiot, specifically by Robert Benchley, one of the Algonquin Wits, referring ironically to someone "talking in connected sentences" as being regarded as a "high class moron" *Vanity Fair* (October 1917, 47). Similarly, *cretin* was originally (from 1779) a specific term for "dwarfed and specially deformed idiots found in certain valleys of the Alps." (Its etymological root is, oddly, in *christian*.) The popular use (dating from the 1930s in D.H. Lawrence and James Joyce) has had the effect of inhibiting the currency of the technical sense. The aforementioned American Association also attempted, perhaps less wisely, to incorporate the established terms *idiot* and *imbecile* for specific categories. According to the *Encylopaedia Britannica* (1999): "The once standard labels—moron, imbecile and idiot—have been abolished." Similarly, *feeble-minded* is no longer a generally acceptable term. While this is understandable, it leaves researchers with a problem of terminology.

Idiot has a complex history, dating from the fourteenth century, including earlier senses of "an ignorant or uneducated man," "an unskilled person," and a professional fool. The principal modern uses are surprisingly ancient: Chaucer's Wife of Bath berates one of her husbands for trying to "make an idiot" of another woman (*Prologue* l. 311), while Macbeth ends his tragedy (1605) with the famous vision of life being "a tale / Told by an idiot, full of sound and fury, / Signifying nothing" (V v 26–28). William Wordsworth showed an unembarrassed acceptance of the term by giving a poem the title of "The Idiot Boy" in the *Lyrical Ballads* (1798), whereas Charles Dickens could use the modern insult "You idiot" in 1840 (*Barnaby Rudge,* chapter 51). These instances show a marked difference from the modern necessity of euphemism.

A sense of the scale and variety of the modern field can be gained from the following sample: addlepate, airhead, BF [bloody fool], berk, brenda, cement-head, clodpoll, clot, clunk, coot, dickhead, dildo, dingbat, dork, drongo, dumbass, dumbell, dumbo, dummy, dweeb, fruitcake, fuckwit, gink, git, goof, ig man, klutz, kook, lamebrain, lunchbox, lunkhead, mut, nit, noodle, nutter, prat, prawnhead, puddinghead, rookie, schlemiel, schmeggege, schmuck, screwball, section eight, shitkicker, sillybilly, spaz, squarebrain, stupe, thickie, thicko, toolhead, twit, and zipalid. These derive from many varieties of global English, so that few people would be familiar with all of them in the sense of "stupid person." The list comprises, incidentally only about one sixth of some 300 terms listed in Jonathan Green's *The Slang Thesaurus* (1988). A field comprising slang terms will inevitably contain items which in some speech communities are also used in other senses. Thus *fruitcake* and *nutter* can also refer to someone who is slightly mad, while *prat, schlemiel, schmeggege,* and *schmuck* show the familiar semantic linkage between stupidity and worthlessness. Although *dildo* is obviously used in other senses, it is notable that sexual terms like prick, tit, twat, and cunt also show this metaphorical extension.

Overall the field shows diminution of specific terms through sensitivity to stigma, but enormous efflorescence of colloquial terms of insult. Several of these have sufficiently complex histories to warrant their own entries. They are listed below.

See also: Berk; Git; Prat; Twat.

Bibliography
Goddard, H.H. *Feeblemindedness, Its Causes and Consequences.* New York: Macmillan, 1923.
Green, Jonathan. *The Slang Thesaurus.* Harmondsworth: Penguin, 1988.

SWIFT, JONATHAN

Jonathan Swift (1667–1745) represents in its most acute form the polarity between the rational and the physical. Regarded as the greatest satirist and exponent of irony in English literature, he was born and bred in Ireland and rose to the position of dean of St. Patrick's Cathedral in Dublin, becoming a great champion of Irish liberty and a national hero. Yet he was intermittently very much part of the London literary and social scene. Although the dominant literary tenor of the Augustan period was that of rationality, politeness, and classic elegance, Swift was a rebellious and eccentric counter-example, together with **Laurence Sterne** and Tobias Smollett. His exploitation of differing registers is as astonishing and unrivaled as are the different literary modes in which he wrote. His huge output contains many insights into swearing and foul language. One can detect three distinct modes in his work: the correct style of the authority figure; the complex ironic uses of the satirist; and the strange regression into childishness and obscenity. Swift was, however, ingenious in the creation of personae or authorial masks, so that the facile identification of narrator with author is not valid.

Ostensibly a conservative in language matters, Swift wrote in 1712 *A Proposal for Correcting, Improving and Ascertaining the English Tongue,* criticizing the poor and declining state of the language down from the court, condemned as "the worst school in England," to common usage. His disturbing masterpiece *Gulliver's Travels* (1727) is model of rational clarity in prose, which he read to his servants to ensure that he had achieved the proper degree of simplicity. Part of the irony of the work is the narrator's determination to tell in a sober, detailed fashion "the whole truth" of his bizarre adventures. Thus in Lilliput, where Gulliver is held prisoner by a race of midgets, his first action is commonplace, but a violation of literary decorum. By using all the standard euphemisms for the necessities of nature, Swift allows the gross truth to dawn on the reader only slowly:

> I had been for some hours extremely pressed by the necessities of nature; which was no wonder, it being almost two days since I had last disburthened myself. I was under great difficulties between urgency and shame. . . . I went as far as the length of my chain would allow and discharged myself of that uneasy load. (Book I, chapter ii).

Later, when the royal palace catches fire, Gulliver becomes a hero in an equally unexpected fashion through "urine, which I voided in such a quantity and applied so well to the proper places, that in three minutes the fire was wholly extinguished" (Book I, chapter v). Throughout *Gulliver's Travels,* Swift maintains this ironic disjunction, between "indecent" actions and polite vocabulary.

454

THE
Swearer's-B A N K:
O R,
Parliamentary Security
F O R
Eftablifhing a new BANK
I N
I R E L A N D.

W H E R E I N
The Medicinal Ufe of OATHS is confidered.

(W I T H
The *Beft in Chriftendom.* A T A L E.)

Written by Dean S W I F T.

Si Populus vult decipi decipiatur.

To which is prefixed,
An E S S A Y upon *Englifh* B U B B L E S.
By T H O M A S H O P E, *Efq*;

D U B L I N:
Printed by T H O M A S H U M E, next Door to the
Walfh's-Head in *Smock-Alley.* 1720. Reprinted at
London by J. R O B E R T S in *Warwick-Lane.*

Jonathan Swift's satiric *The Swearer's Bank* (1720)—written in the year of the South Sea Bubble scandal and England's first great stock market crash—presents the mock financial prospectus of a bank to be funded by one-shilling fines for profanity.

In the surreal fantasy of the last book, Swift even goes so far as to have idiomatic expressions physically enacted. Thus one of the Yahoos literally "licks his master's feet and posteriors," and worse, "the cursed broad" climb up a tree and "began to discharge their excrements on my head." (Back IV, chaptri)

The same technique is used in his *Directions to Servants* (1745), which solemnly advocates the filthiest and most dishonest habits, and in his famous and outrageous "A Modest Proposal" (1714), in which huge social problems of starvation and overpopulation invite a simple, rational but obscene solution: cannibalism.

In his verse, however, Swift discards the façade of decency, becoming the studied violator of Augustan decorum, spectacularly and rudely resuscitating the silenced four-letter words. Thus, "The Lady's Dressing Room" (1730) is an obsessive tour of the less decent intimacies of female life, culminating in the absurd but shocking exclamation:

O, Celia Celia, Celia shits! (l. 118)

This climactic line is repeated in "Cassinus and Peter" (1734). A similar poem, "A Beautiful Young Nymph Going to Bed," describes the hideous striptease of "Corinna, pride of Drury Lane" (notorious for its prostitutes), grimly cataloguing her artificial hair, crystal eye, "flabby dugs" (breasts), "shankers" (chancres, or sores from venereal disease), who awakes to find that "Puss had on her plumpers pissed" (ll. 22, 30, 61). Similarly the wedding night of Strephon and Chloe oscillates between epic romance and crude "carminative and diuretic" details:

Twelve cups of tea (with grief I speak)
Had now constrained the nymph to leak.

Upon hearing the "foaming rill" in the "vessel" (chamber pot) Strephon

Cried out, "Ye gods, what sound is this?
Can Chloe, heavenly Chloe piss?
(ll. 163–64; 179–80)

This "excremental" aspect of Swift has provoked considerable psychological and literary controversy, some participants seeing him as a satirist ruthlessly exposing the hypocrisy of literary preciousness of his time, others regarding him as the victim of an unhealthy obsession with "dirt," technically termed *copromania* or *coprophilia*. The association of these Greek psychological terms with Swift dates from academic articles dated 1900 and 1934 respectively.

The Swearer's Bank was published in 1720, the year when many fantastic financial schemes collapsed in the great stock exchange crash known as the South Sea Bubble. With his characteristically cool irony Swift sets out a perfectly viable financial prospectus. The bank's income will be continuous, deriving from the one-shilling fine exactable by Act of Parliament for profane swearing. Allowing for five thousand gentlemen to swear one oath a day, thus generating £91,250 per annum, and ten thousand farmers to produce £25,000, the rest of the population earning a similar amount, the army would be the greatest source of revenue, generating at least £100,000. Indeed the army might even bankrupt itself, "the militia swearing themselves out of their guns and swords" (1945, 45). After the defrayment of expenses, the profits would be devoted to the erection and maintenance of charity schools.

As these observations indicate, Swift was very aware of the relation between swearing, class, and occupation. The Introduction to *Polite Conversation,* or as it was originally titled, *A Complete Collection of Genteel and Ingenious Conversation* (1737), treats oaths with an ironic earnestness. Swift rejects the supposition that "mean and vulgar people" ("low and common folk") will learn to ape their betters: "A footman can swear; but he cannot swear like a Lord. He can swear as often; but can he swear with equal deliberation, propriety and judgement? No certainly" (1963, 572). Surprisingly, he rejects the traditional view that it is a breach of manners to swear in front of a lady (1963, 570), a point taken up in the entry on **swearing in women**.

There is also the issue of fashion in swearing. Quoting "an antient poet":

For, now-a-days, men change their oaths
As often as they change their cloaths.

He concludes that "Oaths are the children of fashion. . . . I can myself recall about forty different sets. The old stock-oaths, I am confident, do not amount to above forty-five, or fifty at most. . . . But infinitely the greater number hath been so frequently changed and dislocated, that if their inventors were now alive, they could hardly understand them" (1963, 571). Recognizing that "a just collection of oaths, repeated as often as the fashion requires, must have enlarged this volume at least to double the bulk," and that "if I should include all the oaths as are now current, my book would be out of vogue with the first change of fashion . . . I therefore determined with myself to leave out the whole system of swearing" (1963, 571).

Swift nevertheless included in *Polite Conversation* some provocative idioms, such as "Why, Miss you shine this morning like a sh—[shitten] barn-door," according to Eric Partridge "a proverbial saying of the 17th–mid-19th century" (1963, 85). Among the 1074 "flowers of Wit, Fancy, Wisdom, Humour and Politeness, scattered in this volume" are the following: "She rises with her——[arse] upwards" (167); "you hit yourself a devilish box of the ear" (64); "Od so, I have cut my thumb on this cursed knife" (66); and "out upon you for a filthy creater" (66). (This last form shows an interesting link between British *creature* and American *crittur.*)

His *Journal to Stella* (1710–1713, but not published until 1768) is like a transcript of intimate telephone conversations in its affectionate and childish "little language" or baby talk and code names. The nature of Swift's relationship with "Stella" (Hesther Johnson), while clearly intimate, has never been authoritatively defined, but the journal is littered with mild fashionable oaths and demotic idioms: "the dean be poxt" ("damned," letter 4); "slidikins" ("God's little eyelids"); "Agad, agad, agad, agad, agad, agad" ("By God," letter 6); "What the pox!" ("What the hell!"), "What do you mean sirrah? Slids" (*sirrah* was an insulting diminutive of *sir,* while "slids" was a minced version of "God's eyelids"); "a pox on your spelling" ("blast your spelling"); "Who the Devil cares what they think?. . . Rot 'em for ungrateful dogs" (letter 8); "what the D——ailed him" (letter 19); "——Pox take the boats! Amen," (letter 24). He often castigates Stella and her friend, a Miss Dingley, as "rogues," "saucy sluts," and "sirrahs." His comment, "It was bloody hot walking today" (May 8, 1711, letter 22) is one of the earliest instances of *bloody* as an intensive.

While these extracts show the extraordinary diversity of Swift's knowledge, attitude toward, and replication of the oaths and vulgar idioms of both high society and the street, his mastery of the plain register is devastating, never more so than in the condemnation of human society by the civilized King of Brobdingnag: "I cannot but conclude the bulk of your natives to be the most pernicious race of little odious vermin that Nature ever suffered to crawl upon the surface of the earth" (*Gulliver's Travels,* Book II, chapter 6).

See also: Coprolalia; Scatology; Sterne, Laurence.

Bibliography

Brown, Norman O. *Life Against Death.* London: Routledge & Kegan Paul, 1959.
Ehrenpries, Irving. *Swift, the Man, His Works and the Age.* London: Methuen, 1962.
Partridge, Eric, ed. *Swift's Polite Conversation.* London: André Deutsch, 1963.
Rawson, C.J. *Gulliver and the Gentle Reader.* Boston: Routledge & Kegan Paul, 1973.
Rogers, Pat, ed. *Jonathan Swift: The Complete Poems.* New Haven and London: Yale University Press, 1983.
Swift, Jonathan. *The Swearer's Bank.* London, 1720.
Swift, Jonathan. *A Complete Collection of Genteel and Ingenious Conversation* (1738), ed. Eric Partridge. London: André Deutsch, 1963.
Williams, Kathleen, ed. *Swift: The Critical Heritage.* London: Routledge & Kegan Paul, 1970.

SYPHILIS

For the purposes of this entry, syphilis is taken to include gonorrhea, since they are related in the public mind and share a common vocabulary, even though they are technically different diseases, syphilis being caused by *Treponema pallidum* and gonorrhea by *Neisseria gonorrhea*. Both are sexually transmitted diseases with highly visible symptoms such as facial deformities, especially erosion of the nose, and dementia at the latter stages, the principal early cure, mercury, leading to loss of hair. They are thus subject to the stigmas and taboos associated with such afflictions, showing themselves principally in black humor, euphemisms, and xenophobia. The previous high incidence declined with the introduction of penicillin in the 1930s. Comparisons with AIDS are illuminating, as are the differences.

Although syphilis is not generally fatal, it affected many high-profile figures, such as Queen Elizabeth's favorite, the Earl of Essex, King James I (1603–1625) and his favorite, the Duke of Buckingham, the Earl of Rochester (1647–1680), and Lord Randolph Churchill (1849–1895), of whom Lord Rosebery wrote: "There was no curtain. He died by inches in public, sole mourner at his own protracted funeral" (1906, 72). According to D.H. Lawrence in an essay written in 1929, syphilis caused a fundamental rupture, generating "a terror, almost a horror of sexual life" in late-sixteenth-century England (1950, 308). Lawrence's view, although largely intuitive, has been endorsed by a number of studies, as Johannes Fabricius shows in his major work, *Syphilis in Shakespeare's England* (1994). The disease be-

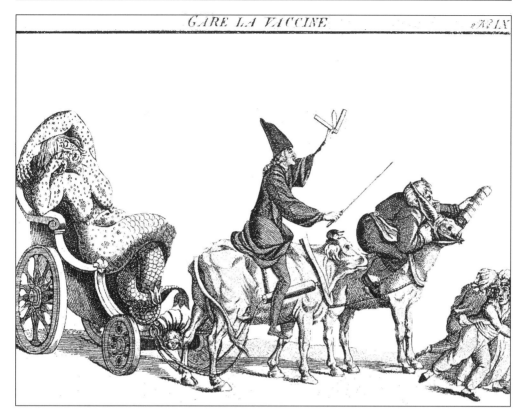

GARE LA VACCINE PL. IX

"Beware the Vaccine," warns this nineteenth-century French cartoon concerning the treatment of syphilis. The term *quack* derives from the practice of treating the disease with quicksilver (mercury), sold by street peddlers known as "quacksalvers." (The Art Archive/Bibliothèque des Arts Décoratifs, Paris/Dagli Orti)

came a significant theme in the plays of Shakespeare and his contemporaries, being referred to via underground slang often laced with savage humor. An earlier school of criticism regarded Shakespeare's *Timon of Athens* (ca. 1608) as a depiction of syphilitic disintegration.

One basic ambiguity in naming arose out of using the general established term *pox* to refer to the plague, to syphilis, and even to smallpox. *Pox* and *pocky* were in use from the mid-fourteenth century, and continued to be current both referentially and as terms of abuse up to the recent past. Thus when Mary Queen of Scots refused to allow "a pokie priest," as she referred to Archbishop Hamilton, to use his spittle in the baptism of James I, which disease would she have had in mind? *Clap*, dating from about 1587, is related to Middle French *clapoir*, "a bubo or swelling," and *clapier*, "a brothel," and technically refers to gonorrhea, but the two terms were often used indiscriminately, as in Alexander Pope's knowing observation on "Time, that at last matures a clap to pox" (*Second Satire of Dr John Donne Versified*, l. 47). Both terms were widely current in major authors through the seventeenth and eighteenth centuries before being driven underground in the Victorian era.

Although there is debate about the demographic origins of syphilis, complicated by references to "venereal leprosy" in Europe in the thirteenth and fourteenth centuries, the first unambiguous evidence of the disease dates from about 1500. Apparently brought back from the New World by Christopher Columbus's crew, the disease spread rapidly through the length and breadth of Europe. One of the standard histories, N.T. Parran's *Shadow on the Land—Syphilis,* traces both the attributions and the origin of the name:

> In the beginning there was no name for the disease. Each suffering nation blamed it on the outlander. To the French it was the Neapolitan disease because they met it in Naples. [Even John Florio called it *mal di Napoli,* probably because he was brought up in England.] The Italians called it the French or Spanish disease. The English, who caught it from the French called it the "French pox." . . . The specific name was acquired in 1530 when an Italian physician, Girolamo Fracastoro, wrote a long poem in Latin hexameters in which the leading character, a shepherd named Syphilus, was stricken with the disease because of an insult to Apollo. The poem was enormously successful and made the word familiar. (1937, 36)

The chain of infection described here makes the nationalist naming of the disease entirely plausible, combined with the desire to project blame elsewhere. At the time France and Italy were already stereotyped in England as hotbeds of vice and promiscuity, as the entries for **French** and **Italians** show. By giving the disease the name *morbus gallicus* ("the French disease"), Fracastoro ensured that this national association remained dominant. Among the English names, *French pox* is found as far back as 1503, followed by *French gout, goods, crown, pig,* and *crust,* culminating in the grisly dysphemism "to suffer a blow over the snout with a French faggot-stick"—that is, to lose one's nose, one of the extreme consequences. All of these are recorded in the seventeenth century and appear in Francis Grose's *Classical Dictionary of the Vulgar Tongue* (1785), which includes many other slang terms, such as *the Frenchman* and *Frenchified* ("the mort is *Frenchified*" = "the wench is infected").

Apart from *French pox,* which emerges in a timely manner in 1503, the other syphilitic specialities, *Great pox* and *Spanish pox,* are recorded well after the outbreaks of the sixteenth century. This may be because they are "underground terms" and thus take longer to emerge in written records. In time, *pox* became widely used as an expletive, like *plague* and *plaguey.* Shakespeare seems to have initiated the use of the term as an imprecation in *Love's Labour's Lost* (1588): "A pox of that jest" (V ii 46). Thereafter it had a long vulgar history such as "pox on it!" or—be poxed!," found in Jonathan Swift, James Joyce, and even Virginia Woolf. There is a more literal royal usage in a letter by William IV in 1784: "Oh, for the pretty girls of Westminster . . . such as would not clap or pox me every time I fucked" (Ziegler 1971, iii, 51).

One early term for a whore with venereal disease are *Winchester goose,* recorded from 1585 and found twice in Shakespeare: *Henry VI, Part I* I iii 53 and *Troilus and Cressida* V x 54–56). The reference is explicated in the entry for **Shakespeare** and by Fabricius (1994, 213–19). Another is *fireship,* alluding to the burning pain of the disease, recorded from 1670 in the Restoration dramatist William Wycherley, followed by *brim* from ca. 1730, *brimstone* from ca. 1751, and *burner* from ca. 1785. Another rarity, *chancre,* from the French term for a venereal ulcer, became a term of insult, first found ca. 1605 in Montgomerie's *Flyting with Polwart* (l. 312).

A note in *American Speech* (1930) observed that *pox* is used of "any kind of venereal disease." Whereas the term has become too generalized and dated, thus petering out, *clap* has had a vigorous history from 1587, remaining current in both British and American English, where it is recorded in the works of such major writers as John Dos Passos, Ernest Hemingway, and Henry Miller. Although syphilis and gonorrhea have shown signs of a recent resurgence, they are now usually categorized under the opaque general style of S.T.D.— that is, "sexually transmitted diseases."

See also: Disease; French, the; Italians; Shakespeare, William.

Bibliography

Bentley, G.W. *Shakespeare and the New Disease.* New York: Peter Lang, 1989.

Fabricius, Johannes. *Syphilis in Shakespeare's England.* London: Jessica Kingsley, 1994.

Lawrence, D.H. "Introduction to his Paintings" (1929), in *Selected Essays.* Harmondsworth: Penguin, 1950.

Parran, N.T. *Shadow on the Land—Syphilis.* New York: Reynall and Hitchcock, 1937.

Rosebery, Archibald. *Lord Randolph Churchill.* London: Humphreys, 1906.

Ziegler, Philip. *King William the Fourth.* London: Collins, 1971.

T

TABOO

Taboo generally describes that which is unmentionable because, on a hierarchical scale, it is either ineffably sacred, like the name of God, or unspeakably vile, like cannibalism or incest. Freud reminds us, in *Totem and Taboo* (originally published 1912–1913) that "Taboo is a Polynesian word, the translation of which provides difficulties for us because we no longer possess the idea which it connotes" (1950, 18). Historically, taboos have tended to move from religious to secular, especially sexual to racial, topics, but they can manifest themselves in relation to a wide variety of things, creatures, human experiences, conditions, deeds, and words. The term is now used somewhat loosely of any social indiscretion that ought to be avoided, since strictly speaking, a taboo action should not be performed nor referred to, and a taboo word should never be uttered.

Although the word itself is Tongan in origin, having been brought into English by the explorer Captain James Cook in his *Voyage to the Pacific Ocean* (1777), the broader notion of prohibition is fundamental and found in all societies. Originally spelled *tabu* in the Melanesian languages, the word had a complex social and anthropological meaning: the adjectival use referred to physical locales that were sacred, set apart for a gods, kings, priests, or chiefs, and therefore prohibited for general use. Cook noted in his account that "the word has a very comprehensive meaning; but, in general, signifies that a thing is forbidden" (II vii). It could also be used as a verb: Cook records that a man had "been discovered with a woman who was *taboo'd*." (Cook's description conforms to the taboos of his own time by not referring explicitly to sexual activity.)

Linguistically taboo is rooted in **word magic,** especially in the belief that certain forces and creatures cannot or must not be named. These have come to include a great range such as the name of God, the Devil, death, damnation, disease, madness, being crippled, the varieties of excretion, and copulation, and in some societies, being fired, being poor, being fat, having a humble occupation, or references to underclothes. Taboos can present themselves in unexpected forms. One of the strangest is that the Germanic ancestors of the English regarded the bear as a creature of such totemistic force that it was referred to only indirectly as "the brown one" or via such metaphors as "the honey wolf." In several religions, such as Brahmanism, Judaism, and Islam, direct reference to the name of God is taboo. This is not the case with Christianity, although there are biblical injunctions, such as the Third Commandment, against "taking the Lord's name in vain" (Exodus 20:7).

Absolute taboos are rare and impractical, since they obviously impede communication and cannot be enforced in an increasingly secular and multicultural world. Consequently, the relationship between taboo and euphemism is symbiotic. As the entry for **euphemisms** shows, some euphemisms are time-honored, such as those for the name of God, while others are comparatively recent, such as those relating to fatness. Historically, there are few areas of continuous taboo. In medieval times, contrary to expectation, the name of God was used very freely in ways that now seem blasphemous, while "four-letter" words were used in certain literary genres and even in medical textbooks. In the Victorian era virtually all the categories listed in the previous paragraph were taboo. The exception was fatness, admired in the male *embonpoint* or paunch. Today taboo increasingly refers to prohibitions against socially unacceptable words, expressions, and topics, especially of a sexual and racist nature. They are also governed by context and medium, being most strictly observed in the press, the printed word, and broadcasting, but less so in oral usage, especially in male-to-male talk. A reminder of the earlier force of taboos occurs in this passage: "If a man had been able to say to you when you were young and in love: 'An' if tha —, an' if tha —, I'd be glad.'" This is from Aldous Huxley's edition of *The Letters of D.H. Lawrence* (1932, 773), quoting a famous passage from *Lady Chatterley's Lover,* from which Huxley had to excise *pisses* and *shits.* Yet both these words figure in proverbs listed in M.P. Tilley's major collection, *A Dictionary of the Proverbs in England in the Sixteenth and Seventeenth Centuries* (1950).

There are also biographical and individual factors governing taboos, especially that of age. Louis MacNeice explores this theme in "The Blasphemies," a poem tracing changing sensitivity through decades of personal maturation. It begins with the child's speculation: "The sin against the Holy . . . though what / He wondered was it?" "Cold in his bed," he is terrified at the prospect that "I shall be damned through thinking Damn." But ten years later he is "Preening himself as a gay blasphemer." "Rising thirty, he had decided / God was a mere expletive, a cheap one." Between forty and fifty "He grew to feel the issue irrelevant." The poem ends with the taboo broken, but the question remaining: "The sin / Against the Holy Ghost—What is it?"

In recent decades the notion of linguistic taboo has shifted from being actual to mythical. Revealingly, in the first linguistic instance given in the *Oxford English Dictionary,* Leonard Bloomfield wrote in his classic study *Language* (1933): "In America *knocked up* is a tabu form for 'rendered pregnant'" (xx ii), thereby breaking the supposed taboo in an example that now seems rather quaint. (In Victorian times even the word *pregnant* was taboo.) A double standard is particularly apparent in modern dictionaries, which commonly employ the usage label "taboo" of sexual and racist terms, even though these words are acknowledged to be in common use. The modern use of corpora, or large bodies of evidence of actual usage, both spoken and written, has enabled lexicographers to make meaningful assessments of word frequency. These clearly show that the notion of "taboo" is a misnomer. Thus the *Longman Dictionary of Contemporary English* (3rd edition, 1995) is based on both the Longman Corpus and the British National Corpus to establish the 3,000 most frequently used words in spoken and written English. Although *fuck* is marked as "taboo," its usage is rated as S3, one of 3,000 most frequently spoken words—while *fucking* is rated even higher as S1, one of the 1,000 most frequently spoken words. *Bastard, bugger,* and *bloody* are rated as S3, while *shit* and *ass* are rated as S2. (None of these words achieves so high a rating in written usage, and the first three are far more common in British than in American English.) Furthermore, it should be noted that usage labels in modern dictionaries tend to be remarkable in their inconsistency.

The increasing use of *taboo* to mean simply "offensive" or "grossly impolite" rather than "strictly forbidden" is also apparent in recent publications actually using the term in their titles. These include *A Dictionary of Obscenity, Taboo and Euphemism* (1988) by James McDonald and *Forbidden American English* (1990) by Richard A. Spears. The latter often rates some words (e.g., *fuck*) as "taboo in all senses," but others (e.g., *cunt*) as merely "very vulgar." However, the work gives quite elaborate caution notes.

In recent decades, as taboos have moved from sexual to racial terms, the lexicographical accommodation of ethnic slurs has attracted much controversy. The Oxford University Press was subjected to protests and eventually a lawsuit in 1972 over the inclusion of opprobrious senses of the word *Jew*. Two years previously the editor in chief of *Webster's New World Dictionary* pointedly omitted what were termed in the Preface "those true obscenities, the terms of racial or ethnic opprobrium." Today, former taboos against religious exclamations are less stringently observed, while gross sexual terms are increasingly current. The category that now most conforms to genuine taboo is that of race.

See also: Abbreviations; Dictionaries; Euphemism; Nigger; *Oxford English Dictionary;* Webster and His Dictionaries.

Bibliography

Freud, Sigmund. *Totem and Taboo.* Trans. James Strachey. London: Routledge & Kegan Paul, 1950.
McDonald, James. *A Dictionary of Obscenity, Taboo and Euphemism.* London: Sphere, 1988.
MacNeice, Louis. *Selected Poems.* London: Faber and Faber, 1964.
Spears, Richard A. *Forbidden American English.* Lincolnwood, IL: Passport Books, 1990.
Steiner, Franz. *Taboo.* Harmondsworth: Penguin, 1967.
Tilley, M.P., ed. *A Dictionary of the Proverbs in England in the Sixteenth and Seventeenth Centuries.* Ann Arbor: University of Michigan Press, 1950.
Ullmann, Stephen. *Words and Their Use.* London: Frederick Muller, 1951.

TELEVISION. *See:* Broadcasting

THOU

This ancient pronoun could be used in various insulting ways in the past. Originally the common form used in addressing a person in Anglo-Saxon, it has now been replaced by *you*. During the Middle English period (1100–1500) the convention developed whereby *thou* was used to address an intimate or an inferior. Although the general and literary uses of *thou* have died out, the form is still used in some British dialects by parents when addressing children, and familiarly between equals. But in the words of the *Oxford English Dictionary,* "in all other cases considered rude." Hence the use of the verbal form "to thou" a person, meaning to show disrespect, as in "Avaunt caitiff, dost thou thou me! I am come of good kin [family]" (from the play *Hickscorner,* ca. 1530, l. 149). At the trial of Sir Walter Raleigh for treason in 1603, the attorney general, Sir Edward Coke, harangued Raleigh insultingly: "for I thou thee, thou Traitor!" (Hargreave *State Trials*, I, 216). The usage is an important indicator of tone and relationship in Elizabethan drama, showing affection, but also contempt, as in Caliban's speech to Ariel: "Thou liest, thou lying monkey thou" (*Tempest* III ii 52). Consequently, when the Quakers started to use *thou* in the mid-seventeenth century as an expression of friendship and equality, it was frequently interpreted as a sign of disrespect. Samuel Pepys noted with amusement in his *Diary* (January 11, 1664): "She thou'd him all along," referring to a Quaker lady addressing King Charles II.

See also: Quakers and Shakers.

TREACHERY

Disloyalty and betrayal have many dimensions and contexts: personal, marital, martial, religious, political, national, and, in recent decades, racial. Consequently, the word-field is made up of hundreds of diverse terms, from the most condemning to the comparatively trivial. The survival of the value of loyalty, even in the most unlikely places, such as among criminals and underworld gangs, is noteworthy. As the entry for **Anglo-Saxon period** makes clear, the value of personal loyalty to the death was upheld both within the *comitatus* or *cynn* (tribal unit) and between the lord and his men. This was the crucial link in the ancient Germanic warrior culture. Those who broke this bond were punished, not by gruesome execution, but by ostracism and exile, the ultimate disgrace. Both *swicere,* the Anglo-Saxon word for "traitor," and *swican,* the verb meaning "to betray," died out in the Middle Ages.

In medieval times the monarch was regarded as embodying the nation, so that treason, technically *high treason*, was a capital offense, being both a personal and a national betrayal. Offenders were typically hanged, drawn (disemboweled), and quartered (cut into four pieces), their decapitated heads being displayed at Traitors' Gate on London Bridge. *Petty treason,* by contrast, was that committed against an ordinary subject: thus in 1763, "Mary Head, convicted at Chester Assizes of petit treason, in killing her husband, was burnt." This is now classified as murder. *Traitor* and *treason,* both dating from about 1225, were in the post-medieval period condemning and gravely insulting terms. They could also be used in intimate contexts: "A, false traitour!" shouts the Miller at the farcical moment in Chaucer's *Reve's Tale* when he discovers that one of his student lodgers has seduced his daughter (l. 4269). Similarly, in his tale the Merchant denounces Damyan, the squire and adulterous lover of May, as "O servaunt traytour" (l. 1785). In Shakespeare's works the word is the third most common noun of opprobrium, with nearly two hundred uses, coming after *villain* and *knave,* which are less specific. "Thou art a traitor and a miscreant" is a typical instance (*Richard II* I i 39), the word being preceded by a great variety of adjectives, such as *monstrous, vile, filthy, viperous,* and even *toad-spotted* (since toads were thought to be poisonous).

The English Civil War created severe problems of authority and terminology, since King Charles I was defeated by the Parliamentary Party under Oliver Cromwell, found guilty of treason, and executed. The famous diarist John Evelyn denounced the judge as "that Arch Traytor Bradshaw" (January 13, 1649) and later acknowledged the "the stupendious [sic] and inscrutable Judgements of God [when] the carkasses of that arch-rebell Cromewell and Bradshaw the Judge were dragged out of their superbe tombs, hanged on the gallows at Tyburn and buried in a deep pit" (November 22, 1658). Henry Hyde, Earl of Clarendon, pointedly called his history of the conflict *A History of the Great Rebellion* (1702–1704). (Incidentally, the title "the Great Rebellion" was also used of the American Civil War.) Today *traitor* and *treason* have been narrowed down to the specific technical sense of betraying one's country, with correspondingly diminished currency, as has *treachery*.

From medieval through to Renaissance times, abandoning or changing one's religion was regarded with detestation. Consequently, powerful terms like *apostate* (ca. 1340) and *recreant* became frequent terms of abuse, joining words like *miscreant* (ca. 1330), originally meaning "infidel," before it acquired the modern sense of "villain" or "scoundrel." Interestingly, the original senses of *pervert* and *perversion* concerned religious betrayal. Today all these words are either obsolete or used in different senses. Contemptuous terms like *turncoat* (ca. 1557) and *renegade* (ca. 1583) came to be used in both religious and political contexts. The same is true of the verb *to defect,* first used (ca. 1596) of those who had defected from the Christian religion before acquiring the political sense of "to desert to a Communist country," current from the 1950s. *Deserter* follows a similar pattern, the first quotation being "the base Desertour of my Mother Church" in Anthony Stafford's life of the Virgin Mary, called, *The Female Glory* (1635, 80). This was followed a few decades later by the military sense. In the highly charged context of war, *collaborator* became a condemning term from 1943, paralleled by the eponym *quisling* (after the Norwegian Vidkun Quisling, 1887–1945), who collaborated with the Germans in World War II).

Various terms condemn breach of loyalty or solidarity in the workforce, stigmatizing those who refuse to join a strike, break a strike, or take over the work of a striker. The strongest term is *scab,* from Elizabethan times a general term of abuse for what the *Oxford English Dictionary* wittily calls "a mean, low 'scurvy' fellow," but later recorded in America in the industrial sense: A notice ending a strike in Bristol, Massachusetts, notes that "The conflict would not have been so sharp had there not been so many dirty scabs " (*Bristol Journal,* July 5, 1777). "What is a scab?" asks a contemporary author. "He is to his trade what a traitor is to his country" (in Arthur Aspinall, *Early Trade Unions* 1949, 84). The other principal term is *blackleg,* recorded in British contexts from 1865. Both terms are rooted in the notion of disease.

In the criminal underworld with its fierce gang loyalties, a whole range of hostile terms has grown up, rather older than expected, with interesting coded origins. The earliest is *snitch* for one who turns state evidence, recorded in Francis Grose's *Classical Dictionary of the Vulgar Tongue* (1785). It is a slang term for *nose,* which had a similar sense in the same period. So has *nark,* possibly a Romany word for "nose" recorded first in John Camden Hotten's *Dictionary of Modern Slang* (1860) for "a police informer" or *copper's nark. Stool pigeon,* originally meaning a decoy, took on a similar sense in the United States from about 1849. All these terms are still current, but in British usage the most prevalent and hostile word is *grass,* used as a noun and verb from the 1930s. Its origin lies in an ingenious piece of Cockney **rhyming slang,** namely *grass* for *grasshopper,* rhyming with *shopper,* since "to shop" is criminal slang for to "sell out, betray."

In the United States perceived racial disloyalty is increasingly stigmatized among blacks. Thus *Jim Crow* took on the sense of "a turncoat" from as early as 1837, followed much later, about 1921, by **Uncle Tom**, seventy years after the publication of Harriet Beecher Stowe's classic novel *Uncle Tom's Cabin.* They have since been joined by the humorous but damning insult *Oreo* from the cookie—that is, dark on the outside but white at the core—thrown up in 1968, during the period when solidarity among American blacks became a major political force.

The essential shift in the dynamic of the word-field is that powerful terms of national significance like *traitor* have generally lost currency and force, whereas group-words like *grass, scab,* and *Uncle Tom* have retained and even increased their vehemence.

See also: Uncle Tom.

Bibliography

Evelyn, John. *The Diary of John Evelyn,* ed. John Bowle. Oxford: Oxford University Press, 1983.
Lockyer, Roger, ed. *Clarendon's History of the Great Rebellion.* Oxford: Folio Society, 1967.

TURD

This ancient term has followed the same basic semantic route historically as *shit,* being first recorded in Anglo-Saxon times in a plain literal sense, leading to various metaphorical extensions of coarse abuse from the medieval period onward. Etymologically the word turns out to be a distant relative of legal *tort,* both rooted in the concept of being twisted or crooked. The early contexts all refer to animal excrement, such as "swines tord" in the Anglo-Saxon *Leechdoms,* ca. 1000. The strangely graphic identification *turd bird* was a provincial name for Richardson's skua even in the nineteenth century. The first metaphorical extension is to phrases like "I don't give a turd," found about 1250 in the polemical poem *The Owl and the Nightingale* (l. 1686). A surprising instance is recorded in the *OED* from the *Minutes of the Archdeaconry of Essex* (1619–1620) when a demand was made for rent from a person holding land bequeathed to the poor of the parish: the person "bid a turde." Insulting personal uses, always exclusively masculine in application, are recorded from about 1450 in the morality play called *Mankind* (l. 127) and are followed by some spirited quotations such as "The foul-mouthed knave will call thee goodman Tord" (1598 in Edward Guilpin's *Skialethia,* 37). Although Shakespeare never used the word in a personal way, Ben Jonson was more robust with the crude dismissive insult "turd i' your teeth" (1614, in *Bartholomew Fair,* I iv). The epithet *turd-faced* occurs in the rich contemporary source of insults, *The Flyting of Mongomerie and Polwart* (1585, l. 787) and in Charles Cotton's *Works* (1678): "Basta! No more, you wrangling turds" (l. 223). Francis Grose's *Classical Dictionary of the Vulgar Tongue* (1785) uses the euphemized form *t—d* but gives many amusing but no insulting uses.

Thereafter there is a curious hiatus in recorded usage until the early twentieth century, when a thriving currency is resumed. *Turd* is now used indiscriminately to mean "a worthless or contemptible person," more commonly in British than American English. Generally speaking, the term is less critical and condemning than *shit.*

See also: Shit Words.

TWAIN, MARK

Mark Twain was, of course, the river-sourced pseudonym of Samuel Langhorne Clemens (1835–1910), who wrote voluminously in many modes besides his famous fictions, including satirical sketches, "tall talk," travel journals, and journalism. His original, imaginative, and frank portrayal of life in the South in *The Adventures of Tom Sawyer* (1876) and most notably in *The Adventures of Huckleberry Finn* (1885) established him as the founding father of American literature: indeed, Ernest Hemingway claimed that all modern American literature comes from *Huckleberry Finn* (*The Green Hills of Africa* 1935, 29). Although both are ostensibly boys' books, Twain's technique of verisimilitude derives from using a naive uncensored narrator and direct idiomatic speech, strongly accented. Furthermore, in *Huckleberry Finn* he daringly depicts the intimate juvenile friendship and intense bond between Huck and the escaped slave Jim, thereby raising the two major issues of slavery and color. By setting the book "some forty to fifty years ago," Twain was placing the story well before the cataclysm of the Civil War. The book has been consistently controversial, called variously "quintessentially American," "original," "daring," "subversive," "a devastating attack on racism," and "racist trash" (Arac 1997, vii–ix, 9).

The popularity of *Huckleberry Finn* has never wavered, but it has a remarkable critical history, running through a cycle of condemnation, idolization, and then sectional rejection. Like *Tom Sawyer,* it has a long record of being legally challenged, especially in the North, being immediately excluded by the Concord (Massachusetts) Public Library Committee in March 1885, condemned as "the veriest trash," as "rough, coarse and inelegant," and "suited to the slums." According to the American Library Association, it remains one of the top ten most frequently challenged books, but on greatly varied grounds.

Recent criticism of *Huckleberry Finn* (post-1950s) has focused on previously neglected aspects of the character of Jim, namely an apparent ambivalence of attitude toward slavery, and especially on the use of the word *nigger,* which occurs 213 times in the novel. In his study, Jonathan Arac (1997) notes furthermore that the title "Nigger Jim" has come to be applied by a whole range of critics, including Leo Marx, Leslie Fiedler, and Ralph Ellison, even though he is never so called in the book. Arac also points out that the title of Fiedler's article, "Come Back to the Raft Ag'in Huck Honey!" (1948), provocatively arguing for a "chaste male love as the ultimate emotional experience," also does not occur in the text.

Ralph Ellison objected as far back as 1958 to Twain's use of the Negro minstrel stereotype in the presentation of Jim. This date coincides with wider opposition: "News about African American protests against the required place of honor held by *Huckleberry Finn* in the classroom . . . began to appear as early as early as 1957" (Arac 1997, 9). One of many offensive passages is Huck's observation that "Niggers is always talking about witches in the dark by the kitchen fire" (chapter 2). The critical defenses of juvenile narration and ironic authorial intention may explain, but do not take away the offensiveness of the term. It has been argued, defensively, that "*Nigger* is what blacks were commonly called in the South until recent times. It is wrong to censure a novel for historical accuracy" (June Edwards, quoted in Arac 1997, 27). However, in Harriet Beecher Stowe's classic *Uncle Tom's Cabin*

Mark Twain's 1885 fictional masterpiece, *The Adventures of Huckleberry Finn*, remains widely criticized—and is banned from some schools and libraries—for its frequent use of the word *nigger*, which appears 213 times. *(Brown Brothers)*

(1852) the callous remark "What's all the fuss about a dead nigger" provokes the comment "The word was as a spark to a powder magazine" (592). An essay under the provocative title "Only a Nigger," which appeared unsigned in the *Buffalo Express* (August 26, 1869) has been reliably attributed to Twain. It is a devastatingly sarcastic commentary on "A little blunder in the administration of justice by Southern mob-law. . . . Only 'a nigger' lynched by mistake." Twain highlights the term by consistently putting it in inverted commas. Huck's unselfconscious use of *nigger* is clearly part of his "sivilization" and the acculturation revealed in the exchange with Aunt Sally in chapter xxxii when Huck explains the reason for their late arrival:

"We blowed a cylinder-head."
　　"Good gracious! Anybody hurt?"
"No'm. Killed nigger."
　　"Well, it's lucky; because sometimes people do get hurt."

A parallel can be drawn with the South African writer Herman Charles Bosman (1905–1951), who employs a similar narrative technique in which a naive Boer narrator uses the deeply offensive term *kaffir* with embarrassing frequency but ironic intention.

In dramatizing the famous psychomachia Huck faces in chapter xxxi, Twain daringly complicates his dilemma by emphasizing a religious dimension. Huck's initial response, to follow his civic duty and turn Jim in gives him a sense of salvation ("I felt good and all washed clean of sin for the first time in my life"). His final decision, to commit to his personal loyalty to Jim, is admirable but expressed in a provocatively wicked idiom for 1885: "All right, then, I'll *go* to hell." On the matter of language, Twain himself issued a typical riposte to the initial censorship from Massachusetts, insisting that Huckleberry Finn was "painstaking and truthfully drawn . . . with but one exception and that a trifling one: this boy's language has been toned down and softened, here and there, in deference to the taste of a more modern and fastidious age" (Norton edition 1977, 286).

Huckleberry Finn remains a controversial text depicting the struggles of innocence to "do the right thing" in a corrupted and unjust society, especially because its direct language, notably the use of *nigger,* has become increasingly provocative and unacceptable. On the latter point the noted theater critic Frank Rich referred in 1995 to "Dropping the N-Bomb."

Twain was a great traveler and recorded his impressions in some very frank *Notebooks & Journals*. In the entries for the Holy Land, he juxtaposed the miserable living conditions with the miracles that had been performed there: "The people of this region in the Bible were just as they are now—ignorant, depraved, superstitious, dirty, lousy, thieving *vagabonds*" (Vol. I, 424–25). "Slept on the ground in front of an Arab house. Lice fleas, horses, jackasses, chickens, and worse than all, Arabs for company all night" (Vol. I, 431). However, such critical passages were omitted from his travelogue, *The Innocents Abroad* (1911).

See also: Kaffir; Nigger.

Bibliography

Arac, Jonathan. *Huckleberry Finn as Idol and Target*. Madison: University of Wisconsin Press, 1997.

Fiedler, Leslie. "Come Back to the Raft Ag'in Huck Honey!" *Partisan Review*, June 1948, 664–71.

Huckleberry Finn: The Norton Critical Edition, ed. Bradley, Beatty, Long, and Cooley. New York: W.W. Norton, 1977.

Mark Twain's Notebooks & Journals, ed. Anderson, Frank, and Sanderson. Berkeley and London: University of California Press, 1975.

Rich, Frank. "Dropping the N-Bomb." *New York Times*, March 16, 1995, A15.

TWAT

Twat, which is usually pronounced to rhyme with "hot" but can rhyme with "hat," is now a well-established slang term meaning a woman's genitals. Included in the *Oxford English Dictionary* in 1916 but marked as "obsolete," it has become quite common as a modern term of abuse for a "worthless male person" in the same fashion as *cunt*, but with less impact. Its origins are complex and confused. Recorded from about 1650, the term is described as "of obscure origin," but was linked to the verb form in a quotation from James Halliwell's *Dictionary of Archaic and Provincial Words* (1847): "The buck or doe twateth, makes a noise at rutting time." However, the *OED* dismisses this as an "error for *troat*," meaning "to cry or bellow, said of a buck at rutting time," recorded from 1611.

The genital sense of *twat* is recorded in Nathaniel Bailey's dictionary of 1727, defined as *pudendum muliebre*, whereafter there is a surprising gap of two centuries until it is resuscitated by such outspoken modern authors as E.E. Cummings, Henry Miller, Norman Mailer, and Germaine Greer. This long hiatus perhaps explains the following curious anecdote. The famous Victorian poet Robert Browning evidently came across this unfamiliar term in a caustic context in a satirical poem called the "Vanity of Vanities" (1660):

They talk't of his having a Cardinall's hat,
They'd send him as soon an Old Nun's Twat.
(ll. 49–50)

Browning committed the hilarious catachresis (serious linguistic error) of using the word in "Pippa Passes" (1848) as the *OED* puts it, "under the impression that it denoted some part of a nun's attire":

Then owls and bats
Cowls and twats
Monks and nuns, in cloister's moods,
Adjourn to the oak-stump pantry.
(IV ii 96–99)

This is a classic instance of the dangers of using an underground slang term without being sure of its meaning. (The Cardinal's Hat was the name of a Bankside brothel in Elizabethan London.)

The use as a term of vulgar personal abuse is fairly recent, being first recorded by Frederic Manning in his war memoir *The Middle Parts of Fortune* (1929) and subsequently taken up by such contemporary authors as Philip Roth and John Updike. A surprising contemporary instance was Britain's Princess Anne's comment that a news reporter who had fraudulently gained access to Buckingham Palace by posing as a servant was "a fucking incompetent twat" (*Daily Mirror,* November 21, 2003).

See also: Berk; Cunt; Genitalia; Instability of Swearing Terms; Victorian Age.

TYNAN, KENNETH

Kenneth Tynan (1927–1980) was a remarkable theatre personality in various important roles, notably as a highly regarded and perceptive drama critic for the *London Observer* (1954–1958 and 1960–1963) and *The New Yorker* (1958–1960). As literary manager for the British National Theatre (1963–1969) he spearheaded the assault on censorship, becoming involved in a number of confrontations with the office of the Lord Chamberlain, whose position was finally abolished in 1968.

Tynan was a witty, provocative, and fearless controversialist, as well as a relentless self-publicist, generating a number of scandals. In 1965 he caused a national furor by becoming the first person to utter the word *fuck* on national television (November 13). In a late-night show called "BBC-3," in which Mary McCarthy was also a guest, Tynan was asked if the National Theatre would allow a play in which sexual intercourse took place. Tynan replied nonchalantly: "Oh I think so certainly. I doubt if there are very many rational people in this world to whom the word 'fuck' is particularly diabolical or revolting or totally forbidden" (Tynan 1988, 236). Despite this context, as his biographer notes, the B.B.C.'s switchboard was jammed by indignant callers, and the episode for a few days

> eclipsed all other news, including the Unilateral Declaration of Independence in Rhodesia and the war in Vietnam; and provoked a barrage of headlines and stories like "That Word On TV . . . "; "Insult to Womanhood"; "Is This Moral?"; The War on BBCnity"; "Sack 4-letter Tynan."
> (Tynan 1988, 237)

Four motions were set down in the House of Commons calling for prosecution on the grounds of obscenity, for the resignation of Tynan, and for the dismissal of the director-general of the B.B.C. None produced any concrete response, but Tynan himself seems to have been genuinely dismayed asking: "Is *that* how I'm going to be remembered?" (Tynan 1988, 236). Others regarded it, albeit later, as an utterance of considerable éclat: "As becomes a great pioneer," wrote Ashley Montagu, "his stock has considerably risen in the world" (1973, 312). However, amid the welter of sermons, cartoons, limericks, and philological discussions, the key question was asked by Stanley Reynolds in the *Guardian,* namely why "that one simple word of four letters can provoke a greater reaction in us than long and complex words like apartheid, rebellion, illegal, police state and treason" (cited in Tynan 1988, 237).

Although this was Tynan's most notorious use of *fuck* in public, it was not the first. During the *Chatterley* trial (1960) he quoted an expert witness, Dr. Richard Hoggart, who claimed that D.H. Lawrence had "striven to cleanse [the word] of its furtive, contemptuous, and expletive connotations, and to use it in the most simple, neutral way: one fucks." This was the first use in a British Sunday newspaper, but as the editor David Astor recalled, "He slid it in and there was no fuss" (Tynan 1988, 178).

Tynan's most famous contribution to popular culture was his association with the erotic review *Oh! Calcutta!,* featuring mass stage nudity and simulated stage sex. (The odd title was a subtle pun on the French "O quel cul t'as" ["Oh what an arse you have."]) However, for legal reasons he conceded that "indecent exposure is out, and so are 4-letter words" (Tynan 1988, 278). Although the show got mixed reviews, it was enormously successful. Tynan's penchant for shock found other outlets: he wittily and outrageously described his friend Orson Welles's performance as Othello as "Citizen Coon" (Tynan 1988, 98).

See also: Lord Chancellor.

Bibliography
Montagu, Ashley. *The Anatomy of Swearing.* London and New York: Macmillan and Collier, 1973.
Tynan, Kathleen. *The Life of Kenneth Tynan.* London: Methuen, 1988.

TOK PISIN. *See:* Pidgin English

U

"U" AND "NON-U"

Linguistic class distinctions have certainly existed in English since the Norman Conquest, when a foreign-speaking élite took over the land, and no doubt before that in the Viking era. Although now greatly diminished, they have continued to show themselves in various features, such as accent, lexis, and differing taboos. The entry for **class and swearing** explores the differing norms either practiced or attributed to the various classes over the centuries. Generally speaking, these class distinctions are peculiar to English society and do not feature in the other global varieties of the language.

The title of this entry comes from the most significant modern contribution made in 1954 by Alan S.C. Ross in an article, "Linguistic Class-indicators in Present-day English," originally published in a learned Finnish journal, *Neuphilologische Mitteilungen*. It reached a wider audience in its popularized form, "U and Non-U: An Essay in Sociological Linguistics" in *Noblesse Oblige* (ed. Nancy Mitford) in 1956. Asserting that "It is solely by its language that the upper class is clearly marked off from the others" (1956, 9), perhaps something of an overstatement, Ross nevertheless posited a fruitful distinction between usages that he designated "U" (upper class) and "non-U" (other class). Ross's analysis and distinctions were not based on the research data and methodology now regarded as necessary for a contribution to sociolinguistics. But they were generally accepted as accurate observations, so that the abbreviations became very fashionable and are still current.

Although Ross did not cover swearing *per se,* his distinctions show clearly that the upper class tend to be very direct and free of euphemisms when dealing with sensitive areas. Thus, Ross noted, *lavatory* is "U" as against "non-U" *toilet,* while *jerry* or *pot* is (or was) used for "chamber pot" rather than "article." More pointedly, *mad* is preferred to *mental.* In contexts of not hearing properly, or as an apology, or "after hiccupping or belching," where *Pardon!* would be the non-U reaction, the normal U responses "are very curt, viz. (1) *What?* (2) *Sorry!*" (3) [silence] (1956, 27). Upper-class terms of disapproval are distinctive but limited: "the antonym of *gentleman* was often *cad* and *bounder*" (1956, 10).

Not surprisingly, a number of similar studies followed, one edited by Ross himself under the title *What Are U?* (1969), and another, *U and Non-U Revisited,* edited by Richard Buckle, in which Ross observed that "the antitheses between U and non-U have *not* changed" (1980, 28). The work contained "A Beginner's Glossary" designating *false teeth* as U, as against non-U *dentures*, similarly *dirty* against *soiled* and *awful smell* against *unpleasant odour*. This was followed by *The Official Sloane Ranger Handbook* (1982), edited by Anne Barr and Peter York, a facetious but perceptive study of upper-class mores, the title deriving from the area of London around Sloane Square with its predominantly upper-class population. The work includes a "Sloane Dictionary" of about 150 items containing most of the same semantic features: crude and colorful metaphors are preferred to euphemisms. Thus *bog* is the typical male Sloane word for "toilet," *pissed* is the basic term for "drunk," and *park a custard* or *shoot a cat* are used as pseudo-euphemisms for "to vomit." *Bang* refers to sexual intercourse, but to *bang one's bishop* is to masturbate (for males). Politically incorrect words are used without embarrassment, for example *spastic* or *thick* for "stupid" and *poncy* for "effeminate." While the euphemism "four-letter man" is common, the offending words themselves often occur in formulas like "he's a real shit" or "the silly cunt." Racism also features in phrases like "Jew's canoe" for an expensive car or "the wogs [foreigners] begin at Dover." Another contemporary comment on being studiedly un-bourgeois is found in Jilly Cooper's *Class:* "I once heard my son regaling his friends: 'Mummy says that *pardon* is a much worse word than *fuck*'" (1981, 39).

A less well known earlier publication on the topic was *Public School Slang* by Maurice Marples (1940). This fairly comprehensive study of the linguistic mores of upper-class private secondary schools in England records the same use of direct, even blunt, terms rather than euphemisms, such as *bogs* for toilet, *bumph* for toilet paper, *jerry* for chamber pot, *batty*, *barmy*, *dippy*, and *dotty* for mad, *thick* for stupid, and the use of racist terms like *Jew* and *wog*. It also cites an interesting source, the "Gradus ad Cantabrigiam," a glossary of Cambridge University slang published in 1803 and 1824, which lists *bogs* for toilet and *to cat* for to vomit. Although the "four-letter words" do not feature, they occasionally surface unrecognized: Marples has an entry under *pintle* explaining it as "cricket played with a narrow bat (also called a *pintle*)." He clearly does not realize that *pintle* is an ancient term for "penis." Under "Terms of Disapproval" are listed many strong epithets, such as *sneak, swine, lout, rotten, putrid, stinking, filthy, lousy, loathsome, ghastly, frightful, beastly, blasted, blooming, blinking,* and others more pungent still" (1940, 60). Two unexpected terms are *wowser*, now Australian in provenance meaning a killjoy, and *gump*, a fool, "now mostly American in its associations, but actually in use in England as early as 1825" (1940, 60).

About half a century after the work of Ross and Marples, there are still many words and phrases such as "this is a damned good show," "the little trollope!," "what a stinking cad!," and "he's a frightful bounder," which are exclusively upper-class in currency. However, linguistic class distinctions are tending to disappear, as a reflection of general trends in British society.

See also: Class and Swearing; Partridge, Eric.

Bibliography

Barr, Anne, and Peter York. *The Official Sloane Ranger Handbook*. London: Ebury, 1982.

Buckle, Richard. *U and Non-U Revisited*. London: Debrett/Futura, 1980.

Cooper, Jilly. *Class*. New York: Knopf, 1981.

Marples, Maurice. *Public School Slang*. London: Constable, 1940.

Ross, Alan S.C. "Linguistic Class-indicators in Present-day English," *Neuphilologische Mitteilungen* LV, 21–49.

———. "U and Non-U: An Essay in Sociological Linguistics." In *Noblesse Oblige*, ed. Nancy Mitford. Harmondsworth: Penguin, 1956.

UNCLE TOM

The long-suffering eponymous hero of Harriet Beecher Stowe's famous abolitionist novel *Uncle Tom's Cabin* (1851–1852) has survived, but as a name of contempt. Initial critical responses to the novel were sharply divided, but the character of Uncle Tom was generally praised for his piety and stoic loyalty. The way that his name has become a label of opprobrium, now referring to "a Black man who is submissively loyal or servile to White men" (*Oxford English Dictionary*) is a remarkable study of stereotyping, racial identification, and the supplanting of religious values by political loyalties.

Several contemporary reviews found Uncle Tom "a paragon of virtue" (unsigned, London *Times,* September 18, 1852) impervious to temptation: "No insult, no outrage, no suffering, could ruffle the Christ-like meekness of his spirit, and shake the steadfastness of his faith. It triumphantly exemplifies the nature, tendency and results of CHRISTIAN NON-RESISTANCE" (William Lloyd Garrison, *Liberator Review,* Boston March 26, 1852). On this point the critics divided, some claiming a sentimental exaggeration which was incredible, others an unseemly pusillanimous subservience. Both critical positions had a racial underpinning. "In attributing perfection to this Negro character Mrs. Stowe not only 'o'ersteps the modesty of nature,' but places in a strong light the absurdity of the whole story" (unsigned, *Southern Literary Messenger Review,* Richmond, October 1852). William G. Allen in the *Frederick Douglass Paper* (Rochester, May 20, 1852) was more militant: "Indeed if any man has too much piety, Uncle Tom was that man." Overtly racism suffused George Graham's review under the scornful title of "Black Letters; Or Uncle-Tom-Foolery," scorning "Sambo's woes" in aggressive terms: "A plague of these black faces! We hate this niggerism," this "woolly-headed literature." For Graham, "Uncle Tom is an exaggeration, a monster of perfection" (*Graham's Magazine Review,* Philadelphia, February 1853). Even the London *Times* protested against the "imbalance of idealised Blacks and blackened whites."

Hugh Rawson notes that among whites "Tom's name was being used within a year of [the novel's] publication in such forms as *Uncle Tomitude, Uncle Tomitized* and *Uncle Tomific.*" (1989, 400). The first recorded usage of *Uncle Tom* as a pejorative label among blacks appears seventy years later, in speeches given by Marcus Garvey in 1921. This considerable time lag reveals how long it took for a "submissively loyal or servile Black man" to be criticized. There is a cross-reference in 1922 to *New Negro* (originally a euphemism for a slave) in the new emancipated sense of one working for black rights: "It does not occur to the Old South, that there is a 'New Negro'; that 'Uncle Toms' are passing" (Alan Dundes, *Mother Wit* 1973, 400–401).

Since then the name has taken on a strong sense of racial loyalty. Clarence Major's definition stresses this point: "a black person who is culturally disloyal; a black person who does not practice racial or cultural loyalty; a pejorative term for any African American who is perceived by other African Americans to be 'middle-class,' to own property, and to have money in the bank" (1994, 492). In Eldridge Cleaver's *Soul on Ice* the assassination of Malcolm X provokes the question: "Why'n't they kill some of those Uncle-Tomming m.f.'s?" (1968, 51). Although the earliest references are naturally to American blacks, the term has since been used generally for one who is politically pusillanimous, especially not loyal to his grouping; for example: "Arafat was always attacked by Marxist-oriented militants as being a Palestinian 'Uncle Tom,' neither sufficiently radical or violent" (*Guardian,* July 15, 1971).

See also: Blacks; Treachery.

Bibliography
Cleaver, Eldridge. *Soul on Ice.* New York: McGraw-Hill, 1968.
Major, Clarence. *Juba to Jive.* Harmondsworth: Penguin, 1994.

UNPARLIAMENTARY LANGUAGE

Although members of the British Parliament have immunity from prosecution, protecting their right to make statements and bring charges that may be in the national interest, there are necessary restraints preventing attacks on the character and dignity of individuals. The basic characterization of unparliamentary language is that in the view of the Speaker of the House of Commons or equivalent chamber, it breaks the rules of respect. The convention of politeness whereby British Members of Parliament refer to each other as "the honourable" and use other artificial formulas of respect extends to not accusing each other of lying, being drunk, misrepresenting, or insulting each other. This last category is, of course, less easy to define. The specific terms to which the Speaker has objected over the years include *blackguard, coward, git, guttersnipe, hooligan, rat, stoolpigeon, swine,* and *traitor.* These vary from the most serious moral condemnations to vulgar abuse. The usual procedure is for the Speaker to demand that the offensive terms be withdrawn, failing which the Member of Parliament will be disciplined or dismissed from the Chamber.

Although *unparliamentary* has been used in a generalized sense from the early seventeenth century, the first record in the *Oxford English Dictionary* of the phrase "unparliamentary language" dates only from 1810: "The Speaker stated that ... a member had used unparliamentary language" (*Sporting Magazine,* XXXV, 302). However, there have been some spectacular earlier breaches. When Oliver Cromwell dissolved Parliament on April 20, 1653, he launched a damning verbal broadside at the incumbents: "Ye are a factious crew, and enemies to all good government. Ye are a pack of mercenary wretches and would like Esau sell your country for a mess of pottage." He pointed at individuals, and called them "whoremasters, drunkards, corrupt and unjust men," adding: "Ye have no more religion than my horse. . . . Perhaps ye think this is not parliamentary language. I confess it is not, neither are you to expect any such from me." Some members protested, more at his language than his unconstitutional action in closing Parliament. (S.R. Gardiner 1903, 262–63).

In spite of the conventional prohibitions, the House of Commons has witnessed some extraordinarily savage insults inflicted in the course of debates. The contests between Charles James Fox and William Pitt in the late eighteenth century were legendary. The debate on the Irish Home Rule Bill (July 27, 1893) degenerated into a fracas and a fight lasting twenty minutes. On May 15, 1846, Benjamin Disraeli attacked Sir Robert Peel in the following terms: "I find that for between thirty and forty years the right honourable gentleman has traded on the ideas and intelligence of others. (Loud cheering.) His life has been a great appropriation clause. (Shouts of laughter and cheers.) He is a burglar of others' intellect . . . there is no statesman who has committed political petty larceny on so great a scale. (Renewed laughter.)" (W.F. Monypenny 1912, Vol. II, 353). Disraeli's rhetorical cunning is to avoid the "unparliamentary" words *thief* and *theft,* using more polite, high-register but equally damaging equivalents. Disraeli used the same rhetorical technique in publicly dismissing his great enemy and rival William Gladstone with withering sarcasm as "a sophistical rhetorician inebriated with exuberance of his own verbosity" (*Times,* July 29, 1878). Perhaps the most famous and witty of these technical evasions was Sir Winston Churchill's use of the phrase "terminological inexactitude" as a substitute for "lie" (February 22, 1906).

In the House of Commons of Commonwealth countries, the definition of "unparliamentary language" is broader. Thus in the Canadian it is interpreted as "any language which leads to disorder in the House." In February 1971 the Prime Minister Pierre Trudeau caused a minor scandal when he allegedly told opposition M.P.s to "fuck off." This was a unique occurrence. In the Australian House of Representatives there is still more latitude, shown in a number of colorful instances, such as this from 1970: "I never use the word 'bloody' because it is unparliamentary. It is a word I never bloody well use" (Hornadge 1980, 145). Some exchanges involve extremely insulting language, such as this in 1975:

Dr. R.T. Gun (Labour):   "Why don't you shut up, you great poofter?"
Mr. J.W. Bourchier (Liberal): "Come round here, you little wop, and I'll fix you up."
(Cited in Hornadge 1980, 166)

The South African Parliament has stricter definitions and rulings over "offensive and unbecoming language." From 1994 (the year of the first democratic election) to 2001, the number of expressions ruled by the Speaker to be "unparliamentary" rose annually from five to thirty. The most common expressions were *lie/liar/lying, shut up,* and *racist,* the last category generating many specific terms commonly heard in the past, such as *boy, monkey, golliwog, ape, baboon,* and other local insulting words for blacks, such as *coconut, hotnot* (a corruption of **Hottentot**), and one newcomer, *token black.*

Rule 19 of the United States Senate prohibits "language unbecoming a senator." Although breaches are not common, according to the *Washington Post* (June 25, 2004), Vice President Dick Cheney, then president of the Senate, told Senator Patrick J. Leahy (Democrat, Vermont) to "fuck yourself" in the course of a widely publicized exchange on the floor of the Senate. However, the Senate was not in session at the time, and Cheney did not apologize.

The term *unparliamentary* has had a minor general currency, being included in Farmer and Henley's dictionary *Slang and Its Analogues* (1890–1904) in the slightly euphemistic senses of "abusive, obscene, unfit for ordinary conversation."

See also: Australia.

Bibliography

Gardiner, S.R. *History of the Commonwealth and Protectorate.* Vol. II. London: Longmans, Green, 1903.
Hornadge, Bill. *The Australian Slanguage.* North Ryde, New South Wales: Cassell Australia, 1980.
Monypenny, William F. *The Life of Benjamin Disraeli.* London: J. Murray, 1910–1916.

URINATION. *See:* Piss

VICTORIAN AGE

Victorian, like many historical terms in English, has both a referential sense, to the reign of one of the great icons of English history, Queen Victoria (1837–1901), and a socially descriptive sense. Throughout her long reign Victoria symbolized the increasing power and prestige of the British Empire, but also epitomized the dignity and family values of the monarchy. From her formidable personality derived the secondary sense, defined by the *Oxford English Dictionary* as "Resembling or typified by the attitudes supposedly characteristic of the Victorian Age; prudish; strict; old-fashioned; out-dated." However, groundbreaking studies by Steven Marcus, *The Other Victorians* (1966), and Ronald Pearsall, *The Worm in the Bud: The World of Victorian Sexuality* (1969), have emphasized the schizophrenic quality of the age, pointing out the sordid realities behind the façade of respectability, especially the vices of prostitution, pornography, "perversion," and homosexuality, all then regarded as crimes. Many studies have followed—for example, Maynard 1993—showing that Victorian attitudes toward sex were complex and not really monolithic. Michel Foucault begins his *History of Sexuality* with an allusion to Steven Marcus ("We 'Other Victorians'"), before questioning "the repressive hypothesis" which, it is commonly argued, derives from the period.

However, the Victorians themselves were well aware of "the Two Nations" alluded to by Benjamin Disraeli in the subtitle of his novel *Sybil* (1845): the rich and the poor, the child labor and extreme poverty of the slums, as well as the riotous hedonism and decadence behind a repressive bourgeois façade. (As the entry for **Jews** shows, Disraeli himself was one target of the open anti-Semitism which was also a feature of the age.) In contrast to the traditional view of decorous Victorian order, the novelist George Gissing wrote in a letter of 1882 that on a typical Bank Holiday, "Places like Hampstead Heath and the various parks and commons are packed with screeching drunkards, one general mass of dust and heat and rage and exhaustion." The Haymarket (the garish hub of prostitution in Victorian London) is described in detail in an article published in *Household Words* (edited by Charles Dickens) in 1857. The social reformer Henry Mayhew was especially shocked by the young: "The precocity of the youth of both sexes is perfectly astounding. The drinking, the smoking, the blasphemy, indecency and immorality that does not call a blush is incredible" (1983, 50). These powerfully impressionistic sketches were endorsed by pioneering sociological studies, such as Henry Mayhew's

London Labour and the London Poor (1851–1862), Dr. William Acton's *Prostitution* (1857), and Charles Booth's *Labour and Life of the City of London* (17 volumes, 1889–1903).

Many of the idols and icons of the period led double or scandalous lives. Some, like Dickens and Thomas Hardy, died with the unedifying secrets of their lives intact; others, like Oscar Wilde, Charles Dilke, and Charles Parnell, were publicly ruined in sensational sex scandals. Some were strangely open in their behavior: the great statesman William Ewart Gladstone, four times prime minister, was in the habit of accosting prostitutes, attempting to reform them, and indulging in self-flagellation (Marlow 1977). The Boulton and Park case of 1871 brought to light bizarre and comic transvestite behavior, explaining the suicide of Lord Arthur Clinton. The Cleveland Street scandal of 1889 publicized not only a homosexual brothel frequented by a number of high-society gentlemen, but a new meaning of the word *gay*. Lesbianism, however, remained off the statute books, essentially because no one was brave enough to explain its nature to Queen Victoria. Yet the young queen and her consort, Prince Albert, exchanged mildly pornographic prints. Her son Edward the Prince of Wales led a life of notorious luxury and had a number of public affairs, most notably with the celebrated beauty and actress Lillie Langtry, as well as Mrs. Alice Keppel. It is thus hardly surprising that some of the most emphasized features in Victorian fiction were hypocrisy and double standards.

Of many such examples, two notable Victorians epitomize the moral divide of the age. The intrepid explorer of Muslim lands, Sir Richard Burton (1821–1890) commented: "For thirty years I served her majesty at home and abroad without acknowledgement or reward. Then I publish a pornographic book [his translation of *The Arabian Nights*] and at once earn £10,000 and fame. I begin at last to understand the public and what it wants." His privately published translation of *The Kama Sutra* (1883) was followed by *The Perfumed Garden* (1886), but an expanded version under the title of *The Scented Garden* (1890) containing a long section in homosexuality was burned by Lady Burton after his death.

The other was Henry Mayhew (1812–1887), the principal and driving force of a team of diligent researchers exploring the Victorian underworld, concretized as the monumental study *London Labour and the London Poor* (published in seven volumes, 1851–1862). Although evangelically motivated, the work itself derived from meetings and interviews with hundreds of prostitutes, "fallen women," thugs, thieves, swindlers, vagrants, tramps, and paupers. With sociological precision distinctions are made between, for example, the various grades of prostitutes, categorizing them as *convives, prima donnas, ladies of intrigue, chères amies,* and even *female operatives.* The juxtaposition of Mayhew's moralistic Victorian analysis conducted in proper gentlemanly style, and the coarse verbatim accounts of his subjects is a sociolinguistic study in itself. The swearing and foul language are comparatively mild, but edited according to the norms of the period: "I'm a drunken old b——if you like, but nothing worser than that"; "[Life's] as sweet for the w——as for the hempress" (Vol. 4, 247); "D——d plucky thing, by Jove to strike a woman" (Vol. 4, 253) Astonishing maps detailed the regional statistics for such offenses as "persons committed for carnally abusing girls," "for keeping disorderly houses," "for attempting to procure the miscarriage of women," for "assaults, with intent to ravish and carnally abuse," for bigamy, and so on. Thus not all sexuality was taboo.

The novelist William Makepeace Thackeray called the period "if not the most moral, certainly the most squeamish." Unlike the verbal robustness of the Elizabethan and Restoration periods, the public language of the Victorian era was celebrated for its propriety and its euphemisms. As the entry for **Charles Dickens** shows, evasions of such words as *damn, hell,* and even *trousers* were very typical of the age, but like **Laurence Sterne**, he enjoyed using obvious euphemisms, actually developing a conniving relationship with his readers. Similarly, Anthony Trollope, whose novels have mainly ecclesiastical settings, shares with the reader the quintessentially Victorian spectacle of self-righteous anger struggling with decorum in Archdeacon Grantly: "'Why not!' almost screamed the archdeacon . . . 'why not!—that pestilent interfering upstart, John Bold—the most vulgar young person I ever met!' . . . And being at a loss for an epithet sufficiently injurious, he finished his expressions of horror by muttering 'Good Heavens!' in a manner that had been found very efficacious in clerical meetings of the diocese" (*The Warden* 1855, chapter 2). In a very different style Thomas Hardy concluded the tragic story of *Tess of the D'Urbervilles* (1891) by referring not to God or Fate, but by the provocative comment that "The President of the Immortals . . . had ended his sport with Tess." Although technically a euphemism, Hardy's divine title is actually blasphemous, amounting to a snub to the Almighty and to notions of Christian Providence.

The Victorian era is famous for its multitudinous sexual euphemisms, preferring "in an interesting condition" to *pregnancy,* "white and brown meat" of a chicken to the *leg* and *breast,* even referring to the *limbs* of a piano. One of Mayhew's informants categorized under the heading of *Bawds,* describes her "fall": "The 'night-cap' was evidently drugged, and during my state of insensibility my ruin was accomplished" (Vol. 4, 247). The use of opaque Latinisms and ingenious metaphors, already developed in the eighteenth century, continued to flourish:

> The tree of Life, then, is a succulent plant, consisting of one only stem, on the top of which is a *pistillum* or *apex,* sometime of a glandiform appearance, and not unlike a May-cherry, though at others seasons more resembling the Avellana or filbeard tree. Its fruits, contrary to most others, grow near the root; they are usually two in number, in size somewhat exceeding that of an ordinary nutmeg, and are both contained in one Siliqua, or purse, which together with the whole root of the plant, is commonly beset with innumerable fibrilla, or capillary tendrils. (from *The Exquisite* 1842)

Not every reader would recognize this as a description of the penis. Those perusing Burton's translation of *The Arabian Nights* (1886) would come across this learned description of the dildo: "Of the penis succadaneus, that imitation of the Arbor vitæ, . . . which the French [call] godemiche" (X, 239).

Within the thriving genre of Victorian pornography the division of registers between rarefied Latin, foreign terms, and frank bawdy is frequently apparent, quintessentially revealed in this description: "I could see the lips of her plump pouting cunny, deliciously feathered, with soft light down, her lovely legs, drawers, stockings, pretty boots, making a *tout ensemble,* which as I write and describe them caused Mr. Priapus to swell in my breeches." The title itself contains the same linguistic mélange: *Sub-Umbra, or Sport Amongst the She-*

Noodles (1879). Other titles were openly salacious: *Lady Pokingham: Or They All Do It* (1880). However, the most notorious work, *My Secret Life* (1890), an extended erotic memoir in eleven volumes by the unidentified "Walter," has all the standard "four letter" words and some unexpected terms like *randy, bumhole,* and *uncunted* set against *love staff* and *spermatic injection* (Mills 1993, 272–73).

There were some notable breaches of decorum by major figures of the age. A composer enthused to Alfred Lord Tennyson: "That's an awfully jolly stanza." "Don't say 'awfully,'" admonished Tennyson. "What shall I say, then?" asked the composer. "Say 'bloody,' replied Tennyson" (Pearsall 1969, 500). (As the entry for **bloody** shows, the word was then extremely improper.) More astonishing is the wild, prurient fantasy found in this letter from Algernon Charles Swinburne to Dante Gabriel Rossetti, dated March 1, 1870:

This is a dildo the Queen used
     Once in a pinch in an office,
Quite unaware that it had *been* used
     First by a housemaid erratic.
Soon, though obese and lymphatic,
     Symptoms she felt all that month as it went on
What sort of parties had used it and spent on.

The spiciness of this wicked scenario is enhanced by *office* being a euphemism for "lavatory" and *spend* including the sense of "ejaculate." Pearsall's study contains a great volume of underground material involving popular bawdy lyrics, obscene puns, and dirty stories involving everybody from the Royal Family down the social scale. Some were obviously designed for the printed page:

C ome love, and dwell with me
U nder the greenwood tree,
N one can more happy be,
T han I shall be if blessed with thee!
(Quoted in Pearsall 1969, 495)

Victorian schizophrenia is symbolized in *The Yellow Book* (1894–1897), a quarterly review containing distinguished literary contributions from Henry James, Max Beerbohm, and Professor George Sainstbury, but also notorious sensual and decadent illustrations by Aubrey Beardsley (1872–1898), famously for Oscar Wilde's *Salome* (1893). Beardsley had worked for one of the major publishers of pornography, Leonard Charles Smithers, to whom he wrote from France where he was dying: "Jesus is our Lord and Judge. I implore you to destroy all copies of Lysistrata and bad drawings . . . by all that is holy all obscene drawings" (cited in Pearsall 1969, 479).

See also: Bloody; Dickens, Charles; Prostitution.

Bibliography

Marcus, Steven. *The Other Victorians*. London: Wiedenfeld and Nicholson, 1966

Marlow, Joyce, *Mr. and Mrs. Gladstone: An Intimate Biography*. London: Wiedenfeld and Nicholson, 1977. 1977

Mayhew, Henry. *London Labour and the London Poor*. London: Charles Griffin and Co., 1851–1862.

Maynard, John. *Victorian Discourses on Sexuality and Religion*. Cambridge: Cambridge University Press, 1993.

Mills, Jane ed. *Bloomsbury Guide to Erotic Literature*. London: Bloomsbury, 1993.

Pearsall, Ronald. *The Worm in the Bud: The World of Victorian Sexuality*. London: Weidenfeld and Nicolson, 1969.

Phillips, K.C. *Language and Class in Victorian England*. Oxford: Basil Blackwell, 1984.

VILLAIN

Originally this very rich term had a class-bound sense, deriving partly from its origin in Latin *villanus,* "a servant at a villa," and partly from its proximity to the cognate term *villein,* "one of the lowest serfs in the Feudal System." Hence the opening of the *Oxford English Dictionary*'s rather class-bound definition: "Originally, a low-born, base-minded rustic; a man of ignoble ideas and instincts; in later use, an unprincipled and depraved scoundrel." The term is a classic instance of C.S. Lewis's brilliant semantic formulation "the moralization of status words" (1960, 21), the process whereby words originally designating low status acquire negative moral senses, and vice versa. Some of the earliest instances are examples of opprobrious address: "Goddys treytour, and ry3t vyleyn!" ("God's traitor, and real villain!") (1303, from Robert of Brunne's *Handlyng Synne,* l. 11,557). Chaucer uses the term extensively some thirty times, often in the phrase "to do a vileynie," while in Shakespeare's works it is by far the most common noun of insult, with nearly three hundred instances, famously in Hamlet's execration of Claudius as a "damned smiling villain" and "treacherous, lecherous, kindless villain!" (I v 106; II ii 617). Such uses extend through to the nineteenth century, the last quotation in the *OED* being from Charles Kingsley's *Westward Ho!* (1855). Since then the personal usage has become obsolete, even in literature.

An early sign of weakening occurs in Shakespeare's *Twelfth Night* (1601), when the libertine Sir Toby Belch says of Maria: "Here comes the little villain" (II v 16). However, in tragic contexts the serious use is still obvious and frequent. The current literary use, as in "the villain of the piece," dates from the early nineteenth century and is still current. Interestingly, in much detective and thriller fiction the villain often turns out to be upper class, seldom "a low-born, base-minded rustic." In recent decades the term has made a minor resurgence, but in slightly coy and self-conscious fashion, such as "We went in search of the villains" or "Beneath his charming exterior, Smith is a bit of a villain." But the old strong personal sense, as in "You damned villain!" has long passed away. The word has never really taken root outside British English.

See also: Moralization of Status Words; Rogue.

Bibliography

Lewis, C.S. *Studies in Words*. Cambridge: Cambridge University Press, 1960.

VIRAGO

The semantic deterioration of this extraordinary term encapsulates the influence of negative stereotypical notions of woman deriving from chauvinist prejudices. Having originally been a personal name of status, *virago* has steadily lost neutrality, becoming first a term for a heroic female warrior or amazon, before acquiring the dominant modern sense of "a bold impudent termagant or scold." *Virago* was in biblical tradition the original name given by Adam to Eve: in the Latin Vulgate version of Genesis 2:23, Adam coins the name from the Latin root *vir* meaning "man," indicating that Eve was "manlike" in the sense of "taken from man," intending no doubt a chauvinist compliment. In the Vulgate the Latin root is obvious: "*Haec vocabitur virago, quoniam de viro sumpta est,*" but this semantic link is lost in the English translation: "She shall be called Virago since she is taken from man." The glossings by Ælfric in Anglo-Saxon about 1000, through John Wycliffe (1388) and William Caxton (1483) up to the Renaissance, show the same problem, so that later translations replaced *virago* with *woman*. However the comment by George Gascoigne in 1576 is significant: "Before she sinned Eva was called Virago, and after she sinned she deserved to be called Eva" (*Droome Doomes Day,* I para. 6).

The positive sense of a female warrior is recorded by the *Oxford English Dictionary* from the fourteenth century to the nineteenth, including this quotation from 1641: "She so ruled as Queen eight years and better; a manlike virago of a stout and noble spirit" (Bishop R. Montagu, *Acts & Monuments,* 361). The negative modern sense has as long a history, being first recorded in Chaucer's *Man of Law's Tale* when the teller launches into a xenophobic and misogynist denunciation:

O Sowdanesse [sultaness], roote of iniquitee!
Virago, thou Semyrame the secounde!
O serpent under femynynytee,
Lik to the serpent depe in helle ybound!
(ll. 358–61)

Semiramis was a quasi-legendary Assyrian queen epitomizing ambition, treachery, and sexual rapacity. The symbolism of the serpent is also significant, drawing on the ancient prejudicial stereotype of Eve and the Devil as co-deceivers of Adam in the Garden of Eden. In some depictions of the Fall, notably that by the Limbourg brothers in the *Tres Riche Heures* of the Duc du Berry (ca. 1350), Eve is painted as a serpent with a woman's face.

All the quotations in the *OED* come from male authors, and most show clear hostility to the notion of a powerful, manlike woman. They include William Cowper's comment in a letter of 1781: "I really think the Russian virago [Catherine the Great] an impertinent puss for meddling with us" (March 5) and Edmund Burke's ironic observation that "No heroine from Billingsgate can go beyond the patriotic scolding of our republican virago" (1770, *Correspondence* I, 230). The most extreme instance is from Jeremy Taylor's comment from 1621: "Like shameless double-sexed *Hermaphrodites,* Virago Roaring Girls" (*Superb Flagellum* C vi). (**Roaring** previously had a special sense.) *Virago* could, rarely, be used of a man, though the instance in *Twelfth Night* is probably a theatrical in-joke: Sir Toby Belch mischievously describes Viola, actually the unwilling participant in a duel, as "a very devil, . . . a firago" (III iv 300). The dramatic irony is that Viola is a male actor in disguise. *Virago,* like *shrew,* now encapsulates all the negative and threatening stereotypes of an aggressive, turbulent woman.

See also: Women, Stereotypes of.

Bibliography

Mills, Jane. *Womanwords*. London: Virago, 1991.

WAR

"War is the greatest excitant of new vocabulary," observed Eric Partridge (1948, 115). Apart from the technical neologisms, it is the social context of war hysteria, especially acute xenophobia, that obviously generates negative stereotypes, opprobrious names, and ethnic slurs for the enemy. Thus a considerable number of prime examples are to be found under the headings for **French, Germans,** and **Japanese.** Others, such as ***gook*** and ***hun*** have their own entries. Of these, *hun* is unique, being first publicized by the Germans themselves, in 1900. A general semantic consequence of war, covered in **soldiers and sailors**, is that slurs and swearwords are given wider currency in society by civilians returning from the hostilities.

The earliest instance, a memorial of the Hundred Years' War, is *goddems,* the revealing nickname given by the French to the English, a point treated further in the entry for **goddam.** The typical generation of nicknames for the enemy is shown in the German group from World War I: *boche* (1914), *Fritz* (1915), *kraut* (1918), and *jerry* (1919). *Hitler* was used as a stereotypical nickname from 1934, often preceded by the demeaning adjective *little,* a description still current in British English. Alternatively, *jap* and *gook* were originally generalized nicknames before taking on an especially xenophobic edge during World War II and the Vietnam War, respectively.

Sometimes words become drawn randomly into a specialized emotive sense by the context of war. Thus *by Jingo!,* a piece of "sonorous nonsense," was variously interpreted as conjurors' gibberish and a minced oath from the seventeenth century. However in 1878 it suddenly became a bellicose rallying cry for supporters of British prime minister Benjamin Disraeli's policy of "active intervention" in the Balkans, largely through the popular music-hall song by George Hunt with its topical refrain: "We don't want to fight, But by Jingo! if we do, We've got the ships, we've got the men, We've got the money too!" The phrase rapidly spawned the related forms *jingo, jingodom,* the verb *to jingo,* as well as *jingoism* and *jingoist,* both still current and critical of aggressive and chauvinist attitudes. During the Boer War (1899–1902) even the uniform term *khaki* took on the symbolic and figurative sense of "possessed by a militant spirit," expanding into other forms and phrases like *khaki election* (of 1902) and to *vote khaki. Chauvinist* itself is an eponym deriving from an idolatrous worshipper of Napoleon, Nicolas Chauvin, whose excessive patriotism was satirized in a play,

Among the categories of new words generated by war are opprobrious names for the enemy, such as *huns* (and others) for Germans during World War I. Such terms are commonly associated with negative stereotypes for propaganda purposes. (Library of Congress, LC-USZC4-10331)

Le Cocarde Tricolore (1831). Both *Chauvinist* and *Chauvinism* were borrowed into English from 1870 referring to exaggerated and bellicose patriotism. Stereotypical national figures like John Bull and Uncle Sam tend to take on martial connotations in times of war. *John Bullism* developed such a currency throughout the nineteenth century when British colonial expansionism was rampant. The iconic figure of Uncle Sam has been used in a similar fashion, both patriotically and xenophobically. **Yankee**, which has its own entry, was first used of the northern states, but as Mencken points out, "During the Civil War, as everyone knows, the Southerners used [*Yankee*], usually contemptuously, of all Northerners" (1963, 122). In times of martial solidarity, treachery and collaboration become obviously detestable, generating eponyms like *Quisling* and *Haw Haw* (the English Nazi propagandist William Joyce) discussed further under **treachery**.

See also: French, the; Germans; Goddam/Goddamn; Gook; Hun; Japanese, the; Treachery; Xenophobia; Yankee.

Bibliography

Hughes, Geoffrey. *History of English Words*. Oxford: Blackwell, 2000.
Mencken, H.L. *The American Language*. New York: Knopf, 1963.
Partridge, Eric. *Words at War, Words at Peace*. London: Muller, 1948.

WEBSTER AND HIS DICTIONARIES

Webster's has become a term of authority in American English and a generic trade name for a whole lexicographical stable deriving from the initiatives of the founding father and great champion of America's linguistic independence, Noah Webster (1758–1843). The major milestones in this huge enterprise were *Webster I*, edited by Webster himself (1828), *Webster II*, edited by William Allan Neilson (1934), and *Webster III*, edited by Philip Gove (1961). Webster in fact styled his first edition *An American Dictionary of the English Language*, while the Second and Third adopted his name, becoming *Webster's New International Dictionary*. (*Websterian* had become an eponym for his enterprise even by 1790.) While the first two editions were greeted with critical acclaim, the third generated a furious controversy involving a number of substantial literary figures and academics.

Noah Webster was astonishingly industrious, producing in addition to his *American Dictionary*, *An American Spelling Book* (1783) and *A Compendious Dictionary of the English Language* (1806), all of which went through numerous editions. He had a great range of interests, being "active as grammarian, lexicographer, essayist, newspaper editor, educator, lawyer, politician, farmer and . . . scientific observer" (Krapp 1925, 368). Sir James Murray, editor of the *Oxford English Dictionary*, praised him in *The Evolution of English Lexicography* as "a great man, a born definer of words" (1900, 43). H.L. Mencken characterized him less favorably: "There was nothing of the traditional pedagogue about him—no sign of caution, policy, mousiness. He launched his numerous reforms and innovations with great boldness, and defended them in a forthright and often raucous manner. . . . It was almost impossible for him to imagine himself in error" (1963, 13). Webster criticized somewhat cavalierly distinguished predecessors like **Dr. Samuel Johnson** and Sir William Jones, and was ignorant of current developments in comparative philology, so that in etymology his work "illustrates the extreme isolation and provincialism of American scholarship in the early years of the nineteenth century" (Krapp 1925, 365).

Webster had written that "The business of the lexicographer is to collect, arrange, and define as far as possible, *all* the words that belong to a language" and had criticized "the man who undertakes to censure others for the use of certain words" for "seeming to arrogate to himself a dictatorial authority" (cited in Warfel, ed., 1953, 350, 367). Yet he had an undoubtedly puritanical streak, criticizing those English dictionaries that "contain obscene and vulgar terms, improper to be repeated before children" (Krapp 1925, 361–62). In particular he castigated Johnson's inclusion of what he called "vulgar words and offensive ribaldry," arguing that "the national language and the national morals are corrupted and debased" (Green 1996, 258). Although Johnson had included most of the "excretory" four-letter words without qualms or comment, he had drawn the line at *fuck* and *cunt*, unlike his predecessor Nathaniel Bailey. Webster proved to be more squeamish—for example, defining *sodomy* euphemistically as "a crime against nature." In his later years he turned to editing the Bible (1833), writing "I consider this . . . the most important enterprise of my life." This he bowdlerized thoroughly, excising words like *womb* and generating such quaint euphemisms as "peculiar members" for *stones* (i.e., testicles), preferring *lewdness* for "fornication," while the graphic phrase *to give suck* became "to nourish." Mencken claimed that "he expunged many verses altogether" (1936, 303). According to his granddaughter, "the words *stink, suck, dung* [and] *belly* . . . fell before his hand." She recorded in some reminiscences: "In my many months of residence with him I never saw him roused to anger but once, and that was when a dubious and rather indelicate word was mentioned before him" (Read 1934, 273).

The *Third Edition* started with the search for an editor upon the death of Neilson in 1946 and took six years. The editor-elect, Dr. Philip Gove, was not a distinguished authority, but had a sound academic background with research on Johnson's *Dictionary*. Unlike Webster and Murray, Gove was not a polymath; like all modern editors, he delegated and expected the team to follow set procedures. He detested time-wasting, severely limited the role of the editorial board in discussion, but brought out the *Third Edition* in ten years as scheduled, a notable feat in lexicography. Gove proposed a "complete and detailed scrutiny of every feature" and a radical reduction of the encyclopedic material to make way for about 100,000 new words and meanings. The policy statement envisioned "primarily a *Dictionary of the Standard Language* as used throughout the English speaking world" (Morton 1994, 62).

The launch of the *Webster III* in September 1961 generated a lexicographical controversy of unique ferocity, mainly deriving from the perception that the dictionary had adopted a *laissez faire* policy in matters of usage, thereby abandoning its assumed role as arbiter and authority in setting the standard. In so doing, the Webster team had, in the eyes of its critics, kowtowed to the current "permissive school" of descriptive linguistics. The treatment of slang was especially criticized on the grounds that "slang labels were not used enough and they were not applied consistently" (Morton 1994, 248). A notably vehement and revealing series of tirades attacked the entry on *ain't*. The details and texts of the main exchanges are collected in an ironically titled casebook, *Dictionaries and THAT Dictionary*, edited by James Sledd and Wilma Ebbitt (1962).

However, there were other inconsistencies indicating that the Third was not truly "permissive" either. The work excluded *fuck*, then starting to emerge in general currency, but included *cunt*, which was (and is) far more taboo, with the curiously mild usage note "usually considered obscene." (In fairness to Gove, *fuck* was excised at galley stage by Gordon J. Gallan, then president of Merriam-Webster.) Less surprisingly, *motherfucker* was also excluded. At the time these omissions attracted little comment, although they showed that there was no clear policy on obscene language.

On another front, the usage markers concerning religious, racial, and ethnic entries were criticized in an article by Philip Perlmutter, "Prejudice Memorialized," in *Frontier* magazine in 1965. Perlmutter noted that entries for *kike, dago, nigger, spick, sheeny*, and *coon* were followed by the usage note "usually taken to be offensive." He objected that this was a "strange explanation" in that it suggested that the word itself is essentially neutral. "Taking offense implies an innocence on the part of the speaker and a sensitivity, if not fault, on the part of the listener," thus carrying the implication that "the words are free of any offending characteristics" (Morton 1994, 237–38). Perlmutter also questioned on what basis the editors had arrived at the distinction between "usually" and "often taken to be offensive."

While Perlmutter's basic observation is sound, there is a semantic distinction between "taking offense" and "usually taken to be offensive." Second, the degree of offense usually depends on the speaker and the context, in view of the phenomenon of **reclamation of opprobrious terms** whereby offensive or stigmatizing labels and ethnic slurs are often used by outgroups within the group in an ironic or affectionate fashion. However, Perlmutter was on stronger ground in preferring the usage marker "usually used disparagingly" found in the entries for *papist* and *wop*. More disturbing were the definitions for *Jesuit*, "one given to intrigue and equivocation," and *Jew*, "a person believed to drive a hard bargain," neither of which carried any usage marker. As Herbert C. Morton sums up the lexicographical problem, "Gove had not set out to offend any minority group. . . . But he had not thought of putting the onus on the speaker rather than the hearer" (1994, 237–38).

The sensitivity surrounding ethnic slurs led to two responses. The editor-in-chief of *Webster's New World Dictionary*, Second College Edition (1970), Dr. David B. Guralnik, simply excluded terms such as *kike, dago, wog*, and *wop*, justifying the policy in the following editorial statement:

> It was decided in the selection process that this dictionary could easily dispense with those true obscenities, the terms of racial or ethnic opprobrium, that are in any case encountered with less frequency nowadays.
> (Foreward, viii)

Outside the Webster stable, Dr. Robert L. Chapman, the editor of *The New Dictionary of American Slang* (1986), instituted usage markers in the form of symbolic triangles, outlined (△) for obscene words and solid black (▲) for taboo terms "never to be used." He categorized "terms of contempt and derision for racial and other groups" as taboo.

In contrast to the serious setback suffered in the launch of *Webster III* in the United

States, the work was well reviewed in Britain by major scholars. In retrospect, it seems to have suffered from a misguided publicity campaign that positioned the work wrongly in a hostile climate of opinion. However, the editor of the *OED Supplement,* Robert Burchfield, commented that Gove had an "over-literal interpretation of the function of a dictionary as a record of usage rather than as a prescriptive guide" (Morton 1994, 248).

See also: Bowdlerization; Dictionaries; Ethnic Insults; Johnson, Dr. Samuel; Reclamation of Opprobrious Terms.

Bibliography

Green, Jonathan. *Chasing the Sun.* London: Jonathan Cape, 1996.
Krapp, George Philip. "American Dictionaries." In *The English Language in America.* 2 vols. New York: Century, 1925.
Mencken, H.L. *The American Language.* Abridged by Raven I. McDavid Jr. New York: Knopf, 1963.
Morton, Herbert C. *The Story of Webster's Third.* Cambridge: Cambridge University Press, 1994.
Murray, Sir James. *The Evolution of English Lexicography.* Oxford: Oxford University Press, 1900.
Perlmutter, Philip. "Prejudice Memorialized." *Frontier,* September 1965.
Read, Walter Allen. "Noah Webster as Euphemist." *Dialect Notes,* Vol. VI, Part VIII, 1934.
Sledd, James H., and Wilma R. Ebbitt. *Dictionaries and THAT Dictionary.* Chicago: Scott, Foresman, 1962.
Warfel, Harry R. *Noah Webster, Schoolmaster to America.* New York: MacMillan, 1936.
———, ed. *Letters of Noah Webster.* New York: Library Publishers, 1953.

WELSH

It is a prevalent feature of the history of the British Isles that as the English have become dominant, they have created stigmatic stereotypes and mildly insulting nicknames for the original Celtic peoples, namely the Scots, the Irish, and the Welsh. In the language of the Anglo-Saxon invaders, the name of the *Welsh,* namely *wealas,* originally meant "a Celt or a Briton," but then, reflecting the changing power relations and considerable arrogance, came to mean "a foreigner," after which a cognate verb *wealian* developed the meaning "to behave immorally." This semantic deterioration is also found in *barbarian.*

The dominant stereotypical qualities attributed to the Welsh are backwardness, slyness, treachery, and dishonesty. The process started early, in Walter Map's description of the people in the twelfth century: "They are treacherous to each other as well as to foreigners, covet freedom, neglect peace" (L'Estrange 2002, 199). The *Description of Wales* by Giraldus Cambrensis ("Gerald the Welshman," 1194) added: "It is because of their sins, and more particularly their detestable vice of homosexuality, that the Welsh were punished by God and so lost first Troy and the Britain." (Giraldus was subscribing to the popular myth that Britain had been founded by Aeneas after the fall of Troy.) A dictionary of 1785 gave Wales the nickname of Itchland, referring ironically to the prevalence of lice. (The same name was subsequently given to Scotland.) Francis Grose's *Classical Dictionary of the Vulgar Tongue* (1796) included the previous definition and *Welsh comb* for "the thumb and four fingers." *Taffy,* the nickname for a Welshman, derived from Daffyd, the Welsh for David, is first recorded in a slang dictionary of 1700, and has become well known in the English nursery rhyme:

Taffy was a Welshman, Taffy was a thief
Taffy came into my house and stole a side of beef.

Self-mocking criticism is a feature of the Welsh, as with the Irish. "This arsehole of the universe . . . this . . . fond sad Wales" comes from a letter by Dylan Thomas (July 17, 1950).

There is, incidentally, no connection with the verb "to welsh" meaning "to swindle or cheat," recorded from about 1857, especially used in the context of horse racing and absconding bookmakers. However, the close connection is such that prominent politicians—for example, former president Bill Clinton—have been known to apologize for any offense that might be caused by using the word.

See also: Blason Populaire; Irish, the.

Bibliography
Cambrensis, Giraldus. *The Itinerary Through Wales.* London: Dent, 1909.
L'Estrange, Julian. *The Big Book of National Insults.* London: Cassell, 2002.

WHITEHOUSE, MRS. MARY

Mrs. Mary Whitehouse (1910–2001) was a moral crusader who mobilized opposition against the increasing volume of sex, violence, and bad language on British television in the post-*Chatterley* era. Insisting on the harmful effects of such material on the young and on the moral fiber of the nation, she mounted a high-profile campaign against the British Broadcasting Corporation (B.B.C.) and the Independent Television Authority (I.T.A.). A retired teacher and housewife, she organized national petitions, Private Members' Bills in Parliament, private lawsuits, and used personal criticism, notably of Sir Hugh Greene, director general of the B.B.C. (1960–1969) whom she attacked as "the man I hold most responsible for the moral collapse in this country." In 1965 she formed an organization initially called "Clean Up TV," which had 165,000 paid-up members, and within a year she claimed to have won the support of "half a million housewives, the Chief Constables of Britain, MPs, bishops, leaders of all churches, city councils and people of standing throughout the country." The following year the organization was renamed the National Viewers' and Listeners' Association, and in 2001 mediawatch-uk.

Historically the stance of Mrs. Whitehouse is paralleled by that of Jeremy **Collier**, the author of the broadside *A Short View of the Profaneness and Immorality of the English Stage* (1698). Mrs. Whitehouse showed the same qualities of determined articulate Puritanism. Although regarded as narrow and obsessional, satirized, and pilloried, she was a formidable opponent and robust debater, who in 1986 carried the motion for debate in the Cambridge University Union that censorship was a lesser evil than pornography by 331 votes to 151. The B.B.C. would not allow her on its programs, and Sir Hugh Greene refused to see her.

She and her organization could claim a number of successes, such as the withdrawal of the sitcom "Till Death Do Us Part" in February 1968 and a conviction against *Gay News* for **blasphemy** in 1977. Her objection to Stanley Kubrick's film *A Clockwork Orange* (1971) led to the director withdrawing the film from showing in Britain. She was influential in the generation of various pieces of legislation, including The Protection of Children Act (1978), the Indecent Displays Act (1981), the Video Recordings Act (1984), and most important, that establishing the Broadcasting Standards Council (1988). The Council monitors programs and issues reports on "the portrayal of violence, sexual conduct and matters of taste and decency." She was awarded the CBE (Commander of the British Empire) in 1980, and in 1989 both the Archbishop of Canterbury and the prime minister publicly thanked her for her "indefatigable work." She represented what the *Daily Telegraph* called in its obituary "the puritan heart of Britain," and to Professor Richard Hoggart she was "the authentic voice of middle England" (*The Guardian,* November 24, 2001).

However, despite these successes and the constant pressure forcing broadcasters to justify their programs, the campaign failed in its general aim to clean up television. The Archive of the National Viewers' and Listeners' Association (NVALA) is held at the Albert Sloman Library, University of Essex.

See also: Blasphemy; Broadcasting; Collier Controversy.

Bibliography

Tracey, Michael, and David Morison. *Whitehouse.* London: MacMillian, 1979.
Whitehouse, Mary. *Cleaning up TV.* London: Blandford Press, 1967.

WHORE AND WHORESON

This ancient and enduring term is one of the few insulting epithets that has never lost its power, whether used in the older narrow sense of "prostitute" or more generally, in the words of the *Oxford English Dictionary* of "an unchaste or lewd woman; a fornicatress or adulteress." Other strong terms like *bitch, bastard,* and *bugger* have all acquired humorous, ironic, or jocular tones, but *whore* remains powerfully condemning. As the entry for **prostitutes** shows, numerous synonyms like *harlot, concubine, strumpet,* and *quean* have become part of the word-field, but most are now archaic. The emotive power of *whore* also explains the need for a steady supply of euphemisms, such as the modern *escort* and the more recent *sexworker* (1982), styling the person neutrally as a labor unit. There are many archaic compounds, such as *whoremonger* and *whoreson,* as well as male forms such as *he-whore.* A recent development has been the extended use to anyone who sells out their principles, found in P.J. O'Rourke's polemical title *The Parliament of Whores* (1991).

Although found in Anglo-Saxon, *whore* is recorded late in comparison with the related Germanic languages. The etymology is fascinating, since *whore* has cognate forms in Latin *carus,* "dear," and Old Irish *cara,* "a friend." It first appears in the form *hore,* subsequently *huir,* indicating the pronunciation "hoor" or "hooer," which continued into the nineteenth century, and as the *OED* noted, "may be adopted . . . when we wish to soften the effect of a coarse word." The spelling with *wh-* became current in the sixteenth century.

Surprisingly, the term occurs only once in the works of Geoffrey Chaucer, but not in the *Canterbury Tales,* where the less critical *concubine* is used. The main concentrations in Shakespeare

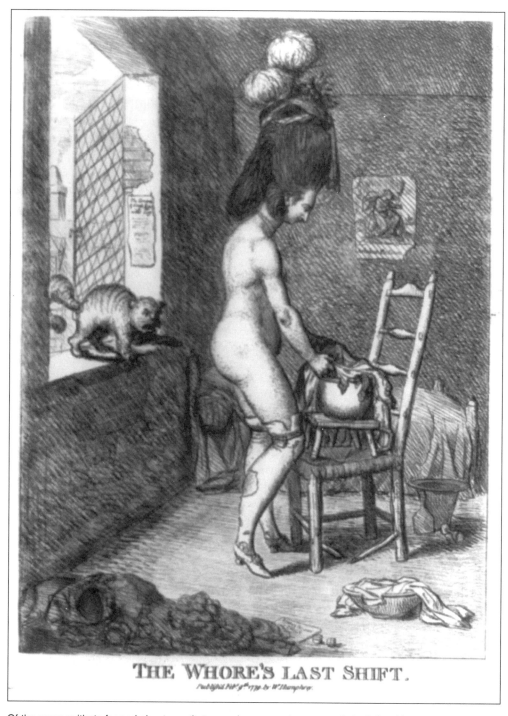

THE WHORE'S LAST SHIFT.

Publish'd Feb'y 9th 1779 by W. Humphrey.

Of the many epithets for and about prostitutes, perhaps none is more enduringly insulting or more emotively powerful than "whore." Only recently has its meaning been extended to anyone who sells out their principles. (Library of Congress, LC-USZ62-85713) are, expectedly, in the tragic context of *Othello* (1604) and the cynical ambiance of *Troilus and Cressida* (1606). The translators of the *King James Bible* (1611) used the term copiously. The generalized sense is recorded from about 1200 in such graphic quotations as this from Layamon: "He slew Zabri . . . His hore binede and him abuven" (*Genesis and Exodus*, l. 4082). The abusive meanings refer to a concubine, kept mistress, or even a catamite. In this context an interesting legal repercussion is recorded in 1547: "Marioun Ray amerciat [fined] for trubling Agnes Hendersoun, calland [calling] her huir and theiff" (*The Borough Records of Stirling* I. 48). However, a judgment of 1703 (still cited in 1817) ruled that "Calling a married woman or a single one a whore is not actionable, because fornication or adultery are subjects of spiritual not temporal censures" (Selwyn, *Law Nisi Prius* II., 1160). In *Troilus and Cressida* the provocatively candid Fool Thersites refers to Patroclus as the "masculine whore" of Achilles (V i 20), while in 1694, Sir Peter Motteux's translation of Rabelais includes the ingenious coinage "he-whore" (*Pantagruel* v. 237).

During the bitter Reformation controversies, the Catholic Church was frequently stigmatized as the "Whore of Babylon." William Tyndale, denouncing the "the greate baude the hore of Babylon," was referring to the Pope (1530, in *Practical Prelates*). Two hundred years later Horace Walpole still mischievously alluded to the phrase, but used the contemporary euphemism *w———*. *Whoredom* became part of the vocabulary of religious abuse, referring to idolatry. Together with *whoremonger* and *whoremaster,* which meant "one who keeps or frequents with whores," it was originally a powerful term of abuse before becoming generalized, especially in the cynical Restoration comedies, and finally obsolete.

Whoreson, dating from the fourteenth century, was originally a strong insult: "He despised the gretteste lordes . . . , and called Sir Robert Clare Earl of Gloucester, 'Horeson'" (Layamon's *Brut,* ca. 1400, I, 207). Being a loan translation of Anglo-Norman *fitz a putain,* "son of a whore," it is first recorded in a literal and highly provocative sense. However, by the late fifteenth century it had clearly lost intensity, for in William Caxton's *Reynard* (1481) there is a reference to "the false horeson the foxe" (xxi l. 53). Thomas Wilson's authoritative *Rhetoric* (1553) gives this amusing and revealing instance: "The mother being merelye [merrily] disposed, wyll saye to her swete Sonne: Ah you little horeson" (79). This is clearly the equivalent of the modern familiar "Ah you little bastard."

The grave digger in *Hamlet* (1604) refers to his dead friend Yorick affectionately as "a whoreson mad fellow" (V i 191), and in *King Lear* there is the amusing personal insult: "Thou whoreson zed, thou unnecessary letter" (II i 64). By the Restoration the term was clearly overused and dated: the revealingly titled *Character of a Town Gallant* (Anonymous 1675) noted: "He admires the Eloquence of Son of a Whore, . . . and therefore applyes it to everything, so that if his pipe be faulty . . . tis a Son of a Whore Pipe" (5).

In American English *whore* was previously avoided, notably by Noah Webster in his edition of the Bible (1833) and was forbidden by the Motion Picture Production Code (1930). H.L. Mencken discusses the taboo in "Forbidden Words" (1963, 360–61) The Black English variant form *ho* (pronounced to rhyme with "hoe") is recorded from 1958 and has become widely used in the generalized sense of "a loose woman," generating a number of compounds.

See also: Promiscuity; Prostitutes.

Bibliography

Fisher, Trevor. *Prostitution and the Victorians.* New York: St. Martin's, 1997.

Mencken, H.L. *The American Language.* New York: Knopf, 1963.

WITCH

The word's earliest application are, surprisingly, to males, a sense recorded from about 890 up to the early twentieth century. It was used of Pharaoh's magicians in the Book of Exodus, of Merlin, and even of Christ in William Langland's account of the Crucifixion in *Piers Plowman* (ca. 1362): "'Crucifige,' quod a cacchepole, 'I warrant him a witch.'" ("'Crucify him,' said a debt collector, 'I guarantee he's a witch,'" (B Text, xviii, l. 46). The male sense is now obsolete, having been superseded by the diverse modern terms *witch doctor, wizard,* and *warlock.* While *wizard* has become entirely positive, *warlock* had in Anglo-Saxon the various senses of "oath breaker," "traitor," "wicked person," "devil," and "the Devil or Satan," leading to the dominant modern meaning of "one in league with the Devil."

The dominant feminine sense of *witch* is almost as old as the male, extending from late Old English to the present. The *Legend of St. Catherine* (ca. 1290) prescribes: "You shall bind a witch fast and immediately strike off her head" (100). However, Joseph Addison, writing in 1711, gives an expectedly rational explanation: "When an old Woman begins to doat, and grow chargeable to a parish, she is generally turned into a Witch" (*Spectator,* 117). The Salem (Massachusetts) witch-hunt, occurring so bizarrely at a time of comparative enlightenment (1692), has left the memorial phrase in New England "to be as nervous as a witch."

Unlike *dragon, harpy,* and *hag,* which show the stereotype of the feminization of the monstrous by means of malicious or humorous metaphor, *witch* is in origin a literal term with a serious diabolical denotation. Thus a woman accused of being a witch faced in the past terrifying consequences, even being burnt alive. According to Jane Mills, "Some estimates put the number of witches burnt, hanged or drowned as high as nine million" (1991, 264).

The historical evidence of the use of *witch* presents a problem of assessing how literally the term is to be taken, in view of the different motives of the observers, varying from early superstition, through the credulous persecution of the Inquisition, to the skepticism of the Enlightenment. Thus witchcraft is specifically prohibited in the Anglo-Saxon *Laws of Athelstan* (ca. 935, I vi), and a medieval text states: "His wife changed him through witchcraft into the shape of a wolf" (ca. 1350, *Will. Palerne,* l. 4044). Thomas Hobbes, skeptical in most things, asserted in 1651: "As for witches, I think not that their witchcraft is any real power" (*Leviathan,* I ii, 7). Yet William Blackstone, the great English legal authority, insisted in 1769: "To deny the possibility of the existence of witchcraft or sorcery, is to contradict the revealed word of God" (*Commentaries,* IV iv, 61). Apart from survivals of the supernatural association in popular culture, the term has now become largely part of folklore. Even so, it remains a powerful and provocative insult.

The stereotype of seductiveness, which the Inquisition and subsequent witch-hunts projected as demoniality or unnatural sexual intercourse with the Devil in the attractive human forms of incubi and succubi, has since been mollified into one of plain eroticism. There has also developed a division on the basis of age: the category of the repulsive *old witch* is recorded from the fifteenth century, joined by the opposing sense of "a young woman of bewitching aspect or manners" from about 1740 in Samuel Richardson's novel *Pamela* (I xxiv 37). Various feminist writers, such as Anne Oakley (1976), have interpreted the persecution of witches as the eradication of paganism and the targeting of female victims by male-dominated callings like the Church and professions, notably medicine.

See also: Feminization of Terms; Women, Stereotypes of.

Bibliography

Durston, Gregory. *Witchcraft and Witch Trials.* Chichester: Barry Rose Law, 2000.
Karlsen, Carol F. *The Devil in the Shape of a Woman.* New York: Vintage Books, 1989.
Kieckfefer, Richard. *European Witch Trials.* Berkeley: University of California Press, 1976.
Mills, Jane. *Womanwords.* London: Virago, 1991.
Oakley, Anne. "Wisewoman and Medicine Man." In *The Rights and Wrongs of Women,* ed. J. Mitchell and A. Oakley. Harmondsworth: Penguin, 1976.

WOG

This highly insulting term for a foreigner is confined almost entirely to British usage, although it has a minor currency in Australian English. Recorded from 1929, it was originally used only of people of color, especially Arabs and blacks. But in recent decades *wog* has subsequently been applied in a general xenophobic way to any foreigner (just as *gook* in American English has been applied to Asians). The common saying "the wogs begin at Dover" encapsulates the worldview behind the usage (*Times Literary Supplement,* April 11, 1958). The aspect of color is important, since *wog* would not be used, say, of Scandinavians or Slavs.

The origin is uncertain, the *Oxford English Dictionary* commenting that the form is "often said to be an acronym" (the principal claimant being "worthy oriental gentleman"), but the authority continues: "none of the many suggested etymologies is satisfactorily supported by the evidence." A remote possibility is the abbreviation of the term *gollywog,* dating from the late nineteenth century. The word is sufficiently inflammatory for personal use to be avoided, as is shown in this instance from 1973: "Judge Sheldon heard that the trouble started when the girlfriends of coloured soldiers . . . were taunted by members of the Royal Scots as 'wog lovers'" (*Daily Telegraph,* May 31, 3). For the same reason, the word has never been "adopted" or "reclaimed" by the targeted foreigners, in the way that *nigger* has.

See also: Blacks.

WOMEN, STEREOTYPES OF

The historical evolution of the word-field for women has produced an extreme dichotomy or binary opposition between a few terms of praise, such as *virgin, maiden, treasure, angel,* and *goddess,* set against a multitude of derogatory terms, of which **bitch, fishwife, quean, queen, scold, shrew, virago, witch,** and **whore** have their own expanded entries. This division, often termed the angel/whore dichotomy, is conspicuously apparent from the Middle Ages onward, and the imbalance has attracted much critical attention in recent decades, notably from feminists. In many ways it continues to this day.

A number of scholars have also noted the trend of deterioration or pejoration in terms relating to women, some attributing it to malicious innuendo, possibly misogynistic in origin, others to false delicacy or tactful vagueness. The first was Michel Bréal, the founding father of the modern study of semantics, in 1897: "The so-called pejorative tendency has yet another cause. It is in the nature of human malice to take pleasure in looking for a vice or fault behind a quality. . . .We remember what a noble signification *amant* [lover] and *maîtresse* [mistress] still possessed in Corneille. But they are dethroned" (1900, 101). (Pierre Corneille (1606–1684) was a major French dramatist.) Stephen Ullmann commented on the same trend in English, French, and German: "Thus the notorious deterioration which has affected various words for 'girl' or 'woman,' such as English *hussy, quean,* French *fille, garce,* or German *Dirne,* was no doubt due to genuine or pseudo-euphemism rather than to any anti-feminine bias" (1964, 90–91). This topic has become part of a broader debate in recent decades in which feminists have argued that the trend derives from language being generated in a "patriarchal" or "phallocratic" dispensation, thus being the product of male prejudices. See especially the cited works by Greer (1970), Sontag, (1973), Schulz (1975), Miller and Swift (1977), Spender (1980), Coates (1986), Cameron (1990), Hughes (1991), and Mills (1991). Most of the definitions in the ensuing discussion are by men.

Resonating behind the angel/whore dichotomy are deeply embedded stereotypes and role models, especially the figures of Eve and Mary, referred to by the medievalist Sheila Delany as "the opposed exemplars of the feminine character" (1974, 68). Significantly, the role of Eve is symbolically continued at the tableaux of the Crucifixion, by the fallen Mary Magdalene, the maudlin prostitute, placed in moral juxtaposition to the Blessed Virgin Mary, the object of *Mariolatry,* or worship of the Virgin to the point of idolatry. The role of Eve in the Fall became the doctrinal root of a great medieval misogynist tradition, taking the form of collections like the "booke of wykked wives" which Chaucer's Wife of Bath found so provocative (*Prologue,* ll. 669–793). Even the amiable Nun's Priest indulges in the *jeu d'esprit* that

Wommennes conseil [advice] broght us first to wo
And made Adam fro Paradys to go.
(*Nun's Priest's Tale,* ll. 3256–66)

Furthermore, the origin of *woman,* which in fact lies in Anglo-Saxon *wifmann,* shows a number of prejudicial interventions or folk etymologies. As the *Oxford English Dictionary* notes, the word was used "in the sixteenth and seventeenth centuries frequently with play on pseudo-etymological associations with *woe.*" The first instance is given from the Chester plays (ca. 1500), where there is a pun on "man's woe," followed by the comment of the noted humanist Sir Thomas More in *Comfort Against Tribulation* (1534): "Man himself that is borne of a woman is indeed a woman, that is full of wo and miserie." Other similar quotations are recorded up to 1653, including a number of chauvinist proverbs, such as: "Woman,

Asse and walnut tree, the More you beat, the better be" (1639, in J. Clarke, *Paraemiologia or Proverbs English and Latin,* 117).

Whereas medieval romance is largely "gynocentric," or centered on love and women, Anglo-Saxon literature was predominantly "androcentric" or male-centered, being preoccupied with war and heroism. Consequently, women do not feature significantly: Beowulf's love life is never touched on, even remotely. By and large, Anglo-Saxon attitudes toward women were feudal: the lower orders are virtually unmentioned, while noblewomen appear principally in the role of queenly consort (*heaslgebedda*), often used as peacemakers in the weaving of diplomatic alliances encapsulated in the terms *freodowebbe,* literally "peace-weaver," and *fridusibb folca,* "peace-pledge of the people." A misogynist tradition was not obvious, although the legend of Orpheus and Eurydice in King Alfred's translation of Boethius has an odd monkish gloss whereby Eurydice is interpreted allegorically as symbolizing the hellish sins that man must renounce. The Anglo-Saxon word-field for women has the positive terms *lady, darling,* and *maiden,* counterbalanced by two negative terms, *whore* and *witch,* although the earliest applications of *witch* are to males. The Anglo-Saxon evidence seems thus to dispute the common feminist view that the prejudicial imbalance of epithets derives in essence from a phallocratic or male dominated dispensation.

From the medieval period onward the profundity of the stereotypical dichotomy becomes very apparent. In the Prologue to Chaucer's *Canterbury Tales* the only two developed portraits of women are binary opposites: the virginal, precious, ladylike Prioress (ll. 118–62) and the much-married, aggressive, heretical, and sexually predatory Wife of Bath, a potent combination of Venus and Mars (ll. 445–76). Furthermore, these opposing stereotypes are also immediately apparent in the heroines of the first two tales, the idealized angelic, virginal Emily of the *Knight's Tale,* and Alison, the vibrantly physical, sly, eager adulteress of the *Miller's Tale.* Within Shakespeare's gallery of women the two antitypes are also clearly apparent: the virginal or purely innocent, exemplified by Hero in *Much Ado About Nothing,* Ophelia in *Hamlet,* Desdemona in *Othello,* Isabella in *Measure for Measure,* and Hermione in *The Winter's Tale.* Contrasted with them are the sexually corrupt Cressida, Goneril and Regan and the various madams, such as Mistress Quickly and Overdone, in the comedies. There are also the ruthless viragos: Tamora in *Titus Andronicus,* Margaret in *Richard III,* Volumnia in *Coriolanus,* and the unmanageable, therefore unmarriageable Katharina the Shrew. In Cleopatra alone, Shakespeare counterpoints two extreme languages, the mythic paean and the insult of the street. The queen who wears the regalia of the goddess Isis (and Antony's "sword Philippic") and who is praised as surpassing both Nature and fancy, is also degraded as a quean, as *strumpet, a dish, a right gypsy* [playing] *at fast and loose* (*Antony and Cleopatra* I i 13; III vi 67; IV xii 13; IV xii 28). In places Shakespeare daringly juxtaposes the two idioms, creating oxymorons like "royal wench" and "my serpent of old Nile" (II ii 235 and I v 25).

The emphasis on promiscuity and its semantic correlatives are covered in the entries for **promiscuity** and **prostitutes,** which detail numerous terms of abuse. Their antitype is the superhuman spiritual creature of salvation, found in terms like *angel, goddess,* and *madonna.* The woman castigated in animal terms is defined in *bitch, vixen, cow,* and *sow,* alternatively patronised as *mouse, pet,* and *lamb.*

A potent stereotype emerging from these words might be called "the feminization of the monstrous": woman is categorized as alien, the recipient or agent of diabolical or unnatural powers, a field that overlaps with the unnaturally aggressive or "manlike" woman, in the terms *amazon, shrew, virago,* and *battle-ax.* In this area credibility is strongly governed by superstition, myth, prejudice, and old wives' tales. Ania Loomba makes the point that "Amazonian homelands always moved to occupy a space just beyond a European horizon, a fantastic or actual locale that symbolized uncharted territory" (2002, 29). The key words in this group are *witch, hag, termagant, tartar, dragon, harpy,* and *siren.*

Witch, the most virulent of these terms, has its own entry. *Hag* is first recorded in the contemporary sense of "a repulsive old woman" in the fourteenth century (William Langland, *Piers Plowman* B Text, V, l. 191) before the appearance of the meaning "an evil spirit, dæmon or infernal being in female form" recorded from 1552: "Hegges, or nyght furyes, or witches like unto old women . . . whyche do sucke the bloude of children in the night." Another contemporary sense is more explicitly infernal: "The hateful hellish hagge of ugly hue" (1587, *The Mirror for Magistrates, Forrex* iii, "How King Forrex was slayne by his brother King Porrex"). Macbeth clearly uses this sense in addressing the "secret black and midnight hags" (IV i 48), but by 1712, Richard Steele is using the modern idiom: "One of those Hags of Hell whom we call Bawds" (*Spectator* 266). *Dragon,* a formidable creature with mythical potency, was applied to Satan from the fourteenth century, then humanized generally before taking on its feminine specialization: "a fiercely or aggressively watchful woman," first recorded in Dr. Johnson's *Dictionary* (1755).

Termagant, also covered in the entry for **Mahomet,** is a major witness word for various kinds of enemy. Its first meaning was xenophobic, being "the name of an imaginary deity held [believed] in medieval Christendom to be worshipped by Mohammedans: in the [medieval] mystery plays represented as a violent and overbearing personage." It is first applied to what the *OED* calls "a virago, shrew or vixen" in 1659, subsequently "a violent, overbearing, turbulent, brawling, quarrelsome woman." Similarly, *tartar,* derived from the name of the savage people of the steppes of Central Asia, was applied to vagabonds and thieves, then to a "rough, violent, irritable or intractable person, especially a woman," first recorded in John Dryden's play *The Wild Gallant* (1663): "I never knew your grandmother was a Scotchwoman: is she not a Tartar too?" (II i). *Harpy* epitomizes in a concentrated form certain misogynist views of woman: "a fabulous monster, rapacious and filthy, having a woman's face and a bird's wings and claws." Although the word has association with the legal profession, and Dr. Johnson referred in 1775 to "the harpies of taxation" in *Taxation no Tyranny* (5), the general use is found in William Makepeace Thackeray in 1859: "Was it my mother-in-law, the grasping odious, abandoned, brazen, harpy?" (*The Virginians,* xviii). *Siren,* dating from about 1340, has a strange semantic history, being initially "an imaginary species of serpent," derived from glossarial explanations of Latin *sirenes* in the Vulgate text of Isaiah 8:22. By Chaucer's time it had evolved into a variety of fabulous, seductive monster, part woman and part bird (sometimes confused with the mermaid), but had developed associations leading to the modern meaning of "a dangerously fascinating woman or temptress."

A number of powerful words show a combination of moral deterioration and sexual specialization: they are *harlot, bawd, gipsy,* and *tramp.* All of these originally referred to immoral males before becoming applied to women. More specifically, *harlot, gipsy,* and *tramp* originally had the senses of "vagabond, rogue, beggar, or rascal" before changing their meanings to that of "sexually promiscuous woman." The previously accepted derivation of *harlot* from Arlette, the mother of the illegitimate William the Conqueror, is now dismissed as a "random conjecture" of William Lambarde in the sixteenth century. Male harlots are recorded from the thirteenth century, while the first use in the sense of "whore" comes from Ranulph Higden (1432–1450) in a fascinating footnote: "The harlottes at Rome were called *nonaria*" (I l. 249), which explains the ironic Elizabethan sense of *nunnery* to mean "brothel," as used by Hamlet of Ophelia (III i 122–42). (The wordplay also has a typical anti-Catholic sting.) The sense of "prostitute" became dominant until the word became obsolescent from Victorian times. *Bawd,* of uncertain origin, first found (ca. 1362) in *Piers Plowman* (A text III l. 42), originally meant a procurer before acquiring the sense defined by Edward Phillips in his dictionary of 1706: "A lewd woman who makes it her Business to debauch others for Gain." Both *harridan* and *jade* originate as contemptuous names for inferior horses before becoming insulting terms for a loose woman. The earlier sense of *jade* is first found in Chaucer; the second in this interesting reference from 1560 combining the vices of prostitution and swearing:

Such a jade she is, and so curst a quean [prostitute],
She would out-scold the devil's dame I ween [reckon].
(*The Nice Wanton, Dodsley* II, 179)

By the eighteenth century the word was widely current as a term of contempt: Joseph Addison gossiped in the *Spectator* (no. 343 of 1712) of one "married to an expensive Jade of a wife." *Harridan* is an underground term first defined in a slang dictionary (ca. 1700) as "half whore, half bawd." Dr. Johnson (1755) preferred the higher register of "a decayed strumpet." Sexual innuendoes associating horses and whores were prevalent in earlier times; they have been superseded by the modern use of *bicycle* as a symbolic referent for "a loose woman." In the analysis of college student speech by Timothy Jay (1992), *whore* was used more frequently by males, but *slut* was more commonly used by women (143).

Generally speaking, the imbalance between favorable and negative terms continues, despite the insights and condemnation of feminists.

See also: Bitch; Fishwife; Promiscuity; Prostitutes; Quean and Queen; Scold; Shrew; Virago; Whore and Whoreson; Witch.

Bibliography

Bréal, Michel. *La Semantique,* trans. Mrs. Henry Cust: *Semantics: Studies in the Science of Meaning.* London: Heinemann, 1900. Reprint. New York: Dover, 1964.

Cameron, Deborah, ed. *The Feminist Critique of Language.* London: Routledge, 1990; 2nd ed. 1998.

Coates, Jennifer. *Women, Men and Language.* London: Longman, 1986.

Delany, Sheila. "Womanliness in *The Man of Law's Tale.*" *Chaucer Review* 9, Summer 1974.

Eckert, Penelope, and Sally McConnell-Ginet, eds. *Language and Gender.* Cambridge: Cambridge University Press, 2003.

Greer, Germaine. *The Female Eunuch.* New York: Bantam, 1970.

Hughes, Geoffrey. *Swearing*. Oxford: Blackwell, 1991. Harmondsworth: Penguin, 1998.

Jay, Timothy. *Cursing in America*. Philadelphia/Amsterdam: Benjamins, 1992.

Loomba, Ania. *Shakespeare, Race, and Colonialism*. Oxford: Oxford University Press, 2002.

Miller, Casey, and Kate Swift. *Words and Women*. London: Victor Gollancz, 1977.

Mills, Jane. *Womanwords*. London: Virago, 1991.

Schulz, Muriel. "The Semantic Derogation of Women." In *Language and Sex: Differences and Dominance*, ed. B. Thorne and N. Henley, 64–73. Rowley, MA: Newbury House, 1975.

Sontag, Susan. "The Third World of Women." *Partisan Review* 40: 2 (1973).

Spender, Dale. *Man Made Language*. London: Routledge & Kegan Paul, 1980.

Ullmann, Stephen. *Language and Style*. Oxford: Blackwell, 1964.

WOMEN, SWEARING IN

The generally accepted traditional norm in English-speaking societies is that it is highly impolite to swear in the presence of a woman and unacceptable or taboo for a woman to swear at all. Although class factors complicate this generalization, the same prohibitions apply to the use foul language. Indeed, they are so taken for granted that they are never articulated, any more than are prohibitions against women spitting or farting. However, these normative notions, confining coarse verbal behavior to the male sex, derive largely from bourgeois Victorian practices that survived through to the mid-twentieth century. They are not upheld historically, since there are notable exceptions in the medieval and Renaissance periods, especially the example of Queen Elizabeth herself. In recent decades swearing in women has become an increasingly notable feature in fact, in fiction, and in popular culture.

Historically one must distinguish between free observation on language behavior and normative pressure. Literary evidence has the important limitation that prior to the eighteenth century virtually all literature was written by men. The emergence in the nineteenth century of major women novelists like Jane Austen, the Brontë sisters, Mrs. Elizabeth Gaskell, and George Eliot (the male pseudonym of Mary Anne Evans) clearly gave more prominence to women characters and their voices. Although these characters are often highly articulate and independent, they are nevertheless usually very restrained verbally, never resorting to strong or foul language, any more than their authors did in real life. It is only in the late twentieth century that women authors create characters unafraid of coarse language.

Women hardly feature in the history and literature of the Anglo-Saxon period, except in religious contexts. Their role is generally regal and ceremonial in works with a prevailing high moral tone, so there are no surviving instances of swearing. However, the cognate Germanic literature provides many examples of formidable and outspoken women in both the Eddic poems and the sagas. Among them are Steingerth in *Kormak's Saga,* the widow Droplaug in *Droplaugarsona Saga,* and Hallgerth in *Njal's Saga*. In *Kormak's Saga,* Steingerth divorces her husband on the grounds of an apparent homosexual attachment; before decamping she says mockingly that he deserves to be nicknamed "Buttocks Bersi" (chapter 13). The saga women are often prime movers in feuds, insisting that insults be avenged, not waiting for men to champion their cause, but egging them on, as does the widow Droplaug in *Droplaugarsona Saga*.

In the medieval period, the growth of the whole literary tradition of courtliness with its attendant notions of politeness created various antitypes. The principal term for a woman of ribald speech or one addicted to abusive language was *scold,* recorded from the thirteenth century. As the entry for **scold** shows, by 1476 this term had extended to the legal category of *common scold,* denoting a woman who disturbed the peace of the neighborhood by constant scolding, behavior so unacceptable as to be subjected to savage public humiliation and punishment. Furthermore, the **fabliaux**, with their emphasis on adultery, reveal a variety of sexually adventurous wives who are both knowing and articulate on sexual matters.

The entry on **Geoffrey Chaucer** discusses the most remarkable literary pioneer, his much-married Wife of Bath, the only secular and self-made woman on the pilgrimage to Canterbury, outrageously liberated in both her flagrant sexuality and her heretical views on religion and marriage. Also highly combative in verbal aggression, she uses in her famous prolonged *Prologue* a great range of four-letter words in berating her successive husbands with wounding insults like "sire olde lecchour." She inverts the medieval obligation of labor, the *servitium debitum,* sexualizes it, and exacts it without mercy: "How pitously a-night I maad them swynke [labor]!" (l. 202). In exacting the husband's sexual obligation she makes him "both my detour and my thral [slave]" (ll. 603–4). Her rebellious response to her fifth husband's repeated readings from a misogynist anthology, "the booke of wykked wives," encapsulates her championship of "experience" over authority: she tears out three pages and punches him so solidly that he falls into the fire (ll. 788–93). The sober pilgrim Clerk ends his tale of the patient Griselda with a powerful riposte mocking "thise archewyves" in the Epilogue (l. 1195).

In the context of medieval femininity, how typical or exceptional is Alison of Bath? F.N. Robinson commented in the standard edition of Chaucer that although "the [Wife's] *Prologue* is highly original in its conception and structure, . . . it shows the influence of a whole series of satires against women" (1974, 698). D.W. Robertson Jr. summarily dismissed the Wife as "hopelessly carnal and literal," consigning her "firmly among the evil who are in the Church but not of it" (1963, 317, 327). Yet in the ongoing debate she is increasingly seen as a militant proto-feminist. Several medieval dramas have outspoken and aggressive women. An altercation in the *Chester Play* (ca. 1400) has the redoubtable challenge: "Whom calleste thou queine, skabt bitch?" ("Who are you calling a whore, you dirty bitch?" l. 181). Noah's wife is a spectacular figure of stubborn aggression, refusing to enter the Ark and even engaging in fisticuffs, shouting "You shall have three blows for two, I swear by God's pain!" (*The Wakefield Noah,* l. 227). In the course of their belligerent altercation, Noah lectures the men in the audience that if they love their wives, they should "chastise their tongue" (l. 398).

Another remarkable text comes at the transition between the medieval and Renaissance periods in the extraordinarily frank disclosures of the *Twa Mariit Wemen and the Wedo* ("Two Married Women and the Widow") by the major Scots poet, William Dunbar (?1460–?1520). The Widow (whose sexual values are unmistakably reminiscent of Chaucer's original) shows total contempt for her dominated husband:

I made that wif carll to werke all womenis werkis
[I made that effeminate bloke do all the house-work]
(l. 351)

I him miskennyt, be Crist, and cukkald him maid
[I deceived him, by Christ, and made him a cuckold]
(l. 380)

The Widow's sexual openness is expressed not only in her predatory opportunism, but in the crudity of her language: the last line shockingly combines sexual infidelity and the name of the Savior. (This is one of the few instances of a religious oath being used in the work.) The entry for **William Dunbar** discusses this remarkable poem more fully.

The type of the verbally aggressive woman emerges strongly in early Elizabethan drama in *Gammer Gurton's Needle* (acted 1566). The play contains a number of violent altercations between Grandma Gurton and Dame Chat, very much in the vein of **flyting** matches:

Gammer: Thou wert as good kiss my tail,
Thou slut, thou cut, thou rakes thou jakes
[You whore, you jade, you bawd, you shit-house]
Chat: Thou skald, thou bald, thou rotten, thou gluttoun
[You scold, you hairless thing, you rubbish, you pig]
(III iii)

It was said of Queen Elizabeth I that she "swore like a man," and as the entry for **class and swearing** shows, many anecdotes attest to her abilities, as well as to her relish for the coarse jest. In these respects she seems be unique in English history. On the stage the female line of the Wife of Bath and Gammer Gurton continues in Shakespeare, although somewhat subdued, in the comic characters of Mistress Quickly and Mistress Overdone, both working-class women, as well as in Margaret of Anjou, the formidable cursing figure of Nemesis in the plays of *Henry VI* and *Richard III*. She is the only character who dominates the villain in the field of verbal combat, and all her curses come true. Her comic equivalent is Kate, who forms the special problematic category of the unmanageable and therefore unmarriageable **shrew**, a key term that has its own entry. Many of the comic heroines participate easily in bawdy exchanges, and there are a number of frankly outspoken women in the tragedies. These include Emilia in *Othello*, the rival sisters Cordelia, Goneril, and Regan in *King Lear*, Tamora, the ruthless Queen of the Goths in *Titus Andronicus*, and Volumnia, the dominant mother-figure in *Coriolanus*. But in general the tragic heroines, most obviously Ophelia and Desdemona, are the passive victims of cursing and verbal abuse. Desdemona cannot even bring herself to utter the accusing word *whore* (*Othello*, IV ii 119–21). After her alarming witchlike invocations, Lady Macbeth cannot cope with their consequences. Virgilia, the wife of Coriolanus, maintains a "gracious silence" throughout. Cleopatra is uniquely both feminine in accepting insults, and masculine in her verbal and physical aggression. Her defiant wearing of Antony's "sword Philippic" is pointed male role-play, not just cross-dressing. She is also unique in appropriating the male idiom of abuse, dismissing Caesar as an "ass unpolicied" (V ii 309).

The most illuminating exchange occurs in *Henry IV, Part I* when Harry Hotspur, the embodiment of aristocratic *sprezzatura,* or heroic insouciance, enjoins his wife to "swear a good mouth-filling oath." Shakespeare's contrived situation gives notable insights into contemporary class norms and expectations. This curious demand is prefaced by a social commentary on degrees of polite oaths, starting when Hotspur says "Come Kate, I'll have your song too," to which she responds "not mine, in good sooth." He roundly mocks her mildness: "'Not yours, in good sooth!' Heart, you swear like a comfit-maker's wife [confectioner's wife]—'Not you, in good sooth!,' 'As true as I live,' and 'As God shall mend me,' and 'As sure as day!'" Then, breaking into verse, he stresses the freedom of speech her status gives her:

Swear me, Kate, like a lady as thou art,
A good mouth-filling oath, and leave "in sooth,"
And such protests of pepper-gingerbread,
To velvet-guards and Sunday citizens.
(III i 257–60)

The meaning is clear, but the allusions are topical and now obscure. In Elizabethan times *gingerbread* had the figurative meanings of "tangy, but not strong"; a *velvet-guard* would wear soft trimmings, while *Sunday citizens* would be those assuming a temporary urbanity, putting on their "Sunday best" and using polite rather than coarse everyday oaths. *Forsooth* and *in sooth* are often satirized for their timidity, as in Richard Brathwaite's *Strappado for the Divell* (1615):

A civill matron, lisping with forsooth,
As one that hath not heart to swear an oath
(ll. 39–40)

Ben Jonson's *Poetaster* contains this advice: "Your citie mannerly word [*forsooth*], use it not too often" (IV i 33–34). The emphasis on "citizen," "civil," and "city" stresses bourgeois respectability, mocked by writers and scorned by the nobility, who conformed more to Sir Thomas Elyot's comment in *The Boke of the Governour* (1531): "They wyll say that he that swereth depe, swereth like a lorde" (I xxvi). Although Elyot recognizes the practice, he disapproves of it, advising that the child of a Gentleman should be brought up exclusively by women in a verbally sanitized environment, without "any wanton or unclene word to be spoken," and that men should not be allowed in the nursery. However, Lady Hotspur remains steadfastly silent.

By contrast, Ben Jonson, more at home in the robust demotic idioms of urban comedy, created within the same stage conventions characters like Dol Common, the formidable whore with a rich vein of profanity in *The Alchemist* (1610), and the "heroine" of the ironically titled play *Epicoene or The Silent Woman* (1609). She shows "Amazonian impudence," being "masculine and loud commanding," and in the final denouement, turns out not to be even a woman, but *epicene* in the sense of having characteristics of both sexes.

The arrival of actresses on the Restoration stage caused a sensation, the most famous or notorious, Nell Gwyn, an "orange wench" born in an alley, making a great impact on Charles II, his court, and the contemporary audience, especially after her celebrated remark, "Good people, be civil, I am the Protestant Whore," alluding to her French Catholic rival, Louise de Kérouaille. The diarist Samuel Pepys, an inveterate playgoer, was both attracted and shocked by her behavior. In his entry for October 5, 1667, he observed: "what base company of men comes among them [the actresses], and how lewdly they talk!," continuing: "But to see how Nell cursed, for having so few people in the pit, was very pretty."

As the entry for the **Restoration** shows, the contemporary comedy produced some wonderfully witty and outspoken women characters who participated readily in sexual innuendo. There was, however, a clear acknowledgment that even they were confined to certain limits. Lady Brute, the central figure of Sir John Vanbrugh's *The Provok'd Wife* (1697), concedes: "Men have more Courage than we, so they commit more Bold, Impudent Sins. They Quarrel, Fight, Swear, Drink, Blaspheme, and the like. Whereas we, being Cowards, only Backbite, tell Lyes, Cheat at cards and so forth" (V ii). In the same year Daniel Defoe, in *An Essay on Projects,* saw the issue in terms of gender development, albeit with some irony: "The Grace of Swearing has not obtain'd to be a Mode yet among the Women; *God damn ye,* does not sit well upon a Female Tongue; it seems to be a Masculine Vice, which the Women are not arrived to yet." Defoe had strong views on swearing, calling it "that Lewdness of the Tongue, that Scum and Excrement of the Mouth," regarding it as "a senseless, foolish, ridiculous practice," and in the *Essay* proposed an academy for the proper education of women (cited in Montagu 1973, 184–85).

The controversial and enigmatic Aphra Behn (1640–1689), the first woman author known to have made a living by her pen, writing sixteen plays, many novels, poems, and translations, was "much attacked for plagiarism and bawdiness" (Todd 1999, 2). Although modern critics concede that "the charge of plagiarism is partially true" (Todd 1989, 2), that for bawdiness is questionable. In *The Rover* (1677), her most famous and discussed play, the character of Willmore, generally agreed to be modeled on the **Earl of Rochester**, is appropriately cynical, but largely lacking the outrageous bawdy for which he was notorious. Her highly successful epistolary novel, *Love-Letters Between a Nobleman and his Sister* (1684), was based on a contemporary scandal, the elopement of Lord Grey and his sister-in-law Lady Henrietta Berkeley in 1682. The passionate participants express their longing and frustration in a mixture of erotic fantasy, melodrama, and euphemism.

The drama and fiction of the Restoration period are almost exclusively concerned with the upper classes. However, the association between swearing and low-class women is encapsulated in the two contemporaneous terms **fishwife** and **Billingsgate***,* both of which have their own entries. In his *Polite Conversation* (1737), **Jonathan Swift** pointedly rejected the traditional view that it was a breach of manners to swear in front of a lady, a view "which, I confess, did startle me not a little; having never observed the like, in the compass of my own female acquaintance, at least for twenty years past" (1963, 30).

The case of Defoe's remarkable sexual and criminal adventuress *Moll Flanders* (1722) is more complex. In the Preface, Defoe makes a clear concession that the style of the narration "is a little altered, particularly she is made to tell her own Tale in modester Words than she told it at first . . . having been written more like one still in Newgate" (the famous London prison). Defoe imposes a structure of modesty by editorial intervention, euphemizing Moll's sexual experiences, preferring the conventional language of strict morality to uphold the taboos regarding the mention of sexual pleasure: "However, tho' he took these freedoms with me, it did not go to that, which they call the last Favour" (21). Moll even concedes her complicity: "Indeed I think I did rather wish for that Ruin, than studied to avoid it" (22). The same "modest" language covers shoplifting, theft, abortion, and the other sordid practices of Moll's various "wicked lives" (268). But other female characters are both violent and voluble: "two fiery Dragons could not have been more furious than they were; they tore my Clothes, bully'd and roared as if they would have murthered me" (213). (The historical sense of **roaring** has its own entry.) Hardened by experience, Moll starts to blur moral categories admitting: "whether I was a Whore or a Wife, I was to pass for a Whore here" (1973, 127), even quoting cynical verses of Rochester.

Henry Fielding, a practiced farceur, created many ingeniously ironic situations in his novels where the traditional balance of sexual power is humorously reversed. These fictional worlds are populated by various sexually predatory upper-class women, such as Lady Booby and Mrs. Slipslop (in *Joseph Andrews,* 1742) and Lady Bellaston (in *Tom Jones* 1749), all practiced in sexual innuendo but avoiding coarse language. That is memorably left to Mrs. Tow-wouse, who goes to the very limit in the "hideous uproar" when she finds her husband *in flagrante* with the maid:

> O you d—ned villain! . . . To abuse my bed, my own bed, with my own servant! Was ever such a pitiful dog, to take up with a mean trollop? If she had been a gentlewoman, like myself, it had been some excuse, but beggarly, saucy, dirty servant-maid! Get out of my house, you w——!" to which she added another name, which we do care to stain our paper with: it was a monosyllable beginning with a b—, and indeed was the same as if she had pronounced the words 'she dog' . . . a word extremely disgustful to females of the lower sort.
>
> Betty had borne all hitherto with patience, and had uttered only lamentations; but the last appellation stung her to the quick. "I am a woman as well as yourself," she roared out, "and no she-dog; and if I have been a little naughty, I am not the first."
>
> (*Joseph Andrews,* Book I, chapter xvii)

Fielding's amusingly obvious allusions to taboo words by accentuating their euphemized printed forms invites the reader into collusion, a technique subsequently developed by his contemporary **Laurence Sterne**. The power of the "monosyllable beginning with a b—" is endorsed by Frances Grose's *Classical Dictionary of the Vulgar Tongue* (1785): "The most offensive appellation that can be given to an English woman, even more provoking than that of whore." However, alongside these ladies, Squire Western produces a crude cascade of coarse language: "to tell you plainly, we have been all this time afraid of a son of a whore of a bastard of somebody's, I don't know whose, not I," recalling that "there was whole room of women. . . . d—n me, if you ever catch me among such a kennel of hoop-petticoat b——s! D—n me." No respecter of persons, Western refers to "that fat a-se b——, my Lady Bellaston" (*Tom Jones,* Book XVII, chapter iii).

Less well known is the witty suggestion by Arthur Murphy in the *Gray's Inn Journal* for June 29, 1754, suggesting a formalization of the flux of verbal fashion by having a Register of Births and Burials of words, adding: "A Distinction might be made between a kind of Sex in Words, according as they are appropriated by Men or Women; as for instance

D—n my blood is of Male Extraction, and *Pshaw, Fiddlestick,* I take to be female" (cited in Tucker 1961, 86).

The **Victorian Age** had the familiar double standard, mainly based on class. On the comic plebeian level is Charles Dickens's creation Mrs. Gamp in *Martin Chuzzlewit* (1843–1844), a disreputable drunken nurse whose favorite oath is "drat!" At another, conforming to the Victorian stereotype of the Angel in the Hearth, is Emily in Anthony Trollope's novel *The Prime Minister* (1876). The entry for **damn** shows the shattering effects on her of her husband's uttering this word in chapter xliv. Figures like Mrs. Gamp appear frequently and are memorably vocal in the grim records of the Victorian social reformers like Henry Mayhew, whereas sensitive characters like Emily are the norm in Victorian novels, especially those written by women. Even rebellious heroines like *Tess of the d'Urbervilles* (1891) who break the chains of marital convention, even committing murder, still use restrained language.

The same restraint can be seen in the women authors of the early twentieth century, several of whom, such as Amy Lowell, Virginia Woolf, Willa Cather, Edith Sitwell, and "H.D." (Hilda Doolittle), sought to establish an alternative tradition, a canon of women writers, countering the traditional male-dominated canon. However, they themselves wrote in a generally genteel fashion.

Part of the scandal surrounding James Joyce's *Ulysses* (1922) was Molly Bloom's uncensored adulterous reverie, which, in Alexander Walker's description of the film version by Joseph Strick in 1967, "bring[s] the film to an amazing close of pure aural orgasm" (1977, 221). Much of the outrage at D.H. Lawrence's **Lady Chatterley's Lover** (1928) was not simply the use of "four-letter" words, but the fact that Mellors the gamekeeper teaches them to the Lady of the Manor. Like Lady Hotspur, Connie Chatterley is, unsurprisingly, reluctant to use such words. Prior to both, George Bernard Shaw had calculatedly exploited the comic violation of another taboo by having the heroine of **Pygmalion** (1914) destroy her elaborate class disguise by uttering the scandalous demotic idiom "Not bloody likely!" However, none of these violations could be regarded as ushering in a new tradition.

A historical survey shows that there have in the past been some signal swearers among women in fact and in fiction, but they have been the exception, not the rule. In recent decades a number of influential sociolinguistic studies have investigated the whole issue of language and women, a topic discussed more fully under **women, stereotypes of**. The argument of Germaine Greer's pioneering study *The Female Eunuch* (1970) is clearly that women have historically been linguistically disempowered. Paradoxically, however, one of the most potent stereotypes has been that of the aggressive or wicked woman, encapsulated in such terms as *witch, hag, amazon, termagant, scold, shrew, virago,* and *vixen,* all of which were established as far back as 1600.

The wave of women's liberation of 1969–1670 was driven by groups propagandizing themselves by semantic shock tactics, using acronyms like SCUM (Society for Cutting up Men) and WITCH (Women's International Terrorist Conspiracy from Hell). Aggressive and provocative language was *de rigueur,* the SCUM Manifesto accusing males of having "made the world a shitpile," reversing received Freudian doctrine, claiming that "men have pussy envy" and advocating revolution by "fucking up the system" (Morgan, ed., 1970, 515–17). The group styled WAR (Women of the American Revolution) even had semantic guidelines in the use of pejorative terms (Morgan, ed., 1970, 524). Stark witness of the racial divide is the radical poem "TCB" by Sonia Sanchez, consisting of three line verses using "incremental repetition":

wite/motha/fucka
wite/motha/fucka
wite/motha/fucka
    whitey

The burden is repeated six times, the only significant variation being in the sequence of insults whereby *whitey* is replaced by other terms of demotic insult, namely *ofay, devil, cracker,* and *honky*. The catalogue of abuse ends with a call for collaboration: "now. That it's all sed / let's get to work."

In her provocative article "The Slag-heap Erupts" in *Oz* magazine, February 1970, Greer argued against the sexual confrontation advocated by militant feminists: "The cunt must take the steel out of the cock and make it flesh again" (1987, 29). In similar vein she wrote in "The Politics of Female Sexuality" (*Oz* May 1970): "Revolutionary woman may join Women's Liberation Groups and curse and scream and fight the cops, but did you ever hear of one of them marching the public street with her skirt high crying 'Can you dig it? Cunt is beautiful!'" (1987, 37). Greer wrote a number of articles in this vein, some collected in *The Madwoman's Underclothes* (1987).

To what extent has there been a gender change in linguistic idiom in recent times? Decades ago, in *Language and Woman's Place,* Robin Lakoff made the point, often repeated, that "If a little girl 'talks rough' like a boy, she will be ostracized, scolded or made fun of" (1975, 5). Tracing the development of this feminine acculturation, Lakoff offered this example:

(a) Oh dear, you've put the peanut butter in the refrigerator again.
(b) Shit, you've put the peanut butter in the refrigerator again.
It is safe to predict that people would classify the first sentence as part of "women's language," the second as "men's language" (1975, 10).

Although Lakoff's thesis (and her example) has a dated air in terms of the current debate, it still applies to the mass of society. Yet one consequence of the feminist movement, notably in America, has been the growth of a more liberated attitude toward swearing. On this point J.L. Dillard observed:

> Another change, towards use of "objectionable" language by women, has taken place as a product of the same [feminist] movement. Erica Jung's [sic] *Fear of Flying* [1973] was a striking example of writing by a woman in a genre which had been almost the exclusive property of men and in which they exercised considerable restraint before World War II. (1985, 215)

Among Jong's richly profane and bawdy novels, *Fear of Flying* (1973) is often cited for being the source of the daring phrase "zipless fuck," but she has also been patronizingly "placed" as "a female Henry Miller," and Paul Theroux dismissed the work in the *New Statesman* as "a mammoth pudenda [sic]." Dillard nevertheless remained skeptical:

> An occasional female speaker at a scholarly conference very pointedly, aggressively and rather self-consciously uses one of the "four-letter" words in order to demonstrate her freedom to do so. In such a case, however, calling attention to the usage is tantamount to an admission that it is not really commonplace for women to use such words in public.
> (1985, 215)

In support of Dillard it can be noted that virtually no women in public life on either side of the Atlantic, even formidable characters like the British prime minister Margaret Thatcher, ever use coarse speech. The analysis of college student speech by Jay (1992) showed that women generally lagged behind men in the use of the most taboo words, but were the more common users of *bastard, goddam, shit, bitch, slut, ass, Jesus Christ,* and *damn* (143–51).

A British perspective was offered by Rosalind Coward's observation that "Women are talking seriously dirty," in a review article in *New Statesman and Society* (June 9, 1989, 42). Although she did not validate the generalization, she reviewed and discussed women's fiction frankly depicting "alternative" forms of female sexual behavior, such as lesbian pornography, fantasies of humiliation, rape, masochism, and sadism, themes that clearly do not conform to the feminist "phallocratic" interpretation of sexual dynamics. Two modern British authors who have decisively broken most taboos of content and language are Angela Carter and Jeanette Winterson. The title of Carter's collection of journalism, *Expletives Deleted* (1992) is mischievously misleading. She acknowledges readily in the Introduction, "I am known in my circle as notoriously foul-mouthed," continuing unexpectedly, "It's a familiar paradox—the soft spoken middle-aged gentlewoman who swears like a trooper when roused" (1992, 1). Carter relishes outrageous epigraphs such as Levi-Strauss's "To eat is to fuck" (1992, 75). Furthermore, her study *The Sadeian Woman and the Ideology of Pornography* (1979) challenges the traditional assumptions of "woman as victim." Winterson shows similar insouciance, especially in *Oranges Are Not the Only Fruit* (1985). Her story title "Why Do You Sleep with Other Girls?" is answered with brutal surrealistic comedy: "My lover Picasso is going through her Blue Period. In the past her periods have always been red. . . . The stench of her, the brack of her, the rolling splitting cunt of her" (1998, 31). The debate has been continued in such works as those by Jennifer Coates, *Women, Men and Language* (1986), and Deborah Cameron's reader, *The Feminist Critique of Language* (first edition 1990, second 1998).

Modern and contemporary American drama still presents swearing and foul language as predominantly an aspect of macho behavior, a form of posturing to establish dominance. There are a few exceptions in the work of Edward Albee and **David Mamet**, apart from Martha, the formidable emasculating "Earth Mother" in Albee's *Who's Afraid of Virginia Woolf?* (1962) and Mamet's *Oleanna* (1992). Paula Vogel's *Desdemona* (1993) is a deconstruction or travesty of Shakespeare's tragedy from the point of view of the three women characters, whereby the heroine becomes a foul-mouthed sexual predator, a reconstruction of Desdemona in terms of misogynist and chauvinist male stereotyping shown in the language of Iago and Othello.

In modern popular culture the spirit of Nell Gwyn has clearly been resuscitated in recent decades, more in the United States than Britain. Frankly bawdy and foul-mouthed female characters assert themselves in the popular television characters of Samantha in "Sex and the City," Carmela in "The Sopranos," Brenda in "Six Feet Under," and the various wives of "The Mind of the Married Man." The British equivalents are less coarse but more literary. The upper-class lady adept at a "good mouth-filling oath" is superbly embodied in the character of Kate Swift, the creation of Michael Aitkins, scriptwriter of the 1990s British television comedy series "Class Act." Her withering denunciations include "you obsequious little turd," "that battered slattern," "troglodytic tart," "expensive mattress," and "miserable tight-fisted old cow." In the area of popular music, obscenities routinely used in male rap performances are increasingly exploited by women artists, especially those intent on seeking publicity. In announcing the winner of Britain's Turner Awards in 2003, Madonna was typically outrageous, saying: "Come on motherfuckers, everyone's a winner!" In the contemporary context, Eve Enslin's stage show, *The Vagina Monologues,* first performed in 1996, is more of a consciousness-raising vehicle, in which the word "vagina" is reiterated to anesthetize the audience and remove its taboo quality. This technique appears tame and programmatic alongside the radical feminism of the 1970s.

The debate about the incidence of women swearing in what is called "natural language" continues. In her brief discussion, Jennifer Coates declared: "There is little hard evidence on male/female differences in swearing" (1986, 108). However, the studies she cited indicate that swearing is still more common among males, although both women and men swear more in the company of their own sex, a point endorsed by Jay (1992, 139).

See also: Billingsgate; Chaucer, Geoffrey; Dunbar, William; Fabliau, the; Flyting; Scold; Shakespeare, William; Shrew.

Bibliography

Behn, Aphra. *Love-Letters Between a Nobleman and His Sister*, ed. Janet Todd. London: William Pickering, 1993.

Cameron, Deborah, ed. *The Feminist Critique of Language*. London: Routledge, 1990; 2nd ed., 1998.

Carter, Angela. *The Sadeian Woman: An Exercise in Cultural History*. London: Virago Press Ltd., 1979.

———. *Expletives Deleted: Selected Writings*. London: Chatto & Windus, 1992.

Coates, Jennifer. *Women, Men and Language*. London: Longman, 1986.

Dillard, J.L. *Towards a History of American English*. London: Routledge & Kegan Paul, 1985.

Greer, Germaine. *The Female Eunuch*. New York: Bantam, 1970.

———. *The Madwoman's Underclothes*. London: Pan, 1987.

Jay, Timothy. *Cursing in America*. Philadelphia/Amsterdam: Benjamins, 1992.

Lakoff, Robin. *Language and Woman's Place*. New York: Harper and Row, 1975.

McConnell-Ginet, Sally, Ruth Borker, and Jenny Furman, eds. *Women and Language in Literature and Society*. New York: Praeger, 1980.

Morgan, Robin, ed. *Sisterhood is Powerful: An Anthology of Writings from the Women's Liberation Movement*. New York: Random House, 1970.

Mugglestone, Lynda. *Talking Proper*. Oxford: Clarendon Press, 1995.

Robertson, D.W., Jr. *Preface to Chaucer*. Princeton: Princeton University Press, 1963.

Robinson, F.N., ed. *The Works of Geoffrey Chaucer*. Oxford: Oxford University Press, 1974.

Spender, Dale. *Man Made Language*. London: Routledge, 1980.

Swift, Jonathan. *A Complete Collection of Genteel and Ingenious Conversation*, ed. Eric Partridge. London: André Deutsch, 1963.

Todd, Janet, ed. *Aphra Behn*. London: Macmillan, 1999.

Tucker, Susie I., ed. *English Examined*. Cambridge: Cambridge University Press, 1961.

Winterson, Jeanette. *Oranges Are Not the Only Fruit*. London: Pandora Press, 1985.

———. "Why Do You Sleep With Other Girls?" In *The World and Other Places*. London: Jonathan Cape, 1998.

WORD-FIELD OF SWEARING

The word-field of the modes of swearing is diverse, being made up of a range of terms deriving from Anglo-Saxon, Latin, and Greek origins. Those in the following discussion styled in bold type have their own entries. The general terms *to swear* and *swearing* derive from Anglo-Saxon *swerian,* which had only the formal sense of "to swear or make an oath," but none of the modern informal senses. It had an unexpected relation *andswarian,* the origin of "answer," indicating the seriousness of the term in the past. We still use the formal sense in the idioms "to answer to a charge." The formal term *oath* similarly derives from Anglo-Saxon *að,* as does *plight* from Anglo-Saxon *pliht,* still used in the archaic wedding formula "I plight thee my troth," in which *troth* is an old personalized form of *truth. Curse,* from Anglo-Saxon *curs,* was often used in medieval religious contexts to mean "excommunication," although the ulterior roots of the word are uncertain.

The most general term deriving from a classical root is *vow,* recorded from the thirteenth century, from Latin *votum,* curiously also the origin of *vote.* In the following century came *pledge* from Latin *plebium.* Most of the more technical legal terms have classical origins. From Latin *jus,* meaning "law" or "right," come *perjury,* "the violation of an oath," and *jury,* the group formally sworn to deliver a true verdict. Less obvious is *injury,* originally meaning a wrongful act or treatment. In earlier times this included intentionally hurtful or offensive speech, recorded from the sixteenth century, as in John Florio's translation of Michel de Montaigne's *Essays* (1603): "He began to raile upon them with a thousand injuries" (I, xlvi). The old sense of the word survives in the South African legal category of **crimen injuria,** the offence of using grossly insulting language. Also deriving from this root is **abjuration,** a formal renunciation under oath. Other classically derived terms are **asseveration, attestation,** and **imprecation.** The various modes of infraction, described by the classical terms **blasphemy, malediction, obscenity,** and **profanity** have their own entries.

Bibliography
Mellinkoff, David. *The Language of the Law.* Boston: Little, Brown, 1963.

WORD MAGIC

The term essentially refers to the belief that words, especially when used ritualistically or in some form of incantation, have the power to unlock mysterious powers in nature and to affect human beings and their relationships. They may be employed benevolently, as in the case of **charms** and prayers, or malignantly, as in the case of **spells** and **curses**. An essential aspect of **taboo** is grounded in the belief that certain forces, creatures, and practices ought not to be named, which results in the suppression of the "dangerous" terms and the generation of pacifying **euphemisms**. In its most fundamental formulations *word magic* (first recorded in Ogden and Richards 1923, ii, 42) derives from anthropological studies of the supposed magical property residing in a name. It is significant that the earliest Germanic alphabet consisted of *runes,* carved alphabetical characters with mysterious or magical powers attributed to them both individually and collectively. Although word magic suggests primitive superstition, the copious and continuing evidence of taboos and euphemisms shows that there is still great respect for the power of words, despite the generally prevalent linguistic philosophy of nominalism, which claims that words have no intrinsic meaning, only that which is generated by convention. The various aspects of word magic are discussed more fully in the cross-referenced headings below.

See also: Charms; Curse and Cursing; Euphemisms; Spells; Taboo.

Bibliography

Ogden, C.K., and I.A. Richards. *The Meaning of Meaning.* New York: Harcourt Brace, 1923.

WORD OF HONOR

This formal phrase, now somewhat out of date, encapsulates the time-honored notion that a person's word represents a serious and binding commitment. Although the phrase *word of honor* is itself recorded only from 1814, the senses in which *word* represents "a promise," still found in the phrases to *keep, pledge,* or *give one's word,* are recorded in the Anglo-Saxon roots of the language. Subsequent formulations dating from the Renaissance are *to take* (a person) *at his word, upon his word,* and *on my word.* The idiom is obviously apparent in the opposite formulations of *to break one's word, to go back on one's word,* and so on. In feudal times, when society was graded hierarchically, there was a corresponding scale of verbal credibility. Thus in his *Chesse* (1474), William Caxton noted: "The simple parole or word of a prince ought to be more stable than the oath of a marchaunt" (II i), a view naturally regarded as insulting in modern egalitarian society. However, this class prejudice is traceable back to the Anglo-Saxon laws, as the relevant entry shows. The modern survival of the phrase serves to indicate the seriousness of a verbal commitment outside contexts of a formal oath.

See also: Anglo-Saxon Period; Formal Oaths.

WRETCH

The word has undergone a notable semantic change, showing three stages of meaning. From its root sense in Anglo-Saxon *wrecca* it originally signified an exile; then from Middle English a miserable or deprived person; and finally a despicable, mean, or contemptible person. This shift in attitude from sympathy at deprivation to contempt is quite a common trend, found in everyday words like *poor* and *fool,* as well as rarer terms like archaic *caitiff,* derived from *captive.* The semantic scholar Stephen Ullmann discusses the latter case in more detail (1962, 231–32).

The Anglo-Saxon condition of being exiled or banished was extremely ignominious, usually a consequence of treachery or cowardice, thus giving the word its initial negative emotive quality. The second sense, memorably used in King Lear's famous expression of sympathy for "poor naked wretches" in the storm scene of Shakespeare's tragedy (III iv 28), is still current. The term could and still can be used without an article in exclamations like "You wretch!," with a variety of tones, including commiseration or even humor. Othello's strange comment to Desdemona is a typical example of problematic tone: "Excellent wretch! Perdition catch my soul but I do love thee" (III iii 90). Usually the preceding adjective rather than the term itself indicates the sense: these can include *poor, little, perfidious, wicked.* The term can also be used simply to express exasperation, as in "That wretch of a plumber has not turned up."

Wretch in the emotive sense has remained largely within the provenance of British English, where it is now rather old-fashioned, being more frequently used by the elderly. It is uncommon in other varieties of English, being unlisted in American dictionaries of slang.

See also: Anglo-Saxon Period; Poverty.

Bibliography

Ullmann, Stephen. *Semantics: An Introduction to the Science of Meaning.* Oxford: Blackwell, 1962.

XYZ

XENOPHOBIA

Although the word itself is surprisingly recent, being a modern coinage recorded from about 1909 based on the classical Greek roots *xenos,* "a stranger," and *phobos,* "fear," the attitudes it describes can be traced historically to time immemorial and have become an obvious feature of many modern societies. The entries for **aliens, ethnic insults,** and **nicknames** trace the causes, social dynamics, and verbal consequences of these attitudes. The word-field, which is dismayingly large, can be divided into *General* and *Specific* terms, and is set out in the entry for **ethnic insults.** Arranged historically, it shows that the motivations behind xenophobia are originally those of religious and martial rivalry, then racist animosity. Indeed the modern sense of *xenophobia* is closer to "hatred of foreigners."

A great number of terms in the word-field have their own entries, as can be seen from the list below as well as the entries for **Chinese, English, French, Germans, Irish, Italians, Japanese,** and **Jews.**

See also: Aliens; Bugger; Coolie; Coon; Ethnic Insults; Gook; Honky; Hottentot; Hun; Kaffir; Nicknames; Nigger; Pom, Pommy; War; Wog; Yankee.

YANKEE

While the etymology of *Yankee* is famously complicated and disputed, being labeled by the *Oxford English Dictionary* as "source unascertained," there is no doubt that the term originated as, and continues to be, a nickname with varying degrees of derision and provocation. It was first applied to inhabitants or natives of New England, then to the northern states generally. It acquired its greatest force when used by the Confederate Army of the Union Army during the Civil War (1861–1865). Mencken, who regards the word as "perhaps the most notable of all the contributions of Knickerbocker Dutch to American," adds: "During the Civil War, as everyone knows, the Southerners used [*Yankee*], usually contemptuously, of all Northerners," adding in a footnote: "After the war the pejorative usually appeared as *damyankee,* and that form still survives in the South" (1963, 122).

English writers and speakers, starting with Lord Horatio Nelson in 1784, used the term generally of an American, usually with an edge of contempt. Even then the name was used stereotypically "with a connotation of cleverness, cunning or cold calculation." Contempo-

Of uncertain origin, the term *Yankee* has been variously used as an epithet, expression of pride, and benign identifier of regional origin. In this British cartoon of the War of 1812, the Yankees (Americans) are depicted as hapless and cowardly. (Library of Congress, LC-USZ62-1557)

raneously Francis Grose informed readers of his *Classical Dictionary of the Vulgar Tongue* (1785) that the word meant variously "A booby, or country lout; a name given to the New England men in North America." When Grose's work was pirated in 1811, the definition was amplified to "A general appellation for an American." The popular song "Yankee Doodle" (composed originally in derision of the provincial troops by Dr. Richard Shuckburg, a surgeon in Lord Jeffrey Amherst's service around 1755) became an ironic cultural marker, leading to the satirical forms *Yankee Doodle Dandy* (1787>) and *YankeeDoodledom* (first recorded, revealingly, in a letter from Thomas Carlyle to Charles Dickens, July 3, 1843): "The last *Chuzzlewit* on Yankeedoodledom is capital. We read it with loud assent." (Dickens's novel *Martin Chuzzlewit* [1843–1844] has a strongly satirical section on America.) Very different in tone is this virulent verse entitled "Death of Lincoln Despotism" (1861), anticipating his assassination:

And hold them Abe Lincoln, and all his northern scum,
Shall own our independence of Yankee Doodledom.

This was three years before Sherman inflicted on the South the strategy of "total war" in his "march to the sea," causing wholesale devastation, culminating in the burning of Atlanta. The policy of annihilation and humiliation left wounds which were slow to heal and enduring bitterness. Despite the passage of time and the diminution of these fierce regional loyalties, *Yankee* retains its emotive edge in parts of the South, as *Boer* and *Hun* do elsewhere. The context of World War II generated the positive message "The Yanks are coming" (from George Cohan's musical *Yankee Doodle Dandy*, 1942) and the rhyming slang allusions *army tank* and *ham shank*. However both *Yank* and *Yankee* continue to be used globally of Americans, usually with insulting intent.

Bibliography

Mencken, H.L. *The American Language*. New York: Knopf, 1963.

ZOUNDS

This quintessentially British oath, now archaic, is a euphemistic abbreviation of the exclamation *God's wounds!* The full form of the oath was common in the sixteenth century and was said to be the favorite of Queen Elizabeth (Montagu 1973, 139). Although *zounds* is first recorded from 1600, it is one of many such forms in which the name of God was excised in response to Puritan pressures and legislation against profanity on the stage. This resulted in equally strange forms like *'sbody* for *God's body, 'snails* for *God's nails,* and many others, covered in the entries for **God** and **minced oaths**. Other variants of *zounds* are *zownes, zoones, zons, dzowns, zownds, zwounds, zauns, zoons,* and *dswounds*. These variations show that people were more used to hearing than writing the form and that the original serious significance of the oath was steadily lost, so that the forms became simple empty exclamations. As early as 1698 the **Restoration** dramatist George Farquhar has the ironic observation in a piece of dialogue showing that the pronunciation had become simply a social distinction: "Zoons is only used by the disbanded [disgraced] Officers and Bullies [prostitutes' protectors]: but

Zauns is the Beaux [fashionable dandy's] pronunciation" (*Love in a Bottle* II ii). His contemporary John Dryden has the verbal sense: "When he loses upon the Square [gambling] he comes home zoundzing and blooding" (*The Kind Keeper,* IV i 39).

In his eccentric novel *Tristram Shandy* (1760–1767), Laurence Sterne builds up mock suspense around "a word of all others in the dictionary the last in that place to be expected—a word I am ashamed to write—yet must be written—must be read—illegal—uncanonical. . . . In short, I'll tell it in the next chapter." This follows immediately:

CHAP. XXVII

ZOUNDS! ————————————————————————————————
——

——————————————————————Z——ds! cried Phutatorius, partly to himself—and yet high enough to be heard—

In Sterne's typically playful fashion, the offending word is printed, but not truly uttered. The last instance recorded in the *Oxford English Dictionary* is from 1883. Perhaps the history of this word, like so much religious swearing, shows a fall from grace.

See also: Euphemisms; God's Wounds; Religious Oaths.

Bibliography

Montagu, Ashley. *The Anatomy of Swearing.* London and New York: Macmillan and Collier, 1973.
Sterne, Laurence. *The Life and Opinions of Tristram Shandy, Gentleman.* 3 vols. Oxford: Basil Blackwell, 1926.

CHRONOLOGY

ca. 450–1100   Anglo-Saxon or Old English Period

673–685   Laws of Hlothhere and Eadric, Anglo-Saxon kings
900   Laws of Alfred
ca. 900   *Beowulf*

ca. 1100–1500 Middle English Period

ca. 1250   *The Owl and the Nightingale*
ca. 1385–1400 Chaucer: *The Canterbury Tales*
ca. 1500   Dunbar: *The Flyting of Dunbar and Kennedy*

ca. 1500 Modern English Period

1552–1592   Underground slang dictionaries by Harman, Greene et al.
1566   *Gammer Gurton's Needle*
1574   Master of the Revels empowered to censor plays
1576   John Burbage builds first public theater in London
1587–1594   Marlowe's creative period
1588–1610   Shakespeare's creative period
1598–1632   Ben Jonson's creative period
1606   Act to Restraine Abuses of Players
1623   Act Prohibiting Swearing and Specifying Fines
1642–1660   Theaters closed by the Puritans
1660   Monarchy restored; theaters reopened;
1660–ca. 1700 Restoration comedy; Rochester's satires
1673   Test Act requiring oaths of religious conformity for public positions
1694   An Act for the More Effectual Suppressing Profane Swearing and Cursing
1698   Jeremy Collier: *A Short View of the Immorality and Profaneness of the English Stage*

1737	Licensing Act censoring all theatrical productions via the Lord Chamberlain
1755	Dr. Johnson's *Dictionary*
1785	Francis Grose's *Classical Dictionary of the Vulgar Tongue*
1828	Noah Webster's *An American Dictionary of the American Language*
1857	Obscene Publications Act (Campbell Act) (U.K.)
1873	Comstock Act suppressing "Obscene Literature" (U.S.)
1884–1928	*Oxford English Dictionary* (Murray, Bradley, Craigie, and Onions)
1890–1904	Farmer and Henley's *Slang and Its Analogues*
1912	British Board of Film Censors established
1930	Hays or Production Code for films in the United States
1934	Federal Communications Commission established in the United States
1959	Obscene Publications Act (U.K.)
1960	Trial of D.H. Lawrence's *Lady Chatterley's Lover*
1961	*Third Edition of Webster*
1968	Theatres Act: Abolition of the Lord Chamberlain's powers of censorship
1968	Code Seal Rating for films in the United States
1984	Video Recordings Act (U.K.)
1994–	*Random House Historical Dictionary of American Slang*
2006	Federal Communications Commission terminated

SELECT BIBLIOGRAPHY

Allen, Irving Lewis. *The Language of Ethnic Conflict*. New York: Columbia University Press, 1983.

Aman, Reinhold, ed. *The Best of Maledicta*. Philadelphia: Running Press, 1987.

Ayto, John, and John Simpson. *The Oxford Dictionary of Modern Slang*. Oxford: Oxford University Press, 1999.

Becon, T. "An Invective Against Swearing." In *The Early Works of Thomas Becon,* ed. Rev. John Ayre. Cambridge: The Parker Society, 1543.

Cameron, Paul. "Frequency and Kinds of Words in Various Social Settings, or What the Hell's Going On?" *Pacific Sociological Review* XII (1969): 101–4.

Chapman, Robert L. *New Dictionary of American Slang*. New York: Harper & Row, 1986.

De Jongh, Nicholas. *Politics, Prudery and Perversion: The Censoring of the English Stage 1901–68*. London: Methuen, 2000.

Farmer, J.S., and W.E. Henley. *Slang and Its Analogues*. 7 volumes, London: Routledge and Kegan Paul, 1890–1904. Reprint, Oxford: Wordsworth Press, 1987.

Flexner, Stuart Berg. *I Hear America Talking*. New York: Van Nostrand Reinhold, 1976.

Freud, Sigmund. "On Obscene Words." In *Sex in Psychoanalysis*, ed. S. Ferenczi. New York: Brunner, 1950.

Graves, Robert. *The Future of Swearing and Improper Language*. London: Kegan Paul Trench Trubner, 1936. (Originally issued as *Lars Porsena or The Future of Swearing,* 1927.)

Green, Jonathon. *A Dictionary of Contemporary Slang*. London: Pan, 1984.

———. *The Slang Thesaurus*. Harmondsworth: Penguin, 1988.

Grose, Francis. *A Classical Dictionary of the Vulgar Tongue*. London: S. Hooper, 1785.

Howell, Alexander. *A Sword Against Swearers*. London: 1611.

Hughes, Geoffrey. *Swearing*. Oxford: Blackwell, 1991. Harmondsworth: Penguin, 1998.

Jay, Timothy. *Cursing in America: A Psycholinguistic Study of Dirty Language in the Courts, in the Movies, in the Schoolyards and on the Streets*. Amsterdam/Philadelphia: J. Benjamins, 1992.

Labov, William. "Rules for Ritual Insults." In *Language in the Inner City*. Oxford: Basil Blackwell, 1972.

Landy, Eugene. *The Underground Dictionary*. New York: Simon & Schuster, 1967.

L'Estrange, Julian. *The Big Book of National Insults*. London: Cassell, 2002.

Lighter, J.E., ed. *The Random House Historical Dictionary of American Slang*. New York: Random House, 1994.

McDonald, James. *A Dictionary of Obscenity, Taboo and Euphemism*. London: Sphere, 1988.

Major, Clarence. *Juba to Jive*. New York/London: Viking/Penguin, 1994.

Maurer, David W. *Language of the Underworld*. Lexington: University Press of Kentucky, 1981.

Mencken, H.L. *The American Language*. New York: Knopf. Four editions: 1919–1936.

————. *The American Language.* Abridged by Raven I. McDavid Jr. New York: Knopf, 1963.

Mills, Jane. *Womanwords.* London: Virago, 1991.

Montagu, Ashley. *The Anatomy of Swearing.* London and New York: Macmillan and Collier, 1973.

Morton, James. *Low Speak.* London: Angus and Robertson, 1989.

Murray, Stephen O. "The Art of Gay Insulting." *Anthropological Studies* 21 (1979).

Paros, Lawrence. *The Erotic Tongue.* London: Arlington Books, 1988.

Partridge, Eric. *A Dictionary of Historical Slang.* London: Routledge & Kegan Paul, 1937–1960.

————. *A Dictionary of Historical Slang.* Abridged by Jacqueline Simpson. Harmondsworth: Penguin, 1988.

————. *Shakespeare's Bawdy.* London: Routledge & Kegan Paul, 1947.

————. *Slang.* London: Routledge & Kegan Paul, 1933–1950.

Rawson, Hugh. *A Dictionary of Invective.* London: Hale, 1991.

Read, Allen Walker. "An Obscenity Symbol." *American Speech* IX:4 (December 1934): 264–78.

Rogers, Bruce. *The Queen's Vernacular–A Gay Lexicon.* San Francisco: Straight Arrow, 1972.

Ross, Thomas W. "Taboo-Words in Fifteenth-Century English." In *Fifteenth-Century Studies,* ed. Robert F. Yeager, 137–60. Hamden, CT: Archon, 1984.

Sagarin, Edward. *The Anatomy of Dirty Words.* New York: Lyle Stuart, 1962.

Sharman, Julian. *A Cursory History of Swearing.* London: J.C. Nimmo and Bain, 1884.

Sheidlower, Jesse, ed. *The F-Word.* New York: Random House, 1995.

Spears, Richard A. *Slang and Euphemism.* New York: Signet, 1991.

————. *Forbidden American English.* Lincolnwood, IL: Passport Books, 1991.

————. *NTC's Dictionary of Slang and Colloquial Expressions.* Lincolnwood, IL: National Textbook Company, 1995.

Travis, Alan. *Bound and Gagged: The Secret History of Obscenity in Britain.* London: Profile Books, 2001.

Wentworth, Harold, and Stuart Berg Flexner. *A Dictionary of American Slang.* New York: Thomas Crowell, 1960.

Wilkes, G.A. *A Dictionary of Australian Colloquialisms.* 2nd ed. Sydney: Sydney University Press, 1985.

Williams, Gordon. *A Glossary of Shakespeare's Sexual Language.* London: Athlone Press, 1997.

INDEX

ABOUT THE AUTHOR

An Oxford graduate, Geoffrey Hughes was an honorary research associate at Harvard, has lectured at various universities and retired as Ad Hominem Professor of the History of the English Language at the University of the Witwatersrand, Johannesburg. His special research interests are historical semantics and sociolinguistics. He has published numerous articles and three books, *Words in Time* (1988), *Swearing* (1991) and *A History of English Words* (2000). He and his wife divide their time between Cape Town and France.

LINCC

Plant City